NP 37

WEST COASTS OF ENGLAND

AND

WALES PILOT

West Coasts of England and Wales, and south coast of Scotland,
from Cape Cornwall to the Mull of Galloway
including the Isle of Man

SEVENTEENTH EDITION
2008

PUBLISHED BY THE UNITED KINGDOM HYDROGRAPHIC OFFICE

Previous editions:

First published 1870
2nd Edition 1876
3rd Edition 1884
4th Edition 1891
5th Edition 1902
6th Edition 1910
7th Edition 1922
8th Edition 1933
9th Edition 1948
10th Edition 1960
11th Edition 1974
12th Edition 1993
13th Edition 1996
14th Edition 1999
15th Edition 2002
16th Edition 2005

PREFACE

The Seventeenth Edition of the *West Coasts of England and Wales Pilot* has been prepared by the late Lieutenant Commander P Jordan, Royal Navy, based on the fully revised Twelfth Edition (1993) compiled by Captain R.P. Stanage, RD (Master Mariner). The United Kingdom Hydrographic Office has used all reasonable endeavours to ensure that this Pilot contains all the appropriate information obtained by and assessed by it at the date shown below. Information received or assessed after that date will be included in *Admiralty Notices to Mariners* where appropriate. If in doubt, see *The Mariner's Handbook* for details of what *Admiralty Notices to Mariners* are and how to use them.

This edition supersedes the Sixteenth Edition (2005), which is cancelled.

Information on currents and climate has been based on data supplied by the Met Office, Exeter.

The following sources of information, other than United Kingdom Hydrographic Office Publications and Ministry of Defence papers, have been consulted:

> *Local Port Authorities*
> *Port Handbooks produced by Port Authorities*
> *Fairplay Ports Guide 2007-2008*
> *Ports of the World 2008*
> *Lloyds Maritime Guide 2007-2008*
> *Whitaker's Almanack 2008*
> *Statesman's Yearbook 2008*
> *Lloyd's List*

Mr M. S. Robinson
Chief Executive of the United Kingdom Hydrographic Office

The United Kingdom Hydrographic Office
Admiralty Way
Taunton
Somerset TA1 2DN
England
19th June 2008

CONTENTS

CONTENTS

CHAPTER 8

CHAPTER 9

CHAPTER 10

APPENDICES

DISTANCES TABLE

INDEX

EXPLANATORY NOTES

Admiralty Sailing Directions are intended for use by vessels of 150 gt or more. They amplify charted detail and contain information needed for safe navigation which is not available from Admiralty charts, or other hydrographic publications. They are intended to be read in conjunction with the charts quoted in the text.

This volume of Sailing Directions will be kept up-to-date by the issue of a new edition at intervals of approximately 3 years, without the use of supplements. In addition important amendments which cannot await the new edition are published in Section IV of the weekly editions of *Admiralty Notices to Mariners*. A list of such amendments and notices in force is published quarterly. Those still in force at the end of the year are reprinted in the *Annual Summary of Admiralty Notices to Mariners*.

This volume should not be used without reference to Section IV of the weekly editions of Admiralty Notices to Mariners.

References to United Kingdom Hydrographic Office publications and *The International Code of Signals*

The Mariner's Handbook gives general information affecting navigation and is complementary to this volume of Sailing Directions.

Ocean Passages for the World and *Routeing Charts* contain ocean routeing information and should be consulted for other than coastal passages.

Admiralty List of Lights or *Admiralty Digital List of Lights* should be consulted for details of lights, lanbys and fog signals, as these are not fully described in this volume of Sailing Directions.

Admiralty List of Radio Signals should be consulted for information relating to coast radio stations, pilotage services, vessel traffic services, port operations, radar beacons and radio direction finding stations, meteorological services, radio aids to navigation, Global Maritime Distress and Safety System (GMDSS) and Differential Global Positioning System (DGPS) stations, as these are only briefly referred to in this volume of Sailing Directions.

Admiralty Digital Radio Signals Volume 6 may also be consulted for information relating to pilotage services, vessel traffic services, port operations and ship reporting systems.

Annual Summary of Admiralty Notices to Mariners contains, in addition to the temporary and preliminary notices, and amendments and notices affecting Sailing Directions, a number of notices giving information of a permanent nature covering radio messages and navigational warnings, distress and rescue at sea and exercise areas.

The International Code of Signals should be consulted for details of distress and life-saving signals, international ice-breaker signals as well as international flag signals.

Remarks on subject matter

Buoys are generally described in detail only when they have special navigational significance, or where the scale of the chart is too small to show all the details clearly.

Chapter index diagrams in this volume show only those Admiralty charts of a suitable scale to give good coverage of the area. Mariners should consult NP 131 *Catalogue of Admiralty Charts and Publications* for details of larger scale charts.

Chart references in the text normally refer to the largest scale Admiralty chart but occasionally a smaller scale chart may be quoted where its use is more appropriate.

Firing, practice and exercise areas. Submarine exercise areas are mentioned in Sailing Directions. Other firing, practice and exercise areas may be mentioned with limited details. Signals and buoys used in connection with these areas may be mentioned if significant for navigation. Attention is invited to the Annual Notice to Mariners on this subject.

Names have been taken from the most authoritative source. When an obsolete name still appears on the chart, it is given in brackets following the proper name at the principal description of the feature in the text and where the name is first mentioned.

Port plans in this book are intended to assist the mariner in orientation and they are not to be used for navigation. The appropriate scale of chart should always be used.

Tidal information relating the daily vertical movements of the water is not given. For this information *Admiralty Tide Tables* or *Admiralty Total Tide* should be consulted. Changes in water level of an abnormal nature are mentioned.
Time difference used in the text when applied to the time of High Water found from the *Admiralty Tide Tables*, gives the time of the event being described in the Standard Time kept in the area of that event. Due allowance must be made for any seasonal daylight saving time which may be kept.

Wreck information is included where drying or below-water wrecks are relatively permanent features having significance for navigation or anchoring.

Units and terminology used in this volume

Latitude and Longitude given in brackets are approximate and are taken from the chart quoted.

Bearings and directions are referred to the true compass and when given in degrees are reckoned clockwise from 000° (North) to 359°
Bearings used for positioning are given from the reference object.
Bearings of objects, alignments and light sectors are given as seen from the vessel.
Courses always refer to the course to be made good over the ground.

Winds are described by the direction from which they blow.

Tidal streams and currents are described by the direction towards which they flow.

Distances are expressed in sea miles of 60 to a degree of latitude and sub-divided into cables of one tenth of a sea mile.

Depths are given below chart datum, except where otherwise stated.

Heights of objects refer to the height of the object above the ground and are invariably expressed as "... m in height".

Elevations, as distinct from heights, are given above Mean High Water Springs or Mean Higher High Water whichever is quoted in *Admiralty Tide Tables*, and expressed as, "an elevation of ... m". However the elevation of natural features such as hills may alternatively be expressed as "... m high" since in this case there can be no confusion between elevation and height.

Metric units are used for all measurements of depths, heights and short distances, but where feet/fathoms charts are referred to, these latter units are given in brackets after the metric values for depths and heights shown on the chart.

Time is expressed in the four-figure notation beginning at midnight and is given in local time unless otherwise stated. Details of local time kept will be found in *Admiralty List of Radio Signals Volume 2*.

Bands is the word used to indicate horizontal marking.

Stripes is the word used to indicate markings which are vertical, unless stated to be diagonal.

Conspicuous objects are natural and artificial marks which are outstanding, easily identifiable and clearly visible to the mariner over a large area of sea in varying conditions of light. If the scale is large enough they will normally be shown on the chart in bold capitals and may be marked "conspic".

Prominent objects are those which are easily identifiable, but do not justify being classified as conspicuous.

Principal marks are marks which qualify for inclusion and are outstanding and clearly visible throughout most of the waterway (or 15 to 20 miles of the waterway for particularly long waterways) as marks by day or lights by night; thereby being associated with the waterway as a whole, rather than being confined to any single set of Directions with it. In particular:
  Landmarks comprise buildings and structures (including lighthouses, whether major lights or not), daymarks and natural features. They may be on the coast or farther inland, provided they are distinctly visible from seaward.
  Offshore marks include light vessels, light floats, lanbys, buoyant beacons, and oil production platforms.
  Major lights is used in Sailing Directions to refer to all lights with a range of 15 miles or over.

ABBREVIATIONS

The following abbreviations are used in the text:

AIS	Automatic Identification System		IMDG	International Maritime Dangerous Goods
ALC	Articulated loading column		IMO	International Maritime Organization
ALP	Articulated loading platform		ISPS	International Ship and Port Facility Security Code
AMVER	Automated Mutual Assistance Vessel Rescue System			
ASL	Archipelagic Sea Lane		ITCZ	Intertropical Convergence Zone
ATBA	Area To Be Avoided		ITZ	Inshore traffic zone
ATLAS	autonomous temperature line acquisition system		JRCC	Joint Rescue Co-ordination Centre
°C	degrees Celsius		kHz	kilohertz
CALM	Catenary anchor leg mooring		km	kilometre(s)
CBM	Conventional buoy mooring		kn	knot(s)
CHA	Competent Harbour Authority		kW	kilowatt(s)
cm	centimetre(s)			
CDC	Certain Dangerous Cargo		LANBY	Large Automatic Navigation Buoy
CVTS	Co-operative Vessel Traffic System		LASH	Lighter Aboard Ship
			LAT	Lowest Astronomical Tide
DF	direction finding		LF	low frequency
DG	degaussing		LHG	Liquefied Hazardous Gas
DGPS	Differential Global Positioning System		LMT	Local Mean Time
DW	Deep Water		LNG	Liquefied Natural Gas
DSC	Digital Selective Calling		LOA	Length overall
dwt	deadweight tonnage		LPG	Liquefied Petroleum Gas
DZ	danger zone		LW	Low Water
E	east (easterly, eastward, eastern, easternmost)		m	metre(s)
EEZ	exclusive economic zone		m^3	cubic metre(s)
ELSBM	Exposed location single buoy mooring		mb	millibar(s)
ENE	east-north-east		MCTS	Marine Communications and Traffic Services Centres
EPIRB	Emergency Position Indicating Radio Beacon			
ESE	east-south-east		MF	medium frequency
ETA	estimated time of arrival		MHz	megahertz
ETD	estimated time of departure		MHHW	Mean Higher High Water
EU	European Union		MHLW	Mean Higher Low Water
			MHW	Mean High Water
FAD	fish aggregating device		MHWN	Mean High Water Neaps
feu	forty foot equivalent unit		MHWS	Mean High Water Springs
fm	fathom(s)		MLHW	Mean Lower High Water
FPSO	Floating production storage and offloading vessel		MLLW	Mean Lower Low Water
			MLW	Mean Low Water
FPU	Floating production unit		MLWN	Mean Low Water Neaps
FSO	Floating storage and offloading vessel		MLWS	Mean Low Water Springs
ft	foot (feet)		mm	millimetre(s)
			MMSI	Maritime Mobile Service Identity
g/cm^3	gram per cubic centimetre		MRCC	Maritime Rescue Co-ordination Centre
GMDSS	Global Maritime Distress and Safety System		MRSC	Maritime Rescue Sub-Centre
GPS	Global Positioning System		MSI	Marine Safety Information
GRP	glass reinforced plastic		MSL	Mean Sea Level
grt	gross register tonnage (obsolete)		MV	Motor Vessel
gt	gross tonnage		MW	megawatt(s)
			MY	Motor Yacht
HAT	Highest Astronomical Tide			
HF	high frequency		N	north (northerly, northward, northern, northernmost)
hm	hectometre			
HMS	Her (His) Majesty's Ship		NATO	North Atlantic Treaty Organization
hp	horse power		Navtex	Navigational Telex System
hPa	hectopascal		NE	north-east
HSC	High Speed Craft		NNE	north-north-east
HW	High Water		NNW	north-north-west
			No	number
IALA	International Association of Lighthouse Authorities		nrt	net register tonnage (obsolete)
			nt	net tonnage
IHO	International Hydrographic Organization		NW	north-west

ODAS	Ocean Data Acquisition System		SSW	south-south-west
			STL	Submerged turret loading
PEC	Pilotage Exemption Certificate		STS	ship to ship
PEL	Port Entry Light		SW	south-west
PLEM	Pipe line end manifold		SWATH	small waterplane area twin hull ship
PMSC	Port Marine Safety Code			
POL	Petrol, Oil & Lubricants		teu	twenty foot equivalent unit
PSSA	Particularly Sensitive Sea Areas		TSS	Traffic Separation Scheme
PWC	Personal watercraft			
			UHF	ultra high frequency
RCC	Rescue Co-ordination Centre		UKC	under keel clearance
RMS	Royal Mail Ship		UKHO	United Kingdom Hydrographic Office
RN	Royal Navy		ULCC	Ultra Large Crude Carrier
RoRo	Roll-on, Roll-off		UN	United Nations
RT	radio telephony		UT	Universal Time
			UTC	Co-ordinated Universal Time
S	south (southerly, southward, southern, southernmost)		VDR	Voyage Data Recorder
SALM	Single anchor leg mooring system		VHF	very high frequency
SALS	Single anchored leg storage system		VLCC	Very Large Crude Carrier
SAR	Search and Rescue		VMRS	Vessel Movement Reporting System
Satnav	Satellite navigation		VTC	Vessel Traffic Centre
SBM	Single buoy mooring		VTMS	Vessel Traffic Management System
SE	south-east		VTS	Vessel Traffic Services
SHA	Statutory Harbour Authority			
SPM	Single point mooring		W	west (westerly, westward, western, westernmost)
sq	square			
SRR	Search and Rescue Region		WGS	World Geodetic System
SS	Steamship		WMO	World Meteorological Organization
SSCC	Ship Sanitation Control Certificate		WNW	west-north-west
SSE	south-south-east		WSW	west-south-west
SSCEC	Ship Sanitation Control Exemption Certificate		WT	radio (wireless) telegraphy

GLOSSARY

Glossary of words of Welsh origin used on charts and in this volume of Sailing Directions.

Welsh	English
aber	estuary
adwy	gap
afon	river
angorfa	anchorage
bach	small, or nook or corner
bae	bay
bâl	summit
bala	outlet of a lake
ban, *pl* bannau	peak
banc, *pl* bencydd	bank
bangor	monastery
blaen, *pl* blaenau	head, end
bod	dwelling
boliog	belly shaped
braich	arm, ridge
bre, bryn	hill
bwlch	gap, pass
bychan	small, little
cae	field, hedge
caer	fort, castle
cafn	boat, or hollow in the land
canol	middle
capel	chapel
carn, *pl* carnau	heap, cairn
carnedd	cairn, mound, tumulus
carreg, *pl* cerrig	stone, rock
carreg trai	sunken rock
castell	castle
cefn, *pl* cefnydd	ridge
cei	quay
cil	recess, corner
cilfach	nook, creek, cove
clegyr	crag, cliff
clogwyn	cliff, crag
clun	meadow
coch	red
coed	trees, wood
cored	weir, dam
cors	bog or marsh
craidd	centre, middle
craig, *pl* creigiau	rock, crag
crib	crest, summit
croes	cross
crug	hillock, cairn
cul	narrow, lean
cwm	valley, glen
cyfrwy	saddle ridge
cyfyng	narrow strait
cymer	confluence
dan	under, below
dau, dwy	two
de	south
dibyn	steep slope, precipice
dinas	hill-fortress
dôl	meadow, dale
du, ddu	black, dark
dwfr, dŵr	water
dwyrain	east
dyfn, dwfn	deep
dyn	man, person
eglwys	church
esgair	long ridge

Welsh	English
gafl, *pl* gaflau	fork
garth	hill, ridge
genau	mouth, opening
glan	bank, shore
glas	blue, green or stream
glyn	valley, glen
gobell	saddle ridge
gogledd	north
gogof, *pl* gogofau	cave
gorllewin	west
gorynys	peninsula
gwastad	flat, level place or plain
gwaun	meadow, moor
gwryd	fathom
gwylfa	lookout point
gwyn, gwên	white
gwynt	wind
gwyrdd, gwerdd	green
hafan	harbour, haven
hen	old
hir	long
is	below, under
isaf	lower, lowest
isel	low
iseldir	lowland, plain
llan	church, village
llech, *pl* llechau	slab, slate
llethr	slope, steep
llwch, *pl* llychau	lake
llwyd	grey, brown
llyn	lake
mab, *pl* meibion	boy, son
maen, *pl* meini	stone
maes	field
mawr	great, big, high
melin	mill
melyn	yellow
merthyr	grave
moel	bare hilltop
morfa	sea-marsh, bog
moryd	estuary, inlet
mynachlog	monastery
mynwent	churchyard
mynydd	mountain
nant	brook
newydd	new
ogof, *pl* ogofau	cave
pant	valley, dent
parc	park, field
pen	head, end, top
penrhyn	promontory
pentir	headland
pig, pigyn	tip (of)
pill	tidal creek
pistyll	waterfall
plas	mansion
pont	bridge
porth	harbour or ferry
pwll	pool
pwll tro	whirlpool
pwynt	point

Welsh	English
rhiw	hill, slope
rhodwydd	embankment
rhos	moor, plain
sarn, *pl* sarnau	causeway
tâl	front, end
tan	under, beneath
ton, *pl* tonnau	wave
traeth	beach, shore
trum	ridge, summit
trwyn	point, cape
twmpath, twyn	hillock, knoll, hill
tŵr	tower

Welsh	English
tŷ, *pl* tai	house
tywyll	dark, black
tywyn	shore, strand
uchaf	higher, highest
y, yr, 'r	the
ynys, *pl* ynysoedd	island
ysgafell	ledge
ysgwydd	shoulder (of the hill)
ystrad	vale

Abbreviation: *pl*......plural

WELSH PRONUNCIATION

Welsh (Cymraeg) belongs to the Brythonic branch of the Celtic languages. The stress is nearly always on the penultimate syllable (though compounded words retain their proper accents).

c = k; *it is never pronounced as* s.

g = *the English hard* g; *it is never pronounced as* j.

ff *and* ph *have the same sound, that of the English* f.

th *has the sound of the English* th *in* thin.

dd *has the sound of the English* th *in* this.

ch *is sounded like the German* ch *in* nach, *and like the Scottish* ch *in* loch.

f = v.

ng *has the sound of the English* ng *in* hanging. *In a few words, such as* Bangor, ng *stands for* ng + g, *as in* finger.

ll *is a voiceless* l, *and bears the same relation to* l *as* th *in* thin *to* th *in* this.

r *is trilled like the Scottish* r.

s = s *in* loss. *It is never sounded* z.

w *and* i *are often consonants, sounded like the English* w *and* y *respectively, as in* with *and* yes.

a *is flat* a *not heard in English, but approximates the* a *in German* nach.

e *when short, has the sound of the English* e *in* pen, *and when long, has approximately the sound of* a *in* face *in Northern pronunciation.*

i *when long, is sounded like the* ee *in English* need. *When short, as in Welsh* dim *(nothing), it has the same sound and not the wider* i *as in English* dim.

o *when long as in Welsh* tôn *(tone) as in English* more. *When short as in* ton *(wave), it is more open, like the* o *in* not.

u *has the sound of the first* y *in English* mystery.

y *has two sounds. (1) In monosyllables and in the ultima it has the same sound as* u.

  (2) In other positions it has the sound of the English y *in* myrtle.

w *when long, equals the English* oo *in* moon, *and when short, equals the English* oo *in* book.

The vowel is short in monosyllables before p, t, c, m, ng, *or before two or more consonants; as* top *(top),* cut *(shed, sty),* lloc *(fold),* cwm *(valley),* llong *(ship),* nant *(brook). The vowel is long in monosyllables if it is final, or followed by* b, d, g, f, dd, ff, th, ch, s; *as* lle *(place),* mab *(son),* gwlad *(country),* teg *(fair),* tref *(town, home),* rhodd *(gift),* rhaff *(rope),* cath *(cat),* coch *(red),* tas *(rick, pile). If the vowel be followed by* l, n *or* r *it may be long or short, and the long vowel is marked with a circumflex; e.g.,* dôl *(meadow),* lôn *(lane),* tŵr *(tower). But* i *and* u *are not circumflexed, as they are almost always long before these consonants; and the long vowel is not marked in the common words,* dyn *(man), and* hen *(old).*

Consonant changes

In Welsh, initial consonants undergo certain regular changes, There are nine mutable consonants and three mutations: the soft, the nasal and the spirant.

Radical	p	t	c	b	d	g	m	ll	rh
Soft	b	d	g	f	dd		f	l	r
Nasal	mh	nh	ngh	m	n	ng	No change		
Spirant	ph	th	ch	No change			No change		

The following points may be noted:

  (i) *The initial consonant of the second element of a compound undergoes the soft mutation. Example:* Brithdir = brith *(speckled, coarse)* + tir *(land).*

  (ii) *The initial consonant of the genitive is often softened after a feminine singular noun, such as* llan *(church, parish),* tref *(town, hamlet, homestead),* pont *(bridge),* rhyd *(ford),* caer *(fort),* ynys *(island, holm, river-meadow). Examples:* Llanbadarn = llan + Padarn *(proper name).* Tregaron = tre(f) + Caron *(proper name).*
        The initial of a personal name in the genitive is sometimes softened in place-names even after a masculine singular noun. Examples: Tyddewi = tŷ *(house)* + Dewi *(proper name).* Cae Ddaffydd = cae *(field)* + Dafydd *(proper name).*

  (iii) *The initial consonant of a feminine singular noun is softened after the article. Examples:* Pen-y-dref = pen *(end, head, top)* + y *(definite article)* + tref *(town, home);* Pant-y-frân = pant *(valley, dent)* + y *(definite article)* + brân *(crow);* Rhobell *for* Yr obell = yr *(definite article)* + gobell *(saddle; ridge between two summits).*

Occasionally the initial consonant of a plural form used as a dual is softened after the article. Example: Yr Eifl = yr *(definite article)* + geifl *(plural of* gafl *fork).*

  (iv) *The initial consonant of an adjective is softened after a feminine singular noun. Example:* Rhyd Goch = rhyd *(ford)* + goch *(red).*

  (v) *The initial consonant of a following noun is softened after the prepositions,* ar *(on, over),* tan (dan) *(under),* tros (dros) *(over). Examples:* Pontardawe = pont *(bridge)* + ar *(on, over)* + Tawe *(name of a river);* Pontarddulais = pont *(bridge)* + ar *(on, over)* + Dulais *(name of a river).*

  (vi) *The initial consonant of a following noun undergoes the nasal mutation after the preposition* yn. *Examples:* Llanfihangel yn Nhywyn, Llanfair yn Neubwll.

WELSH GEOGRAPHICAL NAMES

Many Welsh names have been anglicised, e.g. Caerdydd into Cardiff; conversely some English names have been given Welsh forms, e.g. Bede-house has become Bettws.

Names like Anglesey, Beaumaris, Snowdon, etc are obviously not Welsh. Nearly all the names in South Pembrokeshire are of Norse origin.

NAMES IN CORNWALL AND ISLE OF MAN

Old Cornish was a Brythonic language akin to Welsh and Breton. It has not been spoken for two centuries, and its orthography is very doubtful; but it has left its mark on the names both of places and families in Cornwall.

Manx is a Goidelic language akin to Gaelic, but not much spoken now. Some place-names in the Isle of Man are of Norse origin.

vannstand	sea level	vik	bay, cove, creek, inlet
varde	cairn	viltreservat	nature preserve
værforhold	weather condition	vind	wind
våg	small bay	vindretning	wind direction
våt	wet	vrak	wreck
verksted (mar)	boatyard		
vesle	little		
vestre	west, western	Ytre, yt	outer

Index Chartlet

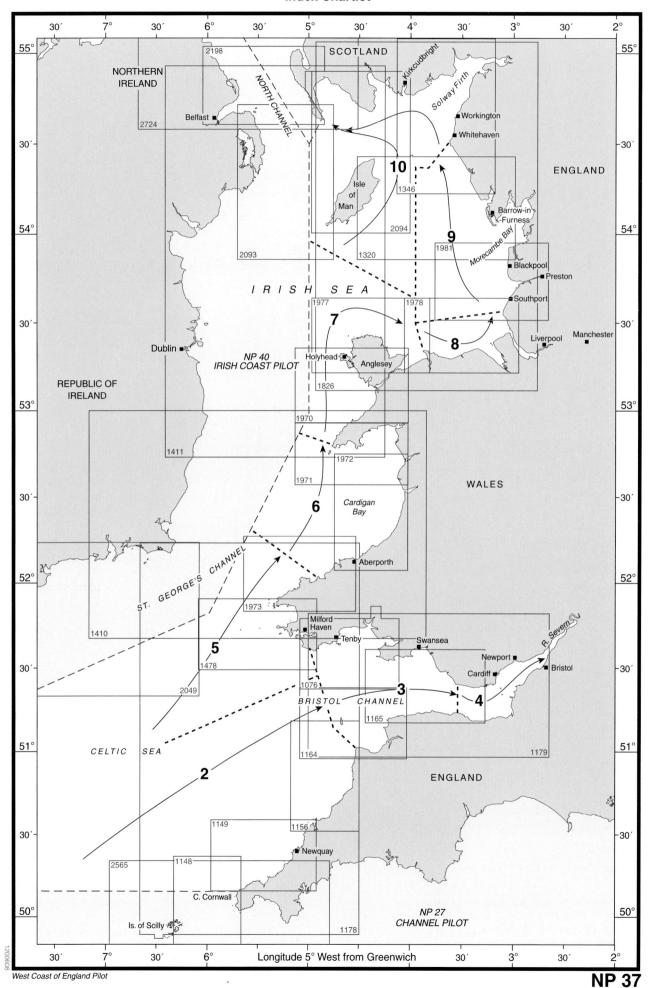

LAWS AND REGULATIONS APPERTAINING TO NAVIGATION

While, in the interests of the safety of shipping, the United Kingdom Hydrographic Office makes every endeavour to include in its hydrographic publications details of the laws and regulations of all countries appertaining to navigation, it must be clearly understood:

(a) that no liability whatever will be accepted for failure to publish details of any particular law or regulation, and

(b) that publication of the details of a law or regulation is solely for the safety and convenience of shipping and implies no recognition of the international validity of the law or regulation.

WEST COASTS OF ENGLAND AND WALES PILOT

CHAPTER 1

NAVIGATION AND REGULATIONS COUNTRIES AND PORTS NATURAL CONDITIONS

NAVIGATION AND REGULATIONS

LIMITS OF THE BOOK

Charts 1123, 1121

Area covered

1.1

1 This volume contains a description of the W coasts of England and Wales and the S coast of Scotland, from Cape Cornwall (50°08′N 5°43′W) to the Mull of Galloway (54°38′N 4°51′W), including Lundy, The Smalls, the Isle of Man and the other islands lying closer inshore.

Also described are the waterways of the River Severn as far as Sharpness; Milford Haven; the Menai Strait; the lower and upper reaches of the River Mersey and the Manchester Ship Canal.

2 The seaward limits of this volume are defined below:

	Lat N	*Long W*
Cape Cornwall (50°08′N 5°43′W)		
W to position	50°08′	10°00′
Thence NE to position	52°00′	6°00′
Thence N through	53°00′	5°00′
to position	54°35′	5°00′
Thence NE to the Mull of Galloway	54°38′	4°51′

1.2

1 The waters N of a line joining Carnsore Point to Saint David's Head and S of a line joining Ballyquintin Point to the Mull of Galloway are known as the Irish Sea and Saint George's Channel. The latter is the stretch of water between Wales and the Irish Coast to the W.

2 The water lying E of a line joining Saint Govan's Head to Hartland Point (51°01′N 4°32′W) is known as the Bristol Channel.

The Celtic Sea lies SW of Saint George's Channel and the Bristol Channel.

NAVIGATIONAL DANGERS AND HAZARDS

Coastal conditions

General

1.3

1 The coastlines of SW England and SW Wales present an area of bold headlands and rocky cliffs which are steep-to; on clear days they can be seen from considerable distances offshore, many of the intervening headlands appearing like islands presenting good radar targets.

A ground swell setting in from the Atlantic is always present; the area N of Saint George's Channel is more or less out of the reach of the Atlantic swell, but it is not exempt from heavy seas with strong winds.

2 Predominant winds are from SW and W though farther N the general wind system is modified by local conditions (1.126); visibility over much of the area is generally good with sea fog affecting the S part most. A well equipped ocean-going vessel with working radio and electronic navigation aids should find no difficulty in making a landfall at any time of the year.

3 The Continental Shelf, which is approximately delineated by the 200 m line (Chart 4102), lies more than 200 miles W of the SW coast of England. It may generally be

recognised in fine weather by the numerous ripplings in its vicinity, and in boisterous weather by a turbulent sea and the sudden alteration in the colour of the water from a dark blue to green.

4   In the approach to the Celtic Sea the shoaling is irregular on account of the banks and ridges described at 1.87; consequently soundings give no exact determination of position.

Routes
1.4
1   A vessel approaching the Bristol Channel from W should make Fastnet Rock (51°23′N 9°36′W) (*Irish Coast Pilot*), which lies directly on the track, and thence pass N of Lundy, guarding against the indraught of the in-going stream into Saint George's Channel, particularly when approaching Milford Haven and ports on the N side of the Bristol Channel.

The tidal streams (1.91) set fairly strongly in and out of the Bristol Channel when E of longitude 5°W.

2   A vessel approaching the Irish Sea through Saint George's Channel should, if coming from W, keep in sight of the Irish coast and pass SE of Tuskar Rock (52°12′N 6°12′W) (*Irish Coast Pilot*), off which there is a TSS, thence if bound for Liverpool, pass through the TSS W of Anglesey; the track lies diagonally across the tidal streams in Saint George's Channel.

3   If coming from SW, and well W of the traffic lanes W of the Isles of Scilly, pass through the deep gully which lies between Nymphe Bank (*Irish Coast Pilot*) and the entrance to the Bristol Channel, and thence W of The Smalls.

Safe harbours and anchorages
1.5
1   In heavy weather, shelter may be found in the lee of Lundy or in Clovelly Road or in Milford Haven; with these exceptions there is no safe roadstead between Cape Cornwall and the E part of the Bristol Channel, the ports in the latter not being available until after half flood.

2   In Cardigan Bay, shelter may be obtained in Fishguard Bay and in Saint Tudwal's Roads.

Farther N, Holyhead provides shelter.

Ice
1.6
1   As a general rule ice does not form in any of the salt water harbours covered by this volume.

TRAFFIC AND OPERATIONS

Traffic
1.7
1   Regular traffic plies between the traffic lanes off Cape Cornwall, The Smalls and The Skerries (1.10) on a N – S axis and between those traffic lanes which diagonally link the Irish and N Scottish coasts to ports within Liverpool Bay.

There is considerable traffic in and out of the Bristol Channel, where there are several large ports in close proximity to each other, and Liverpool Bay, where there is also cross-channel traffic between ports in the Isle of Man, Northern Ireland and the Republic of Ireland.

2   Vessels coasting should expect crossing traffic at some time during their passage.

High speed craft
1.8
1   High speed craft operate in the area covered by this volume. Mariners are advised to maintain a good lookout. Some high speed craft may generate large waves, which can have a serious impact on small craft and their moorings close to the shoreline and on shallow off-lying banks. For further details, see *Annual Notice to Mariners Number 23*.

Traffic separation schemes
1.9
1   Nearly all TSS in United Kingdom waters are IMO-adopted and Rule 10 of the *International Regulations for Preventing Collisions at Sea (1972)* applies.
1.10
1   The following TSS are established in the area covered by this volume:

Off The Smalls 51°45′·7N 5°52′·5W.

Holyhead Harbour entrance 53°19′·5N 4°36′·5W; this scheme is not IMO-adopted.

Off The Skerries 53°22′·8N 4°52′·0W to 53°32′·1N 4°31′·6W.

2   For TSS W of the Isles of Scilly (49°58′N 6°43′W) and off Land's End, between Seven Stones and Longships (50°03′N 5°58′W) see *Channel Pilot*.

For the TSS off Tuskar Rock (52°08′·5N 6°03′·8W) see *Irish Coast Pilot*.

Recreational craft
1.11
1   There are a great number of yacht marinas and other facilities for recreational craft placed at various ports and harbours throughout the coastal limits of this volume; concentrations of small craft therefore are always evident in popular sailing areas such as Milford Haven, the Menai Strait, Morecambe Bay and the Solway Firth, especially during the summer months. Marinas and small craft harbours with VHF facilities are listed in *Admiralty Maritime Communications*.

Fishing

General
1.12
1   The whole area covered by this volume, which lies within British fishery limits, is fished extensively and fishing vessels of many nationalities may be encountered.

Exclusive fishing limits extend up to 6 miles from the baselines of territorial water and for the next 6 miles fishing is limited to countries with established rights; these limits are shown on selected Admiralty charts.

2   Foreign fishing rights in the coastal waters of the British Isles are shown on chart Q6385; British fishery limits are shown on chart Q6353.

The Fishery Limits Act, 1976, extended British fishery limits to 200 nautical miles, or to such other limits as may be specified.

Methods of fishing
1.13
1   The principal methods of fishing in the area covered by this volume are: trawling, which includes the side trawl and twin beam trawl; scallop dredging; seine netting; potting and tangle netting; and diving.

Other methods such as drifting and long-lining may be encountered but these have largely been superseded by the principal methods previously mentioned; hand-lining from small boats may also be encountered, mainly in bays not far from the shore.

2   Care should be taken to keep well clear of vessels engaged in fishing; such vessels are hampered by their gear, may need to make unannounced manoeuvres, and may be unable to take avoiding action.

For details of fishing methods and nets used, see *The Mariner's Handbook*.

Exercise areas

Submarine exercises and operations
1.14

1   Submarines frequently exercise in an area of the Irish Sea which lies between the W coast of the Isle of Man and the E coast of Northern Ireland.

Information concerning submarines and warning signals is contained in the *Annual Notice to Mariners Number 8*.

2   **Subfacts.** Information relating to the activity of both surfaced and dived submarines off the S coast of England (see *Channel Pilot*) is broadcast by Brixham Coastguard and Falmouth Coastguard (Subfacts — South Coast). Information relating to the activity of submarines off the W coast of Scotland (see *West Coast of Scotland Pilot*) is broadcast by Belfast Coastguard, Clyde Coastguard and Stornoway Coastguard (Subfacts — Clyde). See *Admiralty List of Radio Signals Volume 3(1)* for details. In submarine exercise areas mariners may encounter submarines on the surface; a good lookout is essential when transiting these areas.

Firing practice areas
1.15

1   Firing and bombing practice and defence exercises, take place in a number of sea areas around the coasts of the United Kingdom. These areas, many of which are shown on navigational charts, are in use or are available for use, by the Ministry of Defence for practice and exercises, with or without live ammunition, and using a clear range procedure.

2   The designated Range Authorities are responsible for ensuring that there should be no risk of damage to any vessel which may be in a practice area.

For further details see *Annual Notice to Mariners Number 5*.

3   **Gunfacts.** Information relating to gunnery and missile firings of 20 mm calibre and above, and controlled underwater explosions in the South Coast Exercise Areas (see *Channel Pilot*), is broadcast by Brixham Coastguard and Falmouth Coastguard (Gunfacts — South Coast). Details of planned or known activity in the Scottish Exercise Areas is broadcast by Belfast Coastguard, Clyde Coastguard and Stornoway Coastguard (Gunfacts — Clyde). In all other areas, whenever firings are due to take place, warning broadcasts are made on VHF by a "Duty Broadcast Ship". See *Admiralty List of Radio Signals Volume 3(1)* for details. There are no restrictions placed on mariners transiting a firing practice area at any time. Such areas operate a clear range procedure, ensuring that firing will only take place when the area is clear of all shipping.

Limits
1.16

1   The limits of all submarine exercise and firing practice areas lying within the confines of this volume are shown on Practice and Exercise Areas (PEXA) charts Q6402 and Q6403.

Marine exploitation

Development of offshore oil and gas fields
1.17

1   Various types of ships, craft and fixed structures, used in the development of oil and gas fields, may be encountered in the Celtic and Irish Seas in increasing numbers.

Methods of search and production conform in general to those described in *The Mariner's Handbook*. Seismic and other survey vessels carrying out surveys in search of deposits of oil and gas may be encountered throughout the area.

2   Seismic survey methods are outlined in *The Mariner's Handbook*.

For details of fields in Liverpool Bay and Morecambe Bay see 9.4.

3   **Drilling rigs** operate in the Celtic and Irish Seas throughout the year. Buoys, lighters and other equipment associated with drilling operations are often laid near the rigs, and wires may extend up to 1½ miles from them.

4   Drilling rigs are not charted, but their positions are announced by NAVAREA 1 messages, when known, and are listed in *Admiralty Notices to Mariners*.

The positions of buoys laid near rigs are not usually announced, even if known, as the buoys are seldom laid for long enough in one position.

5   **Wellheads.** Wells no longer required for exploratory drilling are sealed off below the seabed, and the sites certified by divers as clear of obstructions. Suspended wells at which pipes and valve gear project, usually from 2 to 6 m and in some cases up to 15 m above the seabed, are charted; they are shown on charts either as obstructions or as a danger circle enclosing the depth over the wellhead, if known, and marked "Well".

Dredging
1.18

1   Dredging for sand and gravel is carried out on the shallow banks of the Bristol Channel.

CHARTS

Admiralty charts
1.19

1   All charts covering the area of this volume are in metric units. Most charts carry a source data diagram indicating the date and scale of the original surveys used to compile the chart. For further details see *The Mariner's Handbook*.

2   Much of the area is covered by recent Royal Navy surveys and data supplied by local harbour authorities. However, it should be noted that in some areas, particularly the North Cornwall Coast and parts of the Irish Sea, the only data available is from nineteenth century leadline surveys.

In some areas of frequent change periodic re-surveys are carried out.

1.20

1   **Horizontal datum.** All British Admiralty charts for the area covered by this book are referred to a WGS 84 compatible datum.

2   **Vertical datum** used for the reduction of soundings equates approximately to LAT. When predicting offshore tidal heights reference should be made to co-tidal Charts.

For an explanation of LAT and other datums see *Admiralty Tide Tables*.

AIDS TO NAVIGATION

Buoyage - General information
1.21

1   The IALA Maritime System (Region A) is in force throughout the area. *The Mariner's Handbook* should be consulted for details of the system.

Some of the coastal areas covered in this volume are subject to rapid and frequent change and buoys may be moved before notice of the move has been promulgated. Areas where this occurs are mentioned in the text.

2   Radar reflectors, fitted to the great majority of the important buoys, are not mentioned in the directions.

Oceanographical Data Buoys
1.22

1   Oceanographical data light buoys and buoys (special), including Ocean Data Acquisition Systems (ODAS) Light Buoys, which gather oceanographic and meteorological data for environmental research purposes, and which may vary considerably in size, may be encountered anywhere in the area. Many are laid temporarily only and not charted.

2   Oceanographical data buoys are described in *The Mariner's Handbook*; those that are permanent are shown on the charts, those temporary are given in *Admiralty Notices to Mariners*.

As the buoys have no navigational significance and as they are liable to be removed at short notice they are not normally mentioned in the text of this pilot. All data gathering buoys should be given a wide berth.

British Isles buoyage
1.23

1   **Authority.** Trinity House is the authority responsible for lights and buoys around the coasts of England, Wales and Channel Islands.

Firing practice areas are marked by buoys (special). Some buoys have the letters DZ and an identifying number painted on the side.

2   **Light vessels** are charted as light floats, or Lanbys, which are described in the *Admiralty List of Lights Volume A*. The smaller buoys are shown on the charts, but are not described in the *Admiralty List of Lights*.

PILOTAGE

General
1.24

1   Every port of any consequence within the area covered by this volume has its own authorised pilots; at minor ports, where no official pilotage organisation exists, local fishermen or boatmen are usually available to act as pilots.

2   Pilotage arrangements are described in the appropriate places in the volume and in *Admiralty List of Radio Signals Volume 6(1)* for places equipped with port radio.

Visual signals requesting a pilot at ports not equipped with VHF radio can be made on arrival.

Passage plans
1.25

1   Every British port is able to use its powers of direction under the Port Marine Safety Code to require that all vessels arriving, departing or transiting the waters of the port use an agreed pilotage passage plan, whether a pilot is embarked or not. Such requirements are generally incorporated in the General Directions for Navigation for the port.

Signals
1.26

1   **General.** With the exception of special signals at certain Bristol Channel ports, the usual signals to be made by a vessel requiring a pilot are those laid down in the International Code of Signals:

By day Flag G and by night Morse letter G ($- - \cdot$) by light.

In low visibility Morse letter P ($\cdot - - \cdot$) by sound.

2   **Bristol Channel.** The following signals in the Morse Code are used as distinctive pilot signals:

Pilotage districts	Number or letter	
Bristol		
Port of Bristol	2	$\cdot \cdot - - -$
Swansea		
Swansea	3	$\cdot \cdot \cdot - -$
Port Talbot	4	$\cdot \cdot \cdot \cdot -$
South-east Wales		
Barry	6	$- \cdot \cdot \cdot \cdot$
Cardiff-Inward	7	$- - \cdot \cdot \cdot$
Cardiff-Outward	N	$- \cdot$
Newport	8	$- - - \cdot \cdot$
Gloucester		
Port of Gloucester	9	$- - - - \cdot$

1.27

1   These signals will be made by the pilot vessel of the authorities in question, when engaged on pilotage duties on their respective stations, as follows:

At night, in clear weather, by flashing light at frequent intervals.

In thick or foggy weather, when the fog signal of a vessel is heard, by whistle.

2   Vessels desiring to embark or disembark a pilot are invited to adopt a similar procedure when approaching any of the pilotage stations concerned.

These signals are in addition to the usual day and night signals made by vessels requiring a pilot on the coasts of the United Kingdom.

Pilot vessels
1.28

1   Most British pilot vessels are black-hulled with the letter "P" or PILOT painted on the hull or superstructure; occasionally the name of the port is shown. Throughout the text of this volume pilot vessels are described where possible.

2   A pilot flag is flown when pilots are embarked. In low visibility a pilot vessel on pilotage duty may identify herself by sounding Morse letter H ($\cdot \cdot \cdot \cdot$).

Deep-sea pilots
1.29

1   Vessels inward bound for ports in NW Europe, including The British Isles and The Baltic, may wish to pick up deep-sea pilots before reaching the complex TSS in the Dover Strait and the North Sea. Such pilots, who are properly licensed, should be requested through one of several agencies based in the British Isles or other European countries.

2   Since deep-sea pilots may have to travel considerable distances to the port of embarkation, as much notice as possible should be given to the pilotage agency.

Outward vessels from ports contained in this volume and vessels coasting from port to port can make similar arrangements.

3   For a list of agencies and pilot authorities who provide deep-sea pilotage see *Admiralty List of Radio Signals Volume 6(1)*.

RADIO FACILITIES

Electronic position fixing systems
1.30

1   Full details of electronic position fixing systems, including satellite navigation systems, are given in *Admiralty List of Radio Signals Volume 2*, and in *The Mariner's Handbook*. Those with a limited applicability are described below.

Loran C. The Icelandic Chain provides groundwave coverage N of 52°N and skywave cover S of that latitude.

Radio aids to navigation
1.31

1   Full details of radio aids to navigation outlined below are given in *Admiralty List of Radio Signals Volume 2*. Individual stations and services which may be of assistance to the mariner are listed as necessary within the text of this volume.

DGPS. Beacons transmitting DGPS corrections cover the entire area of this volume.

2   **Racons** are fitted to many lighthouses, light-floats and buoys.

Automatic Identification System (AIS). For further details see 1.46 and United Kingdom, Ship Reporting Systems in *Admiralty List of Radio Signals Volume 6(1)*. General information about AIS may be found in *The Mariner's Handbook*. Mariners should note that AIS is also being fitted to offshore oil platforms, lighthouses and selected navigational buoys around the coast in order to enhance navigational safety.

VHF direction finding service for emergency use only is operated by UK Coastguard; see 1.70.

Radio navigational warnings
1.32

1   The area lies within the limits of NAV/METAREA I.
Navigation warnings can be obtained via NAVTEX service or from HM Coastguard stations.

Maritime Safety Information (MSI)
1.33

1   All MRCCs broadcast Maritime Safety Information including navigational warnings, gale warnings, shipping forecasts, local inshore forecasts and storm tide warnings. For further details see *Admiralty List of Radio Signals Volume 3(1)*.

Medical aid procedure
1.34

1   HMCG has responsibility for handling Medical Link Calls and PAN PAN MEDICO calls for vessels requiring medical advice or assistance. For further details see *Admiralty List of Radio Signals Volume 1(1)*.

Radio weather reports
1.35

1   Details of radio weather reports are given in *Admiralty List of Radio Signals Volume 3(1)*.

Small craft warnings. A Strong Winds Warning Service, which operates between Easter and October, gives warnings of winds of force 6 or more for sea areas out to 5 miles from many parts of the coast of the United Kingdom. Warnings are promulgated through local broadcasting stations and by UK Coastguard MRCCs on VHF.

2   Persons intending to put to sea can obtain information on current forecasts and warnings in force from the nearest Coastguard Rescue Centre; see 1.62 and *Admiralty List of Radio Signals Volume 3(1)*.

Coast radio stations
1.36

1   For a list of Coast Radio Stations and UK Coastguard MRCCs which are available within or adjacent to, the area covered by this volume, see *Admiralty List of Radio Signals Volume 1(1)*.

Port radio and radar stations
1.37

1   Port Radio Stations are in operation at all but the smallest ports and pilot vessels can also provide radio services.

General details of port radio, radar stations and small craft information (1.11), where applicable for the area covered by this volume, are given within the text; full details are given in *Admiralty List of Radio Signals Volume 6(1)*.

REGULATIONS — INTERNATIONAL

Submarine pipelines and cables

Submarine pipelines
1.38

1   An area W of the entrance to Morecambe Bay is crossed by submarine pipelines, which are shown on the chart with the appropriate legend (Gas), linking the offshore gasfields with the shore. Pipelines may be trenched or stand as much as 2 m proud of the seabed.

2   A charted gas interconnector pipeline lies between the Republic of Ireland and Scotland; its route lies NW of the Isle of Man.

See *The Mariner's Handbook* for a full description of pipelines.
1.39

1   **Caution.** Mariners are advised not to anchor or trawl in the vicinity of pipelines. Gas from a damaged oil or gas pipeline could cause an explosion, loss of a vessel's buoyancy or other serious hazard. Pipelines are not always buried and may effectively reduce the charted depth by up to 2 m. They may also span seabed undulations and cause fishing gear to become irrecoverably snagged, putting a vessel in severe danger. See *Annual Notice to Mariners Number 24* and *The Mariner's Handbook*.

Submarine cables
1.40

1   See *The Mariner's Handbook* for information on the International Convention for the Protection of Submarine cables.

Pollution of the sea

Marpol 73/78
1.41

1   *The Mariner's Handbook* gives a summary of The International Convention for the Prevention of Pollution from Ships 1973, as modified by the Protocol of 1978, and known as MARPOL 73/78.

Pollution reports. Under the Convention, a Master has a duty to report pollution incidents or damage and breakdowns affecting the safety of his vessel. For further details see *Admiralty List of Radio Signals Volume 1*.

2   **Special areas.** Under MARPOL 73/78 designated Special Areas, owing to their sensitive oceanographic and ecological conditions and to their maritime traffic, are provided with a higher level of protection and regulation than other areas of the sea. The North Sea region is regarded as a Special Area in respect of Annexes I (Oil) and V (Garbage from Ships) and, in respect of Annex VI (Air Pollution), it is a special SOx (sulphur oxide) Emission Control Area.

Western European Tanker Reporting System (WETREP)
1.42

1   The *Western European Tanker Reporting System (WETREP)*. It is a mandatory reporting system covering the Western European Particularly Sensitive Sea Area. The objectives of the system are to initiate SAR and measures to prevent pollution.

2   The system applies to every kind of oil tanker of more than 600 dwt carrying a cargo of:

Heavy crude oil.
Heavy fuel oil.
Bitumen and tar and their emulsions.

For limits of the area and further details see *Admiralty List of Radio Signals Volume 6(1)*.

REGULATIONS — EUROPEAN UNION

European Council Directive 2002/59/EC

General information
1.43

1   This Directive establishes a common vessel traffic monitoring and information system throughout European Union (EU) waters. The principal provisions are described below. They apply in general to all commercial vessels over 300 gt but the rules concerning the notification of carriage of dangerous and polluting goods apply to all vessels regardless of size.

2   **Caution.** These extracts are for reference purposes only and are not to be regarded as a statement of the applicable law. The full text of the regulations is the sole authoritative statement of the applicable law and should be consulted. The regulations to which the following refers is *Directive 2002/59/EC* or the appropriate enabling legislation drafted by individual member states, which in the United Kingdom is *The Merchant Shipping (Traffic Monitoring and Reporting Requirements) Regulations 2004*, a copy of which can be obtained from Her Majesty's Stationery Office (www.hmso.gov.uk).

Ship reports
1.44

1   All vessels bound for a port within the EC must report to the port authority at least 24 hours prior to arrival, or, if the voyage is less than 24 hours, no later than the time of departure from the previous port. The report shall include the following information:

Name, call sign, IMO or MMSI number.
Port of destination.
ETA and ETD at port of destination.
Total number of persons onboard.

2   Upon receipt of a ship's report, the port authority will notify the national coastguard authority by the quickest means possible. This information will then be pooled in the European-wide telematic network called SafeSeaNet.

Any amendments to the initial ship report must be notified immediately.

3   **Mandatory ship reporting systems.** All vessels shall report to the coastguard authority on entering an IMO adopted mandatory ship reporting system, the report being made in the recognised format. The coastguard authority is to be informed of any changes to the initial report.

See *Admiralty List of Radio Signals Volume 6(1)*.

VTS and routeing
1.45

1   **VTS.** All vessels are to participate in and comply with VTS systems operated by EC member states and also those systems operated by member states in conjunction with co-operating non-member states. This includes those systems operated by member states outside their territorial waters but which are operated in accordance with IMO guidelines.

2   **Routeing Schemes.** All vessels must comply with IMO recommended TSS and Deep Water route regulations. See IMO publication *Ships' Routeing Guide*.

AIS and VDR
1.46

1   All vessels are to be equipped with AIS and VDR. The systems shall be in operation at all times except where international rules provide for the protection of navigational information.

2   Coastguard stations throughout the EU are required to be able to receive AIS information and to relay it to all other coastguard stations within the EU.

For details see *Admiralty List of Radio Signals Volume 6(1)* and *The Mariner's Handbook*.

Notification of dangerous and polluting goods
1.47

1   All vessels leaving an EU port are to report dangerous and polluting goods as specified within the Directive to the harbour authority. Vessels arriving from outside EU waters must transmit a report to their first EU port or anchorage upon departure from their port of loading. If, at the time of departure, the port of destination in the EU is not known, the report must be forwarded immediately such information becomes known. Where practical, this report is to be made electronically and must include the information described in *Annex 1(3)* of the *Directive*.

2   When a harbour authority receives a dangerous or polluting cargo report, it shall retain the report for use in the event of an incident or accident at sea, forwarding it whenever requested by the national coastguard authority.

Reporting of incidents and accidents
1.48

1   Whenever a vessel is involved with one of the following, the coastguard authority of the EU coastal state is to be informed immediately:

(a) any incident or accident affecting the safety of the ship;
(b) any incident or accident which compromises shipping safety, such as a failure likely to affect a ship's manoeuvrability or seaworthiness;

2   (c) any event liable to pollute the waters or shores of the coastal state;
(d) the sighting of a slick of polluting material or drifting containers and packages.

The owner of a vessel, who has been informed by the master that one of the above has occurred, must inform the coastguard and render any assistance that may be required.

Measures to be taken in the event of exceptionally bad weather or sea conditions
1.49

1 If, on the advice of the national meteorological office, the coastguard authority deems a threat of pollution or a risk to human life exists due to impending severe weather, the coastguard authority will attempt to inform the master of every vessel about to enter or leave port as to the nature of the weather and the dangers it may cause.

2 Without prejudice to measures taken to give assistance to vessels in distress, the coastguard may take such measures as it considers appropriate to avoid a threat of pollution or a risk to human life. The measures may include:

(a) a recommendation or a prohibition on entry or departure from a port;

(b) a recommendation limiting, or, if necessary, prohibiting the bunkering of ships in territorial waters.

3 The master is to inform his owners of any measures or recommendations initiated by the coastguard. If, as a result of his professional judgement, the master decides not to act in accordance with measures taken by the coastguard, he shall inform the coastguard of his reasons for not doing so.

Measures relating to incidents or accidents at sea
1.50

1 The coastguard authority will take measures to ensure the safety of shipping and of persons and to protect the marine and coastal environment. Measures available to EU states include:

(a) a restriction on the movement of a ship or an instruction to follow a specific course;

(b) a notification to put an end to the threat to the environment or maritime safety;

2 (c) send an evaluation team aboard a ship to assess the degree of risk and to help the master remedy the situation;

(d) instruct the master to put in at a place of refuge in the event of imminent peril, or, cause the ship to be piloted or towed.

The owner of the ship and the owner of the dangerous or polluting goods onboard must cooperate with the coastguard authority when requested to do so.

Places of refuge
1.51

1 EU states are required to designate places of refuge where a vessel which has undergone an accident or is in distress can receive rapid and effective assistance to avoid environmental pollution.

Directive 2002/417EC

Single-hull petroleum tankers
1.52

1 This regulation establishes a timetable for the phasing out of all single-hull petroleum tankers of more than 5000 dwt in European waters. Ultimately only double-hull tankers or tankers of equivalent design will be permitted to visit European ports and offshore terminals.

2 The timetable is based upon a vessel's date of build, its design and the types of petroleum carried. The schedule for Category 1 and 2 tankers completed in 2007. Completion for Category 3 tankers will be in 2015.

Regulation 725/2004/EC
Measures to enhance maritime security
1.53

1 In compliance with Regulation 725/2004/EC, all vessels are required to provide security information, as required by SOLAS XI-2 and the ISPS Code, to the appropriate national authority 24 hours prior to arrival.

REGULATIONS — UNITED KINGDOM
Territorial waters
1.54

1 The baselines to be used for measuring the breadth of the territorial seas adjacent to the United Kingdom, the Channel Isles and the Isle of Man are defined in the *Territorial Waters Order in Council 1964* as amended by the *Territorial Waters (Amendment) Order 1998*. See Appendix II and III.

2 The *Territorial Seas Act 1987* enacts that the territorial waters of the United Kingdom, including the Isle of Man, shall extend for a distance of 12 miles from the baselines, while those of the Channel Islands extend 3 miles. See Appendices II and III.

Quarantine and customs regulations
1.55

1 Vessels arriving at any ports or harbours in the United Kingdom are subject to British quarantine and customs regulations.

In British territorial waters, no person is permitted to leave a vessel coming from a foreign place, except in the case of emergency, until pratique has been granted by the local authority.

2 The Master of a foreign-going vessel is required to inform the port health authority if any person onboard is suffering from an infectious disease or has symptoms which may be indicative of an infectious disease, or if there are any circumstances requiring the attention of the port medical officer. This information should be passed not more than 12 hours and not less than 4 hours before arrival. For details of quarantine reports, see *Admiralty List of Radio Signals Volume 1(1)*.

Regulations to prevent the spread of rabies
1.56

1 Stringent regulations are in force to prevent the spread of rabies into Great Britain.

The following is an extract from Article 12 of *The Rabies (Importation of Dogs, Cats and Other Mammals) Order 1974* (as amended 1977). This extract is applicable to any animal which has, within the preceding 6 months, been in a place outside Great Britain, Northern Ireland, the Republic of Ireland, the Channel Islands and the Isle of Man, except one for which an import licence has been issued.

2 It shall be the duty of a person having charge or control of a vessel in harbour in Great Britain to ensure that an animal which is onboard that vessel:

(a) is at all times restrained, and kept securely confined within a totally enclosed part of the vessel from which it cannot escape;

3 (b) does not come into contact with any other animal or any contact animal (other than an animal or contact animal with which it has been transported to Great Britain), and;

(c) is in no circumstances permitted to land.

4 If an animal to which the above extract applies is lost from a vessel in harbour, the person having charge or control of that vessel must immediately inform the Local Animal Health Officer from the State Veterinary Service, an agency of the Department for the Environment, Food and Rural Affairs, or the Police, or an officer of H.M. Revenue and Customs.

5 No native animals or contact animals are permitted to go onboard the vessel on which there is an animal from abroad. This does not apply to dogs belonging to the Police, HM Customs or the Armed Forces and under the constant control of a trained handler, nor to animals being loaded for export.

6 A contact animal is any one of 25 species, listed in an Appendix to the Order, which are not normally subject to quarantine for rabies unless they have been in contact with an animal which is subject to quarantine. For example, a horse, listed as contact animal, could become subject to quarantine if it came into contact with a dog or other animal which is subject to quarantine.

7 Other than in exceptional circumstances, only certain ports are authorised for the landing of animals for which an import licence has been issued; within the limits of this volume there are no such ports.

8 *The Pet Travel Scheme (Pilot Arrangements) (England) Order 1999* amends the above mentioned Order in respect of certain pet animals (cats and dogs only) which may be brought into the United Kingdom without being subject to quarantine provided a number of conditions are fulfilled. The scheme is limited to pets coming from certain designated countries and territories, and operates only on certain sea, air and rail routes to England by designated carriers. Pets may not be brought into the United Kingdom in any private vessel. The scheme is administered by the Department for the Environment, Food and Rural Affairs, from whom advice is available.

Protection of wrecks
1.57

1 In waters around the United Kingdom, the sites of certain wrecks are protected by the *Protection of Wrecks Act (1973)* from unauthorised interference on account of the historic, archaeological or artistic importance of the wreck or anything belonging to it; for further details and a list of protected wrecks, see *The Mariner's Handbook* and *Annual Notice to Mariners Number 16*.

2 To prevent the disturbance of the dead, similar protection applies to certain other vessels, which sank in the last 200 years, including aircraft, both in the United Kingdom and international waters under the terms of *Protection of Military Remains Act 1986*.

Protection of wildlife

General information
1.58

1 There are three government councils responsible for nature conservation in Great Britain: in England, English Nature, headquarters at Northminster House, Peterborough PE1 1VA; in Scotland, Scottish Natural Heritage, 12, Hope Terrace, Edinburgh EH9 2AS; in Wales, the Countryside Council for Wales, Ffordd Penrhos, Plas Penrhos, Bangor LL57 2LQ.

2 These conservation bodies give advice on nature conservation to government and to all those whose activities affect wildlife and wild places. They are also responsible for establishing, maintaining and managing a series of National Nature Reserves and Marine Reserves

and identifying and notifying Sites of Special Scientific Interest. The work is based on detailed ecological research and survey.

3 Information concerning bye-laws, codes of conduct, descriptions and positions of nature reserves and sites of special scientific interest can be obtained from the Councils whose addresses are given above.

National Nature Reserves. In 1999 there were nearly 300 National Nature Reserves in the United Kingdom; only those which can be found on or near the coastlines and river estuaries contained in this volume which may be of direct interest to the mariner are mentioned in the text; reserves are shown on certain charts of the British Isles.

4 **Marine Nature Reserves** provide protection for marine flora and fauna and geological and physiographical features on land covered by tidal waters up to and including the limit of territorial waters; they are shown on the chart. They also provide opportunities for study and research.

Local Nature Reserves. Local authorities in England and Wales and district councils in Scotland are able to acquire and manage local nature reserves in consultation with the conservation councils.

5 Conservation Trusts can also own and manage non-statutory local nature reserves; where necessary, the appropriate Trust name is given within the text of this volume.
1.59

1 **Royal Society for the Protection of Birds (RSPB),** is an organisation whose primary interest lies in the preservation of the many species of wild birds seen in Britain. For the purposes of this volume, only important bird reserves lying in and around the coastal areas which may be of direct interest to the mariner are mentioned.

2 Visiting a reserve in many cases is not encouraged and often not permitted whilst at others it is permitted but under arrangement and strict control.

Lists of important bird reserves can be found within the text to which reference is given as to whether visiting is permitted or not; reserves are shown on certain charts of the British Isles.

3 Further details can be obtained from: Head of Reserve Management, Royal Society for the Protection of Birds, The Lodge, Sandy. Bedfordshire. SG19 2DL.

DISTRESS AND RESCUE

General information

General arrangements for search and rescue
1.60

1 General arrangements for SAR in UK waters are given in *Annual Notice to Mariners Number 4*.

2 HM Coastguard (HMCG) (1.63) is the authority responsible for initiating and co-ordinating all civil maritime SAR operations in the United Kingdom Search and Rescue Region (UK SRR). This includes the mobilisation, organisation and tasking of adequate resources to respond to people either in distress at sea, or at risk of injury or death on the cliffs or shoreline of the United Kingdom.

3 The Ministry of Defence provides units to assist casualties on request from HMCG. RN and RAF SAR resources consist mainly of helicopters and maritime patrol aircraft, supplemented as necessary by other aircraft and surface vessels. The RN provides Explosive Ordnance Disposal Teams to deal with unexploded or suspect ordnance.

4 The Aeronautical Rescue Co-ordination Centre (ARCC) at Kinloss controls the operation of all armed forces SAR air resources within the UK SRR.

The Royal National Lifeboat Institution (RNLI) (1.72) provides all-weather and inshore lifeboats around the coast for saving life at sea.

5 Mariners are reminded that the radio watch on the international distress frequencies which certain classes of ships are required to keep when at sea is one of the most important factors in the arrangements for the rescue of people in distress at sea.

GMDSS
1.61
1 For full details of GMDSS see *Admiralty List of Radio Signals Volume 5*.

HM Coastguard

General information
1.62
1 HMCG is responsible for requesting and tasking SAR resources made available by other authorities and for co-ordinating the subsequent SAR operations unless they fall within the jurisdiction of the armed forces ARCC. Close liaison is maintained with adjacent SAR organisations.

Coastguard network
1.63
1 The UK SRR is bounded by Latitudes 45°N and 61°N (N of the Shetland Isles, 62°N), by Longitude 30°W, and to the E by the adjacent SRRs with whom UK Coastguard maintains a close liaison.

2 The UK is organised into three SRRs each under the authority of a Regional Inspector operating from a MRCC. Each region is divided into six districts with its own MRCC.

3 Each district is divided into sectors. Within each sector there are Coastguard Rescue Teams (CRTs) composed of Auxiliary Coastguards.

4 CRTs are situated at strategic locations around the coast, and are equipped to deal with incidents appropriate to the risks associated with local terrain, activities and conditions. Capability includes cliff and mud rescue, coastal searches and patrols. The smaller CRTs only provide an initial response for investigation, surveillance and reporting. The larger Auxiliary CRTs provide the initial response and additional capability.

Coastguard stations
1.64
1 The coast of Cornwall from the S limit of this book to the border with Devon (Marsland Mouth) is covered by MRCC Falmouth at Pendennis Point, Falmouth. Sectors with responsibility for the area covered by this volume are as follows:

North Cornwall (based at Wadebridge)
West Cornwall (based at Penzance)

2 North of the Cornwall/Devon border, the sea area covered by this volume lies within the Wales and West of England Region. The MRCC is at Tutt Head, Mumbles, Swansea SA3 4HW. This region is sub-divided into four districts, as follows:

Swansea (MRCC).
Milford Haven (MRCC).
Holyhead (MRCC).
Liverpool (MRCC).

3 Coastguard sectors in the Wales and West Region are as follows:

Bideford
Exmoor (based at Ilfracombe)
Severn (based at Clevedon)
Cardiff
Gower (based at Mumbles)
South Pembs (based at Tenby)
4 Preseli (based at Fishguard)
Tremadoc (based at Criccieth)
Clwyd (based at Bangor)
Anglesey (based at Holyhead)
Merseyside (based at Wirral)
Fylde (based at Lytham Saint Annes)
Cumbria (based at Whitehaven)
Solway (based at Kirkudbright)

Coastguard communications
1.65
1 UK Coastguard MRCCs maintain continuous watch on VHF Channel 16 and 70 for distress, urgency and safety calls, covering UK waters. A number of MRCCs also listen on 2187·5 kHz DSC in accordance with GMDSS.

2 The primary method for vessels to alert rescue services is GMDSS VHF or MF DSC. HMCG continue to monitor the R/T VHF distress channel by maintaining a loudspeaker watch.

3 **Note.** Radio and telephone traffic to and from Coastguard Co-ordination Centres is recorded for the purposes of public safety, preventing and detecting crime and to maintain the operational standards of HM Coastguard.

Reports of missing or overdue vessels.
1.66
1 HM Coastguard makes enquiries to determine the whereabouts of any vessel reported as missing or overdue to establish whether the vessel, its crew or passengers are at risk. Enquiries are made to owners, agents, Lloyds of London, port authorities and yacht clubs. If enquiries and broadcasts fail to locate the missing or overdue vessel then SAR operations will be initiated. Assistance may be requested from services outside UK SRR.

MSI
1.67
1 HMCG is responsible for the scheduled broadcast of MSI on VHF and MF R/T and NAVTEX. MSI originates mainly from the UKHO for Navigational Warnings and the Met Office for weather forecasts and warnings.

2 Navigation warnings broadcast by R/T by HMCG are restricted to WZ (Coastal Warnings) and Local Warnings. Navigation warnings broadcast by NAVTEX by HMCG also include NAVAREA ONE Warnings.

MSI broadcasts include Negative Tide Surge Warnings, SUBFACTS (1.14) and GUNFACTS (1.15), ice warnings, and interruption to electronic navigation aids.

Medical link calls
1.68
1 HMCG provides a TELEMEDICAL Advice Service (TMAS). Mariners who need medical advice or assistance should call the nearest coastguard station on DSC (MF of VHF) or VHF Channel 16. The Coastguard will transfer the call to a working frequency and connect the caller to a casualty doctor. The Coastguard will monitor the call, while the doctor assesses the patient, and a decision is made what assistance is necessary.

2   For details see *Admiralty List of Radio Signals Volume 1(1)*.

Voluntary Safety Identification Scheme
1.69
1   HMCG promotes a Voluntary Safety Identification Scheme. Owners complete form CG66 with details of the vessel and its normal area of operation. HMCG puts the detail into a database for easy access later and returns an acknowledgement pack containing safety information and a card explaining how to contact the Coastguard. The owner should give the card to a responsible person. That person should contact the Coastguard if the safety of the vessel is in doubt.

2   Further details can be obtained from any Coastguard Station.

Direction-finding stations for use in emergency
1.70
1   UK Coastguard operate a VHF DF service for SAR purposes at over 40 stations around the United Kingdom. Triangulation from adjacent RCCs can be used to establish the position of a vessel in distress.

Within the limits of this book there are eight stations as follows:

	Station	*Position*	*MRCC*
2	Lands End	50°08′N 5°38′W	Falmouth
	Trevose Head	50°33′N 5°02′W	Falmouth
	Hartland	51°01′N 4°31′W	Swansea
	Saint Ann's Head	51°41′N 5°10′W	Milford Haven
	Rhiw	52°50′N 4°38′W	Holyhead
	Great Ormes Head	53°20′N 3°51′W	Holyhead
	Walney Island	54°07′N 3°16′W	Liverpool
	Snaefell	54°16′N 4°28′W	Liverpool

3   For further details including a full list of stations around the United Kingdom, see *Admiralty List of Radio Signals Volume 1(1)*.

National Coastwatch Institution
1.71
1   National Coastwatch Institution is a voluntary organisation which maintains a visual lookout from coastal vantage points and monitors the VHF radio distress frequency, reporting incidents to the Coastguard. In addition, stations monitor local weather conditions and provide information to mariners on request. Some stations are equipped with radar. Within the limits of this book there are lookout stations at:

2   Cape Cornwall
St Ives
Stepper Point
Boscastle
Barry Island
Worms Head
Rossall Point

Royal National Lifeboat Institution

General information
1.72
1   The Royal National Lifeboat Institution (RNLI) is a voluntarily supported organisation whose headquarters are at West Quay Road, Poole, Dorset BH15 1HZ.

2   The RNLI maintains a fleet of more than 450 lifeboats of various types and there are 220 lifeboat stations around the coasts of the United Kingdom and the Republic of Ireland. Many of the stations operate all-weather (offshore) lifeboats often supported by inshore lifeboats, if not on a permanent basis then during the summer months; some stations operate inshore lifeboats only.

Lifeboat characteristics
1.73
1   **All-weather lifeboats** have the following characteristics:
Length between 10 and 17 m.
Speed: all boats capable of 16 kn or more.
Radius of action of about 140-250 miles.
Equipment: radar; D/F on 2182 kHz and VHF; communications on MF (2182 kHz) and VHF (FM) RT channels 0 and 16.
Blue quick flashing light exhibited at night, when on service.

1.74
1   **Inshore lifeboats** have the following characteristics:
Inflatable or rigid inflatable construction.
Outboard motor(s).
Speed 20 to 30 kn.
RT VHF (FM) multi-channels including 0.

Lifeboat stations
1.75
1   **All-weather lifeboats** are stationed as follows:
Saint Ives (2.40).
Padstow (2.69).
Appledore (3.35).
Ilfracombe (3.50).
Angle (5.41).
Saint Davids (Porthstinian) (5.121).
Barry Dock (4.19).
2   The Mumbles (3.98).
Tenby (3.62).
Fishguard (5.177).
New Quay (6.44).
Barmouth (6.63).
Pwllheli (6.81).
Porth Dinllaen (7.13).
Holyhead (7.60).
3   Moelfre (7.127).
Llandudno (8.19).
Rhyl (8.24).
Hoylake (8.14).
Lytham Saint Anne's (9.25).
Fleetwood (9.47).
Barrow (9.76).
Workington (10.50).
Port Saint Mary (IoM) (10.172).
Douglas (IoM) (10.190).
Ramsey (IoM) (10.212).
Peel (IoM) (10.244).
4   **Inshore lifeboats** are permanently stationed as follows:
Saint Ives (2.40).
Saint Agnes (2.63).
Newquay (2.59)*.
Rock (2.69).
Port Isaac (2.69).
Clovelly (3.45).
Appledore (3.35).
Ilfracombe (3.50).
5   Minehead (4.150)*.
Weston-super-Mare (4.174)*.
Penarth (4.56)*.
Atlantic College, Saint Donat's (4.19).
Porthcawl (3.195).

Port Talbot (3.190).
The Mumbles (3.98).
Horton/Port-Eynon (3.89).
6 Burry Port (3.62).
Tenby (3.62).
Angle (5.41).
Little/Broad Haven (5.121).
Saint Davids (Porthstinian) (5.121).
Fishguard (5.177).
Cardigan (6.29)*.
New Quay (6.44).
7 Aberystwyth (6.46).
Borth (6.63).
Aberdovey (6.69).
Barmouth (6.63).
Criccieth (6.108).
Pwllheli (6.81)*.
Abersoch (6.84).
8 Trearddur Bay (7.44).
Holyhead (7.60).
Moelfre (7.127).
Beaumaris (7.158).
Conwy (7.144).

Llandudno (8.19)*.
Rhyl (8.24)*.
9 Flint (8.33).
West Kirby (8.33).
New Brighton (8.60).
Lytham Saint Anne's (9.25).
Blackpool (9.18)†.
Fleetwood (9.47).
Barrow (9.76).
10 Morecambe (9.38).
Saint Bees Head (9.115).
Silloth (10.63).
Kippford (10.29).
Kirkcudbright (10.111).
Port Erin (IoM) (10.226).
Port Saint Mary (IoM) (10.172).

11 **Inshore lifeboats** are stationed during the summer months only as follows:
Bude (2.92).

* Denotes two similar boats stationed at the same location.

† Denotes three similar boats stationed at the same location.

COUNTRIES AND PORTS

UNITED KINGDOM

General description
1.76

1   The United Kingdom of Great Britain and Northern Ireland is a constitutional monarchy comprising England, Scotland, Wales and Northern Ireland, but does not include the Isle of Man or Channel Islands which are Crown dependencies. The Sovereign is also Head of the Commonwealth.

2   The area and population (2001 Census) of the United Kingdom are as follows:

Country	Area		Population
	Sq miles	Sq km	
England	50 053	130 281	49 138 831
Wales	7 969	20 732	2 903 085
Scotland	29 778	77 925	5 062 011
Northern Ireland	5 206	14 135	1 685 267

History
1.77

1   During the first four centuries A.D., Britain was a province of the Roman Empire, which withdrew its protection in 429. The country then fell into the power of the Saxon invaders from the continent of Europe. There followed a long rivalry for leadership between various Anglo-Saxon kings and invasion by the Vikings from Scandinavia. The various kingdoms were joined into one in the early tenth century and ruled by Saxon kings until the land was conquered by the Danes in 1016. The Saxon house was restored 26 years later.

2   Meanwhile in Europe in the tenth century, a Viking settlement in Normandy was becoming a feudatory in France. It was from this Duchy that the future rulers of England were to come. In 1066, Duke William of Normandy laid claim to the English throne, invaded and conquered the country, and founded the Norman dynasty. The monarchial system of rulers continued by descent, though not without dispute, for nearly 500 years until 1649 when it was overthrown by Oliver Cromwell, who created the Protectorate. With his death in 1658, a reaction against the Protectorate and strife over his successor resulted in the restoration of the monarchy in 1660, which has continued uninterrupted to the present day.

3   The eighteenth century was marked by gradual increase in the power of Parliament, rise of political parties, advances in colonization and trade, and progress of Britain as a sea power.

Wales, Cymru. The earliest inhabitants of Wales were of Celtic origin, and their present descendants, The Welsh, are a distinct nationality with a language and literature of their own.

Conquest of Wales by the Romans, for sometime successfully opposed, was completed in A.D.78, and under them Christianity was introduced in the fourth century.

4   After the withdrawal of the Romans a number of independent Kingdoms emerged. Attempts at unity were made during the ninth and tenth centuries but were only partially successful. Subsequent to the death of Rhodri Mawr (878), King of Gwynedd, pressure was brought to bear by his sons and also by Mercia on the Kings of Dyfed, Brycheiniog, Glywyoing and Gwent which caused them to commend themselves and ultimately render homage

and fealty to the King of Wessex. Finally, the sons of Rhodri submitted to Alfred the Great completing the theoretical subjection of Wales. Turmoil continued, internal conflicts aggravated by Norse, Anglo-Saxon and finally Norman invasions. The last native Prince was killed in 1282. The Statute of Wales, 1284, finally brought the country under the English crown and the Principality was created with the eldest son of Edward I created Prince of Wales, a title which the Monarch's eldest son bears to this day.

5   A National Assembly for Wales, with power to make secondary legislation in the areas where executive functions have been transferred to it, was created in 1999.

Government
1.78

1   The supreme legislative power is vested in Parliament, which is divided into two Houses of Legislature, the Lords and the Commons, and its present form dates from the middle of the fourteenth century, although in 1999 the House of Lords was reformed to exclude the majority of hereditary peers and peeresses.

2   The House of Lords is non-elected and consists of life peers and peeresses, Law Lords, two archbishops and 24 bishops of the established Church of England, and, as an interim measure, 92 hereditary peers and peeresses. The House of Lords has judicial powers as the ultimate Court of Appeal for courts in Great Britain and Northern Ireland, except for criminal cases in Scotland.

3   The House of Commons consists of members representing county and borough constituencies. Every constituency returns a single member. In 2005 there was a total of 659 members, 529 from England, 72 from Scotland, 40 from Wales and 18 from Northern Ireland. Suffrage is limited to men and women of 18 years and above.

4   The executive government is vested nominally in the Crown, but is exercised in practice by the Cabinet, a committee of ministers, which is dependent on the support of the majority in the House of Commons. The Prime Minister presides over the Cabinet and dispenses the greater portion of the patronage of the Crown.

5   In Scotland, where the judiciary and certain other areas of government still differ significantly from those of the remainder of the United Kingdom, the Scottish Parliament, first elected in 1999, has legislative power over all matters not reserved to the United Kingdom Parliament in Westminster, or otherwise outside its powers.

6   **Isle of Man,** with an area of 221 square miles and a population in 2001 of 76 315, is administered in accordance with its own laws by the Court of Tynwald, consisting of the Governor, appointed by the Crown, the Legislative Council comprising official members, members nominated by the Governor, and members elected by the House of Keys, and the House of Keys, a representative assembly.

7   The island is not bound by Acts of Parliament unless specifically mentioned in them.

Language. English is the official language of the United Kingdom but Welsh is spoken by approximately 19% of the inhabitants of Wales.

Coastal features and rivers
1.79

1   Generally speaking, the S, Central and N portions of the coastal area covered by this volume consist of uplands composed of sedimentary rock with outcrops of igneous rock; Wales, the central portion, and the Lake District, in the N portion, contain the highest of the land masses.

2   These uplands are separated by the lowland areas of the River Severn estuary, at the head of the Bristol Channel, and the Lancashire/Cheshire Plain at the head of Liverpool and Morecambe Bays.

2   Numerous rivers flow into the sea; the principal ones are the Rivers Taw, Torridge, Parrett, Avon, Severn, Wye, Usk, Taff, Neath, Tawe, Towy, Cleddau, Dovey (Dyfi), Mawddach, Conwy, Dee, Mersey, Ribble and Lune.

The estuaries of these rivers contain ports of varying size and importance which are described in the text of this volume.

Industry and trade
1.80
1   The United Kingdom is more dependent than most countries on its trade and industries. Major industries are iron and steel, heavy engineering, vehicle manufacture, shipbuilding, aircraft and the processing of imported goods such as wool, cotton and tobacco. With the decline of some of the more traditional industries a new range has emerged such as nuclear power equipment, instruments, electronics, man-made fibres and chemical products.

2   Considerable quantities of crude oil are imported to be refined into petroleum products.

The production of oil and gas from offshore fields plays an ever increasing part in the country's industry and technology.

The country is extensively farmed, mainly for home consumption but an important export trade in agricultural products has been established.

PRINCIPAL PORTS, HARBOURS AND ANCHORAGES
1.81

	Place and Position	Remarks
1	Swansea Bay: Swansea (3.111) (51°37'N 3°56'W)	Large commercial port; petrochemical, bulk and general cargo terminal.
	Neath (3.140) (51°37'N 3°50'W)	Commercial port; chemical terminal.
	Port Talbot (3.163) (51°34'N 3°48'W)	Commercial port for bulk iron ore and coal.
2	Breaksea Point (4.25) (51°23'N 3°24'W)	Deep-draught anchorage.
	Barry Roads (4.25) (51°23'N 3°14'W)	General anchorage.
	Barry (4.26) (51°24'N 3°16'W)	Commercial port.
3	Cardiff (4.69) (51°27'N 3°10'W)	Large commercial port.
	Newport (4.112) (51°33'N 2°59'W)	Large commercial port. Major timber handling terminal.
	Port of Bristol (4.192) (51°30'N 2°42'W)	Major commercial port for the area. Comprises Royal Portbury Dock (4.219) and Avonmouth Docks (4.220).

	Place and Position	Remarks
4	Port of Gloucester (4.278) (51°43'N 2°29'W)	Commercial port at Sharpness. Access to Gloucester and Sharpness Canal.
	Milford Haven (5.50) (51°42'N 5°02'W)	Major oil terminal. Deep-draught berths.
	Port of Pembroke (5.100) (51°42'N 4°57'W)	Small commercial port and ferry terminal within Milford Haven.
5	Fishguard Harbour (5.182) (52°00'N 4°59'W)	Commercial and ferry port. RoRo facilities.
	Holyhead Harbour (7.60) (53°19'N 4°37'W)	Commercial and ferry port. Harbour of refuge.
6	River Mersey: Port of Liverpool (8.68) (53°25'N 3°00'W)	Major commercial port. Comprises Royal Seaforth Dock (8.100), Liverpool Docks (8.101), Birkenhead Docks (8.103) and Tranmere Oil Terminal (8.104).
	Garston Docks (8.115) (53°21'N 2°54'W)	Commercial port.
7	Port of Manchester (8.136) (53°28'N 2°17'W)	Major commercial port. Comprises Eastham (8.154), Ellesmere Port (8.157), Stanlow (8.158), Ince (8.161), Weston Point (8.164), Runcorn Docks (8.166), Partington Basin (8.171), Barton (8.174) and Salford Quay (8.178).
	Fleetwood (9.47) (53°56'N 3°00'W)	Major fishing port and commercial and yachting port. RoRo facilities.
8	Heysham (9.67) (54°02'N 2°55'W)	Commercial port and ferry terminal. RoRo facilities. Supply base for Morecambe Bay Gas Field.
	Barrow-in-Furness (9.76) (54°06'N 3°13'W)	Shipbuilding and commercial port.
9	Workington (10.50) (54°39'N 3°34'W)	Commercial port.
	Isle of Man: Douglas (10.190) (54°09'N 4°00'W)	Commercial port. Ferry terminal. RoRo facilities.

PORT SERVICES — SUMMARY
Docking facilities
1.82
1   The summary below lists ports with docking facilities and where available the dimensions of the largest vessel that can be accommodated. Details of dock sizes are given at the reference.

2   Appledore. Dry dock; 13 000 dwt (3.40).
Newport (South Wales). Dry dock (4.134).
Sharpness. Dry dock; length 103·63 m; beam 14·63 m; draught 4·25 m (4.300).

3   Milford Haven. Dry dock; length 183·0 m; beam 19·0 m; draught 6·0 m; 8000 dwt (5.104).

Liverpool Docks. Four dry docks; length 217·0 m; beam 27·5 m; draught 8·75 m (8.107).

Birkenhead (Riverside). Three dry docks (8.107).

4   Bidston Docks. Dry dock; length 175·0 m; beam 22·86 m (8.107).

Runcorn. Side slipway; length 39·62 m; draught 2·0 m; 170 dwt (8.166).

Manchester. Two dry docks; length 156·0 m; beam 18·0 m; draught 5·05 m; 12 500 dwt (8.179).

5   Fleetwood. Patent slip; length 55·0 m; beam 11·0 to 14·17 m depending on lock invert clearance; 1000 dwt (9.57).

Barrow. Mechanical lift; not normally available for commercial dockings (9.96).

Ramsey. Gridiron; 300 grt capacity (10.220).

Other facilities

Salvage services
1.83

1   Newport (South Wales) (4.135).
Bristol (4.223).
Milford Haven (5.105).
Holyhead (7.92).
Liverpool (8.108).

Compass adjustment
1.84

1   Facilities for compass adjustment usually exist at ports where major repairs or shipbuilding are carried out.

Compass adjusting can be carried out at the following ports:

2   Newport (4.135).
Holyhead (7.92).
Liverpool (8.108).
Fleetwood (9.57).

Ship Sanitation Certificates (SSCs)
1.85

1   The following ports issue Ship Sanitation Certificates (SSCs) and Ship Sanitation Exeption Certificates (SSECs):
Swansea (3.136).
Barry (4.50).
Cardiff (4.96).
Newport (South Wales) (4.135).
Bristol (4.223).

2   Sharpness/Gloucester (4.301).
Milford Haven (5.105).
Fishguard (5.189).
Holyhead (7.92).
Liverpool (8.108).
Manchester (8.180).

3   Fleetwood (9.57).
Glasson Dock/Lancaster (9.59).
Barrow-in-Furness (9.96).
Whitehaven (10.49).
Workington (10.62).
Douglas (IoM) (10.199).

Measured distance
1.86

1   Midway along the E side of Lundy (51°10′N 4°40′W) (3.14).

NATURAL CONDITIONS

MARITIME TOPOGRAPHY

Charts 1123, 1121
Seabed
1.87

1 The Celtic Sea is composed of a series of banks, some of considerable length but of no great breadth, all of which lie in a NE/SW direction. Labadie Bank (50°35′N 8°10′W), in the approach to the Bristol Channel, is the most clearly defined and has a least known depth of 62 m.

Haig Fras (50°12′N 7°56′W), a bank with a depth of 38 m, is the shoalest bank in the Celtic Sea.

The bottom of the Celtic Sea appears to consist of sands, a great deal of broken shell and occasional patches of pebbles, gravel, small stones and possibly mud.

2 The approaches to the Bristol Channel are mainly a featureless area composed chiefly of sands, though to the N, depths increase to over 120 m in the gulley known as the Celtic Deep. The Bristol Channel itself has a mainly sandy bottom at its W end with some mud patches, whereas farther E there are areas of gravel and rock outcrops. The N edge of the channel is characterised by a series of sand banks, the shapes and depths of which are constantly changing.

3 Saint George's Channel and the Irish Sea, W of the Isle of Man, contain a series of depressions with depths of more than 100 m culminating in the Celtic Deep (described above) at the S end. The bottom is mainly composed of sand and gravel though there are areas of mud to the S and E of the Isle of Man. Within Cardigan Bay there are a series of ridges which run NE/SW from the coast. Depths in the E part of the Irish Sea are mainly in the range of 20 to 50 m. The exceptions to this are King William Banks, Ballacash Bank and Bahama Banks, within 12 miles of the NE end of the Isle of Man, where there are depths of less than 2 m. Depths of less than 15 m will also be encountered up to 20 miles SE of the NE end of the island; the bottom again, is mainly composed of sand but with areas of mud and gravel.

Charts 1410, 1978
4 **Sandwaves** some of which reach a height of 7 m above the seabed, exist in Cardigan Bay, off the N coast of Wales and Liverpool Bay. For further details on sandwaves see *The Mariner's Handbook*.

CURRENTS, TIDAL STREAMS AND FLOW

Currents

North Atlantic Current
1.88

1 In the North Atlantic Ocean, E of 46°W, the Gulf Stream ceases to be a well defined current, becoming weaker and broader along the E side of the Grand Banks of Newfoundland. The wide NE and E flow is directed across the ocean towards the British Isles and adjacent European coasts.

Currents diagram
1.89

1 In the currents diagram (1.89) arrows indicate predominant direction, average rate and constancy, which are defined as follows:

Predominant direction. The mean direction within a continuous 90° sector containing the highest proportion of observations from all sectors.

2 **Average rate,** to the nearest ¼ kn, of the highest 50% in the predominant sectors as indicated by the figures in the diagram.

Constancy, as indicated by the thickness of the arrows, is a measure of its persistence, eg low constancy implies marked variability in rate and, particularly, direction.
1.90

1 A current setting NE into the Celtic Sea and Saint George's Channel, then N and NW through North Channel, may follow prolonged S or SW gales. Similarly, S sets may follow prolonged N gales. Strong and persistent E winds may generate a W current from Liverpool Bay across the Irish Sea, passing S of the Isle of Man towards the Irish coast. Its significance is enhanced by the rate of the tidal stream which sometimes sets W from off the S coast of the Isle of Man towards the Irish coast.

For further information see *The Mariner's Handbook*.

Tidal streams

General remarks
1.91

1 The following brief general account is intended to describe only the principal features of the tidal streams in the Celtic Sea, the Bristol Channel, Saint George's Channel and the Irish Sea.

Data for predicting should be obtained from information on the relevant charts and/or *Admiralty Tidal Stream Atlases — The English Channel* and *the Irish Sea and Bristol Channel*.
1.92

1 **Celtic Sea.** In the centre of the Celtic Sea, the streams are generally weak, their rates seldom exceeding ½ kn. Closer inshore, the rates are greater, following the general direction of the coastline.
1.93

1 **Bristol Channel entrance.** The times at which the in-going and out-going streams of the Bristol Channel begin differ greatly from the times at which they begin in Saint George's Channel.

For information see *Admiralty Tidal Stream Atlas — Irish Sea and Bristol Channel*.
1.94

1 **Saint George's Channel and the Irish Sea.** The in-going streams run towards the Irish Sea through Saint George's Channel and the North Channel nearly simultaneously, and the out-going streams run in the reverse directions. The out-going streams run in the reverse directions.

2 Both the in-going streams divide into two branches, W and E. The W branches meet S of the channel between the Isle of Man and Ireland, in a large area SW of the Calf of Man; in this area, the streams are weak and irregular throughout the whole period of the in-going stream. The E branch of the Saint George's Channel stream runs between the Isle of Man and Anglesey to Liverpool Bay and Morecambe Bay; the E branch of the North Channel stream runs between the Isle of Man and Scotland to the Solway Firth and also towards Morecambe Bay and Liverpool Bay, joining the E branch of the Saint George's Channel stream E of the Isle of Man.

3 There are great differences between the streams in the fairways and near the land; data regarding the coastal

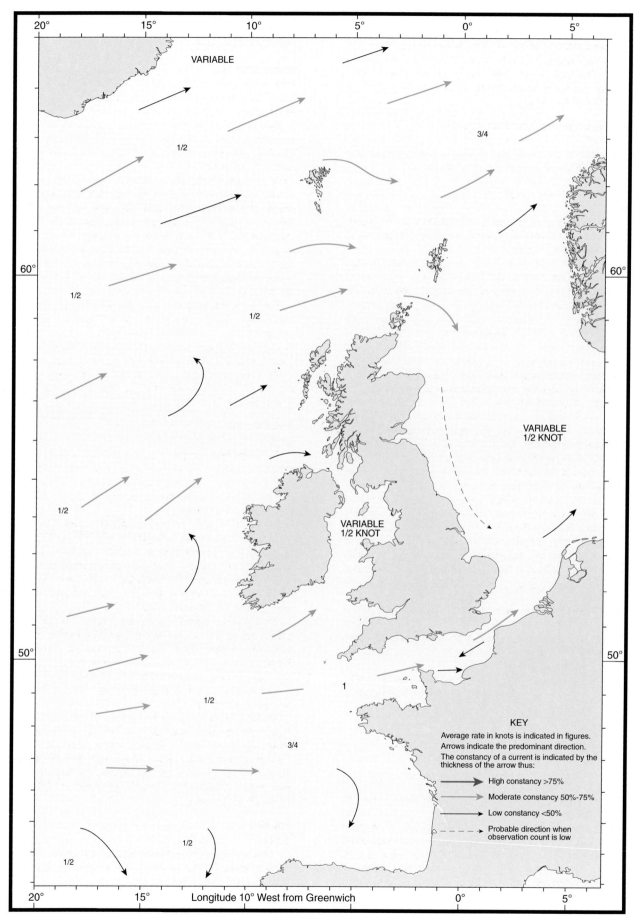

VARIABLE

3/4

1/2

1/2

1/2

1/2

VARIABLE
1/2 KNOT

1/2

VARIABLE
1/2 KNOT

1

1/2

3/4

1/2

1/2

KEY

Average rate in knots is indicated in figures.
Arrows indicate the predominant direction.
The constancy of a current is indicated by the
thickness of the arrow thus:

High constancy >75%

Moderate constancy 50%-75%

Low constancy <50%

Probable direction when
observation count is low

Longitude 10° West from Greenwich

Predominant surface currents JANUARY to DECEMBER (1.89)

streams should be obtained from the descriptions given at the appropriate places in this volume.

4   **Caution.** The in-going streams which meet W of the Calf of Man appear to have a tendency to turn W and set towards the Irish coast. This set may be considerable, especially during E winds. There appears to be no W set on the out-going stream.

Conditions that affect tidal streams
1.95

1   The tidal stream may be affected by both wind-drift currents (1.90) and storm surges (1.99).

Tide races and tide-rips
1.96

1   Tide races and tide-rips are usually marked on the chart, and should be treated with respect; many are dangerous to small craft.

Noticeable tide races and tide-rips within this volume are listed, as appropriate, in each chapter.

Descriptions of tide races and tide-rips are given in *The Mariner's Handbook*.

Flow
1.97

1   The main component of the flow of water contained within this volume is the tidal stream (see 1.91) and tidal rates vary considerably throughout the area.

Midway between Hartland Point and Lundy at the entrance to the Bristol Channel the spring rate is about 3 kn and between Lundy and the S coast of Wales the rate is about half that of the former.

2   Farther E into the Bristol Channel rates generally increase until the entrance to the River Severn is reached where a rate of 8 kn can be attained.

Off the W coast of Wales, spring rates are about 5 kn and are only exceeded by the rates in Jack Sound, Ramsey Sound, and Bardsey Sound.

3   Farther N, rates of between 5 and 6 kn can be expected off South Stack and between The Skerries and Carmel Head (Isle of Anglesey). Similar rates can be attained along the N coast of Anglesey; offshore here the streams are rectilinear.

In the Menai Strait, rates can reach 8 kn through the restricted waterway at its N end.

4   Within the River Dee estuary the spring rate is about 4 kn and in the entrance channels to the River Mersey about 4½ kn.

Elsewhere, in the Solway Firth rates can attain 5 to 6 kn at its inner end whilst off the Isle of Man a rate of about 5 kn is reached in the vicinity of the Calf of Man.

SEA LEVEL AND TIDES

Sea level

General remarks
1.98

1   Observed tidal levels rarely coincide exactly with those published in *Admiralty Tide Tables*. Differences, which are usually small, result from the effect of wind and/or variations in the barometric pressure. Significant events, in the United Kingdom where variations exceed 0·6 m, are termed storm surges (1.99). Strong winds may also cause differences between predicted and actual times of HW and LW. Ports where the effect of strong winds on the tides is noticeable, are mentioned in the text. Tidal streams and

currents are markedly affected by strong winds. See 1.100. For further details see *Admiralty Tide Tables* and *The Mariner's Handbook*.

Storm surges
1.99

1   In deep water, a storm generates long waves which travel faster than the storm so that the energy put into them is soon dissipated. In shallow water, however, the speed of these long waves falls, and in depths of about 100 m their speed is reduced to about 60 kn, which may be near the speed of the storm. If the storm keeps pace with the long waves, it will continuously feed energy into them.

2   The severity of a storm surge depends not only on the speed of advance, size and intensity of the original depression, but also upon its position in relation to the coast and the depth of water in the vicinity. A severe storm surge can be expected when a deep depression moves at a critical speed across the head of a bight or similar area of restricted water with storm force winds blowing into the bight.

3   Positive storm surges, which travel as waves, can attain considerable height and if the peak coincides with HW springs along a stretch of low-lying coastline, serious inland flooding can result; negative storm surges, on the other hand, can considerably reduce sea level.

4   Advance warnings of storm surges are given to the emergency services around the coast of the United Kingdom.

Tidal surges
1.100

1   **Negative tidal surges** are important to the mariner. In a somewhat similar manner to storm surges described above, tide levels can also be lower than the predicted level thereby affecting under-water clearances. Again the cause is usually meteorological.

2   Instances of high barometric pressure and light winds result in a lowering of tidal levels with the change being approximately 1 cm for each hPa of deviation from the average local pressure. Thus pressures exceeding 1040 hPa are likely to reduce tidal levels by 0·3 m. Such events can be expected to occur several times each year and the effect may persist for several days.

3   Strong winds from the NNE are likely to result in even greater reductions of tidal levels. The Morecambe Bay area is prone to this effect. Recent records for Barrow and Heysham show levels reduced by 0·5 m around ten times per year with a reduction of 1 m perhaps once a year.

For details of a warning service see *Annual Notice to Mariners Number 15*.

4   **Positive tidal surges.** Strong winds from the SW drive water into the Irish Sea and raise sea level. The effect is more significant in the shallow extremities such as the Liverpool/Morecambe Bay areas and Severn Estuary. Surges of 1 m or more can be expected perhaps ten times per year. In January 1991 a surge peak of 2·3 m was recorded at Heysham.

Seiches
1.101

1   Abrupt changes in meteorological conditions, such as the passage of an intense depression or line squall, may cause oscillations in sea level.

Small seiches are not uncommon round the coast of the British Isles. The shape and size of certain harbours makes them very susceptible to seiches, especially in winter months. Fishguard is an example of such a harbour.

2   For further information see *Admiralty Tide Tables* and *The Mariner's Handbook*.

Tides

General
1.102

1   The tide is predominantly semi-diurnal off the W coast of England and Wales and entering the area from S progresses NE into the Bristol Channel and the Irish Sea and from N into the Irish Sea and the Solway Firth.

HW is about 7 hours earlier off Cape Cornwall (50°08′N 5°43′W) than off the Mull of Galloway (54°38′N 4°51′W).

2   Where necessary, changes in the actual times at which the streams begin, or in relation between the stream and HW at the named Standard Port, are given in the text of this volume.

Tidal ranges
1.103

1   The mean spring range is greatest, 12·3 m, at the head of the Bristol Channel, and least, 3·8 m, at the SW end of Lleyn Peninsula, Gwynedd.

For information on tidal ranges and equal times of tides, see Chart 5058.

SEA AND SWELL

General remarks
1.104

1   For general information see *The Mariner's Handbook*.

Sea conditions
1.105

1   Sea waves are generated locally and can be variable in direction. The roughest seas are experienced with winds from between S and NW. Strong E winds can also give rise to rough seas on the N coast of Anglesey and the E coast of the Isle of Man. Winter is the stormiest season with 60% of observations over the open sea recording seas of over 2 m; this reduces to 20% by July.

2   Funnelling makes Saint George's Channel especially susceptible to very rough seas in strong S winds, similarly the North Channel with W to NW gales. Strong W winds in the Solway Firth give rise to rough seas as far as Workington.

Swell conditions
1.106

1   Diagrams 1.106.1 to 1.106.4 give swell roses for January, April, July and October. The roses show the percentage of observations recording swell from a number of directions and for various ranges of wave height.

2   In the S of the area the predominant swell waves are from between SW and NW. Over 3 m is recorded on 40% of occasions in winter and 10% in summer. SW swells occur on the N shore of the Bristol Channel as far E as Swansea Bay; these are less frequent on the S shore above Morte Point. In the Irish Sea, the predominant swell is from between S and SW but with an increased frequency of N swells in spring and summer. Swell heights are much reduced to the N of Saint George's Channel with 3 m or more being recorded on 15% of occasions in January and 2% in July. Liverpool and Morecambe Bays are well protected from S swells but, with strong NW winds, a moderate swell occurs on the bar of the River Mersey.

SEA WATER CHARACTERISTICS

Sea surface temperatures
1.107

1   Diagrams 1.107.1 to 1.107.4 show mean sea surface temperatures for selected months.

2   Sea surface temperatures are generally at their lowest in February and highest in August. In the S, off Cape Cornwall, the mean sea surface temperature increases from 9°C in February to 16°C in August and in the North Channel from 7°C to 14°C. The annual variation is generally higher, about 12°C, where there is a major fresh water source, for example in the Solway Firth, Morecambe Bay and the Bristol Channel.

Variability
1.108

1   Sea surface temperatures vary from year to year. Variability tends to be smallest in winter when temperatures are usually within 2°C of the mean. In summer, the variability is greater, especially in shallow coastal waters.

Density and salinity
1.109

1   See *The Mariner's Handbook*. In these coastal waters neither density nor salinity vary appreciably from normal values. The isohalines and isopicnals run approximately E to W. The density of water at selected ports is as follows:

	Port	Dock/Harbour	Density g/cm³
2	Barrow	Buccleuch Dock	1·013
		Walney Channel	1·022
	Barry	Docks	1·021
3	Bristol	Avonmouth Docks	1·012
		Portishead Docks	1·016
		City Docks	1·001
	Cardiff	Queen Alexandra Dock	1·019
4	Fleetwood	River Wyre	1·025
	Liverpool	River Mersey (off Birkenhead)	1·023
		Gladstone Dock	1·022
5	Manchester	Ship Canal	1·001
	Milford Haven	Harbour	1·026
	Newport (South Wales)	Alexandra Dock	1·020
	Swansea	King's Dock	1·020

ICE CONDITIONS
1.110

1   Ice does not normally form in any salt-water harbour. This may not be the case in severe winters where ice forms in harbours, rivers, bays and other shallow inshore locations. In the very severe winter of 1962/63 most harbours reported minor difficulties with ice. Bristol City Docks, however, had serious difficulties with shipping movements in late January and early February 1963.

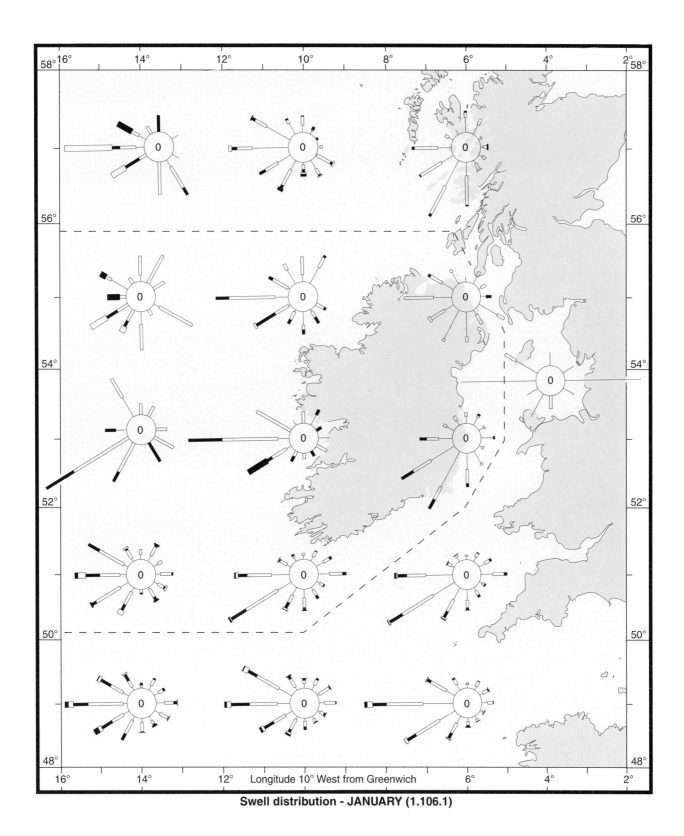

Swell distribution - JANUARY (1.106.1)

EXPLANATION. The frequency of swell from any direction is given according to the scale:

0% 10 20 30 40 50%

This scale is further subdivided to indicate the frequency of swell of different heights (in metres) according to the legend:

3   0.1-2.2   4.3-6.2   8.3+
        2.3-4.2   6.3-8.2

Swell direction is towards the circle centre. The figure within the circle gives the percentage of calms.

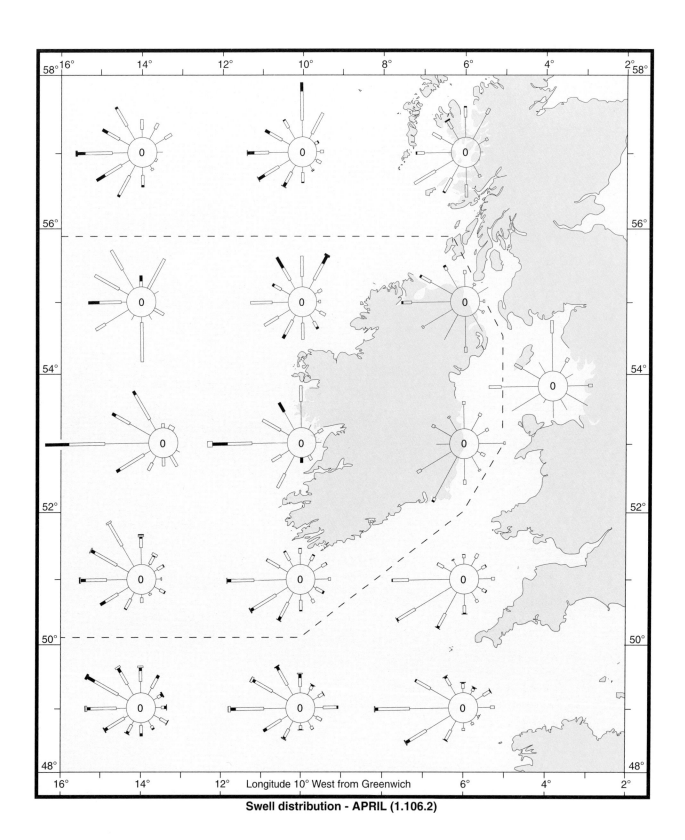

Swell distribution - APRIL (1.106.2)

EXPLANATION. The frequency of swell from any direction is given according to the scale:

0%   10   20   30   40   50%

This scale is further subdivided to indicate the frequency of swell of different heights (in metres) according to the legend:

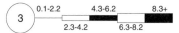

Swell direction is towards the circle centre. The figure within the circle gives the percentage of calms.

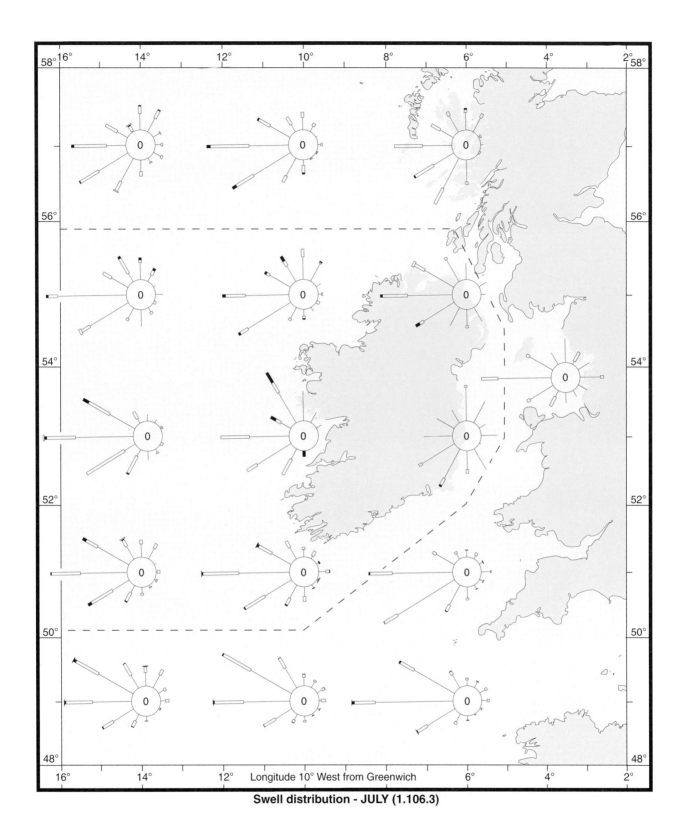

Swell distribution - JULY (1.106.3)

EXPLANATION. The frequency of swell from any direction is given according to the scale:

0% 10 20 30 40 50%

This scale is further subdivided to indicate the frequency of swell of different heights (in metres) according to the legend:

3   0.1-2.2   4.3-6.2   8.3+
    2.3-4.2   6.3-8.2

Swell direction is towards the circle centre. The figure within the circle gives the percentage of calms.

21

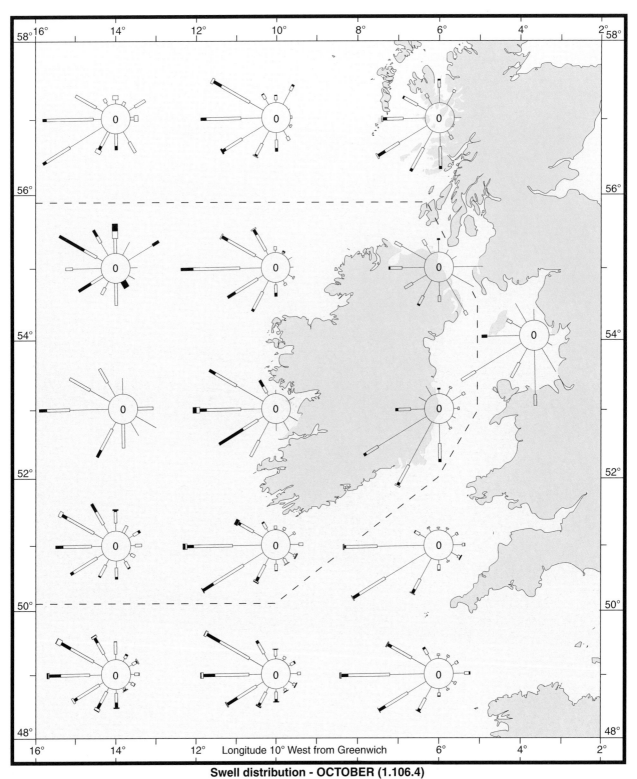

Swell distribution - OCTOBER (1.106.4)

EXPLANATION. The frequency of swell from any direction is given according to the scale:

0%   10   20   30   40   50%

This scale is further subdivided to indicate the frequency of swell of different heights (in metres) according to the legend:

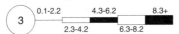

Swell direction is towards the circle centre. The figure within the circle gives the percentage of calms.

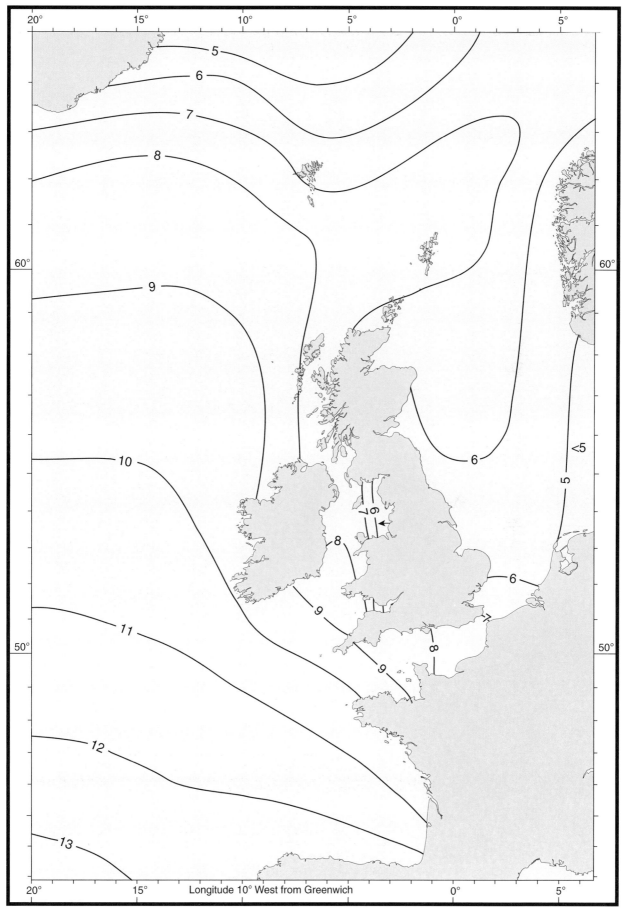

Mean sea surface temperature (°C) FEBRUARY (1.107.1)

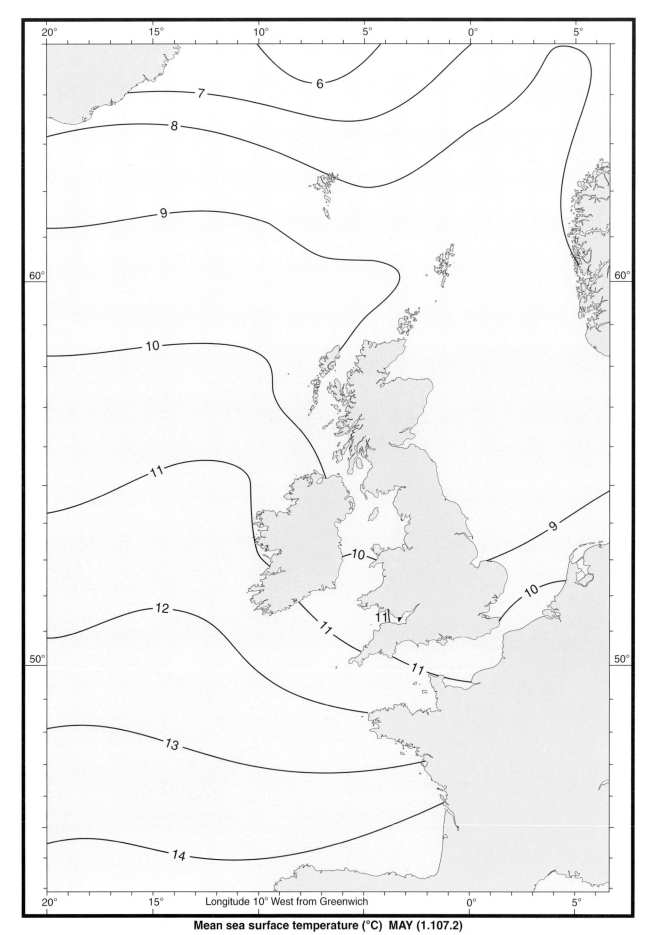

Mean sea surface temperature (°C) MAY (1.107.2)

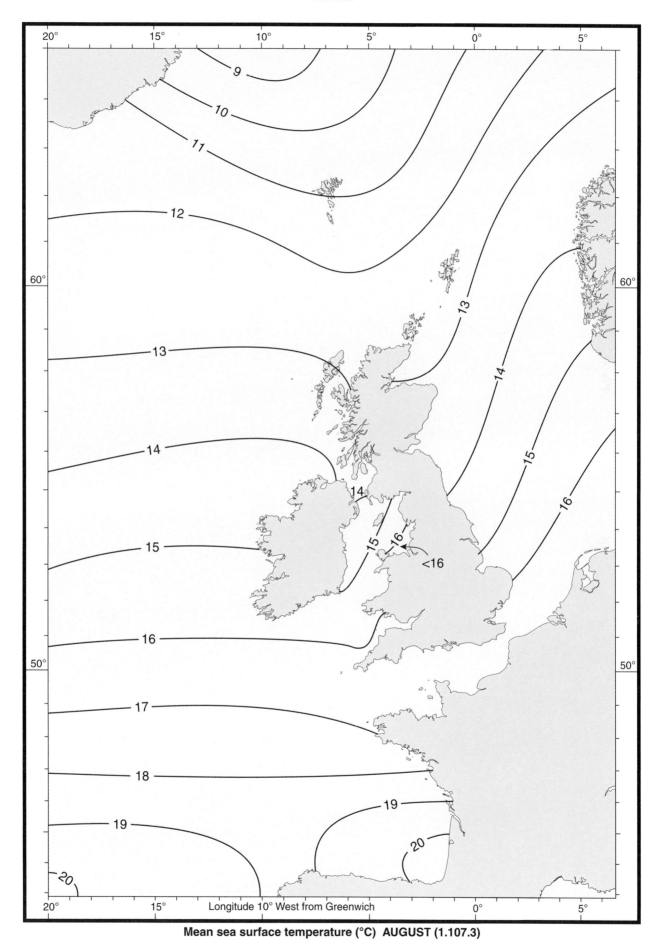

Mean sea surface temperature (°C) AUGUST (1.107.3)

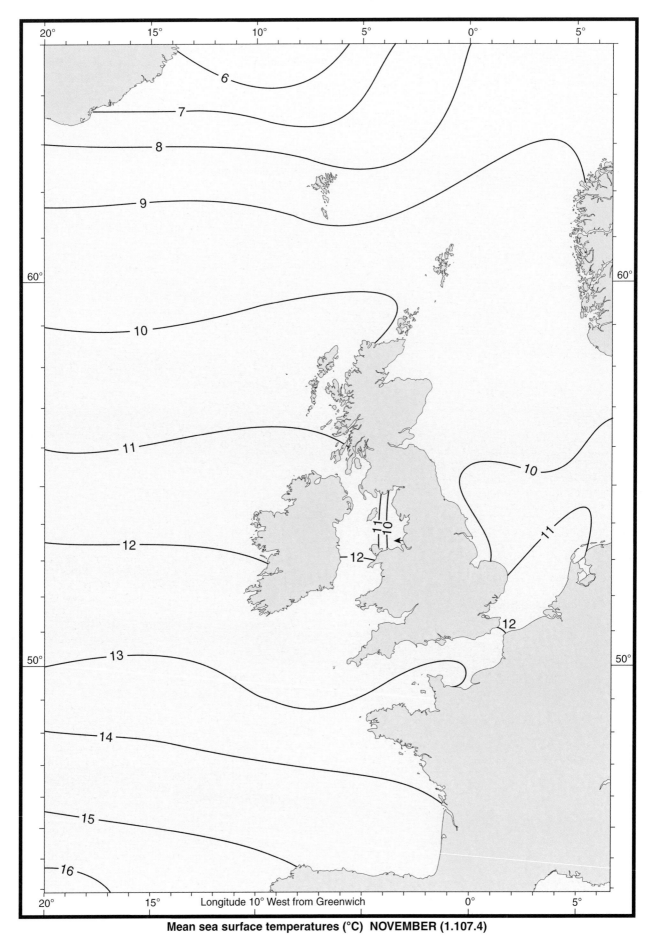

Mean sea surface temperatures (°C) NOVEMBER (1.107.4)

CLIMATE AND WEATHER

General information
1.111

1   The following information should be read in conjunction with *The Mariner's Handbook*.

    Weather reports and forecasts, that cover the area, are regularly broadcast in a number of languages; for details see *Admiralty List of Radio Signals Volume 3(1)*.

General conditions
1.112

1   The region has a mild maritime climate, unsettled at times with periods of strong winds and rough seas. Gales are most frequent in the winter months; winds may reach hurricane strength. Rainfall is plentiful and well distributed throughout the year. The driest period lasts from March to June.

2   It is often cloudy in all seasons, coasts maybe obscured by low cloud and driving rain. Fog at sea is infrequent from November to May and most common in June. Land fog is most frequent in the autumn and winter around dawn. Visibility is generally good, although, marginally less so in the area of the Irish Sea to the E of 4°W in winter.

Pressure

Average distribution
1.113

1   Diagrams 1.113.1 to 1.113.4 show the average pressure distribution, at MSL, for selected months.

    The dominant features of the pressure field are the Azores anticyclone, which is situated to the SW of the area covered by this volume, and the semi-permanent Icelandic low pressure area to the N. The latter results from the many mobile depressions travelling NW, especially in winter.

Variability
1.114

1   The actual pressure pattern will be significantly different from the mean. When deep depressions affect the area, local pressure changes of around 40 hPa in 24 hours have been recorded. Especially in winter, when a high cell becomes established over N Europe, the synoptic chart may show high pressure to the N and relatively low pressure to the S.

Diurnal variation
1.115

1   The diurnal variation is small, about 0.2 to 0.6 hPa peak to peak; it is nearly always masked by other pressure changes.

Anticyclones

The Azores anticyclone
1.116

1   This anticyclone is centred about 35°N in summer and 30°N in winter. In summer, a ridge of high pressure often extends NE towards France and central Europe. This ridge can bring settled weather conditions to the S of the area while forcing the track of E or NE moving mobile depressions farther N.

The Asiatic anticyclone
1.117

1   The Asiatic anticyclone develops over Siberia in winter. On occasions, a ridge may extend W to NW Europe. When this occurs cold dry E winds may affect the area for several weeks. At the same time, mobile depressions are prevented from approaching the area until the ridge recedes.

Depressions

Atlantic depressions
1.118

1   The area lies slightly S of the main low pressure belt of the N hemisphere. Depressions that form over the W North Atlantic, frequently move NE towards the Icelandic area with secondary depressions forming to their rear. These secondary depressions, often in a family of three to five, frequently move E with increasingly S component to affect the area. The interval between depressions can be as short as 24 hours and as long as two to three days, and each depression may give rise to gale or storm force winds, especially in winter.

2   During the hurricane season in the W North Atlantic between July and October, spent hurricanes may curve NE towards the area and re-intensify with winds of force 10 or more.

Polar depressions
1.119

1   Polar depressions generally develop in cold N airstreams in the Norwegian Sea; these bring snow or frequent wintry showers as they move S in winter.

Fronts

Polar fronts
1.120

1   The polar front is a most important feature in the region and plays a dominant role in the weather throughout the year. It marks the boundary between cold air to the N and warm moist air to the S. In winter its mean position is 40°N 40°W to the S coast of England; in summer it lies between 45°N 40°W and the N coast of Wales. The majority of the mobile depressions that affect the area originate in the polar frontal zone over the W North Atlantic.

Arctic front
1.121

1   The mean position of the arctic front in winter is to the N of Scandinavia. Vigorous depressions over the Norwegian Sea, or Scandinavia, occasionally cause the front to move S into the region. Characteristic showery conditions frequently occur in the arctic air behind it. The arctic front is of no importance to the region in summer.

Warm and cold fronts
1.122

1   Warm and cold fronts are generally very active in the area and are responsible for much of the bad weather in the region; see *The Mariner's Handbook* for a full description of warm and cold fronts. Warm fronts usually approach the area from between SSE and NW in summer and from between SW and W in winter. Cold fronts generally approach the area from between NE and SW, through NW, and may bring a sudden shift of wind together with strong winds and squally conditions.

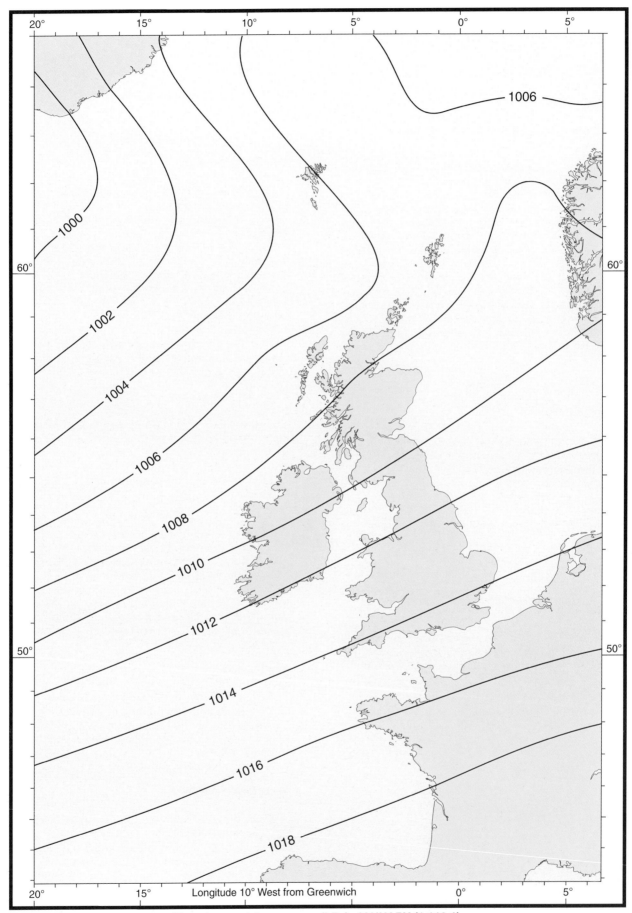

Mean barometric pressure (hPa) JANUARY (1.113.1)

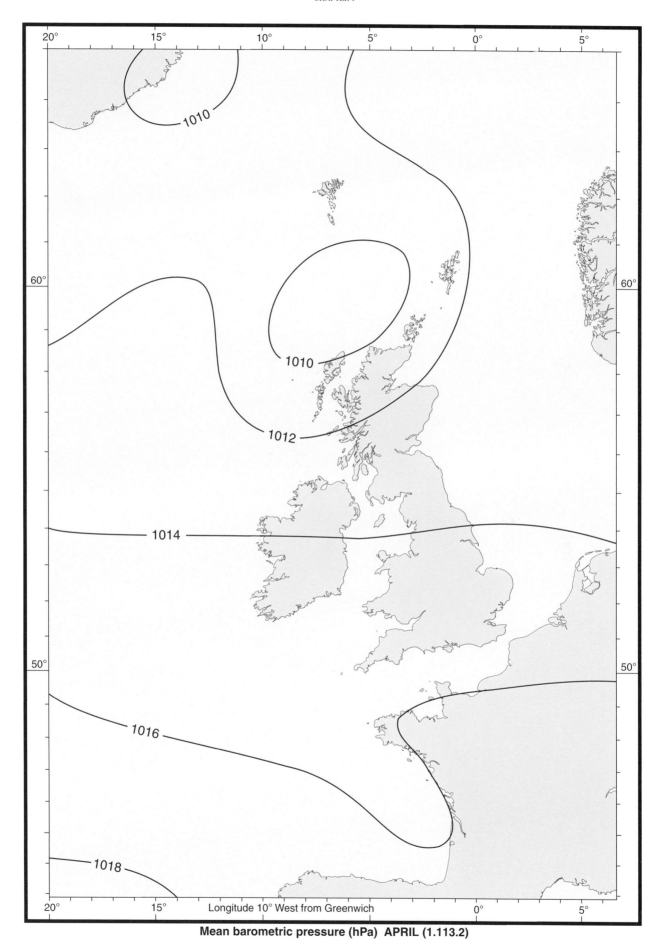

Mean barometric pressure (hPa) APRIL (1.113.2)

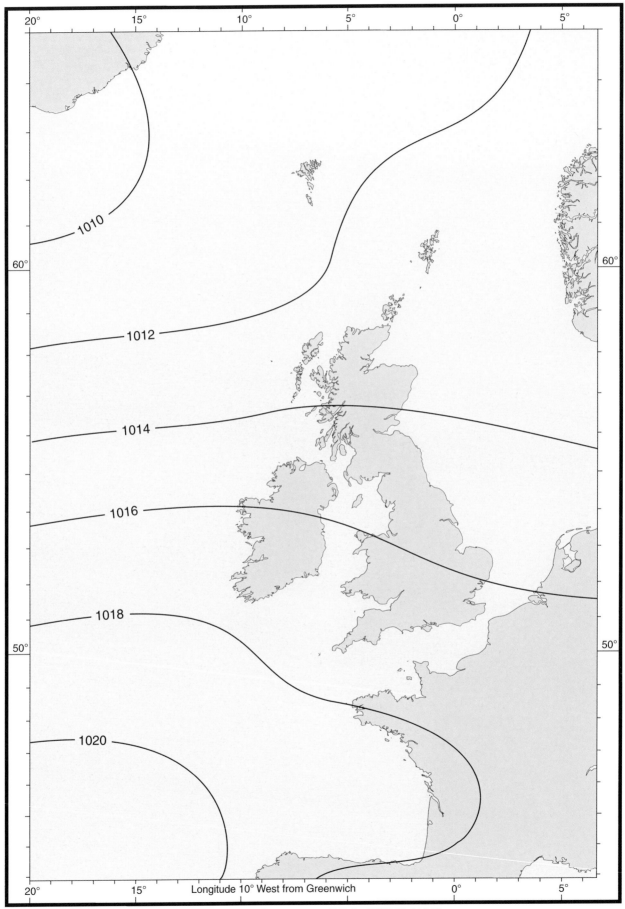

Mean barometric pressure (hPa) JULY (1.113.3)

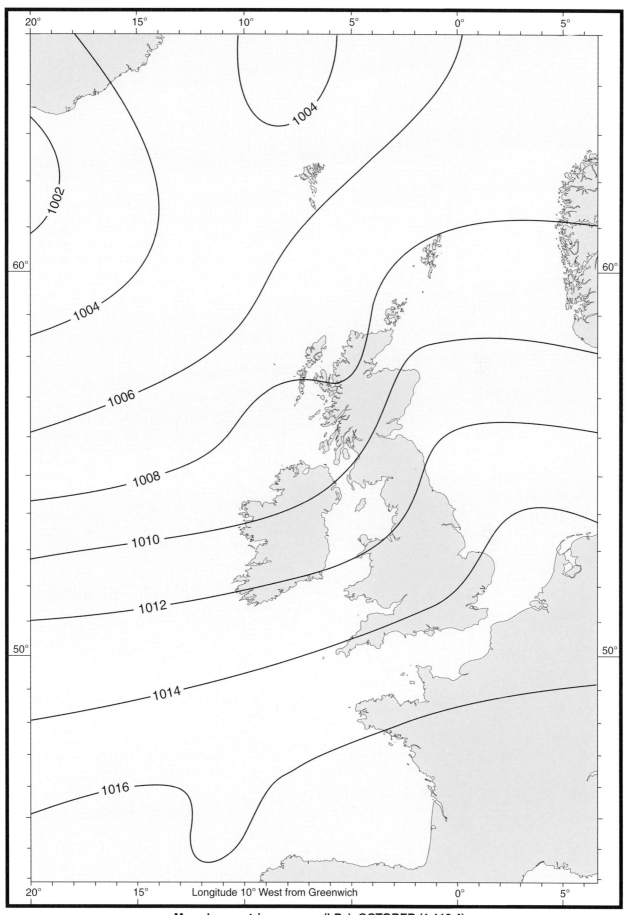

Mean barometric pressure (hPa) OCTOBER (1.113.4)

Winds

Average distribution
1.123
1 Wind roses showing the frequency of winds of various directions and speeds for January, April, July and October are given in diagrams 1.123.1 to 1.123.4.

Variability
1.124
1 Owing to the frequent mobile depressions that affect the area, there are often marked variations in both speed and direction at any location. Late in winter and in early spring, if a high cell becomes established over Central and NE Europe, E to NE winds may persist for several weeks.

Open sea
1.125
1 The predominant winds are from between S and NW. There is an increase in the frequency of N to NE winds in spring and a decrease in E winds in summer. The strongest winds occur during autumn and winter. Winds of force 6 and over occur 40% of the time during December in the N and 35% in the S. In July this frequency is 6% in the N and 9% in the S.

Coastal areas
1.126
1 As over the open sea, the pressure pattern has a major influence on the wind but within about 20 miles of the coast local modifications may be caused by the topography and by land and sea breezes.

  An increase in wind strength, owing to the funnelling effect, is most marked at the following places:

	Locality	*Wind direction*
2	Bristol Channel — E	W
	Bristol Channel — W	SW
	Milford Haven	S to W & N
	Holyhead	NW
3	River Dee estuary	NW or SE
	River Mersey estuary	NW or SE
	Morecambe Bay	SW to W
	Solway Firth	SW
4	Saint George's Channel	S
	Isle of Man to North Channel	NW

Land and sea breezes
1.127
1 Sea breezes are most evident with calm or light wind conditions in late spring, summer and early autumn. Land breezes are more common on calm winter nights, and may increase the incidence of showers at sea. Depending on the direction of the prevailing wind, these breezes may reinforce or moderate the strength of the wind.

2 Land and sea breezes are particularly noticeable on the coasts of Lancashire and Cornwall.

Squalls
1.128
1 Violent squalls are infrequent but are more common with N winds and, especially in winter, near mountainous coasts with offshore winds. Gusts of around 80 to 100 kn have been recorded at exposed sites on the W coasts of England and Wales.

Gales
1.129
1 Diagrams 1.129.1 and 1.129.2 give the percentage frequency of winds with force 7 and over in January and July. Gales (force 8 or greater) are reported on 12% of occasions in December and on less than 2% in July. The most common direction for gales (force 8 or greater) is from between SW and NW. SE gales are less frequent and usually of short duration.

Cloud
1.130
1 In the S the average cloud cover is about 6 oktas in winter and around 4 to 5 oktas in summer. There is slightly more cloud in the N than in the S. Clear skies are most common with E winds from the continent and in the lee of high ground with cold N winds. The W coasts of Cornwall and Wales often experience persistent low cloud, especially in winter, in association with moist SW winds. The N coast of Wales is often clearer and brighter.

Precipitation
1.131
1 The climatic tables (1.143) give the average amounts of precipitation for each month at several coastal stations and the mean number of days in each month when significant precipitation is recorded.

Rain
1.132
1 At sea, rain can be expected on about 18 days per month in winter. In summer, rain occurs on about 10 days per month in the S and about 15 days in the N. The quantity and duration can vary significantly from day to day and from year to year. At coastal stations, rainfall varies according to the prevailing winds and the proximity of high ground. The average annual rainfall is around 1000 mm for exposed sites and 700 mm for those in the lee of high ground. The dry period is during February to July and the wet period October to January.

Thunderstorms
1.133
1 Thunderstorms are relatively infrequent with an average of 1 to 5 per year in the N of the area and 8 to 12 in the S. They usually occur in the summer after a prolonged warm spell, or when a thundery low forms over France and moves NW to affect the area.

Snow
1.134
1 The majority of snow falls at irregular intervals between December and April, with the greatest frequency in the months of February and March. On average there are 3 days of snow-fall per year in the S and 15 days in the N. The snow seldom lies for long near sea level and is usually light but on rare occasions heavy falls can occur, especially on NW facing coasts.

Fog and visibility

Open sea
1.135
1 Sea fog (visibility less than 1 km) is most common with SW winds between April and October and has a maximum frequency of between 2% and 5% of occasions in June. In January the frequency is generally less than 2%, although to the E of 4°W it is between 5% and 10%; see *The Mariner's Handbook* for details on sea and radiation fogs.

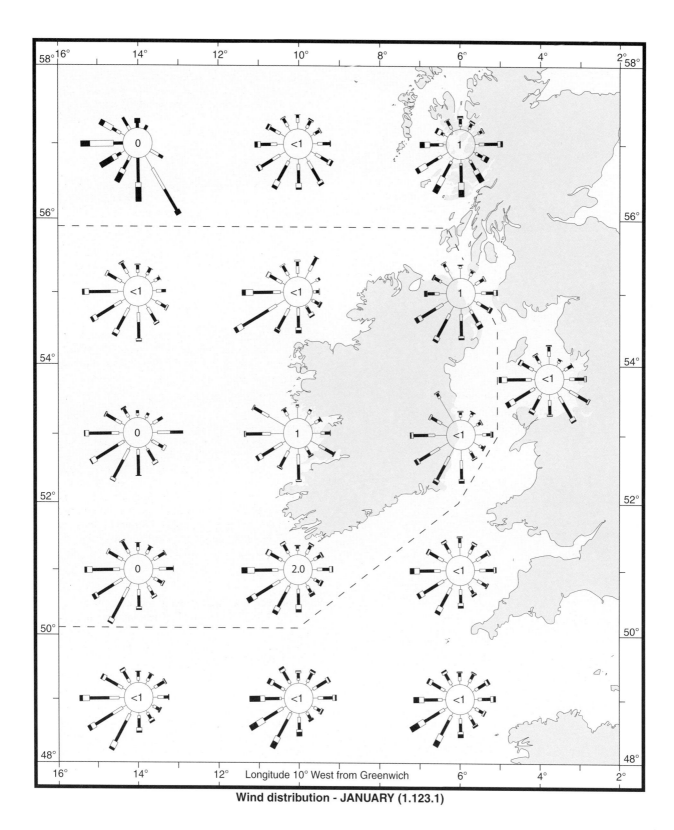

Wind distribution - JANUARY (1.123.1)

EXPLANATION. The frequency of wind from any direction is given according to the scale:

0%   10   20   30   40   50%

This scale is further subdivided to indicate the frequency of winds of different Beaufort force according to the legend:

4   1-3   4   5-6   7   8-12

Wind direction is towards the circle centre. The figure within the circle gives the percentage of calms.

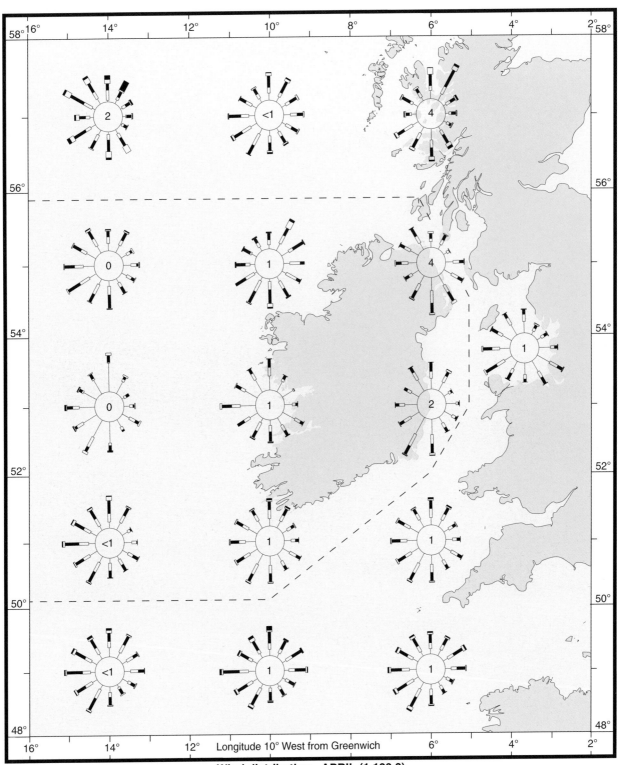

Wind distribution - APRIL (1.123.2)

EXPLANATION. The frequency of wind from any direction is given according to the scale:

0%   10   20   30   40   50%

This scale is further subdivided to indicate the frequency of winds of different Beaufort force according to the legend:

1-3   4   5-6   7   8-12

Wind direction is towards the circle centre. The figure within the circle gives the percentage of calms.

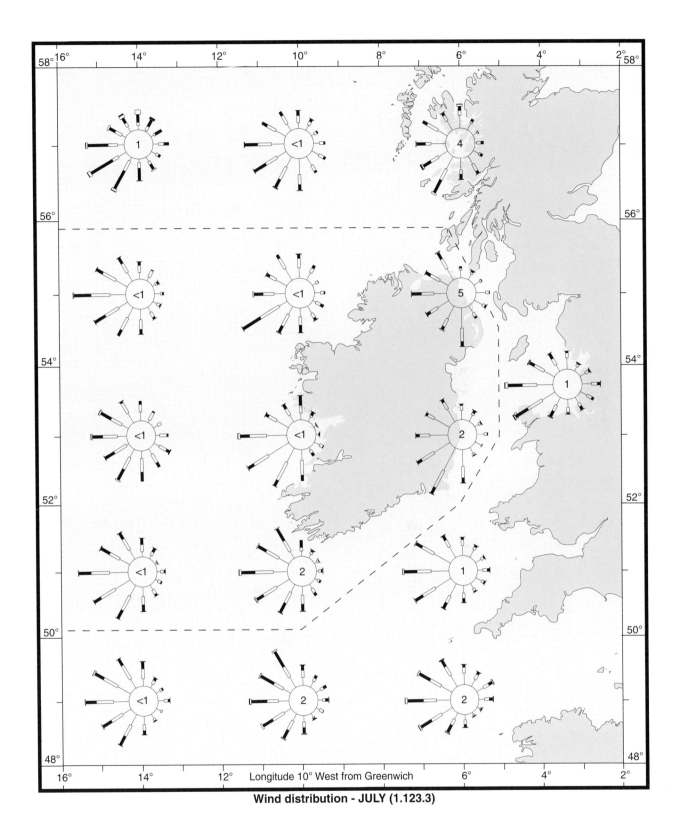

Wind distribution - JULY (1.123.3)

EXPLANATION. The frequency of wind from any direction is given according to the scale:

0%   10   20   30   40   50%

This scale is further subdivided to indicate the frequency of winds of different Beaufort force according to the legend:

4   1-3   4   5-6   7   8-12

Wind direction is towards the circle centre. The figure within the circle gives the percentage of calms.

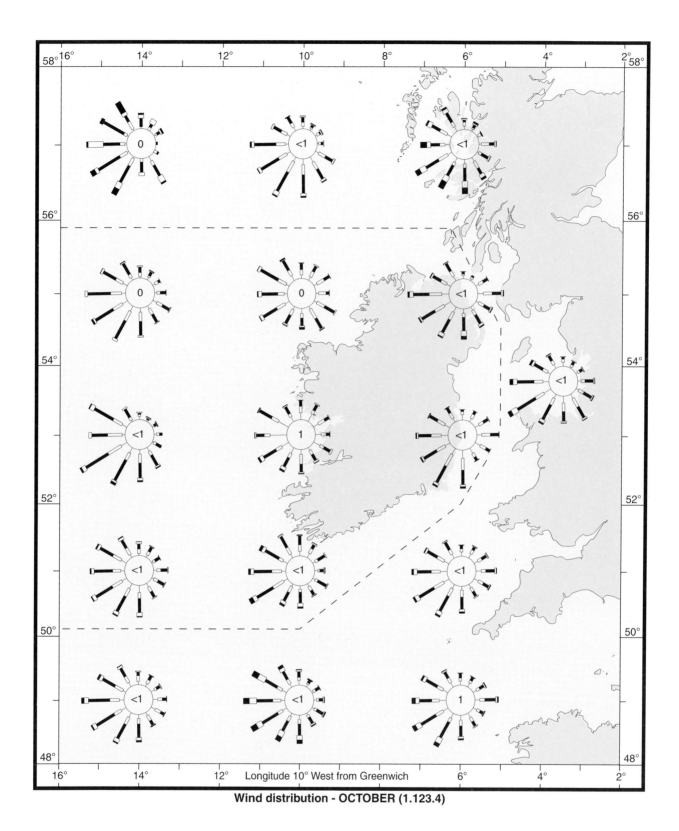

Wind distribution - OCTOBER (1.123.4)

EXPLANATION. The frequency of wind from any direction is given according to the scale:

0%   10   20   30   40   50%

This scale is further subdivided to indicate the frequency of winds of different Beaufort force according to the legend:

1-3   4   5-6   7   8-12

Wind direction is towards the circle centre. The figure within the circle gives the percentage of calms.

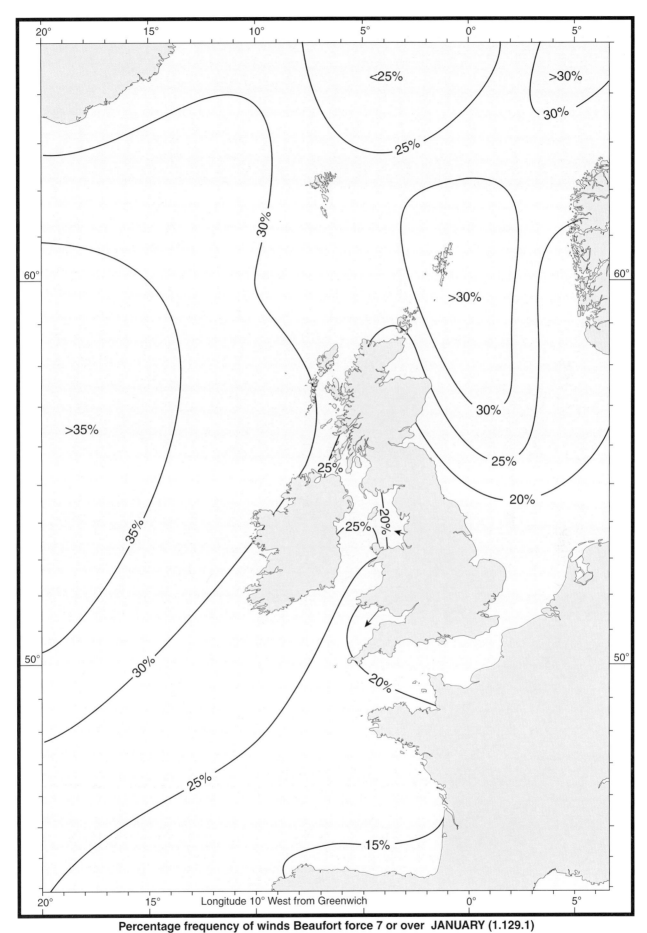

Percentage frequency of winds Beaufort force 7 or over JANUARY (1.129.1)

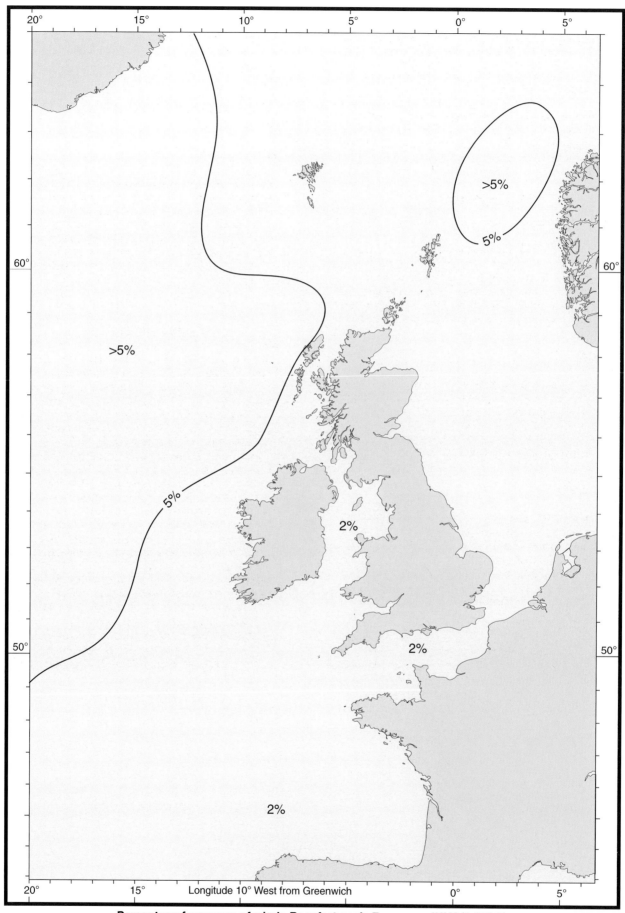

Percentage frequency of winds Beaufort scale 7 or over JULY (1.129.2)

2   The percentage frequency of occasions when the visibility is in excess of 5 miles is between 80% and 85% throughout the year, except for that part the Irish Sea to the E of 4°W, where the frequency falls to about 75% in mid–winter.

Coastal areas
1.136
1   The average number of days with fog for a number of coastal stations is given in the climatic tables (1.143). Liverpool Bay, the head of the Bristol Channel and the area around Silloth are particularly affected by radiation fog in winter.

Air temperature

General information
1.137
1   The coldest time of the year is January and February and the warmest is July and August. The temperature is often very variable, particularly in winter. Numerous passing frontal depressions bring frequent changes of source airstreams. High pressure over N Europe can give rise to very cold periods in winter and warm spells in summer.

Open sea
1.138
1   In the N of the area the mean air temperature in January is about 7°C and in July around 14°C, and in the S about 9°C and 16°C respectively. On average the air is slightly colder than the sea from October to March and slightly warmer from April to August. The average difference is about 1°C, except in the Irish Sea, in winter, where it is around 2°C.

Coastal areas
1.139
1   Air temperatures along the W coasts of England and Wales are generally more variable than over the open sea. The warmest spells often associated with winds from between S and E in summer. In winter the cold spells are mainly associated with winds from between N and E.

Humidity

General information
1.140
1   Humidity is closely related to temperature and generally decreases as the air temperature rises. During the early morning, when the air temperature is normally at its lowest, the humidity is generally at its highest, and falls to a minimum in the afternoon.

Open sea
1.141
1   In winter the mean humidity is about 80% to 82% and in summer around 82% to 85%, with only small variations from one month to the next.

Coastal areas
1.142
1   There are often large fluctuations in humidity along the coast depending on the exposure of the locality to the prevailing wind and its distance from the open sea. In general, areas exposed to SW winds will have higher humidity than those in the lee of high ground or when there is an E or NE wind. Particularly in winter, relatively dry E winds can give rise to significant falls in humidity along the coasts of England and Wales.

CLIMATIC TABLES
1.143
1   The climatic tables which follow give data for several coastal stations which regularly undertake weather observations. Positions of stations are shown in Diagram 1.143.

2   It is emphasised that these data are average conditions and refer to the specific location of the observing station and therefore may not be representative of the conditions to be expected over the open sea or in approaches to ports in their vicinity. The following comments briefly list some of the differences to be expected between conditions over the open sea and those at the nearest reporting station (see *The Mariner's Handbook* for further details).

3   Wind speeds tend to be higher at sea with more frequent gales than on land, although funnelling in narrow inlets can result in an increase in wind strength.

4   Precipitation along mountainous wind facing coasts can be considerably higher than at sea to windward. Similarly, precipitation in the lee of high ground is generally less.

5   Air temperature over the sea is less variable than over the land and in the lee of high ground.
Topography has a marked effect on local conditions.

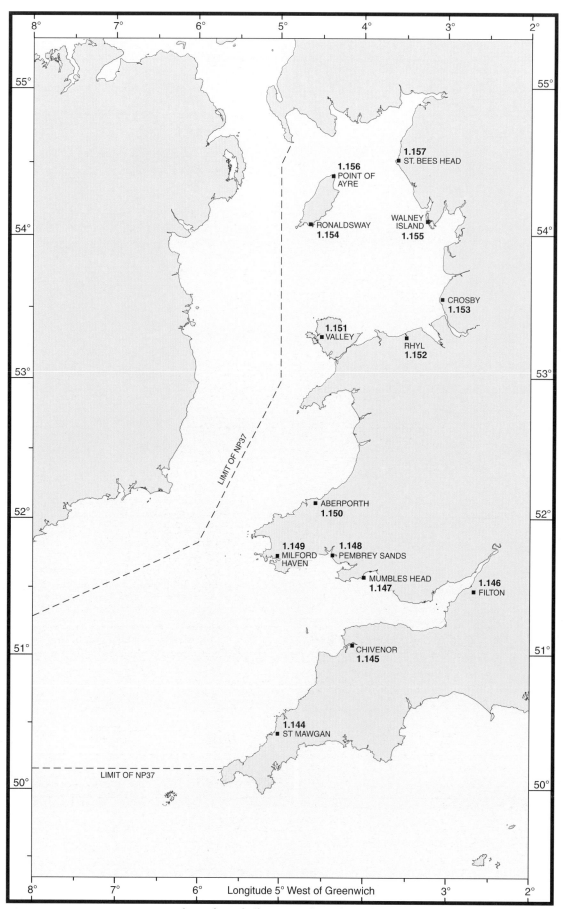

Location of climate stations (1.143)

WMO No 03817 ST MAWGAN

50°26'N 05°00'W.   Height above MSL - 0 m Climate Information for period 1998 - 2008

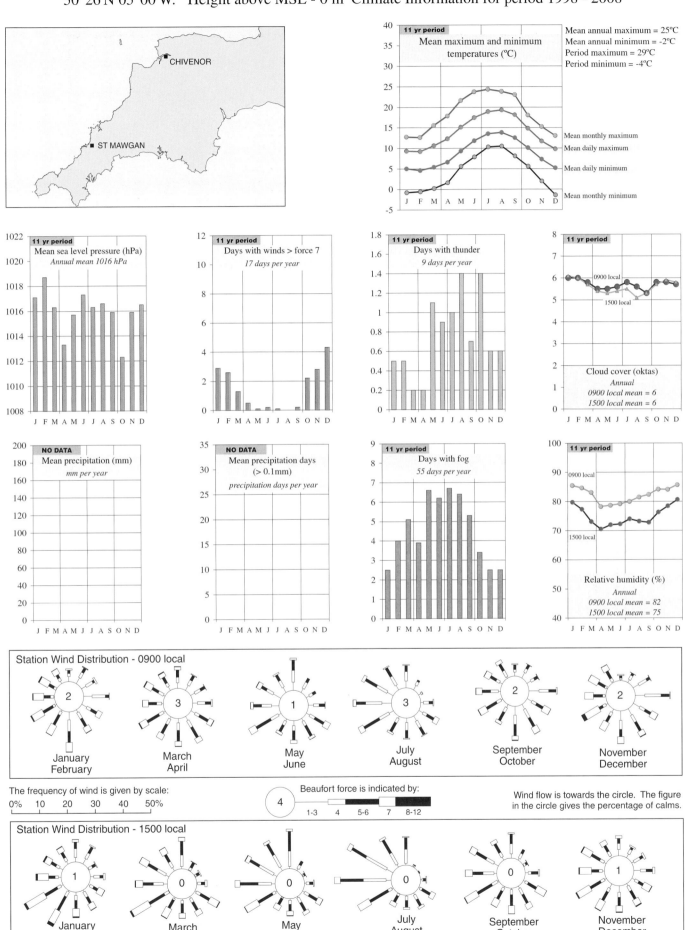

WMO No 03707 CHIVENOR

51°05'N 04°09'W. Height above MSL - 0 m Climate Information for period 1998 - 2008

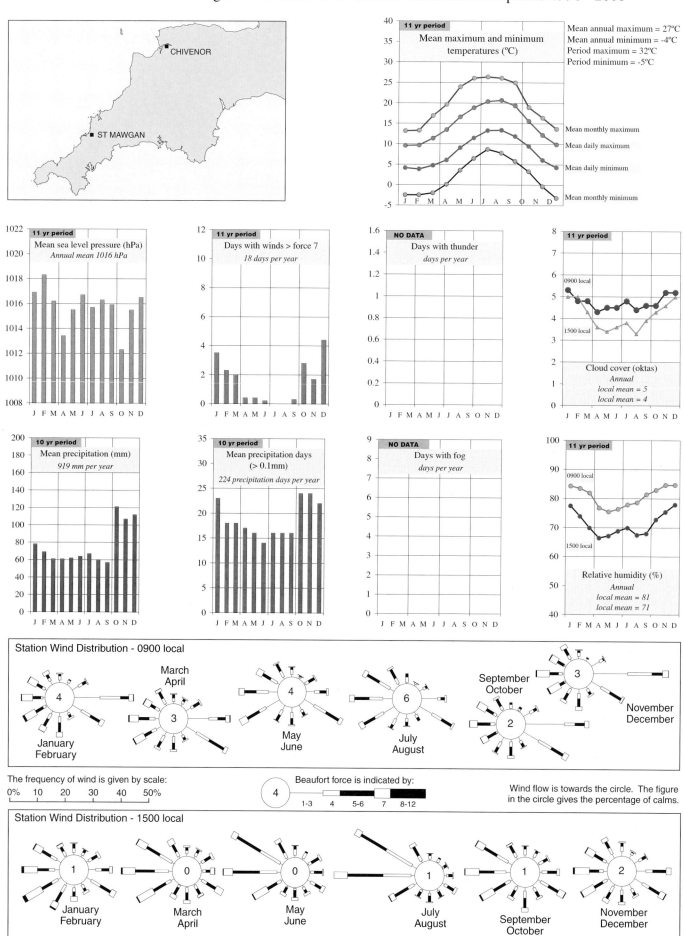

WMO No 03628 FILTON

51°31'N 02°35'W.   Height above MSL - 0 m Climate Information for period 2001 - 2008

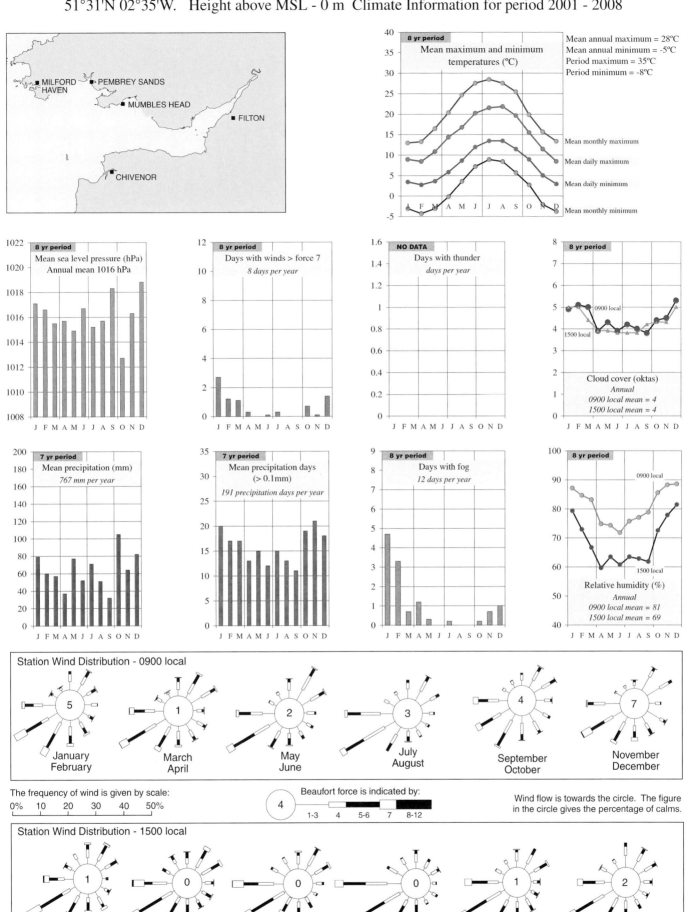

WMO No 03609 MUMBLES HEAD

51°34'N 03°59'W.   Height above MSL - 0 m Climate Information for period 1998 - 2008

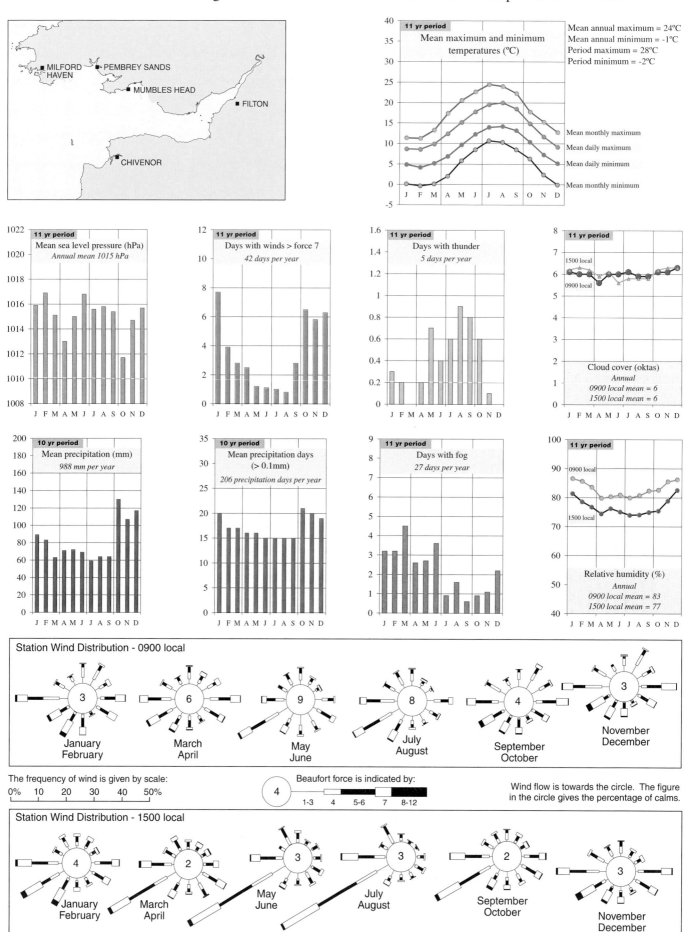

WMO No 03605 PEMBREY SANDS

51°43'N 04°22'W.   Height above MSL - 6 m Climate Information for period 1998 - 2008

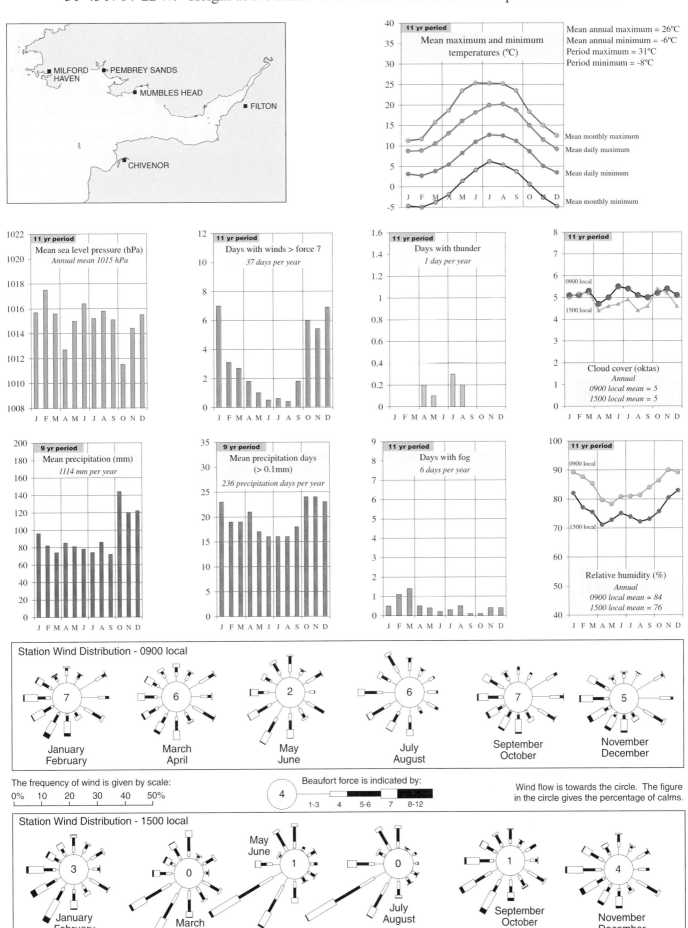

WMO No 03604 MILFORD HAVEN

51°42'N 05°03'W.   Height above MSL - 32 m Climate Information for period 1998 - 2008

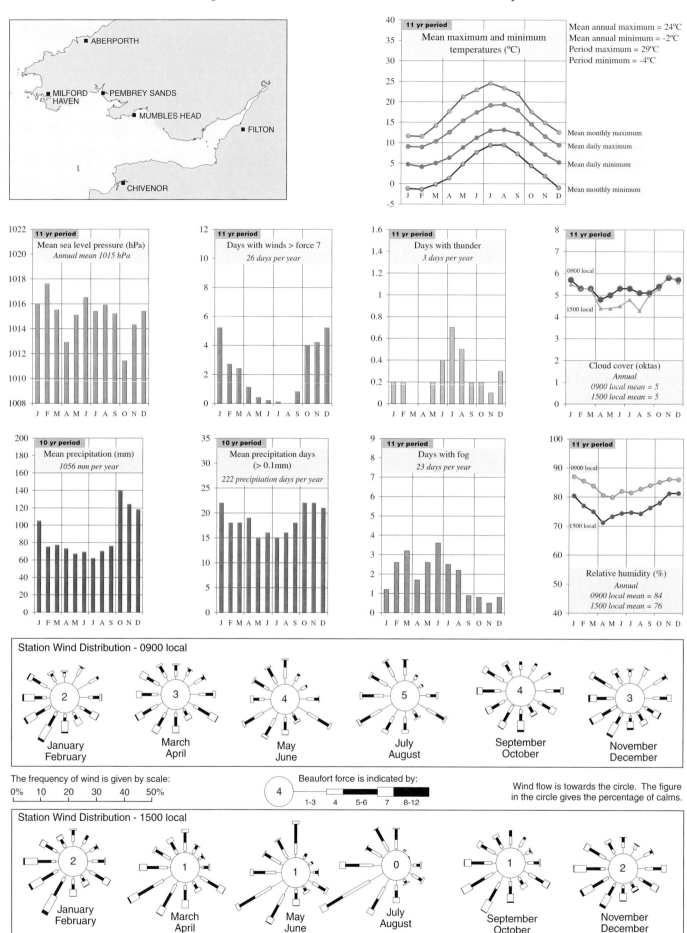

WMO No 03502 ABERPORTH

52°08'N 04°34'W.   Height above MSL - 134 m Climate Information for period 1998 - 2008

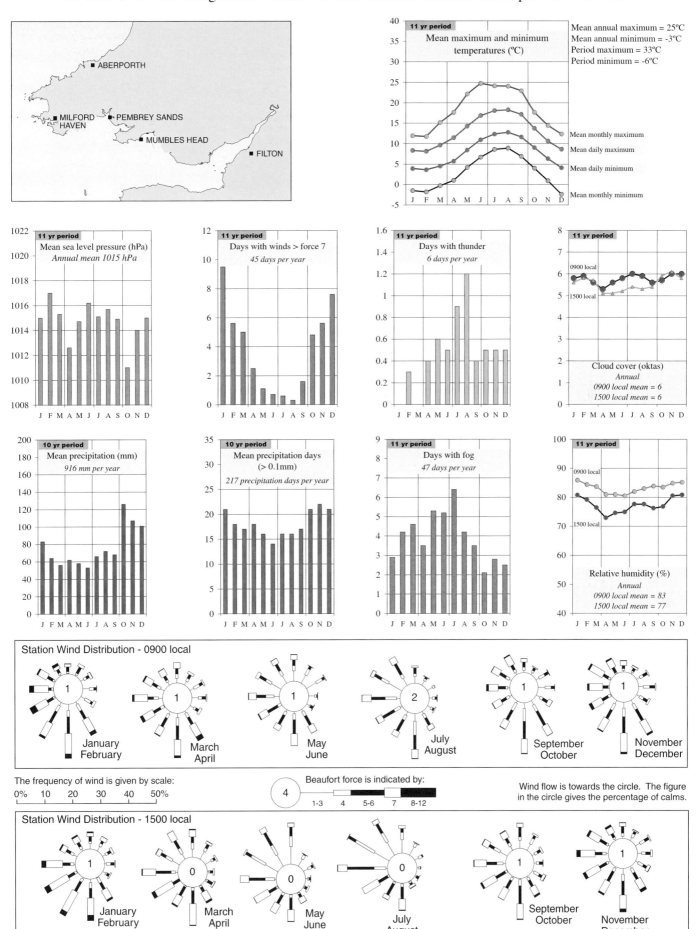

WMO No 03302 VALLEY

53°15'N 04°32'W.   Height above MSL - 10 m Climate Information for period 1998 - 2008

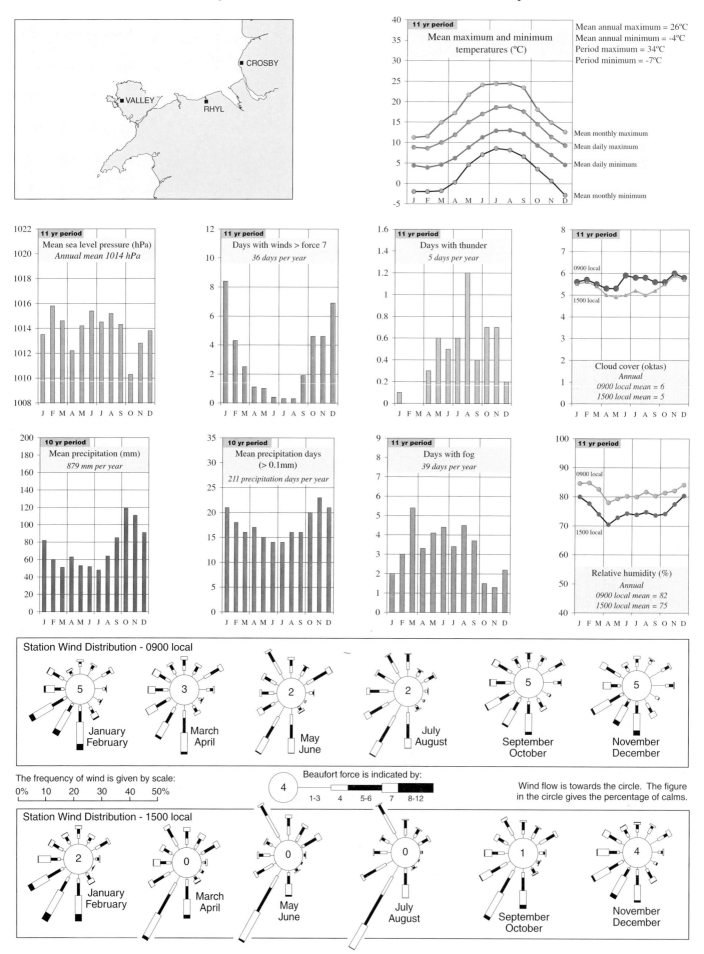

WMO No 03313 RHYL

53°15'N 03°30'W.   Height above MSL - 76 m Climate Information for period 1998 - 2008

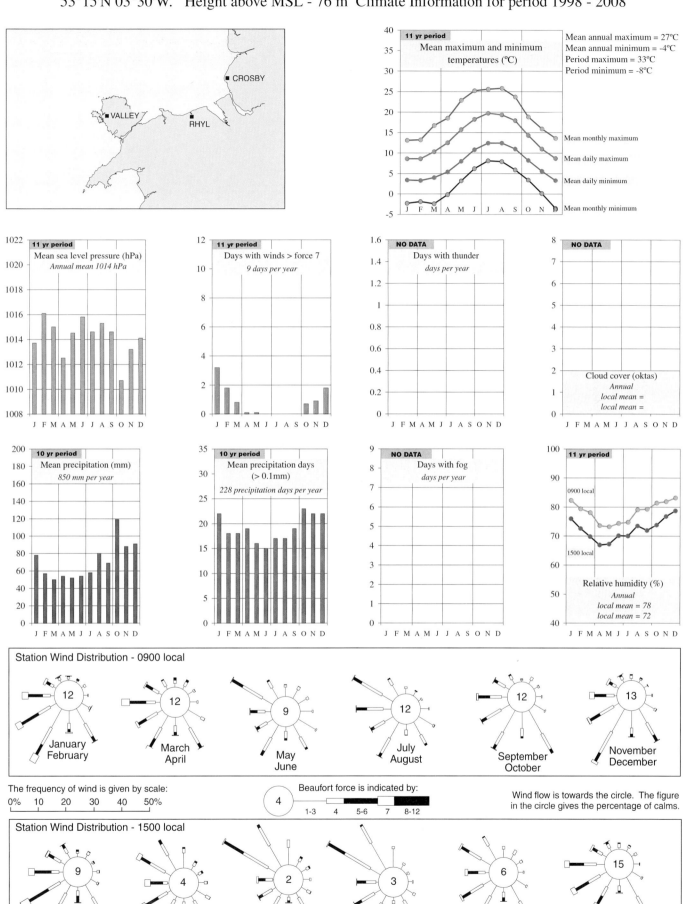

Mean maximum and minimum temperatures (°C) — 11 yr period
Mean annual maximum = 27°C
Mean annual minimum = -4°C
Period maximum = 33°C
Period minimum = -8°C
Mean monthly maximum
Mean daily maximum
Mean daily minimum
Mean monthly minimum

Mean sea level pressure (hPa) — 11 yr period
Annual mean 1014 hPa

Days with winds > force 7 — 11 yr period
9 days per year

Days with thunder — NO DATA
days per year

Cloud cover (oktas) — NO DATA
Annual
local mean =
local mean =

Mean precipitation (mm) — 10 yr period
850 mm per year

Mean precipitation days (> 0.1mm) — 10 yr period
228 precipitation days per year

Days with fog — NO DATA
days per year

Relative humidity (%) — 11 yr period
0900 local
1500 local
Annual
local mean = 78
local mean = 72

Station Wind Distribution - 0900 local
12 January February
12 March April
9 May June
12 July August
12 September October
13 November December

The frequency of wind is given by scale:
0% 10 20 30 40 50%

Beaufort force is indicated by:
4
1-3 4 5-6 7 8-12

Wind flow is towards the circle. The figure in the circle gives the percentage of calms.

Station Wind Distribution - 1500 local
9 January February
4 March April
2 May June
3 July August
6 September October
15 November December

49

WMO No 03316 CROSBY

53°30'N 03°04'W. Height above MSL - 0 m Climate Information for period 1998 - 2008

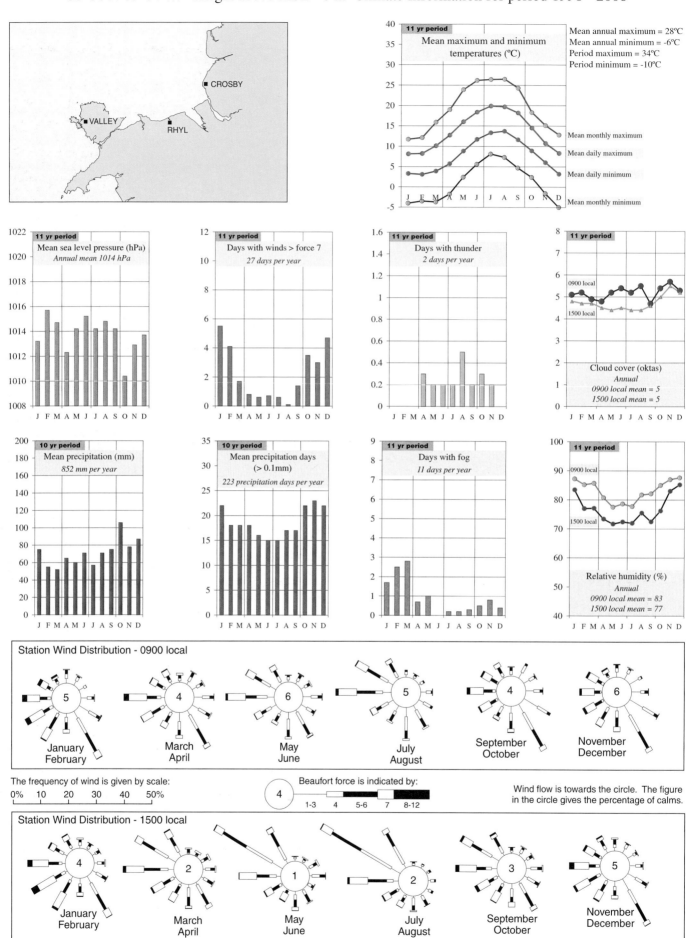

WMO No 03204 RONALDSWAY

54°05'N 04°38'W.   Height above MSL - 16 m Climate Information for period 1998 - 2008

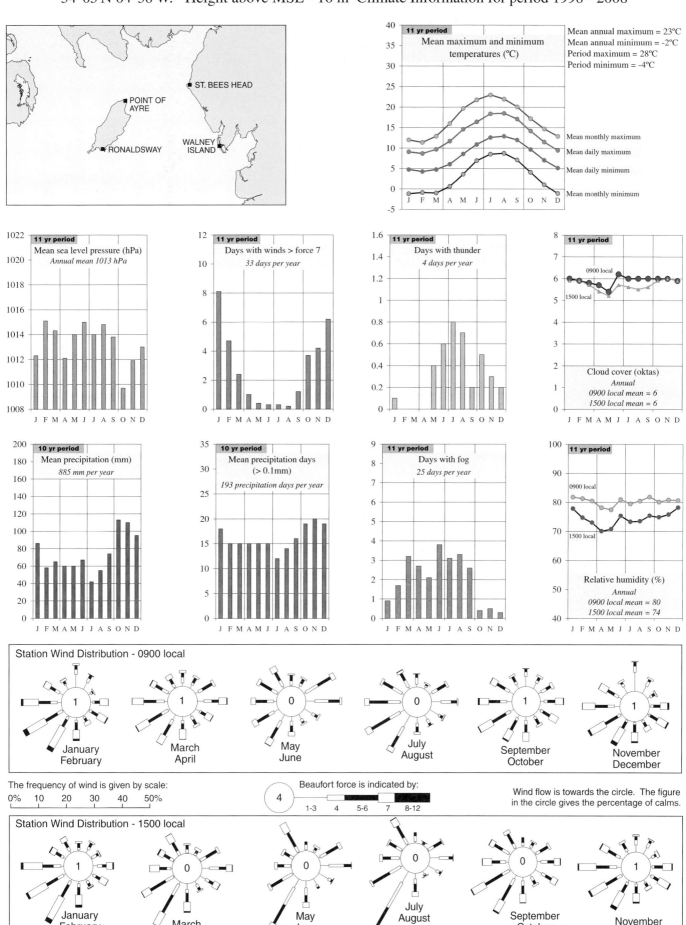

Mean annual maximum = 23°C
Mean annual minimum = -2°C
Period maximum = 28°C
Period minimum = -4°C

The frequency of wind is given by scale:
0%   10   20   30   40   50%

Beaufort force is indicated by:
4   1-3   4   5-6   7   8-12

Wind flow is towards the circle. The figure in the circle gives the percentage of calms.

WMO No 03214 WALNEY ISLAND

54°07'N 03°15'W.   Height above MSL - 14 m Climate Information for period 1998 - 2008

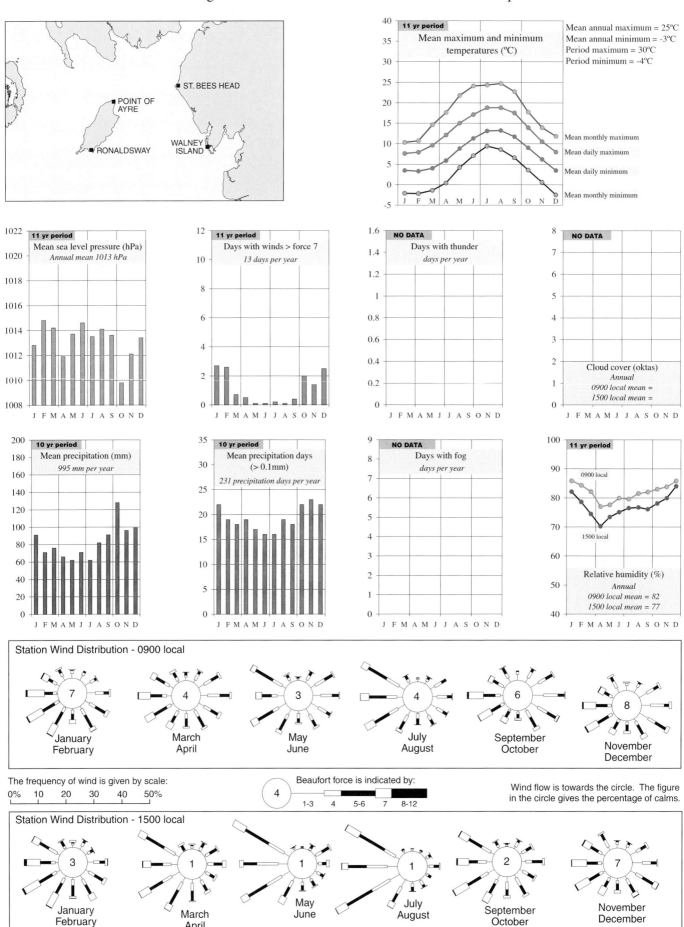

WMO No 03208 POINT OF AYRE

54°25'N 04°22'W. Height above MSL - 9 m Climate Information for period 1998 - 2008

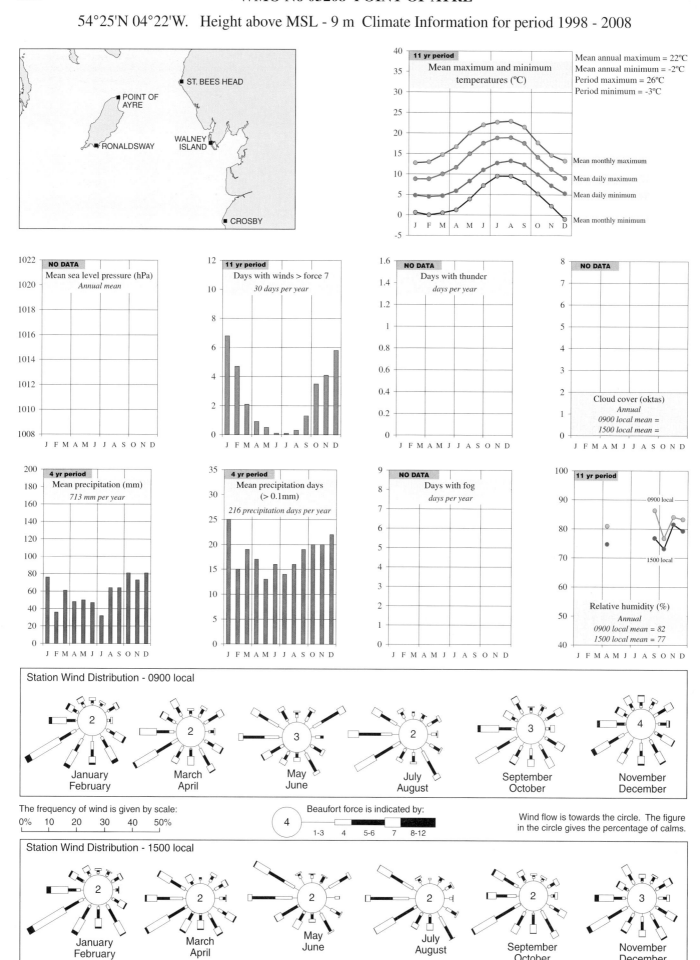

WMO No 03210 ST BEES HEAD

54°31'N 03°36'W.   Height above MSL - 123 m Climate Information for period 1998 - 2008

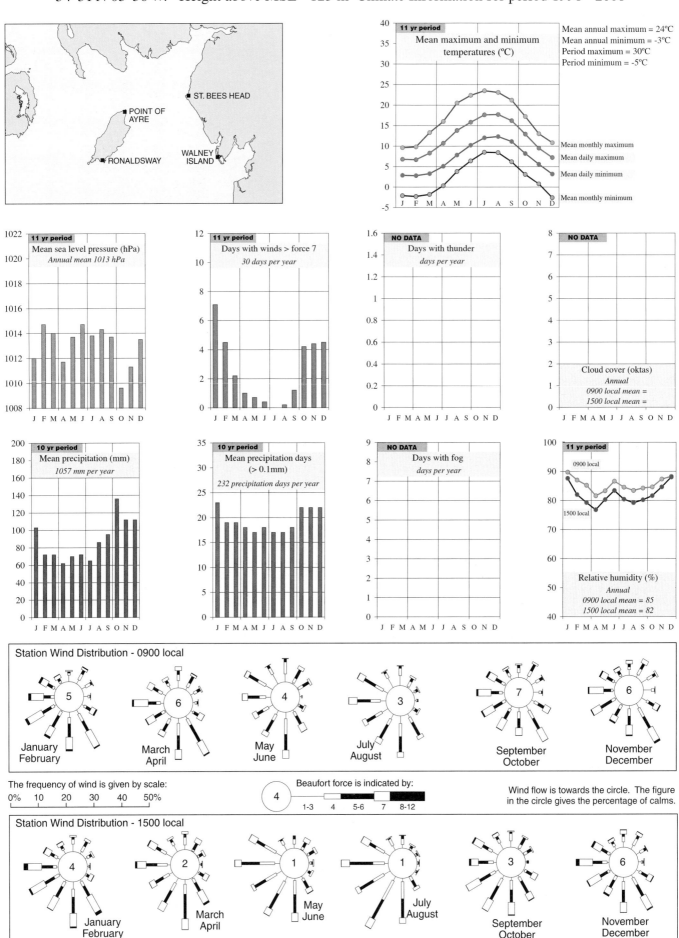

1.158

METEOROLOGICAL CONVERSION TABLE AND SCALES

Fahrenheit to Celsius
°Fahrenheit

	0	1	2	3	4	5	6	7	8	9
°F					Degrees Celsius					
-100	-73.3	-73.9	-74.4	-75.0	-75.6	-76.1	-76.7	-77.2	-77.8	-78.3
-90	-67.8	-68.3	-68.9	-69.4	-70.0	-70.6	-71.1	-71.7	-72.2	-72.8
-80	-62.2	-62.8	-63.3	-63.9	-64.4	-65.0	-65.6	-66.1	-66.7	-67.2
-70	-56.7	-57.2	-57.8	-58.3	-58.9	-59.4	-60.0	-60.6	-61.1	-61.7
-60	-51.1	-51.7	-52.2	-52.8	-53.3	-53.9	-54.4	-55.0	-55.6	-56.1
-50	-45.6	-46.1	-46.7	-47.2	-47.8	-48.3	-48.9	-49.4	-50.0	-50.6
-40	-40.0	-40.6	-41.1	-41.7	-42.2	-42.8	-43.3	-43.9	-44.4	-45.0
-30	-34.4	-35.0	-35.6	-36.1	-36.7	-37.2	-37.8	-38.3	-38.9	-39.4
-20	-28.9	-29.4	-30.0	-30.6	-31.1	-31.7	-32.2	-32.8	-33.3	-33.9
-10	-23.3	-23.9	-24.4	-25.0	-25.6	-26.1	-26.7	-27.2	-27.8	-28.3
-0	-17.8	-18.3	-18.9	-19.4	-20.0	-20.6	-21.1	-21.7	-22.2	-22.8
+0	-17.8	-17.2	-16.7	-16.1	-15.6	-15.0	-14.4	-13.9	-13.3	-12.8
10	-12.2	-11.7	-11.1	-10.6	-10.0	-9.4	-8.9	-8.3	-7.8	-7.2
20	-6.7	-6.1	-5.6	-5.0	-4.4	-3.9	-3.3	-2.8	-2.2	-1.7
30	-1.1	-0.6	0	+0.6	+1.1	+1.7	+2.2	+2.8	+3.3	+3.9
40	+4.4	+5.0	+5.6	6.1	6.7	7.2	7.8	8.3	8.9	9.4
50	10.0	10.6	11.1	11.7	12.2	12.8	13.3	13.9	14.4	15.0
60	15.6	16.1	16.7	17.2	17.8	18.3	18.9	19.4	20.0	20.6
70	21.1	21.7	22.2	22.8	23.3	23.9	24.4	25.0	25.6	26.1
80	26.7	27.2	27.8	28.3	28.9	29.4	30.0	30.6	31.1	31.7
90	32.2	32.8	33.3	33.9	34.4	35.0	35.6	36.1	36.7	37.2
100	37.8	38.3	38.9	39.4	40.0	40.6	41.1	41.7	42.2	42.8
110	43.3	43.9	44.4	45.0	45.6	46.1	46.7	47.2	47.8	48.3
120	48.9	49.4	50.0	50.6	51.1	51.7	52.2	52.8	53.3	53.9

Celsius to Fahrenheit
°Celsius

	0	1	2	3	4	5	6	7	8	9
°C					Degrees Fahrenheit					
-70	-94.0	-95.8	-97.6	-99.4	-101.2	-103.0	-104.8	-106.6	-108.4	-110.2
-60	-76.0	-77.8	-79.6	-81.4	-83.2	-85.0	-86.8	-88.6	-90.4	-92.2
-50	-58.0	-59.8	-61.6	-63.4	-65.2	-67.0	-68.8	-70.6	-72.4	-74.2
-40	-40.0	-41.8	-43.6	-45.4	-47.2	-49.0	-50.8	-52.6	-54.4	-56.2
-30	-22.0	-23.8	-25.6	-27.4	-29.2	-31.0	-32.8	-34.6	-36.4	-38.2
-20	-4.0	-5.8	-7.6	-9.4	-11.2	-13.0	-14.8	-16.6	18.4	-20.2
-10	+14.0	+12.2	+10.4	+8.6	+6.8	+5.0	+3.2	+1.4	-0.4	-2.2
-0	32.0	30.2	28.4	26.6	24.8	23.0	21.2	19.4	+17.6	+15.8
+0	32.0	33.8	35.6	37.4	39.2	41.0	42.8	44.6	46.4	48.2
10	50.0	51.8	53.6	55.4	57.2	59.0	60.8	62.6	64.4	66.2
20	68.0	69.8	71.6	73.4	75.2	77.0	78.8	80.6	82.4	84.2
30	86.0	87.8	89.6	91.4	93.2	95.0	96.8	98.6	100.4	102.2
40	104.0	105.8	107.6	109.4	111.2	113.0	114.8	116.6	118.4	120.2
50	122.0	123.8	125.6	127.4	129.2	131.0	132.8	134.6	136.4	138.2

HECTOPASCALS TO INCHES

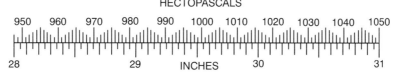

MILLIMETRES TO INCHES

(1) (for small values)

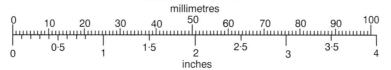

(2) (for large values)

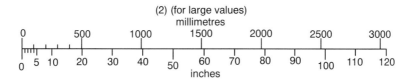

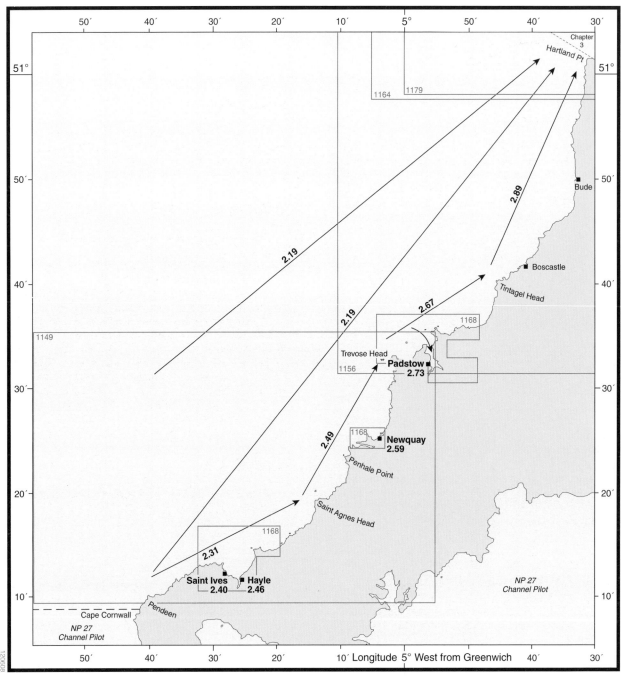

CHAPTER 2

THROUGH ROUTES: CAPE CORNWALL AND THE ISLES OF SCILLY TO THE SMALLS AND MILFORD HAVEN; SOUTH-WEST APPROACHES TO THE BRISTOL CHANNEL

COASTAL ROUTE: CAPE CORNWALL TO HARTLAND POINT

GENERAL INFORMATION

Charts 1178, 2565
Scope of the chapter
2.1

1   This chapter describes the offshore and coastal routes and the harbours and anchorages between Cape Cornwall (50°08′N 5°43′W) and Hartland Point (51°01′N 4°32′W), 70 miles NE. The offshore routes northbound from the TSS off Land's End and the Isles of Scilly are also mentioned.

2   The chapter is divided into the following sections:
     Offshore Routes (2.8).
     Cape Cornwall to Trevose Head (2.30).
     Trevose Head to Hartland Point (2.64).
     The coast S of Cape Cornwall and off-lying dangers are described in the *Channel Pilot*.

Topography
2.2

1   The coastline of SW England is wild and rugged and composed mainly of high cliffs with numerous indentations, and in general is steep-to with rocky fringes and detached rocky outcrops. From a distance many of the intervening headlands appear like islands. In clear weather the land in the vicinity of Cape Cornwall may be seen from a distance of 25 miles.

2   There is very little shelter on this coast and none for larger vessels until the lee of Lundy (51°10′N 4°40′W) is reached. There are only two anchorages of any consequence, Saint Ives Bay (50°13′N 5°27′W) and Newquay Bay (50°26′N 5°05′W); neither offers a harbour of refuge.

Fishing
2.3

1   Trawlers may be encountered in concentrations, between February and April, within 25 miles of Trevose Head. In spring and summer, they are usually found offshore, between Trevose Head and Lundy, often working twin beam trawls.
     Small fishing vessels hand lining for mackerel may be encountered in summer months off the coast between Cape Cornwall and Padstow, especially near Saint Ives and Newquay.

2   Pots and tangle nets may be encountered at any time between Cape Cornwall and Hartland Point, out to 15 miles offshore.
     For details of types of fishing and nets in use, see *The Mariner's Handbook*.

Exercise areas
2.4

1   Submarines exercise throughout the area covered by this chapter; see 1.14. Firing practice area D001 covers offshore waters W and NW of Trevose Head (2.54).

Traffic separation schemes
2.5

1   TSS with their associated inshore traffic zones are established:
     Off Land's End, between Seven Stones and Longships, (50°03′N 5°58′W).
     West of the Isles of Scilly, (49°58′N 6°43′W).
     They are described in the *Channel Pilot*.

2   A recommendation has been adopted by IMO that laden tankers over 10 000 gt using the Off Land's End, between Seven Stones and Longships TSS (50°03′N 5°57′W), should keep at least 3 miles seaward of Wolf Rock (49°57′N 5°49′W), and should not use the scheme in restricted visibility or other adverse weather. For reporting requirements see LAND'S END TSS in *Admiralty List of Radio Signals Volume 6(1)*.

Rescue
2.6

1   For details of rescue organisation and locations of assets see 1.60 and text under Rescue.

Natural conditions
2.7

1   **Tidal streams.** The flow in this area is largely determined by tidal forces. The tidal streams set mainly in the same direction as the coast (NE/SW) at a spring rate of from 1 to 2 kn. They are stronger off Cape Cornwall and Hartland Point, and off salient points, but weaker in the bays between.
     Tidal streams are given on the charts and in *Admiralty Tidal Stream Atlases — The English Channel* and *Irish Sea and Bristol Channel*.

2   **Swell.** Between Cape Cornwall and Hartland Point, a ground swell setting in from the Atlantic Ocean is usually present. This renders the coast unsuitable for anchoring and makes access to the small inlets and harbours difficult and, at times, impracticable.

OFFSHORE ROUTES

GENERAL INFORMATION

Charts 1123, 1178
Area covered
2.8

1   This section describes the offshore routes for traffic bound for Saint George's Channel, Milford Haven or ports in the Bristol Channel from the TSS Off Land's End or W of the Isles of Scilly.

Routes
2.9

1   Two routes are described for traffic north-bound W of The Smalls:

    West of the Isles of Scilly TSS (50°00′N 6°42′W) to Off Smalls TSS (51°40′N 5°51′W), a distance of 103 miles.

    Off Land's End, between Seven Stones and Longships TSS (50°08′N 5°53′W) to Off Smalls TSS, a distance of 92 miles.

2   A single route for Milford Haven traffic is described:

    West of the Isles of Scilly TSS to Milford Haven pilot boarding position, about 4½ miles SSW of Saint Ann's Head (51°41′N 5°11′W), a distance of 108 miles.

For traffic bound for ports in the Bristol Channel two routes are described:

3   Off Land's End, between Seven Stones and Longships TSS to Hartland Point (51°01′N 4°32′W), a distance of 75 miles. This route then continues NE passing between Hartland Point and Lundy (51°10′N 4°40′W).

    West of the Isles of Scilly TSS to Hartland Point, a distance of 100 miles, thence continuing NE to pass NW of Lundy.

The section is arranged as follows:

Cape Cornwall to The Smalls (2.10).

Cape Cornwall to Hartland Point (2.19).

CAPE CORNWALL TO THE SMALLS

General information

Charts 1123, 1178
Routes
2.10

1   There are two main offshore routes which lead N across the entrance to the Bristol Channel to the S end of the traffic lanes W of The Smalls (51°43′N 5°40′W) (5.16):

    From the N end of the traffic lanes W of the Isles of Scilly (49°55′N 6°40′W); this outer route forms an offshore continuation of the ocean passages which end at Bishop Rock (49°52′N 6°27′W), described in the *Channel Pilot*.

2   From the N end of the traffic lanes, 6 miles W of Cape Cornwall (50°08′N 5°43′W).

An offshore route which leads to the approaches to Milford Haven from the N end of the traffic lanes W of the Isles of Scilly is described at 2.18.

Topography
2.11

1   Mainland coasts: see 2.2 and 5.2.

Submarine exercise area
2.12

1   See 2.4.

Rescue
2.13

1   All-weather lifeboats are stationed at Saint Ives (50°13′N 5°29′W) and at Angle, Milford Haven (51°41′N 5°05′W).

Coastguard rescue services covering this offshore area are controlled from Falmouth MRCC.

For details of rescue organisation see 1.60.

Tidal streams
2.14

1   See 2.7.

Directions

Principal marks
2.15

1   **Landmarks:**

    Bishop Rock Lighthouse (grey round granite tower, 49 m in height) (49°52′N 6°27′W) partially and totally obscured from 204° to 259°.

    Round Island Lighthouse (white round tower, 19 m in height) (49°59′N 6°19′W) visible 021° to 288°, obscured from ESE through S to SSW of the light.

    Television mast (50°08′N 5°40′W) (2.35).

    Knill's monument (50°12′N 5°29′W) (2.35).

    Major lights:

    Bishop Rock Light — as above.

2   Round Island Light — as above.

    Seven Stones Light Vessel (red hull, light tower amidships) (50°04′N 6°04′W).

    Wolf Rock Light (grey round granite tower, black lantern, 41 m in height) (49°57′N 5°48′W) also shown in reduced visibility.

    Pendeen Light (50°10′N 5°40′W) (2.35).

    The Smalls Light (51°43′N 5°40′W) (5.14).

Other aids to navigation
2.16

1   **Racons:**

    Seven Stones Light Vessel — as above.

    Wolf Rock Lighthouse — as above.

    Round Island Lighthouse — as above.

    The Smalls Lighthouse (51°43′N 5°40′W) (5.14).

See *Admiralty List of Radio Signals Volume 2*.

Passage
2.17

1   **Outer route.** The offshore route from the N end of the West of the Isles of Scilly TSS (49°55′N 6°20′W), to the S end of the Off Smalls TSS (51°43′N 5°40′W) leads 103 miles NNE; the route lies in deep water and clear of charted dangers.

2   **Inner route.** From the N end of the Off Land's End, between Seven Stones and Longships TSS, 6 miles W of Cape Cornwall (50°08′N 5°43′W), to the S end of the Off Smalls TSS, this offshore route leads 92 miles N passing over the W edge of Cape Cornwall Bank (50°13′N 5°49′W), with a least charted depth of 22 m, but clear W of Bann Shoal (50°19′N 5°46′W), with a least depth of 16·6 m.

3   The sea breaks in strong gales, particularly from NW, over Cape Cornwall Bank and Bann Shoal, which should be avoided at such times by small and heavily laden vessels.

2.18

1   From the N end of the traffic lanes W of the Isles of Scilly an offshore route for deep-draught vessels leads NE for a distance of 108 miles to the pilot boarding position (5.68) for Milford Haven. The route lies in deep water and clear of charted dangers.

For details of prominent features on the Welsh coast at Milford Haven, see 5.74.

(Directions continue for the offshore route off The Smalls at 5.14; directions for the entry to Milford Haven are given at 5.74)

CAPE CORNWALL TO HARTLAND POINT

General information

Charts 1178, 1179
Routes
2.19

1   From the N end of the traffic lanes W of Cape Cornwall (50°08′N 5°43′W), there are two main offshore routes which lead to the entrance to the Bristol Channel NW of Hartland Point (51°01′N 4°32′W) (2.94) and clear of Lundy (3.19), 10 miles NW:

2   From a position at the N end of the traffic lane, about 7 miles W of Cape Cornwall, the inner route leads 75 miles NE.

From the N end of the traffic lane W of the Isles of Scilly (49°55′N 6°40′W), the outer route leads 100 miles NE; this route lies in deep water and is clear of charted dangers.

Topography
2.20
1   See 2.2.

Hazards
2.21
1   **Fishing:** see 2.3.
Submarine exercise area: see 2.4.

Rescue
2.22
1   All-weather lifeboats are stationed at Saint Ives (50°13′N 5°29′W), Padstow (50°33′N 4°56′W) and Appledore (51°03′N 4°12′W).

Coastguard rescue services covering this offshore area are controlled from Falmouth MRCC. East of Hartland Point coverage is controlled from Swansea MRCC.

For details of rescue organisation see 1.60.

Tidal streams
2.23
1   Tidal streams are given on the charts and in *Admiralty Tidal Stream Atlases — The English Channel* and *Irish Sea and Bristol Channel*.

Directions

Principal marks
2.24
1   **Landmarks**:
Round Island Lighthouse (49°59′N 6°19′W) (2.15).
Television mast (50°08′N 5°40′W).
Knill's Monument (50°12′N 5°29′W) (2.35).
Carn Brea Monument (50°13′N 5°15′W) (2.35).
Radio mast (50°13′N 5°14′W) (2.35).
Church tower (50°29′N 5°00′W) (2.54).
2   Trevose Head (50°33′N 5°02′W) (2.54).
Tintagel Head (50°40′N 4°46′W) (2.71) with a conspicuous hotel and tower standing nearby.
Radar aerials (50°53′N 4°33′W) (2.94).
Hartland Point (51°01′N 4°32′W) (2.94).
Major lights:
Round Island Light (49°59′N 6°19′W) (2.15).
3   Seven Stones Light Vessel (50°04′N 6°04′W) (2.15).
Longships Light (grey round granite tower, 35 m in height) (50°04′N 5°45′W).
Pendeen Light (50°10′N 5°40′W) (2.35).
Trevose Head Light (50°33′N 5°02′W) (2.54).
Hartland Point Light (51°01′N 4°32′W) (2.94).
Lundy SE Point Light (51°10′N 4°39′W) (3.17).
Lundy Near N Point Light (51°12′N 4°41′W) (3.17).

Other aids to navigation
2.25
1   **Racons:**
Seven Stones Light Vessel (50°04′N 6°04′W) (2.15).
Wolf Rock Lighthouse (49°57′N 5°48′W) (2.15).
Round Island Lighthouse (49°59′N 6°19′W) (2.15).
See *Admiralty List of Radio Signals Volume 2*.

Passage
2.26
1   From the N end of the traffic lane, about 7 miles W of Cape Cornwall (50°08′N 5°43′W), the route leads 75 miles NE to a position NW of Hartland Point, passing:
SE of Cape Cornwall Bank (50°13′N 5°49′W) (2.17), thence:
NW of Pendeen (50°10′N 5°40′W) (2.36), on which stands a light, thence:
SE of Bann Shoal (50°19′N 5°46′W) (2.17), thence:
2   NW of Saint Agnes Head (50°19′N 5°14′W) (2.35). A wave rider light buoy (special) (50°22′·1N 5°37′·6W), with six marker buoys, is moored 15 miles W of Saint Agnes Head and a radar training light buoy (special) (50°32′·6N 5°23′·1W) is moored 14½ miles NNW. Thence:
NW of Trevose Head (50°33′N 5°02′W) (2.54), on which stands a light, thence:
NW of Tintagel Head (50°40′N 4°46′W) (2.71), thence:
NW of Hartland Point (51°01′N 4°32′W) (2.94), on which stands a light; a tide race extends 2 miles NW of the point.
(Directions continue for the coastal route at 3.17)
2.27
1   The route from the N end of the traffic lane W of the Isles of Scilly (49°55′N 6°40′W) leads 100 miles NE to Hartland Point, passing NW of Lundy,. The route, which can be safely navigated in deep water, passes:
NW of Round Island (49°59′N 6°19′W), thence:

2 NW of Seven Stones Light Vessel (50°04′N 6°04′W) (2.15), thence:

NW of Pendeen (50°10′N 5°40′W) (2.36), thence:

NW of Bann Shoal (50°19′N 5°46′W) (2.17).

The route then continues NE at a greater distance offshore than that described at 2.26.

Hartland Point to Swansea Bay
2.28

1 Vessels proceeding to Swansea Bay ports following either of the offshore routes described at 2.26 and 2.27 can continue NE to the respective pilot boarding stations as shown on the chart.

General directions for Swansea Bay are given at 3.100; deep-draught vessels bound for Port Talbot should follow the directions at 3.184.

Hartland Point to Breaksea Light Buoy
2.29

1 Vessels proceeding to ports E of Breaksea Light Buoy (51°20′N 3°19′W), having followed the offshore routes at 2.26 or 2.27, should follow the directions given for the coastal route at 3.17 or, if having proceeded N of Lundy, at 3.47.

CAPE CORNWALL TO TREVOSE HEAD

GENERAL INFORMATION

Charts 1148, 1149
Area covered
2.30

1 In this section are described the coastal routes, harbours and anchorages between Cape Cornwall (50°08′N 5°43′W) and Trevose Head (36 miles NE).

It is arranged as follows:

Cape Cornwall to Saint Agnes Head (2.31).

Saint Agnes Head to Trevose Head (2.49).

CAPE CORNWALL TO SAINT AGNES HEAD

General information

Charts 1148, 1149
Route
2.31

1 From the N end of the TSS, about 7 miles W of Cape Cornwall (50°08′N 5°43′W), the coastal route leads 24 miles NE to a position NW of Saint Agnes Head.

Topography
2.32

1 The coast, between Cape Cornwall (described in the *Channel Pilot*) and Pendeen, 2¾ miles NNE, is rugged, with cliffs rising to 60 m, and much indented. Between Pendeen and Clodgy Point, 7½ miles ENE, the cliffs rise to over 75 m.

2 From Clodgy Point the coastline is low, and recedes round Saint Ives Bay to Godrevy Point (50°14′N 5°24′W), a bold point with rocky ledges extending 2½ cables, off which lie Godrevy Island (2.37) and The Cleaders (Chart 1168), thence E there are cliffs rising to 90 m at Saint Agnes Head, 7¾ miles NE.

Rescue
2.33

1 All-weather and inshore lifeboats are stationed at Saint Ives (50°13′N 5°29′W) (2.40).

For details of rescue organisation see 1.60.

Tidal streams and tide races
2.34

1 **Tidal streams** are given on the charts and in *Admiralty Tidal Stream Atlas — The English Channel.*

Tide race, centred 2 miles N of Cape Cornwall, is particularly noticeable during SW gales with a SW-going tidal stream. It may be dangerous to small craft.

Directions

Principal marks
2.35

1 **Landmarks:**

Television mast (50°08′N 5°40′W).

Knill's Monument (50°12′N 5°29′W), an obelisk, standing on a hill S of the town of Saint Ives (2.40)

Knill's Monument from N (2.35)
(Original dated 2001)

(Photograph - Air Images)

2 Godrevy Island Lighthouse, (white, octagonal stone tower; 26 m in height) (50°15′N 5°24′W); the lighthouse stands in the centre of the island.

White daymark, (elevation 38 m), (50°16′N 5°17′W), standing on the E entrance point of Portreath Harbour.

Carn Brea Monument (50°13′N 5°15′W), standing on the summit of a hill (elevation 221 m).

Radio mast, (50°13′N 5°14′W), marked by obstruction lights, standing 8 cables SE of the monument on Carn Brea.

Saint Agnes Head (50°19′N 5°14′W), a bold promontory 90 m high, backed by Saint Agnes Hill which is surmounted by a beacon.

Godrevy Island from W (2.36)
(Original dated 2001)

(Photograph - Air Images)

3 **Major light:**

Pendeen Light (white round tower with dwellings, 17 m in height) stands near the watch house on Pendeen (50°10′N 5°40′W).

Passage
2.36

1 From the N end of the TSS, about 7 miles W of Cape Cornwall (50°08′N 5°43′W) the coastal route leads NE to the vicinity of Saint Agnes Head (25 miles ENE), passing (positions given from Pendeen (50°10′N 5°40′W)):

SE of Cape Cornwall Bank (2.17) (6¾ miles NW), thence:

NW of Pendeen, on which stands a light (2.35). The Wra or Three Stone Oar extends 3 cables N with a tide race (2.34) to seaward. Thence:

SE of Bann Shoal (2.17) (10 miles NNW), and:

2 NW of Gurnards Head (3¼ miles ENE), which provides a good radar target, is rugged, bold and fringed by detached rocks; Ebal Rock, the largest of these, lies 1 cable off the headland. Thence:

NW of Carn Naun Point (6 miles ENE); The Carracks, a large group of rocks, lie 5 cables W. Thence:

NW of The Island, also known as Saint Ives Head (8 miles ENE), a low peninsula, fringed with drying rocks and ledges, thence:

3 NW of The Stones (11 miles ENE), three groups of dangerous drying rocks, marked on their N side by a light buoy (N cardinal); Hevah Rock is in the W group. Thence:

NW of Godrevy Island (11½ miles ENE), from which a light is exhibited (2.35), thence:

NW of Gull Rock (15½ miles ENE), 23 m in height, thence:

NW of Saint Agnes Head (2.35).

(Directions continue at 2.54)

Saint Ives Bay

Chart 1168 plan of Saint Ives Bay
General information
2.37

1 Saint Ives Bay is entered between The Island, or Saint Ives Head, (50°13′N 5°29′W) (2.36) and Godrevy Island 3¼ miles ENE, which lies 2¼ cables NW of Godrevy Point

(2.32). The Sound, which lies between Godrevy Island and The Stones (6 cables NW) (2.36), has a least midchannel charted depth of 7·5 m.

2 **Topography.** The shore of the bay between Saint Ives harbour and the entrance to Hayle estuary (1¾ miles SE), at the head of the bay, is composed of bold cliff-fronted slopes, indented by shallow bays. Carbis Bay lies between the headlands of Porthminster Point (50°12′·4N 5°28′·2W) and Carrack Gladden (7½ cables SE) (2.46).

3 Carracks, drying rocks, lie within 1½ cables of Porthminster Point.

Between Hayle estuary and the mouth of the Red River, 6 cables S of Godrevy Point, the coast is fronted by a hard sandy beach which dries to 2 cables offshore, backed by a range of grass-covered sand dunes.

Bessack Rock lies 4 cables offshore, 7 cables SW of the entrance to the Red River; Ceres Rock lies between Bessack Rock and the shore on the edge of the drying contour.

4 **Outfall.** An outfall, terminated by diffusers marked by buoys (port hand) on their E and SE sides, extends 1¼ miles NW from the shore 7¾ cables S of Godrevy Point (2.32).

Obstruction, which dries 1 m, lies in Carbis Bay, 4 cables SSE of Porthminster Point.
2.38

1 **Tidal streams.** In Saint Ives Bay the NE-going stream is very weak; the SW-going stream, though not strong, sets round the bay.

The streams in both directions set fairly strongly past Godrevy Island and across The Stones. Across The Sound they set ENE with the in-going tide and WSW with the out-going.
2.39

1 **Directions.** Approaching Saint Ives Bay from the W there are no off-lying dangers. Approaching from the E give a wide berth to The Stones, with noticeably strong tide-rips, keeping in depths of not less than 20 m. At night do not bring Smeaton Pier light at Saint Ives to bear more than 214° until clear S of the red sector of Godrevy Island Light.

2 The passage through The Sound or inside Godrevy Island should not be attempted without local knowledge. In heavy weather the area is considered dangerous to small craft.

Saint Ives
2.40

1 **Position and function.** Saint Ives has a small tidal harbour, situated on the SE side of The Island (50°13′·1N 5°28′·7W) and is used principally by fishing vessels and pleasure craft.

The town of Saint Ives lies mostly SW of the harbour.

Port limits. A line joining the most E point of The Island to Porthminster Point, 7 cables SSE.

Port Authority. Penwith District Council, Saint Clare, Penzance.

The harbour has the services of a resident Harbour Master whose office is at the root of Smeaton Pier.
2.41

1 **Limiting conditions.** The harbour dries. Depths in the entrance and within the harbour are liable to change owing to silting and erosion.

The deepest water is to be found close to Smeaton Pier.
2.42

1 **Harbour.** The harbour consists of a single basin protected by Smeaton Pier, which extends 200 m S from

Saint Ives Head from NE (2.37)

(Original dated 2001)

(Photograph - Air Images)

The Island, and West Pier which extends 50 m E from the shore towards the outer end of Smeaton Pier. The bottom is sand.

2   The entrance between the piers faces S and is ¾ cable wide. A light (black pole) is exhibited from the head of W pier; a light (white round metal tower, 10 m in height) is exhibited from the head of Smeaton Pier.

The submerged ruins of a breakwater extend SE from the coast, N of the root of Smeaton Pier.

2.43

1   **Landmarks:**

Knill's Monument (50°12′N 5°29′W) (2.35).

Hotel on Pedn Olva, 1½ cables S of the head of Smeaton Pier.

Tregenna Castle Hotel, a prominent building, with two round towers at the extremities of its castellated walls, standing 4 cables S of Pedn Olva.

Viaduct at Carbis Bay, 1¼ miles SSE of The Island.

2.44

1   **Directions.** The harbour is best approached keeping the head of West Pier just open of Smeaton Pier, passing to seaward of a buoy (starboard hand) marking the extremity of a ruined breakwater (2.42), thence rounding Smeaton Pier closely, running a warp to the pier if necessary.

2.45

1   **Berths.** Alongside berths are very limited; shallow draught vessels under 400 tonnes, able to take the ground, can berth at Smeaton Pier.

Facilities: hospital; helicopter landing facilities in the vicinity; slipway.

Supplies: marine diesel (24 hours notice); fresh water at Smeaton Pier.

Hayle

2.46

1   **General description.** The entrance to Hayle estuary, at the head of Saint Ives Bay, lies across Hayle Bar (50°12′N 5°26′W), which dries.

The port of Hayle is used principally by fishing and pleasure craft with local knowledge.

The small town of Hayle lies on the SE side of the estuary.

2   **Harbour limits.** The seaward limits of Hayle Harbour extend from the coast at Carrack Gladden (50°12′N 5°27′W) to a position 4½ cables NNE, thence 9 cables ENE, thence S to the coast at Black Cliff.

Harbour. There are a number of drying quays. The harbour master may be contacted on VHF Channel 16 or by telephone; +44(0)1736 754043 (land line), 07814 010871 (mobile).

3   **Submarine power cables.** Two submarine power cables, marked by beacons, cross the estuary.

Directions. The entrance to the channel is marked by a light buoy (port hand) close N of Hayle Bar. However, sand movement, prevalent during gales, causes the course of the navigable channel to alter and any vessel wishing to

Saint Ives Harbour from SE (2.40)

(Original dated 2001)

(Photograph - Air Images)

4 enter the harbour, and lacking local knowledge, should contact the harbour master before attempting to do so.

A training wall, marked by four light perches (starboard hand) runs N/S close W of the channel towards Chapel Anjou Point, the W entrance point of the estuary and from where a light (metal pole) is exhibited.

Owing to the variable position of the channel the front leading light, ¾ cable S of Chapel Anjou Point, has been discontinued and is no longer visible from seaward. The rear light (pile, red and white lantern, 5 m in height), 1¼ cables S of Chapel Anjou Point, remains.

Vessels may cross Hayle Bar, in favourable weather, at HW ± 1 hour.

Chart 1149
Portreath
2.47

1 **Position and function.** Portreath (50°16′N 5°17′W) is a small tidal harbour, 4 miles ENE from Godrevy Point (50°14′N 5°24′W) (2.32) used by inshore fishing boats and leisure craft.

Limiting conditions. The harbour offers little shelter in strong onshore winds or when there is a heavy ground swell and entry should not be attempted when such conditions prevail.

2 **Approach and entry.** Entered from N at HW ±2 hours. It can be identified by the daymark (2.35) standing close E. Horse Rock lies close N of E side of the entrance and Gull Rock (2.36) lies close W.

Harbour Authority. The harbour is maintained by Kerrier District Council and run by Portreath Harbour Association.

Harbour. A breakwater projects N, forming the W side of an outer basin which leads into two tidal basins, the entrances to which are 8 m wide.

Anchorage
2.48

1 The best anchorage is 5 cables ESE of The Island (2.36) in a depth of 16 m, stiff clay and fine sand, as shown on the chart. N and W winds, however, cause a heavy sea.

SAINT AGNES HEAD TO TREVOSE HEAD

General information

Chart 1149
Route
2.49

1 The coastal route from Saint Agnes Head (50°19′N 5°14′W) to Trevose Head (50°33′N 5°02′W) leads 16 miles NNE.

Topography
2.50

1 To the E of Saint Agnes Head towards Trevose Head, the coastline generally consists of several open bays separated by bold headlands. Watergate Bay, a slight indentation in the coast between Trevelgue Head (50°26′N 5°04′W) and Griffin's Point, 2 miles NNE, is fronted by

Tregurrian or Watergate Beach, a long surf-bound beach which dries to 2 cables offshore. Between Trevelgue Head and Trevose Head, 7 miles N the coast is high, precipitous and indented.

Historic wreck

2.51

1   A restricted area of 250 m radius is established around position 50°20′·1N 5°10′·9W off Cligga Head. For further details see 1.57 and *Annual Notice to Mariners Number 16.*

Rescue

2.52

1   Inshore lifeboats are stationed at Newquay (2.59), Trevaunance Cove (2.63) and Saint Agnes (2.63).
For details of rescue organisation see 1.60.

Tidal streams

2.53

1   Tidal streams are given on the chart and in *Admiralty Tidal Stream Atlas — The English Channel.*

Directions
(continued from 2.36)

Principal marks

2.54

1   **Landmarks:**
        Saint Eval Church tower (50°29′N 5°00′W), tall and square. Several tall radio masts stand close S.

2   Trevose Head (50°33′N 5°02′W), on which stands a lighthouse (white round tower with dwellings, 27 m in height), has the appearance of a rounded island when first seen from W; it is a good landfall. The land within the headland is considerably lower.

    Major light:
        Trevose Head Light — see above.

Trevose Head Lighthouse (2.54)
(Original dated 1997)

(Photograph - Dr. M P Bender)

Passage

2.55

1   From NW of Saint Agnes Head (50°19′N 5°14′W) the coastal route leads NNE to the vicinity of Trevose Head (50°33′N 5°02′W), passing (with positions from Saint Agnes Head):
        Clear of Bawden Rocks (9 cables N), two detached islets, thence:

2   WNW of Penhale Point (5¼ miles NE), with prominent buildings near its summit; Carters Rocks, close NW of the point, appear like a double pyramid when seen from W. A dangerous wreck lies 2 cables W of the rocks. Thence:
        WNW of Kelsey Head (6 miles NE); The Chick, an islet, lies close N. Thence:

3   Clear of Medusa Rock (7 miles NNE); a wreck with a charted depth of 17 m lies close S. Thence:
        WNW of Towan Head (8¼ miles NE), 30 m in height, at the N end of a long peninsula. There is a tide race off the head and a 7 m shoal 9 cables NW. Thence:

4   WNW of Park Head (13 miles NE). Cow and Calf rocks lie within 5 cables WSW. Thence:
        Clear of Diver Rock (14¼ miles NNE), thence:

Trevose Head from W (2.55)
(Original dated 2001)

(Photograph - Air Images)

WNW of Trevose Head (2.54), with The Bull, an above-water rock, and the Quies, above-water rocks lying, respectively, 1 cable and 9 cables W of the headland.

(Directions continue at 2.71)

The Gannel
2.56

1   The Gannel is a long narrow drying creek entered from Crantock Bay (50°25′N 5°08′W), 1½ miles SW of Towan Head. It is navigable only by small craft at MHWS and is entered between two low rocky headlands, Pentire Point West (50°24′·5N 5°08′·1W) and Pentire Point East (4¼ cables ENE). The Goose, a rock 18 m in height, stands 1½ cables W from Pentire Point East.

A ferry crosses the creek 5 cables inside its entrance.

Newquay Bay

Chart 1168 plan of Newquay Bay
General information
2.57

1   Newquay Bay is an open bay entered between Towan Head (50°26′N 5°06′W) (2.55) and Trevelgue Head 1¼ miles E. The indented shores of the bay consist of steep cliffs mainly built up and fronted by sandy beaches which dry to 1½ cables offshore.

2   Porth Beach, a sandy inlet which dries, lies at the E side of the bay on the S side of Trevelgue Head. There is a slipway in the SE corner of the beach.

Fistral Bay, with a wide sandy beach fronting sand dunes at its head, lies on the SW side of Towan Head.

Directions
2.58

1   **Landmarks:**
    Atlantic Hotel (5½ cables SE of Towan Head) with Huers Lookout fronting it, standing on high ground close to the coast in the W part of the bay; a monument in the form of a cross stands close W of the hotel.
    Headland Hotel (3 cables SSE of Towan Head).
    Church tower (1 mile SE of Towan Head).

2   **Approach.** Approaching from the W a wide berth should be given to Towan Head and the rocky shoal 9 cables NW of it. A wide berth should also be given to Old Dane Rock, dries 6·2 m, lying 1 cable N of Huers Lookout (50°25′·2N 5°05′·3W) and Listrey Rock, with a least depth of 0·5 m, extending 1¾ cables E of Old Dane Rock.

Newquay Harbour
2.59

1   **General information.** Newquay is a large holiday resort with a population of about 18 000.

Newquay Harbour from SE (2.59)

(Original dated 2001)

(Photograph - Air Images)

The harbour lies on the SW side of Newquay Bay and is contained within North Pier and South Pier; it is tidal and dries.

It is used only by pleasure craft with local knowledge and fishing vessels; there are considerable numbers during the summer.

2 A light (bracket on wall) is exhibited from the head of N pier; a light (round stone tower, 2 m on height) is exhibited from the head of S pier.

Harbour Authority. Restormel Borough Council, Newquay, Cornwall. There is a full time resident Harbour Master.

Facilities: hospital; small quantities of marine diesel; fresh water; slipway.

2.60

1 **Caution.** No attempt should be made to enter the harbour when there is a ground swell, nor during an onshore gale, as the sea breaks heavily off the entrance and for some distance outside under these conditions; N gales and/or ground swell bring a heavy sea into the harbour and cause uncomfortable conditions.

Anchorages
2.61

1 There is good anchorage in Newquay Bay (50°25′N 5°05′W) (2.57) in fine weather or with offshore winds, in depths of 8·5 m, sand, 6 cables E of Towan Head; as shown on the chart.

Chart 1149
Caution
2.62

1 Mariners are cautioned against anchoring and fishing within an area, marked on the chart, extending 3 miles seaward of Ligger or Perran Bay (50°22′N 5°12′W) owing to the existence of disused instruments and cables. Buoys are moored within the area.

Landing place
2.63

1 Landing is possible at Trevaunance Cove (50°19′N 5°12′W), 1 mile E of Saint Agnes Head, where there is a protected sandy beach.

TREVOSE HEAD TO HARTLAND POINT

GENERAL INFORMATION

Chart 1156
Area covered
2.64

1 In this section are described the coastal routes, harbours and anchorages between Trevose Head (50°33′N 5°02′W) and Hartland Point (34½ miles NNE).

It is arranged as follows:
Trevose Head to Tintagel Head (2.67).
Tintagel Head to Hartland Point (2.89).

Topography
2.65

1 The coast, in general, comprises many open bays which are fringed by dangerous rocks and backed by bold headlands and long stretches of high cliffs, in some places over 200 m high, particularly E of Tintagel Head (50°40′N 4°46′W).

Fishing
2.66

1 See 2.3.

TREVOSE HEAD TO TINTAGEL HEAD

General information

Chart 1156
Route
2.67

1 The coastal route from the vicinity of Trevose Head (50°33′N 5°02′W) to NW of Tintagel Head leads NE for 12 miles giving a wide berth to the dangers N and E of Trevose Head.

Topography
2.68

1 See 2.65. The cliffs between Pentire Point (50°35′N 4°56′W), the E entrance of Padstow Bay, which rises steeply to high ground, and Rumps Point, 6 cables NE, are bold and dark, backed by grassy slopes with outcrops of

rock which, when viewed from the W, have the appearance of a cock's comb.

Rescue
2.69

1 An all-weather lifeboat is stationed at Padstow (50°32′N 4°56′W). The lifeboat slipway is at Polventon or Mother Ivy's Bay, 2½ miles W of the town.

Inshore lifeboats are stationed at Rock (50°33′N 4°55′W) and Port Isaac (50°36′N 4°50′W).

For details of rescue organisation see 1.60.

Tidal streams
2.70

1 For general details see *Admiralty Tidal Stream Atlases — The English Channel* and *Irish Sea and Bristol Channel.*

Directions
(continued from 2.55)

Principal marks
2.71

1 **Landmarks**:
Trevose Head (50°33′N 5°02′W) (2.54).
Daymark (50°34′N 4°57′W), stone tower 12 m in height, standing 3 cables W of Stepper Point.
Hut (50°36′N 4°52′W), a former coastguard lookout, standing on Kellan Head.
Saint Endellion Church tower (50°34′N 4°50′W).
2 Tintagel Head (50°40′N 4°46′W), a prominent bluff headland which rises to an elevation of 79 m, backed by several rounded ridges which are higher than any other part of the coast in the vicinity.
Hotel (2 cables E of Tintagel Head).
Major lights:
Trevose Head Light (50°33′N 5°02′W) (2.54).
Hartland Point Light (51°01′N 4°32′W) (2.94).

Light   Coastguard lookout   Daymark

Stepper Point from NNE (2.71)

(Original dated 2001)

(Photograph - Air Images)

The Mouls   Rumps Point   Pentire Point

Newland from W (2.72)

(Original dated 2001)

(Photograph - Air Images)

Passage

2.72

1   From Trevose Head to Tintagel Head (12½ miles NE), the coastal route leads NE, passing (with positions from Trevose Head):

     NW of Outer Gulland Shoal (2¾ miles NNE); Inner Gulland Shoal lies 1½ miles S and Gulland Rock, which consists of two bold rocky islets almost joined together, lies 1½ miles SSE of the outer shoal. Thence:

2   NW of Stepper Point (3½ miles ENE) from where a light (metal column, 2 m in height) is exhibited; a conspicuous daymark (2.71) stands W of the light. Thence:

     NW of Newland (4¼ miles NE), a bold pyramidal islet, 35 m in height, 5 cables NW of Pentire Point

(2.68); Rainer Rocks extend ½ cable W from the islet; King Phillip Rock lies close E and Villiers Rock lies 1 cable E of the islet (Chart 1168). Thence:

3   NW of Rumps Point (5 miles NE) (2.68). The Mouls, a pyramidal rock, 46 m high, lies 2½ cables ENE of the point and Roscarrock, a below-water rock, lies 2½ cables WNW. Thence:

NW of Kellan Head (7 miles ENE) (2.71), thence:

NW of Varley Head (7¾ miles ENE), a low headland, thence:

NW of Tintagel Head (50°40′N 4°46′W) (2.71); Gull Rock, 41 m in height, lies 3 cables off Dennis Point, 1½ miles S of the headland.

(Directions continue at 2.94)

Padstow Harbour

Chart 1168 plan of Approaches to Padstow
General information
2.73

1   **Position.** Padstow Harbour (50°32′N 4°56′W) is a small port situated 1½ miles within the W entrance to the estuary of the river Camel, which flows into Padstow Bay.

Function. The harbour is used by small vessels of up to 2000 gt. Cargoes handled include: fertiliser, grain, coal, timber and sand. Fishing vessels and pleasure craft also use the harbour.

2   The town of Padstow, which is built up around the harbour has a population of about 2500.

Harbour limits. The seaward limits of the harbour are bounded by a line joining Stepper Point, Gulland Rock, Newland and Pentire Point.

3   **Approach and entry.** The harbour is approached from Padstow Bay and entered via the river Camel.

Port Authority. Padstow Harbour Commissioners, Harbour Office, West Quay, Padstow, Cornwall PL28 8AQ.

Internet. www.padstow-harbour.co.uk

Email. padstowharbour@btconnect.com

The Port Authority is represented by a Port Administrator who is also the Harbour Master.

Limiting conditions
2.74

1   **Depths:** the outer basin dries to firm mud or sand bottom.

Maximum size of vessel handled: 2000 gt, draught up to 4·9 m at MHWS and 3·9 m at MHWN alongside South Dock, dependent upon on the approval of the Harbour Master.

Tidal levels: Mean spring range 6·5 m; mean neap range 3·0 m.

Arrival information
2.75

1   **Notice of ETA required.** Vessels should send their ETA direct to Padstow Harbour Office 12 hours in advance with subsequent amendment, if necessary, up to 2 hours before

Stepper Point   *Pentire Point*

Town Bar   *River Camel*

Padstow from S (2.73)
(Original dated 2001)

(Photograph - Air Images)

original ETA. For further details see *Admiralty List of Radio Signals Volume 6(1)*.

2.76

1   **Outer anchorage.** Padstow Bay is open to W and NW winds and is not recommended as an anchorage if a significant ground swell is running. Considerable alteration to the depths appears to take place from time to time.

2   Anchorage can be obtained in Port Quin Bay, (50°36′N 4°54′W), where the holding is good. Shelter from W winds is obtainable in the W part of the bay. Entered between the promontory of which Rumps Point (2.68) is the W extremity and Kellan Head, 1¾ miles E, the village of Port Quin lies at the head of a narrow inlet situated on the E side of the bay. Cow and Calf, rocks, lie close W of Kellan Head.

2.77

1   **Pilots.** Pilotage is compulsory for all cargo vessels over 30 m and those vessels over 20 m with a draught greater than 3·5 m. The pilot boards 4 cables NE of Stepper Point, or in adverse weather as near to Bar Light Buoy as is practicable.

A pilot is available, if necessary, to Wadebridge (2.86), 4 miles above Padstow.

For further details see *Admiralty List of Radio Signals Volume 6(1)*.

Harbour

2.78

1   The harbour, which fronts the town, comprises an inner harbour and outer basin which lie within New Pier, which extends S from the shore, and South Quay which extends N. South Dock lies on the outer side of South Quay. The entrance, between the heads of New Pier and South Dock, is 90 m wide.

Lights (metal columns, 6 m in height) are exhibited from the heads of the quays.

2   Entry into the inner harbour is through a tidal gate, which, excepting maintenance periods, will allow depths of approximately 3¼ m to be maintained within the basin. The clear distance within the tidal gate passage is 10 m.

A bullnose extends a short distance NW from the head of South Dock.

The deepest water is to be found outside South Dock.

2.79

1   **Tidal streams.** The tidal streams 5 cables NW of Stepper Point are more or less rotary, in a clockwise direction, and rather irregular; see information on the chart.

The in-going stream is strongest in the direction of the channel before The Doom Bar (2.81) covers, after which it gradually decreases and sets inward from all directions. Similarly, the out-going stream is not strong at first, and its direction is uncertain, but as the depth decreases the stream gains strength and sets in the direction of the channel. In the narrow part of the channel the maximum spring rate in each direction is from 3 to 3½ kn.

2   In Port Quin Bay (2.76) between The Mouls (2.72) and the land the streams set ESE for 3½ hours and WNW for approximately 9 hours; it has been reported that the spring rate is approximately 1½ to 2 kn.

Directions

2.80

1   **Approaches.** The best time for entering the harbour is between half flood and HW; at LW spring tides the sea may break over the bar.

The best approach leads ESE from a position midway between Gulland Rock (50°34′·3N 4°59′·9W) (2.72) and

Newland (2¼ miles NE) (2.72) to the pilot boarding position off Stepper Point (2.77).

2   The track then leads S into the buoyed entrance channel avoiding a detached shoal which dries 0·9 m, close NE of the NE corner of Doom Bar.

The approach which leads between Gulland Rock and Gunver Head, 1¼ miles SE, contains several off-lying dangers of which Gurley Rock, 6 cables SSE of Gulland Rock and Chimney Rock, 4 cables NNW of Gunver Head, have depths of 3 m and less over them.

2.81

1   **Entrance channel** to the harbour, is formed by the estuary of the river Camel.

The Doom Bar, an extensive drying sandbank, lies along the W side of the channel, the entrance to which lies 1½ cables W of Trebetherick Point, fringed by rocky ledges on which the sea may break.

2   The channel is 1 cable wide with depths of 0·2 to 1·3 m over the bar and is marked from seaward by light buoys as far as The Pool, in which there are depths up to 3·7 m; thereafter the channel lies close to the W side of the shore.

A light buoy (port hand) is moored close off New Pier at the entrance to the outer harbour.

Caution. The height and shape of the sandbanks in the Camel Estuary are constantly changing and latest details can be obtained from the Harbour Office.

2.82

1   **Useful marks**:

Saint Saviour's Point Lighthouse (green triangle), 3 cables N of Padstow Harbour entrance.

Monument standing close N of Saint Saviour's Point.

Berths and port services

2.83

1   Small vessels berth alongside South Dock, 259 m long, of which 240 m is usable and which has the deepest water alongside; see 2.74.

There are berths for leisure craft within the inner basin and tidal moorings for visiting craft may be available in The Pool. Moorings may also be available at Rock on the E side of the river, opposite Padstow.

2.84

1   **Repairs**: minor repairs; small dry dock situated S of South Dock, can accept vessels up to 20·7 m LOA and beam 7 m, entering from NNE.

Supplies: fuel oil from the N end of South Dock; fresh water and provisions.

Good facilities for visiting yachts.

2.85

1   **Harbour regulations.** Bye-laws are in force for vessels carrying dangerous substances. Copies of the bye-laws should be obtained prior to arrival. The Harbour Master should be informed of the nature and quantity of such cargo; vessels should be anchored or moored only as directed by him.

2   All vessel movements within the harbour must be sanctioned by the Duty Officer (Berthing Master); a speed restriction of 8 kn exists in the approaches to, and within, the harbour.

Chart 1168 plan of the river Camel — Padstow to Wadebridge

Wadebridge

2.86

1   **General description.** Wadebridge, a town in which a road bridge spans the river Camel, lies 4 miles above Padstow. When the height of the tide at Padstow is 6 m or more, vessels drawing up to 2·4 m can navigate this stretch

of the river, which is unmarked, but they must be prepared to lie aground at their berths.

2   Wadebridge has a population of about 5500.

Pilots. See 2.77.

Facilities: several slips and a boatyard lie on the N side of the river; Commissioners Quay on the S side, and part of a tidal defence scheme, contains a slipway.

Harbours

Chart 1168 plan Approaches to Padstow

Port Isaac

2.87

1   **General information.** Port Isaac (50°36′N 4°50′W) lies at the head of a creek open to the N. It is used by small fishing vessels. It is approached from N and entered between Lobber Point, to the W, and Kenewal Rock and Warrant Rock, which both dry and on which the sea frequently breaks, to the E.

The harbour is protected by two breakwaters projecting short distances from either side of the creek with a gap of about 50 m between their heads. A beacon stands on the head of the E breakwater.

2   Drying to a sandy bottom, and accessible only at HW ±2 hours, Port Isaac entrance is impassable in strong onshore winds.

Port Gaverne

2.88

1   Port Gaverne (50°35′·6N 4°49′·4W), a narrow creek open NW with a drying stone and pebble bottom, is entered 2½ cables E of Port Isaac. Sheltered from all except direct onshore winds. There is a slipway.

The houses at the head of the creek are prominent when the entrance opens.

TINTAGEL HEAD TO HARTLAND POINT

General information

Chart 1156

Route

2.89

1   The coastal route from Tintagel Head (50°40′N 4°46′W) to Hartland Point (51°01′N 4°32′W), leads 23 miles NNE.

Topography

2.90

1   See 2.65.

Submarine cables

2.91

1   Mariners are cautioned against anchoring and fishing within an area W of the centre of Widemouth Sand, at the head of Bude Bay, owing to the existence of submarine cables, including transatlantic telephone cables.

Rescue

2.92

1   During the summer months there is an inshore lifeboat stationed at Bude (50°50′N 4°33′W).

For details of rescue organisation see 1.60.

Tidal streams

2.93

1   Midway between Hartland Point and Lundy (51°10′N 4°40′W) the in-going stream begins nearly 6 hours before HW Milford Haven and the out-going stream begins 20 minutes after HW at that port.

The maximum spring rate in each direction is 3 kn.

There is an indraught towards Bude Bay (50°49′N 4°35′W).

Close-up from NW

Hartland Point and Lighthouse from W (2.94)

(Original dated 2001)

(Photograph - Air Images)

Tidal streams are given on the chart and in *Admiralty Tidal Stream Atlas — Irish Sea and Bristol Channel*.

Directions
(continued from 2.72)

Principal marks
2.94

1 **Landmarks**:

Tintagel Head (50°40′N 4°46′W); hotel (2 cables E) and church (4 cables S) (2.71).

Radar aerials (50°53′N 4°33′W), dish shaped, standing close E of Lower Sharpnose Point.

Hartland Point (51°01′N 4°32′W), with a lighthouse (white round tower, 18 m in height), is the termination of a dark brown tableland 107 m high which slopes steeply to the sea; the adjoining cliffs are perpendicular.

2 Radome (51°01′N 4°31′W).

Major lights:

Hartland Point Light — as above; the light is shown continuously.

Lundy SE Point Light (51°10′N 4°39′W) (3.17).

Passage
2.95

1 From a position NW of Tintagel Head to the vicinity of Hartland Point the coastal route leads NNE for 23 miles, passing (with positions from Tintagel Head):

WNW of Penally Point (2½ miles ENE), on which there is a flag staff. Thence:

2 WNW of Cambeak (6 miles NE), a narrow pointed headland with high cliffs, thence:

WNW of Widemouth Sand (10 miles NE), a sandy beach interspersed with rocks at the head of Bude Bay, which extends 1¼ miles N from Foxhole Point with moderately low land behind it, thence:

3 WNW of Lower Sharpnose Point (15 miles NNE) (2.94), thence:

WNW of Higher Sharpnose Point (16 miles NNE), a prominent point fronted by a ledge, thence:

WNW of Knap Head (18 miles NNE), a headland with cliffs over 100 m high and fronted by Knaps Longpeak, a ledge which extends 250 m W, thence:

4 NW of Hartland Point, from which a light (2.94) is exhibited, with a tide race extending 2 miles NW during the strength of the streams in both directions; Tense Rocks, which dry, extend 2 cables NW from the point.

Caution. A shoal with a least depth of 14·6 m lies 3½ miles WNW of Knap Head (50°56′N 4°33′W).

(Directions continue for the coastal passage into the Bristol Channel at 3.17)

Anchorages and harbours
2.96

1 Owing to ground swell and bays being open and exposed, particularly in heavy weather, there are no secure anchorages on this part of the coast. Inlets offer some shelter to small craft, but swinging room may be limited.

Boscastle
2.97

1 **General information.** Boscastle harbour (50°41′·5N 4°41′·7W) lies at the head of a narrow creek, entered between Penally Point (2.95), on the NE side of the entrance, and Willapark (1 cable SW). Meachard, an offshore rock 37 m high, about ¾ cable NW of the entrance, serves to identify it. There are no underwater dangers in the approach.

2 **Harbour.** There are two small breakwaters near the head of the creek. The harbour is accessible only 2 hours either side of HW by small fishing vessels and leisure craft, and then only with local knowledge. It is inaccessible in strong onshore winds.

Bude Haven
2.98

1 **General information.** Bude Haven (50°50′N 4°33′W) is entered from Bude Bay, which lies between the headland of Cambeak (50°44′N 4°39′W) and Lower Sharpnose Point (9¼ miles NNE). The small drying harbour is used by fishing vessels and leisure craft. A lock gate leads into the canal basin.

The harbour authority is North Cornwall District Council, Trevanion Road, Wadebridge, Cornwall PL27 7NU.

2 **Limiting conditions.** Entry is normally limited to 2 hours either side of HW and is not possible when a heavy swell is running or seas are breaking; it is not recommended at night.

Maximum dimensions for vessels using the lock are; length 27·4 m, beam 7·6 m, and draught 2·4 m; a minimum height of tide of 5·5 m is required for locking in. The outer lock gate is normally kept open; since the lock dries, all vessels must be prepared to take the ground.

3 **Harbour.** The harbour, which lies on the SW side of the town is approached through a channel, formed by the river Neet, which leads to a sea lock. The channel is sheltered from SW by a breakwater, which first extends NNW from the shore to Chapel Rock, which lies ¼ mile N of Compass Point, thence continuing a further short distance to Barrel Rock at the harbour entrance.

4 **Berths.** Vessels normally berth inside the sea lock, and between it and a fixed bridge, 2 cables above, where there is 90 m of quay. The canal above the bridge is no longer used for commercial navigation.

Radome　　　　　　　　　　　　　　　　*Hartland Point Light*

Hartland Point from N (2.95)

(Original dated 1996)

(Photograph - Commander J P B Snape, THV Mermaid)

Chapter 3 - Bristol Channel - Western Part

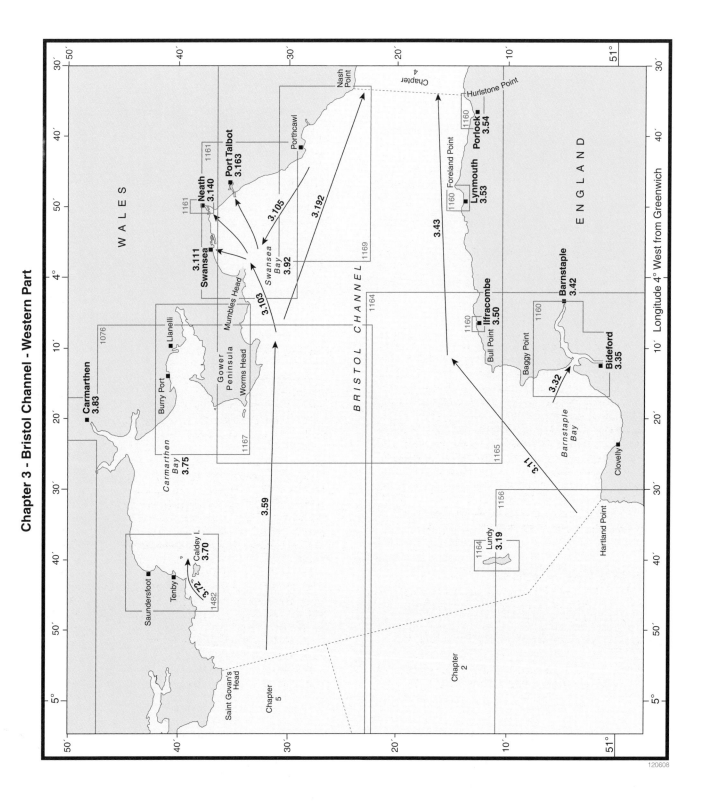

CHAPTER 3

BRISTOL CHANNEL — WESTERN PART

GENERAL INFORMATION

Chart 1179
Scope of the chapter
3.1

1   The area covered is that part of the Bristol Channel lying between Hartland Point (51°01′N 4°32′W) and Saint Govan's Head (38 miles NNW) in the W, and between Hurlstone Point (51°14′N 3°35′W) and Nash Point (10 miles N) in the E.

It is divided into two sections:

2   South side from Hartland Point to Hurlstone Point (3.8), including Lundy (3.19).

North side from Saint Govan's Head to Nash Point (3.55), including Swansea Bay (3.92) and its associated ports.

Topography
3.2

1   The W end of the S shore of the Bristol Channel is deeply indented by Bideford Bay. Between Bull Point (51°12′N 4°12′W) and Hurlstone Point, 24 miles E, the coastline is nearly straight and mainly steep-to. Foreland Point is the most prominent point with Dunkery Beacon, 9 miles SE, at the summit of the highest land visible from seaward on this stretch of coast.

2   The N shore of the Bristol Channel is deeply indented by Carmarthen Bay and Swansea Bay, wide, relatively low backed bays which each have extensive shoals extending W from their E sides, parallel with the main shipping route.

Lundy (51°10′N 4°40′W) is a prominent feature in the approaches to the Bristol Channel. The island is 137 m high at its highest point, where the old lighthouse stands, and consists mainly of steep inaccessible cliffs.

Shelter
3.3

1   In strong W winds the only sheltered roadsteads lie on the E side of Lundy (3.25) or in Clovelly Road (51°00′N 4°23′W) (3.31), there being no other refuge of much value until E of Longitude 3°10′W.

Fishing
3.4

1   Trawlers may be encountered in the summer near, and between, Lundy and Caldey Island (51°38′N 4°42′W), also inshore in Carmarthen Bay, and in the vicinity of Saint Govan's Head.

Pots may be encountered off the Welsh coast W of Mumbles Head, usually within 1 mile of the coast, and off the Devon coast W of Hartland Point and Bude within 15 miles of the coast.

There are cockle fisheries in Burry Inlet and the afon Tywi estuary.

For details of types of fishing and nets used, see *The Mariner's Handbook*.

Rescue
3.5

1   For details of rescue organisation and locations of assets see 1.60 and text under Rescue.

Natural conditions
3.6

1   **Sea and Swell.** There is always a ground swell from the Atlantic Ocean, except when E winds have prevailed. The effect of this swell is apparent on the N shore of the Bristol Channel as far E as Swansea Bay, but on the S shore it rapidly diminishes E of Morte Bay (51°10′N 4°15′W).

3.7

1   **Tidal streams.** In the approaches to the Bristol Channel, the flow of water is largely determined by tidal forces. The in-going stream sets N towards Saint George's Channel. On the S side of the Bristol Channel, the streams set parallel with the coast; on the N side, the streams in Carmarthen Bay and Swansea Bay are irregular and on their E sides set strongly across the shoals which extend W from them.

2   In the central fairway of the channel E of longitude 5°W, the streams set generally in the direction of the deep water channel. From the entrance inwards, the times at which they begin become gradually later and their maximum spring rates increase from 2 kn, between Hartland Point and Saint Govan's Head, to 3 kn S of Nash Point and greater farther E.

For details see information on the chart and *Admiralty Tidal Stream Atlas — Irish Sea and Bristol Channel*.

SOUTH SIDE — HARTLAND POINT TO HURLSTONE POINT

GENERAL INFORMATION

Chart 1179
Area covered
3.8

1   In this section are described the coastal routes, harbours and anchorages between Hartland Point (51°01′N 4°32′W) and Hurlstone Point (51°14′N 3°35′W), including Lundy (51°10′N 4°40′W).

It is arranged as follows:

Hartland Point to Bull Point (3.11).
Bull Point to Hurlstone Point (3.43).

Fishing
3.9

1   See 3.4.

Nature and marine reserves
3.10

1   Lundy Marine Reserve (3.20).
Braunton and Northam Burrows (3.32).
See also Protection of wildlife (1.58).

HARTLAND POINT TO BULL POINT

General information

Chart 1164
Route
3.11

1   From the vicinity of Hartland Point (51°01′N 4°32′W) to N of Bull Point, 16 miles NE, the coastal route passes to seaward of a tide race NW of Hartland Point, SE of Lundy (51°10′N 4°40′W) and NW of Horseshoe Rocks (51°15′N 4°13′W).

Topography
3.12

1   Between Hartland Point (51°01′N 4°32′W) and Morte Point, 15 miles NE, the coast is indented by Bideford Bay which consists mainly of high perpendicular cliffs with rocky foreshore, gradually receding NE towards the estuary of the rivers Taw and Torridge. The coastline on either side of the estuary consists of a succession of low sandhills, which rise N towards Baggy Point (51°09′N 4°16′W), a bold barren bluff, 90 m high.

2   Morte Bay lies between Baggy Point and Morte Point, 2½ miles N, a rocky and barren headland, sloping from its summit to low cliffs.

Firing practice area
3.13

1   Braunton Burrows Range (51°05′N 4°13′W); for further information on practice areas, see 1.15.

Chart 1160 plan of Lundy
Measured distance
3.14

1   A measured distance is charted between Tibbett's Point, midway along the E side of Lundy Island (51°10′N 4°40′W), and the S end of Lundy Road (3.25), marked by two pairs of white posts with diamond topmarks which are difficult to identify. The parameters are:
       Distance 2146·6 m.
       Running track is 350½°/170½°.
       Admiralty Lookout, charted as a conspicuous building, stands at the top of the cliff above the N beacons.

Rescue
3.15

1   An all-weather lifeboat and an inshore lifeboat are stationed at Appledore (51°03′N 4°12′W); the moorings are situated in Appledore Pool.
       For details of rescue organisation see 1.60.

Natural conditions
3.16

1   **Tidal streams** set NE and SW between Hartland Point and Bull Point. Midway between Hartland Point and Lundy (51°10′N 4°40′W) the streams attain a spring rate of 3 kn in each direction; for details see information on the chart and *Admiralty Tidal Stream Atlas — Irish Sea and Bristol Channel*.

2   **Tide races** are particularly in evidence, especially during the strength of the streams, close N and S of Lundy (51°10′N 4°40′W), in the vicinity of Stanley Bank (3.23), and between Horseshoe Rocks (51°15′N 4°13′W) and Bull Point.

Directions
(continued from 2.26 and 2.95)

Principal marks
3.17

1   **Landmarks:**
       Hartland Point (51°01′N 4°32′W), with a lighthouse (2.94).
       Radome, (51°01′N 4°31′W).
       Lighthouse (disused) (51°10′N 4°40′W), (granite tower, 30 m in height), standing on the highest part of Lundy Island, with a church tower 3¾ cables ESE.

Lighthouse – disused (3.17)
(Original dated 1998)

(Photograph - D M Ives)

2   Lundy SE Point Lighthouse (white round tower, 16 m in height) (51°10′N 4°39′W).
       Bull Point (51°12′N 4°12′W), a prominent rocky point with a lighthouse (white round tower with building, 11 m in height).
       Major lights:
3   Hartland Point Light (51°01′N 4°32′W) (2.94)
       Lundy SE Point Light — as above.
       Lundy Near N Point Light (white round tower, 17 m in height) (51°12′N 4°41′W).
       Bull Point Light — as above. A lower light exhibits a fixed red sector light from 058° to 096°.

Passage
3.18

1   From a position NW and to seaward of the tide races off Hartland Point (51°01′N 4°32′W) the coastal route leads 19 miles NE to a position N of Bull Point, passing (with positions from Hartland Point Lighthouse):
       SE of Lundy SE point (9¾ miles NNW), on which stands a light (3.17); Rat Island (3.19) lies close ENE of the point, thence:

Tower   *South-east Lighthouse*

Lundy from SW (3.18)

(Original dated 2001)

(Photograph - Air Images)

NW of Baggy Rock (12¼ miles NE), marked by Baggy Leap Buoy (starboard hand) moored 1 mile WNW of Baggy Point (3.12), thence:

2   NW of Morte Stone (14¾ miles NE), a rocky ledge which dries, marked by Morte Stone Buoy (starboard hand) moored 3 cables W of its W extremity, off which is a heavy tide race. The ledge, which lies in the red sector of Bull Point Light, extends 4 cables W of Morte Point, rocky and barren. Thence:

3   NW of Bull Point (16¼ miles NE), from which lights (3.17) are exhibited. Rockham Shoal, with two rocky heads, lies 8½ cables WSW. Thence:

NW and N of Horseshoe Rocks (17¾ miles NE), marked by Horseshoe Light Buoy (N cardinal).

Caution. Between the shore and a bearing of 056°, the white light exhibited from Bull Point is obscured by high ground.

(Directions continue for the coastal route at 3.47).

Lundy

Charts 1164, 1160 plan of Lundy

General information

3.19

1   **General description.** Lundy (51°10′N 4°40′W), an island 2½ miles in length and ¾ mile wide, rising to a height of 137 m, consists for the most part of granite. It has a bare undulating top with high, steep and inaccessible cliffs on the W side and sloping but steep cliffs indented by tree and vegetation lined hanging valleys on the more sheltered E side. Lundy's climate is milder than the mainland, and the rainfall is lower.

2   Rat Island, a green hummock, lies close off the SE corner of Lundy to which it is joined by a rocky ledge.

The island is leased by the National Trust to the Landmark Trust and is a sanctuary for birds.

A light is exhibited from near the N point and another is exhibited from the SE point of the island (3.17).

Marine nature reserve

3.20

1   The reserve exists to protect the marine habitats and life around the island. The limits of the area are indicated on the chart. In the interests of nature conservancy, vessels should not anchor within 100 m of Knoll Pins, two drying rocks 1½ miles N of the SE lighthouse, because of the many rare and unusual species in this area. See Protection of wildlife (1.58).

2   A statutory No Take Zone (NTZ) is established on the E side of the island. It extends from the coast, between North East Point and Sugar Loaf (2 miles farther S), E to line of longitude 4°39′W. No living natural resources including lobsters, crabs and fish may be removed from the NTZ.

Historic wrecks

3.21

1   Historic wrecks lie off the E side of the island; one about 1½ cables off Tibbett's Point (51°11′N 4°40′W) and another, with a depth of 10 m, 5¾ cables E of the point. For further details see 1.57 and *Annual Notice to Mariners No 16*.

Measured distance

3.22

1   See 3.14.

Natural conditions
3.23

1   **Tidal streams** in the locality of Lundy, clear of the land, attain a spring rate of 2 kn in each direction and begin as follows:

Interval from HW Milford Haven	*Direction*
+0530	ENE
−0030	WSW

2   The E-going stream divides 3 to 4 miles W of the island and thence sets N and S of it, attaining a spring rate of 5 kn off its N and S ends and over Stanley Bank, which lies 2½ miles ENE from North East Point (51°12′N 4°40′W).

The streams turn inwards 3 to 4 miles E of the island, the N branch not until after passing Stanley Bank, they then set together.

3   The W-going stream divides and rejoins at similar distances from the island, the merged streams running towards the S part of the W coast.

The coastal stream off the N three-quarters of the W coast sets N during the E-going stream, but is weak and irregular during the W-going stream. Off the S part of the W coast the stream is rotary and sets SE at the beginning of the E-going stream changing gradually through E to N at its end, during the W-going stream it changes gradually from N through W to S.

4   Off the E coast the stream is S-going for 9½ hours, from −0355 until +0530 HW Milford Haven; it is N-going for approximately 3 hours only.

The coastal streams do not exceed a rate of approximately 1 kn at springs.

Tide races. During the strength of the E-going stream a heavy race extends 1 mile N from the N end of the island and 1½ miles E of Rat Island. A race of exceptional violence, called The White Horses, forms over Stanley Bank which should be given a wide berth.

5   Similar races form during the W-going stream, particularly off the S end of the island extending 1 mile SW of Shutter Point, but the race over Stanley Bank (51°13′N 4°37′W) is considerably less violent than that during the E-going stream.

Landmarks
3.24

1   Lighthouse (disused) (51°10′N 4°40′W) (3.17).
Church tower, conspicuous from S and E, standing 3¾ cables ESE of the disused lighthouse.

Anchorages and landing places
3.25

1   **Lundy Road,** which lies between East Bank, composed of sand and fine shell, and the E side of the island, is a large anchorage, with good holding, out of the strength of tidal streams.

Anchorage may be obtained in position 1 mile NNE of the SE lighthouse in a depth of 20 m, as indicated on the chart. Small vessels may anchor in Inner Anchorage, closer inshore N of the lighthouse.

2   **Cautions.** It is reported that E winds can render anchorage in Lundy Road dangerous, particularly for small craft.

Small vessels making for their anchorage from E on the W-going tide should approach from N to avoid the

Lundy Church (3.24)
(Original dated 1998)

(Photograph - D M Ives)

possibility of being caught in the race (3.23) E of Rat Island.

3   There are two patches of foul ground lying in S part of Lundy Road.

For historic wrecks see 3.21.
3.26

1   There is good shelter in E winds close under the W side of the island in depths of approximately 18 m, but outside that depth the waters shelve rapidly; the best anchorage is in, or close off Jenny's Cove, midway along the W side of the island; if approaching from S, Needle Rock, which lies off the entrance, should be given a wide berth.

Small craft can anchor well inside Jenny's Cove in E winds or obtain shelter from N winds in The Rattles, a small bay on the S side of the island.
3.27

1   **Landing** can be made on a shingle beach in the cove close N of SE Point Lighthouse. A concrete jetty, used by the island's passenger and supply vessel, is at the S end of this cove. A light (metal post, red square topmark, 5 m in height) is exhibited from the head of the jetty.

Landing can also be made at a stage close E of Near N Point Lighthouse, but if there is a W swell this should be used only near LW. Strong E winds may make a landing impossible at either landing place.

2   In emergency during W weather landing could be made on the rocky shore of Gannets' Bay where there is a pathway to the cliff top. The bay is reported to give some shelter during N winds, under the lee of Gannets' Rock. In E weather landing can be made alongside the rocks in Jenny's Cove (3.26) provided there is no swell, but there is a steep climb to the top of the cliffs.

Lundy – Jetty and South-east Lighthouse from N (3.27)

(Original dated 2001)

(Photograph - Air Images)

Bideford Bay

Charts 1164, 1160 plan of Barnstaple and Bideford
General information
3.28

1   Bideford Bay, sometimes known as Barnstaple Bay, entered between Hartland Point (51°01′N 4°32′W) and Morte Point, 15 miles NE, is a large open bay, and includes the smaller Morte Bay and Croyde Bay which lie at the N end. It is backed by high cliffs except in the vicinity of the estuary of the rivers Taw and Torridge which flow into the sea at the head of the bay. On each side of the estuary the land consists of a succession of low sandhills.

2   **Submarine cables.** Two submarine cables exist in Bideford Bay and come ashore at Saunton (51°07′·0N 4°13′·3W).

Pilotage. See 3.37.

Tidal streams. In Bideford Bay the streams are, in general, weak but the NE-going stream is, however, appreciable between Westward Ho!, close NW of Bideford, and Baggy Point where it sets N along the coast; similarly the SW-going stream is appreciable between Clovelly (51°00′N 4°24′W) and Hartland Point where it sets W along the coast.

3   Off Bideford Bar, where coast and river streams meet and separate, the streams are irregular; W winds can raise a heavy sea on the out-going stream; for details, see information on Chart 1160 plan of Barnstaple and Bideford.

In Morte Bay the streams set N and S across the entrance but there is little stream within the bay.

4   The streams in both directions set at a rate of up to 4 kn at springs across Baggy Leap where there may be overfalls or a race.

The N-going stream sets strongly across Morte Stone ledge but the W-going stream from Bull Point sets clear of Morte Stone and turns S, W of the ledge; see information on Chart 1164 for details.

3.29

1   **Landmarks**:

Gallantry Bower (51°01′N 4°25′W), a cliff 110 m high crested by a clump of trees.

Clovelly Court, a prominent mansion, 5 cables NW of Clovelly village (51°00′N 4°24′W).

Hotel (51°07′N 4°13′W) at Saunton, white.

Directions
3.30

1   Within Bideford Bay, passage to the entrance of the rivers Taw and Torridge is generally free of dangers outside 1 mile from the coast.

Clearing bearing. At night Bideford rear light, which is obscured bearing more than 133°, kept in sight clears SW of Asp Rock (51°07′·5N 4°16′·0W).

Anchorages and harbour
3.31

1   **Clovelly Road** (51°00′N 4°23′W), affords sheltered anchorage in S and SW winds; the best berth is 8 cables N of the pierhead at Clovelly, in depths of 10 m, mud. There is a wreck (position approximate), lying about 4 cables offshore, S of this anchorage. The Gore, a drying rocky ridge, extends to about 4 cables offshore 1½ miles E of Clovelly. Small craft can anchor closer inshore NE of the pierhead, clear of a mooring buoy situated 2 cables NNE of the pierhead.

2   Temporary anchorage may be obtained in offshore winds anywhere in Bideford Bay E of Clovelly in moderate depths and good holding.

In offshore winds there is an anchorage for small craft in Croyde Bay (51°08′N 4°15′W). There is also an anchorage in offshore winds for vessels of shallow draught in Morte Bay (51°10′N 4°15′W); the anchorage is 7 cables offshore in depths of 13 m, and is out of the strength of the tidal streams.

3   **Clovelly** (51°00′N 4°25′W), a picturesque village, is built on the face of a thickly wooded slope and is a fairly good mark by day. The small harbour, which dries to a firm bottom of sand and small stones, is formed by a short curved mole extending E which gives little shelter. It is used mainly by fishing vessels and should be entered only near HW.

4   A light is exhibited from a green metal structure on the harbour wall. Depths are up to 3·2 m at MHWS alongside the mole, though less water can be experienced in the harbour mouth owing to a build up of stones. There is a slipway.

Rivers Taw and Torridge

Chart 1160 plan of Barnstaple and Bideford
General information
3.32

1   **General description.** The river Taw (3.41) and the river Torridge (3.35) are entered between the N end of Northam Burrows (51°04′N 4°13′W) and Airy Point (6½ cables N), the SW end of Braunton Burrows. The entrance channel gives access to the Port of Bideford which includes Appledore and Barnstaple.

2   Braunton and Northam Burrows are National Nature Reserves. For further information see 1.58.

Natural conditions. Tidal streams in the entrance to the rivers Taw and Torridge are shown by means of diagrams on the chart. It is reported that the tidal stream off Skern Point (51°03′·5N 4°11′·8W) can attain a rate of 5 kn on spring tides.

A ground swell causes steep and confused seas on the bar.

3   North-west winds can cause seas which make the bar impassable to small craft.

Landing Craft Operations. Royal Marines landing craft operate in the estuary off Instow Sands and Crow Point. Their kedge wires, which extend up to 200 m astern when embarking and disembarking vehicles, can pose a hazard.

Submarine power cables cross the river Torridge, 7 cables above Appledore.

Landmark. A building, standing on the W bank of the river Torridge, 8 cables S of Skern Point, is conspicuous.

Directions
3.33

1   **Entrance channel,** marked by Bideford Bar Light Buoy (starboard hand) and light buoys, crosses Bideford Bar (51°05′N 4°15′W), composed of sand and gravel, and passes through the drying sands at the head of Bideford Bay.

Bideford Fairway Light Buoy (safe water) is moored about 8 cables WNW of Bideford Bar.

2   **Leading lights.** The alignment (118°) of leading lights (51°03′·6N 4°10′·5W) at Instow (3.35), shown continuously, indicates the channel leading inwards between Pulley Ridge, a drying ridge of stones and sand, and Old Wall Rocks, which dry and are frequently covered by sand, 2 cables S of Airy Point.

3   Front light (white framework tower, broad white topmark, 18 m in height) situated near the foreshore.

Rear light (white tower, 9 m in height) 2 cables ESE of front light.

Mariners should then keep in the fairway, passing:

SW of Crow Ridge, a rocky ledge extending W from Crow Point (3.41), on which stands a light, thence:

Crow Point   *Appledore*

North Tail
South Tail

Approach to Barnstaple and Bideford from NW (3.32)
(Original dated 2001)

(Photograph - Air Images)

Instow Leading Lights (118°) from NW (3.33)
(Original dated 2001)

(Photograph - Air Images)

4   E of Grey Sand Hill at the head of Northam Burrows,
thence:
S of Sprat Ridge which extends S from Crow Ridge,
thence into the river Torridge.

3.34

1   **Caution.** The bar and sands are constantly shifting and
the buoys are occasionally moved to allow for this.

Entry should be attempted only 2 hours either side of
HW.

Frequent changes in depths may be expected in the river
Torridge above Appledore. The course and depth of the
river Taw between Fremington Pill and Barnstaple are
subject to daily change. The stakes which mark the
navigable channel are frequently moved to meet the
changing conditions.

Port of Bideford

General information

3.35

1   **Position.** Port of Bideford consists of the broad lower
reach of the river Torridge which is bordered by the towns
of Appledore and Bideford, on its W bank, and Instow
(51°03′N 4°11′W) on its E bank.

Only the berths at Bideford Town Quay accept
commercial cargo.

2   **Function.** The port handles the import of fertilisers and
gravel, and the export of ball clay.

Bideford has a population of about 14 500; Appledore
about 2500.

Port limits. The N limit of the port is a line joining the
N extremity of Skern Point (51°03′·5N 4°11′·8W) and
Instow church tower, 1 mile E. The S limit is Bideford
Bridge (51°01′N 4°12′W).

3   **Traffic.** In 2007 there were 22 ship calls with a total of
62 832 dwt.

Port authority. Torridge District Council, Riverbank
House, Bideford, North Devon EX39 2QG.

Navigational matters should be addressed to the Harbour
Master.

Limiting conditions

3.36

1   **Maximum size of vessels handled:**
Appledore (Bidna Wharf): 7–800 tonnes, depth 5·5 m
at MHWS.
Bideford: 82 m LOA, 12 m beam, draught 5 m at
MHWS.

The berths at Bideford dry at LW, vessels should be
prepared to take the ground.

Torridge Bridge, a road bridge, 7 cables downstream of
Bideford has a vertical clearance of 24 m.

Arrival information
3.37
1   **Notice of ETA required**. ETA should be forwarded 12 hours in advance to the senior pilot. For further details see *Admiralty List of Radio Signals Volume 6(1)*.

Outer anchorage. Vessels waiting to cross the bar may anchor 5 cables W of Bideford Fairway Light Buoy in 13 m.

2   **Pilotage.** The pilotage district of the Port of Bideford lies within a line drawn 270° for 2 miles from Baggy Point (51°09′N 4°16′W), thence 180° to the coast.

Within these limits pilotage is compulsory for all vessels over 350 gt except those exempted by law. The pilot boarding area lies between Bideford Fairway Light Buoy (3.33) and the bar, weather permitting.

Tugs. One small tug.

Directions for entering harbour
3.38
1   Vessels proceeding to Bideford Town Quay from sea should negotiate the preferred shipping channel under the centre span of Torridge Bridge (3.36) which exhibits a flashing orange light on both up and downstream elevations.

The bridge support structures exhibit twin red and green channel marking lights.

Berths
3.39
1   Bideford Town Quay, on the W bank at Bideford, with two berths totalling 164 m, has depths of 5·5 m at MHWS.

There is a quay on the E bank with depths alongside of between 1·8 to 4·3 m at MHWS.

Small craft moorings lie close W of Instow where there is a slip marked by beacons; there are further slips above and below the town. There are pontoon berths at Zeta Berth immediately opposite the covered shipyard at Appledore.

Port services
3.40
1   **Repairs**: can be undertaken for vessels up to 12 m beam; slipway 60 dwt capacity.

Bidna Dry Dock at Appledore is a covered shipbuilding dry dock which can accommodate vessels of up to 13 000 dwt; shipyard.

2   **Other facilities**: SSCC and SSCEC issued for the port but arranged from Plymouth; hospital at Bideford with helicopter landing facilities.

Supplies: small quantities of fuel oil; fresh water.

River Taw
3.41
1   **General information.** The river Taw is entered between Crow Point (51°04′·0N 4°11′·4W), on which stands a light (white framework tower), and Instow at its confluence with the river Torridge.

2   From a wide estuary the river is entered through a narrow channel no wider than 183 m with an average depth 1·5 m at MLWS. Dangerous rocks, some marked by perches, lie on either side of the channel which is navigable with care as far as the disused railway quay at

Appledore   *Instow*

Covered Shipyard   The River Torridge from S (3.41)   *Zeta Berth*
(*Original dated 2001*)

(Photograph – Air Images)

Fremington, nearly 3 miles within the river entrance and by shallow-draught boats as far as Barnstaple, a further 2 miles inland, on the last of the in-going stream.

3   Constant alterations to the sandbanks in the river with the strength of tidal streams, however, render navigation difficult.

River Authority. North Devon District Council, Civic Centre, Barnstaple, EX31 1ED.

Submarine power cables cross the river at Penhill Point (51°05′N 4°07′W) and at a position 8 cables below the point at Fremington. They also cross the river at the entrance to the river Yeo at Barnstaple.

3.42

1   **Yelland Oil Pier** (51°04′·1N 4°10′·8W), is disused.

There is another disused pier, L-shaped and with a light at either end of the pier head, 4½ cables NE of Yelland Oil Pier.

Barnstaple is situated at the junction of the river Yeo and the navigable limits of the river Taw. The port, however, is no longer used for commercial shipping.

BULL POINT TO HURLSTONE POINT

General information

Chart 1165
Route
3.43

1   From Bull Point (51°12′N 4°12′W), N of Horseshoe Light Buoy (N cardinal) to Hurlstone Point (51°14′N 3°35′W), the coastal route leads E for about 24 miles.

Topography
3.44

1   The coast in general consists of stretches of high steep cliffs backed by partly wooded slopes with elevations of more than 350 m in places, intersected by wooded valleys leading to small bays. Foreland Point (51°15′N 3°47′W) is the most prominent point on this coastline. Dunkery Hill (51°10′N 3°35′W), surmounted by Dunkery Beacon (Chart 1179), 514 m high, is the highest land bordering the S shore of the Bristol Channel.

Rescue
3.45

1   An all-weather lifeboat is stationed at Ilfracombe; inshore lifeboats are stationed at Ilfracombe (3.50) and Clovelly (51°00′N 4°24′W).

For details of rescue organisation see 1.60.

Natural conditions
3.46

1   **Tidal streams.** Between Bull Point and Ilfracombe (51°13′N 4°07′W), the streams set in the direction of the coast attaining a spring rate of 3 kn in each direction and beginning as follows:

Interval from HW Milford Haven	Direction
+0540	E
−0025	W

2   Between Capstone Point and Beacon Point the tidal streams begin as follows:

Interval from HW Milford Haven	Direction
+0530	E
−0355	W

A W-going eddy sets for part of the time during the E-going stream.

3   The streams attain a spring rate of 1½ kn E-going and 2 kn W-going.

For tidal streams N of Foreland Ledge (51°16′N 3°47′W), see information on the chart.

See also *Admiralty Tidal Stream Atlas — Irish Sea and Bristol Channel.*

4   **Tide races.** Between Foreland Point (51°15′N 3°47′W) and Foreland Ledge, 7 cables N and between Foreland Ledge and Sand Ridge, 7 cables SW, strong tide races can be experienced, especially during the strength of the streams and during W gales. They may be dangerous to small craft.

In bad weather, heavy seas break over, and N of, Foreland Ledge.

Directions
(continued from 3.18)

Principal marks
3.47

1   **Landmarks:**

     Little Hangman (51°13′N 4°02′W), conspicuous conical hill.

     Foreland Point (51°15′N 3°47′W), the most prominent point on this coastline on which stands a lighthouse (white round tower, 15 m in height). The land rises abruptly 1½ cables within the point to The Foreland, a hill, which is divided from the higher ground S by a saddle which shows up from E and W.

2   Dunkery Hill (51°10′N 3°35′W) (Chart 1179) (3.44).

   Major lights:

     Bull Point Light (51°12′N 4°12′W) (3.17).

     Lynmouth Foreland (Foreland Point) Light — as above; the light is shown continuously.

     Nash Point Light (51°24′N 3°33′W) (3.197).

Passage
3.48

1   From a position N of Horseshoe Rocks (51°15′N 4°13′W) to the vicinity of Hurlstone Point (24 miles E), the coastal route leads E passing (with positions from Lynmouth Foreland (Foreland Point) Lighthouse (51°15′N 3°47′W)):

     N of Capstone Point (12¾ miles W), which is backed by Capstone Hill, an abrupt conical hill, thence:

2   N of Rillage Point (11½ miles W), sloping and broken in outline, with a prominent white cottage standing high above the point, thence:

     N of Hangman Point (9¼ miles W). Little Hangman (3.47) rises from the point; thence:

3   N of Copperas Rock Buoy (starboard hand) moored on the N side of Copperas Rock (8½ miles W). Great Hangman, a cliff with a seaward face deep red in colour, stands 7 cables S of the rock; thence:

     N of Highveer Point (5¼ miles W), with a tide race 5 cables N and clear of a wreck, with a depth of 11 m, 6 cables NNE of the point, thence:

     N of Hollerday Hill (2¼ miles WSW), a steep cliff, thence:

4   N of Sand Ridge Light Buoy (starboard hand), which marks the W end of Sand Ridge (1¾ miles W), a gravel shoal over which there are depths of less than 2 m. Thence:

Close-up from NNW

Foreland Point and Lighthouse from WNW (3.47)

(Original dated 2001)

(Photograph - Air Images)

N of Foreland Ledge with strong tide-rips, which lies parallel with the coast and 7 cables N of Foreland Point (3.47). An underwater turbine fitted with a light beacon (isolated danger) (6 cables NNW) stands inshore of Foreland Ledge. Thence:

5   N of Gore Point (5¾ miles ESE), low with outlying boulders, thence:

N of Hurlstone Point, a craggy point, (51°14′N 3°35′W); a large drying rock lies close W of the point. Nash Point (3.197) lies on the N shore opposite Hurlstone Point.

Useful mark
3.49
1   Lantern Hill Light (white lantern on chapel, 11 m in height) (51°12′·7N 4°06′·8W) (Chart 1160 plan of Ilfracombe).

(Directions continue for the coastal passage on the S side of the Bristol Channel at 4.152; directions continue for the coastal passage on the N side at 4.21)

Anchorages and harbours

Chart 1160 plan of Ilfracombe

Ilfracombe
3.50
1   **General information.** Ilfracombe (51°13′N 4°07′W) is a seaside resort with a small harbour which can be identified by prominent white houses.

The harbour lies on the S side of Lantern Hill and is not visible from seaward. It is used by fishing vessels, local and visiting yachts and, in the summer months, by pleasure craft ferrying passengers on excursions.

The largest vessel handled was one of 629 gt, 60 m in length and having a draught of 2 m.

2   Harbour Authority: Ilfracombe Harbour Master, The Pier, Ilfracombe, EX34 9EQ.

Pilots are not available.

Directions. Approach the harbour after half flood, between Lantern Hill and Hillsborough, an abrupt conical hill, 4 cables E. Buggy Pit, a rocky patch with dangerous tide-rips particularly noticeable with W winds, 7 cables NE of Lantern Hill, and the drying rocky ledges and detached patches fringing Hillsborough should be given a wide berth. Otherwise there are no dangers in the harbour approach.

3   Leading lights:

Front light standing on the foreshore 1¼ cables S of East Face (51°12′·6N 4°06′·7W).

Rear light 20 m behind front light.

The alignment (188°) of the lights leads into the outer harbour passing (positions given from East Face):

W of Broadstrand Beach, (3 cables ENE) thence:

E of East Face.

Quay Head Light (1 cable SW) stands at the entrance to the inner harbour, and opens SW of East Face.

4   **Anchorage.** In fine weather, anchorage may be obtained in The Range, the roadstead between Capstone Point (3.48) and Beacon Point, 7 cables E in depths of 11 m. Within

Ilfracombe Harbour from ESE (3.50)
(Original dated 2001)

(Photograph - Air Images)

The Range, the E-going tidal stream sets for 5 hours and
the W-going stream for 7 hours; see also 3.46.

Harbour and berths. The harbour, which dries, consists
of an inner and outer harbour, divided by a pier which
projects S from the S side of Lantern Hill. Lights are
exhibited from Lantern Hill and from the N and S end of
East Face on the E side of Lantern Hill.

5 At MHWS there are depths of 5·5 m alongside in the
outer harbour, and of 4·9 m alongside in the inner harbour.

There are quays on the N, E and S sides of the inner
harbour. The N side of the outer harbour and East Face
have tidal berths. East Face, which covers at HW, can be
used only at LW ±2 hours.

Repairs: of a minor nature; slipway.

Other facilities: hospital in the town.

Supplies: fresh water; marine diesel; provisions.

Chart 1165
Watermouth Harbour
3.51

1 Watermouth Harbour (51°13'·0N 4°04'·6W) is a narrow
sandy cove situated between Ilfracombe (3.50) and Combe
Martin Bay (3.52). It is entered between Widmouth Head
(not named on chart) and an islet close off the W end of
Burrow Nose (1 cable E).

The harbour, which dries out to a bottom of hard sand,
affords shelter for vessels up to 60 tonnes. Strong NW
winds cause a considerable run of sea into it. An inner

breakwater extends a short distance NE from the shore
affording good protection to small craft moorings.

2 Harbour Authority is Watermouth Harbour Ltd,
Watermouth Cove, Berrynarbor, Ilfracombe, Devon
EX34 9SJ.

Entry into the harbour, which is difficult to see from
offshore, can initially be made on the bearing of 153° by
keeping within the white sector (151½°-154½°) of a sector
light (white triangular topmark on structure, 1 m in height)
standing on the S shore 1¼ cables inside the entrance.

3 A light is also exhibited from the head of the
breakwater.

The white cottage high above Rillage Point (51°13'·0N
4°05'·3W) (3.48) can help to identify the entrance to the
harbour.

Facilities include a boatyard, yacht club and slipway.
Visitors' moorings and diesel fuel are available.

Combe Martin Bay
3.52

1 Combe Martin Bay entered between Burrow Nose
(51°13'N 4°04'W) and Hangman Point 1½ miles E, affords
temporary anchorage in fair weather in depths of
approximately 14 m. The village of Combe Martin lies at
the mouth of the river Umber, a small river which flows
into the SE corner of the bay.

Large waves, which may be dangerous to small craft,
can develop close in to the shore during the last 2 hours of
a rising tide.

Chart 1160 plan of Lynmouth
Lynmouth
3.53

1 **General information.** Lynmouth (51°14′N 3°50′W) and Lynton, small picturesque resorts, lie respectively on the E and W sides of the mouth of the river Lyn which flows into the SW part of Lynmouth Bay. The river scours a narrow channel across a drying shelf of boulders which extends 2½ cables offshore.

2 **Anchorage** can be obtained in Lynmouth Road, S of Sand Ridge (3.48), 5 to 8 cables offshore in depths of approximately 8 m, sand and gravel, out of the strength of the tidal streams; the ridge affords some protection near LW.

Berth. The harbour at Lynmouth is enclosed by two stone jetties which have a depth alongside of 4·6 m at MHWS.

3 A light is exhibited from the head of each jetty.

Caution. Dangerous tide races form in the area; see 3.46.

Chart 1160 plan of Porlock
Porlock
3.54

1 **General description.** Porlock Weir is a small, well sheltered village lying on the W side of Porlock Bay (51°14′N 3°37′W). The foreshore consists of pebbles and boulders through which a narrow drying channel, marked by poles (port and starboard hand), leads SW to a natural dock with dock gates, 9·1 m wide, which are rarely closed. Vessels must be prepared to dry out in the dock; there is however, a quay where a vessel drawing 3·7 m can berth at MHWS.

2 **Anchorage** can be obtained in settled conditions in Porlock Bay, in depths of approximately 8 m out of the strength of tidal streams.

NORTH SIDE — SAINT GOVAN'S HEAD TO NASH POINT

GENERAL INFORMATION

Charts 1179, 1076, 1165
Area covered
3.55

1 In this section are described the coastal routes, harbours and anchorages on the N shore of the Bristol Channel, between Saint Govan's Head (51°36′N 4°56′W) and Nash Point (51°24′N 3°34′W) 52½ miles ESE. The description includes Carmarthen Bay and the ports associated with Swansea Bay.

2 The section is arranged as follows:
Saint Govan's Head to Swansea Bay Approaches (3.59).
Swansea Bay and Approaches (3.92).
Port of Swansea (3.111).
Port of Neath (3.140).
Port Talbot (3.163).
Swansea Bay Approaches to Nash Point (3.192).

Topography
3.56

1 The coastline between Saint Govan's Head and Caldey Island, 9 miles ENE, features several small bays backed in general by sandhills and separated by bold or rocky headlands.

2 The SW side of the Gower Peninsula (15 miles E of Caldey Island) consists of low limestone cliffs up to 30 m high, backed by Rhossili Down, which rises steeply to The Beacon. Between Rhossili Point (51°34′N 4°18′W) and Port-Eynon, 3½ miles ESE, the coast consists of rugged and nearly perpendicular cliffs from 30 to 60 m high. On the S part of the peninsula, the coastline leading to Mumbles Head (51°34′N 3°58′W) is indented by small bays backed by sandy beaches with intervening bold and rocky headlands.

Fishing
3.57

1 See 3.4.

Nature reserves
3.58

1 Saint Margaret's Island (51°39′N 4°43′W).
Whiteford Sands (51°38′N 4°15′W).

Worms Head (51°34′N 4°20′W).
Oxwich Bay (51°33′N 4°07′W).
For further information see 1.58.

SAINT GOVAN'S HEAD TO SWANSEA BAY APPROACHES
General information
Charts 1076, 1165
Route
3.59

1 From Saint Govan's Head (51°36′N 4°56′W) to Swansea Bay, 36 miles E, the coastal route leads E passing S of West Helwick Light Buoy (51°31′·4N 4°23′·6W), marking the W end of Helwick Sands.

Firing practice areas
3.60

1 Eastern part of Castlemartin Range (51°37′N 5°00′W), Manorbier Range (51°39′N 4°47′W) and Penally Range (51°39′N 4°43′W).

2 Within Carmarthen Bay: Pendine Range (51°44′N 4°30′W) and Pembrey Range (51°43′·N 4°21′W). There are a number of DZ light buoys and buoys (special) moored in the bay which mark the practice area associated with Pendine Range. Warning signals, red flags by day and red lights by night, are exhibited from Pendine Burrows and Laugharne Burrows on the N coast and Pembrey Range on the E coast.

For further information on practice areas see 1.15.

Vessel traffic service
3.61

1 A VTS scheme, mandatory for vessels of 50 gt and greater, is in operation for the control of shipping within Swansea Bay and the Bristol Channel. Reporting points are shown on the charts.

Full details will be found in *Admiralty List of Radio Signals Volume 6(1)*.

Rescue
3.62

1 An all-weather lifeboat is stationed at Tenby Harbour (51°40′N 4°42′W); inshore lifeboats are stationed at Tenby, Burry Port (51°41′N 4°15′W) and Port-Eynon Bay (3.89).

For all-weather rescue services within Swansea Bay, see 3.98 and for details of rescue organisation see 1.60.

Natural conditions
3.63

1   **Tidal streams.** See charts for information, also *Admiralty Tidal Stream Atlas for Irish Sea and Bristol Channel.*

Tide races. Strong tide races may be encountered about 4 miles SSE of Saint Govan's Head; in the vicinity of Nash Sands (3.199) and between SE and SW of Oxwich Point (3.66) during the strength of the stream in both directions. They may be dangerous to small craft.

Directions
(continued from 5.26)

Principal marks
3.64

1   **Landmarks:**
Spire (51°38′N 4°59′W) (5.43).
Caldey Island Lighthouse (51°38′N 4°41′W) (3.71).
Monastery (3½ cables N of Caldey Lighthouse) (3.71).
Worms Head (51°34′N 4°20′W), the W of three prominent hummocks on an island separated from Rhossili Point (51°33′·8N 4°18′·5W) by Worms Sound.

2   **Major lights:**
Mumbles Light (51°34′N 3°58′W) (3.100).
Nash Point Light (51°24′N 3°33′W) (3.197).
Lundy Near N Point Light (51°12′N 4°41′W) (3.17).
Bull Point Light (51°12′N 4°12′W) (3.17).
Lynmouth Foreland (Foreland Point) Light (51°15′N 3°47′W) (3.47).

Other aids to navigation
3.65

1   **Racons:**
Saint Gowan Light Buoy (51°31′·9N 4°59′·8W).
West Helwick Light Buoy (51°31′·4N 4°23′·6W).
West Scar Light Buoy (51°28′·3N 3°55′·6W).
See *Admiralty List of Radio Signals Volume 2.*

Passage
3.66

1   From a position S of Saint Govan's Head to Swansea Bay, about 36 miles E, the coastal route leads E, passing:
S of Saint Gowan Shoals (51°33′N 4°58′W) (5.45), which break in heavy weather, thence:
S of Stackpole Head (51°37′N 4°54′W), a bold headland, the extremity of which is nearly detached.
Thence the track continues E, passing (with positions from Worms Head (51°34′N 4°20′W)):

2   S of West Helwick (2½ miles SSW) and East Helwick (3½ miles SE), two shoals, separated by Helwick Swatch (3.69), which extend 6¾ miles W from Port-Eynon Point (5 miles ESE). West Helwick Light Buoy (W cardinal, marked W.HWK) is moored off the W end of West Helwick; see caution. Thence:

3   S of Port-Eynon Point (5 miles ESE), with two low islets (3.89) close E, which rises abruptly; a small stone monument stands on the point. East Helwick Light Buoy (E cardinal) is moored 3 cables S of the point and marks the E edge of East Helwick, thence:

4   S of Oxwich Point (7 miles E), a bluff point fringed by a drying rock ledge. There are strong tide-rips SE and SW of the point.

Caution. West and East Helwick shoals should be given a wide berth not only because of the steepness of their S sides but also because strong W winds against the tide cause a heavy sea in their vicinity and the E-going stream sets NE towards the sands.

Useful marks
3.67

1   White house (51°34′·7N 4°17′·2W).
Mumbles Lighthouse (51°34′N 3°58′W) (3.100).
Nash Point Light (51°24′N 3°33′W) (3.197).
(Directions continue for the coastal route E at 3.197 and for Swansea Bay at 3.100; directions continue for the coastal route W to Milford Haven at 5.43)

Side channels
Helwick Pass
3.68

1   Helwick Pass, the narrow channel which separates the E end of East Helwick from Port-Eynon Point (51°32′·0N 4°12′·5W) has a least depth of 2·4 m in the fairway.
Vessels with suitable draught should attempt the passage only with local knowledge.

Helwick Swatch
3.69

1   Helwick Swatch, the passage midway between West Helwick and East Helwick shoals, has a least charted depth of 5·5 m in the fairway.

Caldey Island
Chart 1482 plan of Tenby and Saundersfoot with Approaches
General information
3.70

1   Caldey Island (51°38′N 4°41′W) is the property of a community of Cistercian Monks and is part of Pembrokeshire Coast National Park; the island forms part of Wildlife Trust of Wales; see 1.58.
Topography. The island is mostly bounded by cliffs of moderate height, the highest being on the S and NE sides. Some detached rocks, or stacks, lie on the E side.
Saint Margaret's Island, bounded on all sides by cliffs, lies 2 cables W of the NW extremity of Caldey Island to which it is connected by a drying rocky reef.

2   **Caldey Sound** lies between the coast W of Giltar Point (51°39′N 4°43′W) and Saint Margaret's Island, 4½ cables S.
Submarine power cables are laid between Caldey Island and the mainland; where they come ashore being marked by beacons.

3   An outfall, marked by a beacon (51°40′·1N 4°42′·2W) on the foreshore, extends 1½ miles ESE from Tenby towards Woolhouse Rocks.
Tidal streams. For tidal streams in the vicinity of Caldey Island see tidal diamonds on the chart.

Directions
3.71

1   **Landmarks:**
Caldey Island Lighthouse (51°38′N 4°41′W) (white round tower, 16 m in height), standing on high ground 1 cable N of Chapel Point, the SE bluff of the island.
Monastery, with a white round tower and red roof, standing near the centre of the island.
Tenby Church spire, (51°40′N 4°42′W).
Penally Church tower (51°39′·6N 4°43′·4W).

Caldey Island from SE (3.70)

(Original dated 2001)

(Photograph - Air Images)

3.72

1   From W of Caldey Island, the passage leads N of the island through Caldey Sound to Caldey Roads or, rounding the island to the S and E, to an anchorage in Man of War Roads.

Passage through Caldey Sound leads (with positions from Caldey Island Light (51°38′N 4°41′W)):

Between Lydstep Point (2¾ miles WNW) and Lydstep Ledge (2¼ miles WNW) or between Sound Rock (2 miles WNW) and the shoal patch W of Saint Margaret's Island (1½ miles NW), thence:

2   Between the port and starboard hand light buoys marking the narrow channel which lies between Eel Spit, a rocky ridge which extends N from Eel Point (1 mile NW), the NW tip of Caldey Island, and the S end of Giltar Spit (1¼ miles NNW), the flat extending E from Giltar Point (1½ miles NW), thence to Caldey Roads anchorage or continuing to positions farther E.

3   **Passage south and east of Caldey Island:**

The alignment (279°) of Old Castle Head (51°38′N 4°47′W) and the centre of Freshwater East (Chart 1076), 3 miles W, astern, passes N of Offing Patches (1 mile SW) and Drift Rock (1½ miles SE).

4   If proceeding to Man of War Roads, the track leads N passing (with positions from Caldey Island Light (51°38′N 4°41′W)):

Between Spaniel Shoal (8 cables ENE), marked by Spaniel Light Buoy (E cardinal) and the shoal patch with a depth of 8·8 m, 4 cables farther E.

5   If proceeding to Caldey Roads from E the track leads round the N edge of Highcliff Bank (1¼ miles N), marked by North Highcliff Light Buoy (N cardinal), passing W of Woolhouse Rocks (2 miles NNE), a narrow reef, the central part of which dries, marked by Woolhouse Light Buoy (S cardinal) or across the S portion of Highcliff Bank.

3.73

1   **Caution.** The sea breaks over the shoals E of Caldey Island in S gales and the W-going tidal stream occasionally causes a considerable sea over Drift Rock.

A dangerous cross sea, locally known as The Fiddlers, breaks over Eel Spit when there is a strong wind against tide.

Anchorages and landing place

3.74

1   **Caldey Roads.** There is an anchorage in the SW part, 3¼ cables ENE of Eel Point, the NW tip of Caldey, in depths of over 5 m; there are greater depths in Bog Hole, stiff mud, in the NW part of the roadstead, but here the tidal streams at springs are strong.

Caldey Sound affords temporary anchorage in depths of 15 m but the holding is poor.

2   **Man of War Roads** off the NE side of the island, affords good anchorage in depths of 12 m, sand over tenacious clay. A good berth is 6½ cables NE of Small Ord Point, the most E point of Caldey Island.

Landing can be made at HW on a slip in Priory Bay on the N side of the island. Permission to land must be obtained from the Abbot of the monastery.

Carmarthen Bay

Chart 1076

General information

3.75

1   **Description.** Carmarthen Bay (51°40′N 4°30′W) is entered between Caldey Island (51°38′N 4°41′W) (3.70) and Worms Head, 14 miles ESE.

The small harbours of Tenby (3.90) and Saundersfoot (3.91) lie on the W side of the bay.

2   The common estuary of the afon Tywi and the afon Taf (3.79) lies at the head of the bay and Burry Inlet, leading to Llanelli (3.86), lies on its E side.

The bay is clear of obstructions outside the 10 m depth contour and the bottom is mainly of sand and shells.

Firing practice areas. See 3.60.

3.76

1   **Topography.** The coastline on the W side of Carmarthen Bay consists of a range of cliffs 50 m high, backed by rising ground. Between Monkstone Point (51°42′N 4°41′W) and Ragwen Point, 4½ miles ENE, the coast is backed by dark cliffs and high ground rising to nearly 150 m and fronted by large boulders. The N shore of the bay, E of Ragwen Point, is composed of a range of sandhills of varying height fronted by Pendine Sands and Laugharne Sands, firm sands which dry to a distance of 2½ miles offshore and lead round to the common estuary of the afon Taf and the afon Tywi. Cefn Sidan Sands, an extensive drying sandbank, occupies the NE corner of the bay.

2　From Tywyn Point (51°44′N 4°23′W), a low sandy point, to The Nose, 4¾ miles SE, the N entrance point to Burry Inlet, the coastline comprises low-lying Pembrey Forest and Pembrey Burrows, fronted by Pembrey Sands, extensive hard sandflats.

3　On the S side of the inlet, the coastline is formed by a range of sandhills of varying heights that continue down to Rhossili Bay, on the W side of the Gower Peninsula. The coastline around the S part of Rhossili Bay leading towards Worms Head comprises limestone cliffs, 30 m high, backed by high ground nearly 200 m high.

Natural conditions
3.77

1　**Tidal streams.** For tidal streams near the E and W entrance points of Carmarthen Bay see the tidal diamonds on the charts.

In the middle of the entrance to the bay the streams set ENE and WSW at an in-going spring rate of 1½ kn and 2 kn out-going.

2　In the NW part of the bay the streams are weak and set N and E, and in the reverse directions.

In the NE part of the bay the streams are weak near the land.

In the centre of the bay the streams are weak, confused and irregular.

Sea. W gales cause a very heavy sea in the bay.

Chart 1167
Anchorage
3.78

1　Anchorage can be found in Rhossili Bay, 1 mile N of Worms Head (51°34′N 4°20′W) in depths of 9 m, but is exposed to the prevailing SW wind. Vessels can anchor 5 cables NE of Worms Head, sheltered from S winds, in 5·5 m, stiff mud.

Chart 1076
Afon Taf and the afon Tywi
3.79

1　Afon Taf and the afon Tywi flow into the sea, through a common estuary, between Ginst Point (51°45′N 4°26′W) and Tywyn Point, 2 miles ESE.

Wharley Point, 1 mile NE of Ginst Point, lies at the bifurcation of the two rivers. A beacon (port hand) stands about 5 cables E of Wharley Point.

2　**Entrance channel.** A channel, navigable 2 hours either side of HW, leads over Carmarthen Bar which lies across the entrance to the estuary. From a position about 2¾ miles SW of Tywyn Point the channel leads NNW for about 2 miles over Cefn Sidan Sands, thence NE passing about 4 cables N of a wreck, marked from June to September by a buoy (N cardinal), 1¼ miles W of Tywyn Point.

3　**Tidal streams.** At Carmarthen Bar, the in-going stream sets first in the channels across the bar, but as the sands cover, it sets inwards from all directions.

The out-going stream at first sets outwards in all directions, but as the sands dry, it sets W and S in the main channel. The streams attain a spring rate of 3 to 5 kn in each direction.

4　**Directions.** Owing to the frequent changes in the channels over Laugharne and Cefn Sidan Sands, directions over Carmarthen Bar cannot be given. The chart therefore must be used with caution.

Without local knowledge no attempt should be made to cross the bar. Pilotage information and directions can be obtained from the Navigation Authority (3.83).

5　**Useful marks:** Towers situated E of Pendine Burrows (3.60) and a tower, 1 mile SSE of Towyn Point are the only useful landmarks in the area.
3.80

1　**Afon Taf** is navigable by unmasted small craft almost as far as Saint Clears, approximately 6 miles within the river entrance. There are moorings situated 2 miles within its entrance off Laugharne and restricted moorings at Saint Clears Boat Club.
3.81

1　**Afon Tywi** is navigable by small craft as far as Carmarthen, 10 miles above the bar, and is tidal for 3 miles above Carmarthen. In general, depths in the river vary between 3 and 5 m (MHWS). There are moorings and anchorage, both drying, within the entrance W of Ferryside at the river Towy Yacht Club. The Towy Boat Club is situated on the W bank about 1 mile upstream with drying moorings. Visitor moorings are available by arrangement.

Overhead power cables cross the river below Carmarthen, the lowest safe vertical clearance being 7·4 m.
3.82

1　**Gwendraeth** (51°44′N 4°21′W) is a drying inlet of extensive sand flats and stony patches on the E side of the confluence of the afon Taf and the afon Tywi. It is fed from the E by two small rivers, Gwendraeth Fach and Gwendraeth Fawr.

Kidwelly, a small harbour lying on the Gwendraeth Fach in the NE corner of inlet, dries and is seldom used.

Carmarthen
3.83

1　**Carmarthen** (51°51′N 4°18′W) lies on the W bank of the afon Tywi. The quay at Carmarthen is not accessible to masted vessels on account of bridges spanning the river below it.

Navigation Authority for Carmarthen Bar, the afon Taf and the afon Tywi is Carmarthen Bar Navigation Committee, 4, The Esplanade, Carmarthen SA31 1NG.

Burry Inlet

Chart 1167
General information
3.84

1　Burry Inlet (51°38′N 4°19′W), through which the river Loughor (afon Llwchwr) flows, is entered between The Nose (51°40′N 4°17′W) and Burry Holms, 3¾ miles SSW. The greater part of the inlet is encumbered with shifting sands. West Hooper, Hooper Sands and Lynch Sands are the principal shoals which obstruct the entrance.

On the N side of the inlet, Pembrey Sands extend E from The Nose to Burry Port.

2　On the S side, sandhills fronted by low cliffs extend 3½ miles NE from Burry Holms to Whiteford Point (51°39′N 4°15′W) with Hills Tor, a cliff, lying midway between them. Whiteford Scar, on which stands a disused lighthouse, lies 5 cables NW of Whiteford Point.

Whiteford Sands front the W side of the point.

Caution. The depths and channels within Burry Inlet are subject to frequent change; hence the chart must be used with caution.

3   **Pilotage.** Pilots for this area are not available. Local knowledge may be obtained from Llanelli Harbour Authority or Burry Port Yacht Club.

Tidal stream information between Whiteford Point and Burry Port can be found on the chart.

When the sands W of the channel in this vicinity are dry the streams run fairly in the channel, but when they are covered they tend to run ESE and WNW across them.

4   **Above Llanelli,** Burry Inlet is almost entirely obstructed by drying sandflats across which lies an old training wall, E of which the inlet becomes the river Loughor (afon Llwchwr). A shallow channel, marked by posts, enables small craft to reach Loughor, a town 2½ miles E of Llanelli, where the river is spanned by two bridges and an overhead power cable, vertical clearance 11 m.

Burry Port
3.85

1   Burry Port (51°41′N 4°15′W) is a small harbour lying 1½ miles ENE of The Nose. It is used by inshore fishing boats and pleasure craft. There is a sand berth for dredgers 1 mile E of the harbour.

2   On the W side of the S facing entrance a breakwater, with a light at its head (grey stone tower with cupola), extends S for 1¼ cables. From the head of this breakwater a training wall, which covers, extends S for a further 1¼ cables and has a barrel post (unlit) at its outer end. The E side of the entrance is formed by a short mole extending SW towards the mid-point of the W breakwater.

3   The harbour, accessible 2 hours either side of HW, is entered through a lock fitted with a flapgate and with a sill depth of 2 m. There are pontoon berths, a slipway and a yacht club within the basin. Diesel fuel and provisions are available.

Harbour master: 01554 835691 or 07817 395710.

Llanelli
3.86

1   **General information.** Llanelli (51°40′N 4°10′W), an industrial town with a drying harbour, lies on the N side of Burry Inlet, 3 miles E of Burry Port.

The harbour, no longer a commercial port, is used only by small fishing boats and pleasure craft. It is protected from the W by a long sand spit extending SSE and enclosing an area encumbered by drying mud flats. It is approached from S of Cefn Padrig Sands and entered between the head of the spit, on which stands an unlit tower, and a light 1½ cables SE, close off the end of an outfall extending SW from the shore.

2   **Caution.** There is a light, marking the outer end of a "fish–tail" groyne, 2¾ cables W from the head of the spit which should not be mistaken as marking the NW point of the harbour entrance.

Further "fish–tail" groynes, marked by beacons, lie N and S of the harbour entrance.

Harbour Authority. Carmarthenshire County Council, 3 Spilman Street, Carmarthen SA31 1LE.

Anchorages and harbours

Whiteford Pool
3.87

1   Anchorage may be obtained in Whiteford Pool, 7 cables NW of Whiteford Lighthouse (51°39′N 4°15′W). The holding is fairly good, but tidal streams run strongly.

Chart 1076
Barafundle Bay
3.88

1   Barafundle Bay, a small sandy cove, lies 5 cables NW of Stackpole Head (51°37′N 4°54′W); anchorage off this bay affords good shelter in depths of 11 m. A private mooring buoy lies within the bay, 2 cables N of Stackpole Head.

Port-Eynon Bay
3.89

1   Anchorage for small vessels can be obtained in Port-Eynon Bay which is entered between Sandy Island, a low sandy hooked point extending from the E side of Port-Eynon Point (51°32′·0N 4°12′·5W) and Oxwich Point, 2¼ miles ENE. Skysea Island, a low islet, stands on a drying rocky ledge which extends 2 cables S from Port-Eynon Point. A wreck (position approximate), with a depth of 2·4 m, lies 5 cables SSE of the island.

2   A recommended berth is 7 cables ENE of Sandy Island, in a depth of 7 m, good holding.

A submarine cable crosses the W part of the bay and a dangerous wreck, marked by buoys (port hand) lies in the NW part of the bay.

Chart 1482 plan of Tenby and Saundersfoot with Approaches
Tenby
3.90

1   **General information.** Tenby (51°40′N 4°42′W), a seaside resort with a small harbour used by fishing vessels and pleasure craft, lies on the W side of Carmarthen Bay. The town stands on a bold promontory which terminates E at Castle Hill, a narrow peninsula of rock, on which stands a monument. Saint Catherine's Island, 28 m in height, surrounded by steep cliffs, lies ½ cable SE of Castle Hill to which it is connected by a drying ridge of sand.

2   The harbour limits are enclosed by a line extending 5¾ cables E from the mainland close S of Saint Cathrine's Island, thence N to Monkstone Point (51°42′N 4°41′W).

The Harbour Authority is Pembrokeshire County Council, Castle Square, Tenby, SA70 7BW.

The tidal harbour, which can be entered at HW ±2½ hours, is formed by a pier, about 120 m long, which extends WNW from the W end of Castle Hill. A light (metal mast, 5 m in height) is exhibited at the head of the pier.

3   A small landing pier projects from the shore SW of the pierhead; within these two piers the harbour is quayed. The harbour dries to a smooth firm sand bottom and is subject to silting.

Tidal stream information will be found on the chart.

4   **Directions:**
Landmarks:
Tall spire of Tenby church, standing close S of the harbour.
Coastguard Lookout (51°41′·7N 4°41′·3W).
From E the alignment (276°) of the N extremity of Saint Catherine's Island with the tall spire of Tenby church, 2½ cables W, leads N of The Yowan (51°40′N 4°38′W), a 4·4 m patch, and DZ2 Light Buoy (special) moored 2½ cables NNE, thence proceed as required for Tenby Roads or the harbour entrance.

5   Useful mark:
Monkstone (1¾ miles NNE of Tenby church), a rock, 15 m in height, lying ¾ cable E of Monkstone Point.
Facilities: slipway; repair grid; diving services; sailing club; hospital.

Supplies: fresh water; electricity; fuel in limited quantities.

Saundersfoot
3.91

1 **General information.** Saundersfoot Harbour, 2 miles N of Tenby, lies within Saundersfoot Bay and consists of a protected harbour; it is used mainly by fishing vessels and pleasure craft.

The harbour consists of a single drying basin enclosed by two moles, one extending ESE from the shore and the other, with a light at its head (stone cupola, 4 m in height), NNE to form a NNE facing entrance, 32 m wide. The bottom in the inner part of the harbour is hard, the remainder being mud and sand with a shelving beach at the N corner.

2 The harbour limit is a line drawn from Coppet Hall Point (51°43′·0N 4°41′·4W) to Monkstone Point (51°42′N 4°41′W).

Harbour Authority is Saundersfoot Harbour Commissioners, Harbour Office, Saundersfoot, Pembrokeshire SA69 9EX.

Bye laws are in force for the harbour, copies of which can be obtained from the Harbour Master.

3 From April to October the line between Coppet Hall Point and Perry's Point (51°42′·3N 4°41′·5W) is marked by buoys (special) to delineate water-skiing areas. Landward of these buoys vessels must not exceed 5 kn.

Directions. Entry can be made only at HW ±2 hours. Landmarks:

4 Hean Castle standing on high ground surrounded by fields and trees, 7 cables N of Saundersfoot Harbour light.

Saint Elidyrs Church tower, standing 2¼ miles NE of the harbour light.

Monkstone, the outer of two islets, lying close E of Monkstone Point 1½ miles NNE of Tenby Harbour.

With a swell setting on to the coast there is a considerable run into the harbour.

5 **Berths.** Craft up to 12 m LOA (15 m LOA by arrangement) and 4 m draught can be accommodated.

Anchorage. Saundersfoot Bay, has, in general, depths of less than 5 m, but there is good holding. An outfall which leads SE out into the bay from the S side of the harbour is marked at its head by a port hand buoy.

Facilities: boatyard; slipway; small craft moorings lie 3 cables E of the inner harbour entrance.

Supplies: fresh water; provisions.

SWANSEA BAY AND APPROACHES

General information

Charts 1165, 1161
Routes
3.92

1 Swansea Bay contains the Port of Swansea, Port of Neath and Port Talbot.

The main approach route into the bay lies between Mixon Shoal (51°33′·4N 3°58′·5W) (3.103) and Scarweather Sands (3.102), 7¼ miles SE, passing W of West Scar Light Buoy (W cardinal) and either N or S of White Oyster Ledge (51°31′N 3°59′W).

2 Deep-draught vessels bound for Port Talbot pass S of Ledge Light Buoy (51°29′·9N 3°58·8′W) before heading towards the harbour; see 3.185.

A navigable channel which lies between Scarweather Sands and Hugo Bank (51°29′N 3°49′W) offers an approach into Swansea Bay from SE by shallow draught vessels; see 3.105.

Topography
3.93

1 The coastline, between Pwlldu Head (51°33′·4N 4°03′·8W) and Mumbles Head, the outer of two islets 3½ miles E, lying close ESE of The Mumbles, consists of broken cliffs, over 60 m high, skirted by ledges, which dry to 2 cables offshore. It is indented by Pwlldu Bay, Caswell Bay and Langland Bay.

2 The coastline of Swansea Bay between Mumbles Head and Sker Point, a low dark and rocky point 9 miles SE, is in general, low, but is backed farther inland by high ground all round. Apart from the indentations of the river Tawe (afon Tawe) and the river Neath (afon Nedd), the coastal area is heavily built up with the W side residential, the N part mainly docklands and the E side mainly industrial as far as Port Talbot.

3 Between Port Talbot and Sker Point, 4 miles SSE, the coast is composed of Kenfig Burrows and Margam Burrows, low sandhills which are intersected by the afon Cynffig, a small river which flows into the sea between them.

4 The foreshore of Swansea Bay for 5 cables W of Mumbles Head is composed of shingle which dries; the W and N shores of the bay are skirted by an extensive drying flat consisting of sand, with patches of stone, bordered by mud, with a coastal bank extending some distance beyond to Green Grounds and Outer Green Grounds (3.131).

Pilotage and tugs
3.94

1 For information on pilotage, pilot boarding positions and tug services within Swansea Bay, see under individual ports.

Vessel traffic service
3.95

1 See 3.61.

Submarine pipelines
3.96

1 Three outfalls with diffusers at their seaward ends extend up to 2 miles from the coast between Swansea and Sker Point.

Spoil grounds
3.97

1 A spoil ground, marked by a light buoy (special) which may be moved without warning, lies 2 miles E of White Oyster Ledge (51°31′N 3°59′W). A further spoil ground, unmarked, lies NE of Outer Green Grounds.

Rescue
3.98

1 An all-weather lifeboat is stationed at The Mumbles (51°34′N 3°58′W); inshore lifeboats are stationed at Mumbles Pier and Port Talbot.

For details of rescue organisation see 1.60.

Tidal streams
3.99

1 For tidal streams in Swansea Bay see the tidal diamonds on the charts.

Tidal streams between Oxwich Point and Mumbles Head set in approximately the direction of the coast, attaining a spring rate of 3 kn off the salient points.

Mumbles Head and Lighthouse from SE (3.93)
(Original dated 2001)

(Photograph - Air Images)

2   The E-going stream sets directly over Mixon Shoal, a branch then turns N round Mumbles Head at +0610 HW Milford Haven and sets for 3 hours towards Swansea at a spring rate of 1 kn. The main body of the stream continues E across Swansea Bay towards Port Talbot where it divides again at –0315 HW Milford Haven, one branch running SSE along the coast, and the other branch running anti-clockwise round the bay for 9½ hours and attaining a spring rate of 3 to 4 kn off Mumbles Head where there may be a race.

3   Tidal streams alongside the head of Mumbles Pier set S except between LW and 2 hours after when the shingle between Mumbles Head and the islet W of it covers.

The streams set obliquely across Scarweather Sands; the directions and rates being subject to great variations; there are eddies and overfalls in their vicinity.

For general details on tidal streams in the area see *Admiralty Tidal Stream Atlas — Irish Sea and Bristol Channel.*

Directions
(continued from 3.67)

Principal marks
3.100

1   **Landmarks:**
Cefn Coed Hospital Tower (51°37′·7N 3°59′·3W).
Guildhall (White Tower) (51°36′·9N 3°57′·6W).
Television Mast (51°37′·8N 3°55′·2W) exhibiting obstruction lights.

Chimney (138 m in height) (51°34′·7N 3°47′·0W) standing at Port Talbot. Another tall chimney (119 m in height) stands 4½ cables NE.

2   Silo (90 m in height) (51°34′·3N 3°46′·4W).
Cooling Tower (74 m in height) (51°33′·9N 3°46′·2W) standing at the Abbey Steel Works, Port Talbot.
Chimney (127 m in height) (51°33′·5N 3°46′·5W). A silo (86 m in height) stands 2 cables E.

Major lights:
Mumbles Light (white octagonal tower, 17 m in height) standing on the summit of Mumbles Head (51°34′N 3°58′W) (3.93).
Nash Point Light (51°24′N 3°33′W) (3.197).

Other aids to navigation
3.101

1   **Racons:**
West Scar Light Buoy (51°28′·3N 3°55′·6W).
Cabenda Light Buoy (51°33′·4N 3°52′·2W).
See *Admiralty List of Radio Signals Volume 2.*

Caution
3.102

1   Scarweather Sands, best seen on Chart 1169, lie across the S approach to Swansea Bay, extending to a position 6¾ miles WSW of Sker Point (51°30′N 3°45′W). The sands, which dry near the E part, are marked on the W side by West Scar Light Buoy (W cardinal), on the S side by South Scar Light Buoy (S cardinal) and on the E side by East Scarweather Light Buoy (E cardinal).

Mumbles Light (3.100)
(Original dated 1996)

(Photograph - Dr. M P Bender)

2   The sands, over which depths are frequently changing, are covered by the red sectors of Porthcawl Light (51°28′·4N 3°42′·0W) and Nash Point Light (3.197).

Heavy seas break over the sands in bad weather.

Approach from south-west
3.103

1   From a position SSE of Oxwich Point (51°33′N 4°09′W), the main approach route to Swansea Bay leads about 8 miles NE between Mixon Shoal and Scarweather Sands (3.102) to the vicinity of Mumbles Head (51°34′N 3°58′W), passing (positions given from Mumbles Head):

> SE of Pwlldu Head (3½ miles W), a bold overhanging bluff, and:
> NW of West Scar Light Buoy (W cardinal) (6 miles SSE) lying at W end of Scarweather Sands, thence:

2

> Clear of White Oyster Ledge (3 miles SSW), the centre of a shoal bank. Ledge Light Buoy (S cardinal) is moored 1¼ miles S of the ledge on the S end of the bank. Thence:
> SE of Mixon Shoal (5 cables SSW), composed of fine white sand, over which depths frequently change; Mixon Light Buoy (port hand) is moored off the SW end of the shoal. Thence:
> To the Swansea pilot boarding area SE of Mumbles Head.

3.104

1   **Useful marks**:
> Mumbles Lighthouse (51°34′N 3°58′W) (3.100).
> Pennard Church tower (51°34′·7N 4°04′·3W).

Saint Thomas Church spire (51°37′·3N 3°55′·7W).
Water Tower (51°37′·7N 3°58′·0W).
West Pier Light (51°36′N 3°56′W).

Chart 1169
Approach from south-east
3.105

1   A navigable channel, with a minimum charted depth of 5·7 m in the fairway, lies between the drying banks of Scarweather Sands (3.102) and Hugo Bank (marked on its S side by Hugo Light Buoy (port hand)) 5 cables NE. There is a wreck, with a depth of 2·3 m, at the E end of the channel, 6½ cables WNW of the East Scarweather Light Buoy (E cardinal) (51°28′·0N 3°46′·8W).

2   **Caution.** Depths frequently change in the area of Hugo Bank owing to shifting sands, and Hugo Light Buoy is moved as necessary to reflect the changes.

> *(Directions continue for Port of Swansea at 3.129, for Port of Neath at 3.157, and for Port Talbot at 3.184)*

3.106

1   **Minor passages.** A navigable passage exists between Hugo Bank (51°28′N 3°48′W) and Kenfig Patches (1 mile NNE), which is composed of rock and fine sand and dries 7 cables NW of Kenfig Light Buoy (E cardinal), moored at the SE end.

2   A passage also exists between Kenfig Patches and Sker Point (51°30′N 3°45′W), though the fairway is encumbered by several shoal patches. Gwely'r Misgl, a rocky outcrop which dries 4½ cables from the shore, lies 5 cables NW of Sker Point. North Kenfig Patches, containing several rocky patches, lie 2 miles N of the passage.

Caution. Depths over Kenfig Patches and North Kenfig Patches change frequently owing to shifting sands.

Chart 1161
Landings
3.107

1   Mumbles Pier, which is unsafe, extends 1¼ cables NE from the mainland 2½ cables WNW of Mumbles Head. Fixed vertical red lights are exhibited from a white framework tower at the head of the pier.

Landing from boats can be made in Caswell Bay (51°34′N 4°02′W) and Langland Bay, 1 mile E. Langland Bay is, however, encumbered by rocks.

Anchorages in Swansea Bay

Outer Roadstead
3.108

1   There is a good anchorage in Outer Roadstead 1½ miles SE of Mumbles Head (51°34′N 3°58′W) in an area centred on 51°32′·7N 3°57′·0W with a radius 7 cables in a depth of 20 m. This anchorage lies S of the pilot boarding position (3.123), and is normally used by vessels awaiting entry to Port of Swansea or Port Talbot Old Dock.

Mumbles Road
3.109

1   Mumbles Road, suitable for vessels of light draught, lies N of Mumbles Head. There is a good anchorage 2 cables NE of Mumbles Head in a depth of 4 m, stiff mud. There is a foul patch 1 cable SSE of the anchorage.

The anchorage suffers from a ground swell in E and in strong W winds, but in the latter case the swell is reduced as the tide falls.

Chart 1165
Port Talbot deep-water anchorage
3.110

1   The deep-water anchorage, with depths of between 25 and 35 m, for vessels bound for Port Talbot Tidal Harbour is centred 7½ miles SSW of Mumbles Head. The Port Talbot pilot boarding station, 6½ miles SW of Mumbles Head, lies within this anchorage.

Caution. A wreck is charted in the N part of the anchorage.

PORT OF SWANSEA

General information

Chart 1161
Position
3.111

1   The docks at Swansea (51°37′N 3°56′W), are situated on the E side of the entrance to the river Tawe which flows into the N side of Swansea Bay.

Function
3.112

1   Swansea handles containers, dry bulk, liquid bulk, timber, general cargo, RoRo, steel and other metals.

Port limits
3.113

1   The outer limit of the Port of Swansea is a line drawn from the coast about 1¾ miles ENE of the harbour entrance to a position about 2½ miles SSW, thence WSW to a position at the outer end of the dredged approach channel, thence WNW to the coast at 51°35′·2N 4°00′·0W. The inner limit lies just seaward of the River Tawe Barrage (51°37′N 3°56′W).

Approach and entry
3.114

1   From the pilot boarding position (51°33′·1N 3°57′·2W) (3.123), the harbour is entered through a dredged channel (3.132), marked by light buoys.

Traffic
3.115

1   In 2007 there were 353 ship calls with a total of 987 981 dwt.

Port Authority
3.116

1   Associated British Ports Swansea, Harbour Office, Lock Head, King's Dock, Swansea SA1 1QR.

The Port Authority is represented by a Port Director. Navigational matters should be addressed to the Dock and Harbour Master.

Port of Swansea from SW (3.111)

(Original dated 2001)

(Photograph - Air Images)

Limiting conditions

Depths
3.117
1   **Controlling depth** is 4·2 m in the entrance channel (2001). For the latest depth information the Port Authority should be consulted.

Berthing is determined by height of tide and vessel's beam.

2   **Deepest berth**: Queen's Dock (3.134).

Tidal levels: mean spring range about 8·5 m; mean neap range about 4·0 m; see *Admiralty Tide Tables.*

Density of water: 1·020 g/cm^3 (King's Dock).

King's Dock Lock
3.118
1   The sea lock gives access to the wet dock system. Normal periods of operation are 4 hours either side of HW, though large deep-draught ships may have to enter at a particular height of the tide. The lock is 266 m long, 27·4 m wide and has a depth over the sill of 12·4 m at MHWS and 10·1 m at MHWN but can be divided into two sections. There is restricted working on public holidays.

Maximum size of vessel handled
3.119
1   The maximum dimensions of vessels handled are: LOA 200 m, beam 26·8 m and draught 9·9 m; approximate tonnage 30 000 dwt.

These vessels are docked over HW period. Any vessel whose dimensions are approaching maximum, should advise the Dock and Harbour Master well in advance. Vessels with a beam of over 26·2 m are not normally accepted unless fitted with a bow thruster.

Arrival information

Port operations
3.120
1   Restrictions on arrival or departure are dependent on the use of the lock and tidal conditions. See 3.119.

Vessels approaching the port should not expect to receive precise information about their movements until they are within 5 miles of the harbour entrance, and they should not attempt to enter harbour until the Dock Master has given permission to do so.

Vessel traffic services
3.121
1   See 3.61.

Notice of ETA required
3.122
1   Vessels should forward their ETA and draught, through their local agents, at least 24 hours in advance.

Pilotage and tugs
3.123
1   **Pilotage district.** The Swansea pilotage district corresponds to the port limits (3.113).

Pilotage is compulsory for vessels over 85 m LOA and all ships carrying 12 or more passengers. Vessels should notify Swansea Docks Radio of final ETA and draught approximately 2 hours before arrival, and on arrival off Mumbles Head, when docking instructions will be given. Vessels can call Swansea Pilots 4 hours either side of HW.

2   Vessels not subject to compulsory pilotage are advised not to enter the harbour without a pilot or local knowledge.

Pilot boarding position is 1 mile SE of Mumbles Lighthouse (51°34'N 3°58'W).

Pilot vessel is *Beaufort*; dark blue hull with orange superstructure. For further pilotage details see *Admiralty List of Radio Signals Volume 6(1).*

3.124
1   **Tugs** are based in King's Dock. Subject to advance arrangements being made through local agents for the tugs to leave the dock during the lock operating period (3.118), they are available on a 24 hour basis.

Regulations concerning entry
3.125
1   Docking instructions will be given on arrival off Mumbles Head and berthing instructions on arrival in the lock.

Quarantine
3.126
1   International health regulations are to be observed. Any vessel which is suspect should inform the Port Medical Officer of Health.

Harbour

General layout
3.127
1   The harbour consists of two wet docks and a tidal RoRo berth on the E side of the river mouth. The approach to the Ferryport Terminal and the entrance lock, King's Lock, to the main docks is protected on either side by breakwaters, each with a light at its head, extending SSW.

2   A barrage, with a lock section, spans the river Tawe approximately 3 cables N of the entrance to the docks.

Swansea Marina lies on the W side of the river Tawe entrance and within the confines of the barrage.

Development. Prince of Wales Dock, formerly part of Swansea Docks, is being redeveloped as a marina, part of Swansea waterfront development. Access will be via a new channel from the river N of the RoRo terminal.

3.128
1   **Approach Jetty,** built of concrete, extends 300 m SSW from the E entrance point of King's Lock forming a lead-in to the lock.

Directions for entering harbour
(continued from 3.105)

Principal marks
3.129
1   **Landmarks**:

Cefn Coed hospital tower (51°37'·7N 3°59'·3W) (3.100).

Guildhall (white tower) (51°36'·9N 3°57'·6W) (3.100).

Water tower (51°37'·7N 3°58'·0W) (3.104).

Television mast (51°37'·8N 3°55'·2W) (3.100).

Major light:

Mumbles Light (51°34'N 3°58'W) (3.100).

Other aid to navigation
3.130
1   **Racon:**

Cabenda Light Buoy (51°33'·3N 3°52'·4W).

See *Admiralty List of Radio Signals Volume 2.*

Approaches
3.131

1　From the pilot boarding position (3.123), the track to the seaward limits of the entrance channel, marked by SW Inner Green Grounds Light Buoy (S Cardinal) (51°34′N 3°57′W), leads 1 mile N through Outer Roadstead (3.108) and between Mumbles Head and Outer Green Grounds, an area containing a large number of shoal patches 2 miles E.

Caution. The depths over Outer Green Grounds are frequently changing.

Entrance channel
3.132

1　From the vicinity of SW Inner Green Grounds Light Buoy, the entrance channel, dredged over a width of 122 m, leads NNE for a distance of 2½ miles across Green Grounds, foul ground which encumbers the greater part of the W side of Swansea Bay with detached patches of rock and stones over which there are frequently changing depths. Light buoys (port and starboard hand) mark the edges of the channel, as shown on the chart.

2　Lights in line, at each end of the approach jetty (3.128), bearing 020°, indicate the E limit of the dredged channel.

At the harbour entrance a light (yellow metal column, 7 m in height) is exhibited at the head of West Pier and at the head of Eastern Breakwater (yellow framework tower, 7 m in height).

Kilvey Hill TV mast

Eastern Breakwater

Port of Swansea entrance from SSW (3.132)

(Original dated 2001)

(Photograph - ABP Swansea and Port Talbot)

Turning area
3.133

1　A turning area, NW of the approach jetty, has been dredged to enable vessels of up to 20 000 tonnes to be swung if required. Lights are exhibited at the S end and close to the N end of the approach jetty.

Basins and berths

Alongside berths
3.134

1　**King's Dock.** A wet dock which is entered directly from King's Lock. The dock is used for handling general, container and dry bulk cargoes, having 3586 m of quay and depth of 10·1 m.

Maximum size of vessel (3.119) can be accepted; height of quay above the water level is normally 1·5 m.

2　**Queen's Dock.** A wet dock with a depth of 10·1m. It is entered from King's Dock through a communication passage 30·5 m wide spanned by a floating oil boom.

Maximum size of vessel (3.119) can be accepted.

3　**RoRo terminal.** Swansea Ferryport, a RoRo terminal with car and passenger services linking the Republic of Ireland, is situated on the E bank of the river Tawe outside the wet dock system, close N of the entrance to King's Lock. The tidal berth, 145 m long and with a dredged depth of 4·9 m alongside (2001), provides a 76 m long linkspan, the nose of which can be lowered through 12·95 m to allow for tide levels and ships' draughts; the S end of the linkspan is marked by lights.

Port services

Repairs
3.135

1　Repairs of all kinds can be effected; diver available.

There is a repair berth at the W end of Queen's Dock which can safely accept the maximum size vessel alongside but with a draught restricted to approximately 4 m forward and 6 m aft.

There are two dry docks:
　No. 1: 204·21 m long; 28·04 m wide.
　No. 2: 170·69 m long; 22·87 m wide.

Other facilities
3.136

1　SSCC and SSCEC; customs; reception of garbage, oily waste, noxious and harmful substances by arrangement; hospitals.

Supplies
3.137

1　Fuel by barge or road; fresh water by hose at most berths; provisions and stores of all kinds.

Harbour regulations
3.138

1　Port of Swansea bye-laws are in force. Copies can be obtained from the Port Authority.

River Tawe

General information
3.139

1　The river Tawe is accessed via a lock in the barrage which crosses the river close N of the RoRo berth and the entrance to Swansea Docks. Traffic lights are mounted on metal posts either side of the approach to the lock.

The lock is 40 m long, 12·5 m wide and is normally operated daily from 0700 to 1900, and 0700 to 2200 during British Summer Time.

2　Above the Tawe Barrage a second lock on the W side of the river gives access to Swansea Marina in Tawe Basin and South Dock.

Marina Authority. Swansea Marina Ltd, Lockside, Maritime Quarter, Swansea SA1 1WG, who also manage Tawe Barrage Lock on behalf of the local authority Swansea City Council.

PORT OF NEATH

General information

Chart 1161
Position
3.140

1　Port of Neath (51°37′N 3°50′W), which includes Briton Ferry, occupies the lower reaches of the river Neath which flows into the NE corner of Swansea Bay; the river estuary lies between Crymlyn Burrows and Witford Point.

Function
3.141
1   The port handles vessels up to 6000 dwt, and comprises several wharves along both banks of the river as far as Skewen, just below the Railway Bridge at Neath Abbey, 2½ miles within the entrance. A large yacht harbour lies on the W bank below the River Neath Road Bridge (3.147).

2   Main commodities traded are steel, scrap, sand and gravel, containers and general cargo.

The town of Neath lies on the E bank of the river 4 miles within its entrance. It has a population of about 46 000.

Port limits
3.142
1   The outer port limit is a line drawn from the shore, about 1¼ miles SE of Witford Point (51°37′N 3°50′W), in a SSW direction for about 9 cables, thence W for 2½ miles and thence NNE to the shore, about 1¼ miles WNW of Witford Point.

Approach and entry
3.143
1   From the recommended positions in the approach through Swansea Bay (3.158), the harbour is entered through a channel, which dries, lying between two training walls.

Traffic
3.144
1   In 2007 the port had 289 ship calls and handled 393 000 tonnes of cargo.

Port Authority
3.145
1   Neath Harbour Commissioners, Bankside, The Green, Neath SA11 1RY.

The Port Authority is represented by a Harbour Manager.

Limiting conditions

Controlling depth
3.146
1   The entrance channel is dredged to 2·0 m above chart datum (1998). Berthing however, is determined by height of tide. There is a least depth of 7·1 m at MHWS, and 4 m at MHWN in the channel as far as Briton Ferry Outer Basin.

2   **Depths** in the river are less than those of the channel by the following amounts:

     Neath Abbey Wharves, 2·1 m less.
     Briton Ferry Shipping Services terminal (Giants Wharf), 1·5 m less.

In the entrance channel SW winds tend to increase the depths and NE winds tend to decrease them.

The river is subject to heavy freshets.

Vertical clearance
3.147
1   **M4 Road Bridge** spans the river 2 cables above Briton Ferry outer basin; it has a vertical clearance of 29 m and a width of 61 m below the centre of the central span. Lights are exhibited from the W pier.

River Neath Road Bridge spans the river close upstream of the M4 Bridge; it has a vertical clearance of 27 m over a width of 61 m below the centre of the central span.

2   Lights are exhibited from the centre of the central span, on both sides of the bridge, to assist vessels passing under the bridge.

Overhead power cables with safe vertical clearances of 42 m and 28 m span the river, respectively, ½ cable below and 4 cables above the River Neath Road Bridge.

Tidal levels
3.148
1   MHWS about 9·7 m; MHWN about 7·4 m. See *Admiralty Tide Tables.* Tide tables are also available from the Port Authority.

Maximum size of vessel handled
3.149
1   LOA 125 m; draught 5·8 m; 5-6000 dwt.

Arrival information

Port operations
3.150
1   The port operates throughout 24 hours subject to tidal conditions and weather.

Vessel traffic services
3.151
1   See 3.61.

Notice of ETA required
3.152
1   No port radio. Vessels can advise ETA and arrival draught by telephone through local agents or by direct communication with the pilot vessel.

See *Admiralty List of Radio Signals Volume 6(1).*

Pilotage and tugs
3.153
1   **Pilotage** is compulsory for all vessels within the port limits.

Pilot boards by prior arrangement through local agents in position 51°35′N 3°53′W.

Tugs. There are no resident tugs at Port of Neath; if required, they can be arranged from Swansea through local agents.

Harbour

General layout
3.154
1   The harbour is formed by the NW and SE banks of the river Neath, from its entrance at Baglan Bay to Neath Abbey Wharves at Skewen, 2½ miles NNE. Wharves consisting of several river berths lie at intervals along both banks of the river.

2   Briton Ferry, a suburb of Neath, 1 mile inside the river entrance has a disused dock and outer basin.

Submarine pipelines
3.155
1   Submarine pipelines cross the entrance channel close below the W end of the slag embankment (3.159).

Turning area
3.156
1   A turning area exists close inside the river mouth; if necessary a vessel can also be turned off the entrance to Briton Ferry outer basin.

Directions for entering harbour
(continued from 3.105)

Principal marks:
3.157

1   **Landmarks**:
      Swansea Guildhall (51°36′·9N 3°57′·6W) (3.100).
      Television Mast (51°37′·8N 3°55′·2W) (3.100).
    Major light:
      Mumbles Light (51°34′N 3°58′W) (3.100).

Approaches
3.158

1   From a position SE of Mumbles Head, vessels bound for Port of Neath should pass between Outer Green Grounds and Green Grounds, clear of two light buoys (special) marking diffusers at the seaward end of an outfall (3.96) extending SSW from the E end of Swansea Docks; or alternatively, S and E of Outer Green Grounds, passing SE of Grounds Light Buoy (E cardinal). The track then generally leads N to the pilot boarding position (3.153) and the entrance of the channel, passing W of the wreck of *Cabenda*, marked on its SE side by Cabenda Light Buoy (S cardinal).

Entrance channel
3.159

1   The entrance to the channel formed by the outlet of the river Neath, lies 1½ miles SW of Witford Point (51°37′N 3°50′W) and is marked by two light buoys (port and starboard hand). The channel leads NE and lies between two training walls 76 m apart. The SE training wall is marked by three light beacons (starboard hand) (green masts), at 5 cable intervals, the outer light being situated 5 cables within its outer end. Unlit green posts stand on the training wall between the lights.

2   A directional light is exhibited from a metal framework tower 4½ cables N of Witford Point.

    The NW training wall, the inner part of which is marked by three light beacons (port hand) (red metal posts), extends seaward to within 2 cables of the light buoys marking the entrance to the channel.

3   From the inner end of the SE training wall a low slag embankment, marked by light beacons (starboard hand), continues ENE to the S entrance to Briton Ferry Outer Basin (dries) and forms the SE side of the channel.

    There are two further light beacons (starboard hand) at the Briton Ferry Shipping Services wharf, on the E bank about 2 cables N of the river Neath Road Bridge.

Basins and berths

Anchorages and moorings
3.160

1   For anchorages, see 3.108.

Berths
3.161

1   The principal berths are shown below (positions given from Neath Road Bridge):
      Neath Abbey Wharves (1 mile N) lie on the W bank of the river at Skewen, below the Railway Swing

Entrance to River Neath from SW (3.159)
(Original dated 2001)

(Photograph - Air Images)

Briton Ferry - Berths N and S of road bridges (3.161)
(Original dated 2001)

(Photograph - Air Images)

Bridge. One wharf is 91·4 m in length and the other is 24·4 m, and are used mainly for steel shipments.

2   Briton Ferry Shipping Services terminal (Giant's Wharf) (3 cables N), on the E bank, consists of three berths with a total length of 274 m; maximum length of vessel 125 m with a draught of 5·8 m on HW (spring tides).

3   South Wales Wharfage (1 cable S), on the E bank; 182·8 m in length, used for general cargo.

Shepherds Wharf (2 cables S), on the E bank, has a length of 42·7 m.

South Wales Sand and Gravel (3½ cables S), also known as Riverside Wharf or Sand and Gravel Wharf, on the E bank; 69·3 m in length.

4   British Dredging Aggregates wharf (Albion Wharf) (4¾ cables S) is disused. Two lights (vertical) are exhibited from Baglan Pumping Station close SW of the wharf.

Vessels should be prepared to take the ground at all berths.

Monkstone Yacht Basin lies on the W side of the river (2 cables S).

Port services
3.162

1   **Repairs:** There are no repair facilities; the nearest available are at Swansea (3.135).

Other facilities: cranes arranged by wharf owners; hospitals at Neath; other facilities are available from Swansea (3.136).

2   **Supplies:** fuel oil; small quantities of fresh water; other supplies available locally or from Swansea.

Harbour regulations: bye-laws and regulations are in force. Copies can be obtained from the Port Authority.

PORT TALBOT

General information
Chart 1161
Position
3.163

1   Port Talbot (51°34′N 3°48′W), lies on the E side of Swansea Bay close S of the entrance to the river Avan. The coastline on either side of the harbour is low-lying with high ground about 1 mile inland rising to an elevation of 250 m.

Function
3.164

1   The port handles general cargo, minerals and ores.

Port limits
3.165

1   An arc of radius about 1 mile centred on the signal station at the root (51°34′·9N 3°48′·2W) of the breakwater, thence extending seaward as a 6½ cables wide corridor to the end of the dredged channel.

Approach and entry
3.166

1   From the recommended positions in the approach (3.185), the harbour is entered through a dredged channel on the alignment of leading lights.

Traffic
3.167

1   In 2007 there were 210 port calls with a total of 12 261 388 dwt.

Port Authority
3.168

1   Port Talbot is administered by the Port Manager at Swansea.

The local harbour office is: ABP Port Talbot, Puckney House, The Docks, Port Talbot, SA13 1RB.

Limiting conditions

Controlling depth
3.169

1   The entrance channel to the Tidal Harbour is dredged to 11·2 m (1999); that to Old Dock is dredged to 0·4 m (1999).

Deepest and longest berth
3.170

1   South Berth on Ore Jetty in Tidal Harbour (3.188).

Tidal levels
3.171

1   Mean spring range about 8·6 m; mean neap range about 3·9 m. For further information see *Admiralty Tide Tables.*

Subject to dredging, there is a least depth at MHWS of 20·8 m in the Tidal Harbour channel, and 10·0 m in the Old Dock channel. At MHWN there is 18·4 m and 7·6 m respectively. The Port Authority should be consulted for the latest information.

Density of water
3.172

1   Tidal Harbour, 1·025 g/cm^3, fresh water in Old Dock.

Maximum size of vessel handled
3.173

1   Tidal harbour: length 290 m, draught 16·7 m, 180 000 dwt.

Old Dock: length 130 m, beam 17·6 m, draught 7·7 m, 8000 dwt.

Arrival information

Port operations
3.174

1   Movements of vessels into and out of Tidal Harbour are affected mainly by vessels draught, but there are also restrictions related to size of vessels and tidal flows across the harbour.

Movement of vessels into or out of Old Dock Lock is restricted to approximately 2½ hours before to 2 hours after HW to ensure safe operation of the lock gates.

2   Berthing of the largest vessels in Old Dock and Tidal Harbour usually takes place up to 1 hour before HW, depending upon draught and height of tide.

Further details may be obtained from the Pilots or the Dock Master.

Vessel traffic service
3.175

1   See 3.61.

Notice of ETA required
3.176

1   Vessels bound for Port Talbot should send their ETA to their local agents 24 hours in advance, with amendments, if necessary, at least 4 hours before arrival.

Outer anchorage
3.177

1   For anchorages, see 3.110.

Pilotage
3.178

1   **Pilotage district.** See Swansea pilotage district (3.123).

Pilotage is provided by Swansea (3.123). Vessels are advised not to enter the Tidal Harbour or Old Dock without a pilot, or local knowledge.

Notice required for a pilot is the same as that for ETA. Amendments to ETA should also be sent direct to the pilots at least 4 hours before arrival.

2   Pilots for vessels entering Tidal Harbour normally embark and disembark in an area 6½ miles SW of Mumbles Head, as shown on Chart 1165. For vessels entering Old Dock the pilot boards at the Swansea pilot boarding position (3.123) 1 mile SE of Mumbles Lighthouse (Chart 1161).

3   **Pilot vessel** is equipped with VHF radio and cruises in the vicinity of the boarding position (see 3.123).

For further details, see *Admiralty List of Radio Signals Volume 6(1).*

Tugs
3.179

1   Tugs, which are usually based in Swansea, must be ordered at least 6 hours in advance through the vessel's appointed agent; they meet vessels as they approach the entrance channel.

Harbour

General layout
3.180

1   Tidal Harbour is protected by two breakwaters; South Breakwater, extended by Lee Breakwater, on the N side and Main Breakwater to the SE. The entrance faces W with the dredged channel passing close to the head of Main Breakwater.

Old Dock (Inner Docks) is approached from W along a dredged channel running, for about ¾ mile, along the N side of South and Lee Breakwaters and entered through a lock.

Traffic signals
3.181

1 Traffic signals (Diagram 3.181) for Tidal Harbour are exhibited from a tower near the root of South Breakwater.

Signal *Meaning*

Vessels may enter Tidal Harbour. (No vessel may enter unless these signals are shown).

Entry is prohibited.

Port Talbot - traffic signals (3.181)

2 There are no visual traffic signals for the river Avan or Old Dock.

Turning area
3.182

1 A turning area, dredged to 11·2 m (1999), exists within the confines of the Tidal Harbour breakwaters, as shown on the chart; the limits of the turning area are marked by steel and wood pile structures from which lights are exhibited.

Swell
3.183

1 A ground swell, particularly when combined with W gales, may cause a heavy sea in the Tidal Harbour and at the entrance to the river Avan; vessels berthed at the Ore Jetty may range, and entry into Old Dock may be restricted.

Directions for entering harbour
(continued from 3.105)

Principal marks
3.184

1 **Landmarks:**
Television Mast (51°37'·8N 3°55'·2W) (3.100).
Chimney (51°34'·7N 3°47'·0W) (3.100).
Silo (51°34'·3N 3°46'·4W) (3.100).
Cooling Tower (51°33'·9N 3°46'·2W) (3.100).
Chimney (51°33'·5N 3°46'·5W) (3.100).
Major light:
Mumbles Light (51°34'N 3°58'W) (3.100).

Approaches
3.185

1 **Tidal Harbour.** From a position outside Swansea Bay and in the vicinity of the pilot boarding area for Port Talbot (3.178), deep-draught vessels bound for Tidal Harbour should pass S of Ledge Light Buoy (51°30'N 3°59'W) (3.103) thence proceed NE towards the entrance channel, passing:
SE of Grounds Light Buoy (E cardinal), moored off the SE end of Outer Green Grounds (3.131), thence:
2 SE of Cabenda Light Buoy (S cardinal) (3.158).
Old Dock. From the vicinity of the Swansea pilot boarding area (3.123), vessels bound for Old Dock should proceed ENE, passing:

NNW of Cabenda Light Buoy, thence:
NNW of Stalheim Light Buoy (W cardinal) (51°34'·6N 3°49'·7W).

Entrance channels
3.186

1 **Tidal Harbour.** The entrance channel to Tidal Harbour, which passes between Lee and Main Breakwaters, is dredged over a width of 183 m and is marked on each side by light buoys. A light (metal framework tower) is exhibited from the head of each breakwater.
Leading lights:
2 Front light (yellow and orange diamond shaped daymark on metal framework tower) situated near the root of the River Avan South Breakwater.
Rear light (similar structure) (400 m ENE of the front light).
The alignment (059¾°) of these lights, which are shown when required, leads through the entrance channel into the Tidal Harbour.
3.187

1 **Old Dock.** The entrance to Old Dock lies at the mouth of the river Avan, which has a channel dredged to a width of about 45 m. Lights (steel columns) are exhibited from the breakwaters on the S side of the channel.
Leading lights:
Front light (orange daymark, steel pile on concrete block) situated on the S bank of the river, about 250 m seaward of the lock entrance.
2 Rear light (orange diamond-shaped daymark on steel post) (450 m E of front light).
The alignment (082°) of these lights, which are shown on request, leads through the entrance channel to a position about 2½ cables from the lock gates, whence the entrance lock can be approached.

Basins and berths
Tidal Harbour
3.188

1 **Ore jetty berths.** South Berth, dredged to 17·2 m (2001), handles the largest vessels; alongside depths 26·8 m at MHWS, 24·4 m at MHWN and 18·1 m at MLWS
North Berth, dredged to 15·0 m (2001), is designed specifically for self-discharge bulk carriers.
Light-beacons standing close N and S of the root of the jetty mark the N and S edges, respectively, of the dredged berths; a light (concrete column on dolphin) is also exhibited at the head of the jetty.

Old Dock
3.189

1 A berth for slag exports is situated in the entrance lock; this berth has also been used for heavy lifts for the steelworks. Slag cement is exported from a berth on the S side.

Port services
3.190

1 **Repairs:** limited repairs afloat; divers available.
Other facilities: arrangements can be made for the reception of garbage, oily waste, noxious and harmful substances; hospital.
Supplies: fuel oil and marine diesel; fresh water; provisions and stores.

Harbour regulations
3.191

1 Port Talbot Harbour Bye-Laws are in force. Copies can be obtained from the Port Authority.

Port Talbot – Tidal Harbour Leading Light structures (059¾°) from SW (3.186)

(Original dated 2001)

(Photograph - Air Images)

Port Talbot Leading Lights (059¾°) – Bridge view from SW(3.186)

(Original dated 2001)

(Photograph - Copyright Granted)

SWANSEA BAY APPROACHES TO NASH POINT

General information

Charts 1165, 1169
Route
3.192

1   From a position S of Oxwich Point (51°33′N 4°09′W) to a position S of Nash Point (51°24′N 3°34′W), the coastal route leads ESE for 23 miles, passing SSW of Scarweather Sands (3.102) and Nash Sands (3.199).

Topography
3.193

1   The coastline between Sker Point (51°30′N 3°45′W) and Porthcawl Point, 2½ miles SE, is low, rocky and mostly flat for more than a mile inland. Rocky ledges extend up to 2 cables offshore from both points.

Between Porthcawl Point and the mouth of the Ogmore River, 2½ miles E, the coast is indented by sandy bays, separated by rocky ledges which dry to 2½ cables offshore, and backed by sandhills.

2   The coast between the mouth of the Ogmore River and Nash Point, 5 miles SE, consists of bold cliffs, 30 to 60 m high, backed by higher land; the foreshore of sand and rock dries to 2 cables offshore.

Port Talbot Ore Jetty from NW (3.188)
(Original dated 2001)

(Photograph - Air Images)

Vessel traffic services
3.194
1   See 3.61.

Rescue
3.195
1   An inshore lifeboat is stationed at Porthcawl (51°28′·4N 3°42′·0W).
    For details of rescue organisation see 1.60.

Natural conditions
3.196
1   **Tidal streams.** See charts for tidal information, and also *Admiralty Tidal Stream Atlas — Irish Sea and Bristol Channel.*
2   **Tide-rips.** During the E-going stream heavy tide-rips can be encountered at the W end of West Nash (3.199) and at the S entrance to Nash Passage (3.201); strong tide-rips can also be encountered off the S side of Middle Nash in the vicinity of a detached shoal, least depth 9·7 m. An area of tide-rips is evident in the vicinity of numerous patches which extend up to 1¼ miles from the coast at Hutchwns Point (51°29′N 3°43′W).
    They may all be dangerous to small craft.

Directions
(continued from 3.67)

Principal marks
3.197
1   **Landmarks:**
    Cooling tower (51°33′·9N 3°46′·2W) (3.100).
    Chimney (51°34′·7N 3°47′·0W) (3.100).

Silo (51°34′·3N 3°46′·4W) (3.100).
Porthcawl Light (51°28′·4N 3°42′·0W) (white hexagonal tower, black base, 9 m in height) standing on the head of Porthcawl breakwater.
2   Water tower (51°30′·5N 3°40′·3W), standing at Newton Down, 2½ miles NNE of Porthcawl Light.
The Rest (51°29′·5N 3°43′·4W), a conspicuous building standing near the shore of Rest Bay, 1½ miles NW of Porthcawl Light.
Sea Bank Hotel (51°28′·6N 3°42′·5W), standing 4 cables NW of Porthcawl Light.
Building (51°28′·5N 3°42′·2W), standing close W of the harbour.
3   Nash Point Lighthouse (white round tower, 37 m in height) standing on flat ground 4 cables ESE of Nash Point (51°24′N 3°33′W); a disused lighthouse (white round low tower) standing close to the edge of the cliff 2½ cables SE of the point is conspicuous.
4   **Major lights:**
    Nash Point Light — as above.
    Bull Point Light (51°12′N 4°12′W) (3.17).
    Foreland Point Light (51°15′N 3°47′W) (3.47).
    Mumbles Light (51°34′N 3°58′W) (3.100).

Other aid to navigation
3.198
1   **Racon:**
    West Scar Light Buoy (51°28′·3N 3°55′·6W).

Nash Point and Lighthouse from W (3.197)

(Original dated 2001)

(Photograph - Air Images)

Passage
3.199

1 From a position S of Oxwich Point (51°33′N 4°09′W) the coastal route leads ESE for 23 miles to a position S of Nash Point, passing (with positions from Porthcawl Point (51°28′N 3°42′W)):

> SSW of West Scar Light Buoy (W cardinal) (8½ miles W), marking the W edge of Scarweather Sands (3.102). An oceanographic data gathering light buoy (special) is moored 2¼ miles S of West Scar Light Buoy. Thence:

2 > SSW of South Scar Light Buoy (S cardinal) (6 miles W), marking the S edge of Scarweather Sands, thence:

> SSW of East Scarweather Light Buoy (E cardinal) (3 miles W), marking the E end of Scarweather Sands, thence:

3 > SSW of West Nash Light Buoy (W cardinal) (3½ miles SW), marking the W edge of West Nash, the W part of Nash Sands which extend nearly 7½ miles ESE from a position 3 miles SW of Porthcawl Point, thence:

> SSW of Mid Nash Light Buoy (S cardinal) (4 miles SSE), marking the S edge of Middle Nash, thence:

4 > SSW of East Nash Light Buoy (E cardinal) (6½ miles SE) which marks the E edge of Nash Sand.

Thence to a position S of Nash Point (3.197).

Useful mark:

> Trywn-y-witch (51°26′·5N 3°36′·4W), a small promontory.

Caution
3.200

1 West Nash, Middle Nash and Nash Sand are subject to frequent change and should be given a wide berth. They are steep-to on their S side and composed of sand and gravel. The Sands are covered by a red sector (100°- 120°) of Nash Point Light.

(Directions continue at 4.21)

Side channel

Chart 1169
Nash Passage
3.201

1 Nash Passage lies between the E end of Nash Sand (3.199) and the rocky ledge which skirts Nash Point (51°24′N 3°34′W); it is 1 cable wide and has depths of less than 7 m in the fairway.

2 **Directions.** Approaching the passage from the WNW, from a position S of Scarweather Sands (51°28′N 3°50′W), the track leads ESE, initially in the white sector (036°- 082°) of Porthcawl Light, passing (with positions from Porthcawl Point (51°28′N 3°42′W)):

3 > Between East Scarweather Light Buoy (E cardinal) (3 miles W) and West Nash Light Buoy (W cardinal) (3½ miles SW), thence:

> Between Tusker Light Buoy (port hand), which is moored SW of Tusker Rock (1¾ miles SE), and the N edge of Middle Nash.

4 The alignment (126½°) of the disused lighthouse (3.197) and the prominent bluff of Nash Point, which lies within a white sector (120°-128°) of Nash Point Light, leads between the coastal bank NW of the point and the NE edge of Nash Sand until within 1 mile of Nash Point. Thence course should be adjusted to pass between East Nash Light Buoy (E cardinal) and the bank extending WSW from Nash Point.

Anchorages and harbour
3.202

1 Anchorage may be obtained temporarily in moderate weather NE of Nash Sands in depths of not less than 10 m. An area of foul ground, owing to the presence of old anchor chain, has been reported (2005) centred on 51°26′·8N 3°42′·6W.

Porthcawl
3.203

1 **General information.** Porthcawl, a holiday resort, with a small tidal harbour, lies close N and E of Porthcawl Point (51°28′N 3°42′W). Porthcawl Light (3.197) stands at the head of a breakwater which extends SE from Porthcawl Point.

Harbour Authority. Bridgend County Borough Council, Civic Offices, Sunnyside, Bridgend, CF31 1LX.

3.204

1 **Harbour.** The harbour is protected by the breakwater extending 1 cable SE from Porthcawl Point. Together with East Pier, a short breakwater extending S from the shore, this forms a small basin. The end of East Pier is marked by a daymark (starboard hand) and covers at HW. On the W side of the breakwater a rocky ledge dries to 1 cable offshore.

Within the breakwater the bottom is gravel and mud and that in the basin is soft mud.

2 The sandy foreshore E of the harbour entrance dries to just beyond the head of the breakwater.

Tidal streams attain a spring rate of 6 kn off the seaward end of Porthcawl breakwater and cause a very strong race.

3.205

1 **Landmarks** (with positions from Porthcawl Light):
Water Tower (2½ miles NNE) standing at Newton Down.
The Rest (1 mile NW), a building standing near the shore of Rest Bay.
Sea Bank Hotel with cupola (4 cables WNW).
Building with dome (3 cables NW).
Building (1¾ cables NW).

3.206

1 **Anchorage** in depths of 7 m can be obtained approximately 3 cables SSE of Porthcawl Light but the holding is poor. Care should be taken to avoid Fairy Rock, a submerged rocky ledge with a drying patch close SW, 6½ cables SSE of Porthcawl Light, and a rocky shoal lying 2 cables NW of the ledge; Fairy Light Buoy (W cardinal) is moored SW of the rocky shoal.

Chapter 4 - Bristol Channel - Eastern Part, including River Severn

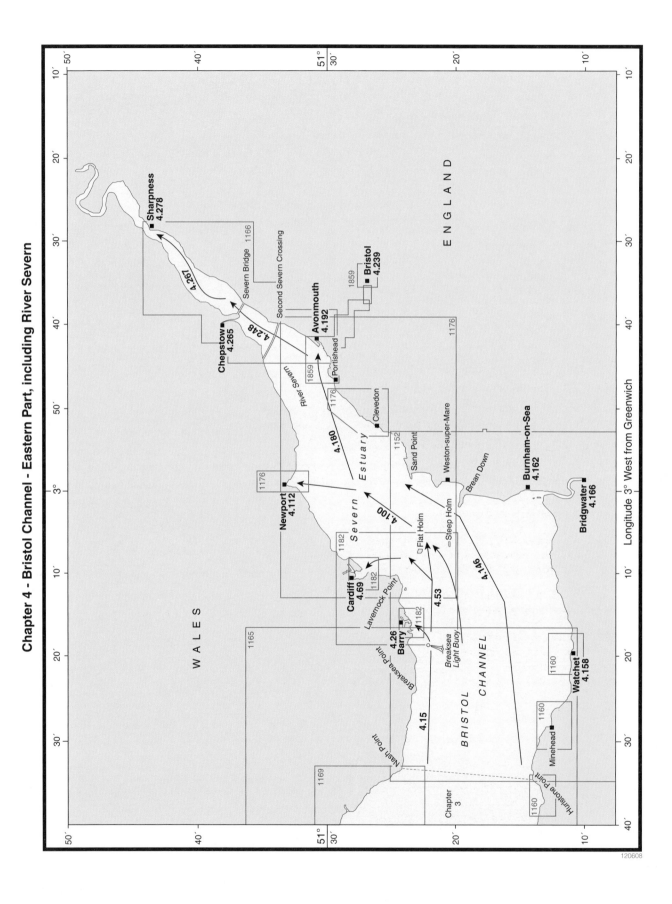

WALES

ENGLAND

BRISTOL CHANNEL

Severn Estuary

Sharpness 4.278

Severn Bridge 1166

Second Severn Crossing

Chepstow 4.265

4.267

4.248

River Severn

1859

Avonmouth 4.192

Portishead

Bristol 4.239

1859

Newport 4.112

1176

4.180

Clevedon

1176

Sand Point

1152

Weston-super-Mare

1176

Brean Down

Burnham-on-Sea 4.162

Bridgwater 4.166

Cardiff 4.69

1182

1182

Flat Holm

4.100

Steep Holm

4.53

4.146

Lavernock Point

Barry 4.26

1182

Breaksea Light Buoy

Breaksea Point

4.15

1160

Watchet 4.158

1160

Minehead

1165

Nash Point

1169

Hurlstone Point

1160

Chapter 3

Longitude 3° West from Greenwich

120608

104

CHAPTER 4

BRISTOL CHANNEL — EASTERN PART INCLUDING THE RIVER SEVERN

GENERAL INFORMATION

Charts 1179, 1152, 1176, 1166
Scope of the chapter
4.1

1   The area covered by this chapter comprises the E part of the Bristol Channel, entered between Nash Point (51°24′N 3°33′W) and Hurlstone Point, 10¼ miles S, and includes the navigable reaches of the river Severn and the Gloucester and Sharpness Canal.

In this chapter are described:
> The passages and routes, together with their ports, harbours and anchorages along the N shore, between Nash Point (51°24′N 3°33′W) and The Bridge, about 23 miles ENE, including the ports of Barry, Cardiff and Newport.

2
> The passage, together with the small ports, harbours and anchorages along the S shore, between Hurlstone Point (51°14′N 3°35′W) and Sand Point, about 25 miles ENE.

> The passage between The Bridge and King Road, about 10 miles ENE, the Port of Bristol and the river Severn above King Road to Sharpness (51°43′N 2°29′W) including the Port of Gloucester.

3   The chapter is divided into the following sections:
> Nash Point to King Road (4.9).

> Rivers Severn and Wye including Gloucester Harbour and the Ports of Sharpness and Gloucester (4.246).

Topography
4.2

1   The coastline for 5 miles E of Nash Point on the N side of the channel consists of cliffs 30 m high, decreasing in height farther E. In general, the N coastline is low-lying, backed by sandhills or rounded slopes, and in places protected by embankments, especially E of Cardiff where land is being reclaimed.

2   On the S side of the channel, the coast close E of Hurlstone Point, rises to an elevation of more than 300 m at Selworthy Beacon decreasing in height farther E. In general, the land, indented by Bridgwater Bay, is low lying with sandy beaches and intermittent areas of higher coastline with bold cliffs.

3   Two small islands, Flat Holm (4.66), and Steep Holm (4.67), lie approximately 16 miles E of Nash Point, in the approaches to the estuary of the river Severn.

Submarine cables
4.3

1   A number of submarine cables, as shown on chart 1179, run on the S side of the Bristol Channel and come ashore 3 miles N of Burnham-on-Sea. Anchoring and fishing in the vicinity of the cables are prohibited. See *The Mariner's Handbook* for information concerning submarine cables.

Pilotage
4.4

1   Breaksea Pilotage Station, the principal pilot boarding station for the area, lies in the vicinity of Breaksea Light

Buoy (safe water) (51°20′N 3°19′W), and is served by pilot launches from Barry. The pilot boarding positions (with positions from Breaksea Light Buoy) are as follows:
> For vessels of 12·5 m draught or greater, 2¾ miles WNW.

> For vessels of less than 12·5 m draught, 1 mile N.

2   Certain vessels may be directed by the Harbour Authorities to a boarding position 2¾ miles NE of the light buoy.

By arrangement with the pilot launch, small vessels may be boarded N of One Fathom Bank (51°21′N 3°12′W), outside the designated pilot boarding area.

A vessel approaching the pilot launch to embark a pilot is advised to maintain a steady course, reduce speed and wait for signals from the pilot launch.

3   Anchoring is prohibited within the designated pilot boarding area, as shown on the chart.

Breaksea Station is used by:
> Bristol Pilotage Authority; see 4.208.

> Associated British Ports, see 4.40.

> Gloucester Pilots; see 4.292.

> Pilotage for Port of Bridgwater, see 4.168.

Vessel traffic service
4.5

1   A VTS scheme, mandatory for vessels of 50 gt and greater, is in operation for the control of shipping within the Bristol Channel. Reporting points are shown on the charts.

See *Admiralty List of Radio Signals Volume 6(1).*

General directions
4.6

1   The channel N of Breaksea Light Buoy (51°20′N 3°19′W) and One Fathom Bank (4.60) is used by vessels approaching Barry and Cardiff. It is also the main route for vessels approaching the estuary of the river Severn, passing N or S of Flat Holm (51°23′N 3°07′W).

2   A side channel S of Breaksea Light Buoy, between One Fathom Bank and Culver Sand (4.154), which later joins the main route, SSW of Flat Holm, is normally used by small vessels proceeding to the estuary of the river Severn, which do not require pilotage.

The channel S of Culver Sand is normally used by vessels proceeding to Bridgwater Bay and Weston Bay.

Rescue
4.7

1   For details of rescue organisation and locations of assets see 1.60 and text under Rescue.

Natural conditions
4.8

1   **Tidal streams.** The flow of water in this area is determined by tidal forces. Tidal streams set generally in the deep-water channel but in the bend (51°21′N 3°07′W) between Culver Sand and the river Severn estuary there is a set towards the SE shore during both the E-going and W-going streams, which at springs attain a rate of 3 to 4 kn.

Bridgwater Bay, Weston Bay and Sand Bay are shallow and the streams do not set into them with any appreciable strength.

2 **Sandwaves.** A number of sandwave areas exist, some close to the main shipping lanes. They are usually concentrated in areas of local eddies. During periods of strong tidal flows, sediment builds up to form sandwaves of varying heights. The main areas are:

The W and E extremities of Culver Sand (51°17′N 3°17′W).
SW of Steep Holm (51°20′N 3°06′W).
3 W and SW of Flat Holm (51°23′N 3°07′W).
SW of Lavernock Point (51°24′N 3°10′W).
N and NE of Monkstone (51°25′N 3°06′W).
Tidal range. The spring tidal range is exceptional and can vary between 4·6 m at Bridgwater (51°08′N 3°00′W) and 12·3 m at Avonmouth (51°30′N 2°42′W). The greatest range at Avonmouth can be as much as 14·8 m.
Bore. The river Severn is subject to a bore (4.304).

NASH POINT TO KING ROAD

GENERAL INFORMATION

Charts 1179, 1152, 1176
Area covered
4.9
1 Described in this section are:
The coastal passages, with the deep-water ports of Barry, Cardiff and Newport, minor harbours and anchorages along the N shore, between Nash Point (51°24′N 3°33′W) and Newport, about 23 miles ENE.
2 The coastal passage along the S shore including the small ports of Watchet (4.158) and Port of Bridgwater (4.166), and other minor harbours and anchorages between Hurlstone Point (51°14′N 3°35′W) and Sand Point, about 24 miles ENE.
The passage between The Bridge (51°27′N 3°00′W) and King Road, about 10 miles ENE.
3 It is arranged as follows:
Nash Point to Breaksea Light Buoy (4.15).
Port of Barry (4.26).
Breaksea Light Buoy to Flat Holm (4.53).
Cardiff (4.69).
Flat Holm to The Bridge (4.100).
Newport (4.112).
Hurlstone Point to The Bridge - South coast route (4.146).
The Bridge to King Road (4.180).
Avonmouth and Royal Portbury Dock (4.192).
River Avon (4.225).

Topography
4.10
1 In the vicinity of Nash Point (51°24′N 3°33′W), the width of the Bristol Channel is approximately 10 miles, and between the longitudes of Nash Point and Rhoose Point (51°23′N 3°20′W) there are no dangers in the fairway of the channel outside 8 cables from either shore. However, E of longitude 3°20′W, there are numerous shoals which appear formidable on the chart, though it should be remembered that the considerable tidal range renders them less of a hazard after half flood.
2 N of King Road, where the river Severn begins, the width of the channel has decreased to about 2 miles.
See also 4.2.

Nature reserves
4.11
1 Flat Holm (51°23′N 3°07′W).
Steep Holm (51°20′N 3°06′W).

Fenning Island (51°13′N 3°02′W), bird reserve.
Stert Flats (51°13′·5N 3°03′·5W), bird reserve.
For further information see Protection of wildlife (1.58).

Channel depths
4.12
1 In the channel N of Breaksea Light Buoy (51°20′N 3°19′W) a deep-water route, with depths generally in excess of 20 m, runs N of One Fathom Bank and S of Mackenzie Shoal and continues within the buoyed channel to EW (English and Welsh) Grounds Light Buoy (51°27′N 3°00′W).
2 In Bristol Deep (4.183) there are depths generally between 10 and 18 m, whilst in Newport Deep (4.132) there are depths of from 5 to 10 m in the fairway.
King Road (4.183) has depths of from approximately 5 to 22 m, but with depths of less than 5 m on the leading line in the approach to Avonmouth Locks.

Vessel traffic service
4.13
1 See 4.5.

Natural conditions
4.14
1 **Tidal streams.** For details see information on the charts and *Admiralty Tidal Stream Atlas — Irish Sea and Bristol Channel.*
Tide races are particularly in evidence, especially during the greatest strength of the streams, in the vicinity of Lavernock Point (51°24′N 3°10′W), the islands of Flat Holm and Steep Holm (SE of Lavernock Point) and Brean Down (51°20′N 3°01′W).

NASH POINT TO BREAKSEA LIGHT BUOY

General information

Charts 1152, 1182 with plan of Barry Docks
Route
4.15
1 The route from Nash Point (51°24′N 3°33′W) to Barry, about 11½ miles E, lies N of Breaksea Light Buoy (51°20′N 3°19′W), and through Breaksea pilotage station. The route is clear of dangers outside 8 cables from the shore as far as Rhoose Point (51°23′N 3°20′W).

Topography
4.16
1   See 4.2.

Wrecks
4.17
1   There are many wrecks in the vicinity of Barry Roads (51°23′N 3°14′W).

Vessel traffic service
4.18
1   See 4.5.

Rescue
4.19
1   An all-weather lifeboat is stationed at Barry Docks (51°24′N 3°16′W); an inshore lifeboat is stationed at Atlantic College, Saint Donat's Bay, 1 mile ESE of Nash Point (51°24′N 3°33′W).

For details of rescue organisation see 1.60.

Natural conditions
4.20
1   **Tidal streams.** Between Nash Point and Breaksea Point (51°23′N 3°24′W), the tidal streams set in the direction of the coast at a spring rate of 3 kn in each direction, beginning as follows:

Interval from HW Avonmouth	Direction
+0535	E
−0035	W

2   Between Breaksea Point and Lavernock Point (51°24′N 3°10′W), the streams set in the direction of the coast and across the entrance to Barry Docks, at a spring rate in each direction of 4 to 5 kn.

3   Tidal streams S of Rhoose Point are shown by means of information on the chart.

Overfalls and race. Overfalls or a tide race may form off Breaksea Point.

Directions
(continued from 3.49 or 3.200)

Principal marks
4.21
1   **Landmarks:**
    Saint Hilary Radio Mast (51°27′N 3°24′W). Painted with red and white bands, the mast, from which obstruction lights are exhibited, can be seen from many miles in clear weather.
    Wenvoe Radio Mast (51°28′N 3°17′W). The mast, from which obstruction lights are shown throughout 24 hours, can also be seen from many miles on a clear day.

2   Lighthouse, and disused lighthouse, standing at Nash Point (51°24′N 3°33′W) (3.197).
    Chimney (51°23′·2N 3°24′·3W).
    Chimneys (Aberthaw Cement Works) (51°24′N 3°23′W), group of four standing on the E bank of

the river Thaw approximately 1 mile within its entrance.
3   Mast (51°24′N 3°21′W), which exhibits an obstruction light.
    Barry West Breakwater Lighthouse (51°23′N 3°16′W) (4.45).
  Major lights:
    Nash Point Light (51°24′N 3°33′W) (3.197).
    Flat Holm Light (51°23′N 3°07′W) (4.58).

Other aid to navigation
4.22
1   **Racon:**
    Breaksea Light Buoy (51°20′N 3°19′W).
For further details see *Admiralty List of Radio Signals Volume 2.*

Nash Point to Barry
4.23
1   From a position S of Nash Point (51°24′N 3°33′W) to Barry, the route leads E about 10 miles, passing (with positions from Nash Point):
    S of Stout Point (3¼ miles ESE), with a square cut appearance, thence:
2   S of Breaksea Point (6 miles ESE), composed of low sandhills, with a low concrete tower, which exhibits a light, 4 cables SSW; Breaksea Ledge, composed of limestone boulders and rocks which dry out to 2½ cables offshore from the point and is covered by a red sector of Nash Point Light. Thence:
3   S of Rhoose Point (8¼ miles E), a limestone cliff 10 m high, thence:
    N of Breaksea Light Buoy (10¼ miles ESE) and within the vicinity of Breaksea pilot station.

Useful marks
4.24
1   Barry West Breakwater Light (51°23′N 3°16′W) (4.45).
    Windmill (white, disused) (51°24′·4N 3°29′·7W).
    Sully Hospital, prominent white building with a tall chimney, standing amidst trees within Hayes Point, 1 mile E of Barry Docks.
(Directions continue for the coastal route at 4.58 directions for entering Barry Docks are given at 4.44)

Anchorages
4.25
1   **Barry Roads.** An anchorage can be found in Sully Bay, out of the strength of the tidal stream, in depths of 7 m, 5 cables W of Sully Island (51°24′N 3°12′W), clear of a wreck, with a depth of 5·4 m over it, which lies 4¼ cables WSW of Sully Island. Anchoring is prohibited within one mile radius of West Breakwater Light of Barry outer Harbour.
2   **Breaksea Point** (51°23′N 3°24′W). An anchorage for deep-draught vessels can be obtained off the point where there is ample room and deep water. Anchoring is prohibited in the pilot boarding area; see 4.4.
  Caution. An area of foul ground has been reported (2008) centred 7 miles SW of Breaksea Point, about 6¼ miles S of Nash Point (51°24′N 3°34′W). Vessels are advised not to anchor within 2 miles of this position.

Barry Docks from SW (4.26)
(Original dated 2001)

(Photograph - Air Images)

PORT OF BARRY

General information

Chart 1182 with plan of Barry Docks

Position
4.26

1   The Port of Barry (51°24′N 3°16′W), is situated on the N and E sides of Barry Island.

Function
4.27

1   Barry's main business is the handling of liquid bulk cargoes in support of the chemical industry. Also handled are; containers, dry bulks, fresh produce, timber and general cargo.

Port limits
4.28

1   The port limits embrace an area up to 2 miles S of Nell's Point (51°23′N 3°16′W), as indicated on the chart.

Approach and entry
4.29

1   Barry Docks are approached from the vicinity of Breaksea Light Buoy in the pilot boarding area and entered from SE.

Traffic
4.30

1   In 2007 there were 211 port calls with a total of 682 201 dwt.

Port Authority
4.31

1   Port of Barry is administered by the Port Manager at Cardiff.

The local harbour office is: ABP Barry, Port Office, Atlantic Way, No. 2 Dock, Barry, CF63 3US.

Navigational matters should be addressed to the Dock and Harbour Master, who is also based at Cardiff.

Limiting conditions

Controlling depth
4.32

1   The channel through Tidal Harbour leading to Lady Windsor Lock has depths of less than 2 m.

The harbour is subject to silting; the Harbour Master should be consulted for the latest controlling depth and maximum draught.

Deepest and longest berth
4.33

1   All three basins can accept the maximum size of vessel.

Tidal levels
4.34
1 Mean spring range about 10·4 m; mean neap range about 4·5 m. See *Admiralty Tide Tables.*

Density of water
4.35
1 Density of water: 1·021 g/cm^3.

Maximum size of vessel handled
4.36
1 Maximum dimensions: length 178 m; beam 23·8 m; draught 9 m.

These vessels are docked before HW through No 3 Dock Basin.

Arrival information

Port operations
4.37
1 Arrivals and departures are restricted by the locks. Use of them from 4 hours HW. Docking and undocking can not be attempted through No 3 Dock Basin after HW.

Notice of ETA required
4.38
1 24 hours, at Breaksea Light Buoy.

Notice of ETD required. Outward-bound vessels should send their ETD to Severn VTS.

See *Admiralty List of Radio Signals Volume 6(1).*

Outer anchorages
4.39
1 See 4.25.

Pilotage
4.40
1 Associated British Ports (ABP) provide the pilotage service for Barry, Cardiff and Newport, including the river Usk. Pilots are based at the Dock and Harbour Master's office, situated on the SW side of West Jetty in Tidal Harbour.

Pilotage is compulsory for all vessels or tows over 85 m in length. Additionally, pilotage is compulsory for vessels or tows of 20 m in length carrying dangerous or noxious substances in bulk, twelve or more passengers, or explosives. For further details see *Admiralty List of Radio Signals Volume 6 (1).*

2 The pilotage district covers those tidal waters within a limit bounded seawards by straight lines joining Hartland Point Light (51°01'N 4°32'W) to Lundy South Light, thence through Caldey Island Light to the mainland.

Notice required for a pilot. Vessels bound for Barry, Cardiff and Newport, including the river Usk, requiring the services of a pilot should give 24 hours notification of their ETA at the pilot boarding position, stating maximum draught and port of destination.

3 Pilots normally board at one of the nominated pilot boarding positions in the vicinity of Breaksea Light Buoy (see 4.4).

Contact should be made with the pilot vessel by VHF at least 2 hours before arrival.

Under certain circumstances, arrangements may be made to board vessels farther to the W within the pilotage area provided at least 24 hours notice is given to Severn VTS.

4 The pilot vessel has a black hull with the word PILOT painted in white letters and puts to sea only when required. There is no cruising or anchored pilot vessel.

For further details, see *Admiralty List of Radio Signals Volume 6(1).*

Tugs
4.41
1 Tugs move between Barry, Newport and Cardiff; requests for tugs should be made when sending initial ETA. Tugs usually join a vessel in Barry Roads.

Regulations concerning entry
4.42
1 **Entry.** Vessels should request permission from the Dock and Harbour Master via VHF before undertaking the following manoeuvres:

Approaching or passing through the entrance to the breakwaters.

Entering Lady Windsor Lock or No 3 Dock Basin from No 1 Dock, or the Junction Cut from No 1 or No 2 Docks.

2 Any movements within the docks.

Vessels are prohibited from anchoring in the entrance to the harbour.

Safety. Vessels carrying dangerous substances must give notice of entry to the Dock and Harbour Master at least 24 hours prior to arrival.

Harbour

General layout
4.43
1 The harbour consists of three wet docks and a tidal basin. The entrance is formed by West Breakwater and East Breakwater leading into Tidal Harbour. The entrance between the heads of the breakwaters is 107 m wide.

Directions for entering harbour

Approaches
4.44
1 From the vicinity of Breaksea Light Buoy to the harbour entrance the route passes S and E of Merkur Light Buoy (port hand) (51°22'N 3°16'W) through an area of many shoals and wrecks.

Caution. A strong W set is generally experienced ¼ mile from the entrance channel at all states of the tide.

Entrance channel
4.45
1 The entrance channel leads between the head of West Breakwater, from where a light (white round tower, 9 m in height) is exhibited, and the head of East Breakwater, also from where a light (mast, 5 m in height) is exhibited.

Lights (white mast, 13 m in height) are exhibited at the head of West Jetty, 1¼ cables within the harbour entrance.
4.46
1 **Useful mark:**

White fluorescent strip light, exhibited from the head of West Jetty for the use of pilots, provides a lead-in between the breakwaters.

Basins and berths

Locks
4.47
1 There are two entrances to the wet docks, namely Lady Windsor Lock, which is that generally used, and No 3 Dock Basin which is used in the event of a breakdown of the former or in the case of a vessel which is too large for it.

Lady Windsor Lock, locally known as Deep Lock, is 197·2 m long and 19·8 m wide. The outer and middle sills

Barry - Tidal Harbour and entrance to Docks from SE (4.43)

(Original dated 2001)

(Photograph - Air Images)

are 4·1 m below the level of chart datum and the inner sill is 0·5 m below that level. The centre of these sills is 0·9 m below these levels.

2   Lady Windsor Lock is open for approximately 7 hours each tide.

No 3 Dock Basin is 183 m long and 24·4 m wide at the entrances, with depths over both the outer and inner sills of 0·5 m below the level of chart datum. The basin gates are closed at HW. When used as a lock the depth is not less than 6·4 m.

Alongside berths
4.48

1   In the NW corner of Tidal Basin the SW wall of Lady Windsor Lock projects SE from the lock entrance to form West Jetty. A lifeboat slip projects into the W side of Tidal Harbour; a yacht club lies close S of the slip. Small craft moorings lie on the inner side of West Breakwater.

In the NE corner of Tidal Harbour, Western Jetty projects SE from the NE wall of Lady Windsor Lock. A dolphin, from which a light is exhibited, and 3 monoliths provide a lead-in to No 3 Dock Basin.

2   Access to the main berths lies through Lady Windsor Lock or No 3 Dock Basin into No 1 Dock which in turn provides access into No 2 Dock through Junction Cut.

Berthing is in accordance with height of tide and vessel's beam.

3   **No 3 Dock Basin.** Semi-tidal, see 4.47 for maximum dimensions. Maximum draught alongside 9·0 m.

No 1 Dock. Length 945 m with a maximum width of 335 m, normally has depths of 9·5 m; total quayage available 2838 m. Enterprise Quays, previously three coal loading stages, at the NW end of the Dock have been developed into hospitality berths to accommodate visiting vessels.

4   **No 2 Dock.** There are no berths on the N side. With the same depth as No 1 Dock, it is entered through Junction Cut; the dock has a length of 1012 m and a width of between 122 to 183 m. Bulk and chemical cargoes are handled in this dock. Total quayage available 2283 m. The tanker terminal has two berths.

Numbered berths are shown on the chart.

Port services

Repairs
4.49

1   The dry dock at SE corner of No 1 Dock is no longer in use.

Most kinds of afloat repairs can be effected, and divers are available. Permission and permits must be arranged through ABP's Cardiff office.

Other facilities
4.50

1   Reception of oily waste, noxious and harmful substances; issue of SSCC and SSCEC; hospital.

Slipway at Barry Yacht Club and a boat hoist at an adjacent repair yard for craft up to 20 tonnes and up to 15 m in length.

Supplies
4.51

1   Fuel by road; fresh water at most berths; provisions; other stores from Cardiff, 6 miles distant.

Harbour regulations
4.52

1 Bye-laws are in force; copies can be obtained from the Dock and Harbour Master's Office.

Vessels laden with petroleum must display International Code B flag, by day, and exhibit a red light at the masthead by night.

Bye-laws for small craft are in force. Small craft are prohibited from anchoring or fishing in the approaches to Barry during tidal periods when larger vessels may be entering or leaving the port.

BREAKSEA LIGHT BUOY TO FLAT HOLM

General information

Charts 1152, 1182, 1176
Route
4.53

1 The principal route to the estuary of the river Severn lies N of Breaksea Light Buoy (51°20′N 3°19′W), passing N of One Fathom Bank and N or S of Flat Holm, about 8 miles ENE. Deep-draught vessels should follow the deeper water route, S of Flat Holm.

A route, generally used by smaller vessels to the estuary of the river Severn, lies S of Breaksea Light Buoy; see 4.64.

Topography
4.54

1 Sully Island (51°24′N 3°12′W), lies 2 miles E of the entrance to Barry Docks, and is connected to the mainland N of it by a drying rocky ledge.

Sully Bay, entered between Hayes Point and Sully Island, is encumbered by a shallow mud bank; the foreshore consists chiefly of rocky ledges and stones.

2 Lavernock Point (51°24′N 3°10′W), 3½ miles E of Barry Island, is a cliff 15 m high; the intervening coast is bounded by low cliffs of from 15 to 30 m in height, backed by rounded slopes.

Penarth Head, 2 miles N of Lavernock Point, rises to an elevation of approximately 65 m; its nearly perpendicular cliff is veined by gypsum.

3 The city of Cardiff stands on very low ground and much is hidden by cranes, oil storage tanks and steelworks at the docks.

The islands of Flat Holm (4.66) and Steep Holm (4.67) lie between Lavernock Point and Brean Down about 7 miles SE.

Vessel traffic service
4.55

1 See 4.5.

Rescue
4.56

1 An all-weather lifeboat is stationed at Barry Docks (51°24′N 3°16′W). Two inshore lifeboats are stationed at Penarth; the lifeboat station is situated close S of Penarth Pier (4.99).

For details of rescue organisation see 1.60.

Tidal streams
4.57

1 For tidal streams in Cardiff and Penarth Roads see tidal diamonds on the chart.

A branch of the main in-going stream sets first N between Lavernock Point and Cardiff Grounds, but as the latter cover the stream sets strongly NE across them; similarly, the out-going stream sets at first SW across Cardiff Grounds but, as they dry, the stream sets S between them and Lavernock Point.

2 During the last two hours of the in-going stream an eddy sets W across Cefn-y-Wrach (4.91) and thence S along the coast up to 3 cables offshore almost as far as Ranny Spit, 5 cables E of Lavernock Point, when it curves E to join the main in-going stream.

The stream sets with great strength over The Wolves (4.61) at springs, and causes turbulence over Ranny Spit.

Near the coast W of Lavernock Point the streams set in the direction of the coast attaining a spring rate in each direction of 4 to 5 kn.

3 Between Flat Holm and Steep Holm, the streams set in the direction of the channel beginning as follows:

Interval from HW Avonmouth	*Direction*
−0610	E
+0015	W

The maximum E-going spring rate is 3 kn and W-going spring rate 4 kn.

Directions
(continued from 4.24)

Principal marks
4.58

1 **Landmarks**:
Wenvoe Radio Mast (51°28′N 3°17′W) (4.21) (Chart 1179).
Flat Holm Lighthouse (white round tower, 30 m in height) (51°23′N 3°07′W).
Steep Holm (51°20′N 3°06′W) (4.67).
Brean Down (51°20′N 3°01′W) (4.152).
Monkstone Lighthouse (51°25′N 3°06′W) (4.104).

2 **Major light**:
Flat Holm Light — as above.

Other aid to navigation
4.59

1 **Racon**:
Breaksea Light Buoy (51°20′N 3°19′W).

Route south of Flat Holm
4.60

1 From a position N of Breaksea Light Buoy (51°20′N 3°19′W) the route towards the river Severn (4.248) S of Flat Holm leads initially E, thence NE, to pass about 6 cables SE of Flat Holm Light, passing (with positions from Flat Holm Light (51°23′N 3°07′W)):
S of Merkur Light Buoy (port hand) (5½ miles W), which marks an area of wrecks on the edge of a coastal bank, thence:

2 N of One Fathom Bank (3¾ miles WSW) marked on its N side by North One Fathom Light Buoy (N cardinal), thence:
S of Mackenzie Shoal (8½ cables SW), on which lies a wreck with a depth of 6·4 m over it. Mackenzie Light Buoy (port hand), is moored about 2 cables SW of the wreck. Thence:

3 NW of Holm Middle Light Buoy (starboard hand) (8½ cables SSE), which marks a rock ledge with a least charted depth of 8·5 m over it.

Cautions. The depths over One Fathom Bank, composed of sand and gravel, are subject to constant alteration.

Very deep-draught vessels should beware of the rock ledge in the vicinity of Holm Middle Light Buoy, when proceeding early on the in-going tide.

Route north of Flat Holm
4.61

1   From a position N of Breaksea Light Buoy the route towards the river Severn N of Flat Holm leads E with Flat Holm Light bearing 077°, passing N of One Fathom Bank until Barry West Breakwater Light (51°23′N 3°16′W) (4.45) bears 317°.

The route then leads NE towards the lighthouse which stands on Monkstone (51°25′N 3°06′W) (4.104) bearing 054°, passing (with positions from Monkstone):

2   NW of Fairway Shoals (3¾ miles SW), with a least depth 4·1 m, thence:

      SE of Lavernock Spit (3¼ miles WSW), a shoal with depths of less than 4 m over it, extending S from Lavernock Point (2¾ miles W). The S extremity of the shoal is marked by Lavernock Spit Light Buoy (S cardinal). Thence:

3   NW of The Wolves (2½ miles SW), three drying rocky heads marked by Wolves Light Buoy (N cardinal).

4.62

1   **Cautions.** When proceeding farther E, mariners should ensure that there is sufficient water over Centre Ledge (51°24′N 3°07′W), where there are depths of less than 3·5 m.

North of Flat Holm the streams, which generally set SW and NE, are strong in both directions.

For vessels approaching from the W, Lavernock Point obscures from view any ships leaving Cardiff on a S course.

Useful marks
4.63

1   Hinkley Point Nuclear Power Station (51°12′N 3°08′W) (4.165).

      Barry West Breakwater Lighthouse (51°23′N 3°15′W) (4.45).

      (Directions continue for entering Cardiff at 4.89
        and for the coastal route at 4.104)

Side channels
South of Breaksea Light Buoy
4.64

1   Between Breaksea Light Buoy and Culver Sand, 3 miles S, a channel exists for vessels with suitable draught and not requiring the services of a pilot, which passes S of One Fathom Bank and which eventually joins the route for deep-draught vessels passing S of Flat Holm.

2   **Directions.** From a position approximately 1 mile S of Breaksea Light Buoy, the channel leads ENE on the line of bearing 070° of Sand Point (51°23′N 2°59′W), passing SSE of One Fathom Bank to a position with Flat Holm Light bearing 027° distant 1½ miles where course is altered to a more NE heading, thence passing between Mackenzie and Holm Middle Light Buoys (4.60) and continuing into the channel leading to The Bridge (4.100).

3   **Caution.** Considerably shallower water than charted is reported (1998) to exist on the NW side of Culver Sand. Mariners are advised to exercise particular caution.

South-east of The Wolves
4.65

1   A passage with depths of less than 10 m lies between The Wolves (4.61) and Flat Holm Shelf, a rocky shoal with a least depth of 2·9 m over it, 2½ cables NW of Flat Holm.

A dangerous wreck (position approximate) lies about ½ cable SE of The Wolves; a further wreck, with a depth of 5·4 m over it, lies 1½ cables S of The Wolves.

Islands of Flat Holm and Steep Holm
Flat Holm
4.66

1   Flat Holm (51°23′N 3°07′W), an island 26 m high, lies between Lavernock Point on the N shore, and Brean Down on the S shore of the Bristol Channel. Drying rocky ledges extend out to 1 cable from the island, and a bank with depths of less than 5 m extends 6½ cables WSW from its W end.

A light (4.58) is exhibited from the SE end of the island. There are some buildings on the N side.

The island is a Local Nature Reserve, see 1.58.

Flat Holm and Lighthouse from SW (4.66)

(Original dated 2001)

Close-up from S

(Photograph - Air Images)

2   **Landing place.** The best landing place on an in-going tide is on a shingle beach on the NE side of the island where there are two ruined jetties, the W of which is a small wooden jetty which dries at half tide. The E jetty is of concrete construction and its outer extremity, consisting of concrete piles, is awash. Out-going tidal streams set strongly round the point and without local knowledge landing is not advised.

3   There is a helicopter landing site on the island.

There is a narrow but deep passage between Flat Holm and New Patch, the SW end of an uneven coastal bank with a least depth of 2·8 m over it, which lies about 2½ cables E of the island.

Anchorage, in 16 m, is obtainable 2½ cables off the NE side of the island.

Steep Holm
4.67

1   Steep Holm (51°20′N 3°06′W), an island 72 m high, lies 2 miles S of Flat Holm; Rudder Rock is at its W extremity and Calf Rock lies close off its SE end. The island, a National Nature Reserve (1.58), is mainly surrounded by steep cliffs and has a few uninhabited buildings.

2   Below-water ledges, with depths of less than 5 m, extend 3 cables NE and SW from the island. A detached rocky patch, with a depth of 5·5 m over it, lies 3 cables WNW of Rudder Rock, but there are depths of 35 m between the patch and the island.

Landing is difficult except at the E end of the island, where a path leads to the summit. There are no public rights of way; access is permitted only to paying visitors.

Anchorage
4.68

1   Should the weather become thick, vessels may anchor anywhere E of the meridian of Swansea (3°56′W), but those anchoring in or near the fairways of the Bristol Channel should remember that there are many vessels outward bound after HW. Vessels should make due allowance for the strong tidal currents in the Bristol Channel.

PORT OF CARDIFF

General information

Chart 1182 with plan of Cardiff Docks
Position
4.69

1   Port of Cardiff (51°27′N 3°10′W) is situated on the E side of the mouth of the river Taff.

Function
4.70

1   The port is capable of accommodating large vessels and is equipped with modern tanker, cargo and container handling equipment.

Cardiff Bay, Barrage and Docks from SSW (4.69)
(Original dated 2001)

(Photograph - Air Images)

Main commodities handled are: containers, dry and liquid bulks, steel and other metals, fresh and perishable produce, and timber.

Cardiff is the capital city of the Principality of Wales.

Port limits
4.71
1 The outer port limit is drawn SSE for about 4½ miles from the shore 1¼ miles NE of the entrance lock, to pass close W of Monkstone (51°25′N 3°06′W), thence SSW to close E of Flat Holm (51°23′N 3°07′W), thence NW to Lavernock Point (51°24′N 3°10′W).

Approach and entry
4.72
1 The harbour is approached through Cardiff and Penarth Roads and entered through a buoyed channel, indicated by a PEL.

Traffic
4.73
1 In 2007, there were 1159 port calls with a total of 4 540 185 dwt.

Port Authorities
4.74
1 The Port Authority for Cardiff Docks is Associated British Ports, Queen Alexandra House, Cargo Road, Cardiff CF10 4LY, who are represented by a Port Director. Navigational matters should be addressed to the Dock and Harbour Master.

Limiting conditions
Controlling depth
4.75
1 The controlling depth is that in the approach channel. For the current situation the Dock and Harbour Master should be consulted.

Berthing is in accordance with height of tide and vessel's beam.

Deepest and longest berth
4.76
1 Queen Alexandra Dock (4.94).
Roath Dock (4.94).

Tidal levels
4.77
1 Mean spring range about 11·3 m; mean neap range about 5·8 m. See *Admiralty Tide Tables.*
Tidal information is available on request.

Density of water
4.78
1 Can be between 1·008 and 1·019 g/cm³ off the sea lock.

Maximum size of vessel handled
4.79
1 LOA 198 m; beam 27 m; draught 10·0 m.

Arrival information
Port operations
4.80
1 Arrivals and departures are restricted by the entrance lock which is open for approximately 7 hours over each HW.

Notice of ETA required
4.81
1 24 hours, at Breaksea Light Buoy.

Outer anchorages
4.82
1 There is an anchorage on the SE side of Cardiff Grounds between Centre Ledge and Monkstone (51°25′N 3°06′W) (4.104), as shown on the chart, in depths of 11 to 15 m, although less water was reported in 1999. This anchorage can be affected by strong tidal streams. The bottom is rocky in places.
2 Good anchorage can be obtained N of Flat Holm (51°23′N 3°07′W), between it and Centre Ledge, in depths of 10 to 18 m. There is an anchorage, shown on the chart, between Flat Holm and New Patch (4.66).
3 Cardiff and Penarth Roads (51°26′N 3°08′W), on the NW side of Cardiff Grounds, afford anchorage in a limited space, in depths from 6 to 10 m. The S entrance to the roadstead lies over a sand bar with depths of less than 5 m over it. The anchorage can be crowded at times and is not comfortable in bad weather or a choppy sea.
4 Two unmarked wrecks with least swept depths of 2·1 and 2·6 m over them lie on the E side of the roads, about 1½ miles E of Penarth Pier (4.99). A patch of mud and rock with a least depth of 1·2 m over it lies 9 cables E of the pier.
Barry Roads (4.25) affords some shelter from the SW and is probably the best anchorage in the vicinity.

Pilotage
4.83
1 Associated British Ports (ABP) pilotage service is based at Pierhead, Barry Docks. Pilotage is compulsory for vessels or tows of 20 m in length carrying dangerous or noxious substances in bulk; twelve or more passengers; or explosives. For details of pilotage, pilot boarding position and pilot vessel, see 4.40. See also *Admiralty List of Radio Signals Volume 6(1).*

Tugs
4.84
1 Tugs may be stationed at Cardiff, Barry and Newport and usually join vessels at the approach to the entrance channel.

Restricted area
4.85
1 The drying area in front of the sluices between the two breakwaters and W of Wrach Channel is an excluded area to all vessels except those which have harbour authority approval. Fishing is prohibited in this area.

Regulations concerning entry
4.86
1 Docking instructions are given on arrival; berthing instructions on arrival in the lock.
Anchorage in the entrance channel is prohibited.
No vessel may attempt to swing in the entrance channel so as to interfere with the passage of other vessels.
2 When the depth of water permits, vessels intended for Queen Alexandra Dock may approach only as far N as Outer Wrach Light Buoy, until directed to proceed by the Dock and Harbour Master.
Vessels carrying dangerous substances must give notice of entry to the Dock and Harbour Master at least 24 hours prior to arrival.

Harbour

General layout
4.87

1   The old harbour formed by the estuaries of the river Ely and the river Taff (4.69) is enclosed within the Cardiff Bay Barrage. Entry into the bay, in which there are several small craft moorings, is through three locks within the breakwaters at the SW end of the Barrage.

Vessels should contact Barrage Control on VHF for locking information, reporting their draught if 2 m or greater. See *Admiralty List of Radio Signals Volume 6(1)*.

2   Penarth Marina lies just within the Barrage, close NW of Penarth Head.

Cardiff Docks, consisting of two large wet docks, are entered through the Queen Alexandra sea lock between North and South Jetties, close to the NE end of the Barrage.

Dredging
4.88

1   Vessels must keep well clear of dredgers and proceed at very slow speed until clear.

Directions for entering harbour
(continued from 4.63)

Landmarks
4.89

1   Monkstone Lighthouse (51°25′N 3°06′W) (4.104).
    Church tower standing on the summit of Penarth Head (51°26′N 3°10′W) (4.54).
    Building (51°29′N 3°11′W).

2   Sails Monument (white) (51°27′·1N 3°09′·9W) standing on the elbow of the barrage.
    Hotel, conspicuous roof structure, (51°27′·6N 3°10′·0W), standing on the N side of the Bay.

Approaches
4.90

1   From W, the directions given at 4.61 should be followed until NW of Wolves Light Buoy. The route then leads NNE to pass between Ranie Light Buoy (port hand) and South Cardiff Light Buoy (S cardinal).

The passage between these light buoys lies in the white sector of Flat Holm Light.

2   **Caution.** An outfall, marked by a light buoy (special), extends 6 cables SE from Lavernock Point (4.54). Strong currents can be experienced in this area, particularly on spring tides.

From E, the route leads midway between Centre Ledge (51°24′N 3°07′W) and New Patch, 1 mile SSE; when N of Flat Holm the track alters WNW, thence NNW to pass between the two light buoys.

3   **PEL.** From a position between Ranie and South Cardiff Light Buoys, the line of bearing 348½° in the centre of the white sector (347°–350°) of Wrach Channel PEL (white metal post) (51°27′·1N 3°09′·8W) leads into the Wrach Channel (4.91).

Entrance channel
4.91

1   Wrach channel is an artificial cut through Cefn-y-Wrach, a bed of stones, which lies across the S end of Cardiff Flats, extensive mud flats. The channel is maintained by dredging as far as the entrance to Queen Alexandra sea lock.

Outer Wrach Light Buoy (W cardinal) and Inner Wrach Light Buoy (starboard hand) mark the E side of the entrance channel; Penarth Head Light Buoy (port hand) moored close E of Penarth Head marks the W side.

2   North Jetty and South Jetty extend from each side of Queen Alexandra sea lock; lights are exhibited from the head of each jetty, and 3 lighted dolphins lie off the SW end of North Jetty.

Close-up from SE

Sails Monument   Directional Light

Cardiff - Entrance to Queen Alexandra Sea Lock from S (4.91)

(Original dated 2001)

(Photographs - Main: Air Images. Inset: Associated British Ports)

From a position close N of Penarth Head Light Buoy, the approach to the new breakwaters and locks at the SW end of the barrage is marked by Light Buoys and leading lights.

Caution
4.92
1 The approach towards Ranie and South Cardiff Light Buoys lies across the very strong NE in-going stream. Great care is necessary to avoid being swept on to Cardiff Grounds, drying banks which lie nearly parallel with the coast between Lavernock Point and the entrance to the Rhymney River, about 4½ miles NE, at a distance of 1 to 2 miles offshore.

2 The bank, which is constantly changing, is marked by South Cardiff Light Buoy (S cardinal) and North Cardiff Light Buoy (starboard hand) which are moored off the SW and NNW extremities respectively, and by Middle Cardiff Light Buoy (starboard hand) and Cardiff Spit Light Buoy (port hand) which are moored off the NW and SE sides respectively.

Basins and berths

Lock
4.93
1 Sea lock gives access into Queen Alexandra Dock and the wet dock system. The lock is 259 m long, 27·4 m wide and has a depth over the sill of 12·8 m at MHWS, and of 9·9 m at MHWN. The lock is divided into two sections. Normal periods of operation are from 4 hours before to 3 hours after HW.

Alongside berths
4.94
1 **Queen Alexandra Dock,** a wet dock entered directly from the sea lock, which is spanned by a roller bridge. It is used for a wide variety of products, mainly fuel oil, timber, and general cargoes. There is an oil berth for tankers, up to the maximum dimensions (4.93), in the SE corner of the dock. King's Wharf, a berth 152 m long for cold storage products lies at the NE end of the dock. There are 2240 m of quay and the normal depth of the dock is 11·6 m.

2 **Roath Dock** is a wet dock entered from Queen Alexandra Dock through a communicating passage 27·0 m wide which is spanned by a swing bridge, with depths over the sill of 10·4 m. The dock can handle maximum draught vessels of 198 m LOA but with beam of no greater than 26·0 m. The normal depth in the dock is 11·3 m. It is used mainly for steel scrap and bulk coal imports and exports. There is an oil berth in the NE corner.

3 **Roath Basin** is a wet dock entered from Roath Dock through a communication passage, 24 m in width and spanned by a swing bridge. It has been developed for residential, leisure and office use. Britannia Quay, 190 m in length, on the NW side of the basin is a hospitality berth for vessels of maximum dimensions 158 m LOA, 21·3 m beam and 8 m draught.

Port services

Repairs
4.95
1 All types of repairs; divers. Permission and permits may be obtained from ABP's Cardiff office.

Other facilities
4.96
1 Issue of SSCC and SSCEC; customs; reception of oily waste, noxious and harmful substances; tank cleaning; hospitals, some with helicopter landing sites; heliport, 500 m NE of the port.

Supplies
4.97
1 Fuel; fresh water; provisions and stores readily available.

Harbour regulations
4.98
1 Bye-laws are in force for vessels entering the port; copies should be obtained from the Dock and Harbour Masters' Office.

There are also bye-laws concerning small craft. Small craft are prohibited from anchoring and fishing in the approaches to Cardiff during tidal windows when larger vessels may be entering or leaving the port.

Landing places

Penarth
4.99
1 **Penarth Pier,** extending 1 cable E from the coast 3½ cables S of Penarth Head, is constructed of iron and has landing stages; lights are exhibited from a brown mast at the pierhead.

When the landing stages are obstructed a red burgee is displayed at the pierhead by day and three red lights vertically disposed, are exhibited by night.

2 **Penarth Yacht Club.** There is a slipway at Penarth Yacht Club, 2 cables S of Penarth Pier; an outer distance barrel buoy (orange), marked PYC and ODM, is moored 2 cables E of the slipway. A conical racing marker buoy (yellow) with the legend PYC Q is moored 3 cables SSE of the slipway.

FLAT HOLM TO THE BRIDGE

General information

Chart 1176
Route
4.100
1 Passing S of Flat Holm, the deep-water route leads to The Bridge (51°27′N 3°00′W), about 8 miles NE, which is the area of water lying at the junction of Newport Deep and Bristol Deep. Vessels of suitable draught can follow the route to The Bridge which leads N of Flat Holm.

2 The coastline between the Rhymney River, on the E outskirts of Cardiff, and the mouth of the river Usk, 6 miles NE, is backed by low, level ground for a considerable distance inland and is protected by embankments.

Mud flats extend up to 1 mile offshore.

For details on English Grounds and the S coastline E of Sand Point (51°23′N 2°59′W) see 4.182.

Vessel traffic service
4.101
1 See 4.5.

Rescue
4.102
1 Two inshore lifeboats are stationed at Weston-super-Mare.

For details of rescue organisation see 1.60.

Tidal streams
4.103
1   For details of tidal streams between Flat Holm and The Bridge see tidal diamonds on the charts.

Directions
(continued from 4.63)

Principal marks
4.104
1   **Landmarks**:

Flat Holm Lighthouse (51°23′N 3°07′W) (4.58).

Monkstone Lighthouse (red column on round masonry tower, 23 m in height) (51°25′N 3°06′W), standing on a rock which lies on a ledge, near the edge of the coastal bank lying off the NW shore.

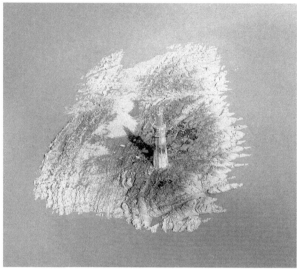

Monkstone and Lighthouse from WNW (4.104)

(Original dated 2001)

(Photograph - Air Images)

2   Steep Holm (51°20′N 3°06′W) (4.67).

Radio mast (51°21′·6N 2°58′·2W) (4.176) with a water tower standing close E.

Radio masts (51°25′·4N 2°51′·8W) (4.188).

Fifoots Point pylon (51°32′·8N 2°58′·8W) (4.129).

Major lights:

Flat Holm Light (51°23′N 3°07′W) (4.58).

Black Nore Point Light (51°29′N 2°48′W) (4.188).

Portishead Point Light (51°29′·7N 2°46′·4W) (4.188).

Other aids to navigation
4.105
1   **Racon**:

EW Grounds Light Buoy (51°27′N 3°00′W).

For further details see *Admiralty List of Radio Signals Volume 2.*

South of Flat Holm
4.106
1   From a position NW of Holm Middle Light Buoy (51°21′·7N 3°06′·7W), and about 7 cables S of Flat Holm Light (51°23′N 3°07′W), the route leads NE for about 6¾ miles to a position SE of EW Grounds Light Buoy,

passing, (with positions from Monkstone (51°25′N 3°06′W)):

SE of Weston Light Buoy (port hand) (2¼ miles S), thence:

2   NW of Tail Patch Light Buoy (starboard hand) (2 miles SE), which marks the W edge of Tail Patch, with depths of less than 3 m, thence:

SE of Hope Light Buoy (E cardinal) (2 miles E), thence:

NW of NW Elbow Light Buoy (W cardinal) (4 miles ENE) marking North West Elbow, the NW edge of English Grounds, thence:

3   SE of EW (English and Welsh) Grounds Light Buoy (safe water) (4½ miles ENE), or W of the light buoy for Newport traffic.

Cautions. A wreck with a swept depth of 8·6 m lies 9 cables SW of EW Grounds Light Buoy.

North of Flat Holm
4.107
1   From a position NW of Wolves Light Buoy (51°23′·1N 3°08′·9W), the route leads generally NE towards The Bridge, passing:

NW of Flat Holm (51°23′N 3°07′W), thence:

Clear of Centre Ledge (4.62), thence:

SE of Monkstone, on which stands a lighthouse (4.104), to join the route described above in the vicinity of the EW Grounds Light Buoy.

Cautions
4.108
1   Depths on The Bridge (51°27′N 3°00′W) (4.100) frequently change. Mariners are advised to consult local pilots or the Port Authority, Port of Bristol, for the latest information.

Depths N of Monkstone are changeable.

Useful mark
4.109
1   Wick Saint Lawrence Church (Tower) (51°23′N 2°55′W) (4.176).

(Directions continue for the coastal route at 4.188; directions for entering Newport are given at 4.129)

Anchorages
4.110
1   In addition to the anchorages at 4.82 tolerably secure anchorage may also be had on the NW side of the fairway between Flat Holm and EW Grounds Light Buoy, in depths of 10 to 20 m, clay and mud.

For anchorages off Newport, see 4.132.

Small boat channel

Orchard Ledges
4.111
1   A small boat channel, marked by stakes and buoys, leads across Orchard Ledges, an extension of Cardiff Flats, to the entrance to the Rhymney River (51°29′·4N 3°07′·3W). The Rhymney River Sailing Club stands on the W bank close inside the entrance.

A light buoy (port hand) which marks the extremity of an outfall 2½ miles NE of Penarth Head, is moored 2¾ cables W of the entrance to the boat channel.

Alexandra Docks, Newport, from SW (4.112)
(Original dated 2001)

(Photograph - Air Images)

PORT OF NEWPORT

General information

Chart 1176 with plan of Newport
Position
4.112
1   The Port of Newport (51°33′N 2°59′W) lies within the entrance to the river Usk.

Function
4.113
1   Newport handles large imports of vehicles and also a wide range of products including; agribulks, steel, solid fuel, minerals, scrap, forest products, general and project cargoes.
   The town of Newport lies 2 miles within the river entrance.

Port limits
4.114
1   The outer harbour limit is a line drawn from Gold Cliff (51°32′N 2°54′W) to a point on the shore 5¼ miles W.
   The inner limits are:
      Newbridge, 10 miles above Newport on the river Usk.
      The railway bridge spanning the river Ebbw.

Approach and entry
4.115
1   The harbour approach is from the S through Newport Deep and entry is through the buoyed channel of the river Usk.

Traffic
4.116
1   In 2007 there were 912 port calls with a total of 3 811 348 dwt.

Port Authorities
4.117
1   The Port Authority is Associated British Ports, Alexandra Dock, Newport NP20 2UW, represented by a Port Director.
   The Harbour Authority is Newport Harbour Commissioners, 125 Lower Dock Street, Newport, who are represented by a Harbour Master.

Limiting conditions

Controlling depth
4.118
1   The entrance channel as far as South Lock has been dredged to 0·7 m below chart datum and this is maintained as far as is practicable. However, for the latest depth information the Dock and Harbour Master should be consulted.

Vertical clearance
4.119
1 An overhead power cable spans the mouth of the river Usk at Fifoots Point (51°32′·8N 2°58′·8W); it has a safe vertical clearance of 64 m.

Deepest and longest berth
4.120
1   South Dock (4.133).

Tidal levels
4.121
1 Mean spring range about 11·8 m; mean neap range about 5·6 m. See *Admiralty Tide Tables*.

Density of water
4.122
1 1·020 g/cm³ but can vary with rainfall.

Maximum size of vessel handled
4.123
1 LOA 244 m; beam 30·1 m; draught 10·4 m, in South Dock.

Arrival information

Port operations
4.124
1 Arrivals and departures are restricted by the opening times of the entrance lock (4.131).

Vessel traffic service
4.125
1 See 4.5.

Notice of ETA required
4.126
1 24 hours at a position 1 mile N of Breaksea Light Buoy.

Pilotage and tugs
4.127
1 **Pilotage.** Associated British Ports (ABP) based at Cardiff, provides pilotage for Newport. Pilotage is compulsory for all vessels or tows over 85 m in length. Additionally, pilotage is compulsory for vessels or tows of 20 m in length carrying dangerous or noxious substances in bulk; twelve or more passengers; or explosives. For further details see *Admiralty List of Radio Signals Volume 6 (1)*. For details of pilotage, pilot boarding position and pilot vessel see 4.40.

2 It is strongly recommended that no vessel without local knowledge or a pilot onboard should attempt to enter Newport.

    Tugs may be based at Cardiff, Barry or Newport and normally join vessels in Newport Deep.

Harbour

General layout
4.128
1 The port consists of two wet docks, North Dock and South Dock, linked by a junction passage, a dry dock, and several drying berths on the river Usk. Access to the wet

Alexandra Docks, Newport, from SE (4.128)
(Original dated 2001)

(Photograph - Air Images)

docks is through a lock (4.131), protected by approach breakwaters extending S from each side of the lock entrance.

The dry dock is entered from the SE corner of North Dock, the smaller of the two wet docks.

Directions for entering harbour

Principal marks
4.129
1   **Landmarks**:

Two pylons supporting an overhead power cable (4.119); one pylon stands on Fifoots Point (51°32'·8N 2°58'·8W), the other 5 cables WNW.

East Usk Lighthouse (white round tower, 13 m in height) (51°32'·4N 2°58'·0W).

East Usk Light from SW (4.129)
(Original dated 2001)

(Photograph - Air Images)

2   West Usk Lighthouse (disused), standing 5½ cables WSW of Fifoots Point.

Major lights:

Flat Holm Light (51°23'N 3°07'W) (4.58).
Black Nore Point Light (51°29'N 2°48'W) (4.188).
Portishead Point Light (51°29'·7N 2°46'·4W) (4.188).

Approaches
4.130
1   From the vicinity of EW Grounds Light Buoy (4.106), the route leads NNE for about 4½ miles across Peterstone Flats on a line of bearing of 023° on East Usk Light; this is the centre line of the white sector of the light. Thence the track joins the entrance channel close W of No 1 Light Buoy (starboard hand) (9¼ cables SSW of East Usk Light).

Entrance channel
4.131
1   The entrance channel, marked by light buoys, runs in a generally NNW direction for 1¾ miles to South Lock.

There is a least depth of 12·5 m at MHWS over the flats in the approach and in the entrance channel as far as South Lock, but this depth is not guaranteed.

2   **Lock.** South Lock, giving access to South Dock, the wet docks, is entered between two approach jetties extending S from each side of the lock. Lights are exhibited from a white framework tower at the head of each jetty.

The lock is 305 m long and 30·5 m wide; it can be divided into two sections, the shorter being 122 m in length. The lock has a depth over the sill of 13·8 m at MHWS and 10·7 m at MHWN. The times of entry to the lock are up to 4 hours either side of HW.

(Directions continue for the river Usk at 4.142)

Basins and berths

Anchorages
4.132
1   There is good anchorage in Newport Deep (51°29'N 2°59'W) in depths of 6 to 9 m, thick clay and mud, or in deeper water W of EW Grounds Light Buoy.

A Anchorage, a designated explosives anchorage, is centred on 51°27'·2N 3°00'·9W, 6 cables W of EW Grounds Light Buoy.

2   **B Anchorage,** a designated explosives anchorage, is centred on 51°28'·6N 2°59'·2W in Newport Deep 1½ miles NNE of EW Grounds Light Buoy.

In Newport Deep the tidal streams are not strong and there is little sea.

Deep-draught vessels awaiting a berth at Newport may find a deep-water anchorage in Barry Roads (4.25) should Newport Deep be considered unsuitable.

Alongside berths
4.133
1   **South Dock,** entered through South Lock, has 3880 m of quay; there are normally depths of 10·2 m in the dock.

South Quay, on the SE side of the dock, has facilities for handling coal, steel products and general cargo.

North Side, on the NW side of the dock, has facilities for handling feedstocks, fertilisers and RoRo vessels.

2   **North Dock,** is entered from South Dock through a passage 17·4 m wide. The dock has 1736 m of quayage, and depths of 8·2 m are normally maintained in the passage and the dock. Vessels of 122 m in length, 17 m beam and having a draught of 7·6 m can be accommodated in the dock.

Port services

Repairs
4.134
1   All types of repairs; dry dock, entered from North Dock, 138 m long, 19·5 m wide at the entrance and has a depth of 6·5 m over the sill. Access to the dry dock is restricted to 17·4 m by the passageway from South Dock to North Dock.

Other facilities
4.135
1   Reception of oily waste, noxious and harmful substances; mobile crane, capacity 45 tonnes; SSCC and SSCEC issued; hospitals; helicopter landing site at Cardiff.

Supplies
4.136
1   Fuel by barge or road tanker; fresh water at most berths; provisions and stores of all kinds.

Harbour regulations
4.137
1   Special bye-laws are in force for vessels carrying carbide of calcium, petroleum or explosives; vessels laden with petroleum when approaching, and whilst in the harbour must display by day a red flag with a white circular centre and at night exhibit a red light at the masthead. Copies of the harbour bye-laws should be obtained from the Clerk to the Harbour Commissioners.

South Lock, Newport, from SSE (4.131)

(Original dated 2001)

(Photograph - Air Images)

River Usk

General Information
4.138

1   The river Usk, which is joined from NW by the river Ebbw off the entrance to South Lock, is navigable by vessels of moderate size as far as Newport Bridge (4.139), although there are no berths suitable for commercial traffic above Southern Distributor Road (SDR) Bridge (4.139). In the lower reaches, large size vessels, which can take the ground, are able to berth at Alpha Steel Wharf (4.144).

2   Birdport Port (4.143) lies 1 mile within the entrance on the E side of the river.

Pilotage. As for Newport (4.127).

Limiting conditions
4.139

1   **Controlling depth** in the river and latest information should be obtained from ABP's Dock and Harbour Master.

Vertical clearance. Bridges span the river Usk in the following positions:

2   Transporter Bridge, 2 cables NE of the N end of North Dock, with a vertical clearance of 54 m. The bridge operates to a limited timetable primarily restricted to weekends and public holidays. Mariners wishing to pass the Transporter Bridge should inform Severn VTS by radio. When 800 m from the Bridge, sound one prolonged blast on the ship's whistle and proceed with caution.

3   Southern Distributor Road Bridge, 5½ cables above the Transporter Bridge, has a vertical clearance of 7 m. A light is exhibited from the bridge.

George Street Bridge, 8 cables above the Transporter Bridge, with a vertical clearance of 13 m for a distance of 46 m either side of the centre of the arch, and with a clear opening between the piers of 137 m. A light is exhibited on the down-stream and up-stream side of the arch centre.

4   Head-clearance indicator lights are exhibited from the E pier of this bridge and from 30 m S of the E end of the Transporter Bridge. The lights show green flashing when the vertical clearance is 13 m or more, and red flashing if the vertical clearance is less than 13 m.

Newport Bridge, 3½ miles within the river entrance and 5 cables above George Street Bridge has a vertical clearance of 9 m; a light is exhibited at the middle of the centre span on its seaward side.

5   **Overhead cables** span the river in the following positions:

Within 2 cables S of the Transporter Bridge with a vertical clearance of 53 m.

Approximately 6 cables above Newport Bridge with a vertical clearance of 9 m.

Two overhead power cables span Julian's Pill (51°33′N 2°58′W). The outer of the two cables has a vertical clearance of 4·3 m; the inner 3·8 m.

Arrival information
4.140

1   For Port operations, VTS, Notice of ETA required, Pilotage and Tugs see 4.124-4.127.

    Submarine cables and pipelines cross the river Usk in the following positions:

2   Gas mains close N of the Transporter Bridge, marked by notice boards on either side of the river.

        Numerous power and telephone cables 1 cable above George Street Bridge.

    Caution. Vessels are prohibited from anchoring in the vicinity of these cables and pipelines.

Harbour
4.141

1   The river Usk as far as Newport Bridge, about 3½ miles upstream from the entrance to South Lock, has a number of drying wharfs along its banks and dry docks at Birdport Port, about 1 mile upstream from the river's entrance.

Directions
(continued from 4.131)
4.142

1   From the directions leading to the entrance to South Lock the channel continues ENE to Birdport (4.143) and the upper reaches of the river Usk.

    Leading marks. The alignment (062°) of Saint Julian's Pill Leading marks (masts, 3 m in height) followed by the line of bearing 149°, astern, of Saint Julian's Pill Front Light lead through the channel in the vicinity of Powder House Point.

Birdport
4.143

1   **General information.** Birdport port, situated on the E side of the river 4 cables N of Saint Julian's Pill, is equipped to handle processed steel cargoes using a 43 tonne gantry crane spanning the dock, and can accommodate vessels up to 10 000 dwt. The dock is 228 m long, 21·3 m wide with depths of 8·5 m at MHWS, 5·2 m at MHWN and is entered between two short jetties. Half-tide gates at the dock entrance are normally kept closed.

2   A green light on the N side of the entrance indicates that they are open, a red light that they are closed. A light is exhibited from the head of the S entrance jetty.

    Facilities: fresh water at both berths.

    Port Authority: see 4.117.

Other berths
4.144

1   **Alpha Steel Wharf,** about 200 m long with a jetty close N of it, is on the E side of the river about 3 cables SSE of Birdport. At MHWS it can accommodate vessels up to 30 000 dwt which can take the ground.

    Dallimore's Wharf, from where a light is exhibited, is situated 4 cables NW of Birdport.

    Lysaghts Works Wharf, from where lights are exhibited, lies on the E bank 4½ cables NE of Transporter Bridge.

Regulations
4.145

1   See 4.137.

HURLSTONE POINT TO THE BRIDGE — SOUTH COAST ROUTE

General information

Chart 1152, 1176

Route
4.146

1   From N of Hurlstone Point (51°14′N 3°35′W), the route leads S of Culver Sand (4.154) to the vicinity of Sand Point, about 24 miles ENE, thence about 4 miles N to the vicinity of EW Ground Light Buoy (51°27′N 3°00′W) at The Bridge.

Topography
4.147

1   See 4.2. The coast between Watchet (51°11′N 3°20′W) and Stoke Bluff, 5 miles E, consists of cliffs of variegated colour.

Firing practice area
4.148

1   Lilstock Range lies off Stoke Bluff (51°12′N 3°12′W) and is marked by DZ light buoys (special). There are targets and buoys moored within 4 miles of Stoke Bluff. For further information on practice areas see 1.15.

Vessel traffic service
4.149

1   See 4.5.

Rescue
4.150

1   Inshore lifeboats are stationed at Weston-super-Mare (51°21′N 3°00′W), Burnham-on-Sea (51°14′N 3°00′W) and Minehead (51°13′N 3°28′W). Hovercraft operate from Burnham-on-Sea in support of the rescue services.

    For details of rescue organisation see 1.60.

Tidal streams
4.151

1   See tidal diamonds on the charts and *Admiralty Tidal Atlas — Irish Sea and Bristol Channel.*

Directions
(continued from 3.49)

Principal marks
4.152

1   **Landmarks:**

        Dunkery Beacon (Chart 1179) (51°10′N 3°35′W) (3.44).

        Conygar Tower (51°11′N 3°27′W) which stands on the summit of a wooded hill 1½ miles SE of Minehead.

        Two radio masts (51°09′·6N 3°20′·9W) marked by obstruction lights, standing SSW of Watchet.

2   Hinkley Point Nuclear Power Station (51°12′N 3°08′W) (4.165).

        Brean Down, conspicuous bold projecting headland, (51°20′N 3°01′W).

        Steep Holm (51°20′N 3°06′W) (4.67).

    Major lights:

        Nash Point Light (51°24′N 3°33′W) (3.197).

        Flat Holm Light (51°23′N 3°07′W) (4.58).

Brean Down from NW (4.152)
(Original dated 2001)

(Photograph - Air Images)

Other aid to navigation
4.153

1   **Racon:**
    Breaksea Light Buoy (51°20′N 3°19′W).

Passage
4.154

1   From a position N of Hurlstone Point (51°14′N 3°35′W) to a position NW of Sand Point, 24 miles ENE, the route leads initially E between Culver Sand (51°18′N 3°17′W) and Graham Banks, 5 miles ESE, passing:

    N of Minehead (51°12′N 3°28′W), thence:

    N of Watchet Harbour (51°11′N 3°20′W), thence:

2   S of Culver Sand, a shoal with depths of less than 2 m; see also Caution at 4.64. Culver Sand is marked by West Culver Light Buoy (W cardinal) and East Culver Light Buoy (E cardinal).

    Leading mark. The line of bearing 064° of the W end of Brean Down (51°20′N 3°01′W) leads between Culver Sand and Graham Banks.

    The track continues ENE, passing:

    NNW of Hinkley Point Nuclear Power Station (51°12′N 3°08′W) (4.165), thence:

3   NNW of Graham Banks (51°16′N 3°10′W) which lie across the NW approaches to the river Parrett (4.166).

    When S of Steep Holm (51°20′N 3°07′W) (4.67) the track alters to a more NE heading, then NNE, passing:

WNW of Brean Down (4.152), (2¾ miles ESE of Steep Holm), with Howe Rock close NW and a strong tide race to seaward of the rock. South Patches lie 1½ miles NW of Brean Down. Thence:

4   WNW of Birnbeck Island (4.175), (4 miles ENE of Steep Holm); Weston Ledge lies 5 cables W of the island, and:

ESE of Flat Holm (51°23′N 3°07′W) (4.66), thence:

Clear of Tail Patch (3 miles E of Flat Holm), with a least charted depth of 2·7 m, thence:

WNW of Sand Point.

The track now continues NNE/NE for a further 3½ miles to the vicinity of EW Grounds Light Buoy at The Bridge.
4.155

1   **Cautions.** The coast beyond Sand Point should not be approached without local knowledge owing to the extensive drying sand and mud flats of English Grounds (4.182).

    There are numerous disused cables on the seabed in the vicinity of South Patches and in an area SW of Steep Holm.

Useful mark
4.156

1   Watchet W Pier Light (51°11′·0N 3°19′·7W) (4.161).
    *(Directions continue for
    points E of Sand Point at 4.188)*

123

Minehead
4.157

1   **General information.** Minehead (51°13′N 3°28′W) is a small, easily accessible, tidal harbour. It is used principally by fishing vessels and pleasure craft. Excursion pleasure vessels also visit.

The harbour is under the jurisdiction of the West Somerset District Council (Statutory Harbour Authority), 20 Fore Street, Williton, Somerset, TA4 4QA. A part-time Harbour Master is located at the Harbour Office, The Quay, Minehead.

2   **Limiting conditions.** Access is possible only for about 2 hours either side of HW. The harbour dries to a muddy bottom, but vessels up to 60 m in length and up to 2·5 m draught, capable of taking the ground, can be accommodated at HW.

Strong SE winds cause a swell at spring tides which produces uncomfortable conditions in the harbour.

3   **Port radio** sets watch 2 hours before HW.

Harbour. The harbour consists of a breakwater, curving E, which provides protection from N winds, but the sea breaks over it in gales at HW springs. A ruined pier, the outer end of which is marked by a beacon (starboard hand), extends ½ cable N from a position ¾ cable NW of the head of the breakwater.

4   A stormwater outfall runs from a position 2 cables S to a position 1¾ cables NNE of the head of the breakwater, and passes ½ cable E of it. Between the latter two positions, the outfall is covered by a protective armouring of rock, rising to 2·8 m above the seabed. The outer end of the outfall is marked by a light beacon (starboard hand).

Five beacons (starboard hand) mark the seaward extremity of sea defences and an outfall which extend from the shore between 4 cables SSE and 7 cables ESE of the head of the breakwater.

5   **Directions for entering harbour.** It is advisable to approach Minehead near HW.

The route from NW leads round the light beacon marking the outer end of the stormwater outfall at a prudent distance, passing 1 cable E of the head of the breakwater, from which a light (metal post) is exhibited, thence towards the harbour entrance passing S of the armoured end of the stormwater outfall.

6   Care should be taken not to cross the protective armouring of rock covering the outer part of the outfall. Vessels approaching Minehead from the E should not cross The Gables, a reef of shingle lying 7 cables ENE of the head of the breakwater, except near HW.

Port services: slipway; boatyard; fresh water; provisions in small quantities. Bye-laws are in force, copies of which can be obtained from the Harbour Master.

Watchet Harbour

Chart 1160 plan of Watchet
General information
4.158

1   **Position.** Watchet Harbour (51°11′N 3°20′W) is a small tidal harbour consisting of two basins, the outer one of which dries.

Function. The harbour is used mainly by pleasure craft. Watchet Harbour Marina occupies the inner harbour.

Harbour Authority. West Somerset District Council, Harbour Office, East Wharf, Watchet, Somerset. There is a Harbour Master.

Local weather
4.159

1   Prevailing winds are from N, NW and NE. Gales from NW and NE bring a heavy sea into the harbour and cause uncomfortable conditions alongside the W breakwater.

Harbour and berths
4.160

1   **Harbour layout.** The harbour, fronted by a drying rocky foreshore, is protected by Western Pier, approximately 210 m in length, which extends NE then ENE from the shore, and Eastern Pier which extends NW from the shore and is about 110 m in length; the entrance between the piers is 28 m wide.

Anchorage can be obtained in Blue Anchor Road; see 4.177.

2   **Watchet Harbour Marina**, in the inner harbour, provides visitors' berths for boats up to 20 m in length.

Tidal streams. See information on the chart.

Directions for entering harbour
4.161

1   It is advisable to approach the harbour entrance near HW. Visiting pleasure craft should not attempt to enter Watchet without recent local knowledge. Fishing stakes may be encountered off the harbour entrance, as indicated on the chart.

Owing to the strength of the tidal streams across the entrance, close attention must be paid to the steering of the vessel.

2   An outfall, terminating in a diffuser, extends 4 cables NNW from the shore 1 cable W of West Pier. A buoy (special with topmark) is moored 9 cables N of the entrance.

Useful mark:

    Western Pier Light (red hexagonal metal tower, white lantern, green cupola, 5 m in height) (51°11′·0N 3°19′·7W).

Bridgwater Bay

Chart 1152
General information
4.162

1   **General description.** Bridgwater Bay, entered between Stoke Bluff (51°12′N 3°12′W) and Brean Down, 9¾ miles NE, is a large open bay backed by low lying ground but encumbered by Stert Flats, Gore Sand and Berrow Flats, extensive sand and mud flats which dry to 5 miles offshore.

The river Parrett (4.166), which gives access to berths within the Port of Bridgwater, flows into the head of the bay.

2   **Burnham-on-Sea,** a seaside resort on the E side of the bay lies N of the mouth of the river Parrett. There is a slip at the S end of the town, whose extremity is marked by a light beacon (port hand).

Fishing
4.163

1   Outside the main approach channels to the river Parrett, fishing methods on Berrow Flats (51°15′N 3°03′W) and Stert Flats (51°13′·5N 3°03′·5W) involve the use of stakes. These stakes may be unmarked, particularly after bad weather.

Tidal streams
4.164

1   The streams E of Watchet (51°11′N 3°20′W) change direction gradually following the trend of the offshore bank. South-west of Cobbler Patch (51°13′N 3°10′W) they begin as follows:

Interval from HW Avonmouth	Direction
+0555	ENE
+0015	WSW

2   The maximum spring rate in the direction ENE is 2 kn and for WSW it is 2¼ kn.

Principal marks
4.165
1   **Landmarks:**
        Hinkley Point Nuclear Power Station (51°12′N 3°08′W) (2½ miles E of Stoke Bluff), the buildings of which are up to 69 m in height.
        Burnham Upper Light Tower (51°15′N 3°00′W) (white round tower, red stripe, 30 m in height); the tower, now disused, formed part of the old leading marks to the river Parrett.
2   Burnham Lower Light Tower (white square tower on piles, red stripe, 9 m in height) stands 2½ cables W of Burnham Upper Light Tower.

River Parrett and Port of Bridgwater

General information
4.166
1   **Position.** The Port of Bridgwater (51°10′N 3°00′W) consists of three wharves, only one of which is in regular use, on the banks of the river Parrett.

Burnham Upper and Lower Light-towers from W (4.165)
(Original dated 2001)

(Photograph - Air Images)

    Function. Serving a mainly agricultural community with several light manufacturing industries, the port handles small vessels up to 2300 dwt and pleasure craft.
2   Main imports are sand and gravel, animal feed, fertilisers, fishmeal, bricks, timber, cement and coal.
    The town of Bridgwater lies 9 miles within the mouth of the river.

Hinkley Point Power Station from N (4.165)
(Original dated 2001)

(Photograph - Air Images)

Topography. The land adjacent to the river is low-lying and the drying banks, which are steep-to, consist mainly of mud with occasional patches of shingle.

Stert Flats and the mouth of the river Parrett are a National Nature Reserve, see 1.58.

3 **Port limit** is a line joining Hinkley Point to the centreline of the river Axe (51°19′·0N 2°59′·5W), keeping a radius of 8 cables from WSW to ENE off the head of Brean Down (4.152).

Approach and entry. The river Parrett is approached through a channel between Stert Flats and Gore Sand, and is entered 5 miles W of Burnham-on-Sea.

4 **Port Authority.** On behalf of Sedgemoor District Council the port is operated by:

C F Spencer & Co Ltd, The Old Malt House, West Street, Banwell, Somerset, BS29 6DB.
Email: harbour.master@sedgemoor.gov.uk
Spencers provide the Harbour Master and pilots.
Web site: www.cfspencerandcoltd.com

Limiting conditions
4.167

1 **Controlling depth.** As most of the approach and the river dry, depths must be ascertained by consultation with the Harbour Authority.

Vertical clearance. Overhead power cables with a safe overhead clearance of 33 m span the river 7 cables below Combwich Wharf (4.171) and with a safe overhead clearance of 31 m, 1½ miles above Dunball Wharf (4.171).

2 **Deepest and longest berth.** Dunball Wharf (4.171).

Tidal levels: at Burnham-on-Sea mean spring range about 11·0 m, mean neap range about 5·5 m; at Bridgwater MHWS is 4·6 m.

Maximum size of vessel handled at Dunball Wharf: 89 m LOA; draught up to 4·5 m at the higher spring tides; about 2300 dwt.

Arrival information
4.168

1 **Port radio:** VHF communications from HW −3 hours when a vessel is expected.

Notice of ETA required: 24 hours, including request for pilot. For further details see *Admiralty List of Radio Signals Volume 6(1)*.

Outer anchorage: Vessels waiting to enter the river Parrett can obtain good, though exposed, anchorage 1¾ miles NNE of Stoke Bluff (51°12′N 3°12′W) in a least depth of 7 m. Attention is drawn to submarine cables which cross Bridgwater Bay N of this anchorage.

2 **Submarine cables** run W from the coast about 2 miles N of Burnham Lower Light Tower (51°14′·9N 3°00′·3W), the closest passing about 1¼ miles N of the above anchorage.

Pilotage is compulsory for all vessels over 30 m LOA. The pilot normally boards off Burnham-on-Sea between No 2 Light Buoy (starboard hand) and Brue Light Beacon (4.170). Directions can be given on VHF from off Gore Light Buoy to the pilot rendezvous; the pilot office is equipped with radar.

3 In bad weather a pilot may be embarked in Barry Roads (4.25) subject to 24 hours notice and availability.

Local knowledge. Vessels which do not fall under the requirement for compulsory pilotage should not attempt to enter River Parrett without recent local knowledge.

Regulations concerning entry. Vessels bound for berths within River Parrett should pass Gore Light Buoy no earlier than 2¼ hours and no later than 2 hours before HW.

Vessels over 30 m LOA should contact the pilot station by VHF before commencing the approach.

Harbour
4.169

1 **General layout.** There are three wharfs, all of which dry, on the banks of the river Parrett.

Natural conditions. The maximum height of tide over the river bed at Dunball is 6 m.

A small bore, of approximately 0·5 m in height at springs, passes Bridgwater about 1 hour 40 minutes before HW on spring tides and about 1 hour 20 minutes before HW on neap tides; excessive freshets reduce the size of the bore.

Directions
4.170

1 **Landmarks:**
Burnham Upper Light Tower (51°15′N 3°00′W) (4.165).
Burnham Lower Light Tower (51°14′·9N 3°00′·4W) (4.165).
Building (51°10′·9N 3°01′·6W) at Pawlett Hill.

2 **Coastal Passage.** From Watchet (51°11′N 3°20′W) to Gore Light Buoy, the approach route leads E for approximately 6½ miles, passing (with positions from Hinkley Point Power Station (51°12′N 3°08′W)):
Clear of DZ No 2 Light Buoy (special) (6 miles WNW), thence:
N of Kilve Patch (4¼ miles WNW), thence:

3 N of the target buoys in Lilstock Firing range (4.148) (3 miles W), thence:
N of Stoke Bluff (2½ miles W), with a prominent flag staff. Stoke Spit, with a detached drying shoal, lies close NW, thence:
S of Gore Light Buoy (safe water) (1¾ miles NW) and across Cobbler Patch, close S of the light buoy.

4 **Approaches.** Depths in the approaches to River Parrett are changeable and navigation lights and buoys may not indicate where the deepest water lies. Moreover, buoys may not be in the positions shown on the chart. See 4.168 for details of assistance by VHF.

The following lights assist in the approach:
Directional Light at Burnham Lower Light (51°14′·9N 3°00′·4W) (4.165).
Leading Lights (112°) on Burnham Seafront (51°14′·4N 2°59′·9W) (Front: Orange stripe on white square on sea wall. Rear: Church Tower.)

Burnham Seafront Leading Lights (4.170)
(Original dated 1996)

(Photograph - Mr. D. James, Port of Bridgwater)

5 **River Parrett.** South of Stert Island the river channel is winding and dries.

The channel leads SSE for a distance of 3 miles above Stert Island and passes through Stert Reach. Brue Light Beacon (white mast, red bands) stands on the E side of the channel, 1½ miles S of Burnham-on-Sea Upper Light Tower, and off the entrance to the river Brue.

6 Marchants Reach, nearly 4 miles within the mouth of the river is its only straight section.

Lights are exhibited from several positions on both banks of the river as far as Cut Point (51°09′·7N 2°59′·4W), opposite Dunball Wharf.

Berths
4.171

1 **Anchorages.** Within the river there are two anchorages for emergency use; off Brue Light Beacon (51°13′·5N 3°00′·3W) in about 2 m at low water springs, and at the W end of Stockland Reach, about 2¾ miles farther up river. Vessels will take the ground at LW in both anchorages.

Alongside berths. Vessels must be prepared to take the ground at Dunball and Combwich where the river almost dries at LW.

Dunball Wharf, 8¼ miles up river from Brue Light Beacon on the E bank, has 150 m of quay. It is the only wharf which can handle general cargo. Vessels up to 2300 dwt can berth alongside.

2 Combwich Wharf, 3¾ miles up river from Brue Light Beacon on the W bank, is 63 m long. It has a RoRo

terminal owned by British Energy. There is no regular traffic but the berth is maintained for possible use by Hinkley Point power station.

Bibby's Wharf, 18 m in length, is close below Dunball Wharf but not currently in use (2008).

Port services
4.172

1 **Facilities**: hospital.
Supplies: fuel; fresh water in small quantities.
Rescue: see 4.150.

Weston Bay

General information
4.173

1 **Description.** Weston Bay is entered between Brean Down (51°20′N 3°01′W) and Anchor Head, 2 miles NE, the W extremity of Worlebury Hill, a ridge 2 miles long which rises to a height of 103 m.

The whole of the bay dries to mud out to a line joining the centre of Brean Down and the W extremity of Birnbeck Island, 2 cables W of Anchor Head.

Fishing stakes, in concentrations, may be encountered within the bay.
4.174

1 **Weston-super-Mare** (51°21′N 2°58′W), a seaside resort, occupies most of the N and E sides of Weston Bay. Grand Pier, on iron piles, extends 2½ cables W from the

Dunball Wharf, Bridgwater, from W (4.171)
(Original dated 2001)

(Photograph - Air Images)

Anchor Head from W (4.173)

(Original dated 2001)

(Photograph - Air Images)

coast, 3 cables SE of Knightstone (51°21'·1N 2°59'·3W); it has no landing place or facilities for boats alongside.

Lights are exhibited from a white post, 2 m in height, on the pierhead.

Facilities: landing facilities are available for helicopters at the hospital in Weston-super-Mare.

Landing place
4.175

1   **Birnbeck Island,** 2 cables W of Anchor Head, is connected to the mainland by a bridge constructed on iron piles. A pier on the N side of the island is used by small passenger vessels on excursions during the summer months.

Bye-laws are in force for vessels using the pier.

Sand Bay

Charts 1152, 1176
General information
4.176

1   **Description.** Sand Bay is entered between Birnbeck Island and Sand Point (51°23'N 2°59'W); the latter lies at the W extremity of Middle Hope, a ridge 1½ miles long, which rises to a height of 43 m. The bay is encumbered by sand banks and mud flats which dry out to a line joining the entrance points.

2   Swallow Rocks extend 1¼ cables W of Sand Point.

Fishing stakes, in concentrations, may be encountered within the bay.

Firing practice area lies off the N side of Middle Hope; see 4.184.

Tidal streams off Birnbeck Island are given on the charts.

3   **Landmarks:**

    Radio mast (51°21'·6N 2°58'·2W) standing on Worlebury Hill (4.173).

    Water tower, standing close E of the radio mast.

    Woodspring Priory (tower) standing at the S foot of Middle Hope, 1¼ miles E of Sand Point and Wick Saint Lawrence Church (tower) standing the same distance farther ESE, are easily distinguishable.

Anchorages
4.177

1   Safe anchorage can be obtained in Blue Anchor Road (51°12'N 3°23'W), 1½ miles NNE of Blue Anchor, in a depth of 7 m, tenacious blue clay.

Tidal streams off Blue Anchor Road are given on the chart. Near the land the spring rate in each direction is 4 to 5 kn.

4.178

1   Vessels with a draught of about 3 m can anchor in moderate weather N of a white mark (best shown on chart 1160 plan of Minehead) on the shore, 6 cables NW of the head of Minehead breakwater on the alignment (145°) of Conygar Tower (51°11'N 3°27'W) (4.152) with the root of Minehead breakwater. A wave recorder light buoy (special) is moored 5¼ cables ENE of the anchorage.

4.179

1   Anchorage can be obtained, out of the tidal stream, in depths of 11 m, approximately 6 cables NW of Sand Point (51°23′N 2°59′W).

THE BRIDGE TO KING ROAD

General information

Charts 1176, 1859

Route

4.180

1   From The Bridge (51°27′N 3°00′W) to Avonmouth Docks, about 11 miles ENE, the route lies through Bristol Deep (4.183), the right arm of the junction at The Bridge, and King Road (4.183).

Topography

4.181

1   The low level ground on the N shore is fronted by Welsh Grounds, extensive drying sand and mud flats which extend S for more than 3 miles between Gold Cliff (51°32′N 2°54′W), a prominent walled point, and Sudbrook Point, 8 miles ENE (Chart 1166).

2   Middle Grounds, which comprise West Middle Ground, Middle Ground and North Middle Ground, form the SW extension of Welsh Grounds.

4.182

1   The S shore from Sand Point (51°23′N 2°59′W) to Clevedon, 5 miles NE, is also low lying. English Grounds, an extensive area of drying sand and mud patches, extends up to 3¼ miles offshore. Closer inshore are Langford Grounds, sand and mud drying to about 1 mile offshore, and Clevedon Flats, with several detached drying patches. Together they form the inshore part of English Grounds between Saint Thomas's Head (51°24′N 2°56′W) and Ladye Point, 4½ miles NE.

2   **Caution.** Depths change frequently and there may be less water than charted in the areas of The Bridge, English Grounds, Langford Grounds, Clevedon Flats and King Road.

    Woodspring Bay lies close E of Saint Thomas's Head; the shore of the bay is backed by low marshy ground through which flows the river Yeo.

3   Between Clevedon Bay and Portishead Point (51°29′·7N 2°46′·4W), 5 miles NE, the coastline consists of higher ground indented by several small bays. A ridge rises steeply from the coast to an elevation of 107 m; Weston Down is the central part of the ridge and Portishead Down its NE end.

4.183

1   Bristol Deep, which extends E between EW Grounds Light Buoy (51°27′N 3°00′W) and Portishead Point, 9 miles ENE, lies between Welsh Grounds and English Grounds.

    King Road lies between Portishead Point and the mouth of the river Avon. It is bounded on its N side by Welsh Grounds and Denny Shoal (4.191).

Firing practice area

4.184

1   Saint Thomas's Head Range (51°24′N 2°56′W) lies to seaward of Middle Hope and Woodspring Bay. A warning light is exhibited from Saint Thomas's Head when the range is in use.

    For further information on practice areas see 1.15.

Vessel traffic service

4.185

1   See 4.5.

Submarine pipelines

4.186

1   There are three disused oil berths, with abandoned submarine pipelines, in the vicinity of Redcliff Bay (51°28′·7N 2°49′·1W). Anchoring is prohibited within an area as shown on the chart.

Tidal streams

4.187

1   At the entrance to Bristol Deep the in-going stream sets NE towards West Middle Ground, thence in the fairway to King Road.

    In the W approach to King Road, approximately 1 mile W of Portishead Point, the in-going stream sets towards Denny Shoal (4.191), the out-going stream inclines towards the N side of the channel.

2   Close inshore in Portishead Pool, which lies between Portishead Point and the entrance to Royal Portbury Dock, there is an eddy on the E-going stream which commences to set W, 3 hours before HW Avonmouth.

    Off Avonmouth the in-going stream sets towards the bank NE of the entrance to Avonmouth Docks, and the out-going stream sets towards the bank between Avonmouth and Portishead.

    Tidal information is shown on the charts.

Directions
(continued from 4.109 or 4.156)

Principal marks

4.188

1   **Landmarks:**
    Radio masts (51°25′·4N 2°51′·8W), standing 7 cables SE of Wain's Hill.
    Church (tower) (51°26′·4N 2°51′·1W), conspicuous from W, standing above the roofs of Clevedon on the S side of Dial Hill.
    Old Nautical School (tower) (51°29′N 2°48′W) standing close to the shore at Portishead.

2   Building (51°29′N 2°47′W).
    Denny Island (51°31′·5N 2°46′·9W).
    Two large white buildings (51°29′·8N 2°42′·9W) on River Quay (4.219).
    Two chimneys (51°30′·6N 2°41′·5W) (4.257).
    Chimney (51°30′·5N 2°41′·0W) (4.257).
    Tower (51°32′·4N 2°39′·6W) (4.257).
    Fifoots Point pylon (51°32′·8N 2°58′·8W) (4.129).

3   **Major lights:**
    Black Nore Point Light (white round tower, 11 m in height) (51°29′N 2°48′W).
    Portishead Point Light (black metal framework tower, white concrete base, 9 m in height) (51°29′·7N 2°46′·4W).

Passage

4.189

1   From the vicinity of EW Grounds Light Buoy (51°27′N 3°00′W) at The Bridge the route to King Road first leads ENE then NE for about 7 miles through Bristol Deep (4.183), passing between the Light Buoys marking each side of the channel until the alignment of the King Road Leading Lights (4.190) standing at the entrance to Avonmouth Docks is reached.

4.190

1 **King Road Leading Lights**:
Front light (white obelisk, red bands, 2 m in height) (51°30′·5N 2°43′·1W), which stands at the foot of North Pier Head Light (round stone tower, 16 m in height).

King Road Leading Lights (072½°) from WSW (4.190)
(Original dated 2001)

(Photograph - Air Images)

Rear light (white disc, black stripes on framework tower, orange bands, 13 m in height) 3 cables from front light.

2 From a position 4 miles WSW of the front light, the alignment (072½°) of these lights leads through the fairway of King Road, passing (with positions from Portishead Point (51°29′·7N 2°46′·4W)):
NNW of Black Nore Point (1¼ miles WSW), on which stands a light (4.188), thence:
3 SSE of Newcome Light Buoy (port hand) (3¾ cables NNW), and:
NNW of Portishead Point, from which a light (4.188) is exhibited, thence:
NNW of Firefly Rocks (7 cables ENE), marked by Firefly Light Buoy (starboard hand) close N, and:
4 SSE of Denny Shoal (7½ cables NE), a detached shoal which constantly changes shape (see Cautions), marked on the S edge by Denny Shoal Light Buoy (S cardinal), thence:
Between Pier Corner (Royal Portbury Dock) (1¾ miles ENE) and Cockburn Rock (1¾ miles NE) marked by Cockburn Light Buoy (port hand) on its SE edge.

4.191

1 **Cautions.** Denny Shoal, a detached shoal, approximately 1 mile in length, lies on the edge of the deep-water channel, 4 cables N of Portishead Pier and is subject to constant change. In some years a large part of the shoal dries and in others there may be as much as 2 m over it; at times the shoal moves S and encroaches the charted shipping channel. Mariners should consult local pilots or the Port Authority, Port of Bristol, for the latest information.

2 Depths in King Road and over Welsh Grounds are also subject to frequent change.

(Directions continue for the river Severn at 4.257. Directions for Port of Bristol Docks are given at 4.215, and for the river Avon at 4.234)

THE PORT OF BRISTOL

AVONMOUTH AND ROYAL PORTBURY DOCK

General information

Charts 1152, 1176, 1859
Position
4.192

1 The Port of Bristol (51°30′N 2°42′W) comprises Avonmouth Docks, Royal Portbury Dock and the tidal river Avon (administered by The Bristol Port Company), City Docks and the non-tidal river Avon (administered by Bristol City Council).

Function
4.193

1 The port is capable of accommodating large vessels and is equipped with modern tanker, bulk and general cargo handling facilities. The main commodities handled by the port are:
Exports: foodstuffs, crude minerals, chemicals, scrap metal, petroleum by-products, manufactured goods, machinery, non-ferrous metals and motor vehicles.

2 Imports: petroleum products, forest products, iron and steel products, motor vehicles, cereals, cement, gypsum, feeding stuffs, fertilisers, ores/minerals, molasses, cocoa, sulphuric acid and coal.
There is a yacht marina, with ample yachting facilities available, within City Docks; these docks, however, are occasionally used for commercial traffic.
4.194

1 The City of Bristol lies largely on the NE bank of the river Avon, 7 miles within its entrance.

Port limits
4.195

1 The port limits embrace the S section of the Bristol Channel between Avonmouth and Steep Holm, as indicated on the chart. They also include:
An area up to 4·6 m above the line of MHWS on both banks of the tidal waters of the river Avon, and its tributaries, up to Hanham Mills, about 5 miles above the entrance to City Docks.
Portishead Dock and all other docks which on 8th August 1977 were within the City of Bristol or abutted on to the port limits.

Bristol – Royal Portbury and Avonmouth Docks from SSW (4.192)

(Original dated 2001)

(Photograph – Air Images)

Approach and entry
4.196

1   The approach to the port is made through Bristol Deep, and King Road. See 4.188.

Entry to the various docks is from King Road; see directions given at 4.215.

Traffic
4.197

1   In 2007 there were 1218 port calls with a total of 20 041 688 dwt.

Port Authority
4.198

1   The Port Authority is The Bristol Port Company, Saint Andrew's Road, Avonmouth, Bristol BS11 9DQ.

The Port Authority is represented by a Managing Director.

Navigational matters should be addressed to The Haven Master, Haven Master's Office, Avonmouth Docks, Bristol BS11 9AT. Web site: www.bristolport.co.uk

Limiting conditions

Controlling depth
4.199

1   Owing to silting the Haven Master, Avonmouth, should be consulted for the latest information on controlling depths. The maintained depths in the entrances to Avonmouth Locks and Royal Portbury Lock are 0·7 m and 4·5 m respectively.

Entry into the individual lock systems is dependent on height of tide and vessel's beam. Fresh E or NE winds can reduce the predicted flood stream significantly and delay the time of HW.

Deepest and longest berth
4.200

1   Royal Portbury Dock, Berths 1–4 (4.219).

Tidal levels
4.201

1   At Avonmouth: mean spring range about 12·2 m; mean neap range about 6·0 m. See *Admiralty Tide Tables.*

Density of water
4.202

1   Avonmouth Docks: 1·012 g/cm^3
Portishead Dock: 1·016 g/cm^3
City Docks: 1·001 g/cm^3

Maximum size of vessel handled
4.203

1   **Royal Portbury Dock:** LOA 300 m; beam 41 m; draught 14·5 m; up to 130 000 dwt.

Avonmouth Lock: LOA 210 m; 30·1 m beam; draught 11 m.

City Docks. See 4.240.

Arrival information

Port operations
4.204

1   Arrivals and departures are restricted by the use of the locks which operate as described at 4.218.

A signal station is situated midway along South Pier at the entrance to Avonmouth Docks and maintains a continuous watch, call sign Avonmouth Radio.

Information concerning berthing, harbour conditions, and safety of navigation is passed by the signal station which is also in constant communications with the pilot launches.

Vessel traffic service
4.205

1   See 4.5.

Notice of ETA required
4.206

1   See 4.209.

Outer anchorages
4.207

1   An anchorage 8 cables W of Newcome Light Buoy (51°30′·0N 2°46′·7W), in a depth of about 11 m, is suitable for small and medium-sized vessels, except on high spring tides. An anchorage for deep-draught vessels is available off Breaksea Point (51°23′N 3°24′W) as given at 4.25.

2   **Prohibited anchorages.** Vessels are prohibited from lying at anchor, except with special permission, in the approaches to Royal Portbury Dock and Avonmouth, in order that the approaches may be kept clear for ships entering or leaving the docks. The prohibited area, as indicated on the chart, encloses a sewer outfall E of Portishead Pool.

3   Prohibition does not cover the use of an anchor as an aid to manoeuvring. A vessel having to anchor in an emergency should report her position through the VTS.

For details of the prohibited anchorage at Redcliff Bay (51°28′·7N 2°49′·1W), see 4.186.

Pilotage
4.208

1   **Bristol Pilotage Area.** The area covers those tidal waters within a limit bounded seawards in the Bristol Channel by lines joining Hartland Point Lighthouse (51°01′N 4°32′W) to Lundy South Lighthouse (51°09′·7N 4°39′·4W), thence through Caldey Island Lighthouse (51°38′N 4°41′W) to the mainland.

2   **Pilotage** is compulsory for the following vessels navigating within the limits of the Port and Harbour of Bristol and the enclosed docks:

    (a) Vessels carrying explosives of 1 tonne or more in quantity.

    (b) Vessels of 70 m LOA or greater carrying dangerous substances in bulk.

3   (c) Vessels of 85 m LOA or greater.

    (d) Tows of vessels, where total length of the vessel(s) towed is 50 m or greater.

    (e) Passenger vessels, with passengers embarked (river Avon only).

4   (f) Any other vessel(s) so specified and/or under circumstances so specified in the Pilotage Directions and General Pilotage Regulations.

Pilotage within Bristol Pilotage Area but outside the limits of Bristol harbour is available to any vessel requiring this service on a non-compulsory basis.

5   Vessels subject to pilotage must be under the direction of an authorised pilot or the holder of a pilotage exemption certificate in respect of the ship and area in question. (A compulsory vessel shifting berth within an enclosed dock and using her mooring lines to do so is not considered to be under way).

6   Through pilotage from sea to berth and berth to sea is the standard service provided.

Pleasure craft of less than 30 m LOA (not being used for profit) can make arrangements for pilotage direct with the Port of the Bristol Channel Pilots Co Ltd.

7   **Pilotage advice for small craft.** The Bristol Port Company has issued pilotage advice to small craft in King Road and the river Avon. Small craft are to keep clear of the main shipping channel by using designated inshore or offshore routes and waiting and crossing areas to seaward of Portishead Marina.

For further details on pilotage, see *Admiralty List of Radio Signals Volume 6(1)*.

4.209

1   **Notice for pilot.** Initial requests for pilotage must be received by the pilotage authority as follows:

    At least 2 hours in advance of any movement within the docks.

    At least 5 hours in advance for vessels sailing from any of the Bristol Docks.

    At least 10 hours in advance for arriving vessels where the pilot is required to board at Breaksea Light Buoy (or any port or place in the estuary E of Breaksea).

2   For arriving vessels where the pilot is required to board at any port or place in the Bristol Channel within the pilot's authorisation W of Breaksea (4.208), prior arrangements to be made through the Haven Master's Office.

3   Requests for pilots can be made by VHF to AVONMOUTH RADIO, or by email to bristolvts@bristolport.co.uk and should include the name of the vessel, draught, the time, date and place where the pilot is to board and the vessel's piloted destination.

4   The passing of an ETA or ETD does not constitute an order for pilotage unless it is also made clear that a pilot is required at the stated time.

Further details can be obtained from *Admiralty List of Radio Signals Volume 6(1)*.

4.210

1   **Pilots board** at the Breaksea pilot boarding station (51°20′N 3°19′W) (4.4). Vessels to be piloted, when approaching the pilot station from seaward, should establish contact with the pilot launch, call sign "Bristol Pilot", approximately 1 hour before arrival and then maintain contact until the pilot is embarked.

The pilot launch, which maintains a 24-hour service, has a black hull and white superstructure with black lettering BRISTOL AND GLOUCESTER PILOTS amidships.

2   For planning purposes vessels should, if possible, aim to embark their pilot at Breaksea about 3 hours before HW Avonmouth so as to ensure that the direction of the tidal stream will be predictable on arriving at the entrance to the lock on the river Avon.

Tugs
4.211

1   Powerful tugs are available. They normally join vessels for Avonmouth Docks to N of the entrance lock on an in-going tide and between Firefly and Cockburn Light Buoys on an out-going tide.

Vessels for Royal Portbury Dock are normally met by tugs E of Cockburn Light Buoy on an in-going tide.

For deep-draught vessels the pilot will issue a specific tug programme on boarding.

Regulations concerning entry
4.212
1 Vessels entering and leaving the port with hazardous goods are to inform the Haven Master, in accordance with the Dangerous Substances in Harbour Regulations; they are not to anchor or moor at any place other than as directed by the Haven Master.

Quarantine
4.213
1 Foreign arrivals are required to complete a Declaration of Health and to report, prior to arrival if possible, to the Port Health Authority any sickness, otherwise report on arrival at dock entrance.

Onus of reporting sickness is the personal responsibility of the Master.

2 All vessels are required to report the presence of animals or birds aboard the vessel and any disease amongst such animals or birds.

Vessels arriving from accepted ports and coastal arrivals need not present a Declaration, but when there is sickness onboard the Port Health Authority is to be informed. See also 1.55.

Harbour
General layout
4.214
1 The general layout is best seen on the chart. Avonmouth Docks are situated on the N side of the entrance to the river Avon and comprise two enclosed docks. They are entered by way of a lock (4.218) protected by North Pier and South Pier.

2 An oil jetty, disused, extends 1¾ cables NW into King Road from a position 1½ cables N of the entrance to the lock.

Royal Portbury Dock lies on the S side of the entrance to the river Avon and is also entered by way of a lock (4.218); its entrance is protected on the N side by an L-shaped breakwater and a short knuckle on the S side.

3 Portishead Dock, home to Portishead Quays Marina, lies almost 2 miles seaward of the entrance to Avonmouth Docks.

Access to City Docks is by way of the river Avon; see 4.225.

Directions for entering harbour

Principal marks
4.215
1 **Landmarks:**
Denny Island (51°31'·5N 2°46'·9W).
Signal Station (51°30'·4N 2°43'·0W), brick building with an adjacent 30 m radar/radio mast, situated ½ cable within the head of South Pier, Avonmouth Docks.
Three wind turbines, showing high intensity obstruction lights, stand, respectively, 2½ cables, 5 cables and 6¾ cables NE of the signal station.
2 White spherical tanks (51°31'·0N 2°42'·0W).

Conveyor standing on Saint Georges Quay, Royal Portbury Dock; an overhead conveyor system connects the quay to a factory standing close SE. Continuous ship unloaders standing at River Quay within the same dock are conspicuous.
Major light:
Portishead Point Light (51°29'·7N 2°46'·4W) (4.188).

Directions for Royal Portbury Dock
4.216
1 Royal Portbury Dock, 1¾ miles E of Portishead Point, is entered from King Road between Portbury Pier which extends NW from the N side of the entrance and a knuckle on the S side, thence through the lock (4.218); there is a tide gauge on the SW side of the pier.

2 From a position about 1½ miles WSW of the front light on the 072½° alignment of the King Road Leading Lights (4.190), the alignment (086¾°) of Seabank Front (51°30'·1N 2°43'·8W) and Rear Leading Lights, exhibited by day and at night, facilitates the approach to the lock entrance.

3 The alignment (099½°) of Knuckle Light (51°29'·9N 2°43'·7W) and a light on the lock control building 1 cable from Knuckle Light provides a leading line which passes approximately ½ cable N of Outer Light Buoy (starboard hand).

On the in-going tide it is customary for vessels to pass the entrance of the lock, turn to port (through more than 180°) and approach the entrance, stemming the tide, from the N.

4 The alignment (191½°) of the lights (grey masts) situated on Portbury Wharf (51°29'·4N 2°44'·2W), also exhibited by day and at night, offers a safe approach to the lock entrance from the N.

Outer, Middle and Inner Light Buoys (starboard hand) mark the S side of the approach to the dock entrance.

Directions for Avonmouth Docks
4.217
1 Avonmouth Docks, 2¼ miles ENE of Portishead Point, are entered from King Road and between North and South Piers.

From the vicinity of Portishead Point, the alignment (072½°) of the King Road Leading Lights (4.190) leads towards the dock entrance.

On the in-going tide it is customary for vessels to pass the entrance, turn to port (through more than 180°) and approach the entrance, stemming the tide, from the N.

Locks
4.218
1 **Royal Portbury Dock.** The lock giving access to the dock is 365·7 m long and 42·7 m wide, with a depth over the outer sill of 17·7 m at MHWS and of 14·3 m at MHWN. The lock normally operates from 4¼ hours before to 3½ hours after HW.

Lights are exhibited from the approach pier (4.216) and from the knuckle at the entrance.

2 **Avonmouth Docks.** The lock which gives access to Avonmouth Docks is 266·7 m long and 30·5 m wide, with a depth over the sill of 14·0 m at MHWS and of 10·8 m at MHWN. The lock normally operates from 4½ hours before to 3 hours after HW, the docking times being dependent on draught.

Lights are exhibited from the pierheads (4.217) and from each side of the lock entrance.

Royal Portbury Dock entrance and Seabank Leading Lights (086¾°) from NW (4.216)

(Original dated 2001)

(Photograph – Air Images)

Basins and berths

Royal Portbury Dock
4.219

1 Entered from the lock the dock has seven numbered berths, all of which can accept vessels of 14·5 m draught, as follows:

> Berths 1 and 2 on W side, 600 m long, forest products terminal.
>
> Berths 3 and 4 on SE side, 605 m long, RoRo terminal, molasses and gypsum terminal, grain export facility.

2 Berths 5 and 6 on NE side, 270 m and 330 m long respectively, served by two continuous ship unloaders and conveyor belt system.

3 Berth 7, L-shaped pier, 270 m berthing length, in the N part of the dock. The limits of the dredged approach area are marked by five light buoys (port hand). A Moiré pattern directional light (320°) is used to assist berthing.

Avonmouth Docks
4.220

1 The docks are entered from the lock and have maintained depths of 8·5 and 11·0 m. A light buoy (special) marks a shallow area at the N end of Eastern Arm.

2 **Oil Basin,** in the W arm of the dock, can accommodate tankers up to 35 000 dwt and there are facilities for the reception of LPG and molasses. There are six numbered berths as follows:

> Nos 1 and 2, 260 m total berthing length, maximum draught 11 m.

3 No 3, 190 m berthing length, maximum draught 10·5 m.

> No 6, 150 m berthing length, maximum draught 10·5 m.
>
> Nos 7 and 8, 360 m total berthing length, maximum draught 11 m.

4 **Eastern Arm,** forms the E portion of the dock and comprises West Wharf, part of which is a container terminal; North Wall, 122 m long, lies at the S end of West Wharf, between it and Oil Basin. The five berths on West Wharf are:

> WW 1, 2 and 3, 470 m total berthing length, maximum draught 11 m.
>
> WW 4 and 5, 380 m total berthing length, maximum draught 11 m.

5 On the E side of Eastern Arm there are five berths, including a dedicated scrap metal berth; they are (from N to S):

> X, W, V and U, 660 m total berthing length, maximum draught 11 m.
>
> Q, 285 m berthing length, maximum draught 10·8 m.

Two berths located farther S are used for general cargoes. On the opposite SW side of the dock there are two berths for general cargo.

6 **South Dock,** in the SE corner of Avonmouth Docks, has a maintained depth of 8·5 m and is entered from the main dock area through Junction Cut, a connecting passage

Avonmouth Docks from NW (4.220)

(Original dated 2001)

(Photograph - Air Images)

165 m long and 25·9 m wide. Vessels with a maximum length 170·7 m, beam 22·8 m and draught 8·1 m can pass through. Lights are exhibited at both ends of Junction Cut.

7   A repair berth (4.222) is situated in the dock; lights are exhibited from the head of the repair jetty and from dolphins.

Lettered berths are shown on the chart.

City Docks
4.221

1   For basins and berths within City Docks, see 4.244. Facilites: fuel; 35 tonnes travel hoist; boat yard.

Port Services
Repairs
4.222

1   Repairs of all kinds; ship repair berth, consisting of a jetty with two off-lying dolphins, lies in the SE part of Avonmouth Docks; divers.

Other facilities
4.223

1   Floating crane, 150-tonne capacity; reception of oily waste through local contractors; issue of SSCC and SSCEC; customs office at Avonmouth; garbage removal facilities through local agents; hospitals; helicopter landing site at Southmead Hospital; salvage services.

Supplies
4.224

1   Fuel oil, most grades with 24 hours notice at Oil Basin or by barge; fresh water at all principal berths; fresh provisions and stores.

RIVER AVON

General information

Chart 1859
Route
4.225

1   The route leads through Swash Channel, thence the river Avon, for a distance of 6 miles to the entrance lock at City Docks, the navigable limit.

Topography
4.226

1   In general on the NE side of the river lie built up residential areas whereas the SW side has a more open, rural aspect. There are several areas of natural beauty on both sides of the river.

Avon Gorge, where the river narrows, 5 cables below the entrance to City Docks, consists of steep cliffs, rising to nearly 100 m in height; the area is also a nature reserve (1.58).

Depths
4.227

1 Chart datum and water levels are shown on a diagram on the chart.

Tidal levels
4.228

1 Avonmouth, see 4.201.

Shirehampton (2 miles within the river): mean spring range 11·5 m; mean neap range 6·1 m.

Sea Mills (3¾ miles within the river): mean spring range 10·9 m; mean neap range 6·2 m.

Cumberland Basin entrance, City Docks: MHWS 10·3 m; MHWN 6·8 m.

Vessel traffic service
4.229

1 See 4.5.

Traffic regulations
4.230

1 Vessels going down river against the in-going tide are to stop above the sharp bends when any vessel coming up the river is rounding such bends, in order to avoid passing at these points.

When vessels are approaching a dredger in the river those proceeding against the tide must reduce speed or stop until those proceeding with the tide are clear of the dredger.

2 The maximum speeds allowed are:

Draught	Speed
1·9 m or more	6 kn through the water 7 kn over the ground.
Less than 1·9 m	9 kn through the water or over the ground

3 Vessels with an overall height in excess of 27 m should take the advice of the Haven Master before attempting the passage from King Road.

Prohibited anchorage. Anchorage is prohibited in the vicinity of the submarine cables and pipelines which cross the river. See 4.231.

4 **Visibility signals.** The following signals are exhibited by day and night, when necessary, from Avonmouth Signal Station from 3 hours before to 1 hour after HW:

Signal	Meaning
Rectangle of white fluorescent light	There is fog in the river, the approximate range of visibility is between ½ and 1 mile.
Two rectangles of white fluorescent light disposed horizontally	Dense fog in the river. The approximate range of visibility is less than ½ cable.

Submarine cables and pipelines
4.231

1 Submarine power cables cross the river at Broad Pill (51°29'·7N 2°42'·0W) and 1¼ miles farther upstream at Hung Road (51°28'·8N 2°40'·7W). The cables are marked by notice boards.

Three submarine pipelines cross the river, below the river bed, 1 cable upstream from Avonmouth Bridge. The two outer pipelines carry high pressure gas, the middle one carries oil. The gas pipeline nearest to the bridge is marked by red poles with red diamond topmarks; the other pipelines are marked by notice boards.

Vertical clearances
4.232

1 Overhead power cables, with vertical clearances of 29 m and 49 m, span the river, respectively, ½ cable and 1½ cables downstream from Avonmouth Bridge.

Avonmouth Bridge, a road bridge which stands nearly 1½ miles within the entrance to the river has a vertical clearance of 29 m. Lights, disposed vertically, are exhibited on either side of each pier of the bridge.

Clifton Suspension Bridge, 3½ cables below City Docks, has a vertical clearance of 71 m.

Natural conditions
4.233

1 **Freshets** bring much sediment down the river Avon. Periodically these can cause a general reduction in mid-channel depths. However the navigable channel, as defined by the 2 m drying contour, is stable.

Cross currents and eddies exist in the vicinity of Black Rocks (51°28'·1N 2°38'·0W) when the storm water sluices are fully open.

Directions

Landmarks
4.234

1 Signal Station (51°30'·4N 2°43'·0W), on South Pier, Avonmouth Lock (4.215).

Two large white buildings (51°29'·8N 2°42'·9W) on River Quay.

Swash Channel
4.235

1 Forming the entrance to the river Avon, Swash Channel is entered close S of South Pier (Avonmouth Docks), and is indicated by lights in line and leading lights.

Lights (white mast, orange square topmark) are exhibited, ¾ cable apart, on the E bank 4 cables SE of the head of South Pier. The alignment (127¼°) of these lights indicates the SW side of the channel entrance. Vessels having negotiated the entrance passing clear of South Pier Light should keep in deeper water close N of the alignment on entry and exit.

2 **Saint George Leading Lights**:

Front light (orange rectangle on white mast, 5 m in height) (51°29'·8N 2°42'·7W).

Rear light (orange rectangle on white mast, 10 m in height) (40 m S of front light).

Within the channel, the alignment, (173¼°), of these lights, on the SW side of the river entrance, leads to a position W of Nelson Point (51°29'·9N 2°42'·5W).

3 The track then leads SE, passing NE of a light buoy (starboard hand) (¾ cable WSW of Nelson Point and the only buoy on the river), and then follows the centre of the river passing under Avonmouth Bridge and the Clifton Suspension Bridge (4.232) to the entrance to City Docks, for which the chart is the best guide.

Lights are exhibited at frequent intervals along the river banks, mostly from white columns.

4.236

1 **Useful marks**:

South Pier Light (round stone tower, 9 m in height) (51°30'·4N 2°43'·1W)

2 Monoliths Light (white and black stripes, fronting white column) (2½ cables ESE from the head of South Pier). The light is an extension of Saint George leading lights and can be used in line, on entering and sailing from the river.

Moorings
4.237
1   Small craft are moored in Crockerne Pill (51°28′·9N 2°41′·0W); Portishead Cruising Club lies at the W entrance where there is a slipway. Small craft are also moored in Chapel Pill (51°28′·9N 2°40′·1W) and Sea Mills Creek (51°28′·8N 2°39′·0W). Vessels should reduce speed when passing these moorings.

Small craft channel
4.238
1   Above Cumberland Basin Entrance Lock, New Cut (4.239) is navigable by small craft for 2½ miles to Netham Weir (51°27′N 2°33′W) using extreme caution. There are several low fixed bridges in this section of the river. Access to the river Avon above Netham Weir and on to the Kennet and Avon Canal at Bath is through Floating Harbour and a feeder canal (4.244).

Bristol — City Docks

General information
4.239
1   **Position.** City Docks (51°27′N 2°36′W) are built on the bed of the original course of the river Avon which was subsequently diverted S of the docks through an artificial cut known as New Cut.
   Function. the docks are used mainly by pleasure craft and the leisure industry. There is a yacht marina.
2   **Approach and entry.** Approached from the river Avon and entered through a lock on the E bank of the river into Cumberland Basin, thence through Junction Lock into the main complex.
   Port Authority. Bristol City Council. The harbour office is in Underfall Yard, Cumberland Road, Bristol, BS1 6XG. The office of the Dock Master is in The Watch House, on the S side of the entrance lock.

Limiting conditions
4.240
1   **Tidal levels.** Cumberland Basin entrance: MHWS 10·3 m; MHWN 6·8 m.

   Maximum size of vessel handled. Length between perpendiculars 99 m; beam less than 15 m. Details of draught limitations can be obtained from the Haven Master, Avonmouth.

Arrival information
4.241
1   **Vessel traffic service.** Port of Bristol (4.204) VTS operates from the river Avon entrance as far as Black Rock Light (51°28′·1N 2°38′·0W). Reporting positions are shown on the chart.
   If using VHF, contact the Dock Master (City Docks Radio) when passing Black Rock Light and again at Hotwells Pontoons, 1½ cables NW of the entrance lock.
2   **Pilotage** see 4.208.
   Unless special arrangements are made with the Dock Master, vessels should arrive off Cumberland Basin entrance not later than 15 minutes after HW to allow time to pass through into Floating Harbour.

Traffic signals
4.242
1   Signals (Diagram 4.242) are exhibited from two positions situated on the E bank of the river, 2 and 2½ cables above Clifton Suspension Bridge; the light nearest the bridge is a high intensity direction light, directed downstream, and the other light is visible all round.

Signal	*Meaning*
	Come ahead with caution.
●	Stop and await orders.

River Avon – traffic signals (4.242)

Harbour
4.243
1   **General layout.** The harbour consists of an interconnecting series of non-tidal basins, including Cumberland Basin, Floating Harbour and Bathurst Basin.
   Bridges. The bridges spanning the locks and Floating Harbour (4.244) are either swing or bascule, giving unlimited vertical clearance as far as Bristol Bridge (vertical clearance 2·6 m).
   Plimsoll Bridge (swing), spans the entrance lock. It has a vertical clearance of 4·3 m when in the closed position. A light is shown upstream and downstream from the centre of the bridge.
2   Junction Lock Bridge (swing) has a vertical clearance of 1·0 m when closed.
   Pero's Bridge (bascule footbridge) spans Saint Augustine's Reach; the centre span is a lifting section 9 m wide. Vertical clearances 1·8 m and 0·7 m when closed.
   Prince Street Bridge (swing) has a clear width of 12 m; vertical clearance 0·7 m when closed.
   Redcliffe Bridge (bascule) has a clear width of 15·2 m; vertical clearance 2·1 m when closed.
3   None of the above bridges is operated on weekdays between 0800 and 0900 and between 1700 and 1800. These restrictions apart, Prince Street Bridge can be operated at fixed times, and with at least one hour's notice, from 0930 to 2200 on weekdays in summer, with additional openings at 0830 and 1715 on weekends and bank holidays. Times of opening and date of commencement of this routine, together with the winter routine, can be obtained from the Harbour Office.
4   Vessels wishing to pass through the various bridges within the harbour should contact the harbour office on VHF or by telephone.

Basins and berths
4.244
1   **Cumberland Basin** is entered through a lock 106·7 m long and 18·9 m wide with a depth over the outer sill of 10 m at MHWS, and of 7 m at MHWN. Lights are exhibited from each side of the lock entrance and from each end. The lock is spanned by Plimsoll Swing Bridge (4.243).
   The basin has 457 m of quay and a maintained depth of 5·5 m.
2   **Junction Lock,** of similar dimensions to the entrance lock and spanned by a swing bridge (4.243), leads from

Cumberland Basin to Floating Harbour. This lock is closed to shipping during periods when the tide is 9·5 m, or greater, on the entrance lock outer sill.

At the E end of the harbour a feeder canal leads to Netham Lock (51°27′N 2°33′W) which can accommodate craft of up to 24·4 m in length having a beam of 5·4 m and draught of 1·9 m.

3   **Caution.** Mariners are warned of strong currents when sluices at Old Junction Lock and Underfall Yard, at the E end of Cumberland Basin, are open to let water out of the harbour. When sluices are in use a red flag is flown at Old Junction Lock and red flashing lights are displayed at Underfall Yard.

Services
4.245
1   Diesel fuel; fresh water and electricity at the principal berths; provisions and stores; refuse and waste oil disposal.

RIVERS SEVERN AND WYE INCLUDING GLOUCESTER HARBOUR AND THE PORTS OF SHARPNESS AND GLOUCESTER

GENERAL INFORMATION

Charts 1176, 1166
Area covered
4.246
1   This section describes the river Severn passages, harbours and anchorages, above King Road to Sharpness (51°43′N 2°29′W) approximately 18 miles NE, allowing for the windings of the river, and Gloucester Harbour, the limits of which embrace part of the estuary of the river Severn above Avonmouth, as shown on the charts, to the weirs at Gloucester and to Bigsweir Bridge on the river Wye.

2   It is arranged as follows:
King Road to Severn Bridge (4.248).
Severn Bridge to Sharpness Point (4.267).
Port of Gloucester (4.278).

Topography
4.247
1   The estuary of the river Severn is considered to begin at a line joining Lavernock Point (51°24′N 3°10′W) and Sand Point (51°23′N 2°59′W) and to extend to a line joining Sudbrook Point (51°35′N 2°43′W) to Cross Hands (not named on chart, but is in the vicinity of the E end of Second Severn Crossing), 2 miles ESE, where the river begins. The coast on the N side and that on the S side of the estuary between Sand Point and Avonmouth are described at 4.181.

2   Between Avonmouth and Cross Hands, 4 miles NNE, the E coastline has been developed as an industrial estate backed with oil storage tanks for a distance of 1½ miles and there are numerous tall chimneys. From Cross Hands to Severn Bridge, 2½ miles NE, the river bank is low lying and rural.

From Sudbrook Point (51°35′N 2°43′W) to Wye Bridge, 3 miles NE, the W river bank is also low lying and rural.

3   From Severn Bridge to Sharpness the land on both sides of the river is immediately low lying and rural, with several stretches of riverbank N of the bridge protected by embankments. On the W bank however, the low ground is backed by considerably higher ground a short distance inland. Sedbury Cliffs, red in colour, 46 m high, rise 1½ miles N of the bridge on the NW side of the river.

KING ROAD TO SEVERN BRIDGE

General information

Chart 1166
Route
4.248
1   The route from the E end of King Road to Severn Bridge leads N thence NE for 7½ miles through the inner part of the Severn Estuary and the outer part of the river between extensive drying banks.

2   Passage through The Shoots (51°34′N 2°42′W) (4.259) must be made between the main pillars of Second Severn Crossing. The principal passage under Severn Bridge lies W of the mid-channel rocks.

Topography
4.249
1   See 4.247.

Depths
4.250
1   A shifting bar, known locally as Severn Bar, with depths of less than 5 m, extends across the channel between shoal banks on either side, about 7 cables N of Avonmouth Docks entrance.

The Shoots (4.259), extending for about 1 mile below Second Severn Crossing, has fairway depths in excess of 10 m.

Dun Sands (4.260), connected to a bank which extends across the river has depths of less than 2 m in the fairway about 1½ miles upriver from Second Severn Crossing.

Tidal levels
4.251
1   Sudbrook (51°35′N 2°43′W): mean spring range about 12·3 m; mean neap range about 6·2 m.
Beachley (Aust) (51°36′N 2°38′W): mean spring range about 12·3 m; mean neap range about 6·3 m.

Vessel traffic service
4.252
1   See 4.5.

Traffic regulations
4.253
1   See 4.289.

To ensure the safety of navigation of all vessels and craft in the river Severn, the fairway between Avonmouth Approaches and Sharpness Old Dock Entrance (4.278) must

Severn Bridges from SW (4.248)

(Original dated 2001)

(Photograph - Air Images)

be recognised as a narrow channel in the context of *International Regulations for Preventing Collisions at Sea (1972)*. The attention of all users of the river Severn is therefore drawn to the provisions of Rule 9 of these regulations. All small craft mariners are reminded that the narrow confines of the navigable channel, and the severe tidal regime, impose considerable restrictions on the navigation of commercial shipping and consequently their ability to take avoiding action might on occasions be severely restricted.

Vertical clearance
4.254
1   An overhead power cable, with a safe vertical clearance of 41 m, spans the river between Beachley Point (51°36'·6N 2°39'·2W) and Aust Cliff on the E side of the river; the cable is supported by two tall pylons, the E pylon, situated on the drying bank 2 cables SW of Aust Cliff, being marked by lights.

Rescue
4.255
1   Inshore lifeboats, operated by the Severn Area Rescue Association, are stationed near the village of Beachley (51°36'·8N 2°38'·9W), close N of Severn Bridge on the W shore, and at Sharpness Point (51°43'·5N 2°29'·0W) on the E shore.

   For details of rescue organisation see 1.60.

Tidal streams
4.256
1   Between King Road and Severn Bridge the tidal streams set directly across the rocks and banks when they are covered but in the direction of the channels when they are dry.

   The in-going stream divides at Beachley Point (51°36'·6N 2°39'·2W), one branch running into the river Wye and the other continuing in the river Severn.

2   The streams at The Shoots and at Severn Bridge begin at the following approximate times:

Position	Interval from HW Avonmouth	Direction
The Shoots	−0430	In-going
	+0045	Out-going

The maximum spring rate in each direction is 8 kn and the maximum neap rate is 3 kn.

Severn Bridge	−0400	In-going
	+0045	Out-going

The maximum spring rate in each direction is 6 kn.

3   The rates mentioned above, for the river between King Road and Sharpness, are approximations for the main body of the stream and may often be exceeded locally. Throughout the area the strength and direction of the streams are greatly affected by the covering and uncovering of the banks, and, to a lesser degree, by the amount of fresh water in the river. There is little or no slack water in the main channels, and the streams may be encountered running in the opposite direction on different sides of the channel near the turn of the tide.

Directions
(continued from 4.191)

Landmarks
4.257
1   Two chimneys (51°30'·6N 2°41'·5W), standing at an elevation of 102 m; a third conspicuous chimney stands 4 cables E with an elevation of 92 m.

Three wind turbines standing close to the coast 1½ to 5½ cables NNE of Avonmouth entrance lock. Tower (51°32'·4N 2°39'·6W).

Other aid to navigation
4.258

1   **Racon:** Second Severn Crossing Centre (51°34'·5N 2°42'·0W) (4.259)

See *Admiralty List of Radio Signals Volume 2.*

Passage
4.259

1   On account of the shifting nature of the sands and of the rate of the tidal streams it is not advisable to attempt to navigate above King Road without a pilot or without recent local knowledge. Vessels should negotiate the channel under Severn Bridge between 1¾ hours before HW when proceeding inwards to 1½ hours after HW when proceeding outwards.

An unmarked wreck, with a least swept depth of 2·2 m over it, lies approximately 1 mile N of the entrance to Avonmouth Docks.

2   **Redcliffe Leading Lights:**

Front light (black metal framework tower, white topmark and white lantern, 10 m in height) (51°36'·2N 2°41'·4W)

Rear light (metal mast, 30 m in height) (320 m from front light)

3   From a position about 4¼ miles SSW of the front light, the alignment (012¾°) of these lights leads through The Shoots, a passage only 1½ cables wide at its narrowest part and bounded by extensive drying reefs, passing (with positions from Sudbrook Point (51°35'N 2°43'W)):

ESE of the edge of Bedwin Sands (2½ miles SSW), an extensive drying bank, thence:

4   WNW of the SW edge of English Stones (1¼ miles SSE), an extensive area of rock, boulders and weed, and marked by Lower Shoots Light Beacon (W cardinal), thence:

ESE of The Mixoms (1 mile S), a detached group of rocks which lie E of Black Bedwins, the N part of Bedwin Sands; a light beacon (port hand) stands on the NE rock. Thence:

ESE of Gruggy (6 cables SSE), a rocky shelf, thence:

5   Between the two main supports of Second Severn Crossing.

Second Severn Crossing, with a vertical clearance of 37 m, spans the the river Severn between positions 51°34'·2N 2°39'·9W and 51°34'·9N 2°43'·9W. All traffic must pass between the two main supports, which are marked by lights. Lights are also exhibited from the centre of the main span indicating the mid point between the supports; these lights are visible on both sides of the bridge.

6   Restricted areas, shown on the chart, are established in the vicinity of the bridge. Unauthorised vessels are prohibited from entering these areas except in an emergency.

Caution. Mariners are advised that under certain conditions and states of the tide, radar equipment may display spurious and misleading echoes in the vicinity of Second Severn Crossing.

The track continues, passing:

7   WNW of Old Man's Head (6 cables ESE), on which stands a light beacon (W cardinal), the NW edge of English Stones, thence:

ESE of Lady Bench (4 cables E), a rocky shelf, on which stands a light beacon (port hand), thence:

WNW of The Dumplings (6½ cables E), a detached group of rocks. The Scars, the N edge of English Stones lies 2 cables SE of The Dumplings.

The leading lights should be kept slightly open W to offset the tendency of the tidal stream to set a vessel E towards English Stones.

8   Charston Rock Light (51°35'·3N 2°41'·7W) (white round stone tower, black stripe, 7 m in height) which stands on Charston Rock, a rock which covers on spring tides, is very slightly open W when Redcliffe Leading Lights are in line.

Caution. The N end of this lead passes over two patches which dry 0·1 m, close W of Old Man's Head and SW of The Dumplings but well clear of a patch which dries 5·6 m on Lady Bench.

4.260

1   **Leading lights:**

Front light Lady Bench Light Beacon (Red concrete pillar, can topmark, 16 m in height) (51°34'·8N 2°42'·2W).

Rear light (mounted on Second Severn Crossing Bridge) (3¾ cables SW of front light).

2   From a position about 2 cables SSW of Charston Rock Light, the alignment (234°) astern of the above lights leads about 2 miles NE, passing between Charston Sands and Dun Sands.

Caution. Mariners are advised to give due regard to height of tide and strength of tidal stream when determining the exact track on which to pass SE of Chapel Rock Light (black metal framework tower, white lantern, 8 m in height) (51°36'·4N 2°39'·2W), which stands on Chapel Rock, a rocky ledge tending 2¼ cables S and SE of Beachley Point (51°36'·6N 2°39'·2W).

3   When Lyde Rock Light (51°36'·9N 2°38'·7W) (black metal framework tower, white bands, 10 m in height) which stands on the edge of Lyde Rock, a rocky ledge, bears 000°, the track leads approximately 010° passing (with positions from Lyde Rock Light):

W of Lower Bench (4¼ cables SSE), a rock, thence:

E of Dod Rock (3¼ cables S), the E end of the rocky shelf of Chapel Rock, thence:

Under the Severn Bridge.

4   **Severn Bridge** is a suspension road bridge with a vertical clearance of 36 m which spans the river Severn between Beachley (51°37'N 2°39'W) and Aust Cliff, 9 cables SE.

Lights, disposed horizontally, are exhibited on both the upstream and downstream sides of the piers supporting the two towers of the bridge, and a light is exhibited in the centre of the arch on both sides of the bridge.

5   Great Ulverstone, the rock on which the E tower of the bridge stands, and Aust Rock lie within 2¾ cables of Aust Cliff.

In the locality, the river is obstructed by rocks which cause severe turbulence in the tidal stream.

The track then continues, passing:

W of Upper Bench (4¼ cables SE), a rock, thence:

W of Leary Rock (4 cables ESE), thence:

6   One cable E of Hen and Chickens Rocks (1 cable S), thence:

E of Lyde Rock.

The track passes very close between Lower Bench and a detached rock which dries 1 m, lying ¾ cable W, which it is not practicable for a stranger to be certain of avoiding.

7　　For vessels passing down-river at night, the alignment (234°) of Lady Bench Light Beacon with the Second Severn Crossing W light (51°34′·6N 2°42′·7W) leads between Charston Sands and Dun Sands to join the leading line S through The Shoots (4.259).

4.261

1　　**Caution.** Both Dun Sands and the connecting bank are constantly shifting, especially during the winter months.

(Directions continue at 4.272)

River Wye

General information
4.262

1　　**Description.** The river Wye flows into the river Severn close SW of Beachley Point (51°36′·6N 2°39′·2W). It is navigable by small vessels as far a Chepstow (4.265).

　　Depths in the river as far as Chepstow, reach 14 m at MHWS and 11 m at MHWN. The tide has been known to rise 0·5 m higher, and the level is marked on the parapet at the W end of the road bridge at the town.

Vertical clearance
4.263

1　　The mouth of the river is spanned by the same overhead power cable which spans the river Severn, 2 cables downstream of Severn Bridge, but here the safe vertical clearance is reduced to 18 m.

　　Wye Bridge, with a vertical clearance of 15 m, spans the river 2 cables NE of this overhead cable. A gauge board on the downstream side of the W pier of the bridge indicates the actual vertical clearance. Lights, disposed horizontally, are exhibited on both upstream and downstream sides of the bridge over the centre of the navigational channel.

2　　Between Wye Bridge and Chepstow the river is spanned by two further overhead cables, the least vertical clearance being 16·8 m.

Directions
4.264

1　　From a position about 6 cables SW of Chapel Rock Light (51°36′·4N 2°39′·2W) the alignment (012°) of the mid point between the two lights on Wye Bridge with Bulwark Beacon (red spar over red structure) (W bank, 1½ cables above Wye Bridge), leads into the river Wye.

Chepstow
4.265

1　　**General information.** Chepstow is a small port which lies 2 miles within the mouth of the river Wye. At Chepstow the river is crossed by a road and railway bridge, immediately below which is a power cable with a vertical clearance of 4 m; 2½ cables farther up it is crossed by a road bridge with a vertical clearance of 3·6 m and with a width between the masonry piers of the central span of 34 m.

2　　The port can handle small vessels of approximately 900 dwt. The Harbour Authority, Gloucester Harbour Trustees (4.282), should be consulted for the latest information.

　　Industries include an ironworks for the construction of railway rolling stock and bridges.

3　　**Limiting conditions.** The port can handle small vessels of approximately 900 dwt. The Harbour Authority should be consulted for the latest information.

　　Pilotage. The port lies within the limits of Gloucester Harbour and pilotage is provided by Gloucester Pilots; for

details see 4.292. In addition to other requirements, vessels are required to state their masthead height and whether masts can be lowered.

4　　For further details see *Admiralty List of Radio Signals Volume 6(1)*.

　　Berths. Two wharves, reported to be heavily silted and in a state of disrepair.

　　Facilities: hospital with helicopter landing site.

Anchorage
4.266

1　　In emergencies, Northwick Roadstead (51°35′·8N 2°38′·8W), NE of Dun Sands, may be used with extreme caution. An obstruction, with a least depth of 6·2 m over it lies within the anchorage 1 mile SSE of Beachley Point (51°36′·6N 2°39′·2W); a foul patch lies approximately 1 cable NE of the obstruction.

SEVERN BRIDGE TO SHARPNESS POINT

General information

Chart 1166
Route
4.267

1　　Between Severn Bridge and Sharpness, a distance of 9½ miles, the river is encumbered by numerous banks and rocky shelves. Oldbury Sands, with Slimeroad Sands at their SW end, lie N of the Severn Bridge and constrict the main channel to the NW side of the river. Farther upstream, N of Narlwood Rocks, at the N end of Oldbury Sands, the channel crosses to the SE side of the river where it is constricted by Sheperdine Sands, Lydney Sands and Saniger Sands.

2　　The main channel passes close to the piers at Sharpness (4.295) and is well indicated by leading lights and other marks.

Topography
4.268

1　　See 4.247.

Vessel traffic service
4.269

1　　See 4.5.

Rescue
4.270

1　　Inshore lifeboats, operated by the Severn Area Rescue Association, are stationed near Beachley (4.260) and at Sharpness (4.278).

　　For details of rescue organisation see 1.60.

Tidal streams
4.271

1　　Between Severn Bridge and Sharpness the tidal streams set directly inwards and outwards across the shoals and rocks when they are covered, but in the direction of the channel when they are dry. See also 4.256.

2　　At Sharpness the streams set strongly across the entrance to the docks, beginning as follows:

Interval from HW Avonmouth	*Direction*
−0200	In-going
+0100	Out-going

　　Maximum spring flood rate 5-6 kn; ebb 4-5 kn.

Directions
(continued from 4.261)

Principal marks
4.272

1   **Landmarks:**

Oldbury Nuclear Power Station (buildings) (51°39′N 2°34′W).

Berkeley Power Station (towers) (51°41′·6N 2°29′·6W).

Grain silo (51°43′·2N 2°28′·6W) (4.296).

Grain silo (51°43′·3N 2°28′·4W) (4.296).

Passage
4.273

1   The recommended track from Severn Bridge to the entrance to Sharpness Docks follows a series of leading lines, shown on the chart.

From a position E of Lyde Rock, the track leads towards Sedbury Light (metal mast, 10 m in height) (51°37′·8N 2°39′·0W), passing through the narrow channel between Lyde Rock and Slimeroad Sand.

Slimeroad Leading Lights:

Front light (white hut) (51°37′·2N 2°39′·1W)

2   Rear light (black metal framework tower, white lantern, 8 m in height) (91 m from front light)

The alignment (210½°) astern, of these lights leads to a position abreast Inward Rocks.

Inward Rocks Leading Lights:

Front light (white round GRP tower, 6 m in height) (51°39′·3N 2°37′·5W)

Rear light (steel mast, 20 m in height) (183 m from front light)

3   The alignment (252½°) of these lights, astern, leads ENE passing NNW of Counts Light Float (N cardinal), which marks the edge of Narlwood Rocks.

With an in-going tide, the turn at Inward Rocks should be made in good time to avoid being set on to Sheperdine Sands.

Sheperdine Leading Lights:

Front light (grey enclosure on black round tower, 8 m in height) (51°40′·1N 2°33′·3W)

4   Rear light (black metal framework mast, white lantern and topmark, 12 m in height) (168 m from front light)

On passing Counts Light Float, the track follows the alignment (070½°) of Sheperdine Leading Lights, thence on the alignment, (225°) astern, of Narlwood Leading Lights, towards Hills Flat Light Buoy (starboard hand) which marks the rocky edge of Hills Flat.

5   **Narlwood Leading Lights:**

Front light (metal mast with gallery, 12 m in height) (51°39′·6N 2°34′·8W)

Rear light (metal mast with gallery, 17 m in height) (198 m from front light)

Ledges Light Buoy (starboard hand) is moored at the edge of The Ledges, a rocky shelf, mid-way between Narlwood and Sheperdine Leading Lights.

6   From a position on the Narlwood leading line about 1¾ miles from the front light and about 1½ cables NW of Hills Flats Light Buoy (starboard hand), the line of bearing 061° on Bull Rock Light Beacon (metal lattice tower, square white topmark, tide gauge), 3 cables NW of Berkeley Power Station (4.272), ahead, leads ENE until the alignment (077½°) of Conigre Leading Lights is reached.

7   From a position on the Conigre leading line 9 cables from the front light, the track passes ½ cable N of

Hayward Rock Light Beacon (N cardinal), which marks the edge of Hayward Rock.

Conigre Leading Lights:

Front light (framework tower, 23 m in height) (51°41′·5N 2°30′·0W)

Rear light (framework tower, 27 m in height) (213 m from front light)

8   The alignment (077½°) of these lights, followed by the alignment, (217¾°) astern, of Fishinghouse Leading Lights leads W of Berkeley Power Station, thence through the narrow passage, blasted to a depth 0·6 m above chart datum, between Bull Rock and Black Rock, lying at the outer end of Bull Rock.

Fishinghouse Leading Lights:

Front light (white GRP cone tower, white and orange X topmark, 4 m in height) (51°41′·0N 2°31′·0W)

9   Rear light (steel mast, white and orange topmarks, 12 m in height) (185 m SW from front light)

Finally, the alignment, (187¾°) astern, of Berkeley Pill Leading Lights leads to the entrance to Sharpness Docks.

Berkeley Pill Leading Lights:

Front light (black metal framework tower, white lantern and topmark, 8 m in height) (51°42′·0N 2°29′·4W)

10   Rear light (black metal framework tower, white lantern and topmark, 12 m in height) (152 m from front light).

Panthurst Pill Light (yellow GRP pillar) is exhibited from a position 7 cables NNE of the leading lights at Berkeley Pill.

Caution. Owing to the strength of tidal streams which may set across the channel when the banks are covered, great attention must be paid to the steering of the vessel.

(Directions continue at 4.296)

Lydney Harbour
4.274

1   **General information.** Lydney Harbour (51°42′·6N 2°30′·5W), formerly a small commercial port which had fallen into disrepair, has been restored (2005) to working condition. The only commercial traffic using the harbour (2007) are small cruise vessels, notably MV *Balmoral*, other traffic being pleasure craft.

2   **Harbour Authority.** The Environment Agency, Riversmeet House, Newtown Industrial estate, Northway Lane, Tewkesbury, Gloucestershire GL20 8JG.

Internet: www.environment-agency.gov.uk/subjects/navigation/747415

Harbour master: telephone 01684 864388 or 07768 861282, out of office hours 0800 807060; VHF Ch 80.

Any vessel intending to enter Lydney Harbour should contact the Harbour Authority well in advance.

4.275

1   **Maximum size of vessel handled:**

Tidal basin only: LOA 55 m; beam 9·5 m; draught 7·6 m (average spring tide), 3·65 m (average neap tide).

Lock: LOA 30·5 m; beam 7·5 m; draught 3·65 m.

Pilotage is provided by Gloucester pilots.

4.276

1   **Harbour.** The harbour consists of a tidal basin and two wet docks. The wet docks are entered from the tidal basin through a lock. The upper dock is connected to the lower dock by a canal 5½ cables long.

Outer entrance; 10 m wide; depths over sill 3·5 m at HW neaps, 8 m at HW springs.

2   Outer basin; 82 m long; 22 m wide.
      Lock; 27 m long; 6·5 m wide; 4·0 m over inner sill.
      Inner basin; 231 m long; 32 m wide; depths up to
         3·0 m.
      Caution. There are very strong currents across the
harbour entrance.

Minor channel
4.277

1   Oldbury Lake runs NE on the SE side of Oldbury Sands
and gives access to Oldbury Pill (51°38'·0N 2°34'·8W),
where there are mud berths and limited facilities for small
craft and yachts. There are depths of 8 m at MHWS
2 cables offshore.

      The channel N of Oldbury Pill diverges from the shore,
passing over Narlwood Rocks, in depths of 6 m MHWS,
before joining the main channel.

PORT OF GLOUCESTER INCLUDING SHARPNESS DOCK

General information

Charts 1166, 1176
Position
4.278

1   Sharpness Dock is entered from the river Severn at
51°43'N 2°29'W and is connected to Port of Gloucester by
the Gloucester and Sharpness Canal (4.305).

Function
4.279

1   Gloucester is no longer used for commercial shipping.
Sharpness handles a diverse range of cargoes, including dry
bulk, minerals, timber, scrap metal, grain, cement, fertilizer,
coal and stone.
      There is a marina in the canal cut immediately N of
Sharpness.

Port limits
4.280

1   The harbour limits embrace part of the estuary of the
river Severn above Avonmouth to the weirs at Gloucester
and to Bigsweir Bridge on the the river Wye. The seaward
limit extends S from the Welsh coast at Gold Cliff
(51°32'N 2°54'W) (4.181) to the limit of the Port of
Bristol.

2   The extent of the Port of Gloucester, which includes
Sharpness Docks and the Gloucester and Sharpness Canal,
is a line between the ends of the piers at Sharpness to the
lock gates at Gloucester.

Traffic
4.281

1   In 2007 there were 180 port calls at Sharpness with a
total of 521 000 dwt.

Port Authority
4.282

1   Jurisdiction of the area within the harbour limits lies
under Gloucester Harbour Trustees, Navigation House, The
Docks, Sharpness, Berkeley, GL13 9UD.
      The Port Authority for Sharpness and Gloucester Docks
is: British Waterways, Navigation House, The Docks,
Sharpness, Berkeley, Gloucestershire GL13 9UD.

      Cargo handling facilities at Sharpness Dock are managed
by the Victoria Group which has a resident dock manager.
E-mail: info@sharpnessdock.co.uk.

Limiting conditions

Depths, clearances and tidal levels
4.283

1   The Port Authority should be consulted for the latest
information on the controlling depth and draught required
for Sharpness, and Gloucester and Sharpness Canal.
      For vessels with maximum dimensions there is a
minimum requirement of 0·91 m clearance under the keel
to clear the outer sill of the tidal basin.
      In order to achieve adequate under-keel clearance,
movements in and out of the lock at Sharpness are timed
close to HW. The majority of vessel movements occur on a
rising tide.

Vertical clearance
4.284

1   For vessels wishing to use the Gloucester and Sharpness
Canal there is a vertical height limitation of 32 m.

Tidal levels
4.285

1   See *Admiralty Tide Tables.* Mean spring range about
8·8 m; mean neap range about 5·6 m. The highest spring
range is 10·4 m.
      Above Inward Rocks (51°39'N 2°37'W) the height of
LW is greatly affected by river flow, and may be increased
by up to 1 m by flood water. The height of HW is hardly
ever affected by river flow.
      Tidal rates are high in the river, with spring rates of up
to 8 kn. A more normal rate is between 4 to 6 kn.

Density of water
4.286

1   Between 1·000 and 1·003 g/cm^3 at Sharpness.

Lock
4.287

1   Access from the tidal basin to Sharpness wet dock is
through a lock, 92·5 m long, 16·15 m wide at the lower sill
level and with a depth of 7·3 m over the upper sill.
      The lock gates are open for about 2 hours, from 2 hours
before HW until HW, but the times vary according to the
draught of vessels in transit. It is recommended that vessels
without a pilot plan to arrive during the hour before HW.
      The walls of the lock chamber and entrance are tapered
from a maximum width of 18·8 m at the coping level to a
minimum of 16·15 at the lock sill. When locking vessels of
maximum beam suitable underkeel clearance is required to
obtain the necessary clearance on the beam.

Maximum size of vessel handled
4.288

1   Maximum dimensions Sharpness: tonnage 6 000 dwt;
16·76 m beam; 6·55 m draught in fresh water; subject to
suitable tides. There is no restriction on length; the tidal
basin is used as a lock when vessels over 91 m in length
are being docked. Permissible draughts within the dock
system vary from 4·5 to 6·5 m.

2   Maximum dimensions Gloucester: 1100 dwt; length
64 m; beam of 10 m and fresh water draught 3·5 m can
navigate to Gloucester. Vessels exceeding these dimensions
are not permitted to do so without the sanction of the
Harbour Master.

Arrival information

Port operations
4.289

1   Arrivals and departures are determined by the depth available over the entrance sill.

Port radio. For details of working hours and communications at Sharpness and Gloucester see *Admiralty List of Radio Signals Volume 6(1)*.

Vessel traffic service
4.290

1   VTS schemes are in operation for the control of shipping. Positions of reporting points are shown on the chart. Vessels should report to Sharpness Radio and to Bristol VTS (4.204). See also *Admiralty List of Radio Signals Volume 6(1)*.

Notice of ETA required
4.291

1   Vessels should send their ETA, Breaksea Light Buoy, at least 24 hours in advance to their Agents, with dwt, fresh water draught and all other information relevant to the navigational status of the vessel. Vessels should contact Avonmouth Radio to confirm ETA at Breaksea Light Buoy 6 hours in advance.

2   For additional requirements for Chepstow see 4.265.

See *Admiralty List of Radio Signals Volume 6(1)* for further details.

Pilotage
4.292

1   **Pilotage.** Gloucester Harbour Trustees (4.282) are the competent Harbour Authority for the purposes of the Pilotage Act 1987. Pilotage is compulsory within the harbour limits (4.280), except within the docks, for the following categories of vessels:

2   Vessels whose deadweight tonnage is 100 tonnes or more, or whose notional superficial area, calculated by multiplying overall length in metres by overall breadth in metres, is greater than 200 m². In the case of towed vessels, the greater of the sum of the deadweight tonnage or notional superficial area of the towing and towed vessels shall determine whether the criteria for compulsory pilotage are met.

3   All vessels carrying dangerous or polluting goods, as specified in current regulations.

All vessels carrying more than 12 passengers.

Pilots normally board in the vicinity of Breaksea Light Buoy (51°20′N 3°19′W) (Chart 1152); vessels should establish contact with the pilot vessel approximately 1 hour before arrival, and maintain contact until the pilot is embarked.

4   Pilotage is not compulsory, but is available, within the docks at Sharpness and Gloucester and on the Gloucester and Sharpness Canal. Dock and canal pilots board in the lock.

Pilot vessel. See 4.210.

For further details on pilotage see *Admiralty List of Radio Signals Volume 6(1)*.

Tugs
4.293

1   There are no tugs stationed at Sharpness. If tugs are required, they should be booked through agents and are

normally picked up off Avonmouth. Pilots will advise if tugs are necessary; 24 hours notice is normally required.

Regulations concerning entry
4.294

1   Masters of vessels carrying dangerous substances are required to give notice of entry into the Gloucester Trustees Harbour Area, to the Harbour Master at Sharpness, at least 24 hours before arrival into the area. In certain circumstances it may be possible for a shorter notice to be acceptable, provided this has previously been agreed with the Harbour Master.

Harbour

General layout
4.295

1   Sharpness Docks are entered between North Pier and South Pier, which project 216 m W and 214 m SW, respectively, from the shore.

A drying mud shoal regularly occurs between North and South Piers; it is dredged as required.

2   The tidal basin, immediately inward of the piers, is 166 m long and 76·2 m wide and the width at the entrance, which has gates, is 17·4 m. There are depths of 8·8 m over the outer sill at MHWS.

Access to the wet dock is through a lock (4.287).

The wet dock has nearly 4000 m of quayage. Access to the dry dock is from the wet dock.

Directions for entering harbour
(continued from 4.273)

Landmarks
4.296

1   Grain Silo (51°43′·2N 2°28′·6W), standing on the W side of the harbour.

Grain Silo (51°43′·3N 2°28′·4W), standing on the E side.

4.297

1   The entrance to the tidal basin leads ENE between North Pier and South Pier, thence into the lock.

Lights are exhibited from the heads of both piers.

Basins and berths

Anchorage
4.298

1   For vessels awaiting a pilot, Barry Roads (4.25) affords the best anchorage.

Alongside berths
4.299

1   **Wet Dock.** There are 10 to 14 available berths depending on the number and length of vessels docked. There is a RoRo berth, with ramp, situated at the seaward end of the S side.

Sharpness marina. There is a yacht marina situated in the N part of Sharpness Docks. The only access to the marina is by way of the wet dock and through two swing bridges. There is a pontoon at the S side of the tidal basin for small craft waiting to proceed through the lock. The old N entrance to the marina, which lies close N of Sharpness Point, is permanently closed by a concrete dam.

2   **Caution.** Sluices in the Old Dock Entrance (51°43′·5N 2°28′·9W) operate automatically and are liable to open at any time without warning. It is therefore inadvisable for small craft to berth in this area.

Canal   *Grain Silo*

Sharpness Docks from WSW (4.295)

(Original dated 1999)

(Photograph - The Citizen, Gloucester)

Port services

Repairs
4.300

1   Most types of repairs are available. Dry dock, operated by Sharpness Shipyard and Drydock Limited: length 110·2 m; entrance width 15·2 m; depth over the sill of 4·6 m at MHWS; breadth of floor 17·9 m.

Other facilities
4.301

1   SSCC and SSCEC issued; limited facilities for the reception of oily waste by prior arrangement; small hospital at Berkeley, 2 miles SE; marina has good facilities.

Supplies
4.302

1   Fuel oil by road tanker, usually requires 12 hours notice; fresh water; provisions and stores.

River Severn above Sharpness

General information
4.303

1   The channel, 2½ cables NW of the entrance to Sharpness Docks, is obstructed by rocks.

There is a pool with depths 5 to 12 m 5 cables NNE of Sharpness Point (51°43'·5N 2°28'·9W). The site of the old Severn Railway Bridge, of which only the piles remain, crosses the pool.

Above this, the river is not charted and is not suitable for navigation other than by small craft at or near MHWS. The channel becomes ill-defined, flowing through drying sandbanks, and it dries in places.

2 **Vertical clearance.** Overhead power cables span the river approximately 5 and 11 miles above Sharpness with a minimum vertical clearance of 21 m. A further cable crossing at Minsterworth (uncharted) has a minimum vertical clearance of about 7 m.

Slimbridge on the SE side of the river, 12 miles below Gloucester, contains a National Wildfowl Refuge.

For the river Severn above Gloucester see 4.307.

4.304

1 Above Sharpness the tidal streams become weaker, but as the channel narrows the river current becomes stronger, and above Framilode, 12 miles above Sharpness, the flow is nearly always downstream except near springs. At Framilode, near springs there is nearly always an in-going stream of 1½ hours duration beginning about half an hour after HW Avonmouth, and at Gloucester, 12 miles farther up river, at springs there is usually an in-going stream for approximately 1 hour beginning two hours after HW Avonmouth. When there is no in-going stream the downstream flow is weaker during the normal in-going period than at other times.

2 **River Severn Bore,** usually occurs when the range of the tide at Avonmouth exceeds 13·5 m. It starts about 2 miles above Sharpness, but does not form a continuous undulation until it reaches Longney, 9 miles below Gloucester, where it rushes up the river with considerable noise and with a front of 1 to 1·5 m high. Under favourable conditions it can reach a height of 2 m and have a maximum rate of up to 13 kn. Opposing winds and high freshwater levels can considerably reduce the height.

3 The bore is highest about the fifth in-going stream after a full or new moon, and usually arrives at Minsterworth (51°51′N 2°19′W) about 45 minutes after HW Avonmouth and at Stonebench (51°50′N 2°18′W) about 15 minutes later.

4 In the centre of the river, unless obstructed by shoal banks, the wave is a simple undulation with a smooth unbroken surface.

It is not dangerous to boats afloat in the centre of the river, head on to the wave, but if they are inshore they are liable to be swamped or stove in as the wave breaks with violence along the river's banks.

Gloucester and Sharpness Canal

General information
4.305

1 The canal, which is no longer used by commercial shipping, is entered from Sharpness wet dock and leads to Gloucester wet dock, 16½ miles distant. There are no locks between the two docks.

The canal is spanned by several swing bridges; there is a vertical clearance limit of 32 m.

The minimum width of the canal is 10·4 m between the masonry piers of the narrowest bridge, but the average width is 26·2 m with a mean depth of 4·4 m.

2 For details of dimensions of vessels which can use the canal see 4.288.

Midway between Sharpness and Gloucester there is a dry dock for repairing small coastal and inland craft.

There are a number of industries on the banks of the canal, and also petroleum installations and large timber yards.

Canal Authority. British Waterways (4.282).

Gloucester Docks
4.306

1 Gloucester wet docks are entered from The Gloucester and Sharpness Canal, and have nearly 3050 m of quay. Depths in the wet docks are similar to those within the canal.

Facilities: two dry docks, largest 50 m in length and 10·7 m breadth; repairs to hull and machinery can be effected.

Supplies: oil fuel, if sufficient notice given; stores and provisions obtainable locally.

River Severn above Gloucester
4.307

1 The river Severn is canalised between Gloucester and Stourport and is used by commercial and pleasure craft.

The canal is entered from Gloucester wet docks through a lock which is 63·4 m long and 6·9 m wide.

Between Gloucester and Worcester, a distance of 30 miles, there are two locks and a minimum vertical clearance of 7 m. The limiting dimensions of craft which can use this section of the canal are: length 41 m, beam 6·4 m, draught 2·4 m.

2 **Worcester,** a town with a population of about 83 000, has ample quayage accommodation for large lighters and boats; there is also a dry dock for repairing boats.

The Worcester to Birmingham Canal joins the river Severn at Worcester.

3 Above Worcester vessels up to 150 tonnes can navigate to Stourport, a distance of approximately 12 miles, at which point commercial navigation ceases. The limiting dimensions of craft which can use this section of the canal are: length 27 m, beam 5·5 m and draught 1·2 m with a minimum vertical clearance of 6·1 m.

4 There is a lock at Stourport which gives access to the narrow gauge canals of the Midlands.

Canal Authority. British Waterways, Dock Office, Commercial Road, Gloucester, GL1 2EB

NOTES

Chapter 5 - South West Coast of Wales, including the Port of Milford Haven

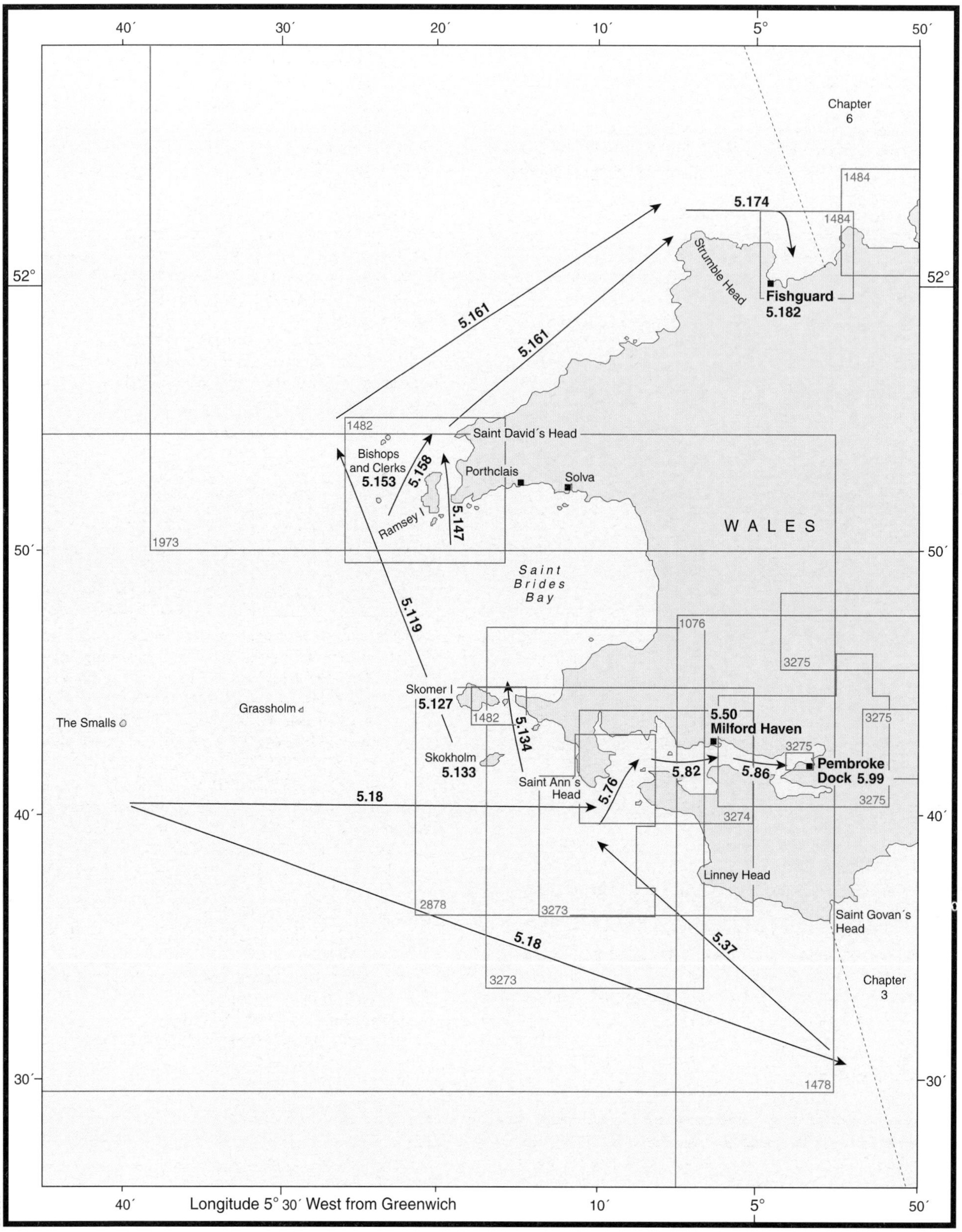

Chapter 6

1484

1484

5.174

Strumble Head

■ **Fishguard**
5.182

5.161

5.161

52°

1482

Saint David´s Head

Bishops
and Clerks
5.153

5.158

Porthclais

Solva

5.147

Ramsey I

1973

W A L E S

50´

*Saint
Brides
Bay*

5.119

1076

3275

Skomer I
5.127

1482

3275

The Smalls

Grassholm

5.134

5.50
Milford Haven

3275

Skokholm
5.133

Saint Ann´s
Head

5.76

5.82

5.86

**Pembroke
Dock 5.99**

3275

5.18

3274

40´

2878

3273

Linney Head

5.18

5.37

Saint Govan´s
Head

Chapter
3

3273

1478

30´

Longitude 5° 30´ West from Greenwich

CHAPTER 5

SOUTH-WEST COAST OF WALES INCLUDING THE PORT OF MILFORD HAVEN

GENERAL INFORMATION

Chart 1178
Scope of the chapter
5.1

1   This chapter covers the waters off the coast of SW Wales between Saint Govan's Head (51°36′N 4°55′W) and Fishguard (52°00′N 5°00′W) about 25 miles N. It includes descriptions of:

> Offshore routes W and S of The Smalls (51°43′N 5°40′W) and offshore dangers.
>
> The coastal routes, harbours and anchorages.

2   Approaches to Milford Haven and Port of Milford Haven.

> The chapter is divided into the following sections:
>
> Offshore Routes West and South of The Smalls (5.6).
>
> Saint Govan's Head to Saint David's Head (5.33).
>
> Saint David's Head to Fishguard Bay (5.161).

Topography
5.2

1   South-west Wales has a coastline consisting mainly of precipitous cliffs of moderate height, indented by several bays, the largest being Saint Bride's Bay (5.137).

Numerous islands and shoals lie off the coast. The hinterland is not particularly high, Carn Llidi (51°54′N 5°17′W) (5.126), a conical hill 179 m in height, being the highest ground.

2   The Smalls (51°43′N 5°40′W) is a group of low rocks marked by a lighthouse (5.14) about 15 miles offshore.

Milford Haven (51°41′N 5°08′W), the shore of which consists chiefly of bold cliffs of moderate height, is formed by the broad, deep outlet of the river Cleddau. The Haven affords excellent shelter and is accessible at all times.

Fishing
5.3

1   Trawlers may be encountered between June and October in the vicinity of Saint Govan's Head (51°36′N 4°55′W); they may also be encountered in Cardigan Bay, particularly in spring.

Inshore trawlers may be encountered at any time in Cardigan Bay in depths of 25 to 35 m. Scallop dredgers operate within these depths.

For details of types of fishing and nets in use, see *The Mariner's Handbook*.

Natural conditions
5.4

1   **Sea and Swell.** On the SW coast of Wales, there is always a ground swell setting in from the Atlantic Ocean, except when E winds have long prevailed. Heavy seas and strong winds can be experienced.

Tidal streams. The flow of water over the area dealt with in this chapter is largely determined by tidal forces. The S-going stream from Saint George's Channel turns E when S of The Smalls and thence sets E into the Bristol Channel; similarly the W-going stream from the Bristol Channel turns N and runs into Saint George's Channel. See 1.91 and 1.94.

2   There is very little difference between the times at which the streams begin at The Smalls and a position 5 miles S of Saint Govan's Head, but great changes occur in the times between the W side of Skomer Island and the mainland, and along the mainland coast S and E to Saint Govan's Head.

3   Near The Smalls the streams begin as follows, attaining a spring rate in each direction of 5 kn near the rocks, decreasing to 3 kn at a distance approximately 2 miles S, W and then N of them:

Interval from HW Milford Haven	*Direction*
+0515	S
−0045	N

For further information see the relevant charts and *Admiralty Tidal Stream Atlas — Irish Sea and Bristol Channel*.

4   **Tide races.** Owing to the exposed nature of the coastline and fast running water through constricted channels, tide races, which may be dangerous to small craft are particularly in evidence in the following areas:

> Around the islands of Skokholm (51°42′N 5°17′W) and Skomer (51°44′N 5°18′W).
>
> Around Grassholm (51°44′N 5°29′W).
>
> Between The Bishops and Clerks and Ramsey Island (51°52′N 5°20′W).

5   Pen Anglas (52°01′·5N 4°59′·5W).

Tide-rips which may be dangerous to small craft are particularly in evidence in the following areas:

> Saint Gowan Shoals (51°33′N 4°58′W).
>
> Between Crow Rock (51°36′·7N 5°03′·3W) and The Toes.
>
> Turbot Bank (51°37′N 5°08′W).

6   Between The Smalls (51°43′N 5°40′W) and Grassholm.

> Between The Bishops and Clerks (51°53′N 5°24′W) and Ramsey Island.
>
> Bais Bank (51°57′N 5°22′W).
>
> Strumble Bank (52°03′N 5°02′W).

Rescue
5.5

1   For details of rescue organisation and locations of assets see 1.60 and text under Rescue.

OFFSHORE ROUTES WEST AND SOUTH OF THE SMALLS

OFFSHORE ROUTE WEST OF THE SMALLS

General information

Charts 1178, 1410, 1478
Route
5.6

1   From the S end of the Off Smalls TSS (51°46′N 5°53′W) to a position in Saint George's Channel, NW of Strumble Head (52°02′N 5°04′W), the offshore route utilises the TSS (5.9) for ships passing W of The Smalls.

Topography
5.7

1   See 5.2.

Offshore fishing
5.8

1   Offshore trawlers may be encountered during the winter months SW of The Smalls as far as Labadie Bank (50°30′N 8°14′W) (see *Irish Coast Pilot*).

Traffic regulations
5.9

1   **Traffic separation scheme.** A TSS is established off The Smalls, centred 51°45′·7N 5°52′·5W. The general flow of traffic lies in the direction NNE-SSW. The scheme is IMO-adopted and Rule 10 of the *International Regulations for Preventing Collisions at Sea (1972)* applies. See 1.9.

2   **Movement of vessels.** Ships navigating in the approaches to Milford Haven should do so with caution as large deep-draught vessels with limited manoeuvrability may be encountered. Passing ships are advised to keep at least 5 miles off Middle Channel Rocks Lighthouse (51°40′·3N 5°09′·8W).

Deep-draught vessels (over 12 m) are advised not to anchor within a radius of 5 miles from Middle Channel Rocks Lighthouse (5.78).

Areas to be avoided
5.10

1   All vessels laden with oil, gas or noxious liquid substances and all other vessels of more than 500 gt, should avoid an area enclosing The Smalls (51°43′N 5°40′W) and Grassholm as shown on the charts.

Laden tankers should avoid the area between the TSS (5.9) and The Smalls.

A recommendation has been adopted by IMO that laden tankers over 10 000 gt should not use the channel between Grassholm and Skomer Island unless moving between Saint Bride's Bay and Milford Haven.

Historic wreck
5.11

1   A restricted area, 100 m radius, is centred on a historic wreck in position 51°43′·2N 5°40′·3W. For further details see 1.57 and *Annual Notice to Mariners Number 16.*

Rescue
5.12

1   All-weather and inshore lifeboats are stationed at Angle (51°41′N 5°05′W); an all-weather lifeboat is stationed at Porthstinian (51°53′N 5°18′W).

For details of rescue organisation see 1.60.

Tidal streams
5.13

1   Information on tidal streams for the area is given on the charts and also in *Admiralty Tidal Atlas — Irish Sea and Bristol Channel.*

Directions
(continued from 2.18)

Principal marks
5.14

1   **Landmark:**
Strumble Head (52°02′N 5°04′W) (5.169).
Major lights:
The Smalls Light (round granite tower, red lantern, 41 m in height, surmounted by a helicopter platform; racon). The light, which is shown throughout 24 hours, stands on the NW rock of the group (51°43′N 5°40′W). An auxiliary light is exhibited under the main light.

2   South Bishop Light (51°51′N 5°25′W) (5.123).
Strumble Head Light (52°02′N 5°04′W) (5.169).
Tuskar Rock Light (52°12′N 6°12′W) (see *Irish Coast Pilot*).

Other aids to navigation
5.15

1   **Racons:**
The Smalls Lighthouse (51°43′N 5°40′W).
South Bishop Lighthouse (51°51′N 5°25′W).
For further details see *Admiralty List of Radio Signals Volume 2.*

Passage
5.16

1   From the S end of the Off Smalls TSS (51°46′N 5°53′W) to a position in Saint George's Channel WNW of Strumble Head (52°02′N 5°04′W) the route leads NNE through the traffic lane, passing:
WNW of The Smalls (5.28) on which stands a light (5.14), thence:
WNW of South Bishop (51°51′N 5°25′W) (5.154), an islet on which stands a light (5.123), thence:

2   WNW of Strumble Head (52°02′N 5°04′W) (5.169), on which stands a light.
In the vicinity of The Smalls the set of the tidal stream (5.4) is an important factor to be considered.
(Directions continue for the offshore route W of Bardsey Island at 6.12; directions for the offshore and inshore routes S of The Smalls are given at 5.23)

The Smalls to the North Channel
5.17

1   A vessel within the traffic lanes W of The Smalls and bound towards the North Channel (see *Irish Coast Pilot*) is

The Smalls Lighthouse from S (5.14)

(Original dated 2001)

(Photograph - Air Images)

recommended to follow a route that leads approximately 80 miles N to a position E of Codling Lanby (53°03′N 5°41′W) and thence proceed as directed in the *Irish Coast Pilot* to the North Channel.

OFFSHORE AND INSHORE ROUTES SOUTH OF THE SMALLS

General information

Charts 1178, 1410, 1478
Routes
5.18

1   Approaching from the S end of the S bound traffic lane W of The Smalls (51°43′N 5°40′W) to the approaches to Milford Haven, the route leads E, passing S of The Smalls and S of an area to be avoided (5.10).

Vessels proceeding E into the Bristol Channel should follow the above route, keeping farther offshore and proceeding directly to a position S of Saint Gowan Light Buoy (S cardinal) (51°32′N 5°00′W), about 38 miles ESE.

Topography
5.19

1   See 5.2.

Fishing
5.20

1   See 5.8.

Rescue
5.21

1   All-weather and inshore lifeboats are stationed at Angle (51°41′N 5°05′W).

For details of rescue organisation see 1.60.

Tidal streams
5.22

1   Information on tidal streams is given on the charts and in *Admiralty Tidal Stream Atlas — Irish Sea and Bristol Channel*.

Directions

Principal marks
5.23

1   **Landmarks**:
    Skomer Island (51°44′N 5°18′W) (5.127).
    Old Lighthouse (Tower) (51°41′N 5°10′W) (5.74).
    Warren Church (Spire) (51°38′N 4°59′W) (5.43).
    Major lights:
    South Bishop Light (51°51′N 5°25′W) (5.123).
    The Smalls Light (51°43′N 5°40′W) (5.14).
    Skokholm Island Light (51°42′N 5°17′W) (5.123).
    Saint Ann's Head Light (51°41′N 5°10′W) (5.74).

Other aids to navigation
5.24

1   **Racons:**

Saint Gowan Light Buoy (51°32′N 5°00′W).

The Smalls Lighthouse (51°43′N 5°40′W).

For further details see *Admiralty List of Radio Signals Volume 2.*

Passage
5.25

1   Approaching from the N and from a position at the S end of the traffic lanes W of The Smalls (51°43′N 5°40′W), the route leads about 27 miles E towards the entrance to Milford Haven, passing:

    S of The Smalls (5.28), from where a light (5.14) is exhibited, thence:

    S of the dangers between The Smalls and Grassholm (51°44′N 5°29′W), thence:

2   S of Grassholm (5.30), with tide-rips extending SE, thence:

    S of Skokholm Island (51°42′N 5°17′W) (5.133), on which stands a light (5.123).

At night the Smalls Auxiliary Light (5.14) covers the dangers between The Smalls and Grassholm.

(Directions for entry to Milford Haven are given at 5.74)

Charts 1178, 1478
5.26

1   Vessels proceeding E into the Bristol Channel should follow the above route, keeping farther offshore and proceeding direct to a position S of Saint Govan's Head (51°36′N 4°55′W), passing:

    SSW of Saint Ann's Head (51°41′N 5°10′W) (5.52) on which stands a light (5.74); an old lighthouse (5.74) stands 1 cable NW of the light, thence:

    SSW of Linney Head (51°37′N 5°04′W) (5.45).

    SSW of Saint Gowan Light Buoy (51°31′·9N 4°59′·8W).

Thence to a position SSW of Saint Govan's Head.

(Directions continue E for the coastal route at 3.64)

Offshore Islands

Chart 1478
Areas to be avoided
5.27

1   See 5.10.

The Smalls
5.28

1   The Smalls (51°43′N 5°40′W), a group of low rocks, lie 13 miles W of Skomer Island (5.127).

North-west Rock, on which stands a light (5.14), is the largest of the group and is ¾ cable in length.

South-west Rock, lies 3 cables SW of the light, at the SW end of the group.

East Rock, lies 2½ cables E of the light; a second rock lies 1 cable W of East Rock.

2   North-east Rock, lies 2 cables N of the light; it is steep-to on its N side.

With the exception of two other rocks which lie close E of the light all the rocks of this group are covered at HW.

Apart from SW Rock there are no outlying dangers W of the light.

Tidal streams W of The Smalls, see 5.4; between The Smalls and Grassholm, see 5.31.

3   **Landing place** on the SE side of the lighthouse receives some protection from the S ledge of rocks which form a

cove at LW, but when the tide is up the water flows through.

A safe landing can seldom be effected.

Helicopter landing, see 5.14.

Hats and Barrels
5.29

1   Hats is the rocky ground 2 miles E of The Smalls; it has a patch with a least depth of 2·1 m, and numerous other shoal heads lying NE.

Barrels is the rocky ground which lies 4¼ miles ESE of The Smalls; two drying rocks lie near its N end and a 3·7 m patch lies 3½ cables S of these rocks.

2   There is a disused explosives dumping ground between Hats and Barrels and foul ground extends 1¼ miles N from the latter.

Hats and Barrels are generally marked by strong tide-rips and the sea breaks over them in bad weather.

Local knowledge is required in this vicinity.

Grassholm
5.30

1   Grassholm, (51°44′N 5°29′W), an island 45 m in height, lies 7 miles E of The Smalls. It has a rugged coast but landing may be effected in fine weather, the place selected being dependent on wind and tide. The island is a bird reserve and as such visiting is not permitted; see 1.58.

2   Mersey Rock lies ½ cable off the NE side of the island, and several rocks lie the same distance off the S and SW part of the island; beyond this distance there are no dangers.

A tongue of foul ground, with a least depth of 20 m, extends 1½ miles SE from the island and causes tide-rips.

Natural conditions
5.31

1   **Tidal streams.** The streams, which attain a maximum spring rate in each direction of 5 kn between The Smalls and Grassholm, are assumed to change regularly, beginning as follows:

Position	Interval from HW Milford Haven	Direction
Between The Smalls and Hats	+0505 −0055	S N
Between Hats and Barrels	+0450 −0115	S N
Between Barrels and Grassholm	+0440 −0135	S N

3   **Tide race.** The tidal streams set directly on to Grassholm from N and S causing a considerable race off both its ends, and a strong eddy or indraught on the opposite side to that on which the tide is setting, for a distance of 5 cables from the island.

Channels
5.32

1   The channel between The Smalls and Hats is 1¼ miles wide and, provided East Rock and Hats are indicated by breakers, there is little danger.

The channel between Hats and Barrels is 2 miles wide and may be taken when they are indicated by breakers.

These two channels are not recommended without local knowledge owing to lack of good leading marks and to the strength of the tidal streams through them.

The channel between Barrels and Grassholm is 2½ miles wide and presents no dangers.

SAINT GOVAN'S HEAD TO SAINT DAVID'S HEAD

GENERAL INFORMATION

Charts 1178, 1478
Area covered
5.33

1   In this section are described the coastal routes, harbours and anchorages between Saint Govan's Head (51°36′N 4°55′W) and Saint David's Head, about 23½ miles NW, including Saint Bride's Bay, Jack Sound, Skomer, Skokholm and Grassholm Islands, Ramsey Island and Sound, and The Bishops and Clerks.

Also described is The Port of Milford Haven, including the upper reaches of the river Cleddau.

2   It is arranged as follows:

Saint Govan's Head to Milford Haven Approaches (5.37).
Port of Milford Haven (5.50).
Milford Haven to Saint David's Head (5.119).

Topography
5.34

1   See 5.2.

Fishing
5.35

1   Inshore trawlers may be encountered during the summer months in the vicinity of Saint Govan's Head (51°36′N 4°55′W).

Nature reserves
5.36

1   Grassholm (51°44′N 5°29′W), bird reserve.
Skomer Island (51°44′N 5°18′W), bird and marine reserve.
Gateholm Island (51°43′N 5°14′W), marine reserve.
Skokholm Island (51°42′N 5°16′W), bird reserve.
Jack Sound (51°44′N 5°15′W), marine reserve.
Ramsey Island (51°52′N 5°20′W), bird reserve.
Martin's Haven (51°44′·2N 5°14′·7W), marine reserve.
For further information see Protection of Wildlife (1.58).

SAINT GOVAN'S HEAD TO MILFORD HAVEN APPROACHES

General information

Charts 1076, 1478, 2878
Route
5.37

1   The coastal route from the vicinity of Saint Govan's Head (51°36′N 4°55′W) to the approaches to Milford Haven, about 14 miles NW, leads S of Saint Gowan Light Buoy (51°31′·9N 4°59′·8W) and W of Turbot Bank Light Buoy (51°37′·4N 5°10′·1W).

2   Passing vessels are advised to keep at least 5½ miles seaward of Middle Channel Rocks Lighthouse (51°40′·3N 5°09′·8W) (5.78), outside the port limits of Port of Milford Haven. Alternatively contact Milford Haven Port Control to obtain advice on movement of shipping in and out of the Port of Milford Haven.

See *Admiralty List of Radio Signals Volume 6(1)* and 5.63.

Topography
5.38

1   The coast between Saint Govan's Head and Linney Head (51°37′N 5°04′W) (5.45), 5 miles W, consists of bold cliffs indented by deep fissures and chasms, with insular masses of cliffs, locally known as stacks, detached only a few metres from the cliff face.

Saddle Head is the W point of a promontory of which Saint Govan's Head is the E point. Bullslaughter Bay and Flimston Bay, separated by Moody Nose (51°36′·5N 4°59′·0W), have boulder beaches, and precipitous cliffs.

2   Freshwater West, a bay, entered between Linney Head and Studdock Point, 4 miles NW, consists of a sandy foreshore on the E side with rocky outcrops at its centre, extending 1¾ miles N from The Pole, a drying reef, which lies in the SE part of the bay.

The N part consists of a coastline with bold cliffs indented by several small inlets which extends WNW towards Studdock Point.

Firing practice area
5.39

1   Castlemartin Range (51°37′N 5°00′W). For further information on practice areas see 1.15 and *Annual Notice to Mariners Number 5*.

Pilotage
5.40

1   For information on Milford Haven pilotage services and pilot boarding positions, see 5.68.

Rescue
5.41

1   All-weather and inshore lifeboats are stationed at Angle (51°41′N 5°05′W) and Tenby (51°40′N 4°42′W). The lifeboat slipway at Angle is situated on the S side of Milford Haven opposite South Hook LNG Terminal.

For details of rescue organisation see 1.60.

Tidal streams
5.42

1   Tidal streams begin as follows at the positions indicated:

Position	Interval from HW Milford Haven	Direction
Saint Govan's Head (2 miles off)	+0400 −0225	ENE WSW

The maximum spring rate in each direction is 3 kn. Closer inshore the stream runs in the direction of the coast and begins ½ hour later.

Saint Govan's Head to Crow Rock	+0400 −0325	SE NW

2   The maximum spring rate in each direction is 4 kn. The SE-going stream runs for 5 hours after which an eddy sets NW.

Turbot Bank	+0400 −0225	SE NW

The maximum spring rate in each direction is 2½ kn.

For spring rates in the vicinity of Saint Gowan Light Buoy (5.45), see information on Charts 1478 and 1076.

3   In Freshwater West (5.38) there is a nearly continuous SSE-going stream which turns S past Linney Head and thence SE or NW according to the direction of the stream off Crow Rock. During the greater part of the NNW-going stream an eddy sets SSE.

See also *Admiralty Tidal Stream Atlas — Irish Sea and the Bristol Channel.*

Directions

Principal marks
5.43

1   **Landmarks:**

Saint Govan's Head (51°36′N 4°55′W), a prominent, bare, perpendicular limestone cliff, 37 m high, with almost level land behind it. The old chapel and well of Saint Govan stand on a shelf, halfway up the cliff, 5 cables W of the head.

Warren Church (Spire) (51°38′N 4°59′W).

Old lighthouse (Tower) (51°41′N 5°10′W) (5.74).

Major lights:

Saint Ann's Head Light (51°41′N 5°10′W) (5.74).

The Smalls Light (51°43′N 5°40′W) (5.14).

Skokholm Island Light (51°42′N 5°17′W) (5.123).

Other aid to navigation
5.44

1   **Racon:**

Saint Gowan Light Buoy (51°32′N 5°00′W).

For further details see *Admiralty List of Radio Signals Volume 2.*

Chart 1478
Passage
5.45

1   From the vicinity of Saint Govan's Head (51°36′N 4°55′W), the coastal route S of Saint Gowan Light Buoy leads about 14 miles NW to the approaches to Milford Haven, passing (with positions from Saint Govan's Head):

S then SW of Saint Gowan Light Buoy (S cardinal), which is moored 7½ cables SSW of the S extremity of Saint Gowan Shoals (3½ miles SW) consisting of several patches, the outermost of which has a depth of 6·7 m over it; a 6·4 m patch lies 1½ miles NE of the outer patch. Thence:

2   SW of Linney Head (5½ miles WNW), dark perpendicular cliffs and flat summit, with Linney Rock, which dries, lying close W off the headland. Crow Rock, which dries and is surmounted by the ruins of a pyramidal beacon, lies 5 cables S. Thence:

3   SW of an ODAS light buoy (special) (8½ miles W), thence:

SW of Turbot Bank Light Buoy (W cardinal) (9¼ miles W), which is moored 4½ cables SW of the N end of Turbot Bank (see Cautions 5.46).

Clearing bearing. The alignment (318°) of the E point of Skokholm Island with the W point of Skomer Island

(51°44′N 5°18′W) passes close W of the W edge of Turbot Bank.

Cautions
5.46

1   There are tide-rips over the uneven ground of Saint Gowan Shoals, which break in heavy weather and which may be dangerous to small craft.

Turbot Bank, with a least depth 9·6 m, lies 2½ miles W of Linney Head (51°37′N 5°04′W), and near the approach to Milford Haven. Bad weather causes a short and dangerous sea over the bank, and there are ripples or tide-rips especially with the wind blowing against the tidal stream.

Useful mark
5.47

1   Saint Twynnells Church (tower) (51°38′·4N 4°57′·9W). *(Directions continue at 5.123; directions for entry into Milford Haven are given at 5.74)*

Anchorages

Charts 2878, 3274
5.48

1   Fair shelter may be obtained in offshore winds in Freshwater West (51°39′N 5°05′W) (5.38), in depths of not less than 16·5 m; closer inshore the bottom is foul.

For details of anchorages in Milford Haven and its approaches see 5.66 and 5.90.

Crow Sound
5.49

1   Crow Sound (51°37′N 5°03′W) is bound on its N side by the coast between Linney Head (51°37′N 5°04′W) and Pen-y-holt Stack, standing on foul ground fronting the coast 7¾ cables ESE, and on its S side by Crow Rock (51°36′·7N 5°03′·3W), which dries. Several straggling below-water rocks lie as follows (with positions from Crow Rock): N.W. Toe (2¼ cables NW), E. Toe (¾ cable E) and S.E. Toe (5½ cables ESE). Tide-rips form in the vicinity of N.W. and S.E. Toe. The sound has a least width of 2 cables and a least charted depth of 6·6 m.

PORT OF MILFORD HAVEN

General information

Charts 2878, 3273, 3274, 3275
Position
5.50

1   Milford Haven (51°42′N 5°02′W), a large sheltered deep-water inlet, cuts deep in to the Pembrokeshire coast from its entrance between Saint Ann's Head (51°41′N 5°10′W) and Sheep Island (2 miles ESE).

NNW   N   NNE   NE   ENE

St. Anne's Head   West Blockhouse Point   Thorn Island   East Blockhouse Point   Sheep Island

Milford Haven from SW (5.50)

(Photograph - Air Images)   *(Original dated 2001)*

Function
5.51
1   The Port of Milford Haven, which includes Pembroke Port, consists principally of oil and LNG terminals and associated refineries.

A container and general cargo terminal operates at Pembroke Dock, together with a RoRo ferry terminal whose service links the area with the Republic of Ireland.

Milford Docks is a base for deep-sea trawlers.

Topography
5.52
1   Milford Haven consists of a deep-water fairway edged by numerous small and medium sized bays, many of which are backed by drying mud and/or sand flats. The waterway itself, one of the finest natural harbours in the world, meanders for over 24 miles into the heart of pastoral Pembrokeshire. Much of the river Cleddau, with its many tributary creeks at the E end of the waterway, passes through dense woodland.

2   Saint Ann's Head, a bold promontory, 37 m high, at the W entrance, projects from a comparatively flat background but is easily identified from a considerable distance; the steep cliff face of the promontory is of a distinctive reddish-brown colour.

3   West Angle Bay, situated on the E side of the entrance, is backed by rocky ledges which extend up to 1 cable offshore.

Angle Bay (51°41′N 5°04′W), on the S shore, entered between Angle Point and Sawdern Point is encumbered by drying mud flats with rocky ledges extending up to 2 cables offshore.

4   Pennar Gut (51°41′N 4°58′W), entered through a narrow passage between West Pennar Point and Pennar Point on the S shore of the haven, is a large enclosed area of drying mud flats. The river Pembroke, flows through Pennar Gut and into the haven.

Dale Flats, on the N shore, is entered between Musselwick Point (51°42′·8N 5°09′·4W) and Black Rock, 4 cables WSW and comprises an area of drying mud and stones.

Port limits
5.53
1   The seaward limits, about 4 miles S and W of the entrance, are shown on Chart 2878. The inshore limits include all tidal waters.

Approach and entry
5.54
1   The harbour is entered through West Channel (5.78), the main deep water approach channel, or East Channel (5.80). At their convergence a single dredged channel leads towards the various berthing areas. The W and combined channels are marked by leading lights and light buoys.

Caution. Vessels navigating in the approaches to Milford Haven should do so with extreme caution, as deep-draught vessels with limited manoeuvrability may be encountered. See 5.10.

Traffic
5.55
1   In 2007 3058 vessels visited the port totalling 51 400 000 gt.

Port Authority
5.56
1   Milford Haven Port Authority, P.O. Box 14, Gorsewood Drive, Milford Haven, Pembrokeshire SA73 3ER.

Web site: www.mhpa.co.uk

E-mail: enquiries@mhpa.co.uk

The Port Authority has its offices at Hubberston Point (5.63) and is represented by a Chief Executive.

Navigational matters should be addressed to the Harbour Master.

For Port Authority details of Pembroke Port see 5.100.

Limiting conditions
Controlling depths
5.57
1   Depth in the West Channel is 16·2 m (2006) and in the main channel it is 16·3 m (2006).

For the latest information on the controlling depths, the Port Authorities should be consulted.

Under-keel clearance
5.58
1   The minimum under-keel clearance allowed is 10% of a vessel's deepest draught reading. However, it should be noted that heavy swell may be experienced until inside Saint Ann's Head and in adverse conditions as far as Angle Light Buoy. As a general rule, the under-keel clearance for deep-draught vessels on the oil terminals is 1 m, but should not be less than 5% of the vessel's draught.

Tidal levels
5.59
1   Mean spring range about 6·3 m, mean neap range about 2·7 m. It is reported that the spring range is occasionally as high as 7·6 m. See *Admiralty Tide Tables*.

Density of water
5.60
1   The density is 1·026 g/cm^3 within the haven.

Maximum size of vessel handled
5.61
1   VLCCs in laden condition up to 20 m draught can be accommodated on most HWs, but for vessels of more than 18·3 m draught special arrangements must be made with the Port Authority.

Vessels up to 168 m LOA can be handled at Pembroke Port.

Local weather
5.62
1   Milford Haven is relatively free of fog but strong winds from any quarter do occur more frequently than in many other British ports.

During or after SW or W gales, a heavy ground swell may be experienced within the haven as far as the berths on South Hook LNG Terminal (5.94), making steering difficult; vessels may yaw up to 20°.

2   At the onset of a gale, it may be prudent for vessels at anchor in the W part of the haven to leave their anchorage and proceed to the open sea, returning when the weather has moderated.

Arrival information
Port operations
5.63
1   Port Control (51°42′·5N 5°03′·2W), situated at Hubberston, call sign: Milford Haven Port Control,

maintains a continuous visual, radar and radio watch. A patrol launch equipped with radar and radio, and at night exhibiting a blue light, works in conjunction with Port Control.

The requirements of the Harbour Master are transmitted by Port Control, which also co-ordinates matters connected with the pilotage service.

2   Information relative to shipping movements, weather and tides can be obtained by vessels approaching, or within, the port.

Requests for berths at buoys or at anchorages should be made to Port Control.

Notices to Mariners, details of any restrictions, passage planning assistance and other information can be accessed on the Port Authority's website: www.mpha.co.uk

Vessel traffic service
5.64

1   A VTS scheme, with full radar surveillance, is maintained for the control of shipping; for details, and list of reporting points, see *Admiralty List of Radio Signals Volume 6(1)*.

The scheme, which is mandatory for all vessels over 20 m in length, operates from Port Control.

Positions of reporting points are shown on the charts.

Remotely controlled radars of the surveillance system are situated at Saint Ann's Head, Great Castle Head, Port Control, Popton Point (51°41'·6N 5°03'·1W) and Patrick's Hill (51°41'·5N 4°57'·5W).

Notice of ETA required
5.65

1   Vessels must send their ETA to Port Control at least 12 hours prior to arrival, or on leaving their last port of call, whichever is the later. Any subsequent amendments must be sent at least 2 hours before arrival.

ETA must be confirmed on VHF when within 20-30 miles of Saint Ann's Head. See also 5.68 and 5.69.

Outer anchorages
5.66

1   Deep draught vessels (more than 12 m) are advised not to anchor within a radius of 5 miles from Middle Channel Rocks Lighthouse (5.78).

Submarine cables and pipelines
5.67

1   There are a great number of disused cables lying on the seabed in the W part of the harbour, the locations of which are best seen on the chart.

An abandoned pipeline extends SSW from the N shore 1½ cables E of Hakin Point (51°42'·5N 5°02'·6W).

2   An outfall which extends 2½ cables SSW from a position on the N shore 1 cable E of Hakin Point is marked at its head by a light buoy (special). A short outfall, close W, is marked by a beacon.

An outfall which lies along the W edge of Carr Rocks (51°41'·9N 4°57'·6W) (5.86), extends 2½ cables NNW from the W side of Pembroke Dock.

Pilotage
5.68

1   Milford Haven Port Authority provides the pilotage for the port of Milford Haven. The pilotage area lies within the confines of the port limits (5.53).

Pilotage is compulsory within the haven for all vessels of 50 m LOA or greater, except HM Ships, vessels moving from one berth to another within a dock and vessels exempted by law.

Accurate times of arrival are required as the pilot vessels do not cruise continuously on station.

2   Vessels should remain at least 5 miles off Saint Ann's Head until contact with the pilot vessel has been established.

Pilots board about 4½ miles SSW of St Ann's Head.

Pilot vessels, green hulls, white superstructures with "Pilot" painted in black are equipped with radar and VHF.

There is a mooring buoy for the use of pilot vessels in Castlebeach Bay, 3 cables SSW of Dale Point (51°42'N 5°09'W).

For further details on pilotage, see *Admiralty List of Radio Signals Volume 6(1)*.

Tugs
5.69

1   There are several tugs which can handle the largest tankers; all these tugs are equipped for fire fighting. Vessels bound for the oil terminals secure tugs on passing Angle Light Buoy (5.80); speed should be adjusted to ensure that all tugs are secured by the time South Hook Light Buoy (5.82) is reached.

Regulations concerning entry
5.70

1   **Entry.** Regulations for Milford Haven will be found in *Entry and Departure Guidlines for Vessels*, published by Milford Haven Port Authority.

It is important to maintain continuous VHF contact with Port Control when within one hour's steaming of Saint Ann's Head, for anchoring or berthing details, and at all times when within the haven and not secured alongside.

2   Vessels should include with their ETA report their pilotage requirement, draught, cargo, PEC number if applicable, previous port of call and any circumstances which may affect the seaworthiness or ability to manoeuvre of the vessel. Any amendment to this information should immediately, and in any case at least 2 hours before arrival, be reported to Port Control.

Vessels towing must report full details of their tow and request permission to enter.

3   **Restricted visibility.** Vessels of 30 000 dwt or greater and all LNG vessels shall not enter or move within the haven if visibility is less than 1 mile.

Vessels less than 30 000 dwt carrying a dangerous substance or polluting cargo in bulk shall not enter or move within the haven if visibility is less than 5 cables.

Vessels greater than 20 m LOA shall not enter or move within the haven if visibility is less than 1 cable.

4   **Escorting** by tugs is compulsory for all loaded tankers of 50 000 dwt or more and certain loaded vessels between 25 000 dwt and 50 000 dwt carrying persistent oil cargo at the discretion of the Harbour Master.

5   **Entry restrictions for large vessels.** VLCCs may enter only between 1½ hours before HW and HW Milford Haven. VLCCs of less than 275 m in length may enter

between 4 hours before and 3 hours after HW Milford Haven at the discretion of the pilot, subject to considerations of underkeel clearance, weather and tidal stream. A VLCC is defined as 65 000 gt and above.

6   **Vessels constrained by their draught.** Within the port limits a vessel with a draught of 12 m or greater should exhibit the shape and lights, and in restricted visibility should make the appropriate sound signal, for a vessel constrained by her draught.

Such a vessel is particularly restricted when in the vicinity of Angle Light Buoy (5.80).

LNG carriers proceeding to South Hook or Dragon LNG Terminals will have a 1 mile exclusion zone, enforced by a patrol boat, ahead and astern when within the buoyed channel.

7   **Dangerous goods.** Masters of vessels carrying dangerous substances are required to send a Schedule 2 Report, in accordance with the *Dangerous Substances in Harbour Areas (DSHA) Regulations 1987*, to Port Control and the berth operator at least 24 hours prior to arrival by one of the following methods:

8   Via the vessel's agent.
      Telephone, followed by fax.
      Fax.
      VHF, followed by fax or email.

Navigation. The following is an extract from Milford Haven Byelaws:

No unauthorised vessel shall enter or navigate within 100 metres of a petroleum berth or petroleum ship moored thereto.

Harbour

Charts 3273, 3274, 3275
General layout
5.71

1   The haven is entered between Saint Ann's Head and Sheep Island, nearly 2 miles ESE. West Channel and East Channel, the two waterways leading into the haven, merge at Angle Light Buoy to form a through channel as far as Cleddau Bridge, nearly 8 miles E. Beyond the bridge the river Cleddau winds its way to the town of Haverfordwest, 6 miles NNE, and is mostly used by small craft.

2   The major part of the haven consists of oil terminals and their respective jetties situated on both N and S sides. In the W part, within the entrance, lie the main anchorages of Dale Roads, Sandy Haven and Stack.

Milford Docks, which lie on the N side of the haven close SW of the town, consist of a wet dock which is entered through a lock (5.98), and a dry dock which is entered from the wet dock. Within the SE corner of the wet dock there is a marina.

3   The Port Control buildings and jetty at Hubberston (5.63) lie 5 cables W of the entrance to Milford Docks.

Newton Noyes Pier (5.102), now disused, lies 1 mile ESE of the docks.

In the E part of the harbour, on the S side, lie Pembroke Dock, Port of Pembroke and a RoRo ferry terminal.

Natural conditions
5.72

1   Across the entrance to Milford Haven the streams set approximately at right angles to the line of approach; within the entrance they set nearly parallel to the channel. There is often a confused sea off the entrance where the streams meet.

2   The times at which these streams begin, differ appreciably from the times of the streams W of Saint Ann's Head (see 5.122), and are as follows in the locality indicated:

Position	Interval from HW Milford Haven	Direction
One mile outside the entrance	+0455	E
	−0125	W

3   The maximum spring rate in each direction is 2¼ kn.

In the entrance	−0555	In-going
	+0030	Out-going

The maximum spring in-going rate is 1½ kn and out-going is 1¾ kn.

Tidal streams within the haven set in the direction of the deep-water channel as far as Wear Point (51°42′N 4°59′W). In the reach above Wear Point the in-going stream is deflected to the N side of the channel by Carr Spit (51°42′·0N 4°57′·8W).

4   In Pembroke Reach the in-going stream runs principally in the channel N of Dockyard Bank; it is weak and irregular in the channel S of this bank, in which it attains a spring rate of ½ kn. The out-going stream runs strongly in the channel S of Dockyard Bank, attaining a spring rate of 2¼ kn. It is weak on the S side of the channel, N of the bank; in the N part of the latter channel an eddy runs strongly during the out-going stream.

5   For details of the tidal streams within the haven see information on the charts and Tidal Stream Atlas available from the Port Authority.

Tidal height. There is an automatic height of tide recording gauge situated at Port Control (5.63).

Swinging areas
5.73

1   A swinging area, primarily for the manoeuvring of large LNG carriers, is established immediately W of South Hook LNG Terminal (51°42′N 5°05′W). The E and W limits of the area are indicated by Qatar Light Buoy (safe water) and South Hook Light Buoy (S cardinal) respectively. The S limit of the area is marked by S1 and S3 Light Buoys (starboard hand) and the N limit by S2 and S4 Light Buoys (port hand).

2   To facilitate the swinging of large tankers in a part-laden state, or in ballast, a swinging area 5¾ cables long and 3¼ cables wide, as shown on the chart, is situated off the Chevron Terminal; the N limit with a control depth of 9·8 m, is marked by Milford Shelf and Cunjic Light Buoys (port hand). Deeper water lies S of the line indicated by the light beacons at Newton Noyes (5.82).

A further swinging area lies off Semlogistics Terminal; see 5.85.

Directions for entering harbour

Principal marks
5.74

1   **Landmarks:**
      Old Lighthouse standing on Saint Ann's Head (51°41′N 5°10′W).
      Fort (51°41′·5N 5°07′·1W) standing on Thorn Island and now used as a hotel.
      Fort (51°42′·2N 5°05′·5W) standing on Stack Rock.
      Chimneys (51°43′·3N 5°01′·8W).
2   Chimneys (51°42′·5N 4°59′·2W), three standing close together within the Semlogistics Refinery.
      Fire station (51°41′·3N 4°56′·5W).

Saint Ann's Head from SE (5.74)

(Photograph - Air Images)

(Original dated 2001)

Major light:

Saint Ann's Head Light (white octagonal tower, 13 m in height) (51°41′N 5°10′W).

Other aids to navigation
5.75

1 **Racons:**

West Blockhouse Front Middle Leading Light Beacon (51°41′·3N 5°09′·5W).

Watwick Point Rear Leading Light Beacon (51°41′·8N 5°09′·2W).

Charts 2878, 3274

Directions for deep-draught vessels
5.76

1 Vessels with a draught of 14·5 m or greater enter harbour through the West Channel (51°40′·0N 5°10′·4W) and normally with a NW-going stream. Under these conditions vessels will be heading about 040° to keep the outer leading lights (5.77) in line bearing 022½°, and will thus be on the right heading for West Channel Leading Lights (5.78) on passing Mid Channel Rocks Light Buoy.

Approach to West Channel
5.77

1 From a position W of Turbot Bank, and in the vicinity of the pilot boarding area (5.68), the route leads NNE.

Outer Leading Lights:

Front light (black rectangular daymark, white stripe, on white concrete tower; 13 m in height) (51°41′·3N 5°09′·6W) on West Blockhouse Point.

2 Rear light (black rectangular daymark, white stripe; 50 m in height) (5 cables NNE of front light) on Watwick Point.

The alignment (022½°) of these lights leads into the centre of the entrance to West Channel, between Saint Ann's and Mid Channel Rocks Light Buoys.

3 Lights (black diamond-shaped daymarks on white concrete towers, 11 and 15 m in height), are situated close NW and SE respectively, of the front leading light. The NW of these lights in line with the rear leading light gives an alignment of 023¾°; the SE of these lights in line with the rear light gives an alignment of 021¼°. These two sets of transit lights help guide the mariner when approaching the West Channel entrance as to the available width of channel.

4 The leading lights are also fitted with high intensity lights for use in daylight in reduced visibility; they will be exhibited on request to Port Control (5.63) at any time.

Small vessels may enter at night keeping in the white sector of West Blockhouse Point Light between the bearings 020° and 036° until the entrance light buoys are passed but it is preferable to keep on the alignment of the leading lights.

5 **Caution.** When West Channel is in use by deep-draught ships, East Channel approach (5.79) should be used by ships of appropriate draught.

West Channel
5.78

1 West Channel, with a minimum depth of 16·2 m (2006), is the main deep-water channel into the harbour. It is separated from East Channel by several detached rocky patches.

Outer Leading Lights (022½°)   *Bridge view*

West Blockhouse Point and Watwick Point beacons from SSW (5.77)

(Original dated 2001)

(Main Photograph - Air Images. Inset - Milford Haven Port Authority)

2   Middle Channel Rocks, with a least charted depth of 5·1 m, together with The Row's Rocks, close E and Chapel Rocks with a least charted depth of 3·0 m farther N lie approximately mid-way between the entrance points of Milford Haven; they all lie within the red sector (285°–332°) of Saint Ann's Light and the red sector (250°–020°) of West Blockhouse Point Light (51°41'·3N 5°09'·5W).

Middle Channel Rocks Light (black round metal tower), 6½ cables SSE of Saint Ann's Head, stands near the W end of Middle Channel Rocks.

3   **Inner Leading Lights and PEL.** From its entrance between Saint Ann's Light Buoy (port hand), which is moored SSE of Saint Ann's Shoal extending S and SW from Saint Ann's Head, and Mid Channel Rocks Light Buoy (W cardinal) (2½ cables E), the channel is indicated by leading lights and a PEL. The PEL, which is intended to assist safe passage on a line of bearing 039¾°, is collocated with the front leading light (see below) on Great Castle Head. It may be obscured when used in conjunction with the front leading light.

4   **Leading lights:**
> Front light (white square tower, black stripe, 5 m in height) (51°42'·7N 5°07'·1W) on Great Castle Head.
> Rear light (white round concrete tower, black stripe, white rectangular topmark, 26 m in height)

(5 cables NE of the front light) on Little Castle Head.

5   The leading lights are fitted with high intensity lights for use in daylight in reduced visibility; they will be exhibited on request to Port Control (5.63) at any time.

The alignment (039¾°) of these lights leads 2 miles NE through West Channel passing (with positions from Saint Ann's Head Light (51°40'·9N 5°10'·4W)):
> NW of Middle Channel Rocks Light (6¾ cables SSE), thence:
6   > SE of Saint Ann's Head from where a light (5.74) is exhibited and on which stands an old lighthouse 1 cable NW of the light, thence:
> SE of Mill Bay Light Buoy (port hand) (6¼ cables ENE) which marks a shallow patch at the entrance to Mill Bay, thence:
> SE of West Blockhouse Point (7¼ cables NE) from where a light is exhibited and on which stand leading light beacons (5.77). Halftide Rock extends 100 m SE from the point. Thence:
7   > SE of Watwick Point (1¼ miles NE) on which stands a leading light beacon (5.77), thence:
> NW and N of Angle Light buoy (N cardinal) (1½ miles ENE). A port entry sector light, centred on the 040° lead, is exhibited on request to Port Control. It is not to be used in conjunction with the front daylight leading light.

Inner leading lights (039¾°)

Great Castle Head and Little Castle Head from SW (5.78)

(Original dated 2001)

(Photograph - Air Images)

8   **Caution.** At night care should be taken to keep in the white sector of West Blockhouse Point Light (5.77), between the bearings 220° and 250°, during the turn off Angle Light Buoy.

(Directions continue at 5.82)

Approach to East Channel
5.79

1   From a position W of Turbot Bank, the route leads NE to the entrance to East Channel which lies between Sheep Light Buoy and Row's Rocks Light Buoy.

There is an experimental light–buoy (special, 18 m in height) moored in position 51°38'·2N 5°09'·0W.

Clearing bearing. The alignment (025°) of Rat Island (51°40'·9N 5°07'·5W) with Thorn Island Fort (7 cables NNE) (5.74) passes NW of Turbot Bank.

East Channel
5.80

1   East Channel, with a minimum depth of 9·6 m. It is entered between Sheep Light Buoy (starboard hand) (51°40'N 5°08'W) which marks the SW edge of Sheep Rock with a least depth of 6 m over it, and Row's Rocks Light Buoy (port hand) (51°40'N 5°09'W), which marks the SE edge of The Row's Rocks (5.78). The channel, which has no leading marks, runs NNE for 7½ cables before turning N to join the main channel, passing (with positions from East Blockhouse Point (51°40'·9N 5°07'·5W)):

2   WNW of Sheep Island (6½ cables S) with a detached islet close W, thence:

    W of Rat Light Buoy (starboard hand) (2¾ cables WSW), which marks shallow water extending 1½ cables SW of Rat Island, thence:

E of East Chapel Light Buoy (port hand) (4¼ cables W), which marks the NE edge of Chapel Rocks, thence:

3   W of East Blockhouse Point, on which stand a series of gun emplacements (disused) and tall radio masts, thence:

W of Thorn Rock Light Buoy (W cardinal) (6 cables NNW), which marks Thorn Rock, thence:

E of Angle Light Buoy (N cardinal) (8½ cables NW), in the vicinity of which, West and East Channels converge.

(Directions continue at 5.82)

Cautions
5.81

1   After a period of severe gales the positions of all light buoys in the West and East Channels should be treated with caution as they may differ from charted positions owing to dragging.

Special care is necessary when navigating in the vicinity of Angle Light Buoy where West and East Channels meet and where vessels may make large alterations of course or cross the fairway to or from an anchorage.

Chart 3274
Approach to the main port area
(continued from 5.78 and 5.80)
5.82

1   The track towards the Chevron Terminal leads E from the vicinity of Angle Light Buoy (51°41'·6N 5°08'·3W) (5.80), and at night within the white sector of Dale Point Light (51°42'·2N 5°09'·0W) (5.83), through the deep-water channel marked by light buoys and indicated by leading

Popton Point Leading Lights from W (5.82)

(Original dated 2001)

(Photograph - Air Images)

lights, passing, (with positions from Thorn Island Fort (51°41'·5N 5°07'·1W)):

N of Thorn Rock Light Buoy (4¼ cables W) (5.80), thence:

2   N of Thorn Island Fort, with drying rocks extending ½ cable NE, thence:

N of Chapel Light Buoy (starboard hand) (2 cables NE), thence:

N of Thorn Point (1¾ cables E), with two detached islets close N thence:

S of Stack Light Buoy (port hand) (6¼ cables NNE), thence:

3   N of an obstruction (5 cables ENE) with a depth of 12 m over it, thence:

S of South Hook Light Buoy (S cardinal) (6¾ cables ENE).

The track then, on an ENE heading, passes through the Swinging Area for South Hook LNG Terminal (5.73), passing:

4   SSE of Stack Rock (1¼ miles NE) surmounted by a fort (5.74), thence following the leading lines as directed below.

Popton Point Leading Lights:

Front light (metal framework tower, black stripe, white disc topmark) (51°41'·7N 5°03'·1W).

Rear light (metal framework tower, black stripe, white triangle topmark) (5½ cables E of front light).

5   The alignment (095°) of these lights leads through deep-water channel passing N of Qatar Light Buoy (safe

water) (2 cables S of the W end of South Hook LNG Terminal jetty).

There is a second front light (black stripe, white diamond topmark) close S of the front light above. The alignment (094°) of this light with the rear light above runs along the S limit of the deep-water channel.

6   Vessels other than deep-draught vessels will normally be required to use the channel passing S of Qatar Light Buoy and N of Al Khor Light Buoy (N cardinal) (51°41'·7N 5°05'·0W) whenever a deep-draught vessel is berthing or un-berthing at South Hook LNG Terminal, as advised by Port Control.

Newton Noyes Leading Lights:

Front light (metal framework tower, black stripe, white rectangular topmark, 10 m in height) (51°42'·2N 5°00'·4W).

7   Common (see below) rear light (similar to front light, 8 m in height) (1¾ cables from front light).

The alignment (080°) of these lights leads through Milford Reach passing N of East Angle Light Buoy (starboard hand) (2 cables S of the E end of the South Hook LNG Terminal jetty) and N of the E section of the Chevron Terminal jetty.

8   There is a second front light (metal framework tower, black stripe, white rectangular topmark, 5 m in height) ¼ cable N of the other light. The alignment (087°) of this light with the common rear light runs 60 m S of, and parallel to, the N edge of the turning area off the Chevron Terminal.

Newton Noyes Leading Lights (080°) from W (5.82)

(Original dated 2001)

(Photograph - Air Images)

The lights on the beacons at Popton Point and Newton Noyes are fitted with high intensity daylight lighting, operated on request.

5.83

1   **Useful marks:**

Dale Point Light (metal column, 3 m in height) (51°42′N 5°09′W).

Radio Mast, Port Control building, (51°42′·5N 5°03′·2W).

Saint Katherine's church (tower) (51°42′·7N 5°01′·7W).

(Directions continue at 5.85)

Approach to Milford Docks

5.84

1   Vessels bound for Milford Docks leave the fairway when abreast Berth 1 of the Chevron Terminal.

The narrow approach channel to the lock entrance has depths of less than 1 m and is marked near its outer end by Milford Dock Light Buoy (preferred channel to starboard), and at its inner end by two buoys (port and starboard hand) situated approximately 1 cable from the lock. The centre line is indicated by leading lights which, during the day, may be difficult to see:

2   Front light (black hut with white circular daymark, 5 m in height) situated on the E side of the lock entrance.

Rear light (black column, white circular daymark; 4 m in height) (1½ cables NNW of the front light).

3   The alignment (348°) of these lights leads from the deep-water channel to the approaches to the lock. There are shoal patches with a least depth of 1 m which lie less than ½ cable on either side of the centre line.

Caution. The tidal streams set across the entrance to the lock.

Chart 3275

Approach to Semlogistics and Dragon Gas LNG Terminals

(Continued from 5.83)

5.85

1   From a position N of the E end of the Chevron Terminal the track continues E, thence ESE, to the Semlogistics and Dragon Gas LNG Terminals (5.97).

The alignment (090°) of leading marks leads in the centre of the channel to pass about 1¼ cables S of Newton Noyes Pier (5.102) on the N shore 1 mile SE of Milford Docks, thence the track continues in the centre of the fairway.

Front mark (51°42′·0N 4°59′·4W).

Rear mark (2½ cables from front mark).

2   The approximate N and S limits of the 21·8 m dredged area off the Semlogistics berths are indicated as follows:

N limit by the alignment (102°) of Wear Spit Light Beacon, front light (black pile, red and white striped triangular topmark) (51°41′·8N 4°58′·8W) and SW Martello Tower Light, rear light (white stripe on tower) (7½ cables from front light).

S limit by the alignment (101°) of Pennar Light Beacon, front light (pile, white stripe, black triangle topmark) (51°41'·6N 4°58'·3W) and Llanreath rear light (similar structure) (640 m from front light)

3 Outfall Light Buoy (N cardinal) (51°41'·7N 4°59'·7W) marks the outer end of an outfall channel which extends NNW across Pwllcrochan Flats.

Approaches to Pembroke Dock
5.86

1 **Channel.** Beyond Wear Point (51°42'N 4°59'W) the channel through Pembroke Reach, which lies N of Pembroke Dock, is marked by light beacons and light buoys; those on its S side also mark the N edge of Carr Spit (51°42'·0N 4°57'·8W) with depths of less than 1 m, and the N and E edges of Dockyard Bank (51°42'N 4°57'W). During the summer months lights are exhibited from a pontoon at Hazelbeach on the shore NW of Carr Spit.

Carr Rocks extend NW from the shore across Carr Spit.

2 **Western approach** to Carr Jetty (5.103) first leads ESE from abreast the Semlogistics Terminal, passing S of Wear Spit Light Beacon (51°41'·8N 4°58'·8W) (5.85), giving a wide berth to the shallow water which extends S of the beacon.

Tug mooring buoy SM1 (orange, 12 m pick up line) is moored about 2 cables NE of the light beacon and vessels are advised to keep well clear.

3 Thence the track continues NE towards Pembroke Reach, passing N of Carr Spit Light Beacon and Carr Spit No 2 Light Buoy (both starboard hand) and S of Hazelbeach Light Buoy (port hand).

Leading lights:
Front light (white diamond topmark, black stripe) (51°41'·8N 4°57'·4W)
Rear light (similar to front) (82 m from front light)

4 The alignment (153°) of these lights leads between Carr Spit and the W edge of Dockyard Bank to Carr Jetty. There is a least charted depth of 6·6 m in the approach channel.

Eastern approach first leads E through Pembroke Reach thence E and S of Dockyard Bank, passing (with positions from the light at the head of Carr Jetty (51°41'·9N 4°57'·5W)):

5 N of Dockyard Bank Light Beacon (starboard hand) (2½ cables NE), which marks the NE edge of Dockyard Bank, thence:
E of DYB No 4 Light Buoy (starboard hand) (3 cables ENE), which marks the E edge of the bank, thence:
S of Traynor Light Buoy (S cardinal) (2½ cables E).
There are depths of less than 8 m on this approach.

6 **Caution.** For vessels berthing and unberthing at Carr Jetty without local knowledge the procedure can be difficult, especially during an out-going tide. For berthing, the most suitable time is just before HW, approaching from the E.

Ships over 100 m in length are advised not to berth or unberth at any time except at slack water.

5.87
1 **Useful mark:**
Church (tower) (51°42'·4N 4°57'·7W).

Approach to Pembroke Dock Ferry Terminal
5.88
1 Vessels bound for the RoRo ferry terminal 2 cables E of Carr Jetty, can proceed as previously directed, using the E

approach to Carr Jetty. On sailing, vessels depart from the berth using the W approach to Carr Jetty.

Approach to Port of Pembroke
5.89
1 Vessels bound for Port of Pembroke should proceed as previously directed at 5.86 using the E approach channel through Pembroke Reach and E of Dockyard Bank.

On passing SE of DYB No 4 Light Buoy (starboard hand) the track towards Nos 2 and 3 Quays leads S towards the berths, keeping clear of the E dolphin of the ferry terminal.

(Directions for the river Cleddau above Pembroke Dock are given at 5.118)

Anchorages

Charts 3274, 3275
Regulations
5.90
1 Vessels wishing to anchor in Milford Haven are required to obtain advice on location from Milford Haven Port Control.

Whilst at anchor ships should keep continuous radio watch.

Dale Roads
5.91
1 There is an anchorage in Dale Roads for vessels of draught up to 12 m, in the area between Stack Anchorage (51°42'N 5°06'W) (5.92) and longitude 5°08'W, N of latitude 51°42'N. The holding is fair with N winds, but poor with winds between SE and SW, and after a persistent period of strong SW winds a ground swell may be experienced in the W part of this anchorage. Mariners should take care not to anchor so as to obstruct the Great and Little Castle Head Leading Lights (5.78).

2 **Wrecks.** There is a wreck, swept by wire to 12·2 m, lying in the SW part of the anchorage, 8 cables E of Dale Point (51°42'N 5°09'W).

Another wreck, depth 1·2 m and marked by Behar Buoy (S cardinal), lies close N of the anchorage, 1 cable S of Great Castle Head.

Other anchorages
5.92
1 **Stack Anchorage** (51°42'N 5°06'W) for medium sized vessels up to 7 m draught lies within the 10 m depth contour about 3 cables W of Stack Rock (51°42'·2N 5°05'·5W). There is a wreck, depth 9·2 m, marked on its SW side by Stack Light Buoy (port hand), lying 6 cables W of Stack Rock (5.82).

2 **Dale Shelf Anchorage,** within the 10 m depth contour between Dale Point (51°42'N 5°09'W) and Watch House Point, 8 cables NE. In the W part of this anchorage weed prevents light anchors from obtaining a good hold. There is a wreck, depth 2·3 m, marked by Dakotian Light Buoy (E cardinal), lying 4 cables E of Dale Point.

3 **Sandy Haven Anchorage,** lies NNW of Stack Rock (51°42'·2N 5°05'·5W).

Montreal Rock (51°42'·6N 5°06'·3W), marked by Montreal Rock Buoy (S cardinal), lies in the WNW part of the anchorage and there are detached shoals at the head of Sandy Haven Bay.

Prohibited areas and anchorages
5.93
1 Anchoring is prohibited within an area extending about ½ cable either side of Milford Docks Channel.

Anchoring and trawling are prohibited within 100 m on either side of submerged oil pipelines which cross the haven between the shore N of Wear Tongue (51°42′N 4°59′W) and West Pennar Point; the pipelines are marked by beacons ashore (special, diamond topmarks, illuminated notice boards).

2   Anchoring, fishing and diving are prohibited in an area of 100 m radius around the wreck of a Sunderland flying boat (51°42′·2N 4°57′·2W).

Alongside berths

Chart 3274
Oil and LNG terminals
5.94
1   **South Hook LNG Terminal** (51°42′N 5°05′W) consists of an approach road jetty with a T-head, extending 1000 m S from Little Wick (51°42′·4N 5°04′·7W).

Lights are exhibited from several positions along the head of the jetty.
5.95
1   **Murco Oil Terminal** (51°42′·0N 5°03′·5W) (formerly the Total Marine Terminal), with an associated refinery, consists of a jetty, 800 m long, extending SSE from the W side of Gelliswick Bay, 5½ cables E of South Hook LNG Terminal. The jetty has a T-head, 700 m long, with Nos 1 and 2 outside berths, for vessels up to 320 m and 201 m LOA, with depths over a width of 80 m of 15·3 m (2006) and 11·4 m (2006) respectively.

2   Inside berth, No 3, for vessels up to 122 m in length, has a dredged depth of 7·5 m (2006) over a width of 61 m off the berth. Two light beacons (white poles) on the jetty, in line 254°, mark the N limit of No 3 Berth swinging area.

Vessels of up to 275 000 dwt can be accommodated at No 1 Berth.

Lights are exhibited at the extreme ends of the jetty and from each end of the berths.

The gap between the heads of Total and South Hook jetties is 275 m wide.

Charts 3274, 3275
5.96
1   **Chevron Marine Terminal** situated on the S side of the haven opposite Milford Haven, consists of an L-head and a T-head jetty.

The W (L-head) jetty, extends N from Popton Point to the deep water channel. The head of the jetty has a length of 1160 m and has three berths on its N side, Nos 8 to 6 from seaward. The deepest, No 6 Berth, has a dredged depth of 20·3 m (2006) and can accommodate vessels up to 275 000 dwt. Nos 7 and 8 Berths have depths of 14·5 and 15·4 m alongside. Fenders allow limited use of No 8 Berth.

2   Lights are exhibited at the extreme ends of the jetty and from each end of the berths.

The E (T-head) jetty extends N to the deep-water channel from a position 8½ cables E of Popton Point and is of similar construction to the W jetty. It is also joined to the W jetty by a walkway, under which there is a boat

South Hook and Total Marine Terminals   Chevron Texaco Terminal

Milford Haven from W (5.94)

(Original dated 2001)

(Photograph - Air Images)

passage (5.108). The T-head has a length of 1100 m and has three berths on its N side, Nos 1 to 3 from seawards.

3   The deepest berth at this jetty, No 1 Berth, has a dredged depth of 19·9 m (2006) and can accommodate vessels up to 275 000 dwt. There are depths of 14·5 m alongside No 2 Berth and 11·6 m alongside No 3 Berth.

Nos 4 and 5 Berths situated on the S side of the T-head, abreast No 3 Berth, have depths alongside of 6·0 m and 6·1 m, and can accommodate smaller vessels of up to 2 500 and 6 000 dwt, respectively.

4   A turning area S of Nos 4 and 5 Berths has a dredged depth of 6·0 m (2006); the NE limit of the area is marked by No 5A Light Buoy (starboard hand) and the S limit is marked by the alignment (268°) of two pairs of lights situated midway along the approach to the head of the jetty.

Lights are exhibited at the extreme ends of the jetty and from the ends of each berth.

A large tank farm and refinery is situated onshore abreast the terminal.

5.97

1   **Semlogistics and Dragon Gas LNG Terminals** consists of three T-headed jetties extending from the N shore, close W of Wear Point (51°42′N 4°59′W). The controlling depth in the approach to the berths is 12·8 m. The berths are:

Dragon LNG (No 1).
Semlogistics No 2; length of face 121 m; depth 15·0 m; maximum size of vessel 165 000 dwt, LOA 283 m.
Semlogistics No 3; length of face 63 m; depth 10·4 m; maximum size of vessel 20 000 dwt, LOA 153 m.

2   Lights are exhibited at the extreme ends of the terminal and from each end of the berths.

A large tank farm is situated onshore abreast the terminal; within this complex there are three prominent chimneys (5.74), 6 cables NNE of the jetties.

Milford Docks

5.98

1   **General information.** Milford Docks (51°43′N 5°02′W), lying on the N side of the haven opposite the Chevron Terminal, are entered through a sea lock and comprise of a wet dock, the greater part of which is dredged to a depth of 10·4 m, and a dry dock. The port is an important centre for the fishing industry. A light is exhibited from the head of the W entrance.

2   The sea lock has a length of 167·6 m and a depth over the sill of 7·9 m. The maximum allowable beam is 18·9 m.

Lock opening times are available from Milford Docks Pierhead on VHF.

Directions. The controlling depth in the approach channel is 1·2 m. For the approach and details of the leading lights, to the E of the entrance, see 5.84.

3   **Berths:**

Hakin Wharf, which lies in the NW corner of the wet dock, is a single cargo berth, dredged to 6·7 m.
Fish quay on the SW side of the dock.
Milford Marina, situated in the SE part of the dock, can accommodate craft up to the limiting conditions for the lock and the depth of water in the wet dock. Facilities include boatyards, boat hoist and slipway, plus the usual marina facilities.

Chevron Texaco Terminal   SemLogistics Terminal

Milford Haven from E (5.97)

(Original dated 2001)

(Photograph - Air Images)

Milford Docks from S (5.98)

(Original dated 2001)

(Photograph - Air Images)

Immediately outside the docks on the E wall, there is a landing stage.

Chart 3275
Berths at Pembroke Dock
5.99

1   **RoRo ferry terminal** (51°41'·9N 4°57'·2W) consists of a traffic pier which extends 130 m N from the shore and a number of dolphins to which vessels lie alongside. A passenger footbridge leads to a floating pontoon situated between the dolphins. The berth has a control depth of 6·85 m (2008) alongside and 7·3 m in the approach. Lights are exhibited from the head of the pier and from the outermost dolphin.

There are daily sailings of car ferries from the terminal to Ireland.

5.100

1   **Port of Pembroke,** consisting of three quays, is situated close E of the ferry terminal.

No 1 Quay, for vessels up to 150 m in length, is 180 m long with a controlling depth of 6·7 m. A light is exhibited from the W corner of the quay.

2   No 2 Quay, with a length of 100 m, and No 3 Quay lie within a basin with a controlling depth of 3·0 m.

There is a least charted depth of 4·3 m in the approaches to all three berths.

Port Authority. Milford Haven Port Authority.
The port is represented by a Port Manager.
Repair facilities. See 5.104.

Other berths
5.101

1   **West Pennar Power Station Wharf** (51°41'·1N 4°59'·1W) is approached through a narrow channel, at the entrance to Pennar Gut (5.52), leading S to Crow Pool. The bar at the entrance to the channel has a least charted depth of 2·8 m over it and is marked by a light buoy (port hand). From Crow Pool a channel, which dries in parts, leads W between buoys (lateral) towards a wharf, which dries alongside, situated on the E side of the power station.

5.102

1   **Newton Noyes Pier,** L–shaped and disused, situated on the N shore of the haven, 1 mile SE of Milford Docks.

Lights are exhibited from each end of the S side of the pierhead.

Carr Jetty
5.103

1   Carr Jetty, at the NW end of Pembroke Dock (51°42'N 4°57'W), is of solid stone construction, having a length of 115 m on its NE side and 50 m on its NW side. The jetty is connected to shore at its root by open piers and there are landing steps on its SW and E sides.

Ships up to 150 m in length can normally be accommodated at the jetty, and in favourable weather those up to 170 m in length can be accepted. Controlling depth on the NE side 8·3 m and 5·4 m on the NW side.

2   The large tidal range makes the jetty unsuitable for small vessels.

Lights are exhibited from each corner of the NE side.
Directions. See 5.86.

Port services

Charts 3274, 3275
Repairs
5.104

1   There is a drydock within Milford Docks: length 180 m, breadth 18·9 m, depth over the sill 10·4 m at MHWS.

All types of repair facilities exist at Pembroke Dock where there is a small graving dock and several slips.

Other facilities
5.105

1   Salvage equipment and services; divers; reception of oily waste at the oil terminals, Milford Docks and Port of Pembroke; oil pollution services; issue of SSCC and SSCEC; customs; hospital at Haverfordwest, 6 miles NNE of Milford Haven; fully equipped medical centres at each oil refinery.

Pembroke Docks from N (5.99)

Carr Jetty

(Original dated 2001)

(Photograph - Air Images)

Supplies
5.106
1 Fuel of all types is available at the oil terminals; small quantities can be obtained within Milford Docks. Fuel can also be supplied by barge or road tanker elsewhere in the haven.

Fresh water is available at the oil terminals, Milford Docks, Pembroke Dock and Port of Pembroke, including Offshore Jetty.

Provisions and stores are available at most berths.

Harbour regulations
5.107
1 Bye-laws for the regulation of navigation within the port limits may be obtained from the Port Authority.

Boat passages
5.108
1 Boat passages can be found at the oil terminals in the following locations:

Inner end of Murco Oil Terminal approach jetty; vertical clearance 1·9 m.

Midway along the Chevron Terminal E approach jetty; vertical clearance 3·8 m.

2 Midway along the Chevron Terminal W approach jetty; vertical clearance 3·5 m.

Under the walkway which links the E and W T-head jetties of the Chevron Terminal; vertical clearance 2·5 m.

Lights indicate all the above boat passages. The jetty legs on either side of the boat passages are painted high visibility orange.

3 The passages provide inshore access through the haven for small craft. However, no craft is permitted to pass between the piles under the jetties other than through these passages.

5.109
1 A boat passage lies between Thorn Point (51°41'·5N 5°06'·8W) and Thorn Island, 1½ cables W; an overhead telephone cable with a vertical clearance of 14 m spans the passage.

Landing places
5.110
1 Landing places suitable for ships' boats, are situated at Hakin, close W of Milford lock entrance, but the steps dry at LW; at Lock Pit, on the W arm of the lock where there is a vertical ladder. There is a seasonal pontoon close E of the lock.

With permission, landing can be made at all states of the tide at the Port Authority Jetty (51°42'·4N 5°03'·1W).

There are landing pontoons at the Total, Chevron and Semlogistics Terminals.

River Cleddau above Pembroke Dock

Chart 3275
General information
5.111
1 From Hobbs Point (51°42'·0N 4°56'·5W) to Haverfordwest, 6 miles NNE, the foreshore of the river is mainly steep-to, though there are several stretches of low lying ground fronted by saltings.

Above Cleddau Bridge (51°42'·4N 4°56'·0W) (5.112) the upper reaches of the river Cleddau are not buoyed and are used mainly by small craft.

2 A wharf 200 m long which dries 1·5 m alongside lies close W of Burton Point, 5 cables E of Cleddau Bridge on the N bank of the river.

Waterloo Quay (51°41′·8N 4°55′·3W), a RoRo facility on the W side of Cosheston Pill (5.113) 5 cables S from its entrance with the river Cleddau, is used to load pre-assembled units for the petro-chemical industry. A buoyed channel leads to the quay from the river.

3　At Lawrenny Quay 2 miles above Cleddau Bridge, the river Cresswell and the river Carew flow into the river Cleddau from E and SE respectively. Between April and September, buoys (special) are laid at Lawrenny to warn boat owners that no planing is permitted above Lawrenny, in the vicinity of Jenkins Point and up the Cresswell and Carew rivers.

4　At Picton Point (51°46′·1N 4°53′·8W) the confluence of the Western Cleddau and the Eastern Cleddau form the river Cleddau.

Neyland Yacht Haven (51°42′·7N 4°56′·5W) lies on the N bank within Westfield Pill opposite Hobbs Point.

Cleddau Bridge
5.112

1　Cleddau Bridge, a road bridge with a vertical clearance of 36 m, spans the lower reaches of the river Cleddau at Pembroke Ferry, a point on the bend of the river, nearly 5 cables NE of Hobbs Point (51°42′·0N 4°56′·5W).

Lights exhibited on the buttresses of the bridge, on both upstream and downstream sides, mark each side of the channel.

Marine farm
5.113

1　A marine farm, with a dolphin berth, lies close W of the entrance to Cosheston Pill (51°42′N 4°55′W), an inlet encumbered by drying mud flats. Lights are exhibited from the dolphin berth and from a position 1¼ cables NW marking the limits of the farm.

Submarine oil pipelines
5.114

1　A submarine pipeline, marked by beacons (special) on each shore, crosses the river at Pembroke Ferry, close E of Cleddau Bridge.

Anchoring and trawling are prohibited within 100 m of the pipeline.

Submarine pipelines cross the river at Beggars Reach (51°44′·1N 4°53′·4W), nearly 3 miles above Burton Point (5.111), and at a position 1 mile S of Haverfordwest.

Submarine cables
5.115

1　A submarine power cable, marked by beacons (special) crosses the river 6 cables above Burton Point.

Another submarine power cable, marked by beacons (special), crosses the entrance to Eastern Cleddau close E of Picton Point (5.111).

Mariners should not anchor in the vicinity of these cables.

Cleddau Bridge from SW (5.112)

(Original dated 2001)

(Photograph - Air Images)

Vertical clearance
5.116

1 An overhead power cable, with a safe vertical clearance of 24 m, spans the river 7 cables above Burton Point (51°42′·3N 4°55′·2W).

In Cosheston Pill (5.113), two overhead power cables with a least vertical clearance of 5 m, span the inlet near its head.

An overhead power cable, with a safe vertical clearance of 3 m, spans the river Carew (51°43′N 4°52′W) in the vicinity of a dam, 2 miles above its mouth.

2 In Llangwm Pill (51°44′·7N 4°54′·4W), 3½ miles above Burton Point, an overhead power cable with a safe vertical clearance of 8 m spans the inlet near its head.

Millin Pill (51°46′·8N 4°54′·5W), 5 cables W of Picton Point (5.111) extends N off Western Cleddau and is spanned by an overhead power cable with a safe vertical clearance of 4 m.

Several overhead power cables span the river S of Haverfordwest. Lowest safe vertical clearance is 9 m.

Tidal streams
5.117

1 There are strong eddies between Hobbs Point and Cleddau Bridge on the out-going tide, especially at springs. Tidal stream information above Cleddau Bridge is shown on the chart.

Directions
5.118

1 From Pembroke Reach, the track passes:

Between Neyland Point Light Beacon (port hand) and Dockyard Bank Light Beacon (N cardinal), thence:

S of a buoy (special can with topmark) marking the S extremity of a line of obstructions, which extend 1¼ cables from Neyland Point, thence:

2 S of Neyland Spit Light Buoy (port hand) marking the S edge of Neyland Spit, which extends 1½ cables S from Neyland Point (51°42′·3N 4°56′·8W), thence:

SE of the entrance to Westfield Pill, which leads to a yacht marina and is marked by buoys, thence:

3 In the fairway under Cleddau Bridge, marked by lights on the bridge, thence:

S of the shallows off Burton Point, and thereafter generally following the centre of the river towards Haverfordwest, for which the chart is the best guide.

MILFORD HAVEN TO SAINT DAVID'S HEAD

General information

Charts 1478, 1973
Route
5.119

1 From the approaches to Milford Haven, W of Turbot Bank, the coastal route to the vicinity W of Saint David's Head (51°54′N 5°19′W) leads about 21 miles NW passing between Grassholm and Skomer Island (51°44′N 5°18′W) and clear SW of The Bishops and Clerks, a group of islets and rocks W and NW of Ramsey Island (51°52′N 5°20′W).

During the summer months, fog can be experienced off the exposed parts of the coast. In poor visibility and strong winds, small craft should keep well offshore as shelter is limited.

Topography
5.120

1 The mainland coastline in general consists mainly of precipitous rocky cliffs, indented with several bays, the largest being Saint Bride's Bay, and numerous narrow inlets and coves. Between Saint Ann's Head (51°41′N 5°10′W) and Wooltack Point, 4½ miles NW, the coast is dark coloured.

2 Within the area there are a large number of inshore islands and shoals, the principal islands being; Ramsey Island (51°52′N 5°20′W), Skomer Island (51°44′N 5°18′W) and Skokholm Island, 1¾ miles S of Skomer Island.

Saint David's Head (51°54′N 5°19′W), 30 m high at its W extremity may be identified by Carn Llidi (5.126). Penberry (5.172), a similar shaped hill, but a few metres lower, lies 1¾ miles ENE of Carn Llidi; care must be taken not to mistake one for the other.

Rescue
5.121

1 An all-weather lifeboat is stationed at Porthstinian (5.151), 1½ miles S of Saint David's Head (51°54′N 5°19′W); an inshore lifeboat is stationed at Little Haven (51°46′·4N 5°06′·4W).

For details of rescue organisation see 1.60.

Tidal streams and races
5.122

1 **Tidal streams.** From outside Bais Bank (51°57′N 5°22′W), the S-going offshore stream at Saint David's Head sets SW before turning S and running clear of The Bishops towards Skomer Island. The N-going stream runs in the reverse direction. For inshore streams, see 5.159.

2 The S-going stream W of Skomer Island divides, one branch running S, W of Skokholm Island, then SE to Turbot Bank, the other turning E into Broad Sound then SE between Skokholm Island and the mainland, towards Saint Ann's Head. The NW and N-going streams set in the opposite direction.

3 The stream in Broad Sound keeps to the N side of the channel; on the S side and over The Knoll it is rotary and weak.

The streams begin as follows at the localities indicated:

Position	Interval from HW Milford Haven	Direction
Approximately 2½ miles W of The Bishops	+0400 −0225	S N
W of Skomer Island	+0400 −0225	S N

4 The maximum spring rate in each direction is 2 kn.

4 The maximum spring rate in each direction is 4 kn.

Broad Sound and E of Skokholm Island	+0430 −0155	E and SE NW and W

The maximum spring rate in each direction is between 2½ to 3 kn.

W of Saint Ann's Head near the land	+0315 −0310	SE NW

5 For tidal information at a position 6 miles SW of Saint Ann's Head see information for tidal diamond B on Chart 1478.

The times at which the streams begin W of Saint Ann's Head differ materially from the times at which they set across and into the entrance to Milford Haven, for which see 5.72.

6   For tidal streams within Saint Bride's Bay see 5.139 and between The Smalls and Grassholm, see 5.31.

See also *Admiralty Tidal Stream Atlas — Irish Sea and Bristol Channel*.

Races. Wild Goose Race, forms W of Skomer and Skokholm Islands during the strength of the streams in both directions. It is especially violent near springs with a strong wind against or across the stream, and it is dangerous to small craft.

7   A race of much less violence extends NE from Skokholm Island when the streams are running strongly.

Off The Bishops and Clerks, a race exists over a detached shoal which lies 2½ miles WSW of South Bishop (51°51′N 5°25′W).

For races off Grassholm, see 5.31.

Directions
(continued from 5.47)

Chart 1478
Principal marks
5.123
1   **Landmarks**:
   Old Lighthouse (Tower) (51°41′N 5°10′W) (5.74).
   Skomer Island (51°44′N 5°18′W) (5.127).
   Roch Castle (51°51′N 5°05′W) (5.140).
   Major lights:
   Saint Ann's Head Light (51°41′N 5°10′W) (5.74).
2   Skokholm Island Light (white octagonal tower, 18 m in height) (51°42′N 5°17′W), which stands at the SW end of the island; the light is partially obscured by higher ground lying ENE.
   The Smalls Light (51°43′N 5°40′W) (5.14).
   South Bishop Light (white round tower, 11 m in height) (51°51′N 5°25′W); the light, shown continuously, stands on the summit of South Bishop (5.154).

Other aids to navigation
5.124
1   **Racons:**
   The Smalls Lighthouse (51°43′N 5°40′W) (5.14).
   South Bishop Lighthouse — as above.
For further details see *Admiralty List of Radio Signals Volume 2.*

Passage
5.125
1   From the approaches to Milford Haven, SW of Turbot Bank, the coastal route continues to a position W of Saint David's Head (51°54′N 5°19′W) about 22 miles NW, passing (with positions from Skomer Island (51°44′N 5°18′W)):
   SW of Saint Ann's Head (6 miles SE) with a light and tower (5.74). Saint Ann's Head Shoals extend 5½ cables SW from the headland. Thence:
   SW of Skokholm Island (5.133) (2½ miles SSE) which exhibits a light (5.123), thence:
2   SW of Skomer Island (5.127), thence:
   NE of Grassholm (5.30) (6¾ miles W), thence:
   SW of South Bishop (5.154) (8 miles NNW), the SW islet of The Bishops and Clerks, from which a light (5.123) is exhibited, with dangerous rocks extending ½ cable NE and NW. Thence:
   SW of North Bishop (5.155) (10½ miles NNW), the N islet of The Bishops and Clerks group, with underwater rocks extending 1 mile SW over which there are tide-rips.
3   The track here alters to a more N heading and continues to a position NW of Saint David's Head (51°54′N 5°19′W), passing W of Bais Bank (51°57′N 5°22′W) (5.171).
5.126
1   **Useful mark**:
   Carn Llidi, a conical hill with steep sides, lies 9 cables E of Saint David's Head (51°54′N 5°19′W) and helps to identify it.
   (Directions continue for the coastal route to Strumble Head at 5.169; directions for the offshore route W of Bardsey Island are given at 6.12)

South Bishop Lighthouse from SE (5.123)
(Original dated 2001)

(Photograph - Air Images)

Skomer, Gateholm and Skokholm Islands

Charts 2878, 1482 plan of Jack Sound

Skomer Island

5.127

1 **Description.** Skomer Island (51°44′N 5°18′W), a prominent feature when viewed from N or S, has a precipitous cliffy coast rising to nearly 60 m; the hinterland is a rough plateau with small rocky peaks, the highest being 76 m. The smaller E part of the island, known as The Neck, is joined to the main part by a low isthmus which forms the common head of North Haven and South Haven (5.129).

2 Garland Stone, a conical rock 29 m high, lies close N of the N point of the island.

Mew Stone, a conical green-capped islet 57 m high, lies off the S point of the island, towards which it overhangs in a singular manner. Three above-water rocks lie 1 cable S of the SW end of Mew Stone.

5.128

1 **Nature reserve.** The island is a national nature reserve, being owned by the Countryside Council for Wales and managed by the Wildlife Trust West Wales. The waters surrounding the island, and extending E across Jack Sound to embrace much of the Marloes Peninsula, are a marine nature reserve. (see also 1.58).

Mariners should keep well offshore in the vicinity of the seabird colonies and, from late August onwards, the seal breeding beaches.

5.129

1 **Anchorages and landing places** can be found in North Haven, where three moorings for day visitors are laid. Vessels not using these moorings should anchor to seaward of them, so as to avoid damage to sensitive seabed plants. Conservation areas, marked by buoys, should be avoided.

South Haven should be used only under stress of weather.

5.130

1 **Directions.** When entering North or South Haven mariners should keep close to the W shores to avoid outlying rocks on the E sides of the bays.

Gateholm Island

5.131

1 **Description.** Gateholm Island (51°43′N 5°14′W), whose W side lies within the Skomer Marine Nature Reserve (5.128), is 37 m high, projects 3½ cables from the coastal cliffs and is fringed by shelving rocks which connect it at LW to the mainland. A detached rock, which dries 1·5 m, lies 1 cable SW of the SW end of the island.

Anchorage. There is an anchorage on the N side of the island in depths greater than 7 m.

5.132

1 **Gateholm Bay** is entered between Gateholm Island and Hooper's Point, 1 mile SE; it is skirted by Marloes Sands which dry to 1½ cables offshore, with some scattered shelving rocks, and bounded by perpendicular dark red cliffs.

The bottom of the bay is mostly foul and anchorage off this exposed coast is not recommended.

Skokholm Island

5.133

1 **Description.** Skokholm Island (51°42′N 5°17′W) lies 1½ miles S of Skomer Island. It is separated from it by Broad Sound, a wide channel partially obstructed in mid-channel by The Knoll, a bank with several rocky heads, over which there is a least charted depth of 7·6 m. The island has a rocky, barren appearance with steep red sandstone cliffs. It attains a height of 50 m near its SW end, but at its E end there is a low neck off which lies The Stack, an isolated rock.

2 Skokholm Island Light (5.123) is exhibited from The Head, the SW extremity of the island.

Close-up from S

Skokholm Island and Lighthouse from SW (5.133)

(Original dated 2001)

(Photograph - Air Images)

Skokholm Spit, consisting of rocks with a least charted depth of 2·1 m, extends 2¾ cables NNE from The Stack. Isolated patches, with a least depth of 6·3 m, lie within 4 cables SE of The Stack.

Crab Bay, opening S, indents the SE corner of the island. An islet, from which drying rocks extend S and E, lies off its E entrance point.

3   **Nature reserve.** The island is a national nature reserve, managed by the Wildlife Trust West Wales, and access is possible only by prior arrangement (see 1.58).

Mariners should keep well offshore in the vicinity of the seabird colonies and, from late August onwards, the seal breeding beaches.

Landing place. There is a landing place in Crab Bay, about 5 cables E of the lighthouse. Landing is also possible in North Haven at Blacksmith's Landing. There is a quay on the W side of Peter's Bay, on the S side of The Neck.

Anchorage can be found, temporarily, in the bay S of The Stack, 1 cable offshore in depths of 13 m, rock.

Jack Sound

Description
5.134

1   Jack Sound lies in the Skomer Marine Nature Reserve (5.127) between Midland Isle (51°44′N 5°16′W) and the mainland 3½ cables E. Anvil Point, 34 m in height, is at the SE end of the sound and Wooltack Point, 3½ cables farther N, is at the NE end. The latter is a dark rugged point backed by Wooltack, a 55 m peak, 2½ cables ESE of the point. The channel is approximately 1 cable wide and has depths of more than 10 m in the fairway, which is bounded on its E side by The Cable, a detached rock, standing 2½ cables SSW of Wooltack Point and 1 cable offshore, and on its W side by Crabstones, drying rocks which extend E from Midland Isle.

Tidal streams
5.135

1   Tidal streams in Jack Sound begin as follows:

Interval from HW Milford Haven	*Direction*
+0200	S
−0425	N

The maximum spring rate in each direction is between 6 and 7 kn. A strong eddy runs round Tusker Rock (1 cable W of Wooltack Point) (5.136), with a considerable tide-rip, and with the S-going stream there is a dangerous eddy near the S side of Midland Isle.

Directions
5.136

1   Jack Sound should be used only with local knowledge. With an adverse tidal stream particular attention should be paid to steering to avoid a sheer towards the rocks on one side or the other.

South approach. From a position in Broad Sound with the W edge of Wooltack Point (5.134) bearing 026°, the track leads NNE passing (with positions from Wooltack Point):

2   Close ESE of Blackstones (6½ cables SSW), rocks, with Western Blackstone, a rock, lying ¾ cable W and a rocky 3·7 m patch lying between Blackstones and Midland Isle, thence:

    WNW of The Anvil (3½ cables S), a rock, which lies close off Anvil Point (51°44′N 5°15′W); Limpet Rocks lie ¾ cable S of the point. Thence, with

Tusker Rock (1 cable W), a black rock, steep-to on its W side, bearing 012°:

    E of Crabstones (¾ cable E of Midland Isle) (5.134).

3   With Garland Stone (51°44′·8N 5°18′·1W) (5.127) open N of Midland Isle the track leads NNW into Saint Bride's Bay giving Tusker Rock a wide berth to avoid the strong eddy which runs round it.

In the SE approach to the Sound, The Bench, a group of rocks, lies 2½ cables SW of Pitting Gales Point (51°43′·8N 5°14′·8W) and a rock with a charted depth of 5·2 m over it lies 1½ cables SW of The Bench.

Saint Bride's Bay

Chart 1478
Description
5.137

1   Saint Bride's Bay, entered between Skomer Island (51°44′N 5°18′W) and Ramsey Island (6½ miles N) (5.146), is free from dangers except near the N and S shores. The bottom is mainly fine sand and mud with good holding, but the bay is too exposed to afford anything but temporary anchorage.

2   Apart from Newgale Sands, 2 miles in length, in the NE corner of the bay, backed by low ground, the coastline is mostly formed by high cliffs with numerous small indentations.

Hand Marks, a rocky bank with a least charted depth of 9·1 m, extends 1½ miles NNW from The Nab Head (51°45′N 5°12′W). Borough Head lies 2¾ miles ENE of The Nab Head, with Stack Rocks lying 5 cables offshore midway between.

3   Green Scar (51°52′N 5°12′W), a grass topped islet, lies 5½ cables S of the entrance to Solva Harbour with The Mare, an above-water rock, lying 1 cable E and Black Scar, an islet, 1¾ cables SW; rocky ground, with depths of less than 9 m extends 5 cables SW from Black Scar.

Half Tide Rock, which dries, lies off the W end of the N shore, 5½ cables S of Porth Clais (51°52′N 5°17′W).

Research area
5.138

1   Oceanographic instruments may be found within the research area, extending WSW, thence W for a total of 8½ miles from Newgale Sands. Vessels are cautioned against anchoring within this area.

Tidal streams
5.139

1   Outside Saint Bride's Bay the streams set N and S beginning at the same times as those W of Skomer Island and W of Ramsey Island (5.122 and 5.159)

In the middle of the entrance to the bay the N-going stream is stated to begin ¼ hour later.

2   In Saint Bride's Bay the streams are weak. A branch of the main S-going stream sets E off the N shore and clockwise round the bay, but there are W-going eddies between Carreg-Frân (51°51′·5N 5°17′·8W) and the S entrance to Ramsey Sound (1 mile W) (5.148). Similarly a branch of the main N-going stream sets E off the S shore and anti-clockwise round the bay.

3   In Goultrop Roads (51°46′·4N 5°07′·8W) the streams begin as follows:

Interval from HW Milford Haven	*Direction*	*Remarks*
−0225	W	Runs for 9½ hours
−0525	E	Runs for 3 hours

4   The times at which the streams are stated to begin outside and within the bay and in Jack Sound and Ramsey Sound differ considerably.

The tidal stream information both inside and outside Saint Bride's Bay is based on incomplete data and should be used with caution.

Landmarks
5.140
1   Roch Castle (51°51′N 5°05′W) (15 m in height).
Water tower (51°52′·2N 5°08′·2W).
Hotel (51°52′·8N 5°15′·5W) standing in Saint Davids.

Chart 1482 plan of Jack Sound
Landings, minor harbours and anchorages
5.141
1   **Martin's Haven** (51°44′·2N 5°14′·7W), a small cove which lies within a marine reserve area (5.128), is situated 3 cables ESE of Wooltack Point (5.134), and affords shelter for boats, except from N winds. The haven is regularly used for communication by boat with Skomer Island and there is a rough road access to a shingle beach.

Chart 1478
5.142
1   **Goultrop Roads**, at the SE corner of Saint Brides Bay, affords anchorage, sheltered from S winds, for small craft in depths of 6 m; in W winds the anchorage is untenable.

Little Haven, an inlet approximately 1 cable long and 60 m wide, lies E of Goultrop Roads and is used by small craft. The foreshore dries to ½ cable W of its W entrance. There is a slipway suitable for hauling out and launching small craft.

Broad Haven, a sandy beach nearly 5 cables long, lies close N of Little Haven.
5.143
1   **Solva Harbour** (51°52′N 5°12′W), lying on the N side of Saint Brides Bay, can accommodate craft which can take the ground, but has very limited facilities. The harbour dries from about 1 cable within the entrance to its head. There are depths of 5 m at MHWS alongside a small wharf on the N shore of the harbour. In bad weather craft berth inside the point opposite the wharf and lie aground on a soft bottom of mud and sand over shingle.

2   Black Rock, an islet from which drying rocks extend ¼ cable W, lies in the entrance to Solva Harbour. The channel on its W side has a depth of 3·7 m, but there are greater depths on its E side between the islet and Saint Elvis Rock, an islet which lies close W of the E entrance point. Water is obtainable at the wharf. Moorings are available for visitors.

3   Anchorage may be obtained in depths of approximately 13 m between Green Scar (5.137) and the entrance to Solva Harbour. This anchorage is subject to a heavy SW swell after W storms.

Chart 1482 plan of Ramsey Sound
5.144
1   **Porth Clais** (51°52′N 5°17′W), an inlet 3 miles W of Solva Harbour, is about ¼ cable wide. It is protected by a stone breakwater on the E side about ½ cable N of the entrance. Within the breakwater the harbour dries. It is suitable for craft able to take the ground, which is hard and stony. There is a landing place on the W side and slipways at the head of the inlet.

2   Carreg-Frân, an islet 18 m high, lies S of the point to which it is connected at LW, 7½ cables SW of the entrance to Porth Clais.

Stodair, a rock, with a least charted depth of 1·9 m, lies 2 cables SE of Carreg-Frân, and a pinnacle rock, with a charted depth of 3·7 m lies 3¼ cables S of Stodair.
5.145
1   **Porthlysgi Bay** (51°51′·7N 5°18′·3W) lies on the E side of Pen Dal-aderyn, the headland forming the SE entrance point to Ramsey Sound. Pen y Foel, a cliffy point on the E side of the headland, forms the SW entrance point to the bay, which is open S. The E side of the bay is formed by Carreg yr Esgob, an islet 20 m high, lying at the SW end of a group of rocks and islets joined to the mainland by a drying rocky ledge. Except during S winds, a secure anchorage may be found in 13 m. An unmarked wreck lies at the head of the bay.

Ramsey Island and Ramsey Sound including Whitesand Bay
Chart 1482 plan of Ramsey Sound
Ramsey Island
5.146
1   **Description.** Ramsey Island (51°52′N 5°20′W), a bird reserve (1.58) where visiting is permitted, is bordered by precipitous rocky cliffs except at Aber Mawr, a small bay on its W coast. The highest hill, Carn Llundain, 134 m high, rises to its summit on the SW side of the island, with Carnysgubor standing near the NW end and Foel-fawr standing at the SE extremity.

2   A number of rocky islets and rocks lie within 1 mile S of Foel-fawr, among which are Ynys Bery, the largest, 70 m in height, Ynys Cantwr, Ynys Eilun and Meini Duon.

Pont yr Eilun, the most E rock, dries 3 m, lies ½ cable E of Ynys Eilun and 3½ cables SSE of Ramsey Island.

3   The only dangers close off the W side of the island are Bancyn-ffald, a drying rock, 1 cable off shore, SSW of Carn Llundain, with an above-water rock 1½ cables SE, and Carreg-gwylan, an above-water rock, situated close offshore W of the summit of Carn Llundain.

Trwyn Ogof Hên is the NE extremity of the island; Gwahan (51°53′N 5°20′W), a rock 3 m high, lies 4¼ cables N and there is a safe channel between with a least charted depth of 5·0 m.

4   The Bitches, a rocky ledge, extends 2 cables E from the middle of the E side of the island; a remarkable rock, 4 m in height, lies at the centre of the ledge, and a similar rock lies close within its E end.

Landing places. There is a concrete jetty, which dries 1·2 m, with an iron ladder, situated close N of The Bitches: the jetty is equipped with a 15-cwt crane.

Landing may also be made in a small cove S of The Bitches.

Anchorages. See 5.150.

Ramsey Sound
5.147
1   **Description.** Ramsey Sound lies between the mainland and Ramsey Island. The channel is straight, with charted depths in the fairway of between 20 and 66 m, and with a least width of 2 cables abreast The Bitches; however, the passage W of Ramsey Island is preferred to that through Ramsey Sound.

2   On the E side of the Sound between Pen Dal-aderyn (51°52′N 5°19′W), the SW point of the headland, and Point Saint John, 1½ miles N the coast is mostly cliffy. Shoe Rock, which has some small heads close N of it, lies 1 cable S of Pen Dal-aderyn.

Horse Rock, with a dangerous wreck close W, lies 6 cables N of Pen Dal-aderyn, its position being generally marked by tide-rips.

5.148

1   **Tidal streams.** In the narrowest part of Ramsey Sound the streams begin as follows:

Interval from HW Milford Haven	Direction
+0300	S
−0325	N

The maximum spring rate in each direction is 6 kn. The rate of the stream decreases N and S of the narrowest part but a spring rate of 5 kn may be encountered on the N-going stream as far N as Gwahan (5.146).

2   **Eddies.** On the S-going stream eddies set N in Whitesand Bay (5.152), and also on both sides of Ramsey Sound, those on the W side extending from Ynys Cantwr to N of The Bitches and those on the E side extending N from Horse Rock.

On the N-going stream eddies set S on both sides of Ramsey Sound, those on the W side between The Bitches and Gwahan, and those on the E side between the narrows and Point Saint John.

5.149

1   **Directions.** The best time for making the passage through Ramsey Sound is at slack water, but it should not be attempted without local knowledge and on no account at night or in low visibility.

Approaching from S, the alignment (005°) of Penmaenmelyn, a bluff close N of Pen Dal-aderyn with Saint David's Head, 2½ miles N passes E of Sylvia Rock, 8½ cables SSE of the S end of Ramsey Island.

2   The track then leads N midway between Shoe Rock and the E side of Ramsey Island, then midway between Penmaenmelyn and the E edge of The Bitches, the narrowest part of the sound, and midway between Carreg-gafeiliog (51°53′·3N 5°18′·9W) (5.152), and Gwahan (7 cables W), passing W of Horse Rock and W of Pont Ywr Wyn Rock, 3 cables N of Horse Rock.

5.150

1   **Anchorages.** There is a berth for coasters at least 1½ cables off the E coast of the island and W of Horse Rock, in a depth of 22 m, sand and shell, out of the strength of the tidal stream, but swinging room is restricted and the engines should be kept at short notice.

A shallower anchorage is approximately 2 cables NNW of The Bitches, 1 cable offshore, in a depth of 9 m, out of the tidal stream. Caution is necessary to avoid small boat moorings in the vicinity.

2   **Directions.** The anchorages are best approached from N during the last hour of the S-going stream when, at the N anchorage, there is a weak NE-going eddy. The alignment of the middle rock of The Bitches with the E extremity of Ynys Cantwr offers the best approach.

If proceeding from S, on the N-going stream, to the S anchorage give a wide berth to The Bitches to avoid the eddy which extends some distance from them.

5.151

1   **Landing** can be effected at any state of the tide in reasonable weather at the lifeboat slip at Porthstinian (51°53′N 5°18′W), 4½ cables SSE of Point Saint John.

Whitesand Bay

5.152

1   Whitesand Bay, or Porth Mawr, is entered between Point Saint John (51°53′N 5°19′W) and Saint David's Head, 1 mile farther N. Carreg-gafeiliog (2½ cables N of Point Saint John), a rock 3 m in height, is connected to the coast SE by a rocky reef. A spit with a least charted depth of

3·6 m extends 2 cables SW of the rock and should be given a wide berth.

2   A drying wreck lies on the foreshore 7½ cables NE of Point Saint John.

Eddies. See 5.148.

Anchorage. There is anchorage for small vessels about 3 cables NE of Carreg-gafeiliog in 10 m, fine sand.

The Bishops and Clerks

Description

5.153

1   The Bishops and Clerks are a group of islets and rocks lying within 2½ miles W and NW of Ramsey Island (51°52′N 5°20′W).

South Bishop

5.154

1   South Bishop (51°51′N 5°25′W), is the SW islet of the group with dangers extending ½ cable NW and nearly 1 cable E from it; the islet is surmounted by a light (5.123).

There is a helicopter landing site at South Bishop.

A shoal, with a least charted depth of 14·3 m over it, lies 3 cables NW of the light.

North Bishop

5.155

1   North Bishop (51°54′N 5°23′W), the N islet of the group, with high rocks extending SW and NE, lies on a narrow ridge of broken and foul ground orientated on the same alignment. Dangerous rocks lie 6½ cables and 9½ cables SW of the centre of North Bishop.

Bell Rock, with a depth of 1·9 m over it lies at the NE end of the ridge 3¼ cables ENE of North Bishop; the rock and the ridge are marked by heavy tide-rips, which are sometimes dangerous, and the whole should be given a wide berth.

Daufraich

5.156

1   Between South Bishop and Ramsey Island there are several islets and dangers.

Daufraich, a flat islet, lies 7 cables NE of South Bishop, with Maen Daufraich, a rock, lying 1 cable farther N.

Moelyn, an above-water rock, lies 3½ cables ENE of Daufraich. Dangerous rocks lie 1 cable W and N of Moelyn. Cribog, a rock which just dries, lies between Daufraich and Moelyn. There is no safe passage between these rocks and there are heavy tide-rips from NE to SE of Moelyn.

2   **Llech Uchaf,** 1·5 m high, and Llech Isaf, a drying rock, lie near the N and S end, respectively, of foul and uneven ground over which there are heavy tide-rips, 6 to 8 cables off the W coast of Ramsey Island. A rocky patch, also marked by heavy tide-rips, lies 6½ cables S of Llech Isaf. Several depths of less than 10 m lie within 4 cables WNW and NW of the rocky patch.

Carreg Rhoson

5.157

1   Carreg Rhoson (51°52′·7N 5°23′·4W), with high rocks extending NE and SW, lies on a narrow ridge, orientated on this alignment, which has a least charted depth of 4·9 m at its NE end and 2·7 m at its SW end. An unmarked dangerous wreck lies close off the S side of Carreg Rhoson, the main islet. Excepting the SW end, Carreg Rhoson may be safely approached as there are no below-water rocks in its vicinity.

2   Maen Rhoson, steep-to, lies 2 cables NW of Carreg Rhoson. An unmarked dangerous wreck lies on its WNW side.

Carreg-trai, with three steep-to drying rocky heads, generally marked by breakers, lies 1¾ miles NE of Carreg Rhoson on a similar but smaller ridge which has a least depth of 4·4 m on its NE portion. An unmarked dangerous wreck lies on the NW side of the rocks.

Navigable channels
5.158

1   There are navigable channels amongst The Bishops and Clerks but none should be attempted at night or in low visibility. Good local knowledge is necessary.

The best channel, though narrower than some others, lies between the W coast of Ramsey Island and Llech Uchaf, Llech Isaf, and the rocky patch 5 cables S. It is safer than Ramsey Sound as the tidal streams are more direct and neither so rapid nor so irregular.

2   There is safe passage between South Bishop and Daufraich, though tide races may be found close to either side of the channel.

There is also a safe passage between Maen Daufraich and Carreg Rhoson; the sea in this passage is usually very disturbed. Between Maen Rhoson and North Bishop, which is also a safe passage, there are strong tidal streams and tide-rips.

Charts 1482 plan of Ramsey Sound, 1973
5.159

1   **Tidal streams.** The inshore S-going stream past Saint David's Head (51°54′N 5°19′W) divides near Gwahan (5.146); one part runs through Ramsey Sound and the other W of Ramsey Island. The N-going stream similarly runs either side of the island, with a tendency for a W set on the N side of Saint Bride's Bay.

2   Between Ramsey Island and The Bishops, the streams begin as follows:

Interval from HW Milford Haven	*Direction*
+0330	SW
−0225	NE

The maximum spring rate in each direction is 5 kn.
Eddies exist in the vicinity of all the islets.
5.160

1   **Directions.** Three alternatives are given for passage NE between Ramsey Island and North Bishop.

From a position SE of South Bishop (51°51′N 5°25′W) to the vicinity of Saint David's Head the track leads N, then NE, passing (with positions from Llech Uchaf (51°52′·3N 5°22′·1W) (5.156)):

W of Meini Duon (1¾ miles SSE), the most S islet off Ramsey Island, thence:

2   W of Carreg-gwylan (8 cables SE), an above water rock, thence:

E of Llech Isaf (4 cables S) (5.156), thence:

E of Llech Uchaf.

In the channel between Ramsey Island and Llech Uchaf vessels should keep closer to Ramsey Island. The track continues, passing:

3   W of Trwyn-drain-du (8 cables ENE), the NW point of Ramsey Island.

About 1 mile NNE of Llech Uchaf the track continues NE on the alignment (225°), astern, of the E edge of Daufraich (1¼ miles WSW) (5.156) with South Bishop, passing:

NW of Gwahan (1½ miles NE) (5.146), thence:

4   SE of Carreg-trai (1¾ miles NNE) (5.157), thence:
NW of Saint David's Head (2¾ miles NE).

Alternatively, from a position NW of South Bishop the route leads ENE between Daufraich and Carreg Rhoson (9 cables WNW), passing at least 2½ cables off Daufraich so as to give a wide berth to Maen Daufraich, thence on the alignment astern as previously directed

5   Or, from a position farther NW of South Bishop, the route leads NE between Maen Rhoson (1¼ miles WNW) and North Bishop, thence on the alignment (208°) astern of Carreg Rhoson with South Bishop, which passes SE of Bais Bank (51°57′N 5°22′W) (5.171).

The main shipping routes and TSS lie approximately 10 miles W of South Bishop.

(Directions for an inshore route to Strumble Head are given at 5.169)

SAINT DAVID'S HEAD TO FISHGUARD BAY

GENERAL INFORMATION

Chart 1973
Area covered
5.161

1   In this section are described:
The coastal and inshore routes between Saint David's Head (51°54′N 5°19′W) and Dinas Head, about 17 miles ENE.
Fishguard Bay including Fishguard Harbour.

Topography
5.162

1   The coastline between Saint David's Head (51°54′N 5°19′W) and Penberry, a hill 2½ miles ENE, is formed by steep-to perpendicular cliffs with no possible landing, but farther E towards Strumble Head (5.169) the coastline consists of moderately high cliffs with numerous bold headlands and small bays.

Fishing
5.163

1   See 5.3.

SAINT DAVID'S HEAD TO STRUMBLE HEAD

General information

Chart 1973
Routes
5.164

1   **Coastal route.** From the vicinity of Saint David's Head (51°54′N 5°19′W) and clear W of The Bishops and Clerks, the coastal route to Strumble Head (52°02′N 5°04′W) leads approximately 20 miles NE, passing NW of Bais Bank (51°57′N 5°22′W).

Inshore route. Small vessels opting to pass SE of Bais Bank are advised to keep at least 1 mile off the coast in order to avoid the dangers of Llechaucochion (5.172), and Bola Bleiddyn (5.172).

Topography
5.165

1   See 5.162.

Offshore buoys
5.166

1   Two light buoys (special) are moored in approximate position 52°10′N 5°04′W, about 8 cables apart.

Rescue
5.167

1   See 5.177.

Natural conditions
5.168

1   **Tidal streams** between Saint David's Head and Strumble Head (11 miles ENE), more than 1 mile offshore, set in the direction of the coast, see *Admiralty Tidal Stream Atlas — Irish Sea and Bristol Channel.*

Closer inshore they may be affected by local conditions. They begin as follows:

Interval from HW Holyhead	*Direction*
+0550	NE
−0010	SW

2   The maximum spring rate in each direction is 2 kn; the tidal stream N of Strumble Bank has been reported to attain a rate of 6 kn at springs, with slack water lasting from 10 to 20 minutes.

Tide-rips are generally in evidence over Bais Bank (5.171), between Bais Bank and the mainland and around the islets of North Bishop (5.155) and drying rocks of Carreg-trai (5.157).

3   **Fog.** During summer months frequent periods of fog can be experienced off exposed areas on this stretch of coastline.

Directions
(Continued from 5.126)

Principal marks
5.169

1   **Landmarks**:
Carn Llidi (51°54′N 5°17′W) (5.126).
Strumble Head (52°02′N 5°04′W), a barren, rugged mass of rock, steep-to, and one of the most conspicuous headlands in South Wales, lies at the NW end of Pen Caer promontory.

2   **Major lights**:
Strumble Head Light (white round tower, 11 m in height) exhibited from the summit of Ynys Meicel (5.171); the light is shown throughout 24 hours.
South Bishop Light (51°51′N 5°25′W) (5.123).
The Smalls Light (51°43′N 5°40′W) (5.14).

Other aids to navigation
5.170

1   See 5.15.

Coastal route
5.171

1   From a position W of Saint David's Head (51°54′N 5°19′W) and SW of Bais Bank, to a position NW of Strumble Head, the coastal route leads approximately

Strumble Head Lighthouse from N (5.169)
(Original dated 2001)

(Photograph - Air Images)

Strumble Head from W (5.171)
(Original dated 2001)

(Photograph - Air Images)

20 miles NE, passing (with positions from Saint David's Head (51°54′N 5°19′W)):

NW of Bais Bank (3 miles NW), a narrow ridge of fine sand and broken shells, which breaks during gales and is marked by strong tide-rips which may be dangerous to small craft, thence:

2   NW of Strumble Head (11¾ miles NE). Carreg Onnen and Ynys Meicel are rocky islets situated close to the W spur of the headland. Strumble Head Lighthouse stands on Ynys Meicel which is accessed from the mainland by a footbridge.

Inshore route
5.172

1   From a position between Saint David's Head and Bais Bank, at the N entrance to the navigable channels through The Bishops and Clerks, a route for smaller vessels which lies farther inshore leads NE towards Strumble Head passing (with positions from Saint David's Head (51°54′N 5°19′W)):

NW of Saint David's Head, the W extremity of a promontory, with Carn Llidi (5.126), a hill, 9 cables E, and:

SE of Bais Bank (3 miles NW), thence:

2   NW of Penberry (2½ miles ENE), a conical hill 173 m in height, which when seen from the W should not be confused with Carn Llidi, thence:

Seaward of Llechaucochion (3¾ miles NE), the collective name for three outer dangers, all of which dry, comprising Llech Isaf, Llech Ganol and Llech Uchaf, thence:

NW of Penclegyr (5¼ miles NE), with Griffiths Rock, 3½ cables W, thence:

3   NW of Pen Castell-coch (7 miles ENE) with Ynys Deullyn, a detached rock, 4 cables NE. Bola Bleiddyn, a rocky patch, lies 8 cables NNE. Thence:

NW of Penbwchdy (51°59′·6N 5°05′·7W), with Carreg Bwch-du, a rock, close W of it, thence:

NW of Pen Brush (52°01′N 5°05′W), with Tri Maen-trai, a group of drying rocks lying 4 cables S, thence:

4   NW of Strumble Head (52°02′N 5°04′W) (5.169). Strumble Rocks, two small rocks close offshore, lie 3 and 5½ cables ENE of the light; they form a danger to small vessels attempting to avoid the tidal stream by closely rounding the headland.

(Directions continue for the coastal route at 6.23; for Fishguard Bay at 5.179)

Harbours and anchorages
5.173

1   **Abereiddi Bay** (51°56′N 5°13′W), 4 miles ENE of Saint David's Head (51°54′N 5°19′W), affords anchorage in depths of 7 m. Trwyncastell forms the N entrance point of the bay with Traeth Rock, which just dries, lying 2 cables W of the point. The dangerous drying rocks of Llechaucochion (5.172) lie offshore in the W approaches to Abereiddi Bay.

2   **Porthgain** (51°57′N 5°11′W), a small artificial harbour, with a quay 150 m long, lies at the head of a small inlet, 15 m wide, 5 cables E of the headland Penclegyr. The bottom is soft mud. There are usually a great number of fishing boats moored within the harbour.

FISHGUARD BAY

General information

Charts 1973, 1484 plan of Fishguard Bay

General description
5.174

1   Fishguard Bay (52°01′N 4°57′W) lies on the E side of Pen Caer promontory, it is entered between Pen Anglas (52°01′·5N 4°59′·5W) (5.180), the NE extremity of the promontory, and Dinas Head (3 miles E) (5.175). The bay, which generally consists of high and steep-to cliffs with many small bays, contains the cross-channel ferry port of Fishguard Harbour, which lies on the W side of the bay 1 mile N of the town of Fishguard.

2   Apart from the Cow, 2 m in height, and the Calf, awash at MHWS, which lie amongst other drying rocks extending 1 cable NNE from Pen-cw at the root of Northern Breakwater, the bay is clear of dangers.

Topography
5.175

1   The N coast of Pen Caer promontory, to the W of Fishguard Bay, is of moderate height, rocky and steep-to with numerous indentations.

Dinas Head (52°02′N 4°55′W), on the E side of the bay, is an impressive headland with a distinctive wedge-shaped appearance. It is the N and highest part of Dinas Island, the name given to a peninsula connected to the mainland by a low swamp.

2   Mynydd Dinas (52°00′N 4°54′W) with Garn-Fawr, a remarkable rock on its summit, lies 2½ miles S of Dinas Head, at the end of the ridge of which Mynydd Carningli (6.23) lies at the E end.

Pilotage
5.176

1   See 5.184.

Rescue
5.177

1   All-weather and inshore lifeboats are stationed in Fishguard Harbour (52°00′N 4°59′W).

For details of rescue organisation see 1.60.

Natural conditions
5.178

1   **Tidal streams** approximately 2½ cables N of Pen Anglas begin as follows:

Interval from HW Holyhead	Direction	Remarks
–0605	E	The E-going stream N of Pen Anglas runs for 3¼ hours.
–0255	W	The W-going stream runs for 9¼ hours.

The maximum E spring rate is 1¾ kn; W is 2¾ kn.

2   Midway between Pen Anglas and Dinas Head the streams begin as follows:

+0530	E	The E-going stream runs towards Dinas Head.
–0120	W	The W-going stream runs towards N Breakwater.

The maximum E spring rate is 1 kn; W is 1½ kn.

There is little or no stream in the harbour.

3   Near the S shore of the bay, outside the harbour, there is no perceptible E going stream but a very weak W-going stream runs between –0310 and +0550 HW Holyhead.

Further details on tidal information within the bay can be obtained from the chart.

Eddy. Between Strumble Head and Pen Anglas an eddy sets W during part of the E-going stream.

Tide races extend 5 cables N from Pen Anglas. There is a strong race 2½ cables N of Dinas Head.

Swell in the bay during N gales is considerable.

Directions
(continued from 5.172)

Principal marks
5.179

1   **Landmarks**:
    Strumble Head (52°02′N 5°04′W) (5.169).
    Dinas Head (52°02′N 4°55′W) (5.175).
    Garn-Fawr (52°00′N 4°54′W) (5.175).
    Mynydd Carningli (52°00′N 4°49′W) (6.23).
Major light:
    Strumble Head Light (52°02′N 5°04′W) (5.169).

Strumble Head to Fishguard Bay
5.180

1   From a position NW of Strumble Head the approach route into Fishguard Bay and to the pilot boarding position (5.184) leads E then SSE, passing (with positions from Strumble Head Light (5.169)):
    N of Strumble Bank (1½ miles ENE), over which there are tide-rips, thence:

2   N of Carregwastad Point (1¾ miles E) lying at the W entrance of an inlet; an inconspicuous stone, commemorating the landing of French forces in 1797, stands on the summit of the point. Thence:
    N and ENE of Pen Anglas (3 miles E), the NE extremity of Pen Caer promontory, on which stands an obelisk 4 m in height.

5.181

1   The approach to Fishguard Bay from the E is clear of dangers. Vessels should keep a distance of at least 3 cables when passing N of Dinas Head to avoid a strong tide race to seaward of the headland.

(Directions continue for Fishguard Harbour at 5.186)

Fishguard Harbour

Chart 1484 plan of Fishguard Bay
General information
5.182

1   **Position.** Fishguard Harbour (52°00′N 4°59′W) lies in the SW part of Fishguard Bay at Goodwick and is protected on its N and E sides by breakwaters.

The town of Fishguard lies at the head and to the W of Aber Gwaun, a small drying inlet on the S side of the bay which forms the harbour of Lower Fishguard (5.190) lying outside the port limits.

2   **Function.** The port is a RoRo ferry terminal operating cross-channel passenger and cargo services to Rosslare in the Republic of Ireland. Container traffic can be handled.

Port limits. The harbour limit extends from Saddle Point (52°00′·0N 4°58′·6W), the NW entry point to Aber Gwaun, to a point 1 cable E of Northern Breakwater head, thence it continues at a radius of 1 cable from the breakwater head and 1 cable off the N side of the breakwater to the group of rocks close by the root of the breakwater.

3   **Approach and entry.** The harbour is approached through Fishguard Bay and entered between breakwaters open ESE.

Traffic. In 2007, in addition to the regular ferry traffic, there were 2 port calls with a total of 2985 dwt.

Fishguard Harbour from E (5.182)
(Original dated 2001)

(Photograph - Air Images)

Port Authority: Stena Line Ports Ltd, Fishguard Harbour, Pembrokeshire SA64 0BU.

The Port Authority is represented by the Harbour Master.

Limiting conditions
5.183

1 **Deepest and longest berth**: Railway Quay (5.188).

Tidal levels: mean spring range about 4·0 m; mean neap range about 1·4 m; there is a tide gauge at the N end of No 1 Berth. See *Admiralty Tide Tables.*

Maximum size of vessel handled. The port can accommodate vessels up to 200 m in length, 28 m beam and 6·5 m draught.

Arrival information
5.184

1 **Notice of ETA required.** ETAs should be forwarded 12 hours in advance, with amendments up to 4 hours before the original ETA to the Harbour Master.

Outer anchorages. Vessels should anchor S of a line drawn ENE from the head of Northern Breakwater. In order not to obstruct the harbour entrance, vessels intending to anchor should maintain a distance of at least 5 cables from the breakwater head.

2 **Restricted anchorage** area lies within the harbour, W of a line drawn between Northern Breakwater Light, a channel marker buoy (special), off the head of East Breakwater, and the RoRo terminal.

3 **Pilotage.** The pilotage district is bounded by a line drawn 090° from Pen Anglas (52°01'·5N 4°59'·5W) to longitude 4°57'W, thence 180° to the coast. Pilotage is compulsory for vessels over 500 gt or drawing over 4·26 m within the pilotage area. Under certain circumstances vessels usually exempt may be required to take a pilot. The pilot boards 8 cables E of Northern Breakwater Light (5.187); the pilot vessel, which carries VHF radio, cruises only when a vessel is expected.

4 See *Admiralty List of Radio Signals Volume 6(1).*

Traffic regulations. Bye-laws, including those regarding vessels carrying petroleum and carbide of calcium, are in force; copies can be obtained from the Port Authority.

Harbour
5.185

1 **General layout.** The single quay is aligned NNE/SSW. It is protected from N by Northern Breakwater, extending 5 cables ESE. There is another breakwater, East Breakwater extending ENE from the shore to form a SE facing entrance 5¾ cables wide.

Natural conditions: see 5.178.

Directions for entering harbour
(continued from 5.181)
5.186

1 When within Fishguard Bay, Northern Breakwater should be given a berth of at least 1 cable as the toe of the breakwater extends just over 60 m seawards of the light (5.187) at its head.

The alignment (282°) of the lights in line (white diamond daymarks on a white mast) situated 1 cable W of Railway Quay (5.188) passes 2 cables S of Northern Breakwater Light.

5.187

1 **Useful marks:**

Northern Breakwater Light (52°00'·8N 4°58'·2W) (octagonal concrete tower, 20 m in height) standing at the head of the breakwater.

East Breakwater Light (metal framework tower, 11 m in height) standing at the head of the breakwater which extends 4 cables ENE from the middle of Goodwick Sands which lie in the SW corner of Fishguard Bay.

2 Hotel (white) (52°00'·5N 4°59'·4W), 1½ cables SW of Railway Quay (5.188).

Fort (ruins) (52°00'·1N 4°58'·2W), at Castle Point.

Berths
5.188

1 **Railway Quay,** with depths of up to 6·0 m alongside and 549 m of quay space, occupies the greater part of the NW side of the harbour.

The area extending to 1½ cables off Railway Quay is foul owing to the presence of disused concrete clumps and chains on the seabed.

2 There are four berths alongside the quay, numbered 1 to 4 from N. No 2 Berth is the lay-by berth; No 3 Berth, 135 m long, is used for general cargo; No 4 Berth, 155 m long is suitable for the maximum size of vessel (5.183) but when clear is available for RoRo traffic.

A stone embankment extends S from No 4 Berth to Goodwick Sands.

3 **Depths** alongside: 3 m between Nos 1 and 2 Berths, 5 m between Nos 2 and 3 Berths and 6·5 m between Nos 3 and 4 Berths. The harbour, however, is susceptible to seiches (see 1.101) which can cause fluctuations in sea level.

Leading Lights (282°)

Northern Breakwater Head

Fishguard entrance from ENE (5.186)
(Original dated 2001)

(Photograph – Copyright Granted)

Fishguard – Railway Quay from SSE (5.188)
(Original dated 2001)

(Photograph – Air Images)

For the latest information on depths alongside and within the harbour the Port Authority should be consulted.

4 There are some private yacht moorings in the S part of Fishguard Harbour, SW of the restricted anchorage (5.184). There are also slipways at each end of Railway Quay and from close to a pier which extends SE from the stone embankment 2 cables SW of the ferry terminal.

Shelter from E gales can be obtained in Pwllgwaelod, a small drying inlet with a slipway, which lies within Fishguard Bay, 8 cables inside Dinas Head. Fresh water at the quay.

5 **Landing places.** The best landing place is at the steps at Railway Quay, 1½ cables N of the ferry terminal. Landing from small boats can also be made from the pier SW of the ferry terminal.

Port services
5.189
1 **Repairs:** minor repairs, 24-tonne fixed crane at No 2 Berth.

Other facilities: issue of SSCC and SSCEC; reception of oily waste by arrangement; hospital at Haverfordwest, 15 miles S.

Supplies: fuel can be delivered by road tanker; fresh water; provisions.

Lower Fishguard
5.190
1 **General description.** Lower Fishguard, a small harbour, is formed by Aber Gwaun, a small drying inlet on the S side of Fishguard Bay. It is entered between Castle Point (52°00′N 4°58′W) and Saddle Point, 1¾ cables farther W.

Outfalls. An outfall, marked at its seaward end by a beacon (starboard hand), is laid down the centre of the inlet. Another outfall, also marked at its seaward end by a beacon (starboard hand), is laid from the SW side of the inlet to a position 60 m off the quay, mentioned below.

2 **Submarine power cable** crosses the inlet near its head.

Berth. A short pier extends from the E side of the inlet 2 cables S of Castle Point and affords a little protection to the harbour; above the pier there is a quay. Fishing vessels up to 24·4 m with a draught of up to 3 m use the quay at MHWS; all vessels can expect to take the ground, mud and clay overlaid by gravel. There is a slipway, limited facilities and berths are available by arrangement.

Caution. Winds from the N cause a considerable sea to set into the inlet; NNW winds cause the worst swell.

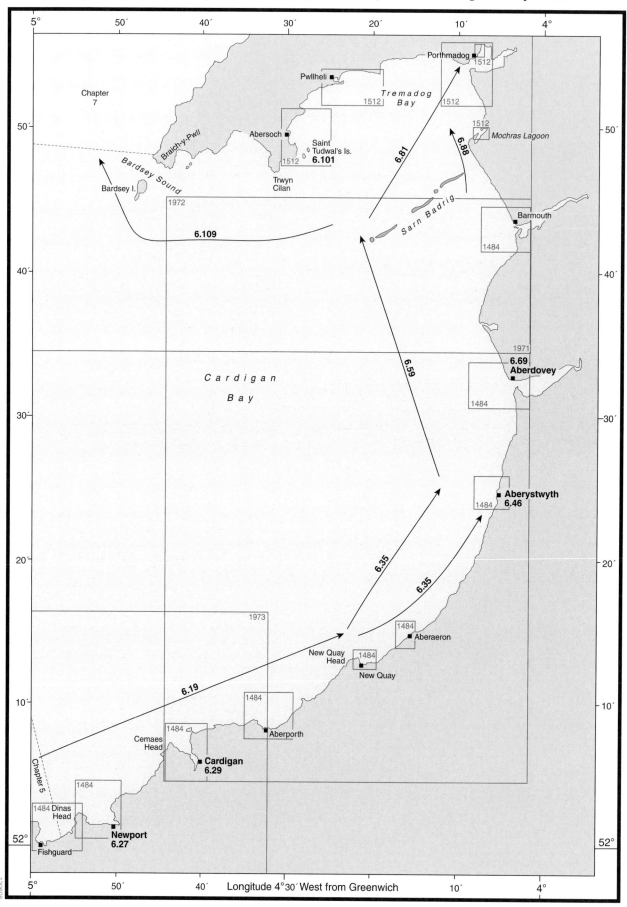

CHAPTER 6

CARDIGAN BAY — FISHGUARD BAY TO BRAICH Y PWLL
INCLUDING BARDSEY ISLAND

GENERAL INFORMATION

Chart 1410
Scope of the chapter
6.1

1   This chapter covers the waters off the coast of Cardigan Bay between Fishguard Bay (52° 01′N 4° 58′W) and Braich y Pwll (52°48′N 4°46′W) the SW extremity of Lleyn Peninsula, 47½ miles N, and includes Bardsey Island (52°46′N 4°47′W), which lies 2 miles SSW of Braich y Pwll.

The chapter is divided into the following sections:
Offshore Route West of Bardsey Island (6.8).
Fishguard Bay to Aberystwyth (6.14).
Aberystwyth to Braich y Pwll (6.55).

Topography
6.2

1   Cardigan Bay is entered between Saint David's Head (51°54′N 5°19′W) and Bardsey Island, 55 miles NNE. The E and NE parts of the bay contain several dangerous shoals of which the most important are Cynfelyn Patches (6.67), which extend nearly 7 miles offshore, and Sarn Badrig (6.66) which extends nearly 11 miles offshore.

2   The bay in general consists of numerous indentations with high and steep-to cliffs and bold headlands. However, the central and N coastline consists of areas of low ground comprising marshland and sandhills backed by higher ground. In the N and SE part of the bay the coastline is backed by high land attaining a height of 200 to 300 m, rising in the NE part to a height of 900 m; this high land is often capped by cloud.

3   Bardsey Island, which lies off the SW tip of the Lleyn Peninsula (7.2) is 165 m high at its highest point.

Traffic separation scheme
6.3

1   A TSS is established 8 miles W of The Smalls (51°43′N 5°40′W). The general flow of traffic lies in the direction NNE-SSW. The scheme is IMO-adopted and Rule 10 of the *International Regulations for Preventing Collisions at Sea (1972)* applies. See 1.9.

Fishing
6.4

1   Trawlers may be encountered in Cardigan Bay, in particular in the spring, where they work in the shelter from E winds.

Inshore trawlers may be encountered at any time in depths of 20 m to 35 m. Scallop dredgers may also be encountered within these depths, sometimes in concentrations.

2   Pots may be found off the coast, occasionally out to 10 miles offshore.

For details of types of fishing and nets in use see *The Mariner's Handbook.*

Dumping ground
6.5

1   Underwater explosives may still remain in an area centred on 52°30′N 4°40′W and bounded by the following positions, which was formerly used as a dumping ground:
52°20′N 4°50′W;
52°40′N 4°50′W;
52°40′N 4°30′W;
52°20′N 4°30′W.

Rescue
6.6

1   For details of rescue organisation and locations of assets see 1.60 and text under Rescue.

Natural conditions
6.7

1   **Tidal streams.** The flow over the area covered by this chapter is largely determined by tidal forces. The streams set N and S across the entrance to Cardigan Bay nearly in the line of the fairway of Saint George's Channel.

In the bay nearer the land, except in the N part, the streams tend to set in the direction of the coast and become weaker. Close inshore the streams may be modified by local conditions.

2   Tidal streams are given on the chart and in *Admiralty Tidal Stream Atlas — Irish Sea and Bristol Channel.*

Tide races and tide-rips which may be dangerous to small craft are particularly in evidence in the following areas:
Devil's Ridge (52°45′N 4°40′W).
Bastram Shoal (52°43′N 4°47′W).
The Devil's Tail (52°38′N 4°42′W).
Around Bardsey Island (52°46′N 4°47′W).

3   **Sandwaves.** Seaward of Cynfelyn Patches (6.67) and Sarn Badrig (6.66), the seabed slopes gently W to depths of 40 m nearly 25 miles offshore but there are a large number of irregular shoals of the sandwave type some of which are up to 7 m proud of the seabed. Gales are likely to alter the shape of these irregular shoals.

OFFSHORE ROUTE WEST OF BARDSEY ISLAND

General information

Chart 1410
Route
6.8

1   From a position WNW of Strumble Head (52°02′N 5°04′W), the offshore route leads about 45 miles NNE in deep water, well W of the entrance to Cardigan Bay, to a position WNW of Bardsey Island (52°46′N 4°47′W).

Topography
6.9

1   See 6.2 and 7.2.

Rescue
6.10

1   All-weather lifeboats are stationed at Porthstinian, 1½ miles S of Saint David's Head (51°54′N 5°19′W) and at Porth Dinllaen (52°57′N 4°34′W).

For details of rescue organisation see 1.60.

Tidal streams
6.11

1   See 6.7.

Directions
(continued from 5.16)

Principal marks
6.12

1   **Landmarks:**
Strumble Head (52°02′N 5°04′W) (5.169).
Cadair Idris (52°42′N 3°55′W) (6.56).
Bardsey Island (52°46′N 4°47′W) (6.115).
Radio Tower (52°50′N 4°38′W) (6.113).
Braich y Pwll (52°48′N 4°46′W) (7.36).

2   **Major lights:**
The Smalls Light (51°43′N 5°40′W) (5.14).
South Bishop Light (51°51′N 5°25′W) (5.123).
Tuskar Rock Light (52°12′N 6°12′W) (See *Irish Coast Pilot*).
Strumble Head Light (52°02′N 5°04′W) (5.169).
Bardsey Island Light (white square tower with red bands, 30 m in height) (52°45′N 4°48′W).

Bardsey Island Lighthouse from WNW (6.12)
(Original dated 2001)

(Photograph - Air Images)

Strumble Head to Bardsey Island
6.13

1   From a position about 20 miles WNW of Strumble Head (52°02′N 5°04′W) and a similar distance NNE of the N end of the traffic lanes off The Smalls (51°43′N 5°40′W), the route leads about 45 miles NNE, in deep water, to a position W of Braich y Pwll (52°48′N 4°46′W).

In thick weather vessels should keep in depths of not less than 75 m.

(Directions continue at 7.15)

FISHGUARD BAY TO ABERYSTWYTH

GENERAL INFORMATION

Chart 1410
Area covered
6.14

1   In this section are described the coastal routes, harbours and anchorages between Fishguard Bay (52°01′N 4°58′W) and Aberystwyth (40 miles ENE).

It is arranged as follows:
Fishguard Bay to New Quay Head (6.19).
New Quay Head to Aberystwyth (6.35).

Topography
6.15

1   The coastline comprises numerous indentations with bold headlands, high and steep-to slate rock cliffs, backed by higher ground. North-east of Cadwgan Point (52°15′N 4°15′W) (chart 1972) the coast recedes and becomes flat and low for about 6 miles, with high ground 5 cables inland, before rising again.

2   Several rivers run into the S part of the bay including the afon Teifi, the largest, which flows through Cardigan (6.29).

Firing practice area
6.16

1   There are about 20 targets, moorings and buoys marking scientific instruments within 20 miles of Pencribach (52°08′·6N 4°33′·5W) (6.24). Some are marked by flashing lights. Their positions are frequently changed and care should be exercised when navigating in the area, especially at night and in poor visibility.

2   The latest information on this practice area and that on the coast at Aberporth, lying on the E side of Pencribach, may be obtained from Aberporth Marine Control, QinetiQ, MoD Aberporth See *Admiralty List of Radio Signals Volume 3(1)*.

For further information on practice areas, see 1.15 and *Annual Notice to Mariners Number 5*.

Fishing
6.17

1   See 6.4.

Nature reserve
6.18

1   Cardigan Island (52°08′N 4°41′W).
For further information see 1.58.

FISHGUARD BAY TO NEW QUAY HEAD

General information

Charts 1973, 1972
Route
6.19

1   From a position NW of Strumble Head (52°02′N 5°04′W) (5.169) the coastal route, leads about 30 miles ENE to a position NNW of New Quay Head. Excepting the firing practice area (6.16), the route is clear of charted dangers when more than 1 mile off the coast.

Topography
6.20

1   See 6.15.

Rescue
6.21

1   An all-weather lifeboat is stationed at Fishguard Harbour (52°00′N 4°59′W) and at New Quay (52°13′N 4°21′W) (6.44); inshore lifeboats are stationed at Fishguard and at Gwybert, within Port Cardigan (52°07′N 4°42′W) (6.29).
       For details of rescue organisation see 1.60.

Tidal streams
6.22

1   See 6.7.

Directions
(continued from 5.172)

Principal marks
6.23

1   **Landmarks**:
       Strumble Head (52°02′N 5°04′W) (5.169).
       Mynydd Carningli (52°00′N 4°49′W) is a bold rugged mountain, situated at the E end of a ridge, 3 miles long, running parallel to the coast 2 miles inland. This ridge is separated from Mynydd Preseli, which rises to more than 500 m 3 miles S, by a deep ravine.

2   Hotel (52°07′N 4°41′W) (6.29).
       New Quay Head (52°13′N 4°22′W) (6.24).
       Major light:
       Strumble Head Light (52°02′N 5°04′W) (5.169).

Passage
6.24

1   From a position NW of Strumble Head (52°02′N 5°04′W), the coastal route leads about 30 miles ENE to the vicinity of New Quay Head (52°13′N 4°22′W), passing (with positions from Cemaes Head (52°07′N 4°44′W)):
       NNW of Dinas Head (8¼ miles SW) (5.175), thence:

2   NNW of Cemaes Head, a bold cape which rises steeply above the cliffs to an elevation of more than 180 m, thence:
       NNW of Cardigan Island (1¾ miles ENE), steep-to except at its W end where drying rocks extend ½ cable offshore; the island is part of Wildlife Trust West Wales (1.58). Thence:

3   NNW of Pencribach (6½ miles ENE), a table headland on which there are a number of pylons and towers, thence:
       NNW of Pen-y-Badell (10¼ miles ENE), a promontory, with a hill resembling an inverted pan

standing close SE. Ynys-Lochtyn, an islet, lies close NE. Thence:

4   NNW of New Quay Head (52°13′N 4°22′W), a high rugged and conspicuous point backed by Pen-y-Castell, 92 m in height, close S. Carreg Draenog, a large rock which is remarkable when viewed from NE or SW, lies 5½ cables WSW of the headland; Carreg Walltog, another rock, lies 1 cable W of the headland and is connected to the coast by a drying ledge. An ODAS light buoy is moored about 15 miles NW of New Quay Head.

Useful mark
6.25

1   New Quay Breakwater Light (52°13′N 4°21′W).
       (Directions continue at 6.40)

Newport Bay

Chart 1484 plan of Newport Bay
General information
6.26

1   **Description.** Newport Bay, which is clear of dangers with depths decreasing regularly to the shore, is entered between Dinas Head (52°02′N 4°55′W) (5.175) and Pen-y-bâl, 2¼ miles E.
       Topography. The coast between Dinas Head and the afon Nyfer, which flows into the SE corner of the bay, consists of slate rock; near Pen-y-bâl the coast is high and steep-to. Carregedrywy, a rock 2 m in height, lies 2 cables N of Pen-y-bâl and is connected to the mainland by a drying ledge.

2   Newport Sands, composed of fine, smooth, hard sand which dries, extend 5 cables N from the entrance to the afon Nyfer.
       Anchorage. Vessels may anchor in any part of the bay, the bottom of which is composed of sand and broken shell, but it affords no shelter in bad weather. Care should be taken to avoid a sewage outfall which extends nearly 4 cables NW from a position close W of the S entrance point to the river.

Newport
6.27

1   **General information.** Newport, a small seaside resort, lies on the S side of the river, at the foot of Mynydd Carningli (6.23).
       The harbour of Newport lies at Parrog, close within the mouth of the afon Nyfer W of Newport. The bed of the river is stony and dries in places. Craft up to 15 m in length with a draught of up to 3 m can be accommodated at MHWS, but should be prepared to take the ground.

2   During onshore winds a considerable sea sets into the bay and renders access to the harbour impossible.
       Tidal streams set round Newport Bay but are very weak.
       Local knowledge is required to enter the harbour. Local fishermen act as pilots.
       Supplies: marine diesel in small quantities; fresh water; provisions.
6.28

1   **Boat harbour.** There is a small boat harbour (52°01′·4N 4°53′·5W), between Trwyn Isaac and Pig y Baw, on the E side of the neck of Dinas Island peninsula (5.175). It is partly protected by some rocks which extend N from Trwyn Isaac.

Chart 1484 plan of Approaches to Cardigan
Port Cardigan
6.29
1   **General information.** Port Cardigan is a bay entered between Cemaes Head (52°07′N 4°44′W) and Cardigan Island, 1½ miles ENE. Except for an unmarked dangerous wreck lying close NW of the W extremity of Cardigan Island, there are no outlying dangers.

2   Cardigan Sound, the narrow passage between the island and the coast, has depths of 3·7 m. Rocks extend from its SE side. The passage is navigable but should not be attempted without local knowledge.

Port Cardigan entrance can be identified by Freni-fawr (51°59′N 4°37′W) (Chart 1973), a mountain, bearing 160° through it.

3   **Tidal streams** are weak in Port Cardigan but set strongly in Cardigan Sound. At the entrance to the afon Teifi the streams begin as follows:

Interval from HW Holyhead	Directions	Remarks
+0325	In-going	
–0330	Out-going	Begins earlier during freshets

4   **Landmark**:
Hotel standing close SE of Craig y Gwbert (52°07′N 4°41′W) on the E side of the bay.

Anchorage. There is good holding in the bay, with Cemaes Head bearing 260° or more. The bottom is generally sandy. Shelter from SW gales may be obtained under the lee of Cemaes Head.
6.30
1   **Landing places.** There is a pier and slipway at Penrhyn on the W side of the bay, below the castellated house of the old coastguard station. When there is any sea running it is usable only after half tide owing to drying rocks which lie off the pier. There is also a landing place at Poppit Sands 5 cables ESE of the slipway. Landing can be effected on the E side of the bay behind the rocks close under Craig y Gwbert (6.29).

Cardigan Harbour
6.31
1   **General information.** Cardigan Harbour is used by fishing boats and pleasure craft up to 12 m in length and a draught of 1·1 m. It is formed by the sand-encumbered estuary of the afon Teifi, the largest river which flows into Cardigan Bay. There are depths of less than 0·3 m over the bar. The entrance channel in the estuary is subject to considerable change. A road-bridge with an adjacent footbridge crosses the river at Cardigan. The centre span of the bridge is marked by a light on both upstream and downstream sides.

2   An overhead cable, with a vertical clearance of 8 m, spans the river 5 cables above the road-bridge at Cardigan. The river is tidal as far as Llechryd Bridge, 3½ miles above Cardigan, and navigable by boats.

Directions cannot be given since the channel is subject to considerable change and is not marked by permanent buoys; local knowledge is required. The river does tend to follow the E side of the estuary as far as Pen yr Ergyd, a sand and shingle point where the river narrows, 1¾ miles ESE of Cemaes Head. A light-beacon (isolated danger) stands 2 cables NNW of Pen yr Ergyd.

3   **Useful mark:** From W, the fixed lights exhibited from the coastguard building standing 1 cable S of the hotel at Craig y Gwbert (52°07′·1N 4°41′·3W).

Caution should be exercised when crossing the bar as high breaking seas may occur even in light winds, particularly at spring tides when the out-going tidal stream is at full strength. Visitors should ascertain the position of the channel across the bar before entering.

4   Berths include Cambrian Quay, on the N bank of the river W of the road-bridge.

There are numerous moorings, mostly drying, in the harbour. Facilities are limited but include two slipways and a boat club.

Chart 1484 plan of Aberporth
Cribach Bay
6.32
1   Cribach Bay is entered between Pencribach (52°08′·6N 4°33′·4W) (6.24) and a point 2 cables SE. There are depths of 3·5 m in the bay to within a short distance of the beach at its head. Small mooring buoys are laid off the bay.

Aberporth Bay
6.33
1   Aberporth Bay (52°08′·2N 4°32′·8W), which dries, is 5 cables SE of Pencribach (6.24), and contains the fishing village of Aberporth. Both Aberporth and Cribach Bays derive some protection from Pencribach during W winds.

A Firing Practice Area exists in the vicinity of Aberporth. See 1.15.

Chart 1972
Pen-y-Badell
6.34
1   On the E side of Pen-y-Badell (52°10′N 4°28′W), there is a small bay which affords temporary anchorage in offshore winds, but a considerable sea quickly sets in on a change of wind.

NEW QUAY HEAD TO ABERYSTWYTH

General information

Chart 1972
Routes
6.35
1   From the vicinity of New Quay Head (52°13′N 4°22′W) the coastal route leads about 11 miles NNE to a position W of Patches Light Buoy (W cardinal) which marks Outer Patch (52°26′N 4°14′W) the W edge of Cynfelyn Patches (6.67).

2   From the former position, an inshore route leads NE for about 14 miles to a position off Aberystwyth, passing S of Cynfelyn Patches, and is clear of charted dangers at a distance of more than 1 mile from the coast.

Topography
6.36
1   See 6.15.

Hazards
6.37
1   **Firing practice area.** See 6.16.
Fishing. A trawling ground, best seen on the chart, lies between New Quay Head (52°13′N 4°22′W) and Aberystwyth (52°25′N 4°05′W).

Rescue
6.38
1   An all-weather lifeboat is stationed at New Quay (52°13′N 4°22′W); inshore lifeboats are stationed at Aberystwyth and New Quay.

For details of rescue organisation see 1.60.

Tidal streams
6.39
1   See 6.7.

Caution. As there is a tendency of both in-going and out-going streams to set towards the coast between Cadwgan Reef and Aberystwyth, vessels should keep in depths of at least 16 m.

Directions
(continued from 6.25)

Landmarks
6.40
1   New Quay Head (52°13′N 4°22′W) (6.24).

Television mast (52°21′·6N 4°06′·2W) standing at an elevation of 346 m and marked by obstruction lights.

Coastal route
6.41
1   From a position NNW of New Quay Head (52°13′N 4°22′W) to a position W of Patches Light Buoy (W cardinal) (52°26′N 4°16′W), moored at the W edge of Cynfelyn Patches (6.67), the coastal route leads about 7 miles NNE, passing WNW of, and farther to seaward of, the features passed and described in the inshore route below.

2   In poor visibility, in the vicinity of Cynfelyn Patches, mariners should keep in depths of not less than 18 m.

(Directions continue for the coastal route at 6.65)

Approaches to Aberystwyth
6.42
1   From a position NNW of New Quay Head, the inshore route to Aberystwyth leads about 14 miles NE, passing (with positions from Pen Pigyn (52°19′N 4°09′W)):

    NW of Ina Point (9 miles SW), a low point, with foul ground and drying rocks extending 3 cables NW, thence:

    NW of Cadwgan Point (5½ miles SW) with Sarn Cadwgan, a rocky ledge, 5 cables offshore, thence:

2   Seaward of Clydan Patch (3¼ miles SW), rock, thence:

    NW of Cadwgan Reef (2¼ miles SW), with depths of less than 5 m which cause a heavy sea in bad weather, thence:

    NW of Pen Pigyn, a high cliff; Carreg Ti-pw, a detached rock, lies close offshore.

Thence the route continues NE for a further 5½ miles to a position NW of Aberystwyth.

Useful marks
6.43
1   New Quay Breakwater Light (52°13′N 4°21′W).
Aberaeron Pier Lights (52°14′·6N 4°15′·9W).
Aberystwyth S Breakwater Light (52°24′·4N 4°05′·5W).

(Directions for Aberystwyth Harbour are given at 6.50)

New Quay Bay

Chart 1484 plan of New Quay
General information
6.44
1   **Description.** New Quay Bay (52°13′N 4°21′W) is entered between New Quay Head (52°13′·1N 4°21′·7W) (6.24) and Ina Point, 1 mile ESE. The head of the bay is backed by clay cliffs. Foul ground and drying rocks extend 3¾ cables NW from Ina Point, terminating in Carreg Ina, a rock which dries.

Shoal water with depths of less than 2 m extends approximately 2 cables W of Carreg Ina. Other than these there are no other dangers within the bay.

2   A discharge, ending in a diffuser, extends 7 cables NNW from a position 1 cable W of Ina Point. The alignment (153½°) of a pair of beacons (special) at the shore end clears close W of the pipeline. Posts, protecting the riser pipes, protrude 1 m proud of the sea-bed over the seaward 50 m of the pipeline.

3   **Tidal streams** set regularly across the entrance to New Quay Bay; the spring rate in each direction is approximately 1 kn.

The streams set round the bay but are weak.

4   **Directions.** Approaching from E the track leads WSW, passing NNW of a buoy (N cardinal) moored 2 cables NW of Carreg Ina, which lies in the green sector (252°–295°) of New Quay breakwater light (52°13′·00N 4°21′·4W). It should be noted that this sector does not completely cover the shoal water between Carreg Ina and the buoy.

5   **Anchorage.** The bay affords shelter with offshore winds in depths of 5 m, sand; NW winds raise a heavy sea and swell rendering the anchorage untenable. The best holding is between 2 and 3 cables NE of New Quay pier.

New Quay Harbour
6.45
1   **General information.** New Quay Harbour, which dries and is used principally by small craft, is protected by a breakwater extending 150 m E from Penwig Point (52°12′·9N 4°21′·5W). A sectored light is exhibited near the head of the breakwater. A light beacon (E cardinal) marks the extremity of the pier extension about 80 m SSE from the head of the breakwater.

2   A beacon (starboard hand), situated 45 m SSE of the light, marks the end of a stone groyne which connects some sunken rocks with the head of the breakwater. A short breakwater extends about 60 m SE from the shore, 1¼ cables S of the main breakwater.

3   **Harbour Authority.** The Harbour Master, Harbour Master's Office, The Pier, New Quay, Ceredigion, SA45 9NW. VHF watch is kept intermittently.

Berths and facilities. Vessels of up to 2 m draught can enter at HW springs and take the ground on a bottom of sand and clay. However, the harbour affords practically no shelter during onshore winds.

4   Craft usually berth stern to the breakwater with anchors ahead. There are no alongside landings for boats except at HW.

There are moorings for local craft S of the breakwater.

Facilities for visiting craft are limited. There are a number of moorings in the bay, and New Quay Yacht Club is situated on the pier.

Supplies: small quantities of fuel, fresh water and provisions.

Wellington Monument

Castle Point

Aberystwyth from NW (6.46)

(Original dated 2001)

(Photograph - Air Images)

Aberystwyth

Chart 1484 plan of Aberystwyth
General information
6.46

1   **Position.** Aberystwyth (52°25′N 4°05′W), a seaside resort and small harbour, and also the seat of the University of Wales, lies close within the mouth of the afon Rheidol, N of its confluence with the afon Ystwyth.

    Function. Aberystwyth Harbour is a busy fishing harbour used at more than half tide by angling vessels and crab and lobster boats. There is a marina on the E side of the river.

2   **Topography.** Castle Point (4 cables N of the harbour entrance), the W extremity of a low promontory at the W end of the town, is fronted by rocky ledges. Castle Rock and Pen Cwningen, detached patches of drying rock, lie 1¾ cables SSW and 1½ cables N respectively, of Castle Point. An iron promenade pier extends ½ cable NW along the E edge of Castle Point ledges. A submerged damaged portion of the pier extends 45 m from its head and boats should keep well clear.

3   **Approach and entry.** Entered from NW across a sandbar and between two breakwater heads.

    Port Authority. Director of Highways, Property and Works, Cyngor Sir Ceredigion, County Hall, Market Street, Aberaeron, SA46 0AT.

    The Harbour Authority is represented by a Harbour Master.

Limiting conditions
6.47

1   **Controlling depth:** minimum charted depth on the bar 0·5 m, however, the harbour for the most part dries.

    Tidal levels: see *Admiralty Tide Tables*. Mean spring range about 4·3 m; mean neap range about 1·7 m.

    Maximum size of vessel handled: 33·5 m LOA; 3·3 m draught.

    Local sea state: a swell nearly always breaks on the bar near LW and often at HW; in strong NW winds conditions over the bar can be dangerous.

Arrival information.
6.48

1   **Outer anchorages.** There is good anchorage in depths of 9 m, sand and clay, 6 cables SW of Castle Point, or in similar depths, mud and stones, 5½ cables NW of Castle Point.

    Local knowledge. See 6.51.

Harbour
6.49

1   **General layout.** The entrance, which is formed by the outlet of the two rivers, is protected from SW by a breakwater which extends 1¼ cables NW from the shore. A submerged portion of this breakwater, half of which dries, extends ½ cable farther NW. A light (metal column, green and white bands, 12 m in height) is exhibited at the head of the breakwater, and from near its root a bridge spans the afon Ystwyth.

2   A mole with a timber jetty at its S end extends S from the N side of the entrance to within ½ cable of the S breakwater. A light (column, red and white bands, 4 m in height) is exhibited from the head of the timber jetty. A tide gauge is situated at the seaward end of the jetty.

Tidal streams are generally weak. There is always a surface current setting out of the harbour at a rate of 1 kn on the in-going stream to 3 kn on the out-going stream. The duration of the in-going stream is 5¾ hours; out-going, 7 hours.

Directions for entering harbour.
6.50
1   **Caution.** Stones and boulders lie near the head of the S breakwater. The Trap, a rocky area dangerous to small craft, lies W of N breakwater.

Leading lights:
> Front light (white topmark) (52°24′·4N 4°05′·4W).
> Rear light (white post, 3 m in height) (close SE of front light).

2   From a position NW of the harbour entrance the alignment (133°) of these lights or, by day, of a beacon (white post (not charted) close NW of front light) with the topmark of the front light, leads through the best water over the bar towards the harbour entrance, passing SW of Castle Rock (3½ cables NNW of front light).

3   When abreast the S breakwater light, the alignment (100°) of a beacon (W cardinal) marking the edge of a stony foreshore on the E side and a yellow daymark on the E shore, leads through the best water between the breakwaters. A groyne, marked at its outer end by a beacon (port hand), projects 18 m E from the N breakwater.

A sandbar lies at the harbour entrance. The harbour and bar for the most part dry, coarse gravel and stones; out of the river current the gravel is overlaid with mud.

4   The afon Rheidol is spanned by a bridge 3 cables within its mouth.

Clearing bearing. The alignment (140°) of the head of the N breakwater (52°24′·4N 4°05′·4W) with Wellington Monument, 4½ cables SE, passes SW of Castle Rock.

Useful marks.
> Tower of Saint Michael's Church and the extensive college buildings which lie close E of Castle Point (52°24′·8N 4°05′·3W).

5
> Wellington Monument (52°24′·1N 4°04′·9W) standing on the summit of Pendinas, a detached hill, which rises between the mouths of the two rivers.
> Welsh National Library (52°24′·9N 4°04′·1W), a rectangular grey building with a conspicuous campanile behind it.
> Constitution Hill (52°25′·5N 4°05′·0W), with its funicular railway, lies near the coast at the N end of the town.

Aberystwyth from SW (6.50)
(Original dated 2001)

(Photograph - Air Images)

Berths
6.51

1   **Alongside berths** can be obtained at Town Quay, 300 m long, the inner section of the mole extending S from the N side. A portion of the river above the N breakwater is quayed for 200 m, but the berths are silted up. Vessels should be prepared to take the ground at all berths.

There is a marina, accessible 3 hours either side of HW, on the E bank of the river opposite Town Quay. However, it is advisable for those without local knowledge to access the marina 2 hours either side of HW.

Port services
6.52

1   **Repairs:** boatyard.

Other facilities: hospital with a helicopter landing site; small craft harbour with narrow entrance and two slipways at inner end of Town Quay.

Supplies: water; petrol and marine diesel in small quantities; provisions.

Rescue: inshore lifeboat.

Chart 1484 plan of Aberaeron
Aberaeron
6.53

1   **General information.** Aberaeron (52°14′·6N 4°15′·9W), a small tidal harbour which dries completely, lies at the mouth of the afon Aeron. It is used only by fishing vessels and pleasure craft. Short piers extend WNW from either side of the river entrance. A sectored light is exhibited from North Pier Head and a light is exhibited from the South Pier Head. An outer breakwater extends approximately 100 m NNW from the root of the N Pier.

2   With strong NW winds there is very little shelter in the harbour.

Harbour Authority is Cyngor Sir Ceredigion (see Aberystwyth (6.46)).

Intermittent VHF watch is kept.

3   **Cautions.** Sarn Cadwgan, a rocky ledge with a 1·8 m patch on it extends 6 cables N of the harbour entrance. The patch, which lies N of the harbour entrance, is covered by the red sector of North Pier Head Light. Carreg Gloyn, a dangerous rock, lies on a patch of foul ground 5 cables WSW of the harbour entrance.

4   **Directions.** Local knowledge is necessary for entering.

The bar at the harbour entrance is obstructed by shingle which is quickly washed away on the occasion of freshets.

Facilities: slipway.

Anchorage

Chart 1972
6.54

1   There is good open anchorage in depths of 19 m between 1 and 2 miles off Aberaeron (52°14′·5N 4°15′·5W); closer in, the bottom is foul with large stones and poor holding. For anchorages off Aberystwyth see 6.48.

ABERYSTWYTH TO BRAICH Y PWLL

GENERAL INFORMATION

Chart 1410
Area covered
6.55

1   In this section are described the coastal routes, harbours and anchorages between Aberystwyth (52°25′N 4°05′W) and Braich y Pwll, 34 miles NW, including Tremadoc Bay, Saint Tudwal's Islands and Bardsey Island.

It is arranged as follows:

Aberystwyth to Mochras Point (6.59).

Tremadoc Bay (6.81).

Trwyn Cilan to Braich y Pwll including Bardsey Island (6.109).

Topography
6.56

1   The coastline consists mainly of low-lying ground with sandhills, marsh or broad sandy strands interspersed with bold rocky cliffs backed by high ground which rises even higher in the NE part of the area. Several small rivers run into the bay including the river Dovey (6.69) and the afon Mawddach.

North of Aberystwyth, there are several dangerous shoals which extend up to 11 miles offshore and dry in places.

2   Borth Sands (52°31′N 4°03′W), composed of fine hard sand interspersed with the remains of an ancient forest, with low marshy ground, extend 3 miles N from Craig yr Wylfa, a bold rock, to Twyni Bâch, the S entrance point to the river Dovey.

3   Moelfre, a mountain, lies 4¼ miles E of Mochras Point (52°49′N 4°09′W), backed 2 miles farther E by a range of four remarkable mountains which, from S to N are; Diffwys, 748 m in height, Y Llethr, the highest at 752 m, Rhinog Fach, table top, and Rhinog Fawr, sharp pointed. This land is often capped with cloud and the aspects of the peaks, Moelfre in particular, changes with the light. It is therefore unwise to rely on them as landmarks.

4   The summit of Cadair Idris (52°42′N 3°55′W), 891 m in height, makes a conspicuous landmark in clear weather.

The estuary of the afon Dwyryd and the afon Glaslyn, in the NE corner of Tremadoc Bay, comprises extensive hard, drying sands.

Saint Tudwal's Islands (52°48′N 4°28′W) (6.101) lie E of the promontory at the E end of the Lleyn Peninsula (52°53′N 4°32′W), which divides Cardigan Bay from Caernarfon Bay to the N.

Bardsey Island (52°46′N 4°47′W) (6.115) lies 1½ miles SW of the SW tip of Lleyn Peninsula.

Fishing
6.57

1   See 6.4.

Nature reserves
6.58

1   Twyni Bâch (52°32′N 4°03′W).

Morfa Dyffryn (52°48′N 4°08′W).

Morfa Harlech (52°53′N 4°07′W).

Bardsey Island (52°46′N 4°47′W).

For further information see 1.58.

ABERYSTWYTH TO MOCHRAS POINT

General information

Charts 1972, 1971
Route
6.59

1   From a position W of Patches Light Buoy (52°26′N 4°16′W), moored off the W edge of Outer Patch, to a position W of Causeway Light Buoy (52°41′N 4°25′W) (6.66) moored at the W end of Sarn Badrig, the coastal route leads about 17 miles NNW.

The route lies clear of charted dangers.

Topography
6.60

1   See 6.56.

Historic wrecks
6.61

1   Restricted areas are centred on positions 52°46′·7N 4°07′·6W and 52°46′·5N 4°11′·0W.

For further details, see *Annual Summary of Admiralty Notices to Mariners.*

Outfall
6.62

1   An outfall, the head of which contains diffusers, extends a short distance from the coast 3½ miles N of Aberdovey. The diffusers are marked by a light buoy (special) (52°35′·4N 4°07′·0W).

Rescue
6.63

1   There is an all-weather lifeboat stationed at Barmouth (52°43′N 4°03′W); inshore lifeboats are stationed at Aberdovey, Barmouth and at Borth (52°29′N 4°03′W), a seaside resort.

For details of rescue organisation see 1.60.

Tidal streams
6.64

1   Off Outer Patch (52°26′N 4°14′W) at the W end of Cynfelyn Patches (6.67), the streams begin as follows:

Interval from HW Holyhead	Direction
+0550	NNE
−0100	SSW

The maximum spring rate in each direction is 1 kn. Between Aberdovey (52°33′N 4°03′W) and Sarn Badrig:

−0605	N
+0020	S

2   The maximum in-going and out-going spring rate in each direction is between ½–1 kn.

Farther inshore, S of Cynfelyn Patches, the streams set NE and SW, but across and N of the patches they set N and S beginning ½ hour earlier than those off Outer Patch. The patches have no noticeable effect on the rate of the streams, but the shallower parts are indicated by ripples.

3   Sarn-y-Bwch (52°35′N 4°12′W) has no appreciable effect on the streams though their rates may be slightly increased over the shallow parts, which may be indicated by ripples.

The N-going stream sets across Sarn Badrig, or Saint Patrick's Causeway, (52°43′N 4°17′W) (6.66) and then turns NE into Tremadoc Bay (6.81); the streams in the opposite directions set SW out of the bay and S across Sarn Badrig.

4   The streams begin as follows:

Position	Interval from HW Holyhead	Direction
South of Sarn Badrig	−0605	N
	+0020	S
North side of Sarn Badrig (6 miles SW of Mochras Point (52°49′N 4°09′W))	+0450	NE
	+0020	SW

5   The spring rate in each direction is approximately 1 kn, but it increases over the shallower parts of the shoals which are indicated by ripples or tide-rips. In calm weather these appear when there is approximately 3 m of water over Sarn Badrig, but in strong winds a heavy breaking sea sets over them at all states of the tide.

For general tidal stream indications in the area, see *Admiralty Tidal Stream Atlas — Irish Sea and Bristol Channel.*

Directions
(continued from 6.41)

Landmarks
6.65

1   Television mast (52°21′·6N 4°06′·2W) (6.40).
Cadair Idris (52°42′N 3°55′W) (Chart 1410) (6.56).
Radio Tower (52°50′N 4°38′W) (6.113).
Bardsey Island Light (52°45′N 4°48′W) (6.12).
Saint Tudwal's West Island Light (52°48′N 4°28′W) (6.87).

Coastal route
6.66

1   From a position W of Patches Light Buoy (W cardinal) (52°26′N 4°16′W), marking Outer Patch, to a position W of Causeway Light Buoy (W cardinal), moored off the SW end of Sarn Badrig, the route leads about 16 miles NNW, passing:
      WSW of Sarn-y-Bwch Light Buoy (W cardinal) (52°34′·8N 4°13′·6W), moored off the W edge of Sarn-y-Bwch, which extends 4 miles WSW from Pen Bwch Point (52°37′N 4°08′W) and is composed of seaweed covered boulders, patches of which dry, thence:
2   WSW of Tail Patch (52°39′N 4°17′W), a narrow shoal extension of Four Fathom Bank which lies 6½ miles W of Barmouth (52°43′N 4°03′W), thence:
3   WSW of Causeway Light Buoy (W cardinal), moored off the W end of West Prong which forms the W extension to Sarn Badrig (Saint Patrick's Causeway), which extends nearly 11 miles offshore and is composed mainly of large loose stones and dries for a considerable part of its length. Near the outer end there is an extensive patch of rock and stones which dries, on the SW tip of which there is a stranded wreck. South Prong extends 1½ miles SSE from a detached drying patch at the outer end of Sarn Badrig.
4   The W part of Sarn Badrig is covered by a red sector (293°–349°) of Saint Tudwal's West Island Light (6.87).

Inshore channel
6.67

1   Main Channel (52°27′N 4°10′W), a navigable channel 3 cables wide with a least charted depth of 6·4 m separates

Sarn Cynfelyn, which extends 2¾ miles W from the coast near Wallog (52°27′N 4°04′W), a deep ravine, and Cynfelyn Patches, with depths of less than 2 m, which extend up to 6½ miles offshore.

2 Sarn Wallog, the inner portion of Sarn Cynfelyn, is formed by a narrow drying spit of shingle and gravel, interspersed with large stones, which extends 3 cables off the shore.

Detached patches with depths of less than 5 m over them lie in the S approach to the channel.

Local knowledge is required before this passage is attempted.

6.68

1 **Clearing bearing.** The line of bearing 159°, astern, of the television mast (52°21·6N 4°06′·2W) (6.40) passes through the fairway of Main Channel.

Clearing mark:

The alignment (158°) of Aberystwyth Castle ruins (Chart 1484, plan of Aberystwyth) with Wellington Monument (6.50), when S of Cynfelyn Patches, passes W of Clarach Patch, foul ground, 2 miles N of the entrance to Aberystwyth Harbour.

(Directions continue at 6.113
and for Tremadoc Bay at 6.86)

Aberdovey

Chart 1972, 1484 plan of Aberdovey
General information
6.69

1 **Position and function.** Aberdovey (52°33′N 4°03′W), a small harbour, used principally as a yachting centre, lies on the N side of the river Dovey estuary. The estuary is entered between Twyni Bâch, the S entrance point, and the low sandy coastline 1 mile W of Aberdovey.

The town of Aberdovey lies close NE of the harbour (6.72).

Twyni Bâch is a National Nature Reserve; see 1.58.

2 **Topography.** The estuary of the river is bounded N by steeply rising high land and S by low marshy ground. It covers a considerable expanse at HW but at LW it is encumbered by sandbanks through which the tortuous and shifting channel of the river flows. The river is navigable by small craft for 12 miles within its mouth.

3 **Port Authority.** Cyngor Gwynedd Council, Council Offices, Fford y Cob, Pwllheli, Gwynedd LL53 5AA.

The harbour has a resident Harbour Master who can be located at the Harbour Office, Aberdovey, Gwynedd LL35 0EB.

Limiting conditions
6.70

1 **Controlling depth.** The channel over the bar has depths of less than 1 m.

Maximum size of vessel handled: 45 m LOA, draught 3 m; on occasions larger vessels can be accepted but the Harbour Authorities should be consulted prior to entry.

Local weather. Strong SW winds raise a heavy sea on the bar particularly on the out-going tide.

Arrival information
6.71

1 **Port radio.** There is a port radio with limited operating hours.

Outer anchorage. There is an open anchorage W of the bar in depths of 8 m, sand over stiff mud.

Submarine cables cross the river entrance; their landing places are marked by beacons, as shown on the chart.

2 **Pilots.** Pilotage is compulsory for all vessels over 50 gt; a pilot is available at tide time, during daylight hours in good visibility and weather conditions, and will board vessels near Aberdovey Outer Light Buoy (6.73). In bad weather a vessel should proceed to Saint Tudwal's Roads (52°49′N 4°29′W) and request the assistance of a pilot.

3 **Local knowledge.** The passage over Aberdovey Bar (6.73) should not be attempted without local knowledge. The depths and direction of the entrance channel are constantly changing and the buoys are moved accordingly without notice.

Aberdovey

River Dovey estuary entrance (6.69)
(Original dated 2001)

(Photograph - Air Images)

Harbour
6.72

1 The harbour lies near the mouth of the estuary and comprises a wharf at the W end of the town and a wooden pier adjacent to and parallel with it.

2 **Tidal streams** begin as follows:

Position	Interval from HW Holyhead	Direction
Aberdovey Bar	+0520	N
	−0040	S

The maximum spring rate in each direction is ¾ kn.

River Dovey entrance	+0520	In-going
	−0155	Out-going

The maximum in-going spring rate is from 2 to 3 kn; out-going from 3 to 4 kn.

3 The in-going stream at first sets E across the bar and into the river but as the sands cover it sets NE across South Bank; the out-going stream from the river at first sets W across North Bank and N with the N-going coastal stream, but later when the S-going coastal stream begins and as the sands dry it sets W across the bar and S with the coastal stream.

4 In the estuary the streams set more or less in the direction of the channels when the sands are dry but across them directly inwards and outwards when they are covered.

It has been reported that the out-going stream on spring tides attains a rate in excess of 6 kn off the pier and over the bar.

Directions for entering harbour
6.73

1 **Approaches.** From the W, the route towards Aberdovey Outer Light Buoy (safe water) leads between Cynfelyn Patches and Sarn-y-Bwch (6.66). There are no off-lying dangers in this approach.

A race mark buoy (special, pillar) is laid about 1½ miles W of the bar from May to September. Other race mark buoys are laid farther inshore to N and S of the entrance.

2 **Entrance channel**, which leads over the bar (52°32′·0N 4°04′·5W), is marked by light buoys (lateral). Bar Light Buoy and South Spit Light Buoy mark the outer and inner limits of the bar respectively.

Within the bar, the channel leads 1 mile ENE between North Bank and South Bank to Aberdovey Harbour having a width of ½ cable just within the bar, to 1 cable near the pier at Aberdovey.

In the approach to the bar the depths are regular with a sandy bottom.

Berths
6.74

1 The wooden pier, 73 m long and with a height of 7 m above chart datum, dries alongside. The wharf, 110 m long, constructed of iron and concrete, dries 1 m alongside. There are depths of 3·5 to 10 m ½ cable SW of the pier.

There are a number of moorings on the N side of the harbour, E of the pier. There are also several berths, which mainly dry, for visiting craft.

Port services
6.75

1 **Facilities**: two concrete slipways for small boats; crane available but notice required.

Supplies: fresh water; provisions and stores; petrol and marine diesel fuel in small quantities.

Harbour regulations are in force within the harbour; copies should be obtained from the Harbour Master.

Ynys-las
6.76

1 Ynys-las (52°31′·1N 4°02′·4W), a small fishing harbour, lies 1½ miles S of Aberdovey, on the S side of the river Dovey estuary.

Barmouth Bay

Chart 1971
General information
6.77

1 Barmouth Bay is entered between Borthwen Point (52°40′N 4°05′W) and Mochras Point (6.81), 9 miles NNW. Bemar Bank, a patch of large stones with depths of less than 1 m, lies 2 miles SSE of Mochras Point in the N part of the bay and an obstruction, with a depth of 6·6 m over it, lies 2½ miles farther S, just to the W of the bay. There is a 4·5 m patch 1½ cables NNE of Borthwen Point.

2 An outfall with diffuser, marked by a light buoy (special), extends 9½ cables WSW from the shore 5½ cables NW of the root of the barrage at Barmouth (52°43′N 4°03′W).

3 **Topography.** The coastline comprises low sandy ground interspersed by high ground which is backed by even higher land.

Morfa Dyffryn, marshland now reclaimed and much built over, fronts the coast SE of Mochras Point.

There is a National Nature Reserve on Morfa Dyffryn; see 1.58.

Historic wreck: see 6.61.
Tidal streams: see 6.64.

Directions
6.78

1 **Approach.** The main approach to Barmouth Bay is from SW between Sarn-y-Bwch (52°36′N 4°11′W) and Sarn Badrig (8 miles NW) (6.66). East Passage, a small craft passage, which lies at the N end of the bay is described at 6.88.

Llwyngwril Shoal, which lies just outside the bay to the S, with a charted depth of 5·8 m over it, extends 1 mile W of Borthwen Point (52°40′N 4°05′W).

Llangelynin Shoal, with a least charted depth 4·5 m, lies 1¾ miles SW of Borthwen Point.

Anchorage
6.79

1 There is an open anchorage W of Barmouth Outer Light Buoy (52°42′·7N 4°05′·0W) in depths of 6 to 10 m.

Afon Dysynni
6.80

1 The afon Dysynni, a small river usable by boats at HW, enters the sea close S of Pen Bwch Point (52°37′N 4°08′W). The village of Tonfanau lies close N of the entrance.

TREMADOC BAY

General information

Chart 1971
Description
6.81

1   Tremadoc Bay lies in the NE part of Cardigan Bay and is entered between Mochras Point (52°49′N 4°09′W), a low sandy point, and Trwyn Cilan (6.87), 14 miles W.

The bay offers shelter from SW winds in Saint Tudwal's Roads (52°49′N 4°29′W) (6.103).

In the NE corner of the bay lies the small harbour of Porthmadog (52°55′N 4°08′W). Pwllheli, a yachting centre containing a large marina, lies 10 miles W of Porthmadog.

Morfa Harlech (52°53′N 4°07′W) is a National Nature Reserve; see 1.58.

Topography
6.82

1   The coastline within the bay comprises several stretches of low sandy land which is backed by higher ground. Harlech Castle, in ruins, stands on steep grassy slopes 2 miles N of the entrance to Mochras Lagoon (52°49′N 4°08′W), a broad sandy inlet. The sandy shore between Mochras Lagoon and Harlech is skirted by large stones which dry.

2   A broad sandy strand fronts Morfa Harlech and becomes merged into extensive sands which encumber the estuary of the afon Dwyryd and the afon Glaslyn (52°55′N 4°8′W).

Saint Tudwal's Islands (6.101), comprising West and East Island, lie off the coast at the W entrance to the bay.

Race marks
6.83

1   Yacht race buoys (special) are moored, May to October, off the N side of Sarn Badrig, 8¼ miles WSW and 3½ miles WNW of Mochras Point (52°49′N 4°09′W).

Rescue
6.84

1   An all-weather lifeboat is stationed at Pwllheli (52°53′N 4°25′W); inshore lifeboats are stationed at Abersoch (52°49′N 4°30′W), Criccieth (52°55′N 4°14′W) and Pwllheli.

For details of rescue organisation see 1.60.

Tidal streams
6.85

1   The N-going stream in Cardigan Bay divides S of Trwyn Cilan (52°47′N 4°32′W) (6.87). One branch sets NE into Tremadoc Bay (6.81) and the other sets NW towards Bardsey Island (6.115).

The S-going stream from Caernarfon Bay sets SE through Bardsey Sound (52°47′N 4°46′W) to S of Trwyn Cilan where it is joined by the SW-going stream from Tremadoc Bay, thence the combined streams set S across Cardigan Bay.

2   Tidal streams on the N side of Tremadoc Bay set in the direction of the coast and are weak, but the times at which they begin vary in different parts.

Off Pwllheli (52°53′N 4°25′W) they begin as follows:

Interval from HW Holyhead	*Direction*
+0430	NE
−0310	SW

The maximum in-going spring rate is ½ kn, out-going ¾ kn. See also 6.101.

Directions
(continued from 6.68)

Principal marks
6.86

1   **Landmarks**:
    Radio tower (52°50′N 4°38′W) (6.113).
    Old Windmill (52°52′N 4°31′W), which has no sails, stands on high ground.
    Carn Fadryn (52°53′N 4°34′W) (7.36), 369 m in height.
    Mynydd Tir-y-cwmwd (52°51′N 4°29′W), rising steeply from low ground within Llanbedrog, is easily identified.

2   Ruins of Criccieth Castle, which contain two complete towers and portions of three more, covering the summit of a promontory on the S side of Criccieth (52°55′N 4°14′W) are a feature of the coastline.
    White House (52°54′·4N 4°09′·1W), a small bungalow standing on Ynys Cyngar.

3   Moel-y-Gest (52°55′·7N 4°09′·6W), an isolated hill, 259 m in height.
    Harlech Castle (52°51′·6N 4°06′·6W) (6.82).

    Major light:
    Bardsey Island Light (52°45′N 4°48′W) (6.12); obscured when bearing less than 260°.

South-west approach
6.87

1   The main approach to Tremadoc Bay is from the SW passing NW of Sarn Badrig.

From a position W of Causeway Light Buoy (52°41′N 4°25′W) (6.66) the route into the bay passes (with positions from Saint Tudwal's West Island Light (52°48′N 4°28′W)):
    NW of Causeway Light Buoy, thence:
    SE of Trwyn Cilan, a bold promontory, (2½ miles WSW), and:

2   NW of West Prong (7¼ miles SSE) (6.66), the W extension of Sarn Badrig with depths of less than 1 m, thence:
    SE of Trwyn yr Wylfa, with a steep rocky face, (9 cables WSW), thence:

3   SE of West Island (6.101), on which stands Saint Tudwal's West Island Light (white round tower, 11 m in height); East Island lies 4 cables NE, thence:
    SE of Carreg y Trai (6.101) (7 cables ENE), thence:
    NW of North Shoals (8 miles ESE), which extends up to 2½ miles NW from the middle and inner portions of Sarn Badrig.

East Passage
6.88

1   East Passage, sometimes called Badrig East Passage, with a least charted depth of 4 m on the line of the leading marks, lies between Bemar Bank (6.77) and the inner end of Sarn Badrig, and between the latter and Mochras Spit, a bank of sand and stones with a least charted depth of 1·3 m over it, which extends 1¼ miles SW from Mochras Point (52°49′N 4°09′W) and parallel with the inner part of Sarn Badrig.

2   The passage is best negotiated 2 hours either side of HW Barmouth.

    Leading marks. The foot of the steep slope at Harlech Castle (6.82) bearing 016° leads between Bemar Bank and the inner end of Sarn Badrig; Moelfre (52°48′N 4°02′W) bearing 081½° astern, leads between the latter and Mochras Spit.

This passage, which requires bold alterations of course, should be used only in settled weather.

Chart 1512 plan of Approaches to Porthmadog and plan of Porthmadog Harbour

Porthmadog Harbour

6.89

1 **General information.** Porthmadog (52°55′N 4°08′W) lies on the N side of the estuary of the afon Dwyryd and the afon Glaslyn. The estuary, which is encumbered by broad expanses of drying sands, Traeth Bach and Traeth Mawr, is entered between Harlech Point (52°53′·7N 4°08′·5W), at the N end of Morfa Harlech, and Ynys Cyngar, a small hill 15 m in height, lying at the SE end of Morfa Bychan, 1¼ miles NNW. The harbour at Porthmadog is mainly frequented by small inshore fishing vessels and pleasure craft, between April and September.

2 **Harbour Authority.** Maritime Officer, Gwynedd County Council, Council Offices, Embankment Road, Pwllheli, Gwynedd LL53 5AA. There is a resident Harbour Master whose office is by the bridge at the head of Porthmadog Harbour.

The Harbour Master can be contacted on VHF radio at prearranged times. See *Admiralty List of Radio Signals Volume 6(1).*

6.90

1 **Pilotage** is compulsory except for vessels exempted by law. Contact with the Harbour Master should be established in advance, usually 3 to 4 days is required because of the restricted and changeable approach conditions.

Pilot boards about 2½ cables NW of the Fairway Light Buoy (52°53′·0N 4°11′·2W) or, in bad weather, at Saint Tudwal's Roads (52°49′N 4°28′W). Small craft can seek shelter in Pwllheli.

Local knowledge is necessary for entering Porthmadog.

6.91

1 **Harbour.** The harbour, in the NW corner of the estuary, is formed by the scour of the afon Glaslyn, channelled along the N side of the estuary by an embankment. It consists of a basin, open S, and a drying wharf on the outer wall on the SE side.

At the N end of the basin the river is crossed by a bridge, above which is an enclosed area, Llyn Bach, of drying mud.

2 A sewer outfall extends 1¼ miles SSW from the coast, 1 mile W of Ynys Cyngar (52°54′·4N 4°09′·1W). Another outfall extends S close to the coast at Borth-y-Gest, 5 cables SSW of the entrance to Porthmadog. The seaward end is marked by a beacon (port hand).

3 **Tidal streams.** On the bar the streams, which are fairly strong, begin as follows:

Interval from HW Milford Haven	Direction
+0515	Flood
−0210	Ebb

The streams run in the direction of the channel when the banks are dry but across them when they are covered. During freshets an out-going stream runs in the harbour from ½ hour before HW and up to 2 hours after LW.

6.92

1 **Directions.** From a position SW of the entrance the track leads to the pilot boarding position (52°53′·2N 4°11′·4W) NW of the Fairway Light Buoy (safe water).

A bar, extending from Harlech Point (52°53′·7N 4°08′·5W) to Morfa Bychan Spit (1¼ miles W), lies across the entrance. The channel is well marked by small buoys, which are moved during the months from April to October to meet the frequent changes in the channel.

2 **Caution.** Seas break on the bar when winds from S to SW exceed 15 kn.

Useful marks:
White house (52°54′·4N, 4°09′·1W) (6.86).
Harlech Castle (52°51′·6N, 4°06′·6W) (6.82).
Moel-y-Gest (52°55′·7N, 4°09′·6W) (6.86).

6.93

1 **Berths:**

Anchorages, sand and mud, but exposed SW, are available in the harbour. Advice should be sought from the Harbour Master before anchoring. Small craft may anchor S of the bar in suitable conditions.

2 **Alongside berths.** There is 1420 m of quay with numerous berths, including the pontoon type. Four drying berths are available for visiting craft but arrangements can be made for deeper draught vessels to berth with prior warning. There are numerous small craft moorings between Borth-y-Gest and Porthmadog.

6.94

1 **Facilities:** repairs to small craft; four slipways.
Supplies: diesel fuel; fresh water; provisions.
Regulations: bye-laws are in force, copies obtainable from the Harbour Master.

Chart 1512 plan of Pwllheli

Pwllheli

6.95

1 **General information.** Pwllheli (52°53′N 4°25′W), whose main trade was once the export of tin and slate is now an expanding yachting harbour, tourist centre and market town which lies at the mouths of the afon Erch and the afon Rhyd-hir, and provides good shelter. The harbour is also a fishery harbour and is frequently used by inshore fishing vessels. It is protected from the E by Glan-y-don Peninsula, 5 cables E of the town and from the S by Morfa'r Garreg, a sandy spit.

2 **Harbour Authority.** Maritime Officer, Gwynedd County Council, Council Offices, Embankment Road, Pwllheli, Gwynedd LL53 5AA.

There is a resident Harbour Master whose office is situated near the Marina Boat Club.

6.96

1 **Limiting conditions:**

Minimum charted depth on bar is 1·4 m. Vessels should be prepared to take the ground out of the limits of the dredged channel and deep water berths.

Maximum size of vessel: length 25 m, draught 2·4 m at outer moorings; length 24·4 m, draught 2·4 m in Hafan Pwllheli.

6.97

1 **Harbour.** There are two basins, inner and outer, accessed via a channel 5 cables long and entered from the ENE. A large marina occupies a dredged area in both basins, the remainder dries. There are moorings in the entrance channel.

Tidal streams. On the bar, at spring tides, the maximum rate of the in-going stream is 3½ kn, out-going is 2 kn. The duration of the in-going stream is less than that of the out-going stream.

6.98

1 **Directions.** The Fairway Light Buoy (safe water, pillar) is moored 4½ cables ESE of Pwllheli Point. From SE, the line of bearing 318° of the light (52°53'·2N 4°23'·7W) at the head of Grib Groyne leads between Outer Shoal and Gimblet Shoals.

Pen-ychain Shoal lies 9 cables SW of Pen-ychain (52°53'·5N 4°19'·5W), a bluff point.

2 **Entry.** The harbour is entered between light beacons (port and starboard hand) situated N of Pwllheli Point. The channel is marked by buoys and beacons, some of which are lit.

6.99

1 **Berths.** Sheltered anchorage from all except S and SE winds can be obtained 2 cables NE of Pwllheli Point, in a depth of 2 m, sand.

Hafan Pwllheli, a marina, situated on the W side of Glan-y-don Peninsula, fronts part of the inner and outer harbours and is accessible at all states of the tide. There are depths of 2·4-3·0 m within the marina basin.

There are also pile and buoyed moorings.

6.100

1 **Services:**

Facilities: boatyards; slipways; 40 tonnes travel hoist; hospital.

Supplies: petrol; diesel; fresh water; provisions.

Saint Tudwal's Islands including Saint Tudwal's Sound and Saint Tudwal's Roads

Charts 1971, 1512 plan of Saint Tudwal's Roads

Saint Tudwal's Islands

6.101

1 Saint Tudwal's Islands, West Island (52°48'N 4°28'W) and East Island (3 cables NE), lie 4 cables and 6½ cables, respectively, E of the promontory that consists of Penrhyn Dû (52°48'·7N 4°29'·3W) at its N end and Trwyn yr Wylfa (6.87), 1¼ miles farther S.

Carreg y Trai, two drying rocks close together, lie 3 cables SE of East Island. Carreg y Trai Light Buoy (port hand) is moored 2 cables E of the rocks.

2 Saint Tudwal's West Island Light (6.87) stands near the centre of West Island; this light is obscured by East Island between the bearings of 211°-231°.

Tidal streams in the vicinity of Saint Tudwal's Islands are strong, and the wind against the tide raises a short cross sea.

Landings. There is a small quay on the E side of the N tip of West Island and a landing exists on the NE side of East Island.

Saint Tudwal's Sound

6.102

1 Saint Tudwal's Sound, a safe channel with a least charted depth of 11·7 m in the fairway, separates West Island from the mainland.

In the passage between the islands a least depth of 5·5 m will be found by keeping on the E side of the channel.

Saint Tudwal's Roads

6.103

1 Saint Tudwal's Roads (52°49'N 4°29'W) lie N of Saint Tudwal's Islands and comprise Inner Road and Outer Road which are divided by Saint Tudwal's Shoal, a narrow sandbank, with depths of less than 5 m over it, extending S from the shore bank N.

The roads are protected from W and N winds but in strong N winds a long scope of cable is advisable; S and E winds raise a heavy sea.

2 In Outer Road there is good holding, sand and shell, in depths of 11 m, 8 cables NE of East Island.

In Inner Road there is better shelter in depths of about 9 m, 4 cables ENE of Penrhyn Dû (52°48'·7N 4°29'·3W); smaller vessels may anchor farther N in depths of 6 m.

The positions of anchorages can best be seen on the chart.

6.104

1 **Directions.** Either road may be entered without difficulty from S through Saint Tudwal's Sound (6.102). The use of this passage is advisable in strong W winds. Care should be taken to avoid the rocky ledge projecting N from West Island and an obstruction (position approximate), lying about 1½ cables N of Penrhyn Dû (52°48'·7N 4°29'·3W).

2 At LW vessels of more than 5·5 m draught proceeding to Outer Road should approach from SE on the alignment (316°) of Old Windmill (52°51'·6N 4°31'·1W) (6.86) with Carn Fadryn (52°53'·2N 4°33'·6W) (7.36) which leads between Carreg y Trai and New Patch, a patch of stones with a least charted depth 5·9 m, 1½ miles ENE of East Island.

3 Carreg y Trai and New Patch are covered by a red sector (243°-259°) of Saint Tudwal's West Island Light (6.87).

Anchorages

6.105

1 There is an offshore anchorage in the centre of Tremadoc Bay in depths of 18 m, mud, but it is untenable in strong SW winds. At such times shelter can be obtained in Saint Tudwal's Roads (6.103). There is foul ground on the W side of the bay.

Chart 1512 plan of Mochras Lagoon

Mochras Lagoon

6.106

1 **General information.** Mochras Lagoon (52°49'·5N 4°07'·5W) is a broad sandy inlet which dries, into which the afon Artro flows. The lagoon is entered between the N tip of Shell Island, which extends NE from Mochras Point, and the S end of a spit extending S from the N side of the lagoon.

2 Within the entrance the channel divides. One channel follows the outfall of the afon Artro and winds generally E for 7 cables to a railway bridge across the river; here there is a slip and a jetty. This channel is marked by stakes. The second channel winds SW close inside Shell Island for 2 cables to a protected boat harbour, where there is a yacht club.

3 **Directions.** Local knowledge is essential for entering Mochras Lagoon.

From March to November a directional light is exhibited from the NE extremity of Shell Island; the white sector (124°-134°) leads across the outer part of Bar Newydd; the inner part is marked by three posts (port hand) fitted with red reflectors.

Landing can be made close to the light.

Chart 1512 plan of Saint Tudwal's Roads
Abersoch
6.107
1   **General information.** Abersoch (52°49′N 4°30′W), a small enclosed harbour, lies on the S side of the mouth of the afon Soch. The inner part of the harbour is accessible to larger craft only at MHWS. Penbennar is the E extremity of a promontory which projects into the bay E of Abersoch. A small breakwater extends N from the coast, 1¼ cables W of Penbennar.

2   There is a jetty, marked at its outer end by a beacon (port hand), ¾ cable S of Penbennar.

A sewer outfall, marked at its outer end by a beacon (port hand), extends 1½ cables ENE from Penbennar.

Charts 1971
Landing
6.108
1   Criccieth (52°55′N 4°14′W), a seaside resort, dominated by the ruins of a castle (6.86) lies 3 miles WNW of Ynys Cyngar (52°54′·4N 4°09′·2W).

Landing from boats can be effected at HW at a disused lifeboat slip, sheltered by a concrete breakwater close S, situated on the E side of the castle promontory.

TRWYN CILAN TO BRAICH Y PWLL INCLUDING BARDSEY ISLAND

General information

Chart 1971
Route
6.109
1   From S of Trwyn Cilan (52°47′N 4°32′W) and W of Causeway Light Buoy (52°41′·2N 4°25′·3W) (6.66), the route leads W along the S coast of the Lleyn Peninsula rounding Bardsey Island to S and W and then continuing NW to a position W of Braich y Pwll (52°48′N 4°46′W).

Topography
6.110
1   The coastline which forms the S side of the Lleyn Peninsula (7.2), consists of several bays, separated by bold headlands, which are open to SW winds. They are mainly backed by high cliffs which, in some places, are backed by even higher ground. The SE part of Porth Neigwl (52°48′N 4°36′W) (6.117), a bay, which lies W of Trwyn Cilan, consists of low ground, which backs a narrow sandy foreshore.

2   Bardsey Island, attaining a height of 165 m at Mynydd Enlli (6.115), lies 1½ miles off the SW tip of Lleyn Peninsula.

Rescue
6.111
1   See 6.84 and 7.34.

Bardsey Island and Lleyn Peninsula from SSW (6.110)
(Original dated 2001)

(Photograph – Air Images)

Natural conditions
6.112

1 **Tidal streams.** From Trwyn Cilan to Braich y Pwll the streams, close inshore set in the general direction of the coast, strongly off salient points.

They begin as follows:

Interval from HW Holyhead	Direction	Remarks
+0350	W	Sets towards W shore of Porth Neigwl.
−0210	E	Sets towards W side of Trwyn Cilan. The onshore sets are strong with S winds.

2 Farther offshore the streams set NW and SE beginning as follows:

Interval from HW Holyhead	Direction
+0550	NW
−0010	SE

The maximum spring rates in both directions are:
Off Trwyn Cilan 1 kn.
Near Devil's Ridge 2½ kn (more over the ridge).
SW of Bardsey Island 4½ kn.
In Bardsey Sound 6 kn (the strongest flow occurs off the headland at the NW end of the Sound).
1 mile W of Braich y Pwll 3½ kn.

3 The NW-going stream divides as it approaches Bardsey Island, running SW of it and through Bardsey Sound, these streams re-unite 1½ miles NW of the island, from which position a strong eddy sets SE towards the island. After uniting the stream sets N with Saint George's Channel N-going stream.

4 The S-going stream in Saint George's Channel turns SE, W of Bardsey Island, similarly dividing and running on either side of the island, re-uniting 2 miles SE and causing a strong eddy to set NW towards the island. After uniting the stream sets SE and S across Cardigan Bay.

5 At a position 2 miles NW of Bardsey Island the stream begins as follows:

Interval from HW Holyhead	Direction
−0455	NNE
+0120	SSW

The maximum spring rate in each direction is 2½ kn.
Tidal stream indications are shown on the chart and in *Admiralty Tidal Stream Atlas — Irish Sea and Bristol Channel.*

6 **Tide races.** There is violent turbulence over Devil's Ridge (2½ miles SE of Pen y Cil (52°47′N 4°44′W)), Bastram Shoal (between 1 and 3 miles SSE of Bardsey Island), The Devil's Tail, a narrow extension of Bastram Shoal, and over all the rocks and inequalities of the bottom in the vicinity of Bardsey Island.

Directions
(continued from 6.68)

Principal marks
6.113

1 **Landmarks**:
Old windmill (52°52′N 4°31′W) (6.86).
Radio tower (52°50′N 4°38′W), carrying obstruction lights, standing on the summit of Mynydd Rhiw.

Carn Fadryn (52°53′N 4°34′W) (7.36).
Mynydd Enlli (52°46′N 4°47′W) (6.115).

2 **Major light**:
Bardsey Island Light (52°45′N 4°48′W) (6.12); obscured in Bardsey Sound.

Passage
6.114

1 From a position W of Causeway Light Buoy (52°41′N 4°25′W) (6.66) and S of Trwyn Cilan (52°47′N 4°32′W) the track leads about 20 miles W, NW and N, to a position W of Braich y Pwll (52°48′N 4°46′W), passing, (with positions from Bardsey Island Light (52°45′N 4°48′W)):
S of Devil's Ridge (4¾ miles E), over which there is violent turbulence which may be dangerous to small craft, thence:

2 S of Bastram Shoal (2 miles SSE) with violent turbulence which may also be dangerous to small craft. The Devil's Tail, over which violent turbulence can be experienced, lies at the S end of a narrow ridge of rock, extending about 7 miles SE from Bastram Shoal. Lighted target floats are moored 2 miles SSE and 6½ miles SSW of the S end of The Devil's Tail (chart 1410); they have no navigational significance. Thence:

3 S and SW of Maen Du (3 cables S) the extremity of the low rocky S point of Bardsey Island, thence:
W of Braich y Pwll (3 miles NNE) (7.36).
(Directions continue for the coastal route at 7.36)

Bardsey Island and Bardsey Sound

Bardsey Island
6.115

1 **Description.** Bardsey Island, or Ynys Enlli, (52°46′N 4°47′W), a National Nature Reserve (1.58), lies 1½ miles SW of the tip of Lleyn Peninsula (7.2). The W side of the island is fronted by foul ground; Carreg yr Honwy, a patch of rock, lies 2½ cables W of Porth Solfach, a small inlet lying 5 cables N of the lighthouse (6.12). The E side of the island has deep water; Ship Ledge lies 3 cables E of Pen Cristin, the SE corner of the island.

2 Mynydd Enlli rises steeply from the E side of the island to a height of 165 m.
The ruins of an abbey stand on the N part of the island.
Landing places. The best landing is near Pen Cristin, the SE corner of the island, in a chasm in the rocks which has been artificially improved; it is marked by a small boathouse. With S winds landing may be made, at more than half tide, on a shingle beach at Bae'r Nant, a small cove midway along the N shore of the island.

3 Near the lighthouse there is a helicopter landing site.
Communication with Bardsey Island is by boat from Porth Meudwy (52°47′·7N 4°43′·5W).

Bardsey Sound
6.116

1 **General description.** Bardsey Sound lies between Bardsey Island and the mainland and has a least charted depth of 23 m in the fairway.
The coast on the NE side of the sound, between Pen y Cil (52°47′N 4°44′W) and Braich y Pwll (52°48′N 4°46′W) is free of danger with the exception of Carreg Ddu, a large above-water rock, situated 1 cable offshore and 3½ cables W of Pen y Cil. The nearly continuous tidal race close to this rock is dangerous to small craft.

2 On the S side of the Sound the only danger is Maen Bugail, a small rock (dries 4·1 m) lying 3½ cables N of the

N end of the island; a heavy tide race extends 5 cables N and W of this rock.

Tidal streams: see 6.112.

3   **Local knowledge** is required for Bardsey Sound except with a favourable tide. Wind against tide produces a strong race round Braich y Pwll.

Anchorages

Porth Neigwl
6.117

1   Porth Neigwl, also known as Hell's Mouth, is entered between Trwyn Cilan (52°46'·7N 4°31'·8W) (6.87) and Trwyn Talfarach (4½ miles WNW), a rocky point. There is a strong indraught into the bay, which is open to the prevailing SW winds which quickly cause a heavy sea.

During offshore winds the bay affords temporary anchorage in depths of 20 m about 1 mile from the shore.

Aberdaron Bay
6.118

1   Aberdaron Bay is entered between Trwyn y Penrhyn (52°47'·7N 4°41'·5W) and Pen y Cil (1½ miles SW); Ynys Gwylan-fawr and Ynys Gwylan-bâch, two islets, lie 4 cables S and 6½ cables SSW respectively, of Trwyn y Penrhyn.

Cautions. Dangerous rocks lie approximately 6 cables WNW of Trwyn y Penrhyn.

2   Though sheltered from W winds, the bay is exposed to S winds which cause a heavy sea and it is not recommended as an anchorage as the holding is bad. Landing from boats can be effected on the shingle beach at Porth Meudwy, on the W side of the bay.

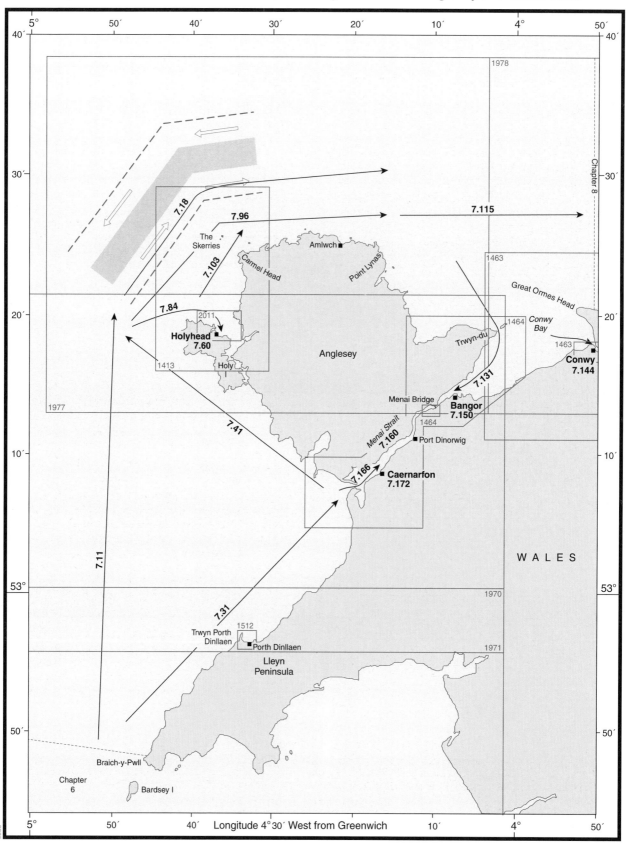

Chapter 7 - North West Coast of Wales, including the Island of Anglesey and Menai Strait

200

CHAPTER 7

NORTH-WEST COAST OF WALES INCLUDING
THE ISLAND OF ANGLESEY AND THE MENAI STRAIT

GENERAL INFORMATION

Charts 1411, 1826

Scope of the chapter

7.1

1   This chapter describes the waters off the NW coast of Wales between Braich y Pwll (52° 48′N 4° 46′W) and Great Ormes Head (53°21′N 3°52′W). It includes the island of Anglesey, Holyhead Harbour and the Menai Strait, the offshore and coastal routes, minor harbours and anchorages.

    The chapter is divided into the following sections:

2   Offshore Route (7.10).

        Braich y Pwll to South Stack (7.27).

        South Stack to Great Ormes Head (7.57).

        Menai Strait (7.160).

Topography

7.2

1   The SE side of Caernarfon Bay, which is entered between Braich y Pwll (52°48′N 4°46′W) and Holy Island (27½ miles N) is formed by the NW coast of Lleyn Peninsula which is bold, rocky and mainly steep-to, rising inland to mountainous country of which Snowdon (Chart 1121), sometimes covered by cloud, is the highest peak at 1082 m. The NE side of the bay is formed by the SW coast of Anglesey and is indented by many small bays with ledges and rocks extending 1½ miles offshore.

2   The island of Anglesey, the general aspect of which is slightly undulating, is separated from the mainland by the Menai Strait (7.161), a narrow navigable waterway.

    Holy Island which lies close off the W side of Anglesey forms the S side of Holyhead Bay (7.58).

3   The Skerries (7.103) lie off the NW extremity of Anglesey.

    The N coast of Anglesey is bold, rocky and mainly steep-to with off-lying dangers within 2 miles of the coast.

    Conwy Bay is entered between Trwyn Du (53°19′N 4°02′W) and Great Ormes Head, 6 miles ENE.

Shelter

7.3

1   Shelter is available at all times in Holyhead Outer Harbour (7.79).

Traffic separation schemes

7.4

1   The Off Skerries TSS (53°22′·8N 4°52′·0W to 53°32′·1N 4°31′·7W) is established for vessels rounding the NW coast of Anglesey. The scheme is IMO-adopted and Rule 10 of *The International Regulations for Preventing Collisions at*

Sea (1972) applies. An unadopted TSS is established at the entrance to Holyhead Harbour (7.60).

7.5

1   Laden tankers should avoid the area between the SE boundary of the scheme and the coast.

Fishing

7.6

1   Trawlers may be encountered in Caernarfon Bay, in particular in the spring when they work in the shelter from E winds.

    Inshore trawlers may be encountered at any time in depths of 25 to 35 m.

    Pots may be found off the Welsh coast, occasionally up to 10 miles offshore.

    For details on types of fishing and nets used see *The Mariner's Handbook.*

High speed craft

7.7

1   High speed ferries operate between Liverpool and Dublin; between Holyhead and Dublin; and between Holyhead and Dun Laoghaire. See 1.8.

Natural conditions

7.8

1   **Tidal streams.** The flow over the area dealt with in this chapter is largely determined by tidal forces. The tidal streams across the entrance to Caernarfon Bay set N and S, but they set round the bay in the direction of the coast.

    The streams change direction NNE and SSW off the NW coast of Anglesey; they set E and W off the N coast.

    Tidal streams are given on the charts and in *Admiralty Tidal Stream Atlas — Irish Sea and Bristol Channel.*

2   **Tide races,** which may be dangerous to small craft, are particularly in evidence off Bardsey Island (52°46′N 4°47′W), Braich y Pwll (52°48′N 4°46′W), South Stack (53°18′N 4°42′W) and North Stack (53°19′N 4°41′W).

    Overfalls. Heavy overfalls can be experienced in the vicinity of Langdon Ridge (53°23′N 4°38′W) (7.102), between The Skerries and Carmel Head (53°24′N 4°34′W) and The Tripods (7.37).

Rescue

7.9

1   For details of rescue organisation and locations of assets see 1.60 and text under Rescue.

OFFSHORE ROUTE

GENERAL INFORMATION

Charts 1411, 1977
Area covered
7.10

1   This section describes the offshore route from Braich y Pwll (52°48′N 4°46′W) to Great Ormes Head (53°21′N 3°52′W) via the Off Skerries TSS (53°29′N 4°41′W).

It is arranged as follows:
Braich y Pwll to Off Skerries TSS (7.11).
Off Skerries TSS to Great Ormes Head (7.18).

BRAICH Y PWLL TO OFF SKERRIES TSS

General information

Chart 1411
Route
7.11

1   From W of Braich y Pwll (52°48′N 4°46′W) the route leads about 34 miles N across Caernarfon Bay to the Off Skerries TSS (53°29′N 4°45′W) (7.4). This is a continuation of the route through Saint George's Channel from the Off Smalls TSS (51°40′N 5°51′W).

Topography
7.12

1   See 7.2.

Rescue
7.13

1   All-weather lifeboats are stationed at Porth Dinllaen (52°57′N 4°34′W) and at Holyhead New Harbour (53°19′N 4°38′W).

For details of rescue organisation see 1.60.

Tidal streams
7.14

1   Tidal streams approximately 7 miles W of South Stack begin as follows:

Interval from HW Holyhead	Direction
–0520	NNE
+0050	SSW

The maximum spring rate in each direction is 2½ kn.
For tidal stream indications in the area, see *Admiralty Tidal Stream Atlas — Irish Sea and Bristol Channel.*

Directions
(continued from 6.13)

Principal marks
7.15

1   **Landmarks:**
Bardsey Island (52°46′N 4°47′W) (6.115).
Radio tower (52°50′N 4°38′W) (6.113).
Bwlch-Yr-Eifl Quarries (52°59′N 4°26′W) (7.36).
Radio mast (53°01′N 4°16′W) (7.36).
Radio mast (53°18′·6N 4°40′·1W) (7.83).

2   **Major lights:**
Bardsey Island Light (52°45′N 4°48′W) (6.12).
South Stack Light (white round tower, 28 m in height) (53°18′N 4°42′W); the light is shown throughout 24 hours.
The Skerries Light (53°25′N 4°36′W) (7.23).

South Stack Lighthouse from NW (7.15)
(Original dated 2001)

(Photograph - Air Images)

Other aid to navigation
7.16

1   **Racon:**
The Skerries Lighthouse (53°25′N 4°36′W).
For further details see *Admiralty List of Radio Signals Volume 2.*

Braich y Pwll to Off Skerries TSS
7.17

1   From a position W of Braich y Pwll (52°48′N 4°46′W) (7.36), the route leads NNE for 36 miles, passing:
WNW of Braich y Pwll, which provides a good radar echo, thence:
WNW of Penrhyn Mawr (53°17′N 4°41′W) (7.47), thence:
2   WNW of South Stack (53°18′N 4°42′W) (7.47), on which stands a light (7.15).
The track then continues to the S end (53°22′N 4°49′W) of the N-bound Off Skerries TSS.

(Directions continue at 7.23;
directions for the approach to
Holyhead Harbour are given at 7.83)

OFF SKERRIES TSS TO GREAT ORMES HEAD

General information

Charts 1411, 1826, 1977
Route
7.18

1   From the S end (53°21′·8N 4°49′·4W) of the Off Skerries TSS the route continues through the traffic lanes, thence continues E on exiting the lanes to a position N of Great Ormes Head (53°20′N 3°53′W), a distance of 38 miles.

Topography
7.19
1   See 7.2.

Pilotage
7.20
1   In bad weather or at the request of a vessel's master, Liverpool pilots (8.85) will board off Point Lynas (53°25′N 4°17′W). The boarding position is shown on the chart.

For further details on Liverpool Pilots, see *Admiralty List of Radio Signals Volume 6(1)*.

Rescue
7.21
1   All-weather lifeboats are stationed at Holyhead New Harbour (53°19′N 4°38′W) and at Moelfre (53°21′N 4°14′W).

For details of rescue organisation see 1.60.

Tidal streams
7.22
1   Tidal streams are given on the charts and in *Admiralty Tidal Stream Atlas — Irish Sea and Bristol Channel*.

Directions
(continued from 7.17)

Principal marks
7.23
1   **Landmarks:**
    Radio mast (53°18′·6N 4°40′·1W) (7.83).
    Wylfa Power Station (53°25′N 4°29′W) (7.100).

    Point Lynas (53°25′N 4°17′W) (7.100).
    Radio mast (53°18′·4N 4°07′·7W) (7.121).

Major lights:
2   South Stack Light (53°18′N 4°42′W) (7.15). The light is obscured by North Stack (7.102) when E of The Skerries.

    The Skerries Light (white round tower, red band, 23 m in height) (53°25′N 4°36′W); the light is shown throughout 24 hours.

    Point Lynas Light (53°25′N 4°17′W) (7.100).

Other aid to navigation
7.24
1   **Racon:**
    The Skerries Lighthouse — as above.

For further details see *Admiralty List of Radio Signals Volume 2*.

Off Skerries TSS to Great Ormes Head
7.25
1   The offshore route follows the Off Skerries TSS, running parallel to the coastal route farther inshore. The directions for the coastal route (7.100 and 7.121) should be used taking account of the greater distance to seaward and the requirements of the TSS (7.4).

Anchorage

Ynys Moelfre
7.26
1   There is a deep water anchorage about 2 miles NE of Ynys Moelfre (53°21′·5N 4°13′·5W) in a depth of 20 m, taking care to avoid the patches of foul ground shown on the chart. See 7.127.

The Skerries Lighthouse from N (7.23)
(Original dated 2001)

(Photograph - Air Images)

BRAICH Y PWLL TO SOUTH STACK

GENERAL INFORMATION

Chart 1411
Area covered
7.27

1   This section describes the coastal routes, harbours and anchorages between Braich y Pwll (52°48′N 4°46′W) and South Stack (53°18′N 4°42′W) (30 miles N).

It is arranged as follows:
Braich y Pwll to the Menai Strait (7.31).
Menai Strait to South Stack (7.41).

Topography
7.28

1   See 7.2.

Fishing
7.29

1   See 7.6.

Nature reserves
7.30

1   Llanddwyn Island (53°08′N 4°25′W).
Newborough Warren (53°08′N 4°22′W).
For further information see Protection of wildlife (1.58).

BRAICH Y PWLL TO THE MENAI STRAIT

General information

Charts 1971, 1970
Route
7.31

1   The coastal route from Braich y Pwll (52°48′N 4°46′W) to the Menai Strait leads about 27 miles NE.

Topography
7.32

1   Between Braich y Pwll and Trwyn Porth Dinllaen, 12 miles NE, the coast is bold and rocky and, with the exception of The Tripods (7.37), there is deep water when more than 1 mile offshore.

2   A further 10 miles NE, between Trwyn Porth Dinllaen and Trwyn Maen Dylan (53°03′N 4°21′W) the coast lies at the foot of a range of mountains which slope gradually towards the sea. Bwlch-Yr-Eifl, a remarkable landmark described at 7.36, slopes rapidly down to a cliff at Trwyn y Gorlech. The cliffs at Penrhyn Glas, 1¼ miles SW, rise almost perpendicular from the sea to an elevation of 120 m.

3   Fort Belan (53°07′N 4°20′W), lies at the N end of a promontory which forms the S side of the SW entrance to the Menai Strait. Morfa Dinlle (Morfa Dinlleu), the intervening coast, is low lying. The foreshore between Trwyn-y-Tâl (7.37) and Fort Belan consists of coarse shingle and large stones.

Seasonal buoyage
7.33

1   Between April and October, Poole Light Buoy (special) (53°00′N 4°34′W) is moored within Caernarfon Bay.

Rescue
7.34

1   An all-weather lifeboat is stationed within Porth Dinllaen (52°57′N 4°33′W); two red can buoys mark its moorings on the W side of the bay.

For details of rescue organisation see 1.60.

Tidal streams
7.35

1   From Braich y Pwll to Llanddwyn Island (53°08′N 4°25′W) the streams set in approximately the direction of the coast beginning between Braich y Pwll and Trwyn Porth-Dinllaen as follows:

Interval from HW Holyhead	Direction
+0550	NNE
−0010	SSW

2   The maximum spring rate in each direction is 2 kn, but probably more off salient points; 3 kn is attained over The Tripods (7.37) where tide-rips are in evidence.

Between Trwyn Porth Dinllaen and Llanddwyn Island:

+0550	N
−0010	S

The maximum spring rate in each direction is 1½ kn. See *Admiralty Tidal Stream Atlas — Irish Sea and Bristol Channel* for general tidal stream indications in the area.

Directions
(continued from 6.114)

Principal marks
7.36

1   **Landmarks:**
Braich y Pwll (52°48′N 4°46′W), a bold steep-to rocky point which lies at the SW extremity of Lleyn Peninsula. Close within the point two hills Mynydd Mawr and Mynydd Anelog, rise to an elevation of more than 150 m.
Radio tower (52°50′N 4°38′W) (6.113).
Carn Fadryn (52°53′N 4°34′W); this prominent mountain is surrounded by low ground.

2   Bwlch-Yr-Eifl (52°59′N 4°26′W), is one of the best landmarks in Caernarfon Bay. It can be easily recognised by the white patch formed by quarries extending from sea level for two-thirds of its height and appears from N as two, and in very clear weather, three sharp peaks.
Radio mast (53°01′N 4°16′W), elevation 596 m, marked by obstruction lights.

3   Belfry (53°10′N 4°22′W).
Llanddwyn Island (53°08′N 4°25′W).
Major lights:
Bardsey Island Light (52°45′N 4°48′W) (6.12); obscured close inshore by the island between the bearings 198°–250°.
South Stack Light (53°18′N 4°42′W) (7.15).

Braich y Pwll to Llanddwyn Island
7.37

1   From a position W of Braich y Pwll to the entrance to the Menai Strait, SW of Llanddwyn Island (53°08′N 4°25′W), the route leads about 27 miles NE, passing (with positions from Trwyn Porth-Dinllaen (52°57′N 4°34′W)):
NW of The Tripods (10 miles SW), a steep-to bank of sand and shells, 1½ miles in length, which lies parallel to the coast 1 mile N of Braich y Pwll. There are tide-rips on the bank and with wind against the tidal stream a considerable sea is raised. Thence:

2   NW of Penrhyn Mawr (8 miles SW), a headland, with Maen Mellt, an above-water rock lying 2 cables SW of the headland, thence:

NW of Trwyn Porth Dinllaen, the N extremity of a rocky point which projects 6 cables N from the coast. An occasional light is exhibited from the NE side of the point. Carreg-y-chad, a dangerous rock, lies 7 cables SW of Trwyn Porth Dinllaen with drying rocks between it and the shore. Thence:

3   NW of Trwyn-y-Tâl (5½ miles NE), a rocky promontory, with Bwlch-Yr-Eifl (7.36) 1½ miles S, thence:

NW of Trwyn Maen Dylan (9¾ miles NE), a low point. Gored Beuno, a drying rock, lies 2 cables offshore 1 mile SW; Caer Arianrhod, a drying patch, lies 1¼ miles NNW.

4   The track continues NE to a position S of Llanddwyn Island (53°08'·3N 4°24'·7W) at the start of the buoyed channel leading to the Menai Strait.

Clearing bearing. The line of bearing 188°, or less, of Bardsey Island Light (52°45'N 4°48'W) and open W of the NW extremity of the island passes W of The Tripods.

Useful marks

7.38

1   Dinas Dinlle (Dinas Dinlleu) (53°05'N 4°20'W), a small hill surrounded by low land.

Llandwrog Church (spire), 8 cables E of Dinas Dinlle.

Llanddwyn Island Light (53°08'N 4°25'W) (7.171).

(Directions continue at 7.46; directions for the SW entrance to the Menai Strait are given at 7.168)

Anchorages

Chart 1512 plan of Porth Dinllaen

Porth Dinllaen

7.39

1   **General information.** Porth Dinllaen is a bay lying between Trwyn Porth Dinllaen (52°57'N 4°34'W) and Penrhyn Nefyn, 1¼ miles ESE. The foreshore of the bay is flat and a broad margin of sand dries along its S shore.

Carreg Ddu, a rock with less than 2 m over it, lies close N of Trwyn Porth Dinllaen.

Careg Oysters, a detached rocky ledge which dries lies in the SW part of the bay. A rocky ledge which dries ½ cable offshore fronts Penrhyn Nefyn.

2   Careg y Chwislen, a rock marked by a metal beacon (isolated danger) is situated 2 cables ENE of Trwyn Porth Dinllaen. A pinnacle rock with a depth of 2·4 m over it lies ½ cable E of Careg y Chwislen and a detached shoal with a depth of 4·3 m over it, on which the sea breaks during NW gales, lies 1¾ cables farther ENE.

Tidal streams run strongly across the entrance to Porth Dinllaen, but are weak in the bay where they run E for 5¼ hours and W for 7¼ hours.

3   Bye-laws restricting the speed of pleasure craft to not more than 8 kn within 100 m of the coast in the vicinity of Porth Dinllaen are in force during the summer months.

At LW, when all dangers are uncovered, the passage in mid-channel between Careg y Chwislen and Trwyn Porth Dinllaen, in which there is a least charted depth of 6·1 m, may be taken without difficulty.

4   **Anchorage.** The best anchorage is approximately 3½ cables ESE of the light (52°56'·8N 4°33'·9W) on Trwyn Porth Dinllaen, in a depth of 6 m.

Moorings. There are numerous moorings, some of which are available for visitors, maximum draught about 2·4 m. Craft that can take the ground may find a berth clear of private moorings.

Charts 1512 plan of Porth Dinllaen, 1970

Porth Nefyn

7.40

1   Porth Nefyn (52°56'·4N 4°31'·9W) lies close E of Porth Dinllaen. Frequented by pleasure craft it is entered between Penrhyn Nefyn and Penrhyn Bodeilas, 1¼ miles ENE. The bottom of the bay and the beach skirting it are sandy.

On the W side of the bay there is a breakwater extending SE and a slipway.

MENAI STRAIT TO SOUTH STACK

General information

Charts 1970, 1413

Route

7.41

1   From the vicinity of the SW entrance to the Menai Strait, SW of Llanddwyn Island (53°08'N 4°25'W) to a position W of South Stack (53°18'N 4°42'W), the coastal route leads about 17 miles NW.

Topography

7.42

1   On the NE side of Caernarfon Bay, the coast between Llanddwyn Island and Penrhyn Mawr (7.47), the SW extremity of Holy Island, 13½ miles NW, is indented by many small bays into which several small rivers flow. Many of these bays are separated from each other by bold headlands. Ledges and detached rocks, some of which dry, extend up to 1½ miles offshore in places; the sea breaks over them in bad weather.

2   Malltraeth Bay (7.49) the largest inlet, is surrounded by low land.

Holy Island, which rises to a height of 217 m near its NW end, lies close off the W coast of Anglesey and is separated from it by a narrow drying channel, the S entrance of which lies at the head of Cymyran Bay (7.53). The N part of the island, on which Holyhead Harbour is situated, forms the S side of Holyhead Bay.

South Stack (7.47) lies close off the W extremity of Holy Island.

Submarine cables

7.43

1   A submarine cable runs from Porth Dafarch (53°17'N 4°39'W), on the S coast of Holy Island, across Saint George's Channel to Ireland.

Rescue

7.44

1   An all-weather lifeboat is stationed at Holyhead Harbour; inshore lifeboats are stationed within Trearddur Bay (53°16'·7N 4°37'·2W) at Holyhead Harbour.

For details of rescue organisation see 1.60.

Tidal streams

7.45

1   Between Llanddwyn Island (53°08'N 4°25'W) and Rhoscolyn Head, 10 miles NW, the streams set generally in the direction of the coast at the rates and beginning at the times at 7.35 for between Trwyn Porth Dinllaen and Llanddwyn Island.

The rates are probably stronger off salient points but less in the bays between them.

A W-going eddy forms off the N shore of Cymyran Bay (53°14′N 4°34′W) during the S-going stream.

2 Between Rhoscolyn Head and Penrhyn Mawr, 3½ miles NW, the streams set generally in the direction of the coast, strongly off both promontories but weaker in Penrhos Bay.

The NW-going coastal stream is joined by the N-going stream from Caernarfon Bay tending to set towards the land; the stream turns NNE round South Stack. The rates increase NW from Cymyran Bay.

3 The SSW-going stream from North Stack turns S across Caernarfon Bay and SE round South Stack and Penrhyn Mawr.

A W-going eddy forms off the coast E of Penrhyn Mawr during the SE-going stream and there are eddies in Abraham's Bosom (7.56) and in Gogarth Bay (53°19′N 4°42′W) during the streams in both directions.

4 Tidal streams in the vicinity of South Stack begin as follows:

Interval from HW Holyhead	Direction
–0605	NNE
+0020	SSW

The maximum spring rate in each direction is 5 kn.

There are tide races off Rhoscolyn Head and Penrhyn Mawr.

The tidal stream cycle for the area is shown in *Admiralty Tidal Stream Atlas — Irish Sea and Bristol Channel*.

Directions
(continued from 7.38)

Principal marks
7.46

1 **Landmarks**:
Bwlch-yr-Eifl Quarries (52°59′N 4°26′W) (7.36).
Radio mast (53°18′·6N 4°40′·1W) (7.83).
Major lights:
South Stack Light (53°18′N 4°42′W) (7.15).
The Skerries Light (53°25′N 4°36′W) (7.23).

Passage
7.47

1 From a position at the SW entrance to the Menai Strait, S of Llanddwyn Island (53°08′N 4°25′W), to a position W of South Stack, the route leads NW and N for about 17 miles, passing (with positions from Rhoscolyn Head (53°15′N 4°37′W)):

SW of Pen-y-parc (8¼ miles SE), a rocky point. A shoal, on which lies the stranded wreck of the *Kimya* (dries 1·9 m), is situated 2¾ cables NW of the point and is marked on its SW side by a buoy (starboard hand). Thence:

2 SW of Braich-lwyd (6¼ miles SE), with a drying reef (7.50) 3 cables SW, thence:
SW of Ynys Meibion, an islet (5¼ miles SE), thence:
SW of Ynysoedd Gwylanod (8 cables SSE), a cluster of islets and rocks with tide-rips marking the outer extremity of the rocks; a beacon (stone tower, 14 m in height) stands on the largest islet. Thence:

3 SW of Rhoscolyn Head, the NW extremity of the bold promontory which forms the S end of Holy Island; Maen Piscar, a steep-to rock which dries, lies 8 cables NW of the headland. Thence:

Clear of Careg Hen (2¾ miles WSW), a steep-to rock marked by tide-rips, over which the sea breaks occasionally in bad weather.

4 **Caution.** Deep-draught vessels should not pass between Careg Hen and the mainland coast near LW.
The track continues:

SW and W of Penrhyn Mawr (3½ miles NW) with a tide race which should be given a wide berth. Ynysoedd Y Ffrydiau, above-water rocks, lie close S off the S extremity and The Fangs, two drying rocks, lie 1 cable farther S.Thence:

5 To a position W of South Stack, a rocky islet with dangerous tide races in the vicinity, surmounted by South Stack Light (7.15), which lies close off the W extremity of Holy Island and is connected to it by means of a bridge. The islet is a bird reserve where visiting is permitted (1.58).

Useful marks
7.48

1 Llanddwyn Island Light (53°08′N 4°25′W) (7.171).
Valley Airfield Aero-Light (occasional) (53°14′·9N 4°31′·5W).
(Directions continue for the coastal routes at 7.100; directions for Holyhead Harbour are given at 7.83)

Anchorages

Charts 1970, 1464
Malltraeth Bay
7.49

1 Malltraeth Bay is entered between Llanddwyn Island (53°08′N 4°25′W) and Pen-y-parc, 1½ miles NW; Careg Malltraeth, a rocky islet, lies close SE of the latter point. The bay is clear of dangers and provides sheltered anchorage in offshore winds.

A wreck, swept depth 12·7 m, lies 8 cables WSW of Pen-y-parc.

Afon Cefni flows through Malltraeth Sands, which dry, into the N corner of the bay.

Aberffraw Bay
7.50

1 Aberffraw Bay is entered between Braich-lwyd (53°11′N 4°29′W) and Dinas Bâch, an islet, 1½ miles SE. Carreg-y-trai, a drying reef, extends 3 cables SW of Braich-lwyd. The bay offers temporary anchorage in offshore winds in depths of 7 m.

Porth Trecastell
7.51

1 Porth Trecastell (53°12′·3N 4°30′·2W), an inlet very exposed to winds from SW to W, requires local knowledge. The approach to the anchorage, in the entrance, is marked by tall posts (red, diamond topmarks).

Crigyll Bay
7.52

1 Crigyll Bay (53°14′N 4°32′W) is entered between a ridge of rocks extending nearly 1½ miles SSW from the shore at Rhosneigr and terminating in Careg Goch, a steep-to rock, and another similar ridge, 1 mile NNW, which includes Ynys Feirig (7.53).

The bay is very exposed to winds from SW to W. Careg Goch and the below-water rocks seawards of Ynys Feirig are sometimes marked by tide-rips.

Cymyran Bay
7.53

1   Cymyran Bay (53°14′N 4°34′W), lies on the NW side of a ridge of rocks which extends 7 cables SSW from Ynys Feirig, an above water rock lying 5 cables offshore. The S coast of Holy Island forms the N shore of the bay; a drying rock and a below-water rock lie close together 5 cables offshore in the centre of the bay and a wreck, dries 1 m, lies 5 cables farther E.

Temporary anchorage can be found in the bay, clear of these dangers, in depths of 11 to 15 m, sand and stiff clay.

Borthwen
7.54

1   Borthwen, a small cove at the NW end of Cymyran Bay (7.53), provides shelter from all but S winds for craft of less than 2 m draught. There are moorings in the cove and a disused lifeboat house stands on the W entrance point.

A drying shoal lies in the approach to the cove 1½ cables S of the islet in the entrance.

Chart 1413
Trearddur Bay
7.55

1   Trearddur Bay (53°16′·5N 4°37′·8W) lies at the head of Penrhos Bay and affords temporary anchorage in offshore winds. Moorings are laid in the bay. It should be noted that South Stack Light (7.15) may be obscured within Penrhos Bay by the high land of Penrhyn Mawr (53°17′N 4°41′W).

Abraham's Bosom
7.56

1   Abraham's Bosom, a small bay, lies between Penrhyn Mawr (53°17′N 4°41′W) and South Stack, on the W coast of Holy Island. Pen-las Rock, a below-water rock, lies close to the N entrance point of the bay and foul ground extends 1 cable SW from the rock.

The bay affords anchorage, as shown on the chart, in offshore winds.

SOUTH STACK TO GREAT ORMES HEAD

GENERAL INFORMATION

Charts 1977, 1826
Area covered
7.57

1   This section describes Holyhead Harbour (53°19′N 4°37′W) and its approaches, and the coastal route between South Stack (53°18′N 4°42′W) and Great Ormes Head (53°21′N 3°52′W), a distance of about 30 miles.

It is arranged as follows:
Holyhead Harbour (7.60).
South Stack to Point Lynas (7.96).
Point Lynas to Great Ormes Head (7.115).
Conwy Bay (7.131).

Topography
7.58

1   This section of Anglesey coastline is generally bold, rocky and steep-to, with numerous islets and dangers lying within 2 miles of the N shore. It is heavily indented by numerous rocky bays, of which Holyhead Bay (53°22′N 4°37′W), Dulas Bay (7.126) and Red Wharf Bay (7.129) are the largest.

2   Holyhead Mountain, with an elevation of 218 m, is situated near the NW end of Holy Island at the W extremity of Anglesey.

The land surrounding Holyhead Bay, E of Holyhead Mountain, is low as far as Church Bay, also known as Porth Swtan (53°22′N 4°34′W), whence the cliffs increase in height to Carmel Head (53°24′N 4°34′W).

3   The cliffs in the N part of Church Bay are of a red colour; brown cliffs, which rise up to 50 m, form the W headland of the precipitous promontory of which Carmel Head is the N headland.

At the E end of Anglesey the coast consists of limestone cliffs terminating at Trwyn du (53°19′N 4°02′W).

4   Conwy Bay (7.131) lies between the E point of Anglesey and Great Ormes Head (53°21′N 3°52′W), a prominent landmark.

The Skerries, a cluster of islets and detached rocks which lie off the NW extremity of Anglesey are described at 7.103.

Nature reserves
7.59

1   South Stack (53°18′N 4°42′W), bird reserve.
The Skerries (53°25′N 4°36′W), bird reserve.
Puffin Island (53°19′·1N 4°01′·5W), bird reserve.
Lavan Sands (53°15′N 4°03′W).
For further information see Protection of wildlife (1.58).

HOLYHEAD HARBOUR

General information

Charts 1413, 2011
Position
7.60

1   Holyhead Harbour (53°19′N 4°37′W), situated on Holy Island, lies on the S side of Holyhead Bay.

Function
7.61

1   The port operates conventional and high speed cargo and passenger ferry services, including RoRo, to Dublin and Dun Laoghaire in the Republic of Ireland. There are also facilities for handling aluminium, marine diesel oil and petroleum coke at a deep-water berth.

Port limits
7.62

1   The N limit is a line drawn W from the coast at 53°20′·12N 4°34′·25W to a position 2·6 cables N of the breakwater head; thence it curves round the breakwater head at a distance of 2·6 cables to meet the breakwater on its outer side. The S limit is a line joining the coast at Penrhos (53°18′·06N 4°35′·13W) with Trwyn-gwyn to the E.

Approach and entry
7.63

1   Approach to the pilot boarding position (7.75) is made through Holyhead Bay; entry is E of the breakwater following the TSS and fairways leading into either New or Inner Harbour, as shown on the chart.

Traffic
7.64
1   In 2007, in addition to the normal ferry traffic, the port handled 123 vessesl with a total of 800 398 dwt.

Port Authority
7.65
1   Stena Line Ports Ltd, Stena House, Holyhead, Anglesey LL65 1DQ.

The port is represented by a Harbour Master, to whom navigational matters should be addressed.

For the Aluminium Jetty the Authority is: Anglesey Aluminium Metals Ltd, Penrhos Works, P.O. Box 4, Holyhead, Anglesey LL65 2UJ.

Navigational information concerning the jetty should be addressed to the Purchasing Agent.

Limiting conditions

Controlling depths
7.66
1   The approach to Terminals 3 and 5 in Outer Harbour is dredged to 8·0 m (2003). Inner Harbour has a maintained depth of 5·5 m, but is liable to silting and the harbour authority should be consulted for the current status.

For depths in the approach to and at Anglesey Aluminium Jetty the harbour authority should be consulted. See 7.90.

Deepest and longest berth
7.67
1   Anglesey Aluminium Jetty (7.90).

Tidal levels
7.68
1   Mean spring range about 4·9 m, mean neap range about 2·4 m. See *Admiralty Tide Tables.*

Density of water
7.69
1   Density of water in the harbour: 1·025 g/cm^3.

Maximum size of vessel handled
7.70
1   **Aluminium Jetty:** 40 000 dwt; LOA 235 m; beam 29 m; draught 11 m.

Inner Harbour: 7500 dwt; LOA 125 m; beam 20 m; draught 5·0 m.

Arrival information

Port operations
7.71
1   All vessels arriving at the port must establish contact with Holyhead Port Control, situated on Admiralty Pier, not less than 1 hour before arrival to update their ETA, and again when 3 miles from the breakwater to request permission to enter.

Vessels leaving, or manoeuvring within, the Inner and Outer Harbours must contact Port Control 10 minutes before their ETD.

2   Messages relating to the movement of vessels, the safety of persons and emergencies of any nature can be accepted by Port Control.

For further details see *Admiralty List of Radio Signals Volume 6(1).*

Speed limits apply as follow:
New Harbour and Outer Harbour, 12 kn.
Inner Harbour, 8 kn.

Notice of ETA required
7.72
1   All vessels should send their ETA to Port Control 24 hours in advance, either via their agents or by e-mail. Email: holyheadportcontrol@stenaline.com

For further details see *Admiralty List of Radio Signals Volume 6(1).*

Outer anchorage
7.73
1   Holyhead Bay affords an anchorage in offshore winds.

Submarine cables
7.74
1   Disused submarine cables run from Holyhead Bay down the E side of Outer Harbour to come ashore in Towyn Bay, 1 mile SSE of the ferry terminal.

Pilotage
7.75
1   **Pilotage** is available throughout 24 hours and is compulsory for all vessels over 40 m in length. Whenever possible, a minimum of 24 hours notice should be given to Holyhead Port Control when requesting a pilot.

Pilot boarding position. The pilot boards from the pilot boat, which has a black hull, 1½ miles NW of the breakwater head as shown on the chart.

For further details see *Admiralty List of Radio Signals Volume 6(1).*

Tugs
7.76
1   A small tug is available throughout 24 hours. Additional tugs from other ports may be made available if requested.

Traffic regulations
7.77
1   **TSS.** All vessels, except small craft, entering or leaving Holyhead Harbour are required to follow the TSS (7.86).

Restricted area. Vessels, except small craft, entering or leaving harbour should not pass within 1 cable of the breakwater head.

Precautionary area. Small craft must not impede large vessels which are required to use the inbound and outbound traffic lanes.

2   **Inner Harbour.** All vessels are prohibited from using Inner Harbour unless proceeding to the Fish Dock or to their allocated berth. All vessels entering or leaving Inner Harbour, including the fish dock, must do so only when clearance has been obtained from Port Control.

Between April and September an amber flashing light is exhibited to the SW from Breakwater Lighthouse for 5 minutes before the arrival at the breakwater of a ferry from seaward.

Regulations concerning entry
7.78

1   **Berthing** instructions are usually given by prior arrangement from Port Control once clearance for entry to the port has been given.

  Special bye–laws are in force for vessels using the Inner and New Harbours, also for those carrying explosives, petroleum and carbide of calcium. When nearing harbour and during the time the vessel remains in harbour, such vessels should show the following signals:

2   If carrying explosives. By day, a red flag not less than 1 m square. At night, a red light at the masthead.

    If carrying petroleum products. By day, a red flag not less than 1 m square with a white circular centre 0·2 m in diameter. By night, a red light at the masthead. See 7.95.

Harbour

General layout
7.79

1   The harbour comprises Outer Harbour, New Harbour and Inner Harbour and is best seen from the chart. It is protected by a breakwater which extends 1¼ miles ENE in a double curve, from Soldiers Point (53°19'·1N 4°38'·9W).

2   **Outer Harbour** lies S of an E/W line drawn from 2½ cables N of the head of the breakwater to Twyn Cliperau, 1¼ miles E. To the W the Harbour limit is defined by a curve of radius 2½ cables as shown on the chart. It forms a harbour occupying the whole space within the breakwater with the exception of New and Inner Harbours. Creigiau Cliperau, a group of rocks, many of which dry, with foul ground near their W extremity, extends 7 cables W from Twyn Cliperau.

3   Anglesey Aluminium Jetty (7.90) extends from the N end of Salt Island (53°19'N 4°37'W) also known as Ynys Halen.

  Salt Island Ferry Terminals 3 and 5 lie on the NE side of Salt Island.

  New Harbour is situated within the breakwater W of Outer Platters (7.86).

4   A wharf (7.90) lies at the root of the breakwater and Terminal 4 (7.90) extends out into the harbour from the W side of Salt Island. There are numerous yacht moorings in the S part of the harbour and a marina in the SW corner.

  Mackenzie Pier lies 3 cables W of Salt Island.

5   **Inner Harbour** is entered between Admiralty Pier, which projects 2 cables E from the S end of Salt Island, and South Pier, which extends 1¼ cables N from the shore 1 cable S of Admiralty Pier.

  The harbour consists of a fish dock (7.91) and ferry terminals.

6   **Landing places.** Landing steps, which dry, are situated at regular intervals along the inner side of the breakwater; the innermost steps comprise a landing slip.

  There are landing steps at Mackenzie Pier, with depths of 1 m alongside, suitable for use by small boats.

  After consulting Port Control, landing steps within Inner Harbour may be used.

New Harbour   *Outer Harbour*

Inner Harbour   *Skinner's Monument*   *Fish Dock*

Holyhead – Inner Harbour and Salt Island from SSW (7.79)
(Original dated 2001)

(Photograph - Air Images)

Dredging
7.80

1 Vessels are cautioned to go slow, to keep clear of, and to exercise extreme care when passing dredging plant or moorings. Dredgers will display the signals in Diagram 7.80.

By Day	By Night	Meaning
		Dredging operations are in progress.

Holyhead – dredger signals (7.80)

Traffic signals
7.81

1 Signals (Diagram 7.81) are displayed from Old Lighthouse (7.88) at the E end of Admiralty Pier.

Signal	Meaning
	Entrance to Inner Harbour is not permitted.
	Entrance to Inner Harbour is clear.

Holyhead Harbour – traffic signals (7.81)

Tidal streams
7.82

1 Within Holyhead Bay the streams begin four cables NNE of the breakwater as follows:

Interval from HW Holyhead	Direction
+0600	E (sets for 4 hours)
–0115	W (sets for 4½ hours)

2 The spring rate is generally 1 to 2 kn, with up to 3 kn being experienced in the vicinity of the pilot boarding position.

Close N of the breakwater:

–0240	W (sets for 6 hours)

3 A weak N-going stream sets along the coast between South Porthwan Point and Carmel Head (53°24′N 4°34′W).

The ingoing stream in Holyhead Bay tends to create a weak clockwise flow within Outer Harbour until - 0100, when the outgoing flow begins.

4 Close inside the W breakwater a rate of 4 kn may be experienced from - 0115 to + 0300.

For tidal stream information outside Holyhead Bay see 7.99.

Directions for entering harbour

Principal marks
7.83

1 **Landmarks**:
Radio mast (53°18′·6N 4°40′·1W) elevation 146 m (charted 113 m), marked by obstruction lights.
Skinner's Monument (53°18′·5N 4°37′·6W).

Chimney (53°18′·0N 4°36′·3W) marked by obstruction lights.

2 Monument (53°23′N 4°32′W), standing on Mynydd y Garn.

Major lights:
South Stack Light (53°18′N 4°42′W) (7.15), until obscured by North Stack (7.102).
The Skerries Light (53°25′N 4°36′W) (7.23).

Charts 1977, 1413
Approaches
7.84

1 **West approach.** From a position W of South Stack (53°18′N 4°42′W) the track to the pilot boarding position, 1½ miles NW of the breakwater head, leads NE into Holyhead Bay, noting the strong tide races (7.99) off South Stack and North Stack (1 mile NNE).

2 **North approach.** Approaching the pilot boarding position from the N the track leads W of Langdon Light Buoy (W cardinal) (53°22′·8N 4°38′·6W), marking the outer extent of Langdon Ridge (7.102).

Bolivar Rock, marked by a light buoy (starboard hand), and a wreck, swept by wire to 8·5 m and marked by a light buoy (port hand), lie, respectively, 2 miles and 7¾ cables NE of the breakwater head.
7.85

1 **Useful marks**:
Holyhead Breakwater Light (white square stone tower, black band, 19 m in height) (53°20′N 4°37′W).
Church (Spire) (53°22′·5N 4°32′·9W) overlooking Church Bay (7.58).

Chart 2011
Entering New Harbour
7.86

1 From the pilot boarding position the track to New Harbour leads round the breakwater head, noting that the W-going stream (7.82) of 6 hours duration, sets onto it, in the inbound lane of the TSS. Shoal water lies close off the outer side and a bank of drying boulders lies close off the inner side of the breakwater head. Spit Light Buoy (starboard hand), moored ½ cable S of the breakwater head, marks the spit extending SE from close inside the breakwater head.

2 If bound for Terminal 4, the track leads SW within the limits of the fairway, passing NW of two light buoys (port hand) marking the N and NW edge of Outer Platters, a group of shoals lying between the breakwater and the N end of Salt Island. Without local knowledge vessels should not pass through the buoyed channel close W of the Aluminium Jetty, NE of Terminal 4.

3 If bound for Anglesey Aluminium Jetty, vessels should proceed direct to the berth. See also 7.90.

Caution. A wreck, with a swept depth of 12·3 m, lies ¾ cable E of the breakwater head, within the restricted area (7.77).

Entering Inner Harbour
7.87

1 From the inbound lane of the TSS, the track towards Inner Harbour leads SE thence SW in the fairway.

The SE side of the fairway is marked by three light buoys (port hand).

Inner Harbour is entered between the heads of Admiralty Pier and South Pier (1 cable SSW).

Aluminium Works Chimney

Holyhead from N (7.86)
(Original dated 2001)

(Photograph - Air Images)

Old Lighthouse

Inner Harbour Leading Lights (222°) — Dolphin light and Skinner's Monument from NE (7.87)
(Original dated 2002)

(Photograph - Stena Line Ports Holyhead)

2   There is a dolphin, from where a light (starboard hand) is exhibited, ¾ cable E of Admiralty Pier.

Vessels should not pass between the dolphin and the head of Admiralty Pier.

Stag Rock lies close NW of the fairway, 7¼ cables SSE of the breakwater head, and Peibio rocks lie 2 cables E of South Pier.

Useful mark
7.88

1   Old Lighthouse (white round tower, 15 m in height) (53°18′·9N 4°37′·2W) standing at the head of Admiralty Pier.

Basins and berths

New Harbour anchorage
7.89

1   Sheltered anchorage can be obtained in New Harbour W of the fairway. However space is limited by small craft moorings and Holyhead Marina in the SW of New Harbour.

Alongside berths in Outer Harbour and New Harbour
7.90

1   **Anglesey Aluminium Jetty.** The jetty extends nearly 900 m NNE from the N end of Salt Island (53°19′N 4°37′W). A berth, 184 m long, is situated on the NW side of the jetty near its seaward end. Depths in the approach to

and at the berth are maintained as required by Anglesey Aluminium.

Lights are exhibited from the jetty head and from a walkway tower support at its seaward end.

2   **Salt Island Terminal 4.** This former RoRo berth extends about 300 m NW from the W side of Salt Island and is now used by tankers delivering fuel oil to the small tank farm close W of the Irish Ferries Terminal.

Lights, disposed vertically, are exhibited from a dolphin at the outer end of the berth.

3   **Salt Island Terminals 3 and 5.** These RoRo berths, Terminal 3 on the W side and Terminal 5 on the E, extend about 430 m NNE from the NE side of Salt Island. The depth in the approaches and alongside is dredged to 8·0 m (2003).

There is a group of four light beacons close W of Terminal 3 ramp.

4   The N light beacon in line with the SE light beacon (190°) marks that W limit of the dredged area which lies on a similar bearing; see chart.

The N light beacon in line with the SW light beacon (204°) marks the E extremity of a rocky outcrop lying ½ cable NNW of the ramp; see chart.

Lights are exhibited from two dolphins at the outer end of the berths.

5   **New Harbour – West.** A camber 23 m long, 5·5 m wide and slipway lie close E of Mackenzie Pier (53°19′N 4°38′W) where there are boatyard facilities and a crane.

Holyhead Marina and RNLI base are in the SW corner of New Harbour. A floating concrete pontoon breakwater extends NNE and NW to protect pontoon berths. Lights, disposed vertically, are exhibited from the outer end of the breakwater.

6   The Holyhead Sailing Club slipway extends N from the shore, ½ cable E of the marina shorebase. A second slipway lies SSW of the marina shorebase.

There are numerous moorings off the S shore between Graig Ddu, a drying ledge 1 cable W of Salt Island, and Holyhead Marina.

Soldiers Quay situated at the root of the breakwater; length 280 m, dries alongside. The quay must not be used without the permission of the port authority.

Alongside berths in Inner Harbour
7.91

1   **Admiralty Pier Terminal 2** which lies close inside Inner Harbour at the S end of Salt Island, has a RoRo ramp which projects 13 m S from the root of the pier. The berth, with charted depths alongside of between 2·6 and 5 m, can accommodate vessels up to the maximum dimensions given at 7.70.

Terminal 1, for the use of High Speed Service craft, lies on the E side of Inner Harbour; lights are exhibited at the berth. A road bridge, with lights exhibited from its piers, crosses the harbour close SW of the terminal.

2   **Layover berth,** 120 m long with a least depth alongside of 5·0 m, lies on the W side of Inner Harbour, 1 cable N of Terminal 1.

Public Quay, situated within Inner Harbour; length 95 m; depth alongside 3·3 m.

Fish Dock is situated on the S side of the entrance to Inner Harbour. It is entered between the head of South Pier, from which lights (metal mast) are exhibited, and the head of a floating Y-shaped pier.

3   The dock, which can take up to 30 fishing vessels, has a tendency to silt up; charted depths are less than 3 m and less than 1 m alongside South Pier.

Facilities include a refrigerated store.

Dock Authority: Ynys Mon (Isle of Anglesey) Borough Council, Shire Hall, Llangefni.

Dolphin

Holyhead – Fishdock from NE (7.91)

(Original dated 2001)

(Photograph - Air Images)

Port services

Repairs
7.92

1　Limited repair facilities.

Other facilities
7.93

1　SSCC and SSCEC issued; compass adjusting; fire-fighting and salvage facilities; customs.

Supplies
7.94

1　Marine fuel and diesel oil supplied by arrangement, normally by road tanker, including at Aluminium Jetty; fresh water available at all berths except No 4; provisions by barge or road.

Harbour regulations
7.95

1　Copies of regulations and bye-laws for the harbour which are in force should be obtained on arrival from the Port Authority.

SOUTH STACK TO POINT LYNAS

General information

Charts 1413, 1977
Route
7.96

1　From a position W of South Stack (53°18′N 4°42′W) to a position N of Point Lynas (53°25′N 4°17′W) and within the Liverpool Pilots boarding area (8.85), the coastal route rounds The Skerries at a distance of at least 1 mile offshore.

Passages inside The Skerries may be taken by day when there are offshore winds and clear weather. These passages, the directions for which are given at 7.106, are unsuitable for deep-draught vessels and should not be used by any vessel at night.

Topography
7.97

1　See 7.58.

Rescue
7.98

1　All-weather and inshore lifeboats are stationed at Holyhead Harbour (7.60).

For details of rescue organisation see 1.60.

Natural conditions
7.99

1　**Tidal streams.** Across the entrance to Holyhead Bay the streams set NNE and SSW. The SSW-going stream probably turns SE in the vicinity of Langdon Ridge (53°23′N 4°38′) and sets towards South Porthwan Point (53°21′N 4°34′W).

For tidal streams within the bay see 7.82.

2　The streams change direction round The Skerries and Carmel Head (53°24′·5N 4°33′·7W), see 7.105, and set E and W along the coast to and from Point Lynas. The E-going stream probably turns S in the vicinity of Ethel Rock (53°26′·4N 4°33′·6W) and Coal Rock (6½ cables ESE) and sets towards Hen Borth (1 mile E of Carmel Head). Between Hen Borth and Carmel Head there is a nearly continuous W-going stream.

3　The coastal streams along the N coast of Anglesey attain a maximum rate off the salient points, where there are races and tide-rips, but the rates are less in the bays between. The streams begin inshore as follows:

Interval from HW Holyhead	*Direction*
−0605	E
+0020	W

4　The maximum spring rate in each direction is 5 kn. Offshore, 4 miles N of Llanlleiana Head:

−0500	E
+0100	W

The maximum spring rate in each direction is 3½ kn. Tidal streams are given on the charts and in *Admiralty Tidal Stream Atlas — Irish Sea and Bristol Channel.*

5　**Tide races.** Holyhead Race extends from South Stack (53°18′N 4°42′W); that on the N-going stream extends 1½ miles NW and is most violent up to 4 cables NW of the islet; that on the S-going stream extends 5 cables W.

A race also extends 5 cables W from North Stack during the N-going stream.

The races off both North Stack and South Stack are dangerous to boats.

6　There is a considerable race off Point Lynas (53°25′N 4°17′W) on the E-going stream, extending 5 cables offshore. Rates of up to 7 kn may be experienced.

Eddies occur in Cemlyn Bay (53°25′N 4°30′W) and Cemaes Bay (53°25′·3N 4°27′·7W) but the rates are not strong. In Bull Bay (53°25′N 4°21′W) they attain a rate of 2 kn at springs during the strength of the coastal stream in both directions, which is much greater in the offing.

7　**Caution.** It has been reported that the race off South Stack can attain a rate of 6 kn and, in certain conditions, can create a confused sea, with 2 m high breaking waves, with wind strength of only force 3.

It is also reported that, in bad weather at spring tides, the race can extend for 7 miles.

Directions
(continued from 7.48)

Principal marks
7.100

1　**Landmarks:**
　Radio mast (53°18′·6N 4°40′·1W) (7.83).
　Monument (53°23′N 4°32′W) (7.83).
　Wylfa Power Station (53°25′N 4°29′W).
　Windmill (disused) (53°23′·3N 4°20′·5W) on Parys Mountain.
　Point Lynas (53°25′N 4°17′W), prominent when viewed from both E and W.

2　**Major lights:**
　South Stack Light (53°18′N 4°42′W) (7.15). The light, however, is obscured by North Stack (7.102) when E of The Skerries.
　The Skerries Light (53°25′N 4°36′W) (7.23).
　Point Lynas Light (white castellated tower, 11 m in height) (53°25′N 4°17′W), shown throughout 24 hours.

Other aid to navigation
7.101

1　**Racon:**
　The Skerries Lighthouse (53°25′N 4°36′W) (7.23).
For details see *Admiralty List of Radio Signals Volume 2.*

South Stack and Lighthouse from SW (7.102)

(Original dated 2001)

(Photograph - Air Images)

Passage
7.102

1   From a position W of South Stack (53°18′N 4°42′W) (7.47) to a position N of Point Lynas (53°25′N 4°17′W), the coastal route rounds The Skerries at a distance of at least 1 mile, passing (with positions from Carmel Head (53°24′N 4°34′W)):

    NW of South Stack (7¾ miles SW) (7.47), thence:

2   NW of North Stack (6½ miles SW), an islet with dangerous tide races in the vicinity, which lies close off the NW extremity of Holy Island. A prominent white building (disused signal station) stands on the point of land E of the islet. Thence:

    NW of Langdon Light Buoy (W cardinal) (3½ miles WSW) which marks Langdon Ridge, a rocky shoal with a least charted depth of 9·1 m, over which there are tide-rips, thence:

3   NW and N of The Skerries (1¾ miles NW) (7.103) on which stands a light (7.23), thence:

    N of Ethel Rock Light Buoy (N cardinal) (2¼ miles N) moored near the NW edge of a rocky bank on which Ethel Rock lies, and N of Carmel Head, which lies at the NE end of the bold and precipitous promontory which forms the NW extremity of Anglesey, thence:

4   N of Archdeacon Light Buoy (N cardinal) (3 miles NE) moored on the NW side of Archdeacon Rock, thence:

    N of Wylfa Head (3½ miles ENE), with a power station close SW, thence:

    N of Middle Mouse (5 miles ENE), an islet which is steep-to. Llanlleiana Head, a steep-to headland which forms the N point of Anglesey, lies 5 cables SE. Thence:

5   N of Trwyn Melyn (7 miles ENE), a rocky point, thence:

    N of Point Lynas (53°25′N 4°17′W) (7.100). Lynas Bank, steep-to on both sides, lies parallel with the coast 5 cables offshore, between Amlwch Harbour (7.112) and the point; the bank is generally marked by tide-rips.

6   Ethel and Archdeacon Rocks lie within the red sector (231°–254°) of The Skerries Light.

(Directions continue at 7.121)

The Skerries and inshore passages

Chart 1413
Description
7.103

1   The Skerries (53°25′N 4°36′W) are a cluster of dark coloured rugged islets and detached rocks which lie 1¾ miles NW of Carmel Head (53°24′N 4°34′W) (7.102), on the N side of Holyhead Bay. The Skerries Light (7.23) stands on the highest islet of the group. The islets are a bird reserve; visiting is not permitted.

2   West Platters, two rocks, lie ½ cable S of The Skerries.

    African Rock lies 2½ cables NW of The Skerries; its position is generally indicated by tide-rips.

    Between The Skerries and the coast at Carmel Head, lie the following dangers; East Platters, a drying reef, Middle

Point Lynas from NW (7.102)
(Original dated 2001)

(Photograph - Air Images)

The Skerries from SW (7.103)
(Original dated 2001)

(Photograph - Air Images)

Rock, Passage Rock, North Carmel Rock and Carmel Rocks.

Dangerous and historic wrecks
7.104
1   The wreck of the SS *Castilian* lies close off the NW side of East Platters. Owing to the presence of unstable explosives the wreck is considered to be a potential danger to life and property and a 500 m radius prohibited area has been established around it. See *Annual Notice to Mariners Number 16.*

2   A restricted area, 100 m radius, centred on a small islet close off the W extremity of The Skerries contains the historic wreck of King Charles II's Royal Yacht *Mary.* Within this area, diving, dumping, trawling and anchoring is prohibited at all times. When authorised diving and

salvage operations are in progress, navigation in the close vicinity should be avoided.

Natural conditions
7.105

1   **Tidal streams.** Between The Skerries and Carmel Head, the streams begin as follows:

Interval from HW Holyhead	Direction
+0550	NE
−0010	SW

The maximum spring rate in each direction is between 5 and 6 kn.

One mile NW of The Skerries:

−0505	NE
+0120	SW

2   The maximum spring rate in each direction is 4½ kn. Off Carmel Head, rates up to 7 kn may be experienced. Tidal streams are given on the chart and in *Admiralty Tidal Stream Atlas — Irish Sea and Bristol Channel.*

Tide races. In the vicinity of The Skerries there are races over and near all the rocks and shoals. There are probably eddies E and SE of The Skerries and Carmel Head.

Inshore passages
7.106

1   **South-east of The Skerries.** During daylight hours and only in good weather and favourable offshore winds, small vessels may pass SE of The Skerries, passing (with positions from Carmel Head (53°24′N 4°34′W)):

NW of Langdon Light Buoy (3½ miles WSW), thence:

2   On the alignment (211°), astern, of North Stack with South Stack which leads NW of Carmel Rocks (1 mile WSW), NW of Middle Rock (8 cables WNW) and SE of East Platters (1¼ miles WNW) (7.103). The wreck of an explosives ship lies close NW of East Platters, see 7.104. Thence:

3   On the line of bearing (258°), astern, of The Skerries Light which passes N of West Mouse (7 cables NNE), an islet, on which stands a beacon (white, pyramid; ball topmark), with Saint Vincent Rock lying 2½ cables W, thence:

4   Between Coal Rock (1¾ miles NNE), which lies near the NE edge of a rocky bank and is marked by a light buoy (S cardinal), and Victoria Bank (1½ miles NE), steep-to, marked by a light buoy (N cardinal), thence as directed at 7.102 from N of Middle Mouse.

5   If heading N a continuation of the alignment (211° astern) passes nearly 2 cables W of Ethel Rock.

The alignment (199°) of the two beacons (white pyramids, 10 m in height) near Carmel Head with the beacon on West Mouse, crosses the position of Coal Rock; the rock is also covered by the red sector (233°-253°) of The Skerries Light, shown at night and in times of poor visibility.

6   **East of Carmel Rocks.** A good route also exists which lies parallel to, but closer inshore, than that described above, passing E of Carmel Rocks, but close to Passage Rock (3 cables NNW of Carmel Head).

After rounding the point 4¼ cables WSW of Carmel Head (53°24′·4N 4°33′·7W) at a distance of about 2 cables the track leads ENE, passing (with positions from Carmel Head):

7   SSE of Passage Rock (2¾ cables NW), thence:

SSE of West Mouse (6¾ cables NNE), thence:

NNW of Craig yr Iwrch (1½ miles ENE), a detached rock, thence:

SSE of Victoria Bank (1¾ miles NE), thence:

NNW of Harry Furlong's Rocks (2 miles ENE), a rocky ledge marked by Furlong Light Buoy (starboard hand).

8   The route then follows the directions given at 7.102 from N of Middle Mouse.

Caution. There is a short, steep and confused sea between Carmel Rocks and the coast when a fresh wind is against the tidal stream.

South of Middle Mouse. A clear passage with deep water exists between Llanlleiana Head (53°25′·8N 4°25′·6W) and Middle Mouse, 5 cables NW.

Useful marks
7.107

1   Jetty lights (53°25′·5N 4°29′·3W) at Wylfa Power Station.

Llanbadrig Church (53°25′·4N 4°26′·7W).

Outer breakwater lights (53°25′·0N 4°19′·8W) of Amlwch Harbour.

Mynydd Eilian (53°24′N 4°18′W), a hill surmounted by a beacon with radio masts close E and four more radio masts 5 cables S.

Anchorages and harbours

Cemlyn Bay
7.108

1   Cemlyn Bay entered between Trwyn Cemlyn (53°25′·0N 4°30′·5W) and Cerrig Brith, a rocky ledge, 4 cables ESE, affords good shelter for small coasting vessels with winds between W and SE, out of the strength of the tidal stream, in depths of 7 m, but it should not be used in N winds.

A causeway with a shingle beach lies at the head of the bay.

Cemaes Bay
7.109

1   Cemaes Bay is entered between Wylfa Head (53°25′N 4°28′W) and Llanbadrig Point, 8 cables E, and offers good shelter with winds between W and SE, but it should not be used in E winds. It is however, necessary to guard against a sudden N shift of the wind which is a common occurrence and often preceded by a swell from that direction.

If anchoring, care should be taken to avoid the cable (below).

2   A pier at Cemaes, at the head of the bay, with depths of 3 m alongside at MHWS, affords additional shelter.

Submarine cable. A disused submarine cable is laid through the centre of the bay and comes ashore at its SE corner near the village.

Cautions. When entering or leaving the bay it is advisable to pass well clear of Llanbadrig Point on account of drying rocks which extend off the point. A rock, with a depth of 0·7 m over it lies 1½ cables W of the point.

Porth Wen
7.110

1   Porth Wen (53°25′·4N 4°24′·0W) is a small cove skirted by cliffs 12 m high and bounded by sloping rocky ledges. Graig Wen, a hill with a remarkable white top, lies close to the coast on the W side of the cove. A smooth shingle beach lies close within its W entrance. A wharf, with some disused brickworks also lies on the W side.

When approaching the beach, an outlying arched rock should be left to starboard.

Bull Bay
7.111

1 Bull Bay, bounded by rocky cliffs, is entered between Trwyn Melyn (53°25'·4N 4°22'·0W) and Trwyn Costog, 1 mile ESE, and provides a good anchorage in offshore winds between W and SE, in depths of 9 to 11 m, sand, out of the strength of the tidal stream (see Tide races 7.99).

Caution. Bull Rock, with a depth of less than 4 m over it, lies 3 cables W of Trwyn Costog.

Amlwch Harbour
7.112

1 **General information.** Amlwch Harbour (53°25'N 4°20'W) lies at the head of an inlet and is protected by outer and inner breakwaters, from the heads of which lights are exhibited.

Quays within the harbour are available to small leisure and commercial craft.

2 A submarine pipeline extends 1½ miles N from the shore close W of the harbour, at the head of which lies a patch of foul ground, being the remains of the seabed moorings of an SBM.

Anchoring and fishing are prohibited in the vicinity of the pipeline as shown on the chart.

3 **Facilities.** Fuel and fresh water are available.

Caution. A rock, which dries 2 m, lies ½ cable offshore, 3 cables ESE of Trwyn Costog, on the W side of the approach to the harbour.

Porth Eilian
7.113

1 Porth Eilian is a small inlet, whose shores are steep-to, which lies on the W side of Point Lynas (53°25'N 4°17'W) and is protected from E by the same point of land.

There is a mooring buoy in the centre of the inlet and a slipway at its head. The inlet provides good anchorage for small craft in offshore winds, in depths of 15 m, mud and sand. An uncomfortable sea may occur when the tide is running strongly.

Side channel
7.114

1 A narrow passage exists between Trwyn Costog (53°25'·2N 4°20'·3W) and East Mouse, a rocky islet, 2 cables N with depths of 9·4 m in the fairway. Shoal ground extends SE from East Mouse and rocks and ledges skirt Trwyn Costog. It is therefore necessary to maintain a mid-channel course if proceeding between East Mouse and the coast.

POINT LYNAS TO GREAT ORMES HEAD

General information

Charts 1977, 1978
Route
7.115

1 The route towards Liverpool Bay leads E from Point Lynas (53°25'N 4°17'W) to Great Ormes Head, a distance of about 15 miles.

Topography
7.116

1 See 7.58.

Pilotage
7.117

1 Pilots for Liverpool board off Point Lynas, see Liverpool Pilots (8.85).

Transfer of cargo operations
7.118

1 Transfer of liquid cargo operations frequently take place in the deep water anchorage (7.26) approximately 4 miles ESE of Point Lynas (53°25'N 4°17'W). Vessels engaged in these operations may be at anchor, or otherwise unable to manoeuvre, and should be given a wide berth.

Rescue
7.119

1 An all-weather lifeboat is stationed at Moelfre (53°21'N 4°14'W), at the head of Moelfre Bay; an inshore lifeboat is also stationed at Moelfre.

For details of rescue organisation see 1.60.

Tidal streams
7.120

1 Between Point Lynas and Trwyn-du (53°19'N 4°02'W), at the entrance to the Menai Strait, the streams set SE and NW with a maximum spring rate of 1¼ kn in each direction; they are weak in Dulas and Redwharf Bays and in Moelfre Road, though fairly strong off Ynys Moelfre (53°21'·5N 4°13'·5W).

2 In Table Road (53°19'·5N 4°05'·5W) (7.130) the streams begin as follows:

Interval from HW Holyhead	Direction
−0535	SE
+0035	NW

The maximum spring rate in each direction is 3 kn.
Tidal streams are given on the charts and in *Admiralty Tidal Stream Atlas — Irish Sea and Bristol Channel*.

For information on tidal streams within Conwy Bay, see 7.139.

Directions
(continued from 7.102)

Principal marks
7.121

1 **Landmarks**:
   Point Lynas (53°25'N 4°17'W) (7.100).
   Radio mast (53°17'·7N 4°08'·7W).
   Radio mast (53°18'·4N 4°07'·7W) marked by obstruction lights.
   Great Ormes Head (53°21'N 3°52'W) (8.16).
   Major light:
   Point Lynas Light (53°25'N 4°17'W) (7.100).
   Trwyn-du Light (white round castellated tower, black bands, 29 m in height) (53°19'N 4°02'W).

Other aid to navigation
7.122

1 **Racon**:
   West Constable Light Buoy (53°23'N 3°49'W).

Passage
7.123

1 From a position N of Point Lynas (53°25'N 4°17'W) the route towards Liverpool Bay, leads E, in deep water, to a position N of Great Ormes Head (53°21'N 3°52'W), passing:
   N of Trwyn-du (53°19'N 4°02'W). A light (white round castellated tower, black bands; 29 m in

height) is exhibited from a rock close N of the point; Puffin Island (7.143), lies 3½ cables ENE of the light. Thence:

2 N of Great Ormes Head (8.16), with a radio mast and hotel standing on the highest point of the headland.

There are no dangers adjacent to the route to Liverpool or other W coast ports.

(Directions continue for Liverpool Bay at 8.16; directions for the NE entrance to the Menai Strait are given at 7.140)

Anchorages and harbours

Chart 1977
Fresh Water Bay
7.124

1 Fresh Water Bay 5 cables SE of Point Lynas (53°25′N 4°17′W), affords shelter in W winds, with anchorage in depths of 17 m. A bank, which lies 5 cables offshore with a least depth of 7·7 m over it, fronts the bay.

Landing can be effected in a small creek at the head of the bay.

Porthygwchiaid
7.125

1 Porthygwchiaid, a bay 5 cables S of Fresh Water Bay, also affords shelter in W winds, with anchorage in depths of 8 m, sand. The shore of the bay is composed of shingle with drying ledges extending from it.

Dulas Bay
7.126

1 Dulas Bay, including Traeth Lligwy, is entered between Ynys Dulas (53°23′N 4°15′W), a detached drying rocky patch on which stands a beacon (staff, vane topmark), and Ynys Moelfre, 2 miles SSE. It is suitable only as a temporary anchorage in offshore winds; at LW Ynys Dulas and the shallow flat on which it stands afford little protection. Garreg Allan, a detached drying rocky patch, lies close E of Ynys Dulas.

2 Traeth Dulas is an inlet at the head of the bay which dries completely. The S entrance point of the inlet consists of a shingle beach and low sandhills.

Passage. Between the coast and Ynys Dulas there is a navigable channel with a least depth of 3·7 m. A rock which dries lies midway in the channel 1 cable W of the N tip of Ynys Dulas.

Local knowledge is necessary.

Moelfre Road
7.127

1 Moelfre Road, close S of Ynys Moelfre (53°21′·5N 4°13′·5W), an islet which lies close offshore at the entrance to Moelfre Bay, affords good shelter in W winds with anchorage in depths of 6 m, mud and sand. The tidal stream in Moelfre Bay is negligible.

Deep water anchorage. See 7.26.

Traeth Bychan
7.128

1 Traeth Bychan, which lies in the bight 1 mile S of Ynys Moelfre (7.127) contains a small harbour with a slipway, originally constructed for the use of vessels loading from the now disused quarries. The whole bight dries but vessels can take the ground on a clean sandy bottom.

In offshore winds anchorage may be found in the bight in shallow water.

Chart 1464
Red Wharf Bay
7.129

1 Red Wharf Bay, also known as Traeth-coch, is entered between Trwyn Dwlban (53°19′N 4°12′W) and Carreg Onnen, 2¾ miles E. It is fronted by Four Fathom Bank which extends E towards Puffin Island. Trwyn Dwlban is crowned by Castell-mawr, a steep, abrupt and regular mass of rock which resembles the remains of a castle when viewed from a distance. The shore at the head of the bay consists of a low ridge of sandhills which continues E to within 1 mile of Carreg Onnen where the coast becomes rugged with cliffs rising to about 90 m.

2 The bay dries almost as far as the line joining the entrance points. A wreck lies on the drying sands 7 cables SE of Trwyn Dwlban.

In SW gales violent gusts come off the land through the deep ravine which extends nearly across Anglesey to Red Wharf Bay.

A narrow channel marked by seasonal buoys gives access to Porthllongdy, with a slipway, which is situated close S of Castell-mawr. Boats with a draught of 1 m can enter the channel from half tide.

3 The remains of a ruined pier, which dry, lie close W of Carreg Onnen.

Outfalls. An outfall extends 3 cables ENE from the shore 6¼ cables NW of Trwyn Dwlban. Its root is marked by a beacon (special, diamond topmark) and its extremity by a buoy (starboard hand).

A second outfall, the extremity of which is marked by a buoy (special), extends 1 mile NE from the shore 3 cables NW of Trwyn Dwlban.

Table Road
7.130

1 Table Road, which fronts the limestone cliffs between Carreg Onnen (53°19′N 4°07′W) and Trwyn Dinmor, 2¼ miles E, affords anchorage, with offshore winds, in depths of 11 to 16 m.

A disused pier extends NW from the coast at Parc Dinmor Quarry, 2 cables SE of Trwyn Dinmor (53°18′·8N 4°03′·5W). The pier is in an advanced state of disrepair and should not be used except, perhaps, in an emergency.

CONWY BAY

General information

Charts 1463, 1464
Description
7.131

1 Conwy Bay is entered between Trwyn-du (53°19′N 4°02′W) and Great Ormes Head, 6 miles ENE, and extends about 8 miles SW to Bangor (53°14′N 4°07′W) at the NE entrance to the Menai Strait. The bay is occupied over the greater area by the drying sands of Dutchman Bank and Lavan Sands, also known as Traeth Lafan, broken only by Midlake Swatch and Penmaen Swatch, with The Pool lying farther E having depths of up to 16·5 m. Four Fathom Bank, with depths of less than 6 m, lies W of Great Ormes Head fronting the entrance to the bay.

2 A navigable channel, which lies on the W side of the bay, links the Menai Strait and its approaches with the open sea at Puffin Island (7.143).

In the NE part of the bay, Conwy (53°17′N 3°50′W) (7.144) with its massive castle, lies on the W bank of the river Conwy. Conwy Sands, which dry, occupy much of the river Conwy estuary which lies between Great Ormes Head and Penmaen-bach Point, 3 miles S.

Puffin Island and Lavan Sands are nature reserves; for further information see 1.58.

Topography
7.132

1   The immediate coastline on both sides of the bay is low, backed by high ground. However, the high ground on the E side is considerably higher than that on the opposite side. Particularly noticeable are the quarry workings above Penmaenmawr Point (53°16′N 3°57′W). A railway line closely follows the E shoreline.

2   The coast N of Deganwy Point (53°18′N 3°50′W), at the entrance to the river Conwy, is formed by a low-lying isthmus, on which stands the town of Llandudno, which connects Great Ormes Head with the mainland.

Fish weirs
7.133

1   Bangor Flats (7.154) which lie close E of the NE entrance to the Menai Strait are partly occupied by salmon weirs and mussel banks; the W weir is marked at its N end by a beacon.

Within Friar's Bay (53°16′·5N 4°05′·0W), a fish weir lies close to the main channel, SW of the underwater remains of a groyne 1½ cables S of Tre-castell Point (53°16′·9N 4°04′·6W). It is marked at its S end by a beacon.

Submarine pipelines
7.134

1   A submarine pipeline crosses the bay from a position 53°16′·3N 4°05′·2W to a point close to the mouth of the afon Aber, 2¾ miles SE. It is buried to a depth of 1 m under Lavan Sands and 3 m below the navigable channel (7.142) on the W side of the bay, although some shoaling has taken place along its length.

7.135

1   **Outfalls** extend 7 cables W and 2 miles WNW from the shore 1½ miles and 1 mile, respectively, N of the entrance to the river Conwy. The S, and longer, outfall is marked by a buoy (special).

2   Outfalls extend 8 cables and 2½ cables NW from the shore approximately 6½ and 7½ cables, respectively, SW of Penmaen-bach Point (53°17′·4N 3°52′·8W). The longer outfall is marked by a light buoy (special) and the shorter by a beacon (starboard hand).

An unmarked outfall extends for 7½ cables across Lavan Sands towards The Pool from a position 1 mile WSW of Penmaenmawr Point (53°16′N 3°57′W).

Foul areas
7.136

1   Penmon Bay (53°18′N 4°03′W), which lies between Penmon Point and Trwyn-y-Penrhyn (7 cables SW), consists of an area of foul ground. The bay dries for 1½ cables outside the line joining the entrance points, and there is a drying reef close off Trwyn-y-Penrhyn.

2   The wreck of the dredger *Hoveringham 11*, stranded in 1971, lies off the entrance to Penmon Bay, 3 cables S of Penmon Point. The wreck is awash at MHWS and is marked on its E side by a buoy (starboard hand).

The bay between Trwyn-y-Penrhyn (53°17′·8N 4°03′·5W) and Tre-castell Point, 1 mile SW, dries in places at a distance of 3 cables from the shore. The foreshore consists of stones and rocks which are dangerous to boats.

Careg Duon, a rock 1 m high, stands ½ cable offshore at the head of the bay.

Pilotage
7.137

1   Pilotage for North-West Entrance to the Menai Strait is arranged from Caernarfon (53°09′N 4°16′W) (7.172); boarding positions are shown on the chart.

For further details see *Admiralty List of Radio Signals Volume 6(1)*.

Rescue
7.138

1   Inshore lifeboats are stationed at Conwy (53°17′N 3°50′W) and Beaumaris (53°16′N 4°05′W).

For details of rescue organisation see 1.60.

Tidal streams
7.139

1   On the W side of Conwy Bay the stream is rotary clockwise; when strong, the E-going stream sets SE towards Penmaen-bach Point (53°17′N 3°53′W), and the W-going stream sets NW, well N of Puffin Island.

In the north-west entrance off Perch Rock the streams begin as follows:

Interval from HW Holyhead	Direction
−0510	S
−0025	N

2   The maximum spring rate in each direction is 3½ kn. North-east entrance, off Puffin Island:

−0340	SW
+0220	NE

The maximum spring rate in each direction is 4 kn. Outer Road (7.156):

−0545	SW
−0100	NE

3   On the E side of Conwy Bay, about 2½ miles SW of Great Ormes Head, the E-going stream probably sets towards the latter, and the W-going stream towards Lavan Sands.

4   In the entrance to the river Conwy the streams begin as follows:

Interval from HW Holyhead	Direction
−0410	In-going
+0020	Out-going

The maximum out-going spring rate is 5 kn.
Tidal streams are given on the charts and in *Admiralty Tidal Stream Atlas — Irish Sea and Bristol Channel*.

Directions

Principal marks
7.140

1   **Landmarks:**
Ruined tower (53°19′·1N 4°01′·5W) standing on Puffin Island.
Perch Rock Light Beacon (conical concrete, red, can topmark) (53°18′·8N 4°02′·2W).
Trwyn-du Lighthouse (53°19′N 4°02′W) (7.121).

2   Chimney (53°18′N 4°03′W), at Penmon Point.
Saint Seiriol Church (tower) (53°18′·3N 4°03′·4W).
Radio mast (53°17′·4N 4°04′·7W) marked by obstruction lights.
Bulkeley Memorial (53°16′·4N 4°06′·9W).

3 Tower (53°13'·7N 4°07'·8W) of Bangor University.

Penrhyn Castle (53°13'·5N 4°05'·7W) standing on high ground.

Hotel, standing at the highest point of Great Ormes Head (53°20'N 3°52'W) (8.16).

Chart 1464

Approaches
7.141

1 The Menai Strait is approached on the W side of Conwy Bay near the Anglesey shore. There are two approach channels: North-West Entrance and North-East Entrance, of which the former, being more direct and better marked, is the one generally used.

2 At the entrance to North-West Entrance a bar, consisting of a rocky patch which connects the coast 1½ cables S of Trwyn-du Light (53°18'·8N 4°02'·5W) with the drying spit extending SSE from Perch Rock (1¾ cables E of Trwyn-du Light), has a least depth of 4 m over it. An inner bar, 3 cables farther S, which lies between a patch of deep water, Pool, and Outer Road (6 cables SSE of Trwyn-du Light), has a least charted depth of 2·8 m.

North-West Entrance
7.142

1 From a position NW of Trwyn-du Light (53°19'N 4°02'W) the line of bearing 137° of Perch Rock Light Beacon (53°18'·8N 4°02'·2W) (7.140) leads SE passing (with positions from Trwyn-du Light):

2 Between Dinmor Bank (5½ cables NW), the NW portion of foul ground marked by Dinmor Light Buoy (starboard hand) moored off the NW end of the bank, and Ten Feet Bank (7 cables N), which lies at the E end of Four Fathom Bank (7.129) and is marked by Ten Feet Light Buoy (port hand) off its SW edge, thence:

NE of a 2 m shoal patch (3 cables WNW), thence:

NE of Trwyn-du Light.

3 The track then leads S into Outer Road (7.156), thence for a further 5 miles in a generally SW direction towards Bangor Pool, passing (with positions from Penmon Point (53°18'·3N 4°02'·7W)):

W of Perch Rock Light Beacon (5½ cables NE), thence:

Close W of B2 Light Buoy (port hand) (4 cables E), which is moored on the inner bar (7.141), thence:

E and SE of B1 Light Buoy (starboard hand) (3 cables SE), thence:

4 Between B3 Light Buoy (starboard hand) (6 cables S) and B4 Buoy (port hand) (7¼ cables S). A wreck with a depth of 3 m over it lies close S of this buoy. Thence:

NW of Light Buoys B6 and B8 (port hand) (1¼ miles and 2 miles, respectively, SSW), thence:

E of a buoy (starboard hand) (2¼ miles SSW), marking a diffuser with a depth of 7 m over it, thence:

5 Through Friar's Road (2¼ miles SSW), passing E of a 0·9 m shoal patch (2½ miles SSW), caused by

North-East Entrance　　　*Puffin Island*　　　*North-West Entrance*

Menai Strait entrances from NNE (7.141)

(Photograph - Air Images)　　*(Original dated 2001)*

Perch Rock   Trwyn du

North-West Entrance and Conwy Bay from NNW (7.142)

(Original dated 2001)

(Photograph - Air Images)

the existence of a submarine pipeline (7.134), which lies about 6 cables NE of Beaumaris Pier Light (53°15′·7N 4°05′·4W).

The track continues S, passing (with positions from Beaumaris Pier Light):

E of a beacon (starboard hand) (3½ cables NE), thence:

6   E and SE of B5 Light Buoy (starboard hand) (3 cables ENE), thence:

Between Beaumaris Pier and B10 Light Buoy (port hand) (1 cable ESE), thence:

NW of B12 Light Buoy (port hand) (2½ cables SSW), thence:

SE of Gallows Point (5½ cables SW), thence:

7   SE of B7 Light Buoy (starboard hand) (7 cables SW).

On passing B7 Light Buoy, the track continues SW into Bangor Pool (53°14′N 4°08′W), passing NW of Garth Point (1¾ miles SW).

The light buoys and buoys in the channel are fitted with retroreflective material.

Caution. Depths in the Menai Strait are continually changing, the buoys are moved accordingly to meet the changes in the channel.

(Directions continue for Garth Point to Caernarfon at 7.193)

North-East Entrance
7.143

1   The channel, with depths of less than a 1 m, leads SW between Puffin Island (53°19′·1N 4°01′·5W), a low-lying rocky grass-topped island on which stand the ruins of a tower, and Irishman Spit, a drying bank, 2 cables SE, thence through a narrow swashway, which separates the drying spit (7.141), from a drying sandbank ½ cable SE, and thence into Outer Road.

2   The channel is not buoyed and should not be attempted without local knowledge.

Puffin Island is a nature and bird reserve; for further information see Protection of wildlife (1.58).

Conwy

Chart 1463
General information
7.144

1   **Position.** Conwy (53°17′N 3°50′W) lies on the W bank 1 mile within the entrance to the river Conwy.

Function. The harbour, no longer used for commercial purposes, is mainly used by pleasure craft and fishing vessels.

2   **Approach and entry.** The harbour is approached through Conwy Bay and entered through a buoyed channel.

Port Authority. Conwy County Borough Council, Harbour Office, The Quay, Conwy LL32 8BB.

The harbour is represented by a Harbour Master.

Limiting conditions
7.145

1   **Tidal levels.** Mean spring range about 6·8 m; mean neap range about 3·6 m. See *Admiralty Tide Tables*.

Maximum size of vessel handled. The harbour can accept vessels up to 45·7 m in length with a draught of up to 4 m, 1½ hours either side of HW; smaller craft can gain access between 2 to 4 hours either side of HW.

Arrival information
7.146

1   **Port radio.** The harbour master can be contacted during office hours on VHF channel 16, working channel 14.

Prohibited anchorage area lies 50 m either side of a road tunnel under the river Conwy, which lies 4 cables N of the bridges previously mentioned.

Pilotage is not compulsory but local knowledge is desirable.

It is advisable for vessels to arrive at the Fairway Buoy at half flood tide.

Harbour
7.147

1   The harbour entrance lies between the NE extremity of Conwy Morfa (53°18′N 3°51′W), fronted by low-lying sand dunes, and Deganwy Point, which is low-lying and fronted by a shingle beach, on the opposite side.

2   The ruins of an ancient castle are situated on Deganwy Point and the area behind the beach is occupied by the town of Deganwy. A jetty, consisting of a fixed walkway with a pontoon section, extends 76 m NE from the E side of Conwy Morfa and is marked by starboard hand daymarks. There are quays at Deganwy and Conwy. The town of Conwy is enclosed by old walls and towers, and fronted by a seawall which dries. Conwy Castle stands at the S end of the town; the river here is spanned by three bridges, lying close together, having a vertical clearance of 3·6 m.

3   Conwy marina is on the W bank of the river and 3 cables E on the opposite bank is Deganwy Quay Marina.

    Both marinas are entered via tidal gates; access, controlled by traffic signals, being made when height of tide exceeds 3·5 m at Conwy Marina and 4·0 m at Deganwy Quay Marina.

    Tidal streams in the approach channel to the harbour are strong; see 7.139.

Directions for entering harbour
7.148

1   **Landmarks**:

    Light beacon (black metal column, 11 m in height) (53°18′·1N 3°50′·8W) standing on a drying bank on the S side of the river entrance.

    Tower, standing on high ground at Deganwy (53°18′·4N 3°49′·4W).

2   **Approach channel.** From a position S of the Fairway Light Buoy (safe water), moored 1¾ miles WNW of Penmaen-bach Point (53°17′N 3°53′W), a bold point, the track leads generally E through a narrow buoyed approach channel across Conwy Sands, passing (with positions from the light beacon above):

    N of Llys Elisap Clynnog (2¾ miles WSW), a rocky patch, thence:

3   S of a rocky patch which dries (1¾ miles W), thence:

    S of West Bwrling Rock (1¼ miles W), a collection of drying boulders, with further drying boulders and Bwrlingau Rock 2 cables N, thence:

    N of the light beacon.

    On rounding the light beacon and C11 Light Buoy (starboard hand) (½ cable farther E) the track leads SE into the harbour.

4   **Cautions.** The approach channel, marked by light buoys (port and starboard hand), is constantly changing. The buoys are moved to meet the changes; details of current positions are available from the Harbour Master (telephone 01492 596253).

Berths and services
7.149

1   **Berths.** The quay at Deganwy is 182 m long and has a depth of 5·8 m alongside at HW; Town Quay, at Conwy, 1 cable N of the bridges, is 90 m long; both are 1·5 m above MHWS and both dry at LW.

2   **Services**: repairs to craft of up to 20 m; mobile cranes are available to handle small craft in and out of the water; marine diesel by road; fresh water in small quantities; provisions.

Bangor

Chart 1464
General information
7.150

1   **Position.** Bangor, a university city, lies on the SE side of the entrance to the Menai Strait; Porth Penrhyn (53°14′N 4°07′W) (7.153), the port of Bangor, lies on the NE side of the city.

    Function. The port handles mainly sand dredgers, commercial coasters and pipe-pulling barges. Inshore trawlers and pleasure craft frequent the harbour.

2   **Approach and entry.** See 7.154.

    Port Authority. Port Penrhyn Plant Ltd., Port Penrhyn, Dock Office, Bangor, Gwynedd LL57 4HN.

    The port is represented by a Harbour Master.

Limiting conditions
7.151

1   **Controlling depth.** The approach to the port dries 2 hours either side of LW.

    The port is workable 2 hours before HW to 1 hour after HW, depending upon height of tide; vessels take the ground.

    Maximum size of vessel handled: 150 m LOA; beam 18 m; draught 5·2 m spring tide, 3·66 m neap tide.

Arrival information
7.152

1   **Pilotage.** For details, see 7.174 under Caernarfon.

    Tug. One small tug available but larger tugs can be supplied with 24 hours notice.

Harbour
7.153

1   The tidal harbour at Porth Penrhyn, which dries, has depths of 3·4 m at MHWS. On the E side, New Dock, which is a tidal basin 2 cables in length, is situated between two privately owned piers and has alongside depths of up to 5·2 m at MHWS. The W pier head is marked by two vertically disposed lights.

2   Bangor New Pier, an iron pile pier, extends 2½ cables NNW from Garth Point (53°14′N 4°07′W) on the NW side of the city; Bangor Buoy (port hand) lies close NNW off the pierhead.

    A small harbour, contained between breakwaters, lies on the W side of the tidal harbour and is sheltered from all directions. Facilities include a boatyard for repairs; two slipways; fresh water and fuel.

    There are moorings on the inner wall of New Dock.

Directions for entering harbour
7.154

1   Vessels should follow the directions given at 7.142 as far as Bangor New Pier, thence follow the channel across Bangor Flats, which are the SW extension of Lavan Sands, to the entrance to the new dock.

Berths and port services
7.155

1   **Berths.** Within the new dock, there is a RoRo berth with a ramp to take 300 tonnes. Vessels up to 2300 gt are regularly berthed. Facilities also exist for handling a variety of bulk cargoes.

    Services: fresh water and moderate supplies of stores; fuel by road; hospital at Bangor with helicopter landing facilities.

Anchorages and harbours

Outer Road
7.156

1   Outer Road (53°18′N 4°02′W), lies between B2 and B1 Light Buoys, and below the Pool, an area of deep water, and is well protected by the banks lying to seaward. The best anchorage, as indicated on the chart, is 4 cables E from Penmon Point (53°18′N 4°03′W) in depths of from 3 to 5·5 m, sand and shell.

Porth Penrhyn outer anchorage
7.157

1   Vessels awaiting a berth at Porth Penrhyn (7.153) usually anchor outside the NW entrance in open water.

Beaumaris
7.158

1   Beaumaris (53°16′N 4°06′W) fronts the shore on the W side of the channel. Beaumaris Castle, a historic ruin, stands at the NE end of the town, and the church, with a square tower, stands near the town centre.

A pier, suitable only for small craft, extends 1 cable SE from the coast abreast the town. Depths of 4 m are found alongside the pierhead, from which a light is exhibited.

2   Anchorage, with good holding, can be found in depths of 2 m, 2½ cables SSE from the head of Beaumaris Pier. However, this anchorage is exposed to NE winds and can be uncomfortable in SE winds when the banks are covered.

Temporary anchorage can be found in the channel abreast Beaumaris (53°15′·7N 4°05′·3W) in depths of 7 to 13 m. See also 7.199.

Other anchorages and facilities
7.159

1   **Lighthouse Cove and Puffin Island.** Temporary anchorages can be found in Lighthouse Cove, a small bay close W of Trwyn-du Light (53°18′·8N 4°02′·4W), opposite a small beach, and on the E side of Puffin Island, in depths of 4 m, sand. Both anchorages, shown on the chart, are untenable in strong E winds. Landing may not be made on Puffin Island, which is a nature reserve.

2   **Gallows Point.** A boatyard, at which repairs to small craft can be effected, lies on the S side of Gallows Point (53°15′N 4°06′W). A slipway at the boatyard is marked at its seaward end by a beacon (black, green cone topmark).

Moorings. There are numerous moorings and slipways on the W side of the channel between Trwyn-y-Penrhyn (53°17′·7N 4°03′·5W) and Garth-y-don (53°14′·6N 4°07′·7W), 4 miles SW. Moorings continue along the shore to about ½ mile N of Menai Suspension Bridge.

MENAI STRAIT

GENERAL INFORMATION

Chart 1464
Area covered
7.160

1   In this section are described the passages, harbours and anchorages between SW entrance to the Menai Strait, S of Llanddwyn Island (53°08′N 4°25′W) and Garth Point (53°14′N 4°07′W) at Bangor.

It is arranged as follows:
Menai Strait — Approaches to Caernarfon (7.166).
Caernarfon to Garth Point (7.181).

Topography
7.161

1   The navigable waterway of the Menai Strait which separates Anglesey from the mainland covers a distance of about 10 miles, the channel being narrow throughout. The distance between the entrances of the approach channels at either end is 20 miles.

2   The SW entrance consists of a low-lying sandy spit, backed by large drying flats on the N side (7.169), and a low sandy promontory on the S side. Foryd Bay, a long inlet of drying flats lies on the E side of the promontory. farther N the immediate land on either side of the strait is low with higher ground a short distance inland, being interspersed with areas of woodland.

3   However, between Port Dinorwic (53°11′N 4°12′W) and Garth Point (7.153), at the NE end, the strait becomes narrower and winding with a width of less than 1½ cables in places and assumes the character of a gorge with wooded slopes dropping steeply to rocky shores. At the town of the Menai Bridge, the narrowest point, the strait is crossed by two bridges (7.188).

4   Between Craig-y-don and Garth-y-don which lie on the Anglesey shore at the NE entrance of the strait, the shore is rocky and steep-to.

Several small rivers flow into the strait mainly near the SW end.

Marine farms
7.162

1   Oyster, mussel and clam fisheries, in which there are a number of obstructions, are situated on both sides of the Menai Strait, above the MLWS tide line. The locations are shown on the chart.

Mariners are advised not to anchor within the fisheries, the limits of which are marked by perches.

Pilotage
7.163

1   The pilotage service for the SW and NE entrances to the Menai Strait is maintained from Caernarfon (7.172). The boarding positions are shown on the chart.

Vessels with a draught exceeding 2 m should not attempt the passage through the SW entrance without the aid of a pilot.

2   Local knowledge is essential owing to the great strength of the tidal streams and constant changes in the channel.

The passage is suitable for vessels up to 80 m in length but should be attempted only near slack HW.

Natural conditions
7.164

1   **Sea level.** The tide is about one hour later, and its range at springs is about 2·7 m greater, at the NE end of the Strait than at its SW end. Computations from tidal data show that the greatest differences in sea levels occur about one hour after HW at the NE end, when the level here is more than 1·8 m higher than at the SW end, and about 4¾ hours before, or 7¾ hours after, HW at the NE end, when the relation between the levels is reversed, and the level is more than 1·8 m higher at the SW end.

Menai Strait from SW (7.161)

(Original dated 2001)

(Photograph - Air Images)

2   **Tidal streams** in the the Menai Strait are caused primarily by differences in sea level at the ends, but are modified by natural forces and local conditions.

Although they mostly set through the strait between Fort Belan and Garth Point, there is a period when the streams separate between Garth Point and The Swellies.

3   The normal times and directions of the streams are as follows:

Interval from HW Holyhead	Direction
−0040 to +0420	SW between Garth Point and Fort Belan.
+0420 to +0545	from about the Swellies, NE towards Garth Point SW towards Fort Belan.
+0545 to −0040	NE between Fort Belan and Garth Point.

The streams set generally in the direction of the channel, but at bends a set towards the outer side must always be expected.

4   The spring rate of the stream in each direction is about 3 kn in the wider parts of the channel, but more in the narrower parts.

In the SW entrance, between Fort Belan and Abermenai Point, the spring rate is about 5 kn in both directions; NE of the Menai Suspension Bridge, and SW of the Britannia Bridge, the spring rate increases to 6 kn, and between the bridges, in the channel in The Swellies, to about 8 kn, in both directions.

5   The streams in The Swellies, and to a lesser extent in the strait NE and SW of the bridges, are affected by winds at sea outside the entrances. With strong S and SW winds, both the duration and the rate of the NE-going stream are increased, and the stream may begin about a quarter of an hour earlier and end about a quarter of an hour later than usual, with corresponding reductions in the duration and rate of the SW-going stream. Strong NE winds have the opposite effect.

6   Within 5 cables N of the Menai Suspension Bridge, an eddy generally sets near the Anglesey coast in the reverse direction to the main stream in the centre and E of the strait.

Tidal stream information is given on the chart.

Buoyage
7.165

1   The direction of buoyage is inward from either end, meeting at Change Light Buoy (S cardinal) (53°09′N 4°17′W). The buoys are moved from time to time to meet changes in the channel.

MENAI STRAIT — APPROACHES TO CAERNARFON

General information

Chart 1464
Route
7.166

1   From the vicinity of Llanddwyn Island (53°08′N 4°25′W), the route first leads through a buoyed approach

channel approximately 3 miles long, before entering the Menai Strait between Fort Belan on the S side and Abermenai Point, on the N side, then continues for a further 2 miles NE to Caernarfon.

Tidal streams
7.167

1 Within Caernarfon Bar the N-going coastal stream gradually changes direction to that of the E-going entrance stream and increases in rate. Similarly, the W-going stream from the entrance gradually changes direction outwards across the bar to that of the S-going coastal stream and decreases in rate.

Near LW, the streams set generally in the direction of the channel across the bar, but near HW they set across the sands more in the direction of the coastal streams. See also 7.164. For further details, see information on the chart.

Directions

Landmarks
7.168

1 Llanddwyn Island (53°08′N 4°25′W).
White Cottage (53°07′·7N 4°18′·6W).
Saint Peter's Church belfry (53°09′·8N 4°21′·9W).
Celtic cross (53°08′·6N 4°16′·2W), standing on Twt Hill at Caernarfon.

7.169

1 **Approach.** From the pilot boarding position (7.174) S of Llanddwyn Island, the approach track leads over Caernarfon Bar, which lies 3 miles W of the entrance to the strait, thence through a buoyed channel which separates South Sands and North Sands, extensive drying sandbanks, passing:

Between C1 Light Buoy (starboard hand) and C2 Light Buoy (port hand), thence:
Through the buoyed channel towards the entrance to the strait.

2 Mussel Bank, composed of stones which dry, and on which stands a ruined beacon which dries 2 m, lies on the N side of the approach channel, 7 cables W of the entrance. It is marked by Mussel Bank Light Buoy (port hand), moored off the SE part of the bank.

Cautions. The depth over Caernarfon Bar is constantly changing. The bar should not be crossed at any time other than 3 hours either side of HW.

3 The light buoys in the approach channel are moved as necessary to meet the frequent changes in the channel and adjacent banks. For the latest controlling depth over the bar, and information concerning the latest positions of the buoys, the Harbour Master at Caernarfon should be consulted prior to entry.

A wreck (position approximate), with a safe clearance of 5·0 m, lies about 1 mile S of Llanddwyn Island Light. The stranded wreck *Grampian Castle* lies 1¼ miles SE of Llanddwyn Island Light.

7.170

1 **Entry.** On passing between Abermenai Point, on which stands a light (7.171), on the N side, and Fort Belan (53°07′N 4°20′W), on the S side, the track continues through a buoyed channel which leads a further 2 miles NE to Caernarfon.

Traeth Melynog and Traeth Gwyllt, large drying flats lying on the NW side of the channel, extend over 3 miles NE from Abermenai Point and occupy the greater portion of the NW side of the strait.

7.171

1 **Useful marks**:

Llanddwyn Island Light (white tower) (53°08′N 4°25′W).
Abermenai Point Light (white mast, 5 m in height) (53°08′N 4°20′W).

(Directions continue at 7.193)

Caernarfon

General information
7.172

1 **Position and function.** Caernarfon (53°09′N 4°16′W), has a small harbour which lies on the SE side of the Menai Strait, 2 miles within its SW entrance, and on the NE bank of the mouth of the afon Seiont which flows into the strait.

Caernarfon Castle and walls surrounding the town are in a good state of preservation and are prominent from seaward.

2 Caernarfon caters mainly for leisure craft and fishing vessels.

Caernarfon

Abermenai Point   *Fort Belan*

Menai Strait entrance from WSW (7.170)
(Original dated 2001)

(Photograph – Air Images)

Caernarfon from WSW (7.172)

(Original dated 2001)

(Photograph - Air Images)

Caernarfon from NW (7.172)

(Original dated 2001)

(Photograph - Air Images)

Extensive harbour works front the town along the shore of the strait and along the NE shore of the river.

Caernarfon has a population of about 10 000.

Port Authority. Caernarfon Harbour Trust, Harbour Office, Slate Quay, Caernarfon, Gwynedd LL55 2PB.

The port is represented by a Harbour Master.

Limiting conditions
7.173

1 **Controlling depth.** See Caution at 7.169.

Tidal levels. Mean spring range about 4·6 m; mean neap range about 2·1 m. See *Admiralty Tide Tables.*

Maximum size of vessel handled. Vessels up to 75 m in length can be berthed at Caernarfon Pier (7.175).

Local weather. During winter gales, the approach channel is often impassable and vessels should wait outside until conditions moderate.

Access to Inner Harbour and the tidal basin is possible only three hours either side of HW.

Arrival information
7.174

1 **Pilotage.** Within the Menai Strait, between Puffin Island and Caernarfon Bar, pilotage is compulsory for the following categories of vessels:

Vessels over 1500 gt.

Passenger vessels over 20 m LOA.

Vessels carrying hazardous cargo.

In addition, pilotage is compulsory for the following categories of vessels if passing through The Swellies (7.196):

2 Vessels carrying passengers, unless holding an exemption certificate.

Vessels over 3·5 m draught, and/or 50 m LOA, and/or greater than 500 gt.

Requests for pilots should be sent 24 hours in advance.

Pilot boarding positions are situated S of Llanddwyn Island in the vicinity of 53°07′N 4°25′W (for N-bound vessels) or at North-West Entrance to the Menai Strait (53°19′N 4°03′W) (for S-bound vessels).

For further details on communications and pilotage see *Admiralty List of Radio Signals Volume 6(1).*

Harbour
7.175

1 The harbour consists of Caernarfon Pier, a tidal basin known as Victoria Dock, and Inner Harbour.

Caernarfon Pier is a T-headed landing stage extending 37 m into the Menai Strait from a position 1¼ cables NE of the entrance to Victoria Dock. The head of the landing stage, from which lights are exhibited, is 12·5 m in length; dolphins at either end give an overall frontage of 40 m. There are five levels, to allow boarding and landing at any state of the tide, and there is a minimum depth alongside of 3 m.

2 Victoria Dock is entered from the strait between two short piers and contains several alongside and pontoon moorings. A flap gate across the entrance maintains a minimum depth of 2 m within the dock.

Inner Harbour, which dries at LW, is situated at the mouth of the afon Seiont and is entered through a narrow cut which is spanned by a swing bridge. Slate Quay lies on the NE side of Inner Harbour.

3 **Traffic signals** are exhibited at the swing bridge.

Vessels should sound one long blast followed by three short blasts for the swing bridge to be opened.

Main signals No 2 and No 4 of the International Port Traffic Signals are exhibited from the SW side of the entrance to Victoria Dock. For traffic signals see *The Mariner's Handbook.*

Directions for entering harbour
7.176

1 The track into Inner Harbour rounds C9 Light Buoy (starboard hand) moored at the edge of the drying bank which extends N from the river entrance, thence follows the buoyed channel, passing W of the buoy (E cardinal) moored close to the shore SW of Victoria Dock, towards the swing bridge cutting.

2 When NW of C9 Light Buoy, vessels can proceed as necessary towards the tidal basin entrance or general purpose berth.

Berths
7.177

1 **Anchorage.** There is good anchorage in the strait in depths of 5 to 9 m, 2 cables W of the tidal basin entrance.

Alongside berths:

Victoria Dock: 530 m of quay and a landing place; least depth 4·3 m at MHWS at the entrance. Used mainly by leisure craft and fishing vessels up to 30 m LOA, beam 9 m and draught 3 m. There is a marina, with some facilities, in the S part of the dock.

2 Inner Harbour: Slate Quay, 600 m in length which dries at LW; there is a depth of 4 m at MHWS but suitable only for small craft.

Port services
7.178

1 **Repairs:** minor repairs; patent slip in Victoria Dock, capacity 20 tonnes, 15 m LOA, beam 5 m.

Other facilities: hospital.

Supplies: fresh water; marine diesel by road; provisions.

Harbour regulations are in force. Copies of bye-laws are obtainable from the Harbour Master.

Anchorages

Llanddwyn Island
7.179

1 **General information.** Llanddwyn Island (53°08′N 4°25′W), on which stands a light (7.171), lies 3 miles WNW of the SW entrance to the Menai Strait and forms the W side of Llanddwyn Bay. In reality the island is a peninsula connected by a narrow isthmus to the S coast of Anglesey and is a good landfall when approaching the vicinity of the entrance to the Menai Strait.

2 There is a tower at the SW extremity of the island which should not be mistaken for the light tower. The island is a nature reserve and access above the HW mark is prohibited; see Protection of wildlife at 1.58.

The W side of the island is exposed to the prevailing winds and is inhospitable. Seaward of the S extremity lie small stacks and out-lying drying rocks, marked on their SW side by a buoy (S cardinal). A drying rock 2 cables E of the light is marked on its SE side by a buoy (S cardinal).

3 **Anchorages.** On the E side of the island, Pilots Cove, close N of the light, offers temporary anchorage in fine weather or offshore winds whilst waiting for the tide to cross Caernarfon Bar, but caution is necessary in approaching it on account of the rocks previously mentioned. See also caution below. Anchorage with good holding can be found off the entrance in about 5·5 m but is subject to swell. Boats can anchor inside for a few hours only as the cove practically dries at MLWS.

4   Mermaid Cove, about 2 cables NNE of Pilots Cove, also provides fair weather anchorage in depths of 2 m in the vicinity of Ynys y Clochydd, a large above-water rock, 3·8 m in height, which lies off the entrance to the cove.

Local knowledge. Between the two coves there are several drying rocks and local knowledge is essential.

5   **Cautions.** In the approach to the E side of the island, an unmarked drying rock lies 4 cables SSE of the light. In 1992 users of Pilots Cove reported the inside anchorage as dangerous and unsafe for shelter owing to shifting sands; this phenomenon may also apply to Mermaid Cove.

Abermenai Point and Fort Belan
7.180

1   Temporary anchorage, sand, can be found 1½ cables NNE of Abermenai Point, at the SW entrance to the Menai Strait. The anchorage is untenable in E winds.

An anchorage also exists on the S side of the SW entrance point at Fort Belan where there is a private landing jetty and open dock. A private mooring buoy lies off the dock.

CAERNARFON TO GARTH POINT

General information

Chart 1464
Route
7.181

1   From Caernarfon to Garth Point, at the NE entrance of the Menai Strait, the route leads NE for about 8½ miles, passing through The Swellies (7.196), an area of the strait encumbered with rocks and islets.

See 7.165 for information on the direction of buoyage.

Topography
7.182

1   See 7.161.

Depths
7.183

1   The buoyed channel on the W side of the bar between Caernarfon and Port Dinorwic has depths generally greater than 2 m. However, the greater extent of the bar, extending from the E side of the strait to within 1¼ cables of the W shore, has depths of less than 2 m.

Above and below the bar there are depths in the fairway of more than 6 m.

Ferry services
7.184

1   A ferry service operates between the Menai Bridge and Bangor New Pier.

Marine farms
7.185

1   See 7.162.

Historic wreck
7.186

1   A historic wreck lies on the S side of the strait, 4 cables SW of Britannia Bridge (53°13′N 4°11′W) (7.188). Unauthorised approach within 150 m is prohibited. See 1.57 and *Annual Notice to Mariners Number 16*.

Pilotage
7.187

1   Owing to the rocks and islets, the narrowness of the channel, and the strength of the tidal streams, with very little slack water, navigation through The Swellies (7.196) is dangerous and should not be attempted without an experienced pilot. Pilotage is compulsory for certain categories of vessels; see 7.174.

Bridges
7.188

1   **Britannia Bridge,** a rail and road bridge, situated 2¼ miles NE of Port Dinorwic (53°11′N 4°13′W), has a vertical clearance of 26 m under the centre of the S arch, but less on either side of the centre. A light is exhibited from the centre of the S span, and a light is exhibited on the span 30 m on either side of the centre light. There is a vertical clearance of 21·3 m under each of these side lights.

2   Leading lights (7.196) for S-bound craft are situated on the S shore close to the bridge.

Menai Suspension Bridge, situated 8 cables ENE of the Britannia Bridge, has a vertical clearance of 29 m and is without lights. The small town of Menai Bridge is situated on the Anglesey shore close N of the bridge.

Menai Suspension Bridge from W (7.188)

(Original dated 1992)

(Photograph - Mr. D C Williams)

Submarine cables
7.189

1   Submarine power cables cross the strait 5 cables and 1½ miles SW of Port Dinorwic; the points where they come ashore are marked by beacons.

Submarine cables cross the strait close E of the Menai Suspension Bridge; each shore end is marked by a beacon (white, diamond topmark).

Vertical clearance
7.190

1   An overhead power cable with a safe vertical clearance of 21 m spans the strait close W of the Britannia Bridge (7.188).

Foul ground
7.191
1   An area of foul ground, which is shown on the chart, lies 5 cables N of Port Dinorwic.

Tidal streams
7.192
1   See 7.164 and also tidal information on the chart.
Tidal streams in Bangor Pool (53°14′N 4°08′W) begin as follows:

Interval from HW Holyhead	Direction
−0040	SW
+0420	NE

2   The maximum spring rate in each direction is about 3 kn.

Directions
(continued from 7.171 or 7.142)

Landmarks
7.193
1   Celtic cross (53°08′·6N 4°16′·2W) (7.168).
Column, white in colour (53°13′·2N 4°11′·8W).
Tower (53°13′·7N 4°07′·8W) (7.140).

Caernarfon to Port Dinorwic
7.194
1   From Caernarfon to Port Dinorwic the track leads 3½ miles NE in the buoyed channel, passing SE of Change Light Buoy (53°08′·8N 4°16′·7W) (7.165) and between Traeth Gwyllt (7.170) and the mainland coast. The track then passes over a bar which is situated midway between the two ports.

Port Dinorwic to The Swellies
7.195
1   In the reach between Port Dinorwic and the entrance to The Swellies, 2 miles NNE, the only danger is Careg Ginnog, a rocky ledge which occasionally dries, situated near the E shore, 1¼ miles N of Port Dinorwic.
Foul ground. See 7.191.

The Swellies
7.196
1   The Swellies, the reach between the Britannia Bridge (53°13′N 4°11′W) and the Menai Suspension Bridge (8 cables ENE) is encumbered with rocks and islets; a channel leads through the S side of the reach. The best time to negotiate The Swellies is at HW slack, which normally occurs at about 1¼ hours before HW at Holyhead.
Sound signals. A long blast should be sounded on passing under either bridge when approaching The Swellies from W or E, since a vessel approaching from the opposite direction is obscured from view by the land.

2   **Approaching from west** vessels should proceed via the channel which lies near the S shore.
From a position W of the Britannia Bridge (7.188), the track, which follows the line of bearing 080° of a white concrete pyramidal beacon (53°13′·0N 4°10′·9W), leads E, passing (with positions from the beacon):

S of Britannia Rock (1½ cables W) and under the S arch of the Britannia Bridge, thence:

3   SE of Cribbin Rock (½ cable NW), on the line of bearing 062° of Price's Point Light (white beacon, 5 m in height) (2½ cables NE) until the alignment of the leading lights is reached.

Leading lights:
Front light (metal framework tower; 5 m in height) (E side of the Britannia Bridge)
Rear light (similar structure) (45 m from front light, W side of the bridge)

Britannia Bridge Leading Lights from NE (7.196)
(Original dated 1992)

4   The alignment (231°) of the lights (seasonal, 1st April to 30th September), astern, leads NE until the light at Price's Point is abeam, thence the track leads generally E passing (with positions from Price's Point Light (53°13′·1N 4°10′·5W)):

Price's Point Light Beacon (7.196)
(Original dated 1992)

(Photograph - Mr. D C Williams)

5   N of Price's Point Light on the line of bearing 087° of the lower part of the roof of Glan-aethwy

House (5½ cables E), just open N of the S pier of the Menai Suspension Bridge, thence:

S of Swelly Rock (¾ cable NNE), marked by a light beacon (S cardinal), standing on the SW side of the rock, thence:

S of a rock which dries 1 m (1¼ cables NE).

6   The track then leads on a line of bearing 074° of the N pier of the Menai Suspension Bridge, then alters to 084° on the beacon (red metal beacon, 8 m in height) (53°13′·2N 4°09′·6W) to pass:

N of Platters Rock (3 cables ENE), thence:

Under the mid point of the centre arch of the bridge.

By night the track lies within the white sector of Price's Point Light.

7   **Approaching from east** the track initially leads SW towards the centre arch of the Menai Suspension Bridge on a heading of 227°.

Under the bridge the track changes direction to follow the line of bearing 263°, within the white sector of Price's Point Light Beacon, of the S chimney of the cottage on Gored Goch (53°13′·1N 4°10′·9W), two rocky islets surrounded by a salmon weir. The track passes:

8   N of Platter's Rock, thence:

S of the drying rock close E of Swelly Rock, thence:

S of Swelly Rock, thence:

N of Prince's Point Light Beacon.

The track then changes direction to the alignment (231°) of the Britannia Bridge Leading Lights until abreast the concrete pyramidal beacon, 1½ cables NE of the lights, thence:

Through the centre of the S span of the bridge.

Gored Goch from NNW (7.196)
(Original dated 1992)

(Photograph - Mr. D C Williams)

9   **Caution.** An outfall extends SE into the navigable channel from the W side of the promontory on which the town of Menai Bridge stands.

The Swellies to Garth Point
7.197

1   From a position close NE of the centre span of the Menai Suspension Bridge, the track leads NE to Bangor Pool, a distance of about 1½ miles, passing (with positions from the bridge):

Midway between a beacon (starboard hand) (1½ cables NE), which marks Half Tide Rock, a drying rocky ledge on the NW shore of the strait, and the edge of drying rocks on the SE shore, thence:

2   SE of Saint George's Pier (3½ cables NNW), on which stands a light (7.198). Another light (7.198) stands close SSW of the pier. Thence:

SE of the small craft moorings in Bangor Pool and two unlit mooring buoys (orange) 1¾ cables E of Ynys y Bíg (53°14′·0N 4°09′·1W), a rock standing on the drying W bank.

Useful marks
7.198

1   Nelson's Statue (stone, 13 m in height), standing on a rock close to the N shore, 2 cables W of the Britannia Bridge.

Saint George's Pier Light (mast) (53°13′·5N 4°09′·5W).

Light (pile) (53°13′·51N 4°09′·57W) close SSW of Saint George's Pier.

(Directions for the NE entrance to the Menai Strait are given at 7.140 and for Bangor, Porth Penrhyn at 7.154)

Anchorages and harbours
7.199

1   **Anchorage.** There is an anchorage, for vessels waiting to pass through the strait, off Bangor New Pier (53°14′·4N 4°07′·6W) in depths of from 5 to 14 m.

Port Dinorwic
7.200

1   **General information.** Port Dinorwic (53°11′N 4°13′W) is a small harbour lying on the SE side of the strait, about 3 miles SW of Menai Bridge and was at one time used for shipping slate from nearby quarries. The harbour consists of a tidal basin, known as the Outer Harbour, with a landing jetty close SW, and Vaynol Dock.

The harbour authority is NWS Dock Management Ltd., Dinorwic Marina, Y Felinheli, Gwynedd, LL56 4JN.

2   The Outer Harbour dries at MLWS; vessels must be prepared to take the ground. The entrance to Vaynol Dock is by way of a lock 54·9 m long and 9·7 m wide, with a depth over the sill of 5·2 m at MHWS. The lock is opened on demand 3 hours before and up to 3 hours after HW. Craft up to LOA 22·8 m, beam 4·6 m and draught of 3·5 m can be accommodated.

3   Radio contact with Vaynol Dock can be made using the call sign: Dinorwic Marina.

Berths. Outer Harbour, 157 m long and 53 m wide with depths of 4·3 m at MHWS, is entered from the strait. The width at the entrance to the harbour is 21·3 m. Visitors berths are available.

Vaynol Dock, which lies close NE of Outer Harbour, is a yacht harbour nearly 345 m in length and ranges in width from 18·3 to 30·5 m with a normal depth of 4·6 m. Visitors berths are available.

4   **Repairs:** repairs, cranes, tugs and divers can be arranged; slipway, width 6 m, in the SW corner of Outer Harbour; dry dock, 58·5 m long, 9·7 m wide, entered from Vaynol Dock, depth over sill 3 m.

Other facilities: hospital at Bangor.

Supplies: fresh water; fuel.

Menai Bridge
7.201

1   **General information.** Menai Bridge (53°13′N 4°10′W) is a small town occupying the high ground of a promontory on the Anglesey shore which is connected to the mainland by the Menai Suspension Bridge (7.188). At the N end of the waterfront of Menai Bridge, 3½ cables NNE of the

bridge, Saint George's Pier, an iron pier with a floating landing stage at its head, projects 100 m from the shore to the edge of the navigable channel, where there is a depth of 3 m. A light (7.198) is exhibited from a mast at the head of the pier and another light (7.198) is exhibited from a pile close SSW of the pier.

2   **Tidal stream** off the pier generally runs in the opposite direction to that of the main stream; see 7.164. Moorings lie between Saint George's Pier and Princes Pier, 1 cable SSW, where craft can take the ground.

Foel
7.202

1   Anchorage can be obtained at Foel (53°09'·5N 4°16'·6W), a small hamlet on the Anglesey shore, N of the tidal basin at Caernarfon (7.172), in depths of 2 to 4 m, off the ruins of a ferry landing jetty which extends 150 m SE from the shore and is marked at its head by a perch.

    The approach to the anchorage is made through Foel Swatchway (6 cables NE) as shown on the chart.

Moorings
7.203

1   Moorings lie in the anchorage off Fort Belan (53°07'·4N 4°19'·9W), off the E bank of the strait midway between Fort Belan and Caernarfon and close W of the entrance to the afon Seiont at Caernarfon. Other moorings lie off the E bank at Waterloo Port (53°09'·2N 4°15'·8W), a small hamlet, off the W bank opposite Waterloo Port and close S of Port Dinorwic (53°11'N 4°12'W).

2   Bangor Pool (53°14'·3N 4°08'·0W), which lies between Craig-y-don and Garth-y-don, points on the Anglesey shore opposite Bangor, contains small craft moorings lying off the NW shore. Other moorings lie close SE off Bangor New Pier (53°14'·3N 4°07'·5W).

Landing place
7.204

1   There is a landing place on the SE shore, 4 cables NNE of Waterloo Port (53°09'·2N 4°15'·9W).

Chapter 8 - Liverpool Bay, including the Ports of Liverpool and Manchester

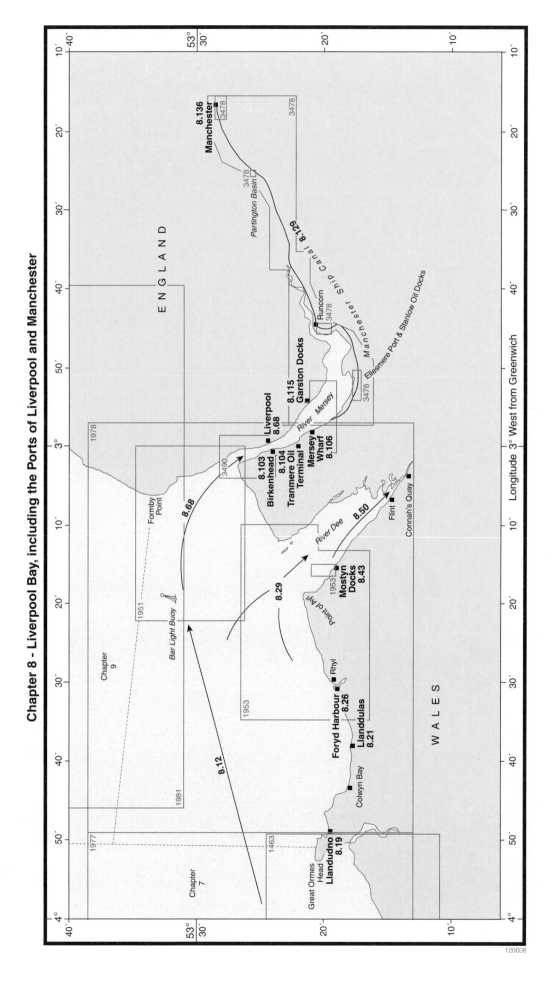

Longitude 3° West from Greenwich

120608

232

CHAPTER 8

LIVERPOOL BAY INCLUDING PORTS OF LIVERPOOL AND MANCHESTER

GENERAL INFORMATION

Charts 1978, 1826
Scope of the chapter
8.1

1   This chapter covers the waters of Liverpool Bay, entered between Great Ormes Head (53°21′N 3°52′W) and Formby Point, 30 miles ENE, and includes the river Dee estuary, the navigable reaches of the river Mersey and the Manchester Ship Canal.

    The description includes the routes and passages of the area, and the ports, harbours and anchorages; of these the most important are the deep water ports of:

2   Liverpool (53°25′N 3°00′W), which includes Birkenhead and the port of Garston.
        Manchester (53°28′N 2°17′W), which includes the oil terminals at Eastham and Stanlow.
    The chapter is divided into the following sections:
        Liverpool Bay including the river Dee estuary (8.10).
        River Mersey (8.59).

Offshore route
8.2

1   An offshore route runs between the North Channel (see *Irish Coast Pilot*) and the Bar Light Buoy (53°32′N 3°21′W), passing SW of the Calf of Man (54°03′N 4°50′W); for details see 10.154.

Topography
8.3

1   Between the bold promontory of Great Ormes Head (8.16) and the low-lying Point of Ayr, the W entrance point of the river Dee estuary, the coastline of North Wales is mainly backed by high land, except for 3 miles either side of Rhyl (53°19′N 3°29′W) where it is low-lying. The remaining coastline to Formby Point (53°33′N 3°06′W), which includes the land at the entrance to the river Mersey, consists mainly of low-lying ground with heavily built up residential areas. The Liverpool Docks complex begins at Seaforth on the E side of the entrance to the river.

2   Much of the waters lying between Great Ormes Head and Formby Point are shoal and encumbered by banks which extend up to 8 miles offshore.

Hazards
8.4

1   **Marine exploitation.** Drilling rigs and production platforms for the recovery of oil and gas are situated in the approaches to Liverpool Bay. For details see 9.4.
    Fishing. Offshore trawlers may be encountered within Liverpool Bay during April and May, and inshore trawlers at any time.
    Pots may be found off Great Ormes Head.
    For details of types of fishing and nets in use, see *The Mariner's Handbook*.

Wrecks and obstructions
8.5

1   Many wrecks and obstructions exist in Liverpool Bay. Some are marked by light buoys.

High speed craft
8.6

1   High speed ferries operate between Liverpool and the Isle of Man, Dublin and Belfast. See 1.8.

Great Ormes Head from NW (8.3)
(Original dated 2001)

(Photograph - Air Images)

Offshore pilotage
8.7

1   Liverpool Pilots offer a pilotage service, if requested or in bad weather, from Point Lynas (53°25′N 4°17′W) inwards and also to ports within the river Dee. For details see 8.85 and *Admiralty List of Radio Signals Volume 6(1)*.

Rescue
8.8

1   For details of rescue organisation and locations of assets see 1.60 and text under Rescue.

Natural conditions
8.9

1   **Tidal streams.** The flow of water over the area dealt with in this chapter is largely determined by tidal forces.

Between Great Ormes Head and the river Dee estuary the stream sets mainly in the direction of the coast; see also 8.15.

The E-going stream in the Irish Sea divides off Formby Point and runs into the estuaries of the river Mersey and the river Ribble; the streams from the estuaries unite off Formby Point thence set W.

2   Tidal streams are given on the charts and in *Admiralty Tidal Stream Atlas — Irish Sea and Bristol Channel*.

Swell. In Liverpool Bay there is considerable swell on the bar of the river Mersey during strong NW winds.

Sandwaves. Fields of sandwaves, some of which reach heights in excess of 8 m above the seabed after periods of calm weather at neap tides, extend up to 20 miles offshore in Liverpool Bay and its approaches.

LIVERPOOL BAY INCLUDING RIVER DEE ESTUARY

GENERAL INFORMATION

Chart 1978
Area covered
8.10

1   In this section are described the coastal route, harbours and anchorages between Great Ormes Head (53°21′N 3°52′W) and Bar Light Buoy (20 miles ENE).

Also described are the passages, channels, harbours and anchorages within the river Dee estuary and the navigable section of the river Dee as far as Chester (8.50).

It is arranged as follows:
    Great Ormes Head to Bar Light Buoy (8.12).
    River Dee Estuary (8.29).

Topography
8.11

1   See 8.13.

GREAT ORMES HEAD TO BAR LIGHT BUOY

General information

Chart 1978
Route
8.12

1   The coastal route between Great Ormes Head (53°21′N 3°52′W) and Bar Light Buoy (53°32′N 3°21′W) leads about 20 miles ENE.

Deep-draught vessels should keep to seaward of the numerous banks and shoal waters encumbering the North Wales coast.

Topography
8.13

1   Much of the North Wales coastline between Great Ormes Head and Point of Ayr, at the entrance to the river Dee estuary, 20 miles E, is low and flat. East of Rhos Point (53°19′N 3°44′W) the foreshore is mostly shingle fronted by sand which dries to 5 cables offshore. Between Abergele and the mouth of the river Clwyd (8.24), 3 miles E, the coastline is backed by low-lying marshland.

2   A series of groynes, each marked by a beacon (starboard hand), extend NW from the coastline fronting Prestatyn (53°20′N 3°25′W).

A railway line closely follows the coastline.

Rescue
8.14

1   All-weather lifeboats are stationed at Llandudno (53°20′N 3°50′W), Rhyl (53°19′N 3°29′W) and Hoylake (53°24′N 3°10′W). Inshore lifeboats are stationed at Llandudno and Rhyl.

For details of rescue organisation see 1.60.

Tidal streams
8.15

1   Tidal streams between Great Ormes Head and Point of Ayr start running E and W beginning as follows:

Interval from HW Liverpool	Direction
+0600	E
−0015	W

The maximum spring rate in each direction is 3 kn.
Tidal streams are given on the chart and in *Admiralty Tidal Stream Atlas — Irish Sea and Bristol Channel*.

Directions
(continued from 7.123)

Principal marks
8.16

1   **Landmarks:**
    Great Ormes Head (53°21′N 3°52′W), is a promontory and one of the best landmarks on this stretch of coast. The N face is a steep bold limestone cliff. At its highest point stands a radio mast, a cable car station and a hotel. The old lighthouse, white square castellated stone tower, is situated on the steep cliff of North Toe, the NW extremity of the promontory. The area lies within a local nature reserve; see 1.58.

2   Dome, approximate position 53°17′·5N 3°42′·6W.
    Church tower (53°18′N 3°32′W).
    Tower standing at Rhyl (53°19′N 3°29′W), exhibits an obstruction light.
    Spire, situated 3 cables E of the tower.

3   Saint Elmo's Summerhouse (ruins) (53°19′·5N 3°22′·6W) and a framework radio mast close N standing at an elevation of 234 m on the ridge of a hill. Two radio masts standing close W of the ruins are also conspicuous.
    Old Lighthouse (53°21′·4N 3°19′·3W) (8.35).
    Radio masts (53°22′N 3°10′W) (8.35).

Other aids to navigation
8.17
1   **Racons:**
     West Constable Light Buoy (53°23′N 3°50′W).
     Bar Light Buoy (53°32′N 3°21′W).
     For further details see *Admiralty List of Radio Signals Volume 2.*

Passage
8.18
1   From a position N of Great Ormes Head (53°21′N 3°52′W) to the vicinity of Bar Light Buoy (53°32′N 3°21′W) the route leads about 20 miles ENE, passing:
     NNW of Constable Bank marked by W Constable Light Buoy (W cardinal) (53°23′N 3°49′W); the bank extends W from Rhyl Flats (8.37) and lies parallel with the coast 3½ miles offshore with depths of less than 5 m. Thence:
2   NNW of Rhyl Flats Offshore Wind Farm (53°23′N 3°39′W), marked by light buoys. A light buoy (special, wave recorder) is moored 3½ miles N of the wind farm. Thence:
     NNW of N Hoyle Light Buoy (N cardinal) (53°27′N 3°31′W) marking shoal ground N of Chester Flats (53°22′N 3°28′W) (8.37) and moored 1¾ miles NW of North Hoyle Wind Farm (8.39), thence:
3   NNW of Gwynt Y Mor meteorological mast (53°28′·8N 3°30′·5W). There is a light-buoy (special, wave recorder) 2¼ miles W of the mast. Thence:
     SSE of the Douglas/Hamilton Oil/Gas Field platforms (53°32′N 3°35′W and 53°34′N 3°27′W) (9.4) to the pilot boarding position close E of Bar Light Buoy (53°32′N 3°21′W). Light buoys (special) are moored 5 cables W and 2½ cables NW of Bar Light Buoy.

(Directions continue for entry to the river Mersey at 8.92; directions for entry to the river Dee are given at 8.35.)

Llandudno Bay
8.19
1   **General information.** Llandudno Bay, also known as Ormes Bay, is entered between Pen-trwyn, the NE extremity of Great Ormes Head (53°21′N 3°52′W) and Little Ormes Head, 2 miles ESE, which somewhat resembles the former though much smaller. The land at the head of the bay is low-lying.
     The W side of the bay is fronted by ledges which dry to 2 cables offshore but farther E the foreshore is shingle fronted by sand at LW. A coastal bank with depths of less than 5 m extends to a line joining the entrance points of the bay.
2   Llandudno, a seaside resort with a population of about 15 000, is situated on a low marshy isthmus which joins the promontory of Great Ormes Head to the mainland.
     Llandudno Pier, which has not been in use since 1987, extends 2 cables NE from the W shore at Llandudno. There is a light at the head of the pier.
     Two jetties, the heads of which are marked by beacons (starboard hand), project from the shore close S of the pier.
3   **Tidal streams** are negligible in the bay.
     Anchorage may be found close outside the bay, with reasonable holding of fine sand and mud, inside the 10 m depth contour.
     Caution: 5 m shoal 1 mile E of Llandudno Pier.

Facilities: helicopter landing site near Llandudno hospital.

Colwyn Bay
8.20
1   Colwyn Bay is entered between Rhos Point (53°19′N 3°44′W), low and flat, and Tan Penmaen Head, 2½ miles ESE. The foreshore of shingle fronted by sand dries to a distance of 3 cables offshore. There are some loose rocks and stones round the head of the bay. A drying rock lies 4 cables offshore in the middle of the entrance.
     The town of Colwyn Bay is a large seaside resort.
2   A detached breakwater, 200 m in length, nearly parallel to the shore and about 200 m from it, is situated close SE of Rhos Point. A short breakwater extends E from the shore towards the S end of the detached breakwater and forms a small harbour which dries.
     A stranded wreck which lies 3 cables NE of Rhos Point is marked by Rhosneigr Buoy (starboard hand) moored close NE.
     Tidal streams in Colwyn Bay are negligible.

Llanddulas
8.21
1   **General information.** Llanddulas, a small town and port which includes Llysfaen, is situated near the coast, 1½ miles E of Tan Penmaen Head (53°17′·7N 3°40′·8W). Two jetties extend from the coast close W of Llanddulas and are used for loading crushed limestone and granite from the quarries nearby.
     Traffic. In 2007 there were 96 ship calls with a total of 295 787 dwt.
2   **Pilots** are available for berthing at either jetty by arrangement with the respective operating authority. They are supplied by Liverpool Pilotage (8.85), and board vessels at Bar Light Buoy (53°32′N 3°21′W) or off Point Lynas (53°25′N 4°17′W).
     Anchorage. Vessels awaiting a berth at either jetty can anchor in the vicinity, 2 miles offshore, in depths of at least 5 m, good holding.

Raynes Jetty
8.22
1   **General information.** Raynes Jetty (53°17′·6N 3°40′·3W) extends 218 m N from the shore at Llysfaen, 5 cables W of Llanddulas. Lights are exhibited from the head of the jetty.
     Vessels up to 92 m in length can be loaded on either side of the jetty, at a rate of up to 1100 tonnes per hour; the largest vessel that can be handled being one of 4500 dwt.
2   Vessels usually stay on the berth between 3 hours before until 1 hour after HW when there are depths of about 7·5 m alongside. The maximum draught accepted at HW is 6 m. Depending on tide the jetty can dry out at LW.
     Owing to the exposed position of the jetty vessels cannot be worked when winds reach force 5 or over.
     The operating authority is RMC Aggregates North West Ltd, Raynes Quarry, Llysfaen, Colwyn Bay, Conwy LL29 9YW.
3   The operating authority is represented by the Quarry Manager.
     Supplies: fuel available.

Llanddulas Jetty
8.23
1   **General information.** Llanddulas Jetty (53°17′·6N 3°39′·5W), also known as Llysfaen Jetty, extends about 204 m NNW from the shore at Llanddulas and dries

Llanddulas from WNW (8.21)
(Original dated 2001)

(Photograph - Air Images)

alongside at LW. A light is exhibited from the head of the jetty.

Vessels up to 4000 dwt, having a length of up to 100 m and draught of 5·9 m can be accommodated on either side of the jetty in depths of about 6·7 m at MHWS.

2   A loading rate of 1000 tonnes per hour can be achieved.

Vessels should not approach the berth until 3 hours before HW and only with permission from the operating authority: ARC Northern Ltd, Llanddulas Quarry, Llanddulas, Abergele, Conwy.

The operating authority is represented by a Harbour Master.

3   Night berthing signals are in operation: For berthing on the W side, a red light is shown from the head of the jetty and for the E side, a green light.

Supplies: limited; fresh water. There are no facilities.

For further details on port operations at both jetties, see *Admiralty List of Radio Signals Volume 6(1).*

River Clwyd

Chart 1953
General information
8.24

1   **Description.** The river Clwyd enters the sea at the W end of the town of Rhyl (53°19′N 3°29′W). The entrance to the river at HW, which gives access to the small harbour (8.26) lying close inside, is formed by a promenade to the SE and sandhills to the W. Although the river is tidal to

Rhuddlan, a small town 2 miles within its entrance, it is suitable only for light pleasure craft.

2   Rhyl, a seaside resort, with a population of about 25 000, occupies 1¾ miles of the coastline E of the river entrance; the town, with conspicuous buildings (8.16) is prominent from seawards.

Outfalls. A buoy (starboard hand), marking the seaward end of an outfall, is moored 2 cables NW of the entrance to the channel.

3   An outfall also extends 2 miles NW from the shore at Kinmel Bay, 5 cables SW of the entrance to the river Clwyd, and is marked at its seaward end by Kinmel Bay Buoy (starboard hand) (Chart 1978).

Vertical clearances. A fixed road bridge, with a vertical clearance of 1 m at MHWS, spans the river 2 cables within the entrance; 3 cables above the road bridge the river is crossed by a railway bridge with a vertical clearance of 1 m at MHWS.

Directions
8.25

1   **Cautions.** In the approaches to the river Clwyd, at half tide, there are depths of less than 1 m over the sandbanks either side of the entrance channel and up to 3 cables seaward of the lighted beacon.

A drying obstruction lies about 5½ cables WNW of the river entrance, as shown on the chart.

Local knowledge for vessels entering the river Clwyd is advisable; visitors unfamiliar with the harbour should wait until HW before entering on account of the strong in-going tide which can run at up to 6 kn.

2   The channel leading to the river entrance dries; it lies close W of a revetment which extends N from the E entrance point of the river and is marked by beacons. A light, which at night can be obscured by background shore lights, is exhibited from the beacon at the seaward end of the revetment, and the remaining beacons are each surmounted by a broom, which, owing to bad weather, may be missing.

The harbour becomes inaccessible in heavy onshore winds particularly after HW.

Foryd Harbour
8.26

1   Foryd Harbour, which dries, lies on the W bank inside the entrance to the river Clwyd. In the past the harbour accommodated small commercial coasters but is now principally used by fishing vessels and pleasure craft up to 12 m in length which can take the ground; the harbour can become congested with uncontrolled moorings.

2   There being no Harbour Authority, mariners requiring information about the harbour should contact Rhyl Yacht Club, whose premises are situated on the upper W side of the harbour; Rhyl Coastguard will also offer advice.

Facilities in the harbour are limited: two slipways for boats; fresh water from Rhyl Yacht Club; helicopter landing site on the promenade near Rhyl hospital.

Anchorages
Chart 1978
Liverpool Bay
8.27

1   For anchorages in Liverpool Bay see 8.82 and in Llandudno Bay 8.19.

Abergele Road
8.28

1   A temporary anchorage for small vessels during offshore winds can be obtained in Abergele Road which fronts the coast abreast Abergele (53°17′N 3°35′W). The road consists of flat shallow ground with depths of from 2 to 4 m, but there are patches with a least depth 0·5 m close W of the road within 2 miles of the coast N of Gwrych Castle, a large building surrounded by trees which stands on the E face of a hill.

RIVER DEE ESTUARY

Charts 1978, 1953
General description
8.29

1   The estuary of the river Dee, most of which dries, is entered between Point of Ayr (53°21′N 3°19′W), a low sandy point on which stands a disused lighthouse (8.35), and Hilbre Point, composed of low sandhills, which lies 4½ miles ENE. Red Rocks, a drying ledge, extends 3 cables NW from Hilbre Point.

Hilbre Island from NW (8.29)
(Original dated 2001)

(Photograph - Air Images)

A group of three small islands lie on the NW part of Lime Wharf, a drying bank, which extends 1¼ miles W and 2 miles S from Hilbre Point.

2 The NW, and largest of the group, is Hilbre Island (53°23′N 3°14′W), from where a light (8.41) is exhibited, and on which stand a beacon (8.41) and several buildings.

About 1 cable SE of Hilbre Island is Little Hilbre and Little Eye lies 5 cables farther SE.

Tanskey Rocks, which dry, lie 4 cables SE of Little Eye.

3 Much of the estuary of the river Dee is a statutory Site of Special Scientific Interest (1.58). There is a bird observatory on Hilbre Island.

In the summer months a large number of pleasure craft are moored S of West Kirby Marine Lake (53°22′N 3°11′W) and there is much sailing activity in the estuary and its approaches.

4 Above Mostyn Docks (53°19′N 3°16′W), a navigable channel leads between drying sandbanks to the entrance to the river Dee at Connah's Quay, 9 miles SE (Chart 1978).

Topography
8.30
1 The coastline on both sides of the estuary is generally low and flat. The W side is backed by higher ground whilst the E side comprises low marshland. Along the E entrance, the land is heavily residential.

A railway line skirts the W coastline.

The estuary of the river Dee is encumbered by drying banks, the largest, West Hoyle Bank, separates Welsh Channel (8.38) in the W from Hilbre Swash (8.41) in the E.

Historic wreck
8.31
1 A historic wreck lies 9 miles WNW of Point of Ayr. The wreck is protected against unauthorised interference. See 1.57 and *Annual Notice to Mariners Number 16*.

Pilotage
8.32
1 Pilotage for Mostyn Docks and ports in the river Dee and its estuary is compulsory for all vessels of more than 20 m LOA, and is provided by Mostyn Pilots (8.45).

Rescue
8.33
1 Within the estuary, inshore lifeboats are stationed at West Kirby (53°22′N 3°11′W) and Flint (53°15′N 3°08′W) (Chart 1978).

For details of rescue organisation see 1.60.

Tidal streams
8.34
1 For tidal information 6 miles N of Point of Ayr see the tidal diamond on the chart.

At the E end of Welsh Channel off Point of Ayr, the tidal streams set as follows:

In-going stream:

Interval from HW Liverpool	Direction
–0545	NE – E
–0255	E
–0030	N

2 The maximum spring rate in the E direction is 2½ kn.

The in-going stream sets towards Salisbury Middle but farther W and SE the stream sets more in the direction of the channel.

Near springs between –0345 and –0145 HW Liverpool there may be sudden rushes of short duration with rates up to 4 kn.

3 Out-going stream begins as follows:

Interval from HW Liverpool	Mean direction
HW	WNW – NW

The maximum spring rate is 2 kn.

The out-going stream sets towards West Hoyle Bank, but towards the end of the stream the direction changes N and ends NW.

4 In the estuary above Point of Ayr the tidal streams set strongly in the direction of the channels when the banks are dry, but directly inwards and outwards when they are covered.

For offshore streams see also *Admiralty Tidal Stream Atlas — Irish Sea and Bristol Channel*.

Directions

Principal marks
8.35
1 **Landmarks:**
  Old Lighthouse, white with red top, disused (53°21′·4N 3°19′·3W) standing at Point of Ayr.
  Two radio masts (53°22′N 3°10′W) standing at West Kirby.
  War Memorial (obelisk) (53°22′·5N 3°10′·5W).
  Grange Monument, column surmounted by a sphere, standing 4 cables SE of the war memorial.

Cautions
8.36
1 The approaches to the river Dee estuary are barred by shifting banks which dry in places and extend out to 6 miles seaward.

Local knowledge. Because of the shifting nature of the dangers in the approaches, vessels without local knowledge should not enter the estuary without contacting Mostyn Harbour Master to obtain information and advice; see *Admiralty List of Radio Signals Volume 6(1)*.

2 It is dangerous to ground in the channels on an out-going tide as the sand washes away so quickly that the vessel is liable to keel over.

In Welsh Channel, Hilbre Swash, Outer Passage, Mid Hoyle Channel and the river Dee, the channels are liable to frequent change and the buoys are moved accordingly.

3 **West Hoyle Bank,** which dries, occupies a considerable area off the entrance to the estuary. It is crossed by Mid Hoyle Channel (8.39) and narrow and unnavigable swashways. The bank is steep-to on its S and E sides but its N part shelves gradually though irregularly.

West Hoyle Spit is the W extremity of the bank.

East Hoyle Bank, which dries, is a continuation N of Lime Wharf (8.29). Its W side is moderately steep-to for 2 miles N of Hilbre island, thence it turns W shelving gradually and terminating in East Hoyle Spit.

Approach from the west
8.37
1 **Inner Passage** lies between Rhyl Flats with depths of less than 1 m, which extend 4 miles offshore abreast Rhyl (8.24), and Chester Flats, a continuation W of West Hoyle Bank with Tail of Middle Patch at its W end. It has depths of less than 2 m, and Middle Patch partly dries at its E end.

2 From a position NNE of the North Constable Light Buoy (53°23′·8N 3°41′·4W) (N cardinal) the track leads

Point of Ayre Lighthouse (disused)

River Dee Estuary from NW (8.36)
(Original dated 2001)

(Photograph - Air Images)

ESE for about 5 miles, thence SE and E for a further 4 miles to the outer end of the dredged channel leading into Welsh Channel, passing (with positions from Point of Ayr Old Lighthouse (53°21′·4N 3°19′·3W)):

3   NNE of the Rhyl Flats Offshore Wind Farm site (12 miles W), which extends ESE for about 3 miles from the North Constable Light Buoy. Its N extremity is marked by RFWF No2 Light Buoy (starboard hand) and RFWF No1 Light Buoy (N cardinal) is moored at its NE corner. Thence:

SW of Middle Patch Spit Light Buoy (port hand) (8 miles W), moored at the W end of Tail of Middle Patch, thence:

4   NE of Rhyl Flats (8 miles W), a series of shifting sandbanks with depths of less than 1 m over them (see information on sandwaves at 8.9), thence:

SW of Tail of Middle Patch, (7½ miles W) marked by Inner Passage Light Buoy (port hand), moored 5 cables SW of Tail of Middle Patch. In the fairway between Middle Patch Spit and Inner Passage Light Buoys there is a least charted depth of 3·1 m, with depths of less than 2 m close SW of the fairway.

5   Thence the line of bearing 096½° in the white sector (096°-097°) of West Hoyle Spit (Earwig) Outer Directional Light (perch pile) (53°21′·2N 3°24′·1W) leads into the channel S of West Hoyle Spit. This PEL is remotely operated by a person authorised by Mostyn Harbour Authority. The perch pile contains monitoring equipment to broadcast wind, tide and current information to Mostyn and to suitably equipped vessels. The channel is marked by light buoys and leads E and ENE into Welsh Channel. Although dredged to 4·7 m (2001), a more recent survey (2003) revealed two 4·1 m patches as shown on the chart.

8.38

1   **Welsh Channel** lies between the coastal bank, fronting the shore W of Point of Ayr, and West Hoyle Bank. The dredged channel (8.37) crosses a bar (53°21′·4N 3°23′·5W) which joins the shore bank to West Hoyle Spit at the W end of the channel. A patch, drying 2·1 m, lies close NW of the dredged channel and 2¾ miles W of Point of Ayr.

2   The track, continues ENE thence E and SE, passing:

S of East Hoyle Light Buoy (port hand) (1¼ miles WNW), thence:

N of Air Light Buoy (starboard hand) (4½ cables N), thence:

SW of Dee Light Buoy (S cardinal) (7 cables NNE), into Wild Road (8.55), to Mostyn inner pilot boarding position.

8.39

1   **Outer Passage** lies N of Chester Flats with depths of 4 m over Chester Bar (1½ miles NE of Chester Flats).

From a position about 9½ miles WNW of Point of Ayr Old Lighthouse (53°21′·4N 3°19′·3W), the track leads ESE over Chester Bar, passing (with positions from Point of Ayr Old Lighthouse):

239

SSW of North Hoyle Wind Farm, centred on 53°25′N 3°27′W. An anemometry mast, 61 m in height, stands close off the NW corner.

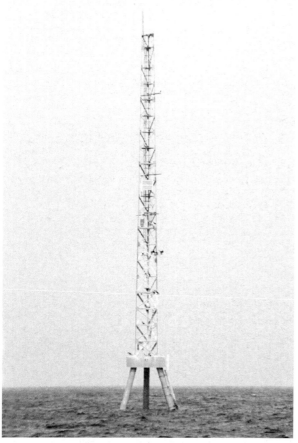

N Hoyle anemometry mast from S (8.39)
(Original dated 2000)

(Photograph - HMSML Gleaner)

2   **Mid Hoyle Channel,** which leads E and S across West Hoyle Bank has depths of less than 1 m where it crosses West Hoyle Bank (4 miles E of Chester Bar). From a position about 4½ cables S of NW Hoyle Light Buoy (port hand) (3½ miles NW), moored at the W end of the drying patches extending W from West Hoyle Bank, the track leads E and S passing (with positions from Point of Ayr Old Lighthouse (53°21′·4N 3°19′·3W)):

3   S of Hoyle Light Buoy (port hand) (2 miles NNW), which marks the S edge of the drying patches extending W from West Hoyle Bank, thence:
SW of Mid Hoyle Light Buoy (port hand) and E of East Hoyle Spit Light Buoy (starboard hand) (1½ and 1¼ miles N respectively), marking the channel where it crosses West Hoyle Bank, thence:

4   SW of Dee Light Buoy (S cardinal) (6 cables NNE).
Submarine gas pipeline. A charted submarine pipeline lies across Chester Bar and close along part of the passage above.

Approach from the north
8.40

1   Vessels bound for Mostyn Docks may enter the Mid Hoyle Channel at NW Hoyle Light Buoy (8.39). Vessels bound for Connah's Quay or Shotton Jetty may use the Hilbre Swash (8.41).

8.41

1   **Hilbre Swash** (53°25′N 3°15′W), with a least charted depth of 1·4 m in the fairway, lies between West Hoyle Bank, on its S side, and East Hoyle Spit and East Hoyle Bank on its N and E sides.
The channel, which is entered SW of HE1 Light Buoy (W cardinal) (53°26′·3N 3°18′·1W) moored off the W edge of East Hoyle Spit, 4¾ miles NW of Hilbre Point (8.29), leads ESE thence S passing (with positions from Hilbre Point (53°23′N 3°12W)):

2   N and E of HE2 Light Buoy (E cardinal) (2 miles NNW) which marks the drying spit extending NE from the NE end of West Hoyle Bank, thence:
E of HE3 Light Buoy (starboard hand) (1¾ miles NNW), which marks the W side of the channel, thence:

3   E of a wave recorder light buoy (special) (1½ miles W), thence:
W of Hilbre Island Light (white metal framework tower, 3 m in height) (1 mile W), which stands at the NW end of the island. A tall prominent beacon (lattice, black and white) stands close S of the light. Thence:
To the vicinity of HE4 Buoy (starboard hand) (1¾ miles WSW).

Welshman's Gut
8.42

1   Welshman's Gut (53°22′N 3°16′W) lies between the S edge of West Hoyle Bank and the N edge of Salisbury Middle and connects the inner ends of Welsh Channel and Hilbre Swash. The channel is no longer used for navigation; it is unmarked and dries to nearly 5 m in places.

(Directions continue at 8.47)

Mostyn Docks
Chart 1953
General information
8.43

1   **Position.** Mostyn Docks (53°19′N 3°16′W) is a small port with a RoRo terminal and river wharf on the W side of the river Dee estuary, 2¾ miles SE of Point of Ayr.
Function. The port is a ferry terminal for Ireland and also handles bulk cargoes.

2   **Port limits** enclose the immediate area of the docks.
Approach and entry. See 8.47.
Traffic. In 2007 the port was used by 121 vessels totalling 315 427 dwt.

3   **Port Authority.** The Harbour Authority for the Dee Conservancy area is Environment Agency Wales. The Dee Conservancy is represented by a Harbour Master. The Port Authority for Mostyn is Mostyn Docks Ltd, Mostyn, Holywell, Flintshire CH8 9HE. The Port Authority is represented by a Harbour Master.

Maximum size of vessel handled
8.44

1   The river wharf can accept vessels up to 6500 dwt; with 120 m LOA; beam 20 m; 6·5 m draught, at all states of the tide.

Arrival information
8.45

1   **Port operations.** For details see *Admiralty List of Radio Signals Volume 6(1).*
Notice of ETA required is at least 24 hours prior to arrival at at North Rhyl Anchorage (53°23′N 3°33′W).

The report should include the vessel's maximum draught, confirmation that a corrected to date copy of Chart 1953 is carried and that the vessel has no defects affecting her safe navigation.

2 A subsequent report should be made on arrival at North Rhyl Anchorage.

Outer anchorage. The North Rhyl Anchorage is centred at 53°23′N 3°33′W, close N of Mostyn-Outer pilot boarding position. This is an open anchorage with only reasonably good holding and where vessels have been known to drag in moderate weather conditions. An alert anchor watch is essential.

3 Anchorage may also be obtained in Wild Road (53°22′N 3°18′W) (8.55) and Mostyn Deep (53°21′N 3°17′W) (8.56).

Pilotage is generally compulsory for all vessels over 20 m LOA bound for Mostyn or the river Dee. Other seagoing vessels are recommended to obtain information and advice from the Harbour Master on VHF. See *Admiralty List of Radio Signals Volume 6(1)*.

For Mostyn Docks pilots usually board near Dee Light Buoy (53°22′·0N 3°18′·7W) (8.38).

4 However, a vessel of greater than 95 m LOA whose master does not have recent local knowledge of the approaches to Mostyn will embark a pilot at Mostyn-Outer pilot boarding position (53°22′·5N 3°33′·3W).

All vessels bound for Mostyn Docks should await pilotage instructions at North Rhyl Anchorage, either at anchor or under way as appropriate.

Harbour
8.46

1 The harbour consists of a rubble training wall which extends 3½ cables NE from the shore, a RoRo terminal and a river wharf. Lights (vertically disposed) are exhibited from the head of the training wall.

The RoRo terminal is SE of and parallel to the training wall and the river wharf extends 2 cables farther SSE. There is a turning basin, marked on its E side by M8 and M10 Light Buoys (port hand) moored 2½ cables NE and E of the RoRo terminal respectively.

Tidal streams. See 8.34.
Anchorage. See 8.55 and 8.56.

Directions for entering harbour
(continued from 8.42)
8.47

1 From Dee Light Buoy (53°22′·0N 3°18′·7W) to the entrance to Mostyn Docks, the track leads, in a buoyed channel, 3 miles generally SSE through Wild Road (8.55) and Mostyn Deep to Mostyn Docks, passing (with positions from Point of Ayr Old Lighthouse (53°21′·4N 3°19′·3W)):

NE of North East Mostyn Light Buoy (starboard hand) (9 cables E), moored at the NE edge of Mostyn Bank, thence:

2 NE of an obstruction (1¼ miles E), with a depth of 3·3 m over it, thence:

SW of Salisbury Middle Light Buoy (port hand) (1½ miles E), moored at the NW extremity of Salisbury Bank, thence:

NE of M1 Light Buoy (starboard hand) (1¾ miles ESE), moored at the entrance to Mostyn Channel.

Thence the track continues S, and thence SSE, through the buoyed channel into the turning basin.

3 A PEL, located ashore 5¼ cables SW of the breakwater head, indicates the centre line of the initial S leg of the buoyed channel.

Caution. The Harbour Master should be consulted for the latest depth information in Mostyn Channel and alongside berths. The buoys are moved to best mark the channel.

(Directions continue at 8.51)

Berths
8.48

1 Berth 1 is the RoRo terminal.
Berths 2, 3 and 4 are on the river wharf, total length 310 m. Berth 4 dredged to 7·0 m (2000).

Port services
8.49

1 **Repairs:** minor repairs can be carried out alongside; heavy lifts up to 60 tonnes can be handled.
Other facilities are limited.
Supplies: fuel oil at 24 hours notice; fresh water; supplies.
Harbour regulations: bye-laws regulate the conveyance, loading and unloading of explosives within the port.

River Dee

Charts 1978, 1953
General information
8.50

1 **Description.** The river Dee flows into the estuary between two training walls at Connah's Quay (53°14′N 3°04′W) (8.53), a small town on the S side of the river. The N training wall is approximately 7 cables long and the S training wall 4 cables long. A light (metal framework tower) is exhibited at the seaward end of each training wall with regularly spaced perches along its length.

2 Vertical clearance indicators, referenced to the road bridge about 2 cables downstream from Shotton Wharf, are situated at Flint Point (53°15′N 3°08′W) on the N training wall and the upstream end of the S training wall

Above Connah's Quay the river is canalised and used by a specialist transportation barge, survey craft, dredgers, fishing and pleasure craft.

3 Boats can reach Chester (53°12′N 2°52′W) passing beneath the bridges at Hawarden and Queensferry, ¾ and 1¾ miles respectively above Connah's Quay. The minimum width of the passage under the bridges is 37 m with a maximum vertical clearance of 8·85 m. A footbridge, with a vertical clearance of 9 m spans the river at Saltney, 4 miles farther up river. There is little water at Chester at MLWS.

Chester, a city with a population of about 90 000, stands on the N bank of the river approximately 7 miles above Connah's Quay.

4 **Pilotage.** See 8.45.
Vertical clearance. A number of power cables, least safe vertical clearance 24 m, and a bridge, vertical clearance 15 m, span the river in the vicinity of Connah's Quay.

Another power cable, safe vertical clearance 15 m, spans the river 1 mile above Connah's Quay.

5 **Tidal streams.** Above Mostyn Docks the in-going stream begins as follows:

Position	Interval from HW Liverpool	Duration
Holywell Bank	–0500	5 hours
Connah's Quay	–0110	2 hours
Chester (Chart 1826)	HW	1¾ hours

6 **Bore.** A bore forms on spring tides approximately 1 mile below Connah's Quay and attains a height of 0·5 m. When the bore has passed, at the beginning of the in-going stream, the after-rush may momentarily attain a rate of as much as 8 kn.

Directions

(continued from 8.47)

8.51

1 Vessels may navigate the HW channel above the port of Mostyn at appropriate states of the tide. The channel leads through the estuary, entering the canalised section between the N and S training walls. The channel is marked by light buoys (lateral).

Because of the changing nature of the sandbanks and channels, local knowledge is essential.

8.52

1 **Useful marks:**

Tall buildings (53°15′N 3°08′W) standing at Flint.

Berths

8.53

1 **Connah's Quay** (53°14′N 3°04′W) lies on the S side of the mouth of the river Dee. This is extensively used by fishing vessels.

A power station with 4 cooling towers stands on the W bank of the river near the bridge (8.50).

There is a disused tidal dock.

2 **Shotton Wharf,** which exhibits lights, lies on the N bank of the river opposite Connah's Quay. It is 180 m long and is only used by commercial traffic on an irregular basis.

3 **Port Authority.** The Harbour Authority for Dee Conservancy area is Environment Agency Wales. The Dee Conservancy is represented by a Harbour Master.

For navigational matters, enquiries should be directed to Environment Agency Wales, Chester Road, Buckley, Flintshire, CH7 3AJ.

Regulations

8.54

1 Within the river Dee, bye-laws are in force with regard to vessels carrying petroleum and carbide of calcium.

Anchorages and harbours

Chart 1953

Wild Road

8.55

1 Short term anchorage can be obtained in Wild Road (53°22′N 3°18′W), in depths of about 17 m. There is little protection from weather and tidal stream and vessels should use this anchorage only in slight to moderate weather conditions and be prepared to move at very short notice.

Mostyn Deep

8.56

1 Anchorage can be obtained in Mostyn Deep (53°21′N 3°17′W), which has depths of from 5 to 10 m. Whilst more sheltered in SW winds than Wild Road similar precautions should be observed (8.55).

Lime Wharf

8.57

1 Small craft can find temporary anchorage in the channel off Lime Wharf (53°22′N 3°13′W).

Moorings

8.58

1 There are moorings at West Kirby (53°22′N 3°11′W) and at Caldy (Chart 1978), 1 mile S, where vessels can take the ground. There are several slips at both locations. Other moorings exist farther E along the coast.

RIVER MERSEY

GENERAL INFORMATION

Charts 1978, 1951, 3490, 3478

Area covered

8.59

1 In this section are described the approaches to the river Mersey including the entrance channel, the Port of Liverpool which includes Birkenhead and the oil terminal at Tranmere, Garston Docks, the Manchester Ship Canal and the Port of Manchester.

2 Also described are the navigable reaches of the upper Mersey and Inland Waterways associated with the river.

It is arranged as follows:

Port of Liverpool and Approaches, including Garston Docks and the upper Mersey (8.68).

Manchester Ship Canal (8.129).

Port of Manchester (8.136).

Topography

8.60

1 The coast between Hilbre Point (53°23′N 3°11′W) and Rock Lighthouse (unlit) (53°27′N 3°02′W), which stands at the entrance to the river Mersey on the W side, is composed of low sandhills fronted by East Hoyle Bank

(8.36) and Mockbeggar Wharf, drying sandflats. At the W end of this stretch of coast stands the town of Hoylake (53°24′N 3°10′W) and at the E end is New Brighton (53°26′N 3°03′W), a suburb of Wallasey.

2 The coast from Formby Point (53°33′N 3°06′W) (9.14) to Royal Seaforth Dock, 5½ miles SE, at the entrance to the river Mersey on the E side, also consists of low sandhills. The town of Crosby lies close N of the dock.

3 Queens Channel and Crosby Channel, which form a continuous channel through which the river Mersey discharges, lie between Taylor's Bank and Formby Bank, both of which dry and form the N side of the channel, and Great Burbo Bank, which also dries, and which extends NW from the E end of Mockbeggar Wharf and forms the greater part of the S side.

4 Above the entrance to the river, on the E bank, lies the City of Liverpool with its extensive system of docks and basins.

The W bank of the river is occupied successively by the towns of Wallasey, with its suburbs of New Brighton, Liscard, Egremont and Seacombe, then Birkenhead with its extensive dock complex, Rock Ferry and Tranmere Oil Terminal and Eastham (53°19′N 2°57′W).

Upper Mersey is described at 8.124.

River Mersey from NW (8.59)
(Original dated 2001)

(*Photograph - Air Images*)

Firing practice area
8.61

1   Altcar Rifle Range (53°31'·5N 3°04'·5W), see information on the charts.

For further information on practice areas see 1.15.

Vessel traffic services
8.62

1   A VTS scheme is maintained for the control of shipping in the approaches to, and within, the river Mersey, see 8.80.

Buoyage
8.63

1   Within Queens Channel and Crosby Channel all buoys and light floats, with the exception of those named, bear the initial letter of the channel which they mark and are numbered from seaward.

The N and S sides of the entrance to the channel are marked by Q2 and Q1 Light Floats respectively.

Formby and Crosby Light Floats are moored mid-channel, the former on the bar near the outer end of Queens Channel, and the latter 11½ cables WSW of Crosby Beacon (8.92).

Wrecks and obstructions
8.64

1   There are many wrecks and obstructions in the approaches to the river Mersey.

Rescue
8.65

1   An inshore lifeboat is stationed at New Brighton (53°26'N 3°03'W).

For details of rescue organisation see 1.60.

Tidal streams
8.66

1   Tidal stream information in the approaches and within the river Mersey is shown on the charts.

In general the streams set in the direction of the channels when the banks are dry but across them directly to and from the river entrance when they are covered.

In the entrance to Queens Channel a SE set will be experienced during the in-going stream and a W set during the out-going stream.

2   Between the bend in Crosby channel and the river entrance, when the banks are covered, an E set will be experienced on the in-going stream and a NW set during the out-going stream; these sets may be very strong at springs.

The rate of the tidal stream increases inwards, attaining approximately 5 kn on spring tides in the river entrance.

3   Near Newcombe Knoll (53°28'N 3°14'W) when the banks are dry there is little stream.

See also *Admiralty Tidal Stream Atlas — Irish Sea and Bristol Channel*.

Regulations
8.67

1   **Mersey Channel Collision Rules.** The Mersey Docks and Harbour Company have adopted certain regulations for vessels navigating the river Mersey and the sea channels and approaches thereto; for details see Appendix I.

Bye-laws are also in force for vessels carrying dangerous substances.

2   No ballast, ashes or other bulky substance, or rubbish may be jettisoned in the river or any of the sea channels, or from any pier or quay.

Copies of bye-laws may be obtained from the Port Authority (8.73).

PORT OF LIVERPOOL AND APPROACHES, INCLUDING GARSTON DOCKS AND UPPER MERSEY

General information

Charts 1951, 3490
Position
8.68

1   The Port of Liverpool (53°25'N 3°00'W) consists of seven miles of docks, on both banks of the river Mersey, including Royal Seaforth Dock, Liverpool Docks, Birkenhead Docks and Tranmere Oil Terminal.

Function
8.69

1   There are regular shipping services to and from most parts of the world, and distribution services from Liverpool by rail, road, canal and coasting vessels.

There are regular shipping services to and from most

The port is equipped with modern cargo handling facilities, a large oil terminal and facilities for dry docking and repair of large vessels.

2   Cargoes handled are; general, bulk and oil, container and RoRo traffic. There is considerable trade in scrap metals.

The industries of the port include flour milling, ship repair, seed crushing, artificial fibre manufacture, engineering and telecommunications.

3   **Free port.** Superimposed on the port is Liverpool Freeport, an area on the Liverpool side of the river comprising Royal Seaforth Dock, Gladstone, Alexandra, Langton and Canada Docks; an area within Birkenhead Docks has also been given free port status.

Liverpool and the towns bordering the river Mersey, known collectively as Merseyside, have a total population of about 1½ millions.

Charts 1978, 3478
Port limits
8.70

1   The port limits extend about 18 miles W and 14 miles N from the river entrance and include the river Mersey and up river to Warrington Bridge (53°23′N 2°35′W), excluding any waters belonging to the Port of Manchester.

Customs limits. A line, shown on the chart, drawn between Dungeon Point (53°20′N 2°50′W) and a point on the opposite bank of the river at Ince separates the customs control areas of Port of Liverpool from that of Port of Manchester.

Charts 1951, 3490
Approach and entry
8.71

1   The port is entered through Queen's Channel and Crosby Channel (8.60), the approach to which lies through Liverpool Bay. The channel is encumbered by banks on either side which extend up to 8 miles offshore, but these dangers and the channel are well marked by light floats and light buoys.

2   The approach to Queen's Channel is marked by the Bar Light Buoy (safe water) (53°32′N 3°21′W), moored 3 miles WNW of the entrance to the channel.

An ODAS light buoy (special) is moored 2½ cables NW of the Bar Light Buoy and a waverider light buoy (special) is moored 5 cables W.

Traffic
8.72

1   In 2007 there were 3594 ship calls with a total of 56 000 706 dwt.

Port Authority
8.73

1   The Port Authority is Mersey Docks and Harbour Company, Maritime Centre, Port of Liverpool, Liverpool L21 1LA.

The port is represented by the Director Port Services.

Navigational matters should be addressed to the Marine Operations Manager.

Limiting conditions

Depths
8.74

1   **Controlling depths.** The Port Authority should always be consulted for the latest information on controlling depths in the river and at the entrances to the river locks, as these depths change frequently.

Channel depths. The depths in the Queens and Crosby Channels are maintained at or near 7·0 m; a channel 5 cables wide has been dredged through the bar at the outer end of Queens Channel.

2   With this depth vessels with a draught of 12·8 m can enter the port at any HW and vessels of up to 14·1 m draught at 75% of HWs during the year. Occasionally, these draughts have been slightly exceeded by arrangement and permission of the Port Authorities.

Charted depths. Between the entrance to the river and Liverpool Landing Stage (53°24′N 3°00′W) there are depths of from 6·0 to 21·0 m in the fairway; thence as far as Tranmere Oil Terminal depths vary from 11·4 to 19·1 m.

3   Between the Tranmere Oil Terminal and the entrance to Eastham Channel there is a least depth of 0·7 m.

The depth in Eastham Channel (8.98) leading to Eastham Locks, varies and can be obtained from the Harbour Master, Port of Manchester.

4   **Dock water levels.** The water in the docks on the Liverpool side is impounded at a level approximately 9·7 m above chart datum. The water in Birkenhead Docks is impounded at a level approximately 10 m above chart datum. The level of water is apt to vary more or less from time to time and vessels must therefore take precautions whilst berthed alongside. In both docks, however, the levels are maintained so far as circumstances permit by pumping from the river.

Deepest berths
8.75

1   Royal Seaforth Dock (8.100).
Liverpool Docks (8.101).
Birkenhead Docks (8.103).
Tranmere Oil Terminal (8.104).

Density of water
8.76

1   Birkenhead 1·023 g/cm³; Gladstone Dock 1·022 g/cm³.

Tidal levels
8.77

1   Mean spring range about 8·4 m; mean neap range about 4·5 m. For further information see *Admiralty Tide Tables.*

Strong NE winds reduce tidal height and SW winds increase tidal height.

The heights of tide at Hilbre Island (for Liverpool Bay), Gladstone Dock river entrance, Alfred Dock river entrance and Eastham Lock are available on request.

Tide gauges are sited at the entrances to Gladstone, Alfred and Eastham Locks.

Entrance locks
8.78

1   **Gladstone Lock,** entered 5 cables SE of Royal Seaforth Dock, operates throughout 24 hours giving direct access into Gladstone Dock thence into Royal Seaforth Dock. The lock is 326·1 m long and 39·6 m wide; the sill is 5·6 m below the level of chart datum.

On sailing, a considerable scend can be experienced when the dock gates are opened.

2   **Langton Lock,** entered 1¼ miles SSE of Royal Seaforth Dock, operates throughout 24 hours depending on tide,

giving direct access into Langton Dock thence into Alexandra, Brocklebank, Canada and all other Liverpool docks as far as Trafalgar Dock. The lock is 251·5 m long and 39·6 m wide; the sill is 5·29 m below the level of chart datum.

When using Langton Lock, some flexibility for shallower draught vessels can be given in the times of operation.

3 **Alfred Lock** on the W side of the river gives access to Birkenhead Docks, and is entered 2½ miles within the river entrance. The lock, which operates for large vessels 2 hours before HW until HW, and for other vessels 4 hours either side of HW, is 146·3 m long and 30·3 m wide; the sill is 2 m below the level of chart datum.

4 For ships which are longer than the lock, the whole of Alfred Dock is used as a lock, with the vessel secured either alongside the N wall or on four hawsers in the centre of the dock. Under these circumstances vessels should allow 2½ hours from locking to berth.

Maximum size of vessel handled
8.79
1 The largest vessel handled was one of 322 912 dwt; 346·3 m LOA; beam 57·4 m; draught 12·5 m, which berthed at Tranmere Oil Terminal.

Arrival information

Port operations
8.80
1 **Port radio.** Routine broadcasts include disposition reports, movements of very large tankers, weather reports, local navigation warnings and, every 30 minutes in fog, visibility reports.

Control Centre. The control centre for communications relating to port operations and pilotage is situated in The Mersey Docks and Harbour Company's headquarters at Seaforth, Bootle.

Email: vts.portoperations@merseydocks.co.uk

2 **VTS** scheme, which operates from the Control Centre with radar surveillance being operated from the Port Radar Station (53°28′N 3°02W) (8.92), is maintained for the control of shipping. The radar coverage extends over Liverpool Bay for a radius of 20 miles from the station, and in the river Mersey as far S as the approaches to Manchester Ship Canal and Garston Docks.

3 Vessels of more than 50 gt navigating within the Port of Liverpool must be equipped with VHF communications and should establish contact with the Control Centre, call sign: MERSEY RADIO, when approaching Bar Light Buoy inward-bound or before sailing, and maintain a continuous listening watch when under way or at anchor within the port.

4 For further details see *Admiralty List of Radio Signals Volume 6(1)*. Positions of reporting points are shown on the chart.

For details of dock traffic signals, see 8.90.

Notice of ETA required
8.81
1 Vessels should send their ETA at the nominated pilot boarding position (8.85) at least 24 hours in advance (48 hours in advance for vessels carrying a dangerous cargo) or on leaving the last port, whichever is later, to Port Operations Control Centre.

Email: vts.portoperations@merseydocks.co.uk

For further information required see *Admiralty List of Radio Signals Volume 6(1)*.

Outer anchorages
8.82
1 In the event of berths not being readily available, there is ample good anchorage outside the river Mersey in the open roadstead of Liverpool Bay. When anchoring it is essential that vessels do so well clear of the buoyed channel and Bar Light Buoy.

Vessels over 50 gt may not anchor inside the river Mersey, except in an emergency, without permission from Mersey Radio.
8.83
1 **Prohibited anchorage.** In order to avoid obstructing shipping in the approach to the river Mersey, vessels may not anchor within an area shown on the chart, W from Q2 and Q1 Light Floats and extending to 3 miles W of Bar Light Buoy.

Anchoring within the river Mersey is generally prohibited except with the permission of the Port Authority or in an emergency.

2 **Prohibited fishing and anchoring areas,** indicated on the charts, are situated in the following positions:

Within 1 cable S of Tower Light Buoy; foul ground.

In an area W of Liverpool Landing Stage; foul ground.

In an area N W and S of Dukes Light Buoy (3½ cables S of Liverpool Landing Stage) considered by the Mersey Docks and Harbour Company as a prohibited anchorage; ground tackle.

3 Abreast Tranmere Oil Terminal; foul ground.

In an area adjacent to the N end of Garston Channel (8.120); submarine pipelines.

Prohibited dredging and anchoring area lies 1½ miles W of Garston Docks (8.115); submarine cables.

Submarine pipelines
8.84
1 At the entrance to Garston Channel (53°22′·6N 2°58′·9W) (8.120), a submarine pipeline extends SW from the shore at Dingle and is marked at its head by Dingle Light Buoy (special). Anchoring and fishing are prohibited within an area, which encloses the pipeline, shown on the chart.

Disused submarine pipelines lie between the Tanker Cleaning Jetty (8.105) at Rock Ferry (53°22′·5N 3°00′·0W) and the NW end of the training wall, 8 cables SE, as shown on the chart.

Pilotage
8.85
1 Pilotage is compulsory, except for HM Ships, within the port for all vessels of more than 82 m in length and for all other vessels carrying hazardous cargoes or with defective equipment affecting their safe navigation.

Notice required for a pilot is the same as that for ETA. If a vessel will not arrive within 3 hours of its ETA, an amended ETA must be received at least 12 hours before arrival and 6 hours before the original ETA and should be confirmed when within VHF range. Email: vts.pilotage@merseydocks.co.uk

2 **Pilot boarding position.** Pilots normally embark or disembark in the vicinity of Bar Light Buoy (53°32′N 3°21′W) or in the case of bad weather or at the request of a vessel's master, off Point Lynas (53°25′N 4°17′W) (Chart 1977).

A Communications Officer boards with the pilot for vessels of 100 000 dwt or more.

3   In extreme cases of poor weather, a pilot may leave an outward vessel anywhere in the river, providing there is agreement with Port Control to do so.

Pilot vessels are operated by the Control Centre, and have the words Liverpool Pilot painted on the superstructure.

For further details on pilotage, see *Admiralty List of Radio Signals Volume 6(1)*.

Tugs
8.86

1   There are numerous tugs stationed at the port. Tugs usually join vessels in the vicinity of Rock Lighthouse (8.92).

Regulations concerning entry
8.87

1   **Dangerous cargo** regulations for vessels within the river Mersey, see *Admiralty List of Radio Signals Volume 6(1)*.

There are heavy penalties for failure to conform with the regulations. Vessels carrying a dangerous cargo are also required to report to Control Centre (8.80) when passing Bar Light Buoy inward-bound.

2   **Restricted visibility.** Laden tankers bound for Tranmere Oil Jetty and passenger vessels will not normally be allowed to navigate within the port when visibility is reported to be less than 5 cables in any area through which the vessel intends to navigate.

Harbour

General layout
8.88

1   On the Liverpool side of the river the docks are divided into two divisions, lying N and S of Liverpool Landing Stage and the Cruise Ship Terminal.

Within the N division it is possible, subject to depths, for a vessel, if necessary, to be transferred from one end to the other without having to enter the river. The S limit is Trafalgar Dock.

2   The S division consists of docks used mainly by leisure craft and includes Liverpool Marina. Craft can move from one end to the other but this is dependent upon the vertical clearances under the bridges in the system.

The Cruise Ship Terminal (53°24′N 3°00′W) (8.102) extends N from Liverpool Landing Stage.

Liverpool Landing Stage fronts the river W of the Royal Liver Building, S of the Cruise Ship Terminal.

3   Birkenhead Docks, which form part of Port of Liverpool, occupy approximately 1 mile of the river frontage on the W bank of the river. They consist of a series of wet docks at the N end, and the Cammell Laird Shipyard complex of dry docks, Tranmere Basin (8.107) and slipways fronting the river.

Tranmere Oil Terminal lies 1 miles S of the entrance to Birkenhead wet docks.

4   Mersey Wharf (8.106), which fronts the former Bromborough Dock, lies 1½ miles above Tranmere Oil Terminal.

Liverpool and Birkenhead are connected by rail and road tunnels under the river.

For details of the upper Mersey, see 8.124.

Hazards
8.89

1   **Dredgers** are constantly operating in the approach channels and within the river Mersey. For signals displayed, see Appendix I.

Ferries. There are regular ferry services in the vicinity of Liverpool Landing Stage to points on the opposite side. High speed ferries to Dublin and the Isle of Man also operate from the Landing Stage.

2   **Traffic.** A great number of vessels navigate the river at all times. Large tankers may be met entering or leaving the port. Other vessels should avoid meeting or passing them between Formby and Crosby Light Floats.

Information concerning large vessel movements is included in the routine disposition reports broadcast by the Port Radar Station and will be given at any time.

Traffic signals
8.90

1   At the entrance to Gladstone Lock, Langton Lock and Alfred Lock, signals (Diagram 8.90) are shown.

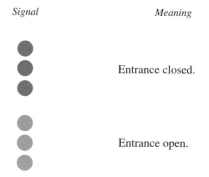

Signal	Meaning
● ● ●	Entrance closed.
● ● ●	Entrance open.

Liverpool – docking signals (8.90)

Tidal streams
8.91

1   See information on the chart. The in-going stream sets off from Liverpool Landing Stage, more strongly at its N end, the S end of the Cruise Ship Terminal.

The out-going stream sets on to Liverpool Landing Stage, more strongly at its S end.

Directions for entering harbour
(continued from 8.18)

Principal marks
8.92

1   **Landmarks:**

Crosby Beacon (red ball over diamond topmark, 22 m in height) (53°31′·4N 3°04′·7W).

North Inner Mark (diamond topmark) (53°29′·8N 3°03′·6W).

Port Radar Station (white, 25 m in height) (53°28′·0N 3°02′·4W), conspicuous from most directions. Six wind turbines are situated along the dock wall SE of the Radar Station.

Rock Lighthouse (white granite tower) (53°26′·7N 3°02′·5W), disused.

Approach channels
8.93

1   The route, from the pilot boarding area S of Bar Light Buoy (53°32′N 3°21′W) to the entrance to the river Mersey and docks complex, generally leads E through Queens Channel then SE through Crosby Channel, a distance of approximately 14 miles, passing (with positions from Crosby Beacon (53°31′·3N 3°04′·7W)):

Between Q2 Light Float (port hand) (53°31′·5N 3°15′·0W), moored off the W edge of Taylor's Spit, an extension of Taylor's Bank (8.60) S of Zebra Flats (4 miles WSW), and:

Radar Station   *N wind turbine*

Liverpool Port Radar Station from WSW (8.92)

(Original dated 2001)

(Photograph - G. Kirk mv Logos II)

2   Q1 Light Float (N cardinal), 1 mile WSW, and moored close N of a wreck with a least depth 6·8 m over it which lies on the N edge of Three and Four Fathom Tongue, a spit which extends W from Little Burbo (53°30′N 3°12′W). An obstruction, the remains of Burbo Towers (53°30′·3N 3°17′·4W), lies on the NW part of the tongue and is marked by BT Light Buoy (starboard hand). Thence:

3   S of Formby Light Float (safe water) (53°31′·1N 3°13′·5W), thence:

N of C5 Light Buoy (N Cardinal) (2½ miles W) moored close NE of Askew Spit which dries and which extends N from Great Burbo Bank. C9 Light Buoy (starboard hand) (1·8 miles W) marks the E side of the spit.

4   Burbo Offshore Wind Farm stands on Little Burbo and Great Burbo Flats. The most N turbine mast is about 1 mile S of the Formby Light Float. All masts are lit. Three high voltage submarine cables come ashore in the vicinity of 53°25·6N 3°05·5W. Thence:

W of Crosby Light Float (safe water) (11½ cables WSW), thence:

5   NE of a light buoy (E cardinal) (2½ miles S) which marks Burbo wreck, thence:

SW of Port Radar Station (53°28′N 3°02′W) (8.92), thence:

NE of Brazil Light Float (starboard hand) (53°27′N 3°02′W) which lies at the entrance to the river and about 7 cables W of Gladstone Dock.

6   **Cautions.** Training banks, which cover, have been constructed on each side of the channel. Their levels above chart datum vary between 2 and 3 m. It is not safe to navigate between the channel light buoys, or light–floats, and the training banks.

7   There is considerable swell on the bar during strong NW winds. Due allowance must be made by large deep draught vessels when entering or leaving the river.

The depths in the entrance channel and river are liable to change and buoyage is altered as necessary.

Approach to Gladstone Lock
8.94

1   From a position E of Brazil Light Float (53°27′N 3°02′W), vessels bound for a berth within Royal Seaforth Dock or Gladstone Dock should proceed towards Gladstone Dock river entrance, which is aligned NNW/SSE. Vessels are presented bow first having been swung into position using tide and/or tugs. The lock operates throughout 24 hours. Large vessels usually berth at or near HW.

2   The S limit of the dredged approach to the lock is indicated by a sectored light standing 2 cables SSE of the lock entrance.

Two further sectored lights on the dock wall SSE of the entrance indicate distances of 122 m and 213 m from the entrance.

Approach to Langton Lock
8.95

1   From a position E of Brazil Light Float (53°27′N 3°02′W), vessels bound for either Alexandra, Langton, Brocklebank, Canada or any other dock in the northern division (8.88), should proceed to Langton Lock river entrance, aligned N/S 7 cables S of Gladstone Lock. As for Gladstone Lock, vessels are manoeuvred to enter bow first.

2   The S limit of the dredged approach to the lock is indicated by a sectored light standing 2¼ cables S of the lock entrance.

Two further sectored lights on the river wall S of the entrance indicate distances of 122 and 213 m from the lock entrance.

Caution. There are obstructions in an area, indicated on the chart, close N of the lock entrance; Canada Light Buoy (port hand) is moored off their W extremity.

Approach to Alfred Lock and Twelve Quays RoRo Terminal
8.96

1   From a position E of Brazil Light Float (53°27′N 3°02′W), the track generally leads SE then S for a distance of about 3 miles to the entrance to Alfred Lock, which gives access to Birkenhead Docks, passing (positions from Langton Lock (53°26′·4N 3°00′·5W)):

E of Tower Light Buoy (E cardinal) (6 cables WSW), which marks an area of foul ground, thence:

E of Egg Light Buoy (starboard hand) (1 mile SSW), thence:

2   W of Victoria Tower (1 mile S), which stands on the river wall at Salisbury Dock (53°25′·3N 3°00′·3W). Millhouse Rocks project W from the river bank in the vicinity of the tower. Thence:

E of Seacombe Ferry Landing Stage (1¾ miles S), used by passenger traffic only, and from which

Twelve Quays Project   *Alfred Lock*

Birkenhead – Alfred Dock and East Float from ENE (8.96)
(Original dated 2001)

(Photograph - Air Images)

lights are exhibited, thence to the entrance of the lock.

3 Vessels enter the lock, from the river, bow first using tide and/or tugs; on leaving, large vessels leave the lock stern first.

Caution. There is a strong out-going stream across the entrance to the lock after HW on spring tides.

Twelve Quays RoRo terminal has two berths. Lights are exhibited from the ferry pontoon and from the N and S dolphins (green triangle point downwards). A sectored light is exhibited from the river wall adjacent to the N berth.

Approach to Tranmere Oil Terminal
8.97

1 From a position off Seacombe Ferry Landing Stage (53°24′·6N 3°00′·9W) (8.96), the track continues up-river a further 2 miles towards the terminal, passing (with positions from Liverpool Landing Stage (53°24′N 3°00′W)):

W of the Cruise Ship Terminal, which extends N of Liverpool Landing Stage, thence:

W of Liverpool Landing Stage, which exhibits lights (metal columns) at each end, thence:

E of Twelve Quays RoRo Terminal (5 cables WSW).

2 W of Dukes Light Buoy (port hand) (4 cables S), which marks the N edge of Pluckington Bank, mentioned below, thence:

E of Woodside Ferry Landing Stage (6½ cables SSW), used by passenger traffic only, and from

where lights (metal columns) are exhibited at each end, thence:

3 E of former Cammell Laird's yards (1¼ miles SSW), from the S corner of which, a light (white structure, 9 m in height) is exhibited, thence:

W of Pluckington Bank Light Buoy (W cardinal) (1¼ miles S) marking the SW edge of Pluckington Bank, which dries to 1½ cables from the bank, and fronts the S division of docks; thence to the berth.

4 **Docking** at the terminal is normally carried out on the out-going tide up to 1½ hours after HW. Undocking takes place 4 hours before HW up to HW; on occasions undocking can be after HW according to tide and weather. All vessels swing before proceeding down river.

Channel width between Tranmere and Pluckington Bank is only 500 m wide, all of which is required when unberthing.

Approach to Eastham
8.98

1 **Caution.** Depths in the river are subject to change and the buoys are moved accordingly. Depths in Eastham Channel vary and can be obtained from the Harbour Master, Manchester Ship Canal Company.

From a position off Tranmere Oil Terminal (53°22′·7N 2°59′·9W), the track leads a further 4 miles through Eastham Channel to the vicinity of Eastham Locks or Queen Elizabeth II Dock, within the Port of Manchester,

248

passing (with positions from the light (53°20'·8N 2°58'·1W) at the S end of the river wall at the N end of Eastham Channel, or otherwise stated):

2   NE of the disused jetty (8.105) 2 cables SE of the oil terminal, thence:

SW of Dingle Light Buoy (special) (1·3 miles NNW), which marks the SW limit of a prohibited anchorage, thence:

NE of Brombro Light Buoy (E cardinal) (10½ cables NNW), thence:

3   Between E2 Light Buoy (port hand) (5 cables N) and E1 Light Buoy (starboard hand) (6 cables NNW) which lie at the entrance to Eastham Channel, thence following the channel, marked by light buoys, to the locks.

4   Inward vessels should time their arrival to approach Eastham Locks at HW or just on the start of the out-going tide, so as to avoid the E set across the face of the locks on the in-going tide.

Maximum draught outward vessels should leave the lock ½ hour before HW against the in-going tide. Similar procedures should be adopted for Queen Elizabeth II Dock.

Useful marks
8.99

1   Royal Liver Building (W spire) (53°24'·3N 2°59'·8W), standing 1 cable E of Liverpool Landing Stage.

Birkenhead Town Hall (dome) (53°23'·6N 3°00'·9W), standing 9 cables SW of Liverpool Landing Stage.

(Directions for Garston Docks are given at 8.120)

Alongside berths

Royal Seaforth Dock
8.100

1   Situated in the port area of Seaforth, N of the Liverpool Docks system, Royal Seaforth Dock (53°27'·6N 3°01'·6W) provides ten modern deep-water berths and is entered from Gladstone Dock through a passage 39·6 m wide with a depth of 5·6 m below chart datum over the sill and a similar depth in the dock.

2   There are 3170 m of quay including grain, container and forest product terminals; RoRo facilities include a terminal with services to Belfast.

Vessels up to 75 000 dwt with a maximum length of 260 m and having a draught of 12·8 m can be accommodated at the grain terminal.

Liverpool Docks
8.101

1   **Gladstone Dock** (53°27'·3N 3°01'·2W), adjacent to the S side of Royal Seaforth Dock, is one of the principal wet docks, and includes three branch wet docks. Entered from the river through Gladstone Lock it contains general cargo berths and a dedicated coal terminal in Branch No 1; RoRo and bulk facilities within Branch No 2; a RoRo terminal handling services to the Republic of Ireland, situated in Branch No 3.

2   Bulk liquid facilities exist alongside N Branch No 2, and a steel terminal is served by berths in Branch No 1 and Branch No 2.

Royal Seaforth Dock from WSW (8.100)

(Original dated 2001)

(Photograph - Air Images)

Gladstone Lock   Langton Lock

Gladstone, Alexandra, Langton and Brocklebank Docks from S (8.101)

(Original dated 2001)

(Photograph - Air Images)

The maximum draught permissible in the dock is 12·8 m alongside the bulk liquids berth. Vessels having a draught of up to 11·5 m can berth at the steel terminal.

Alexandra Dock (53°26'·8N 3°00'·8W), which is connected to Langton Dock, adjacent S, by a passage 27·3 m wide, contains RoRo facilities and berths for feedstuffs and bulk ores. Maximum draught 8·8 m.

3   **Langton Dock,** entered from Langton Lock gives access to the remaining docks within the N division. There is a general cargo berth on the W side of the dock.

Brocklebank Dock, which includes a branch dock, lies S of Langton Dock. The dock contains a freight ferry terminal with services to and from Belfast.

4   **Canada Dock** (53°26'·2N 3°00'·3W), entered from Brocklebank Dock through a passage 39·6 m wide, contains three branch wet docks. There are RoRo facilities and berths for scrap metal and bulk liquid. Vessels up to 30 000 dwt, maximum draught 10·0 m, can berth within the dock in certain areas.

Huskisson Dock, entered from Canada Dock through a passage 27·3 m wide, contains two branch wet docks for handling general and bulk cargoes including grain and timber. Maximum draught 9·5 m.

8.102

1   **Sandon Half-tide Dock** (53°25'·7N 3°00'·3W), entered from Huskisson Dock, gives access to the smaller docks in the system.

Wellington and Bramley Moore Docks handle small shipments of bulk commodities. Access into Wellington Dock from Sandon Half-tide Dock is via a cut 21·3 m wide, and into Bramley Moore Dock through a cut 18·3 m wide.

2   **Nelson Dock,** entered from Bramley Moore Dock through a cut 18·3 m wide, is used for the handling of

wines and spirits through RoRo facilities. Vessels up to 99·1 m in length, 15·5 m beam and draught 7 m can be accommodated alongside.

3   **Salisbury Dock.** Entered from Nelson Dock through a cut 18·2 m wide, can accommodate small vessels with bulk commodities. A narrow cut leads into Collingwood Dock thence Stanley Dock and the inland waterway system of the Leeds and Liverpool Canal. A second cut leads S into Trafalgar Dock and gives access to Clarence Graving Dock (8.107). In 1999, plans to construct a RoRo terminal at Trafalgar Dock were under discussion, and work had begun on filling in the dock to create a traffic marshalling area.

4   **Cruise Ship Terminal:** fronts the river on its E side between the two dock complexes, 2 cables NW of the Royal Liver Building (53°24'·3N 2°59'·8W). It is about 270 m long with alongside depths of 9 to 10 m and a light at its N end.

Liverpool Landing Stage is a floating structure 350 m long and 24 m wide, held in position to the shore by a number of bridges and booms. A vehicle and passenger service to Dublin and the Isle of Man, using high speed ferries, operates from a pontoon linkspan on the N section of the stage.

Birkenhead Docks

8.103

1   **Alfred Dock,** entered directly from Alfred Lock (53°24'·3N 3°01'·0W) (8.78) has facilities for handling edible oils on the N side. Maximum draught alongside 8·6 m. Scrap metal is handled on the S side.

East Float is entered from Alfred Dock by the former N passage. The width of the passage is 30·5 m.

Grain and animal feedstuffs are handled alongside with draughts of up to 8·7 m.

Twelve Quays works in progress

Birkenhead and Wallasey from SE (8.103)

(Original dated 2001)

(Photograph - Air Images)

2   **Vittoria Dock** which lies within East Float, contains berths at Vittoria Wharf and S Vittoria Dock for handling mainly forest products. Vessels up to 25 000 dwt can berth at S Vittoria Dock.

    West Float is entered from East Float by Duke Street Passage, having a width of 30·1 m.

3   Bulk ore vessels of up to 192 m in length, with a beam of 26·5 m and a having a draught of up to 8·7 m, can berth alongside Duke Street Wharf and Cavendish Wharf. On the N side of West Float, bulk fertilisers, bulk oils and chemicals are handled.

    Twelve Quays RoRo Terminal (53°24'·0N 3°00'·6W) consists of a large pontoon, with RoRo berths for ferries at N and S ends, moored in the river fronting Birkenhead Docks.

Tranmere Oil Terminal
8.104

1   Tranmere Oil Terminal (53°23'N 3°00'W), which consists of a U-headed pier, can accommodate tankers in excess of 200 000 dwt. The pier projects NE from the shore embankment 3 cables S of the slipways of the former Cammell Laird's Shipyards, S of Tranmere Basin.

    The approach arms carry pipelines and a roadway.

2   At the head of each arm, on which there is a hose-handling gantry, there is a floating landing stage, 111 m long, and 14 dolphins for vessels berthing alongside.

    A light is exhibited from the N dolphin, and lights are exhibited at each end of both floating stages.

    Gangways connect the landing stages to the heads of each arm.

3   There are swept depths of 12·6 and 11·7 m alongside the N and S stages respectively. Vessels having a draught of up to 14 m can, when conditions permit, berth alongside the N stage of the terminal.

    A tank farm is situated close to the root of the terminal. Much of the foreshore between the terminal and Rock Ferry Pier (8.105) has been reclaimed.

Rock Ferry Pier
8.105

1   Rock Ferry Pier, 2 cables S of Tranmere Oil Terminal, projects ENE from the shore embankment for 305 m thence ESE for 200 m.

    It is no longer used and is considered unsafe.

    The foreshore for a distance of 1 mile SE of Rock Ferry Pier dries to 2 cables from the bank, thence for a distance of 1 mile SE the river is fronted by a training wall from which lights are exhibited at the NE and SW corners.

Mersey Wharf
8.106

1   **General description.** Mersey Wharf (53°21'·5N 2°58'·5W) lies 1½ miles SE of Tranmere Oil Terminal and fronts the former Bromborough Dock.

    The wharf, which handles general and bulk cargoes, is 230 m long and vessels take the ground when alongside. The berth, which has a maximum depth on spring tides of

Tranmere Oil Terminal from N (8.104)
(Original dated 2001)

(Photograph - Air Images)

Mersey Wharf from E (8.106)
(Original dated 2001)

(Photograph - Air Images)

7·5 m, can accommodate vessels up to 6000 dwt with no beam or vertical clearance restrictions.

2   **Notice of ETA required:** 24 hours. See *Admiralty List of Radio Signals Volume 6(1)*.

Approach. On an in-going tide, vessels round E1 Light Buoy to berth port side to; out-going tide, vessels berth starboard side to.

3   **Facilities:** repairs; fresh water; fuel and supplies by prior arrangement.

Wharf Authority. Mersey Wharf, Dock Road South, Bromborough, Merseyside. L62 4SF.

The Wharf Authority is represented by a resident Port Manager.

Port services

Repairs
8.107

1   There are several dry docks within Port of Liverpool; some are privately run, others are leased to various ship repairers. Repairs of every description can be carried out. Divers are available.

Princess Dry Dock (No 5) (53°23'·3N 3°00'·6W) is the largest, having a length of 289·5 m and an entrance width of 42·7 m, the sill of which is 1·0 m below the level of chart datum. Depth on the sill 10·3 m at MHWS. It has been constructed primarily for large tankers.

2   Two smaller dry docks, No 6 which has a length of 200 m and a width of 23·3 m, the sill of which is 0·2 m above the level of chart datum, and No 7 which is 253 m long and 26·3 m wide, the sill of which is 0·5 m below the level of chart datum, lie close S of Princess Dry Dock.

Tranmere Basin, a fitting out basin, lies 1½ cables S of Princess Dry Dock, and is entered from the river through a gateway 42·7 m wide, the sill of which is 2·5 m below the level of chart datum. The least depth in the approach to the gateway is 1·5 m above the level of chart datum.

3   **Canada Graving Dock** (53°26'·1N 3°00'·1W), within Liverpool Docks, is entered from Canada Dock and has a length of 282·2 m and a width at the entrance of 28·6 m; blocks level with the sill.

Clarence Graving Docks (53°25'·2N 3°00'·1W), within Liverpool Docks, are entered from Trafalgar Dock. The largest of the three graving docks has a length of 135·3 m and an entrance width of 15·9 m; blocks level with the sill.

4   **Bidston Graving Dock No 3,** within West Float, Birkenhead Docks, has a length of 228·7 m and an entrance width of 25·9 m; level of sill 1·5 m above chart datum; blocks are 0·4 m above the sill.

Other facilities
8.108
1   Issue of SSCC and SSCEC; customs; reception of oily waste; salvage facilities and fire fighting vessels; medical services and hospitals with helicopter landing site in vicinity; sea-going floating crane of up to 250 tonnes capacity; compass adjustment by swinging, with 24 hours notice, in Liverpool Bay.

Supplies
8.109
1   Fuel oil and marine diesel up to a maximum quantity of 850 tonnes. The principal bunkering centre is at Birkenhead, but vessels may bunker with fuel oil in any of the docks subject to certain bye-laws. Fresh water at all docks by arrangement; provisions and stores in ample quantities.

Harbour regulations
8.110
1   Copies of bye-laws which might affect a vessel's stay in port can be obtained from the Port Authority (8.73) and include the disposal of waste food products ashore into special containers.

South docks
8.111
1   The S division of docks consists mainly of marinas and enclosed berths used by pleasure craft and the leisure industry. The status of the docks is constantly under review as new developments continue to take shape.

Canning River Entrance gives access from the river into Canning Half-Tide Dock through a set of dock wall gates, thence either into Canning Dock or Albert Dock with depths of 6 m.

2   Maximum width at the river entrance 13·3 m.

Brunswick River Entrance, a lock, maximum length 30 m, entrance width 8 m, sill 4·5 m above chart datum, gives access from the river into Brunswick Dock

and Liverpool Marina, approximately 2 hours either side of HW.

Docking signals. Lights vertically disposed (Diagram 8.111) are exhibited from a pole at Canning River Entrance and at Brunswick River Entrance.

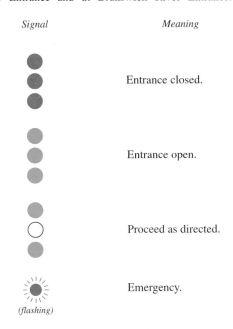

Signal	Meaning
	Entrance closed.
	Entrance open.
	Proceed as directed.
(flashing)	Emergency.

Canning and Brunswick River entrances – docking signals (8.111)

8.112
1   **Albert Dock,** restored and re-developed in 1986, with marina facilities, is entered over a sill 3·5 m above chart datum and can accommodate small vessels up to 55 m LOA, 11·5 m beam and 4·5 m draught, utilising Canning River Entrance and Canning Half-Tide Dock.

Entrance to the dock from the river is 2 hours before HW up to HW, by arrangement. Facilities include access to several slipways.

Dock Authority. Merseyside Development Corporation, Royal Liver Building, Pier Head, Liverpool L3 1JH.

2   The dock is under the supervision of a resident Harbour Master.

Liverpool Marina occupies the former sites of Brunswick and Coburg Docks. The marina, with a depth of 3·5 m, is entered through Brunswick Lock and can accommodate vessels of up to 25 m LOA, maximum draught 2·5 m.

3   **Marina Authority.** Liverpool Marina, Harbourside Marine plc, Coburg Wharf, Sefton Street, Liverpool L3 4BP. The marina is under the supervision of a resident Harbour Master.

Leeds and Liverpool Canal
8.113
1   The Leeds and Liverpool Canal is entered from Stanley Dock (53°25'·3N 2°59'·9W) at Liverpool through four locks each of which is 24·7 m long and 5·0 m wide.

The canal is used by pleasure craft, in particular the Leigh Branch between Wigan and Leigh where it connects with the Bridgewater Canal (8.182) giving access to Manchester. At Leeds the Canal links with Aire and Calder Navigation, details of which are contained in the *North Sea (West) Pilot.*

2   Limiting dimensions of craft using the canal are: LOA 21·9 m (but 18·3 m between Wigan and Leeds); beam 4·3 m; draught 1·0 m. The minimum vertical clearance on the canal is 2·2 m.

Canal Authority. Waterways Manager, British Waterways, Pottery Road, Wigan. Lancashire. WN3 5AA.

Chart 1978, 1951
Side channel
8.114

1   **Rock Channel** (53°27′N 3°07′W), parts of which dry, gives access to the river Mersey from Liverpool Bay. The channel, roughly parallel with and about 1 mile off the coast, leads between North Bank, which dries and extends seawards from Mockbeggar Wharf (53°26′N 3°04′W), and Brazil Bank (53°27′N 3°04′W) which also dries, at the SE end of Great Burbo Bank.

Rock Gut, which dries, lies at the inner end of Rock Channel.

2   Local knowledge is necessary for this channel which is passable only near HW.

Directions. The track leads generally E over Great Burbo Flats, which occupy a large area extending 2 miles W from Great Burbo Bank and with depths of less than 5 m, passing (with positions from Rock Lighthouse (53°26′·7N 3°02′·5W)):

3   N of a light buoy (special) (5 miles W), which marks the head of a sewer outfall extending NW from the shore, and:

S of Burbo Wind Farm (6 miles WNW), thence:

Through Rock Channel (W end 3 miles WNW), thence:

Between Mockbeggar Wharf (1 mile W) and Brazil Bank (1¼ miles NW) to enter Rock Gut (1 mile W), thence:

4   S of the S end of Crosby West Training Bank (5¼ cables NW), thence:

N of the light beacon (starboard hand) (1¾ cables NW) which marks the N end of a training wall running NW from Rock Lighthouse, thence:

Into the river in the vicinity of Brazil Light Float (2½ cables NE).

Light beacons (starboard hand) also mark the ends of training walls ESE and SE of Rock Lighthouse.

Garston Docks
Chart 3490
General information
8.115

1   **Description.** Garston Docks (53°21′N 2°54′W), lie on the N bank of the river Mersey, at the head of Garston Channel (8.120), approximately 4 miles SE of Liverpool South Docks. The docks consist of three interconnected wet docks; Stalbridge Dock, Old Dock and North Dock.

2   **Function.** The port specialises in the handling of steel, coal and dry bulk products.

Traffic. In 2007 there were 101 ship calls with a total of 344 117 dwt.

Port Authority. Associated British Ports, Port Office, Dock Road, Garston, Liverpool L19 2JW.

The Port Authority is represented by a Port Manager.

Limiting conditions
8.116

1   **Controlling depths.** For the latest information on controlling depths within the river Mersey, the Port Authority, Liverpool (8.73) should be consulted.

Depths within Garston Channel can be obtained from Associated British Ports, Garston.

Density of water: 1·023 g/cm^3 within the docks.

Maximum size of vessel handled: LOA 152·4 m; beam 19·2 m; draught 8·3 m; approximately 10 000 dwt.

8.117

1   **Stalbridge Lock,** through which the docks are entered, is 84·12 m long, 19·81 m wide, sill 0·7 m below the level of chart datum. A light (blue tubular steel tower) is exhibited from the W entrance wall.

Entry and departure for vessels up to 75·0 m in length can take place 3 hours either side of HW. Vessels over this length enter or leave when the river and dock are level, approximately 1 hour before to ½ hour after HW.

2   Vessels usually enter the lock from the river at slack water or with the out-going tide flowing, owing to the presence of cross currents in the lock entrance during the in-going tide.

Garston Docks from WNW (8.115)
(Original dated 2001)

(Photograph - Air Images)

Arrival information
8.118

1 **Port operations.** See Liverpool Port Operations 8.80. When approaching Garston Docks, communications can be carried out direct with the port; for details see *Admiralty List of Radio Signals Volume 6(1)*.

Outer anchorage. See 8.82.

Pilots and Tugs. See Liverpool Pilotage 8.85.

Regulations concerning entry. See Liverpool Entry Regulations 8.87.

Harbour layout
8.119

1 The docks are approached from Garston Channel and entered through Stalbridge Lock into Stalbridge Dock. A jetty projects NW from the NE side of the approach to the lock.

Stalbridge Dock is connected NW to Old Dock thence North Dock. A large development area lies N of North Dock.

Dredging. A dredger is often at work in Garston Channel during tidal periods.

2 **Traffic signals** (Diagram 8.119) are displayed at night from a blue tubular steel tower on the W side of the lock entrance.

At night	Meaning
▬▬▬▬	Dock full or entrance blocked.
▭	Vessels may proceed direct to the dock.

Garston Docks – traffic signals (8.119)

No vessel shall enter Garston Channel or proceed beyond G6 Light Buoy (53°21′·9N 2°56′·5W) when the entrance to the Stalbridge Dock is blocked.

Directions for entering harbour
8.120

1 From a position W of Pluckington Bank Light Buoy (W cardinal) (53°23′·0N 2°59′·6W) the track to the entrance to Garston Docks leads approximately 4 miles SE, through Garston Channel, passing (with positions from the entrance to Brunswick Dock (53°23′N 2°59′W)):

2 Between G2 Light Buoy (port hand) (5 cables S) and G1 Light Buoy (starboard hand) (7¼ cables SSE) which mark the entrance to Garston Channel, thence between the light buoys marking the channel.

Leading lights:

Front light (vertical orange rectangle) (53°20′·8N 2°54′·3W).

Rear light (similar structure) (175 m SE of front light).

3 On passing G8 Light Buoy (port hand) (4¾ cables NW of the lock), the alignment (125°) of the leading lights leads through the fairway, passing between the N edge of Garston Rocks, a drying rocky ledge, marked by a light–structure (mast on black dolphin) (2 cables NW of front leading light), and the head of the jetty (8.119), marked by a light, ½ cable NNE of the dolphin.

Caution. The depths in Garston Channel, which is bordered on its S side by Devil's Bank, which dries, are frequently changing and the buoys are moved as necessary.

Alongside berths
8.121

1 **Stalbridge Dock,** the largest dock, is entered from Stalbridge Lock and contains a coal terminal on the W side and a steel terminal on the E side. The depth within the dock varies with the height of HW but can accommodate the maximum size of vessel (8.116).

2 **Old Dock** is entered from Stalbridge Dock through a cut 19·8 m wide. The sill of the former gates in this cut is 1·4 m above chart datum. The depth within the dock varies with the height of HW. The maximum sized vessel can be accommodated but with a reduced maximum draught of 5·5 m.

3 **North Dock** is entered from Old Dock through a passage 27·5 m wide. The sill of the former gates in this passage is 1·5 m above the level of chart datum. The depth within the dock also varies with the height of HW; the maximum sized vessel with a reduced draught of up to 5·5 m can be accommodated.

Port services
8.122

1 **Facilities** are available for the reception of oily waste, noxious and harmful substances, by arrangement.

RoRo traffic can be handled though there are no designated berths.

Supplies: fuel oil; diesel oil; fresh water; provisions.

Harbour regulations
8.123

1 Except under the direction or permission of the Dock Master, no vessel shall moor alongside the wooden jetty at the entrance to Stalbridge Dock.

No vessel shall anchor in the entrance channel to Stalbridge Dock except in emergency.

Upper Mersey

Chart 3478
General information
8.124

1 The upper Mersey is that part of the river Mersey which lies above a line joining the old Eastham Ferry, situated 4½ cables NNW of Eastham Locks (53°19′·4N 2°56′·9W), and the S end of Garston Docks.

East of Garston Docks the river widens considerably before narrowing again at Runcorn (8.126). The upper reaches of the river, which almost dry, are less compact and whilst there are areas of heavy industry on both banks there are also rural and less populated areas.

2 Liverpool Airport is on the N bank of the river between Garston Docks and Dungeon Point (53°20′N 2°50′W) (8.70).

Hale Head, on which stands a disused lighthouse, lies at a sharp bend on the N side of the river, 1½ miles E of Dungeon Point; Seldom Seen Rocks, which dry, lie 5 cables ENE of Hale Head.

3 Stanlow Point, fringed by drying rocks, projects N from the S bank of the river, opposite Dungeon Point.

Much of the upper Mersey is a statutory Site of Special Scientific Interest, mainly for the study of birds.

Warrington (53°23′N 2°36′W), a large industrial town with a population of about 83 000, lies on the N bank of the river, 5 miles above Runcorn Bridge.

Channels
8.125

1   The navigable channels and their depths vary so frequently that is it impracticable to describe them. No reliance can be placed on the buoys marking these channels since they are frequently dragged out of position by the strong tides.

Above Dungeon Point, the channel is unmarked.

Limiting conditions
8.126

1   **Controlling depth.** Vessels of 3·5 m draught can reach Warrington at MHWS.

Vertical clearance. Runcorn Railway Viaduct and Runcorn High Level Road Bridge, which lie close together, span the river between Runcorn and Widnes at Runcorn Gap where it narrows to a width of 2 cables. There is a least vertical clearance of 24·2 m.

Tidal streams
8.127

1   The duration of the in-going stream at Widnes is 2½ hours, and at Warrington is approximately 1¾ hours.

Berth
8.128

1   **Bank Quay** (53°23·2N 2°36·5W) at Warrington is accessible to vessels of suitable draught (see 8.126).

MANCHESTER SHIP CANAL

General information

Chart 3478
General description
8.129

1   The Manchester Ship Canal, which links Eastham Locks (53°19′N 2°57′W) (8.130), at the seaward end, with Salford Quays, is 36 statute miles in length; figures on the canal bank denote distance from its seaward end, in statute miles.

The Canal is approached through Eastham Channel and entered at Eastham Locks, which is the only entrance from the river Mersey in use.

2   Between Eastham and Manchester there are four sets of locks giving a total lift of 17 m (see 8.135). Much of the canal passes through low lying ground on either side consisting of industrial and residential areas with stretches of rural land in between.

There are approximately 5500 vessel and barge movements in and out of the canal annually and this accounts for over half of the traffic which uses the river Mersey.

3   **VTS.** A VTS system (8.146) operates throughout the length of the canal.

Fog. In the Frodsham area, between Ince (53°17′N 2°49′W) and the entrance to the river Weaver, 2½ miles NE, the canal suffers high incidence of fog or poor visibility.

Chart 3490
Eastham Locks
8.130

1   Eastham Locks consists of three locks, side by side, of which the E, and smallest, lock is permanently closed.

The W lock is 183 m long and 24·4 m wide, the centre lock is 106·7 m long and 15·2 m wide; the lower sill of both locks is 3·5 m below the level of chart datum, with the upper sill of the W lock is 0·7 m below chart datum.

The E side of the approach to the locks from Eastham Channel is marked by a light beacon (port hand).

2   The locks operate for 4 hours either side of HW at Eastham. The two larger locks are usually closed during levelling tides (8.134).

Docking signal lights (Diagram 8.130.1) are exhibited by day and night from a horizontal platform, mounted on a metal mast, situated at the outer end of the centre lock island.

3   Five lights, disposed horizontally on the platform, consist of two Red outer lights, two White inner lights and one Green centre light; the Red and White lights at the E end of the platform control entry to the centre (15 m) lock and those at the W end control entry to the W (24 m) lock.

Signal	Meaning
☼ *(occulting)*	Lock indicated is available.
● *(occulting)*	Lock indicated is not available; vessels are to keep well clear.
☼ *(occulting)*	Lock gates are open. Water levels in River and Canal are equal.

Eastham Locks – docking signals inbound (8.130.1)

4   For outward bound traffic similar signal lights (Diagram 8.130.2) are exhibited by day and at night from a concrete column at the inner end of the centre lock island.

Signal	Meaning
☼ *(flashing)*	Lock indicated is available.
☼ *(flashing)*	Lock indicated is not available; vessels are to keep well clear.
●	Lock gates are open. Water levels in River and Canal are equal.

Eastham Locks – docking signals outbound (8.130.2)

Emergency signal, consisting of an amber flashing light and two white balls, disposed horizontally, is shown from a mast on the W side of the W lock to indicate that the lock is inoperative.

Queen Elizabeth II Dock and Eastham Locks from S (8.130)
(Original dated 2001)

(Photograph - Air Images)

Chart 3478
Limiting conditions
8.131

1 **Depths.** The canal between Eastham and Ince Oil Berth (53°17′N 2°48′W) (8.161) has been excavated to a depth of 9·75 m; thence to Latchford to a depth of 9·14 m; thence to Manchester, including the dock, to a depth of 8·53 m.

Widths. At water level the width of the canal generally varies between 40 and 64 m, but the minimum width at water level occurs in the passage under the Runcorn bridges (8.126) where it is 25·9 m wide.

2 The bottom width is generally 36·6 m, but only 27·4 m between Warburton High Level Bridge and Millbank Paper Mills, and the channel through Barton Swing Bridge and Barton Swing Aqueduct.

The banks of the canal are marked by light beacons, and the bend, at the junction of the river Weaver, by light buoys.

Maximum size of vessel handled:

3 Between Eastham Locks and Ince Oil Berth (53°17′·2N 2°50′·6W):

Length	Beam	FW Draught	Mast height
170·7 m	21·9 m	8·78 m	No limit

Between Ince and Runcorn Lay-by (53°20′N 2°45′W):

161·5 m	19·4 m	8·07 m	No limit

4 Between Runcorn Lay-by and Mode Wheel Locks (53°28′N 2°18′W):

161·5 m	19·4 m	7·31 m	21·3 m

Between Mode Wheel Locks and Salford Quays Marina (No. 6 Dock):

161·5 m	19·4 m	5·48 m	21·3 m

Mariners should always obtain the latest information from Manchester Port Operations (8.146).

Vertical clearances
8.132

1 Several bridges and overhead cables span the canal; vertical clearances are shown on the chart; the least vertical clearance of any fixed bridge is not less than 22 m and the safe vertical clearance of any power cable not less than 25·8 m, above normal water level. Above Runcorn, there are also a number of swing bridges, which give a passage 36·6 m wide. All vessels and craft must obtain permission from the Lock Master (Upper Locks) before transiting any of these bridges.

2 Gauge wires span the canal before the bridges and any vessel failing to clear these wires should not attempt to pass under the bridge.

Maximum permitted air draught above Runcorn Docks is 21·3 m. Masts and funnel tops can be reduced at Ellesmere Port by arrangement.

Traffic signal lights (Diagram 8.132) are exhibited by day and night on the downstream and upstream sides of all swing bridges.

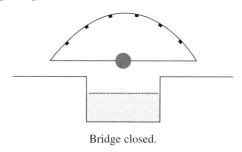

Bridge closed.

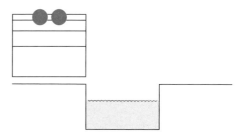

Bridge open.
Vessel must not approach bridge which is open for vessel from opposite direction.

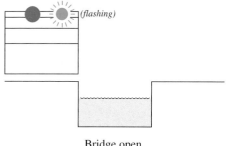

(*flashing*)

Bridge open.
Vessel may proceed.

Red flashing light in any position.
Emergency signal. Bridge not fully open. Do not approach.

Swing bridges - traffic signals (8.132)

3   **Lifting bridges.** Centenary Lift Bridge, about 8 cables downstream of Mode Wheel Locks, is a vertical lift bridge over the canal. Clearance above normal water level is 22·44 m when raised, and 6·975 m when lowered. Lowry Footbridge, about 8 cables upstream of Mode Wheel Locks, is a vertical lift footbridge over the canal. Clearance above normal water level is 22·59 m when raised, and 5·49 m in the centre of the fairway, 4·77 m at the sides, when lowered.

4   The signals (Diagram 8.132) are exhibited by day and night from both bridges.

Emergency signals
8.133
1   In the event of an emergency situation in the Ince "B" Berth area resulting from a spillage of ammonia, the following signals will be made:
1. Three flashing red lights in a vertical line will be displayed both by day and night from beacons situated 1 kilometre upstream and downstream from Ince "B" Berth.

Signal	Position	Meaning
●	Centre of lifting section.	Mark for centre of bridge.
●	Upstream side of NE tower and downstream side of NW tower.	Bridge lowered.
☀ (*flashing*)	Towers (as above) in direction from which vessel is approaching.	Bridge raised.
☀ (*flashing*)	Upstream side of NE tower and downstream side of NW tower.	Emergency Signal.

Lifting bridges - traffic signals (8.132)

2   2. In conjunction with (1) above, a continuous sound signal will be sounded from a siren located on Ince "B" Berth.
Should these signals be made vessels must avoid passing through this area.

3   In the event of an emergency situation in the Runcorn Lay-by Berth area the following signals are made:
1. Three flashing red lights in a vertical line will be displayed both by day and night from beacons situated at the upstream and downstream ends of Runcorn Lay-by Berth.

4   2. In conjunction with (1) above a continuous signal will be sounded from sirens located on Runcorn Lay-by Berth.
Should these signals be made vessels must avoid passing through this area and should pay close attention to advice relayed via the appropriate radio channel.
When operations involving cargo with a low flash-point are taking place at the berth the upper light of both beacons will display a flashing red light.

Storm gates
8.134
1   When Eastham Locks are used as storm gates they will be closed as the water level in both the river Mersey and Manchester Ship Canal becomes the same on the in-going tide, and they will be reopened when these levels are the same on the out-going tide. Throughout the period of closure, shipping will be excluded from both locks at Eastham.

2   The storm gates may be closed for that part of any tide exceeding a height of 9·08 m above chart datum.
When for any reason the storm gates are not in use, then when the tide rises to a height of 9·08 m above chart datum in the river Mersey, Eastham Locks are opened to the river and the canal thus becomes tidal as far as Latchford Locks (53°23′N 2°33′W), causing an appreciable flow of water from Eastham towards Latchford Locks.

3   Vessels navigating with this tide astern should exercise great caution.
When the levelling out-going tide starts, Eastham Locks are closed and the excess water is returned to the river Mersey through Weaver Sluices, 10 miles above Eastham. This induces a flow of water from Eastham and from Latchford towards the sluices.

4   In the canal above Latchford Locks excess water is carried off by sluices at each lock to the section below.

Should it become necessary to return water to the river Mersey in this area, sluices at Woolston Weir (53°23′N 2°31′W) are used.

Vessels should approach the locks with great care when the sluice gates are open.

Canal locks
8.135

1   Between Eastham and Manchester there are four sets of canal locks, namely at Latchford (21 mile mark; see 8.129), at Irlam (between 28 and 29 mile marks), at Barton (between 30 and 31 mile marks), at Mode Wheel (34 mile mark) and at the entrance to Manchester Docks Basin and Salford Quays. All the locks are manned when required.

The rise at each set of locks is indicated on the chart.

2   Each set of locks consist of two locks, side by side, of the following dimensions:

    N Lock 183 m long and 19·8 m wide.
    S Lock 106·7 m long and 13·7 m wide.

The upper sills of all the larger locks have a normal depth of 8·5 m over them.

Traffic signals. At the downstream and upstream side of each lock signal lights (Diagram 8.135) are exhibited by day and night from a concrete column on the lock wall.

Signal	Meaning
(flashing)	Lock available.
(flashing)	Lock not available.

Canal locks – traffic signals (8.135)

PORT OF MANCHESTER

General information

Chart 3478
Position
8.136

1   The Port of Manchester (53°28′N 2°17′W) includes the whole of the Manchester Ship Canal and Queen Elizabeth II Dock at Eastham (53°19′N 2°57′W).

Function
8.137

1   Most of the cargo within the port is handled between Eastham and Runcorn, only a very small amount being handled at the dock in Manchester. Major commodities handled include petroleum and chemical products, timber, grain, scrap and general cargo.

The port contains container, RoRo and heavy lift facilities.

2   The City of Manchester has a population of about 400 000; Greater Manchester has a population of about 2½ millions.

Port limits
8.138

1   The limits of the Port of Manchester commence at the inner limit of the Port of Liverpool (8.70) at Warrington Bridge and include the river Mersey N and E of the bridge and the river Irwell, so far as they are navigable, the river

Weaver to Frodsham Bridge, and the Manchester Ship Canal from the entrance at Eastham, where it touches the Port of Liverpool, to Hunts Bank in the City of Manchester.

Charts 1951, 3490
Approach and entry
8.139

1   The port is approached through the river Mersey and from Eastham Channel, the directions of which are given at 8.98 and is entered close NNW of Eastham Locks; vessels then proceed to either Queen Elizabeth II Dock or the Manchester Ship Canal.

Chart 3478
Traffic
8.140

1   In 2007 there were 91 ship calls with a total of 375 115 dwt.

Port Authority
8.141

1   The port is owned, maintained and operated by the Manchester Ship Canal Company, Collier Street, Runcorn, Cheshire WA7 1HA.

Navigational matters should be addressed to the Harbour Master, Manchester Ship Canal Company, Marine Operations, Administration Building, Queen Elizabeth II Dock, Eastham, Wirral CH62 0BB.

Limiting conditions

Controlling depth
8.142

1   The Port Authority should always be consulted on the controlling depths for Eastham Channel and within the Manchester Ship Canal.

Deepest berths
8.143

1   Queen Elizabeth II Dock, Eastham (8.154).
    Ellesmere Port (8.157).
    Stanlow Oil Docks (8.158).
    Ince (8.161).
    Weston Point Docks (8.164).
    Runcorn Docks (8.166).
    Partington Basin (8.171).
    Barton (8.174).
    Salford Quay (8.178).

Density of water
8.144

1   The water in the lower section of the Ship Canal between Eastham and Latchford Locks is fresh to brackish, above Latchford the water is fresh, 1·001 g/cm^3.

Maximum size of vessel handled
8.145

1   The size of vessel is governed by the limiting conditions in the Ship Canal (8.131 and 8.132); for Queen Elizabeth II Dock, the limitation is the entrance to the lock (8.154).

Arrival information

Port operations
8.146

1   VTS. A VTS scheme operates from Eastham (53°19′N 2°57′W). A continuous listening watch is maintained.

Inward-bound vessels for the canal or Queen Elizabeth II Dock should establish contact with the Harbour Master,

Eastham, call sign: EASTHAM, prior to arrival to make arrangements for canal transit and/or berthing and provision of tugs.

2 **Traffic control.** The Marine Supervisor at Eastham is responsible for regulating traffic between Eastham and Old Quay Swing Bridge, Runcorn (53°20'·6N 2°43'·3W); the Lock Master at Latchford Locks is responsible for regulating traffic between Old Quay Swing Bridge, Runcorn and Manchester Docks.

There is a radio station at Latchford Locks.

For further details see *Admiralty List of Radio Signals Volume 6(1)*.

Notice of ETA required
8.147

1 Vessels should send their ETA Bar Light Buoy at least 24 hours in advance as per entry for Liverpool (8.81) in the first instance with details of any service requirements.

Outer anchorages
8.148

1 The anchorages are outside the river Mersey, see 8.82.

Pilotage
8.149

1 **Pilotage** is compulsory in the Ship Canal and for entry into Queen Elizabeth II Dock. In addition to the procedures required for the river Mersey given at 8.85, Eastham pilots and assistant pilots should be ordered at least 6 hours in advance. All communications should be addressed to the Harbour Master (8.146).

2 **Pilot boarding positions.** For Ship Canal, pilot boards inward vessels at Eastham Locks; for Queen Elizabeth II Dock, at the entrance lock.

Tugs
8.150

1 Four powerful tugs are available.

Within the Manchester Ship Canal tugs accompany vessels and are attached throughout the transit from Eastham to the berth.

For further details on pilotage see *Admiralty List of Radio Signals Volume 6(1)*.

Regulations concerning entry
8.151

1 See 8.87.

Quarantine
8.152

1 See 1.55. Any vessel bound for a berth within the Port of Manchester which is suspect should inform Manchester Port Health through the ship's agent, preferably not more than 12 hours and not less than 3 hours before arrival.

Harbour

General layout
8.153

1 The harbour consists of numerous basins and berths along the length of the canal between Eastham (53°19'N 2°57'W) and the City of Manchester. Most of the traffic bound for the area is handled between Eastham and Stanlow at the seaward end of the canal.

Basins and berths between Eastham and Runcorn

Chart 3490
Queen Elizabeth II Dock
8.154

1 Queen Elizabeth II Dock at Eastham (53°19'N 2°57'W) is entered through a lock 246 m long and 30·48 m wide; depth over the sill 5·6 m below chart datum. The lock is operated 3 hours either side of HW.

The dock is designed for the handling of bulk petroleum and liquid chemicals, including liquids with a flash point below 23°C.

2 There are oil berths, the numbers of which are shown on the chart, on each of the four sides of the dock with lengths varying from 221 to 274 m.

Vessels of approximately 40 000 dwt, having a length of up to 208·7 m, beam 28·3 m and draught of 10 m can be accommodated.

Docking signals (Diagram 8.154) consisting of three lights in the form of a triangle, are exhibited from a mast, at the E entrance to the lock.

Signal	Meaning
●	Vessels may not enter the lock.
●	Vessels may enter the lock.
☀ (flashing)	Sluicing in progress.

Queen Elizabeth II – docking signals (8.154)

Chart 3478
Eastham Basin
8.155

1 Eastham Basin, immediately inside Eastham Locks, has lay-by berths on either side; the W lay-by 475 m long has depths of 9·1 m alongside; the E lay-by, 197 m long, has depths of 8·5 m alongside.

Vessels of up to 79 m in length and of not more than 6·1 m draught can be swung in the basin immediately above the locks.

Fresh water is available at the W lay-by only; advance notice of requirements is necessary.

Manisty Wharf
8.156

1 Manisty Wharf, previously called Bowaters Wharf, lies opposite Mount Manisty on the SW side of the canal 1¾ miles above Eastham, and is principally equipped to handle forest products for the nearby paper mill. It is 335 m long and can accept vessels with a restricted beam of up to 20·7 m.

Chart 3478 plan of Ellesmere Port and Stanlow Oil Docks
Ellesmere Port
8.157

1 Ellesmere Port (53°17'N 2°54'W) on the S side of the canal, 2¾ miles above Eastham, is the terminus of the Shropshire Union Canal (8.184).

Queen Elizabeth II Dock and Eastham Locks from N (8.154)

(Original dated 2001)

(Photograph - Air Images)

Ellesmere Port Quay, which fronts the canal close NW of the entrance to the former Ellesmere Docks, now principally a boat museum, has a length of 700 m.

2 There are 6 berths, all capable of accommodating vessels with the maximum dimensions for this section of the canal (8.131). At the E end of the quay there is a RoRo berth for heavy lifts, and at the W end a RoRo berth for light vehicular traffic.

3 **Supplies**: fresh water; fuel oil; provisions.

Stuart's Wharf, 119 m long, lies 3 cables SE of Ellesmere Port Quay.

Associated Octel Wharf, 183 m long with depths for full canal draught alongside (8.131), lies 4 cables E of Stuart's Wharf.

Stanlow Oil Docks
8.158

1 Stanlow Oil Docks (between 4 and 5 mile marks (8.129)) and lying on the N side of the canal, consists of berths for three tankers. The docks can accommodate vessels with the maximum dimensions for this section of the canal (8.131).

The docks are used for handling petroleum spirit and other liquids with a flash-point below 23°C. There is large tankage accommodation for storage of oil and spirit.

2 Dimensions of the docks are as follows:

No 1 Dock: 183 m long, 30·5 m wide.
No 2 Dock: 198 m long, 54·9 m wide.

Supplies: fresh water; fuel and diesel oil.

Stanlow Turning Basin, at the entrance to Stanlow Oil Docks, can accommodate the largest vessels using the canal.

8.159

1 **Stanlow Chemical Berth** lies at the head of a short pier which extends 25 m from the shore on the S side of the canal close W of the entrance to Stanlow Oil Docks. The pier has a length of 40 m with a least depth of 6·4 m alongside. Vessels of up to 110 m in length can lie alongside the pierhead.

8.160

1 **Stanlow Lay-by,** on the S side of the canal opposite Stanlow Oil Docks, is used for the handling of fuel and other oils with a flash-point above 23°C. The berth is 183 m long and will accommodate vessels with the maximum dimensions for this section of the canal (8.131).

Ince
8.161

1 **Ince Coaster Berth,** on the S side of the canal above Stanlow Lay-by, is used for the handling of petroleum products with a flash-point below 23°C. The berth is 107 m long. Vessels of up to 80 m in length and of not more than 6·4 m draught can swing off the berth.

Ince Oil Berth (between 5 and 6 mile marks (8.129)), on the S side of the canal, is used for handling petroleum and petroleum products with a flash-point above 23°C.

2 The berth, 183 m long alongside a wharf 91 m long, is capable of accommodating vessels with the maximum dimensions for this section of the canal (8.131).

Stanlow Oil Docks from ENE (8.158)

(Original dated 2001)

(Photograph - Air Images)

Ince Tying-up Berth, on the S side of the canal, 2 cables above Ince Oil Berth, is a dolphin berth 375 m in length; it can accommodate the maximum size of vessel permitted in the canal.

Chart 3478
8.162

1   **Ince Powergen Berth** (Ince "B" Berth), with a length of 183 m, lies on the SE bank of the canal adjacent to the power stations at Ince (53°17'N 2°49'W). Vessels of up to 147·8 m in length, 21·3 m breadth and 8·07 m draught in fresh water, with the capability of achieving a forward ballast draught of 4·5 m to enable the vessel to be swung, can be accommodated.

Emergency signals. See 8.133.

River Weaver
8.163

1   Entrance to the river Weaver lies 4¾ miles above Stanlow Oil Docks, at its junction with the Ship Canal at Frodsham Marsh; Spike Island (53°18'·9N 2°45'·0W), a lighted man made feature consisting of four piles supporting a platform, stands close outside its entrance. Vessels of up to 150 m in length having a maximum draught forward of 4·5 m in fresh water can be turned at this location.

The channel in the vicinity is marked by light buoys.
For Weaver Navigation Canal see 8.183.

Chart 3478 plan of Runcorn and Weston Point Docks
Weston Point Docks
8.164

1   Weston Point Docks (53°20'N 2°46'W), at the terminus of Weaver Navigation Canal, lie on the E side of the Ship Canal from which they are entered through a passage, 18·3 m wide, leading to Delamache Dock, formerly Delamere and Tollemache Docks. Other docks and basins are connected to Delamache Dock, all of which can accommodate vessels of up to 2500 dwt, length 76 m, beam 10·7 m and up to 4·6 m draught. There is 625 m of quay.

2   The docks were used as a terminal for small bulk cargoes and containers.

Docks Authority. British Waterways, Chester Way, Northwich CW9 5JT.

8.165

1   **Salt Berth,** lies 1 cable N of the entrance to Delamache Dock. The berth is approximately 183 m long with depths of up to 6·4 m alongside.

Runcorn Docks
8.166

1   Runcorn Docks, which lie 7 cables NE of Weston Point, consists of three principal wet docks which are entered from the Manchester Ship Canal through a passage leading into Francis Dock. Vessels of up to 115 m in length, 16 m beam and 7·0 m draught can be accommodated. The numbered berths are shown on the chart.

The dimensions of the principal docks are as follows:

Oil Berth   Coaster Berth
Ince from NW (8.161)
(Original dated 2001)

(Photograph - Air Images)

Francis Dock: Entrance width 42·5 m, dock width
53 m, quay length 111 m.

2 Alfred Dock: Entrance width 39·3 m, dock width
39·3 m, quay length 200 m.

Fenton Dock: Entrance width 39·3 m, dock width
45 m, quay length 190 m.

The docks handle dry bulk cargoes, containers and
general cargoes.

Facilities include a slipway at Old Quay, having a
length of 39·6 m and lifting capacity of 178 dwt.

8.167

1 **Runcorn Lay-by,** 4 cables NE of Weston Point, on the
S bank, is 168 m long with depths to accommodate vessels
up to 8·0 m draught alongside. The berth is used for
loading/discharging tankers, molten sulphur being the main
commodity handled. Caustic soda liquor from the nearby
ICI works is exported from the berth.

Emergency signals. See 8.133.

Basins and berths between
Runcorn and Latchford Locks

Chart 3478
Lay-by berths
8.168

1 Lay-bys between Runcorn and Latchford Locks, all
capable of accommodating vessels with the maximum
dimensions for this section of the canal (8.131), are situated
as follows:

Old Quay Wall, 4 cables above Runcorn Bridge on
the N bank, 457 m long.

Moore Lane, 3¼ miles above Runcorn Bridge on the
NW bank, 220 m long.

Latchford Lower, dolphin berth on the S bank, 183 m
long.

Wigg Wharf
8.169

1 Wigg Wharf (53°21′N 2°43′W), used for handling bulk
stout, is situated on the N bank of the Canal, approximately
8 cables E of Runcorn Bridges. Suitable for vessels of up
to 100·5 m LOA; 12·2 m beam; 5·5 m draught.

Basins and berths between Latchford Locks
and Irlam Locks

Lay-by berths
8.170

1 **Latchford Upper:** on the S bank at Latchford Locks,
length 158 m, capable of accommodating vessels with the
maximum dimensions for this section of the canal (8.131).

Chart 3478 plan of Partington basin
Partington Basin
8.171

1 Partington Basin (53°25′·6N 2°25′·3W) occupies both
sides of the canal, 1 mile below Irlam Locks; it has a quay
frontage of 950 m with depths alongside for vessels with
up to 7·3 m draught.

Partington Basin from SW (8.171)
(Original dated 2001)

(Photograph - Air Images)

On the NW side there are facilities for discharging bulk liquid chemicals and petroleum products at No 1 berth.

No 7 berth is a lay-by berth.

On the SE side there are facilities for the loading and discharge of bulk liquid chemicals and oil cargoes at three berths.

2   **Supplies:** fuel; fresh water.

Caution. When vessels are loading or discharging inflammable liquids, a red flashing light (metal tripod) is exhibited at the NE corner of the basin; in these circumstances other vessels should pass through the basin at the slowest possible speed.

Chart 3478
Irlam
8.172

1   **Irlam Wharf,** on the W bank of the canal, 5 cables below Irlam Locks, is 183 m long with depths alongside for vessels with up a maximum draught of 7·3 m.

Basins and berths between
Irlam Locks and Mode Wheel Locks

Lay-by berths
8.173

1   **Barton Locks** lie between mile marks 32 and 33. Immediately above the locks on the SE bank there is a berth 148 m long which can accommodate vessels with the maximum dimensions for this section of the canal (8.131).

Weaste Wharf, 91·4 m in length, lies 4 cables below Mode Wheel Locks (mile mark 34) on the NW bank.

Barton Oil Berth
8.174

1   The berth (mile mark 32), 155 m long, on the S bank of the canal 1¼ miles above Barton Locks, can accommodate vessels with a maximum draught of 7·3 m.

Irwell Park Wharf
8.175

1   Situated on the N bank of the canal, between mile marks 32 and 33, approximately 1½ miles above Barton Locks. The wharf, which is 335 m long, is equipped for the handling of scrap metal and can accept a vessel with a maximum draught of 7·3 m.

Cerestar Wharf (CPC Wharf)
8.176

1   Cerestar Wharf (CPC Wharf), lies on the S bank of the canal 7 cables E of Barton Oil Berth and close W of mile mark 33, and is privately owned.

The wharf is 213 m long and can accommodate a vessel having a maximum draught of 7·3 m.

Bulk maize is discharged to nearby works.

Southern Oil Wharf
8.177

1   Southern Oil Wharf, on the NW bank, below Mode Wheel Locks (mile mark 34), is 152 m long and can accommodate vessels with a maximum draught of 7·3 m.

Mode Wheel Locks, Dry Docks and Salford Quay from WNW (8.178)

(Original dated 2001)

(Photograph - Air Images)

Chart 3478 plan of Manchester Docks
Salford Quays
8.178

1   Much of the area within the former Manchester Docks, now known as Salford Quays, has undergone redevelopment and accepts only limited commercial traffic.

Salford Quay, situated on the N bank of the canal close above Mode Wheel Lock, 335 m in length with a depth of 5·5 m alongside, is the only commercial berth.

The entrance to No 9 Dock is designated for swinging vessels within the basin.

2   The Lowry Footbridge crosses the Ship Canal between Salford Quays and Trafford Wharf. Traffic lights control the transit of vessels under the bridge. Vertical clearances above normal water level are:

Lowered: 4·77 m at sides, 5·49 m in centre of fairway.
Raised: 22·59 m.

The current water level should be obtained from Eastham Control Room. For details see *Admiralty List of Radio Signals Volume 6(1)*.

3   The maximum permissible overall height of a vessel passing under the bridge is 21·33 m.

Salford Quays Marina is situated in South Bay (52°28'·1N 2°17'·2W). Craft lie to floating pontoons and there is a removable boom at the entrance to the marina.

Marina Authority. Salford Quays Marina, Clippers Quay, Trafford Road, Manchester M17 1EY.

Port services

Repairs
8.179

1   **Dry docks:** There are three dry docks within Salford Quays, the largest being No 1 Dock; length 163·1 m, width 19·8 m with a depth of 6·17 m of water on the blocks.

Large repairs to hull and machinery can be undertaken. Vessels arriving for dry docking purposes only do not have to pay canal dues.

Other facilities
8.180

1   Reception of oily waste; issue of SSCC and SSCEC; hospital and other medical facilities.

Supplies
8.181

1   All grades of fuel oil; fresh water; stores and provisions can be supplied to vessels in the Manchester Ship Canal by arrangement with the Port Authorities and/or agents.

Inland waterways

Chart 3478
Bridgewater Canal
8.182

1   Bridgewater Canal is entered at Pomona Lock, Manchester, the only lock in the canal. It has a branch at

Trafford Park, 2 miles W of Pomona lock, which connects with the Leigh Branch of Leeds and Liverpool Canal and crosses the Manchester Ship Canal by means of a swing aqueduct at Barton (53°28′N 2°21′W).

2   Limiting dimensions of craft using the canal are: length 21 m, beam 4·3 m, draught 1·2 m, but 1·5 m between Manchester and Trafford Park. The minimum vertical clearance in the canal is 3·0 m but 2·5 m in the branch connecting with the Leigh Branch.

Canal Authority. The Manchester Ship Canal Company, Quay West, Trafford Wharf Road, Manchester, M17 1HH.

Weaver Navigation Canal
8.183

1   Weaver Navigation Canal is entered from the Ship Canal through Weston Marsh Lock, near Weston Point Docks (53°20′N 2°46′W) (8.164), which is 69·8 m long and 13·0 m wide with a depth of 3·2 m.

The canal serves Northwich and Winsford and is used by both commercial and pleasure craft; it has access also to Runcorn and Manchester.

2   Limiting dimensions of craft using the canal from Weston Point Docks to Anderton Depot, Northwich are: tonnage 1000 dwt, length 60·0 m, beam 10·1 m, draught 3·0 m. The minimum vertical clearance in the canal is 18·3 m.

From Northwich to Winsford limiting dimensions are: LOA 40·0 m; beam 10·7 m; draught 3·0 m. The minimum vertical clearance in the canal is 9·1 m.

3   **Facilities** include a dry dock 30·5 m long; breadth 6·0 m.

Vessels intending to enter or leave Weaver Navigation Canal should establish contact with Weaver Navigation Port.

Canal Authority. Waterways Manager, British Waterways, Lighterage Yard, Chester Way, Northwich. CW9 5JT. Cheshire.

There is a resident Wharf Superintendent at Anderton.

Shropshire Union Canal
8.184

1   Shropshire Union Canal is entered from the Ship Canal through locks at Ellesmere Port (53°17′N 2°54′W).

The canal serves Chester and Nantwich at which place it becomes narrower.

Limiting dimensions of craft using the canal as far as Nantwich are: length 21·4 m, beam 3·0 m, draught 1·0 m. The minimum vertical clearance in the canal is 2·4 m.

Canal Authority. Waterways Manager, British Waterways, Lighterage Yard, Chester Way, Northwich. Cheshire. CW9 5JT.

NOTES

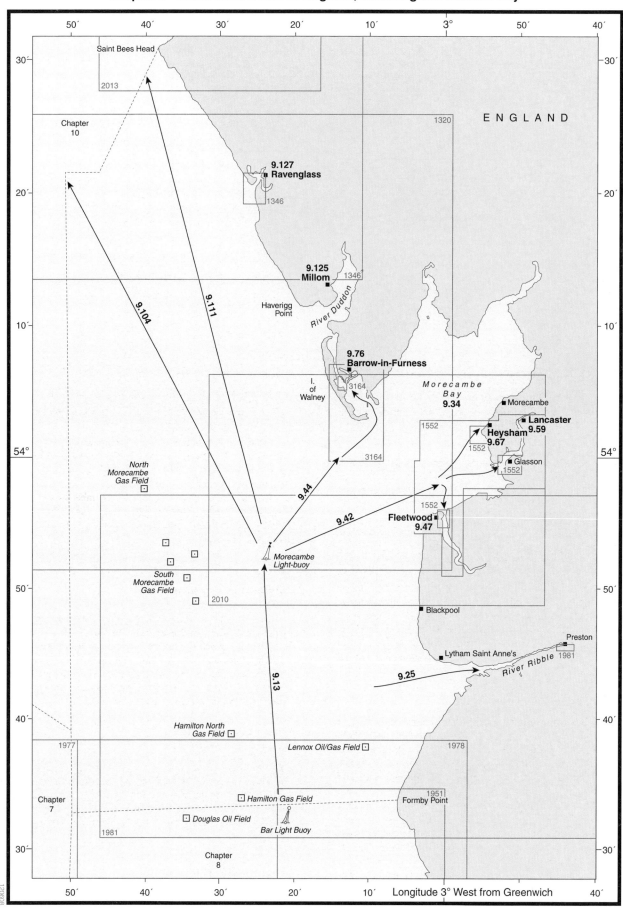

CHAPTER 9

NORTH WEST COAST OF ENGLAND INCLUDING MORECAMBE BAY

GENERAL INFORMATION

Chart 1826
Scope of the chapter
9.1

1 This chapter describes the waters off the coast of North West England between Formby Point (53°33′N 3°06′W) and Saint Bees Head, 60 miles N, and includes the estuary of the river Ribble and Morecambe Bay.

The description also includes the routes and passages of the area, together with their ports and harbours; of these the more important are:

2 Barrow-in-Furness (54°06′N 3°13′W), a deep-water port.

Heysham (54°02′N 2°55′W), an artificial harbour.

The chapter is divided into the following sections:

Formby Point to Morecambe Bay (9.10).

Morecambe Bay to Saint Bees Head (9.99).

Offshore route
9.2

1 The initial stage of an offshore route (9.110) which passes NE of the Isle of Man, lies in deep water between a position NNW of Morecambe Light Buoy (53°52′N 3°24′W) and a position SE of King William Banks (10.20).

Topography
9.3

1 In general the coast between Formby Point (53°34′N 3°06′W) and Morecambe Bay is low-lying. The Isle of Walney (54°05′N 3°14′W), fronts the coast between the N entrance to Morecambe Bay and the S side of the estuary of the river Duddon (9.121).

Barrow Wind Farm (9.34) is centred about 5 miles SW from the S end of the Isle of Walney.

2 For a distance of 7 miles N of the river Duddon estuary the coast consists of reddish cliffs which gradually diminish in height on each side of the entrance to Ravenglass Harbour (54°21′N 3°25′W) which is bordered by sandhills; the sandhills continue a further 3 miles N of the entrance, the coast then rising towards Saint Bees Head (9.117).

Inland between Barrow-in-Furness and Saint Bees Head the land rises to a range of mountains which attain an elevation of 974 m.

Hazards
9.4

1 **Exercise areas.** Firing and other defence exercises in which surface warships, submarines, aircraft and shore establishments participate take place up to 30 miles from the coast at Ravenglass (9.127). For further details regarding firing practice and exercise areas, see 1.15 and information on the charts.

2 **Fishing.** Offshore trawlers may be encountered in large concentrations up to 35 miles W or SW of Lune Deep Light Buoy (53°56′N 3°13′W) during April and May, smaller numbers during August to October; inshore trawlers may be encountered at any time.

For details of types of fishing and nets in use, see *The Mariner's Handbook*.

3 **Marine exploitation.** Drilling rigs and production platforms for the recovery of oil and gas are situated in the approaches to Liverpool and Morecambe Bay. All structures are protected by safety zones extending to 500 m around them. Pipelines linking the structures to each other are marked on the charts.

For further information concerning offshore oil and gas fields including types of platforms and structures, safety zones, signals made, markings displayed, lights exhibited and fog signals sounded, see *The Mariner's Handbook*.

4 The fields within this area are:

Name	Position		Remarks
	Lat N	*Long W*	
Calder	53°48′	3°40′	
Douglas	53°32′	3°34′	Production complex
Hamilton	53°34′	3°27′	
Hamilton North	53°39′	3°29′	
Lennox	53°38′	3°10′	
Millom	54°02′	3°52′	
North Morecambe	53°58′	3°40′	
South Morecambe	53°51′	3°35′	Development Area

5 **Offshore Loading Facility.** An offshore loading facility, consisting of a mooring buoy and a storage barge, lies in position 53°41′N 3°33′W. A safety zone of 800 m is established around this installation.

Development Area. South Morecambe Gas Field has been designated a Development Area; for details see *The Mariner's Handbook*. Mariners are strongly advised to keep outside this area.

Submarine pipelines
9.5

1 Gas pipelines run S from the Douglas production complex to the coast near Point of Ayr (53°21′N 3°19′W) (8.29). Gas pipelines run NE from the North Morecambe, South Morecambe and Calder Gas Fields to the coast on the Isle of Walney (54°04′N 3°14′W). An oil pipeline runs 9 miles N from the Douglas production complex to the offshore loading facility. See also 1.38.

Wrecks
9.6

1 There are many wrecks situated in the area covered by this chapter. Some are marked by light buoys and some may need to be avoided depending on draught; the positions of wrecks can best be seen on the chart.

High speed craft
9.7

1 High speed ferries operate between Liverpool and the Isle of Man, and between Heysham and Belfast. See 1.8.

Rescue
9.8

1   For details of rescue organisation and locations of assets see 1.60 and text under Rescue.

Tidal streams
9.9

1   Off the coast between Formby Point and Morecambe Bay the E-going stream sets towards the land and into Morecambe Bay and the estuary of the river Ribble. The W-going stream sets in the reverse direction.

2   Between Morecambe Bay and Saint Bees Head the E-going stream sets E off the N end of the Isle of Man and then SE between the island and the coast towards Morecambe Bay. The W-going stream sets in the reverse direction.

    Tidal streams are given on the chart and in *Admiralty Tidal Stream Atlas — Irish Sea and Bristol Channel*.

FORMBY POINT TO MORECAMBE BAY

GENERAL INFORMATION

Chart 1826
Area covered
9.10

1   In this section are described the coastal route, harbours and anchorages between Formby Point (53°33′N 3°06′W) and Rossall Point, 22 miles N.

    Also described are the navigable reaches of the river Ribble as far as Preston (53°45′N 2°43′W) and the harbours and anchorages of Morecambe Bay.

2   It is arranged as follows:
    Formby Point to Rossall Point (9.13).
    Morecambe Bay including the Port of Barrow-in-Furness (9.34).

Topography
9.11

1   See 9.3

Nature reserves
9.12

1   Ainsdale Sands (53°36′N 3°04′W).
    For further information see Protection of wildlife (1.58).

FORMBY POINT TO ROSSALL POINT

General information

Charts 1981, 2010
Route
9.13

1   From the vicinity of Bar Light Buoy (53°32′N 3°21′W) to a position W of Rossall Point, and seaward of Shell Flat (53°51′N 3°20′W) (9.22), a coastal route leads approximately 23 miles N.

    The route is clear apart from a number of wrecks lying in the approaches to Bar Light Buoy and a submarine production well (53°53′N 3°28′W), E of South Morecambe Gas Field.

Topography
9.14

1   Between Formby Point (53°33′N 3°06′W), low-lying and sandy, and Southport, 5 miles NE, the coastline is composed mainly of sand dunes which are backed by rural and residential areas.

    The foreshore here consists of Mad Wharf Sands, Ainsdale Sands and Birkdale Sands which dry up to 1 mile offshore and contain areas of foul ground,.

    Formby Spit extends W of Mad Wharf Sands.

2   Between Stanner Point (53°45′N 3°01′W) and Rossall Point, 10 miles N the coast is mainly occupied by the towns of Lytham Saint Anne's (9.25) and Blackpool, a large seaside resort with many prominent buildings.

    The coastline for 3½ miles N of Stanner Point is low and sandy but rises at Blackpool to red clay cliffs decreasing in height and succeeded 1½ miles N by a sandy bank.

3   Rossall Oyster Grounds extend 3½ miles W and 6½ miles SW from Rossall Point (9.34) and Rossall Scar, an extensive drying rocky patch, lies close off the same point.

    Behind the built-up coastal area the land is mainly flat and well cultivated.

Marine exploitation
9.15

1   For details of oil and gas fields see 9.4.

Submarine cables
9.16

1   A submarine cable extends W from a position on the coast 2½ miles S of Blackpool Tower (9.20) linking the mainland with the Isle of Man. Another submarine cable, from Lytham Saint Anne's to Portmarnock in the Republic of Ireland (see *Irish Coast Pilot*), extends W from Stanner Point (9.14).

2   A submarine cable is laid from Southport leading towards the North Channel (see *Irish Coast Pilot*) passing SE of the Isle of Man (10.137). Further S, two submarine cables are laid from Ainsdale linking the Republic of Ireland (see *Irish Coast Pilot*).

Outfalls
9.17

1   Outfalls extend W for short distances from the coast in the vicinity of Blackpool (53°49′N 3°03′W); a buoy (starboard hand) is moored at the head of each outfall. From positions on the shore, lights in line indicate the direction of the outfalls.

    An unmarked outfall extends W from the shore from a position 2 miles S of Blackpool Tower (9.20).

Rescue
9.18

1   An all-weather lifeboat is stationed at Lytham Saint Anne's (53°44′N 2°58′W); inshore lifeboats are stationed at Lytham Saint Anne's and Blackpool (53°49′N 3°03′W).

    For details of rescue organisation see 1.60.

Tidal streams
9.19

1   Tidal streams along the coast between the estuary of the river Ribble and Morecambe Bay are weak and uncertain, and are affected by wind and other circumstances.

    Tidal streams are given on the chart and in *Admiralty Tidal Stream Atlas — Irish Sea and Bristol Channel*.

Blackpool Tower and North and Central Piers from SW (9.20)
(Original dated 2001)

(Photograph - Air Images)

Directions

Principal marks
9.20
1   **Landmarks:**
White tower, conspicuous, (53°44′N 2°59′W) (9.30).
Blackpool Tower, conspicuous, (53°49′N 3°03′W) standing between the resort's North and Central Piers is similar in construction to the Eiffel Tower in Paris; it provides a good radar echo.
2   Chimney (53°53′N 3°00′W) (9.52).
Isle of Walney Lighthouse (54°03′N 3°11′W) (9.40).
Major light:
Isle of Walney Light (54°03′N 3°11′W) (9.40).

Other aids to navigation
9.21
1   **Racons:**
Bar Light Buoy (53°32′N 3°21′W).
Lune Deep Light Buoy (53°56′N 3°13′W).
Halfway Shoal Light Beacon (54°01′·5N 3°11′·8W).
For further details see *Admiralty List of Radio Signals Volume 2.*

Charts 1951, 1981
Bar Light Buoy to Morecambe Light Buoy
9.22
1   From the vicinity of Bar Light Buoy (53°32′N 3°21′W) to Morecambe Bay, the route leads approximately 23 miles N, passing:
2   W of Jordan's Spit (53°34′N 3°15′W), an extension of shoal ground W from Formby Spit (9.14) with depths of less than 3 m. Jordan's Spit Light Buoy (W cardinal) is moored off the NW edge of the shoal water. An area of spoil ground marked by a

light buoy (special) lies off the W edge of Jordan's Spit. An obstruction, the remains of Formby Towers, lies at the NE tip of the Spit, and is marked by FT Light Buoy (N cardinal). Thence:
3   E of South Morecambe Gas Field (53°51′N 3°35′W) (9.4). A submarine gas pipeline extends ENE from the field to a production well, which is marked on its SW side by a light buoy (special). And:
W of Shell Flat (53°51′N 3°20′W) extending 11 miles W from the coast, with depths of less than 10 m, being the tongue-like extension of Rossall Oyster Grounds (9.14). Two anemometry masts (metal lattice framework mast on yellow pile) stand on Shell Flat. Thence:
4   W of Morecambe Light Buoy (W cardinal) (53°52′N 3°24′W) which is moored off the NW edge of Shell Flat.

9.23
1   Vessels of suitable draught bound for Lune Deep (9.42) can take an inside route over Shell Flat, in depths of not less than 6 m.
After passing W of Jordan's Spit Light Buoy the route leads approximately 20 miles NNE.
Clearing bearing. The line of bearing 009° of the tower of Saint Michael's Church (54°06′N 3°10′W) (Chart 2010) open W of the Isle of Walney Light (9.40) passes over Shell Flat and W of Rossall Patches (9.42).

Useful marks
9.24
1   Gas-holders (53°38′·5N 2°57′·9W), three in number, prominent, standing near Southport.
South, Central and North Piers, Blackpool (53°49′N 3°03′W) extend from the coast abreast the centre

part of the town; the N pier is approximately 3 cables in length. Lights are exhibited from the head of each pier.

(Directions continue for coastal route at 9.117,
for offshore route at 9.108 and
for Morecambe Bay at 9.40)

River Ribble estuary

Chart 1981
General description
9.25

1   The estuary of the river Ribble is entered between Formby Point (53°34′N 3°06′W) and Stanner Point, 11 miles N. The narrow navigable channel (9.26) of the river Ribble leads through the estuary as far as the town of Preston, approximately 15 miles inland, which is no longer used by commercial traffic.

On the S side of the channel the whole of the estuary is encumbered by drying sandbanks; namely Angry Brow, Horse Bank, Great Bank, Foulnaze and Georges Brow.

2   Southport (53°38′N 3°00′W), a popular seaside resort, lies on the S side of the estuary entrance; a pier extends 3 cables NW from the coast near the centre of the town.

The foreshore and the coastal sand dunes between Formby Point and the river Ribble constitute statutory Sites of Special Scientific Interest and there is a National Wildfowl Refuge near Southport.

A helicopter landing site is situated on Birkdale Sands, close NW of Southport, as shown on the chart.

3   On the N side of the estuary, the town of Lytham Saint Anne's, consisting of Lytham, in the S part, and Saint Anne's, in the N part, occupies approximately 4 miles of the low sandy coastline in the vicinity of Stanner Point (53°44′N 3°01′W). Crusader Bank and Salters Bank, both of which dry, extend up to 3 miles from the coast abreast the town; the latter forms the N side of the navigable channel.

4   **Marine exploitation.** Lennox Oil and Gas Field (9.4) lies W of Southport in the approaches to the Ribble estuary.

Tidal stream information off the estuary is shown on the chart. See also *Admiralty Tidal Stream Atlas — Irish Sea and Bristol Channel.*

Gut Channel
9.26

1   Gut Channel is the navigable channel, with drying patches, formed by the river Ribble. It is confined on both sides by training walls marked by perches, many of which are lit, and leads through the N part of the wide estuary to Preston (53°45′N 2°43′W). The S training wall is marked near its outer end by 14¼ mile Light Perch (green solid steel perch 12 m in height, supported by a tripod).

2   A stranded wreck lies close N of the S training wall 2 cables SSW of the 13 mile Light Perch (red solid steel mast, 12 m in height, supported by a tripod).

Gut Light Buoy (safe water) (53°42′N 3°09′W) is moored NW of the entrance to South Gut.

In 1989, owing to severe siltation at the seaward end, the entrance to the original navigable channel could be used only at HW.

3   South Gut, an unmarked channel, has developed through a gap in the S training wall at 12 mile Perch and is now used to gain access to Gut Channel. The wreck of the *Zealandia* (53°39′·9N 3°05′·6W), which dries, lies at the seaward end of South Gut and is marked on its W side by a light buoy (W cardinal).

4   Depths in Gut and South Gut Channels are not maintained and are liable to change.

Caution. It has been reported that the aero light (53°44′·3N 2°53′·6W) at Warton Airfield may be confused with the lights marking the S training wall.
9.27

1   **Vertical clearance.** Overhead power cables span the channel within 1 mile of the entrance to Preston Riversway Docklands (53°45′N 2°45′W). The lowest safe vertical clearance is 39·0 m.

Submarine pipelines, marked by beacons, cross the channel 2½ miles W of the entrance to Preston Riversway Docklands.
9.28

1   **Tidal streams.** In Gut Channel the in-going stream attains a rate of 1½ kn and the out-going stream 1¾ kn.

There are tide gauges at the 11½ mile light beacon (53°43′·5N 3°01′·5W) (S cardinal) and at the 5 mile light perch (53°44′·1N 2°51′·6W) (tide gauge not shown on the chart).
9.29

1   **Local knowledge** is needed to navigate Gut Channel, South Gut and the river Ribble in which the depths are not maintained. The use of South Gut at night requires local knowledge and great caution.

The alignment (057°) of 11½ mile light beacon (S cardinal) (53°43′·5N 3°01′·5W) with a light exhibited from the conspicuous white tower (see below) at Lytham Saint Anne's passes through the gap in the S training wall.

2   An obstruction, the stump of an old perch, is visible at MLWS at a height of 2·3 m above chart datum in position 53°42′·5N 3°06′·0W at the outer end of the S training wall; a further obstruction, the position of which is approximate, lies 8 cables WSW of 13 mile Light Perch.
9.30

1   **Useful marks:**

    White tower (53°44′N 2°59′W), from which a light is exhibited, at Lytham Saint Anne's.

    White windmill (53°44′N 2°57′W), standing on the coast at Lytham.

    Southport Pier Light (white post, 6 m in height) (53°39′N 3°01′W).

Anchorages

Gut Channel
9.31

1   There is good anchorage, in offshore winds, about 1 mile WSW of Gut Light Buoy (53°42′N 3°09′W), in depths of 13 m, good holding.

Temporary anchorage in depths of 4 to 7 m may be obtained near the entrance to South Gut.

There is also temporary anchorage within Gut Channel near the training wall 8 cables WSW of the white windmill (9.30) in depths of less than 1 m; vessels should be prepared to take the ground.

River Douglas
9.32

1   The river Douglas, also known as the river Asland, joins Gut Channel S of Naze Mount (53°44′·4N 2°51′·9W), approximately 4 miles W of Preston; this river flows through Tarleton (53°41′N 2°50′W) at which place it is joined by the Leeds and Liverpool Canal.

A marina is situated 2 miles within the entrance to the river.

5 mile Light Perch stands at the confluence of the river Douglas with the river Ribble.

Landing places
9.33

1   Landing can be made at the head of Southport pier (9.25) which dries out; a train, which operates from the pier head throughout the year excepting winter months, can be taken to the mainland.

Boats can secure alongside the pier.

MORECAMBE BAY INCLUDING THE PORT OF BARROW-IN-FURNESS

General information

Chart 2010
Description
9.34

1   Morecambe Bay, is an extensive inlet which is entered between Rossall Point (53°55′N 3°03′W), a low lying sandy point backed by residential land, and the Isle of Walney (9.82), 9 miles NW.

It is occupied by a very considerable area of drying sands intersected by a number of channels, of which Lune Deep (9.42) at the SE entrance to the bay is the principal channel through which direct approach can be made to Fleetwood Harbour and the Port of Lancaster.

2   Shoals (9.72) divide Lune Deep channel into two parts, the N part known as Lancaster Sound which is bounded W by Fisher Bank and Scars, which dry, lying in the E edge of Morecambe Flats (9.42), and the E part as Heysham Lake (9.72), which leads to Heysham Harbour (54°02′N 2°55′W).

The port of Barrow-in-Furness (9.76) lies inside the NW entrance to the bay and is approached through a buoyed channel from Lightning Knoll Light Buoy (54°00′N 3°14′W).

3   **Barrow Wind Farm** (53°59′N 3°17′W) covers an area of about 3 square miles to seaward of Lightning Knoll and close NW of the leading line for the Lightning Knoll buoyed channel. The vertical clearance of the blade discs is 25 m.

National Wildfowl Refuge. The Wyre-Lune Sanctuary has been established on the sands fronting the coast between the mouths of the rivers of the same names

Pilotage
9.35

1   Vessels bound for Barrow-in-Furness embark their pilots in the vicinity of Lightning Knoll Light Buoy (54°00′N 3°14′W) and vessels for Heysham embark their pilots SE of Lune Deep Light Buoy (53°56′N 3°13′W).

For either Fleetwood or Lancaster, pilots embark off the entrance to the port.

For further details, see 9.50 (Fleetwood), 9.61 (Port of Lancaster), 9.69 (Heysham) or 9.80 (Barrow).

Submarine cables and pipelines
9.36

1   There are numerous cables, some disused, and pipelines in the area. Gas pipelines come ashore on the Isle of Walney (54°04′N 3°14′W) and a high voltage cable, part of which is exposed on the seabed, runs from the Barrow Wind Farm to Heysham.

Fishing
9.37

1   Large concentrations of static fishing gear are laid within Barrow Wind Farm and E and NE of the wind farm See also 9.4.

Rescue
9.38

1   All-weather lifeboats are stationed at Fleetwood (53°55′N 3°00′W) and Barrow-in-Furness (54°04′N 3°10′W); inshore lifeboats are stationed at Fleetwood, Morecambe (54°04′N 2°52′W) and Barrow-in-Furness

For details of rescue organisation see 1.60.

Tidal streams
9.39

1   The tidal stream follows the principal approach channel until the banks are covered, then sets E on the in-going stream and W out-going.

The maximum spring rate in each direction within the channel is 4 kn.

Tidal streams are given on the chart and in *Admiralty Tidal Stream Atlas — Irish Sea and Bristol Channel.*

Directions
(continued from 9.24)

Principal marks
9.40

1   **Landmarks:**
  Blackpool Tower (53°49′N 3°03′W) (9.20).
  Chimney (53°53′N 3°00′W) (9.52).
  Silo (53°57′N 2°51′W).
  Power Stations (54°02′N 2°55′W) (9.72).
  Isle of Walney Lighthouse (stone tower, 24 m in height) (54°03′N 3°11′W); prominent.

2   Monument surmounting Oubas Hill (54°09′·5N 3°05′·5W) (132 m high) (Chart 1826) visible from the greater part of Morecambe Bay.

Major light:
  Isle of Walney Light — as above. The light is obscured between the bearings 122°–127° when within 3 miles of the shore.

Isle of Walney Lighthouse (9.40)
(Original dated 1996; verified 1999)

(Photograph - Associated British Ports, Barrow)

Other aids to navigation
9.41

1   **Racon:**
  Lune Deep Light Buoy (53°56′N 3°13′W).

For further details see *Admiralty List of Radio Signals Volume 2.*

South-west approach through Lune Deep
9.42

1   From a position W of Morecambe Light Buoy (53°52′N 3°24′W) to a position NW of Fleetwood Fairway Light Buoy, about 16 miles ENE, moored at the entrance to the river Wyre, the route to ports lying on the E side of Morecambe Bay leads ENE and NE through Lune Deep, a steep gully with depths in excess of 60 m in places, passing (with positions from Rossall Point (53°55'N 3°03'W)):

NNW of Morecambe Light Buoy (53°52'N 3°24'W), thence:

2   NNW of Shell Flat (53°51'N 3°20'W) (9.22), thence:

SSE of Lune Deep Light Buoy (S cardinal) (6 miles W), which is moored at the SW end of Lune Deep off the S edge of Morecambe Flats (3 miles NW), an extensive shoal ground, thence:

NW of Shell Wharf Light Buoy (starboard hand) (3½ miles W) marking the W side of Boulder Banks, and:

SE of Fisher Bank Light Buoy (port hand superbuoy) (4 miles WNW), thence:

3   NW of a group of banks and flats consisting of North West Boulders (2¾ miles W), Rossall Patches (2½ miles W) and South Boulders (2½ miles WSW), which dries. A rock, awash, lies 3½ cables NW of South Boulders. Thence:

NW of a light buoy (special) (2¾ miles WNW) marking an obstruction at the seaward end of an outfall. The outfall is encased in rock, which dries, and is marked by three beacons (special) along its length. Thence:

4   SE of Fisher Bank Patches (3 miles NW) with depths of less than 5 m over them, and:

NW of a drying patch, (1¾ miles NW), thence:

5   Between Danger Patch (2¾ miles NW), marked by Danger Patch Light Buoy (port hand), and King Scar (1½ miles NNW), a drying rocky patch which lies near the N end of North Wharf (9.52) and is marked by King Scar Light Buoy (starboard hand). Fisher Bank Spit which forms the SE edge of Morecambe Flats lies 1 mile NNE of Danger Patch. Thence:

NW of Fleetwood Fairway Light Buoy (N cardinal) (2¼ miles N).

9.43

1   Vessels of suitable draught approaching from S may pass over Shell Flat following the directions given at 9.23.

South-west approach to Barrow-in-Furness
9.44

1   From a position WNW of Morecambe Light Buoy (53°52'N 3°24'W) the route to the pilot boarding position W of Lightning Knoll Light Buoy (54°00'N 3°14'W), which lies at the entrance to the channel leading to the port of Barrow-in-Furness, leads about 10 miles NE, passing:

2   NW of Lune Deep Light Buoy (53°56'N 3°13'W) (9.42), thence:

SE of Barrow Wind Farm (9.34).

Deep-draught vessels should pass between Lightning Knoll Light Buoy and Sea 1 Light Buoy so as to enter the buoyed channel on the leading line (9.86).

Cautions
9.45

1   Owing to frequent changes in the channels, banks and buoys, the chart must be used with caution.

Navigation in the upper parts of the channels in Morecambe Bay should not be attempted without local knowledge.

(Directions continue for Fleetwood at 9.52, Port of Lancaster at 9.63, Heysham at 9.72 and for Barrow-in-Furness at 9.86)

Anchorages

Chart 2010, 1552 plan of Approaches to Fleetwood
9.46

1   Vessels can find open anchorage about 1¾ miles NNW of Wyre Lighthouse (disused) (53°57'N 3°02'W) (9.52), as shown on the chart, in depths of about 18 m. An area of foul ground lies 1 mile NW of the lighthouse.

Vessels of less than 50 m in length can anchor in Heysham Lake (9.72) at its SW end, approximately 2¾ miles NNE of the disused Wyre Lighthouse and 5 cables WNW of No 1 Light Buoy (53°59'·4N 2°59'·1W) (9.72), in depths of about 12 m.

Fleetwood

Chart 1552 plan of Fleetwood
General information
9.47

1   **Position.** Fleetwood Harbour (53°56'N 3°00'W) is situated on the W side of the mouth of the river Wyre.

Function. Fleetwood is a major fishing port with most of the fish landed from inshore and middle distance trawlers. The port operates a RoRo terminal with regular services to Northern Ireland.

2   **Port limits.** That part of the river Wyre extending 2 miles N of Rossall Point on the W side, and 3 miles N of Knott End on the E side; and from the extreme SW point of a headland of which Hay Nook (53°54'N 2°59'W) lies at the N end, W to the opposite shore. Included is the area comprising the docks at Fleetwood. Full details are contained in the harbour bye-laws.

3   **Approach and entry.** Approach is made from Lune Deep and entry through a narrow channel, formed by the river Wyre.

Port Authority. Associated British Ports, Dock Office, Fleetwood, Lancashire FY7 6PP.

The port authority is represented by a Port Manager. Navigational matters should be addressed to the Harbour Master.

Limiting conditions
9.48

1   **Controlling depths.** A depth of approximately 2·5 m is maintained over the bar and in the channel as far as the river berths. The turning area off the RoRo terminal is dredged to 2·0 m (2006); a depth of 3·5 m is maintained at the berth.

2   Depths within Fleetwood Harbour, the river Wyre and approaches are subject to frequent change owing to siltation, and continuous dredging is carried out. The channel buoys are adjusted accordingly. For the latest information on controlling depths, the Port Authority should be consulted prior to arrival.

Density of water. The density at the river berths is 1·015 g/cm^3 at half tide and 1·025 g/cm^3 at HW.

3   **Maximum size of vessel:** 5000 dwt, length 152 m, beam 20·3 m, draught 4·2 m at the RoRo berth; within the dock system, vessels of up to 1500 dwt, 58 m in length, beam 14·1 m and draught 6·5 m can be accepted. However, a vessel with a draught over 5·5 m may only enter the port 1 hour either side of HW springs.

9.49

1   **Lock.** Wyre Lock, which gives access to Wyre Dock and Fish Dock, is 76·2 m long, 15·2 m wide with depths of 7·4 m at MHWS over the sill.

Under normal circumstances the lock gates are open 1½ hours before and after HW. Vessels can be locked in

Fleetwood Fish Dock and Wyre Dock from SSW (9.47)
(Original dated 2001)

(Photograph - Air Images)

and out before or after these times by special arrangement if conditions are suitable.

2 Within the locking times the time of entry for vessels of 11·3 m beam, or over, has to be adjusted because the width of the lock is narrower at the bottom than at the top.

Vessels of more than 13·7 m beam can only enter at HW.

There is a tide gauge at the entrance to the lock.

Arrival information
9.50

1 **Port operations.** The port does not maintain a continuous listening watch, but from 2 hours before HW to 1½ hours after HW a watch is maintained on VHF.

Vessels entering or leaving the harbour must make a "Securite" broadcast on VHF; for details, see *Admiralty List of Radio Signals Volume 6(1)*.

2 Vessels carrying dangerous substances should advise the Harbour Master at least 48 hours prior to arrival, or in the case of a voyage of less than 48 hours, such notification should be given as long as reasonably practicable before the vessel enters the harbour.

Vessels proceeding to the enclosed docks and marina should call Fleetwood Docks at locking times, call sign: Fleetwood Docks; communications are carried out from a small office located at the entrance to Wyre Dock.

3 Vessels should forward their ETA and draught 24 hours in advance to their agents. Amendments may be made not less than 12 hours before the original ETA.

Outer anchorage. Vessels waiting to enter Fleetwood should anchor about 1¼ miles NNW of Fairway Light Buoy.

4 **Pilotage and tugs.** Pilotage is compulsory for all vessels of 50 gt and over and is arranged through the Harbour Master. Vessels of not more than 1500 gt regularly trading on the British coast and not carrying passengers are exempt. Visitors to the port should indicate to the Harbour Master if they require a pilot or not, before entering the approach channel.

5 The pilot boarding position is situated in the vicinity of Fairway Light Buoy (53°58′N 3°02′W) (9.42).

Regulations concerning entry. Special bye-laws are in force, see 9.58.

Harbour
9.51

1 **General layout.** The harbour entrance lies between the E side of a headland of which Rossall Point (53°55′N 3°03′W) forms the W point, and Knott End-on-Sea, 3 cables opposite on the E shore.

Tidal berths line the W bank for 3 cables within the entrance. The non-tidal berths (9.49) are approached through a channel 4 cables in length. This channel, which dries, is entered off the S end of the tidal berths.

2 Jubilee Quay, situated in Inner harbour, lies on the W bank between the tidal berths and the lock.

A sailing school pier, 95 m long, is situated 3½ cables S of the ferry pier at Knott End-on-Sea. Its seaward end is marked by a beacon (port hand).

Victoria Pier, a promenade pier, extends a short distance NW from the N coast fronting the town.

The river Wyre above Fleetwood is used by small craft and contains a marina and several moorings.

3   **Ferry service.** During the summer months a ferry service operates from the ferry dock situated on the W bank at the harbour entrance to Knott End-on-Sea pier (2¼ cables W).

Shellfish beds. Mussel beds lie on each side of the entrance to the river Wyre. Larger concentrations however, lie on the E side.

Dredging takes place continually in the harbour channels. Vessels are cautioned to give the dredgers a wide berth and to pass them at slow speed.

4   **Docking signals** (Diagram 9.51) are exhibited at Wyre Dock.

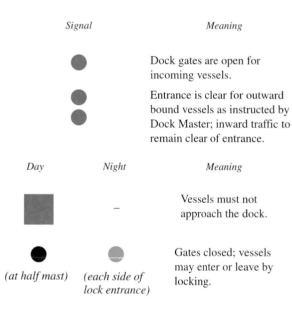

Signal	Meaning
⬤	Dock gates are open for incoming vessels.
⬤ ⬤	Entrance is clear for outward bound vessels as instructed by Dock Master; inward traffic to remain clear of entrance.

Day	Night	Meaning
◼	–	Vessels must not approach the dock.
⬤ *(at half mast)*	⬤ *(each side of lock entrance)*	Gates closed; vessels may enter or leave by locking.

Wyre Dock - traffic signals (9.51)

5   **Tidal streams** near Fairway Light Buoy are shown on the chart. In the approach channel the streams set in the direction of the channel when the banks are dry, but across the channel when they are covered.

The spring rate off Fleetwood is 3 kn; within the channel the spring rate is about 4 kn.

Directions for entering harbour

(continued from 9.45)

9.52

1   **Landmark:**

     Chimney (53°53′N 3°00′W) standing within the ICI complex at Thornton.

2   **Approach channel.** From the vicinity of the pilot station off Fairway Light Buoy (9.42), the track leads SE then 2 miles SSE through the buoyed approach channel which separates two large areas of drying sandflats; North Wharf, which extends 1¾ miles N from the coast between Rossall Point (53°55′N 3°03′W) and Fleetwood, and Bernard Wharf, which extends 2½ miles N from the coast E of Fleetwood.

3   The channel buoys, all of which are lit, are numbered from seaward.

Caution. Depths in the channel are subject to frequent change owing to siltation and the buoys are moved accordingly. The Harbour Authority should be consulted for the latest information.

The track passes (with positions from Wyre Lighthouse (disused) (53°57′N 3°02′W)):

4   NE of No 3 Light Buoy (starboard hand) (3 cables N), thence:

     ENE of Wyre Lighthouse (disused) (black metal structure on piles) which stands close within the NE corner of North Wharf, thence:

     ENE of No 11 Light Beacon (starboard hand) (1 mile SSE), situated on Black Scar, thence:

5   NNE of Steep Breast Perch (platform on black wooden post, black base, 8 m in height) (1½ miles SSE, within ½ cable N of the front leading light (see below)), on which stands a light, thence:

     Between Fleetwood and the head of Knott End-on-Sea ferry pier, from where a light (platform on column, 10 m in height) is exhibited.

6   **Leading lights.** The alignment (156°) of the lights marking the general axis of the channel can be effectively used only between No 8 Light Buoy and No 11 Light Beacon:

     Front light (stone tower, 12 m in height) (on the E end of the esplanade close to the W entrance point to the harbour) which is visible on the bearing only.

7   Rear light (stone tower, 25 m in height) (1½ cables SSE from the front light) visible on the leading line only.

Both lights are shown throughout 24 hours.

9.53

1   **Dock Channel**, which is buoyed and entered between No 23 Buoy (starboard hand) and No 24 Buoy (port hand), leads SSE from the RoRo berth towards the entrance to Fleetwood Docks.

Slade Slip Corner, 2 cables NNE of the dock entrance and from which lights are disposed vertically from a metal post, marks the turning point SW for the docks.

2   On the SE side of Dock Channel East Jetty and a breakwater, known as East Bund, the outer end of which dries 7·0 m, extend parallel to the channel for 2 cables from the dock entrance.

9.54

1   **Cautions.** For the benefit of other port users, vessels berthing at the RoRo berth on an in-going tide always swing with bow to quay and on an out-going tide, stern to quay.

If entering on the in-going tide, care is necessary to guard against the E-going stream (9.51) as the harbour is approached. See also Regulations at 9.58.

2   Mariners should exercise special care in the vicinity of the lifeboat station at the entrance to the harbour, and Knott End Ferry Pier (9.51) so as not to cause damage by wash or displacement.

The most dangerous winds for the bar are those from between NW and NE.

Berths

9.55

1   **Wyre Dock** lies at the head of Dock Channel and is 293 m long, 116 m wide and has a maintained depth of 5·5 m. It is entered through Wyre Lock (9.49). There are

Ro-Ro Terminal *Leading Lights (circled)*

Fleetwood from NNW (9.52)

(Original dated 2001)

(Photograph - Air Images)

lights on either side of the approach, about ½ cable from the lock entrance.

Fleetwood Harbour Village Marina lies on both sides of the dock.

2 A channel, bound by piles and with a minimum width 31·7 m, leads through the centre of the dock from the entrance lock to the entrance to the fish dock.

Fish Dock, entered from Wyre Dock through a passage, is 274 m long and 213 m wide. There is a maintained depth of 5·5 m, and is used mainly by local fishing vessels. The fish market, with 180 m of quay length, occupies the W and S sides of the dock.

3 **RoRo berth** lies on the W side of the river entrance at Norwest Terminal, 4 cables NE of Wyre Dock. The berth, controlled by Stena Line Ferries, the Irish Sea unit load operator, lies within a maintained depth area of 3·5 m and can be used by vessels 152 m in length having a draught of 4·2 m.

There is a tide gauge situated at the berth and lights are exhibited from both ends.

4 **Isle of Man Berth,** which forms part of Norwest Terminal, lies close seaward of the RoRo berth within the maintained depth area. The berth is 91 m long and can accommodate car and passenger ferries up to 107 m in length having a draught of 4·2 m. The ferries operate, mainly on a seasonal basis, to Douglas.

There is a tide gauge at the S end of the berth and lights are exhibited from both ends.

9.56

1 **Fleetwood Harbour Village Marina** (53°55'·0N 3°00'·7W) lies on both sides of Wyre Dock with berths for craft up to 12 m LOA. The docks must not be entered without the prior permission of the Harbour Master.

Wardley's Yacht Club (53°52'·7N 2°57'·9W), with marina facilities, lies on the E side of the river Wyre at Hambleton, nearly 3 miles above Fleetwood. Overhead

power cables with a safe vertical clearance of 27 m span the river between pylons close N of the yacht club.

Port services
9.57

1 **Facilities:** reception of oily waste, noxious and harmful substances and galley waste; issue of SSCC and SSCEC; compass adjustment; hospital at Blackpool, 13 km S.

Supplies: all grades of fuel and diesel oil; fresh water; provisions.

Harbour regulations
9.58

1 Bye-laws and notes for masters, copies of which can be obtained from the Harbour Master, are in force, from which the following regulations have been extracted:

The Master of a vessel must pass the Fairway Light Buoy on the starboard hand when entering the river Wyre from the sea and must not cut through between the Fairway Light Buoy and Wyre Lighthouse.

2 The Master of a vessel shall navigate within the harbour with care and caution and so as not to cause obstruction, damage, risk of displacement or backwash, or inconvenience to any vessel or property, or to any vessel in tow, dredger, tug, lighter or other craft working within the harbour.

3 In the event of any vessel grounding in any part of Fleetwood Harbour the Master shall not attempt to refloat the vessel by reversing the engines, or by any other means whatsoever, until all vessels following have passed the stranded vessel and the channel is clear of shipping.

No commercial diving operations may take place within the port and harbour limits without the prior permission of the harbour authority.

Glasson Dock and Glasson Basin Yacht Harbour from S (9.59)
(Original dated 2001)

(Photograph - Air Images)

Port of Lancaster

Chart 1552 plans of the river Lune and Approaches to Heysham and Glasson

General information

9.59

1   **Position.** Port of Lancaster embraces Lancaster (54°03′N 2°49′W) and Glasson Dock (54°00′N 2°51′W) (9.65), which are situated 7 miles and 2 miles respectively, within the mouth of the river Lune.

    Function. Nearly all the trade in the port is handled at Glasson Dock with only the occasional vessel berthing at Lancaster.

    Topography. The river in this area is bordered mainly by marshland with low lying and rural land beyond.

2   Inshore fishing vessels also work out of Glasson Dock at certain times of the year.

    Approach and entry. Approach is made from Lune Deep and entry through a narrow channel formed by the river Lune.

    Traffic. There are regular services to and from the Isle of Man, Northern Ireland and Europe.

3   In 2004 there were 156 port calls with a total of 134 738 gt.

    Port Authority. The Lancaster Port Commission, West Quay, Glasson Dock, Lancaster LA2 0DB.

    The port is represented by a Port Manager who is also the Harbour Master.

Limiting conditions

9.60

1   **Controlling depths.** The banks and channels within the river Lune and approaches are subject to frequent change. Buoyage is often moved to reflect changes to the channel, but occasionally the river Lune navigational channel does not lie between the buoys. For the latest information on controlling depths and channels, the Port Authority should be consulted prior to arrival.

    Vessels arriving with more than 2·4 m draught should not leave the vicinity of River Lune Light Buoy (53°59′N 3°00′W) until 1 hour before HW.

2   **Vertical clearance.** Overhead power cables, with a vertical clearance of 29 m, span the river 1½ miles above Glasson Dock.

    Maximum size of vessel handled: at North or East Wall, Glasson Dock, approximately 3000 dwt, length 92 m, beam 14 m beam, having a draught of up to 5·2 m at MHWS. Vessels berthed alongside North or East Wall always take the ground.

    Within Glasson Dock: approximately 1900 dwt, length 85 m, beam 14 m and draught 4·5 m MHWS.

Arrival information

9.61

1   **Port operations.** For details, see *Admiralty List of Radio Signals Volume 6(1)*.

    Outer anchorage. Vessels waiting for a tide to Glasson Dock should anchor off River Lune Light Buoy. See caution on wreck (9.63).

Anchorage is prohibited E of Sunderland Point (53°59'N 2°53'W) in the vicinity of a submerged pipeline, as shown on the chart.

2 **Pilotage** is not compulsory but is highly recommended. All vessels must forward their ETA and draught 12 hours in advance to their local agent or Harbour Master.

The pilot boarding position lies 1 cable S of river Lune Light Buoy. Vessels should be underway on the arrival of the pilot boat, blue hull and white superstructure, which carries VHF radio. In bad weather, vessels should be prepared to follow the pilot boat into the river.

Tugs. There are no tugs at the port.

Harbour
9.62

1 **General layout.** The harbour comprises the river Lune from Lancaster (54°03'N 2°49'W) downstream to the river mouth where it opens into Morecambe Bay between Sunderland Point (53°59'N 2°53'W) and Plover Scar (9.63), 5 cables S.

Training walls, which are shown on the chart, are situated at several locations along the course of the river.

An approach channel, which gives access to the harbour entrance, separates several areas of drying sandflats and foul ground.

2 Glasson Dock, which lies on the S side of the river close E of Fishnet Point (9.63) comprises a wet dock with access to a large enclosed basin and marina into which runs an arm of the Lancaster Canal. River berths, which dry, lie either side of the entrance to the dock.

Lancaster (54°03'N 2°49'W) comprises a single riverside quay which dries out, 5 cables W of Carlisle Bridge, a rail bridge, at the W end of the town.

3 **Shellfish beds** lie at the entrance to a bay 6 cables NE of Sunderland Point.

Traffic signals are displayed from a white structure at the W entrance gate of Glasson Dock.

Signal	Meaning
●	No access from direction exhibited.
●	Access clear from direction exhibited. Pleasure craft must give way to commercial traffic.

Glasson Dock - traffic signals (9.62)

4 **Tidal streams.** The in-going stream sets strongly SE across the approach channel towards the entrance to the river Cocker (53°57'N 2°50'W) (Chart 2010) when the flats on either side are covered.

In Abbey Hole (53°59'N 2°53'W), the in-going stream sets strongly SE, and in Sunderland Hole (9.63), 6 cables NE, it sets strongly E towards Crook Skear, on the E side of the channel, 4 cables NE of Sunderland Point; off the latter it attains a spring rate of 5 kn.

5 An eddy sets W across the entrance to Glasson Dock during the last 2 hours of the in-going stream.

Above Glasson Dock the duration of the in-going stream decreases and off Lancaster is only approximately 2 hours.

Tidal stream information at the entrance to the river Lune is given on the chart.

Directions for entering harbour
(continued from 9.45)
9.63

1 **Landmarks:**
Power stations (54°02'N 2°55'W) (9.72).
Pylons (54°01'N 2°50'W).
Chimney (53°53'N 3°00'W) (Chart 2010) (9.52).

2 **Approach.** From a position NW of Fleetwood Fairway Light Buoy (9.42) the track leads a further 1½ miles ENE to the vicinity of the pilot boarding position close S of River Lune Light Buoy (W cardinal) (53°59'N 3°00'W).

Caution. A wreck, position approximate, with unsurveyed clearance depth of 3 m lies about 2 cables S of River Lune Light Buoy.

3 **Channel.** From the pilot boarding position, the track leads about 4 miles E through a channel marked on both sides by light buoys, formed by the river Lune, which separates Sunderland Shoulder, a drying sandflat which extends 5 miles W from the coast encumbering the N side, and Bernard Wharf (9.52) and Pilling Sands, which dry, on the S side, passing:

4 Half a cable N of Plover Scar, rocks which extend 2½ cables NW from the shore and which are marked on their N side by Plover Scar Light (white stone tower, black lantern) (53°59'N 2°53'W).

Caution. The banks and channels at the entrance to the river Lune are constantly changing and the buoyage is frequently moved to reflect this. The chart must be used with caution.

5 **Entry.** From a position N of Plover Scar Light, the track towards Glasson Dock, 2 miles upstream, continues through a channel marked by light buoys and light beacons, passing (positions from the light):

W of Crook Perch Light Beacon (starboard hand) (7 cables NNE), which stands on the E edge of Sunderland Hole with depths of up to 4 m, thence:

6 S of Bazil Perch Light Beacon (port hand) (1½ miles NE), which lies ½ cable S of Bazil Point, thence:
NE of Fishnet Point (54°00'N 2°51'W), a low lying point.

Mariners should be aware of the E set of the in-going stream in Sunderland Hole and if entering Glasson Dock, against the W eddy off the entrance, see 9.62.
9.64

1 From Glasson Dock to Lancaster, the channel is not buoyed and should only be undertaken with local knowledge. Except for small craft, this part of the river is only occasionally used.

Berths
9.65

1 **River berths.** North Wall, 100 m in length, lies directly outside the entrance to Glasson Dock; East Wall, 122 m in length, lies on the outer side of the E entrance. Both berths can accommodate the maximum size vessel (9.60).

Glasson Dock, 156 m long and 61 m wide with depths of 5·5 m at MHWS or 3·5 m at MHWN consists of East Quay, 152 m in length, and West Quay, 122 m in length.

Dock entrance: 15 m wide, depth on the sill 6·6 m at MHWS, 4·5 m at MHWN.

2 The dock may be entered ¾ hour before HW until HW The dock gate is manned only on one tide per day, being the tide closest to midday. A vessel wishing to enter or leave the basin at another time must give at least 12 hours notice to the Harbour Master (01524 751724 or

07774 773189) between the hours of 0900 and 1700, Monday to Friday.

3   **Lancaster.** New Quay (9.62), with a length of 146 m can accommodate a vessel having a draught of 3·8 m at MHWS. All vessels take the ground.

Glasson Basin Yacht Harbour, operated by Glasson Basin Yacht Company Ltd, is situated in British Waterways Basin, entered from Glasson Dock through a lock 30·5 m long, 7·6 m wide with a depth of 4·3 m over the sill.

The Lancaster Canal is entered from the sea at Glasson Dock; it is suitable only for pleasure craft.

Port services
9.66

1   **Facilities** are limited; issue of SSCC and SSCEC can be arranged; divers; hospital at Lancaster.

Supplies: fresh water at all quays; fuel and diesel oil by road tanker; provisions.

Heysham

Charts 1552 plans of the river Lune and Approaches to Heysham and Heysham harbour, 2010

General information
9.67

1   **Position.** Heysham (54°02′N 2°55′W), is an artificial harbour situated 1 mile SW of Throbshaw Point and is accessible at all states of the tide.

Function. The harbour handles regular passenger and freight traffic to and from Northern Ireland, the Republic of Ireland and the Isle of Man; there are RoRo and general cargo facilities.

2   There is a regular though small general cargo trade with South America, Europe and the Mediterranean.

The harbour is the support base for the South Morecambe Gas Field and oil and gas fields in Liverpool Bay (9.4).

Approach and entry. The approach to the harbour lies through the channels of Lune Deep (9.42) and Heysham Lake (9.72). Entry is made from Heysham Lake on the leading line passing between North and South Pierheads.

3   **Traffic.** In 2007 there were 554 ship calls with a total of 2 955 622 dwt.

Port Authority. Heysham Port Ltd, Port of Heysham, Heysham, Lancashire LA3 2XF.

The port is represented by a General Manager who deals with navigational matters.

Limiting conditions
9.68

1   **Controlling depths.** For the latest information on controlling depths, the Port Authority should be consulted.

Charted depths:
> In the entrance channel, which is dredged on a regular basis, there is a least depth of 4·1 m.
>
> In the harbour there is a general depth of 4·1 m; alongside the RoRo berths there is a least depth of 5·1 m.

2   Depths within the entrance channel and harbour are liable to change.

Heysham from E (9.67)

(Original dated 2001)

(Photograph - Air Images)

Depending on draught, vessels should be prepared to take the ground alongside South Quay.

Maximum size of vessel handled: the largest vessel handled was one of 25 000 dwt, having a length of 160 m, beam 26 m and draught 9 m.

Arrival information
9.69

1   **Port operations.** For details of Heysham Port Control, see *Admiralty List of Radio Signals Volume 6(1).*

Anchorage. Vessels awaiting a pilot should, if necessary, anchor in the charted anchorage, which is 3 cables N of the pilot boarding position (see below).

Vessels of less than 50 m in length can anchor in Heysham Lake, see 9.46 for details.

2   **Pilotage** is compulsory for all vessels over 50 m in length except HM vessels and foreign naval vessels. Notice required for a pilot is 24 hours in advance; ETA should be sent to the local agent through any coast radio station. Subsequent amendments should be made direct with the pilot station or Port Control.

The pilot boarding station is in position 53°58′·5N 3°03′·0W; the pilot boat, black hull and white superstructure, is only on station when vessels are expected.

Regulations concerning entry
9.70

1   **Quarantine.** See 1.55. International health regulations are to be observed.

Harbour
9.71

1   **General layout.** The tidal harbour is 730 m long and 213 m wide having an entrance width of 91 m. Entrance to the harbour lies between South Pier head, at the W end of West Quay, and the W extension of North Quay, ½ cable N; the entrance is protected by South Jetty, which extends 1½ cables W from South Pier.

There are several alongside berths together with facilities at the E end of the harbour for RoRo traffic.

2   West Quay, close inside the S entrance, is linked by road to the near-by nuclear power stations (9.72); dolphins at the SE end of the quay protect the water intake to the power stations.

Submarine cables. See 9.36.

Tidal stream information is given on the charts; in Heysham Lake the streams set in the direction of the channel.

Directions for entering harbour
(continued from 9.45)
9.72

1   **Landmarks:**

Power Stations (54°02′N 2°55′W). Two power stations, each comprising a conspicuous building, stand close together on the SE edge of Heysham Harbour.

Chimney (53°53′N 3°00′W) (9.52).

Radio Mast (54°02′N 2°55′W), from which lights are exhibited, stands close N of Heysham Harbour.

2   **Approach.** From a position NW of Fleetwood Fairway Light Buoy (9.42) the approach to the harbour leads a further 5½ miles through Heysham Lake, a continuation NE

Heysham entrance from WNW (9.71)
(Original dated 2001)

(Photograph - Air Images)

of Lune Deep, with depths of over 5 m in the buoyed channel, and which is bounded on its SE side by Sunderland Shoulder (9.63) and on its N side by Clark Wharf and Clark Wharf Spit, both of which dry, passing (with positions from the head of South Jetty (54°01′·9N 2°55′·7W)):

3   Between No 2 Light Buoy (port hand) (4½ miles SW), moored on the SE side of shoals, composed of rock mainly overlaid by sand, and River Lune Light Buoy (9.63), 7½ cables ESE, moored at the entrance to the river Lune, thence:

NW of the NW side of Sunderland Shoulder with a foul area, marked by No 1 Light Buoy (starboard hand) (3·2 miles SW) and No 3 Light Buoy (starboard hand), 1 mile NE, thence:

4   SE of No 6 Light Buoy (port hand) (2 miles SW) which marks the edge of shoal water with depths of less than 5 m, thence:

Caution. The shoals S and SE of Clark Wharf have gradually encroached into the W side of the fairway between Nos 6 and 8 Light Buoys; in consequence the deeper water of the channel in this area lies towards the starboard hand light buoys. In recent years however, the channel has remained in a stable condition. Thence:

5   WNW of Middleton Sands, a drying bank with a foul area, marked by No 5 Light Buoy (starboard hand) (1·4 miles SSW) and No 7 Light Buoy (starboard hand) (8 cables SSW).

ESE of No 8 Light Buoy (port hand) (4 cables WSW), and:

WNW of light beacons (metal posts) (½ and 2 cables S) marking the W end of 2 outfall culverts, thence:

6   WNW of South Jetty from which a light (white metal framework tower, 6 m in height; radar reflector) is exhibited, thence following the leading lights into the harbour entrance.

Leading lights. The alignment (102¼°) of the leading lights indicates the centre of the dredged channel which leads from the approaches into the harbour between North and South Piers:

7   Front light (orange and black diamond on post) (54°01′·9N 2°55′·2W).

Rear light (similar structure) (137 m from front light).

A light (mast, 5 m in height) is exhibited from the head of North Pier but is obscured from seawards.

Two obstructions, marked by light buoys (W and N cardinals), lie approximately 4 cables NNW of the harbour entrance.

8   On the N-going stream, on passing South Jetty, course should be altered in good time to pass ½ cable N of its head, completing the turn on to the leading line before entering the still water within South Jetty.

On the S-going stream, vessels should keep well clear of the head of South Jetty, but guard against back eddies from the jetty, which may cause a sudden reversal of the direction of the stream across the harbour entrance.

9   The best time for entering is on the last of the in-going stream when the stream has weakened.

Strong W winds cause a steep and awkward sea near the harbour entrance; if the draught permits, the best time to enter harbour under these conditions is at LW when the banks in the vicinity, which dry, afford some protection.

Directions for leaving harbour
9.73

1   If leaving harbour during the N-going stream, vessels should round the head of South Jetty to within ½ cable or

it may not be possible to complete the turn before running on to the bank on the E side of Clark Wharf.

Useful marks:
Chimneys (54°01′N 2°54′W) standing at an oil refinery SE of the harbour.

2   Near Naze Lighthouse (disused) (54°02′·3N 2°54′·7W) standing on Near Naze, a small outcrop of rocks, NE of the harbour entrance.

Alongside berths
9.74

1   **South Quay,** 460 m long, with a least depth 4·1 m alongside, having No 1 RoRo berth at its E end, can accommodate the maximum size vessel (9.68) alongside General Cargo Terminal. Depending on draught vessels should be prepared to take the ground whilst alongside the quay.

2   **North Quay** is 290 m long. The outer 140 m of the quay forms part of a marine supply base which services the South Morecambe Gas Field and is mostly used by supply vessels. The inner section of the quay is a general purpose berth.

Nos 2 and 3 RoRo berth. Between North and South Quays, two further RoRo berths extend up to 90 m into the harbour from the E shore. At the seaward end of the linkspans lie 4 dolphins which are linked by a walkway; the outer dolphin exhibits a light.

3   **West Quay,** 170 m long, situated on the S side of the harbour entrance, is available to new port users. Heavy lift vessels carrying machinery for the power stations occasionally use this quay.

Fish Quay, 100 m long, is situated on the N side of the harbour entrance and is used for the discharge of sea dredged aggregates.

Port services
9.75

1   **Repairs**: minor repairs; divers.

Other facilities: helicopter landing site close NE of North Quay; hospital at Morecambe.

Supplies: fresh water at all berths except West Quay; fuel oil by road tanker only; provisions.

Barrow-in-Furness

Chart 3164
General information
9.76

1   **Position.** Barrow-in-Furness (54°06′N 3°13′W), referred to hereafter as Barrow, is situated on the NW side of Morecambe Bay. The port and its inner approaches are protected from seaward by the low-lying Isle of Walney. It is the only port between Liverpool and the river Clyde (see *West Coast of Scotland Pilot*) which can accommodate vessels with a draught of up to approximately 10 m, having one of the greatest tidal ranges in the United Kingdom.

2   **Function.** The port specialises in the handling of the products of high technology, including nuclear fuel and gas condensates. Purpose built berths for both these activities are situated in Ramsden Dock (9.95).

In addition to these specialised functions, there is a considerable trade in bulk aggregates, paper pulp and traffic servicing offshore developments.

A large section of the port is devoted to shipbuilding, principally the BAE SYSTEMS shipyard at Devonshire Dock (9.95).

Barrow-in-Furness from SSE (9.76)
(Original dated 2001)

(Photograph - Air Images)

Barrow – Ramsden Dock Basin and Ramsden Lock from SSW (9.77)
(Original dated 2001)

(Photograph - Air Images)

3 **Harbour limits** (Charts 1320, 3164) extend from Lightning Knoll Light Buoy (54°00′N 3°14′W) to Scarth Channel (54°09′N 3°15′W) and include Piel and Walney Channels.

Approach and entry. Barrow is approached from the SW, passing SE of Barrow Wind Farm (9.34), and entered through a narrow channel, indicated by leading lights and marked by light buoys.

4 The docks are entered from Walney Channel through Ramsden Dock Basin and a lock system.

Traffic. In 2007 the port was used by 205 vessels.

Port Authority. Associated British Ports, Port Office, Ramsden Dock Road, Barrow-in-Furness, Cumbria LA14 2TW.

The port is represented by a Port Manager, a Port Operations Manager and a Harbour Master.

Limiting conditions
9.77

1 **Controlling depths.** Depths in the channel between Lightning Knoll and Deep Water Berth are constantly changing; dredging takes place at intervals. The Port Authority should be consulted for the latest information on depths, which may be less than charted, prior to entering the channel.

2 **Tidal levels:** see *Admiralty Tide Tables*. At Ramsden Dock Basin entrance mean spring range about 8·2 m; mean neap range about 4·3 m. At Halfway Shoal mean spring range about 7·9 m; mean neap range about 4·1 m.

Tidal height information is available from the Harbour Master's Office through Barrow Port Control.

3 **Density of water.** Buccleuch Dock, 1·013; Walney Channel, 1.022. However, the density in the enclosed docks varies with the amount of fresh water inflow from Cavendish Dock compared with the inflow from Walney Channel on spring tides; Walney Channel has minimal fresh water streams feeding it and is therefore predominantly salt water.

4 **Maximum size of vessel handled.** Vessels of up to 230 m LOA, 35 m beam and 10 m draught can be accommodated in Ramsden Dock Basin. Vessels of up to 200 m LOA, 29 m beam and 8 m draught can be accommodated in Ramsden Dock. Vessels in excess of these dimensions may be able to enter Ramsden Dock; prior consultation with the Harbour Master is required.

5 **Winds.** Strong winds from between N and E can reduce the height of tide in Walney Channel; winds from SW and W can have the opposite effect. The most dangerous winds that can be experienced are those from W which raise a considerable sea in the outer channel.

Lock. Ramsden Lock, which lies at the inner end of Ramsden Dock Basin, gives access to Ramsden Dock. The lock is 213·4 m long and from 28·8 to 30·4 m wide.

6 Ramsden Dock Basin entrance gate (9.95) is normally open from about 2½ hours before HW to HW, and up to 1 hour after HW by arrangement. The outer gates of Ramsden Lock can be open at the same time as the entrance gate into Ramsden Dock Basin. Only under exceptional circumstances at MHWS is Ramsden Dock directly open to the Walney Channel.

Arrival information
9.78

1 **Port operations.** A compulsory reporting system is in operation for all vessels over 20 m LOA, vessels carrying 12 or more passengers or vessels carrying dangerous cargo. Such vessels should report to Barrow Port Control when abeam Haws Point (9.86), both in-bound and out-bound. A Port Operation and Information Service is located at the pierhead of Ramsden Dock Basin, call sign : Barrow Port Control. For further details see *Admiralty List of Radio Signals Volume 6(1)*.

2 **Outer anchorage** is available SW of the Isle of Walney Light (9.40) to seaward of Barrow Wind Farm (9.34) and clear of the submarine cables shown on the chart. The holding is poor in strong winds. In adverse weather conditions from W, shelter may be obtained in Ramsey Bay (10.214) or, for vessels of suitable size, in Lancaster Sound (53°58′·8N 3°03′·0W).

3 **Prohibited anchorages.** Anchoring is prohibited in an area of the Walney Channel, between 1 mile and 1¾ miles downstream from Ramsden Dock gate, where it is crossed by submarine gas pipelines and a power cable see 9.79, and also in Piel Channel off the lifeboat slipway on the S point of Roa Island (54°4′·5N 3°10′·5W).

9.79

1 **Submarine cables and pipelines.** Three gas pipelines and a power cable cross the Walney Channel between 1 and 1½ miles SE of Ramsden Dock Entrance. The directions of run of the pipelines and cable are indicated by pairs of light beacons standing on the drying banks on the NE side of the channel.

2 Submarine power cables cross the channel close and ¾ cable N of Jubilee Bridge (1 mile NW of Ramsden Dock entrance) and another submarine power cable and telephone lines cross the channel 6 cables N of the bridge at North Scale. Each shore end of the cables is marked by a beacon. A submarine cable crosses the E end of Devonshire Dock. A submarine cable and gas pipeline cross the E end of Buccleuch Dock.

9.80

1 **Pilotage** is compulsory, available day or night, for vessels 50 m or greater LOA, all vessels carrying dangerous substances or more than 12 passengers, when navigating within the limits of Barrow Harbour and its approaches.

Vessels should forward their ETA at the pilot boarding position, either direct or through their local agent, to the Harbour Master via Barrow Port Control at least 24 hours in advance, 36 hours if due to arrive during a weekend or public holiday. If necessary, later corrections to ETA should be given direct to Barrow Port Control.

2 Vessels with an ETA between 1600 on Friday and 0745 the following Monday (or Tuesday on Bank Holiday weekends) must give at least 36 hours notice of ETA to ensure the availability of a pilot.

The pilot boarding position is situated close W of Lightning Knoll Light Buoy (54°00′N 3°14′W); the pilot, who also covers the in-dock berthing, boards approximately 2 hours before HW at Ramsden Dock entrance.

3 Vessels awaiting a pilot should keep S of the boarding position in at least 10 m of water and E/SE of Barrow Wind Farm (9.34).

The pilot boat, black hull with white superstructure with the words Harbour Master written on each side, is equipped with radio.

Tugs. Small tugs and work boats are normally available. Larger tugs can be obtained from Liverpool with adequate advance notice.

Speed limit within the port is 8 kt.
9.81

1 **Regulations concerning entry.** Special bye-laws are in force for vessels carrying dangerous substances; signals required to be shown by such vessels in or near the port are given at 9.97.

2 Vessels arriving before tide time are prohibited from anchoring off Ramsden Dock entrance, or from going alongside the pierhead before the gates are open, without permission from Barrow Port control. The lead-in jetty N of the entrance may be used in adverse weather to assist entry.

Before entering the dredged channel vessels should contact Barrow Port Control for instructions.

Harbour
9.82
1 **General layout.** Much of the water area in and around the S and main approach to the harbour, through which the deep water approach channel runs, is encumbered by extensive drying sandbanks and sandflats which dry in places of which Mort Bank and Mort Flat, occupying the NW part of Morecambe Bay, border the SE side of the outer section of the deep water channel.

2 The docks, situated in the N part of the harbour are built on and around Barrow Island and are entered through Ramsden Dock Basin (9.95) from Walney Channel, the inner section of the deep-water channel, which is prone to silting.

The main shipbuilding area lies on the NW side of Barrow Island.

3 The SW side of the harbour is enclosed by the Isle of Walney (54°05′N 3°14′W); on the E side lie several small islands of which Roa Island, which lies 2 miles SE of the docks, and Foulney Island (54°04′N 3°09′W) are joined to the mainland by narrow causeways.

Piel Island (9.86) lies 4 cables S of Roa Island, and is separated from it by Piel Channel.

Piel Harbour (54°04′N 3°10′W) lies between Piel, Roa and Foulney Islands.

4 Walney Channel continues N above the entrance to the docks through Jubilee Bridge as far as Walney Meetings (54°08′N 3°15′W) where it meets the waters of Scarth Channel (9.126) at the N entrance to the harbour (Chart 1320).

9.83
1 **Dredging** between Lightning Knoll and Ramsden Dock Basin entrance takes place at intervals. Dredger moorings may be laid near the latter position; in other areas trailer suction dredgers will operate.

9.84
1 **Traffic signals.** International Port Traffic Signals Numbers 2 and 5 are exhibited from a mast, 15 m in height, on the S pierhead of Ramsden Dock entrance.

For detials of traffic signals see *The Mariner's Handbook.*

9.85
1 **Tidal streams.** In Walney Channel, the tidal water flows in from both ends of the channel, meeting at Walney Meetings (9.82), N of Barrow Island. Tidal streams in the channel continue to flow N for a period after HW.

For details of tidal streams near Lightning Knoll see information on the chart.

Between Lightning Knoll and the Bar, the in-going and out-going streams set across the leading line of the channel.

2 Near Bar Light Buoy the stream sets generally in the direction of the channel; see information on the chart.

Between Bar Light Buoy and Piel Harbour it has been reported that the tidal streams are at least 30% stronger than those between Outer Bar and Lightning Knoll Light Buoys.

In Piel Harbour the tidal streams set towards the NW side of the harbour at the bend of the channel; for details see information on the chart. The NW-going stream turns at HW.

3 Off East Elbow Light Beacon, 6 cables SSE of the dock basin, the stream attains maximum rates of 2½ kn at springs; the N-going stream continues for ½ hour after HW.

Off Ramsden Dock Basin entrance the N-going stream continues for 1½ hours after HW, and attains a maximum rate of 1½ kn at springs.

4 North of Jubilee Bridge, the N-going stream continues for nearly 2 hours after HW; approximately ¾ hour before HW there is a comparative "slack" in the tide which lasts for ½ hour, after which the stream continues N and attains its maximum rate ½ hour after HW gradually decreasing until it turns S.

Strong SW and W gales increase the duration and rate of the NW-going stream in Walney Channel and reduce the SE-going stream; strong N and E winds have the opposite effect.

Directions for entering harbour
(continued from 9.45)
9.86
1 **Landmarks:**
>Isle of Walney Lighthouse (54°02′·9N 3°10′·6W) (9.40), which stands at the SE end of the Isle of Walney.
>
>Flagstaff (54°02′·9N 3°11′·9W) near Hilpsford Point, the S extremity of the Isle of Walney.
>
>Hare Hill Beacon (orange, triangular in shape) (1 mile NW of Hilpsford Point).

2 >Castle (ruins) (54°03′·8N 3°10′·4W) situated at the S point of Piel Island.
>
>Saint Michael's Church (tower) (54°05′·8N 3°09′·9W).

Outer Channel Leading Lights on Foulney Twist. From the pilot boarding area off Lightning Knoll Light Buoy (safe water) (54°00′N 3°14′W), the alignment (040¾°) of the leading lights on Foulney Twist leads 3¾ miles through the buoyed outer channel:

3 >Front Light, (black rectangular topmark on pile) (54°03′·2N 3°09′·2W).
>
>Rear Light, (similar structure) (6 cables NE from front light), situated on Foulney Twist, drying rocky ground.

Rear   Front

Outer Channel Leading Light-beacons (9.86.1)
(Original dated 1996; verified 1999)

(Photograph - Associated British Ports, Barrow)

4 The track passes (with positions from South East Point (54°02′·8N 3°10′·4W)):

Between Lightning Knoll Light Buoy and SEA 1 Light Buoy (starboard hand), 1½ cables SE, thence:

5 Between Halfway Shoal Light Beacon (red and yellow chequered rectangular daymark on framework beacon) (1½ miles SW) and SEA 5 Light Buoy (starboard hand) moored 1½ cables SE, thence:

Isle of Walney Light

Halfway Shoal Light-beacon (9.86.2)
(Original dated 1996; verified 1999)

(Photograph - Associated British Ports, Barrow)

Between Bar Light Buoy (port hand) (3 cables S) and SEA 9 Light Buoy (starboard hand), 1½ cables SE, thence the track alters to a more N heading on the alignment of Inner Channel Leading Lights.

6 **Caution.** On in-going tides, vessels inward bound should be prepared to give port helm before approaching Bar Light Buoy, so as not to overshoot the mark of the Inner Channel leading lights in line and, similarly on approaching Piel West Light Buoy and rounding on the line of Walney Channel leading lights; on out-going tides vessels should be aware of a possible opposite effect at these points.

7 **Inner Channel Leading Lights on Rampside Sands.** The alignment (005°) of the leading lights leads through the buoyed Inner Channel:

Front Light, (white round GRP tower) (54°04'·4N 3°09'·8W).

Rear Light, (red brick column, white face) (7¾ cables N of the front light).

Rear

Front   *Piel East Light-buoy*

Inner Channel Leading Light-beacons (9.86.3)
(Original dated 1996; verified 1999)

(Photograph - Associated British Ports, Barrow)

The track passes (with positions from Isle of Walney Light (54°03'N 3°11'W)):

8 E of South East Point (1¾ cables ESE), with the ruins of a groyne extending S from the shore, thence:

E of the Isle of Walney Light (9.40), thence:

Between Haws Point West Light Beacon (white rectangular daymark, black band, on piled beacon) (3¼ cables ENE) and Haws Point East Light Beacon (similar structure), 1 cable E, standing at the W edge of Seldom Seen, a bank of boulders, thence:

9 E of Piel Island (9 cables N) on which stand the ruins of a castle (see above).

From here the track alters WNW onto the alignment of Walney Channel Leading Lights, passing:

Between Piel East Light Buoy (starboard hand) and Piel West Light Buoy (port hand), moored on the E side of Barnet Scar, a drying bank lying 1¾ cables ENE of Piel Island.

9.87

1 **Walney Channel Leading Lights (Nos 5 and 6) on Biggar Sands.** The alignment (297½°) of the leading lights leads for 1¾ miles through the buoyed Piel and Walney Channels:

Front Light, (white triangular daymark, apex down, on black pile) (54°05'·2N 3°13'·6W).

Rear Light, (white triangular daymark, apex up, on black pile) (5¾ cables from front light).

Rear
Front

West Elbow Light-buoy

Walney Channel Leading Light-beacons (9.87)
(Original dated 1996; verified 1999)

(Photograph - Associated British Ports, Barrow)

The track passes (with positions from Ridge Point, Piel Island (54°04'·0N 3°10'·4W)):

2 NNE of Piel Ridge, a drying bank which extends N from Piel Island and is marked by Ridge Light Buoy (port hand) (1½ cables NNE); Roa Light Buoy (starboard hand) lies 1 cable NNE, thence:

SSW of Roa Island (4 cables N), on which there is a jetty and lifeboat slip, thence:

3 Between Pickle Scar Light Beacon (red and yellow chequered rectangular topmark) (6½ cables NW) and Head Scar Light Beacon (white rectangular topmark, black band), 1 cable NNE, thence:

NNE of Long Rein Point (1¾ miles WNW), protruding E from the Isle of Walney. The track now alters to a more NW heading with the alignment of Ramsdan Dock Entrance Leading Lights on Snab Sands astern.

9.88

1   **Ramsden Dock Entrance Leading Lights on Snab Sands.** The alignment (143¼°), astern, of the leading lights leads for about 4¾ cables to a position about 2½ cables S of the entrance to Ramsden Dock Basin and 5 cables SSE of Deep Water Berth.

    Front Light, (red triangular topmark, apex up) (54°04′·6N 3°12′·5W).

    Rear Light, (red triangular topmark, apex down) (3 cables from front light).

2   The track passes (with positions from Ramsden Dock Basin entrance):

    Between East Elbow Light Beacon (white rectangular topmark, black band) (6 cables SSE) and West Elbow Light Buoy (port hand), thence:

    NE of No 10 Light Buoy (port hand) (5 cables S), thence:

    Between West Pile Light Beacon (white topmark) (3½ cables S) and East Pile Light Beacon (white rectangular topmark, black band).

Rear

Front

Walney Channel Leading Light-beacons (9.88)
(Original dated 1996; verified 1999)

(Photograph - Associated British Ports, Barrow)

9.89

1   **Leading lights at Ramsden Dock Basin.** Vessels entering Ramsden Dock Basin approach the dock gate on the alignment (031¼°) of the leading lights at the NE corner of the basin:

    Front light (orange triangular topmark, apex down) (54°05′·8N 3°13′·3W). Also fitted with a Moiré pattern indicator, activated on request to assist berthing.

    Rear light (orange triangular daymark, apex up) (65 m from front light).

Directions for leaving harbour
9.90

1   **Piel Channel Leading Lights on Foulney Twist.** When leaving harbour via the Walney Channel the directions for entry are followed in reverse to a position NNE of Long Rein Point (54°04′·8N 3°13′·2W), thence the alignment (117½°) of the leading lights on Foulney Twist lead through the Walney and Piel Channels.

    Front light, (black rectangular topmark on framework tower) (54°03′·8N 3°09′·0W).

2   Rear light, (black rectangular topmark on pile) (2¾ cables from front light).

Ramsden Dock Basin Leading Lights (9.89)
(Original dated 1996; verified 1999)

(Photograph - Associated British Ports, Barrow)

At a position NNE of Ridge Point, the N point of Piel Island, the directions rejoin the reverse of those for entry.

Useful marks
9.91

1   Chimney (elevation 67 m) (54°06′·3N 3°11′·4W) standing at Roosecote Power Station.

    Chimneys (54°05′·5N 3°11′·1W) standing at the Centrica HRL Gas Terminal at Westfield Point.

Upper reaches of the Walney Channel
9.92

1   **Local knowledge** is required for the upper reaches of the Walney Channel, which are suitable only for small craft at HW. Vessels must negotiate the opening span of Jubilee Bridge.

    Jubilee Bridge, a double bascule bridge which connects the Isle of Walney with Barrow Island near the BAE SYSTEMS shipyard, is marked by port and starboard fixed lights on both N and S sides.

2   The bridge is closed to vessels from November to April inclusive. During the period from the beginning of May until the end of October the bridge may, as a general rule, be opened during the period HW ± 2 hours. There is a vertical clearance of 8·0 m commensurate with a tide height of 6·8 m

3   **Traffic signals.** During the period when the bridge is manned the following fixed light signals are shown by day and night from the E side of the channel above the level of the roadway.

Signal	*Meaning*
	Bridge is closed.
	Bridge is open.

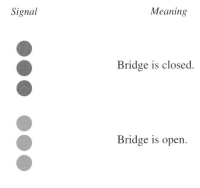

Jubilee Bridge - traffic signals (9.92)

Basins and berths

9.93

1 **Anchorage.** Piel Harbour (54°04′N 3°10′W) which lies between Piel, Roa and Foulney Islands provides temporary anchorage for small vessels, except at MLWS; anchored vessels should not obstruct the fairway or lifeboat slipway on Roa Island.

9.94

1 **Tidal berths.** There are two tidal berths on the E side of Walney Channel, N of Ramsden Dock Basin entrance.

Belfast Quay, 183 m long, is available for cargo operations over the HW period but is not suitable at LW when vessels would take the ground. The berth is mainly used by offshore wind farm support craft.

2 **Deep Water Berth,** 259 m long and 30·5 m wide, is used by BAE SYSTEMS Marine Ltd. Lights are exhibited from a platform at the SE end of the berth.

For the latest alongside depth information, the Port Authority should be consulted.

9.95

1 **Barrow Docks** consist of three principal enclosed basins, Ramsden Dock, Buccleuch Dock and Devonshire Dock, which are interconnected and provide a continuous waterway; the depth in the fairway varies between 8·5 to 9·1 m. Depths at individual berths vary; the port authority should be consulted.

2 **Ramsden Dock Basin,** with a lead-in jetty extending from the NW side of the entrance, is entered from Walney Channel though a gate 36·5 m wide with a depth of 3·0 m plus the height of tide over the sill at MHWS. Vessels of up to 10·0 m draught can lie within the basin alongside pile fendering on the S side. Lights are exhibited from the E side of the entrance.

3 The gate at the entrance to the dock basin is a single flap gate, which is hinged at the bottom and is opened by lowering it inwards on to the dock bottom. It is essential that no vessel attempts to pass in or out of the dock until given the appropriate signal (9.84) and via VHF.

Ramsden Dock, with depths of from 7 to 9·1 m, is entered from Ramsden Dock Basin through Ramsden Lock (9.77). The SE side of the dock is used by International Nuclear Services at their twin berth marine terminal. There is a gas tanker loading jetty and condensate tank farm on the N side of the dock.

4 **Anchor Line Basin** at the W end of Ramsden Dock has four berths; the longest is 275 m long and can accommodate vessels up to 7·0 m draught with RoRo facilities.

Buccleuch Dock entered from Ramsden Dock through a narrow passage 50 m wide with a depth of 9·1 m. There are depths alongside from 4 to 9·1 m. The fitting out berth of BAE SYSTEMS lies on the S side of the dock.

5 **Devonshire Dock** is entered from Buccleuch Dock through a passage 24·1 m wide with a depth over the sill of between 8·5 to 8·9 m; this passage is spanned by a lifting road bridge.

The BAE SYSTEMS shipyard with its large construction hall stands on reclaimed land which was formerly the W part of the dock.

6 **Cavendish Dock,** adjacent to the NE side of Ramsden Dock, has never been completed and is not in use for shipping.

Moorings, which dry, lie off Roa Island where there is a slipway and landing place. Small craft can lie afloat at moorings outside the navigable channel, off the E side of Piel Island where there is also access to a landing place.

7 Moorings, which mostly dry, lie N of Jubilee Bridge. There is a slipway close N of the bridge.

Caution. Training walls, which cover, as shown on the chart, lie outside the buoyed section of Walney Channel; those on the NE side vary in height from 8·2 to 5·2 m above chart datum, and those on the SW side from 5·2 to 3·7 m.

Port services

9.96

1 **Repairs** of all kinds can be carried out; divers; shiplift 161·8 m long and 21·7 m wide, nominal capacity of 16 200 tonnes, not normally used for commercial purposes.

Other facilities: hospital; reception of oily waste, noxious and harmful substances.

Supplies: marine diesel by road tanker; fresh water at most berths; provisions.

9.97

1 **Harbour regulations.** Bye-laws are in force and masters of vessels should make themselves acquainted with them immediately on arrival; copies may be obtained from the Harbour Master.

Vessels shall be moored in any place that the Harbour Master may direct, and shall not shift berth without permission.

Charts 1552, 2010

Morecambe

9.98

1 **General information.** Morecambe (54°04′N 2°52′W), a large coastal town, occupies nearly 4 miles of coastline NE of Heysham Harbour.

The harbour, which dries, is used only by inshore fishing boats and pleasure craft which can take the ground. It is protected from SW by Stone Pier, which extends 1¼ cables NW from the coast abreast the centre of the town. A light is exhibited from the pierhead.

2 **Outfall.** A metal dolphin from which a light is exhibited, marks the seaward end of a sewer outfall which extends 6½ cables NW from the shore 4 cables SSW of Stone Pier.

Tidal streams in Grange Channel (54°02′N 3°00′), between the drying banks of Yeoman Spit and Clark Wharf Spit, run in approximately the direction of the channel with a spring rate in each direction of 3 kn. For times at which they begin see information on the charts.

3 Off Morecambe the streams run in about the direction of the channel when the banks are dry but across the banks when they are covered.

Depths in the area are constantly changing.

Directions. Local knowledge is essential. The approach to Morecambe lies through Grange Channel, thence Kent Channel. Visiting craft must have clear weather and suitable state of tide to reach the harbour.

4 The alignment (090°) of lights (green masts) near the root of Stone Pier leads N of the outfall.

The channel N of Morecambe disappears amongst Lancaster Sands and other sands which encumber Morecambe Bay.

Facilities. There are no facilities other than landing stages and slips for use by small craft.

MORECAMBE BAY TO SAINT BEES HEAD

GENERAL INFORMATION

Chart 1826
Area covered
9.99

1   In this section are described the routes, harbours and anchorages between the Isle of Walney (54°05′N 3°15′W) and Saint Bees Head, 29 miles NNW.

    The description includes an offshore route between Morecambe Bay and King William Banks (54°27′N 4°06′W) off the NE coast of the Isle of Man.

2   It is arranged as follows:
        Offshore Route (9.104).
        Coastal Route — Isle of Walney to Saint Bees Head (9.111).

Topography
9.100

1   See 9.3.

Marine exploitation
9.101

1   See 9.4.

Submarine cable
9.102

1   A submarine cable is laid between the E side of the Isle of Man and a point on the coast 2 miles N of Haverigg Point (54°11′N 3°19′W).

Nature reserves
9.103

1   Hodbarrow (54°13′N 3°16′W).
        Drigg Dunes (54°21′N 3°26′W).
        Saint Bees (54°30′N 3°36′W), bird reserve.
    For further information see Protection of wildlife 1.58.

OFFSHORE ROUTE

General information

Charts 1320, 1346
Route
9.104

1   The offshore route runs NNW for about 34 miles from the vicinity of Morecambe Light Buoy (53°52′N 3°24′W) to a position SW of Saint Bees Head (54°31′N 3°38′W) (9.117), passing ENE of South Morecambe, North Morecambe and Millom Gas Fields (9.4).

Marine exploitation
9.105

1   For details of South Morecambe, North Morecambe and Millom Gas Field see 9.4.

Rescue
9.106

1   An all-weather lifeboat is stationed at Barrow-in-Furness (54°04′N 3°10′W).

    For details of rescue organisation see 1.60.

Tidal streams
9.107

1   Tidal streams are given on the charts and in *Admiralty Tidal Stream Atlas — Irish Sea and Bristol Channel.*

Directions
(continued from 9.24)

Principal marks
9.108

1   **Landmarks:**
        Blackpool Tower (53°49′N 3°03′W) (9.20) (Chart 1826).
        Black Combe (54°15′N 3°20′W) (9.117).
        Saint Bees Head Lighthouse (white round tower, 17 m in height) (54°31′N 3°38′W) standing on Saint Bees Head (9.117), prominent.

2   **Major lights:**
        Isle of Walney Light (54°03′N 3°11′W) (9.40).
        Saint Bees Head Light — as above.
        Maughold Head Light (54°18′N 4°18′W) (10.204).

Other aids to navigation
9.109

1   See 9.21.

Directions
9.110

1   From a position W of Morecambe Light Buoy (53°52′N 3°24′W) to a position SW of Saint Bees Head (54°31′N 3°38′W), the route leads NNW, passing:
        Clear of a well head (53°52·5N 3°28·1W), with a depth of 12·3 m over it and marked by a light buoy (special), thence:

2   ENE of Calder and South Morecambe Gas Fields (53°51′N 3°35′W) (9.4).
        WSW of Barrow Wind Farm (54°00′N 3°18′W) (9.34), thence:
        WSW of the Isle of Walney (54°05′N 3°14′W), on which stands a light (9.40), and:

3   ENE of North Morecambe Gas Field (53°58′N 3°40′W) (9.4), thence:
        ENE of Million Gas Field (54°02′N 3°52′W) (9.4), thence:
        WSW of Selker Point (54°17′N 3°25′W) (9.119), thence:

    (Directions continue for the offshore route NE of the Isle of Man at 10.18)

COASTAL ROUTE — ISLE OF WALNEY TO SAINT BEES HEAD

General information

Charts 1320, 1346
Route
9.111

1   The coastal route from a position W of Morecambe Light Buoy (53°52′N 3°24′W) to a position W of Saint Bees Head (54°31′N 3°38′W) leads approximately 40 miles NNW.

Topography
9.112

1   Much of the foreshore between Selker Point (54°17′N 3°25′W) and Saint Bees Head, 15 miles NNE, consists of sand and stone, and dries out 5 cables in places. Several rocky scars and out-lying drying rocks extend SW from the shore throughout this stretch of coast. See also 9.3.

Marine exploitation
9.113

1   See 9.105.

Saint Bees Head and Lighthouse from SW (9.108)
(Original dated 2001)

(Photograph - Air Images)

Firing practice area
9.114

1   Eskmeals Range (54°19′N 3°24′W); see information on the chart.

For further information on practice areas, see 1.15.

Rescue
9.115

1   An all-weather lifeboat is stationed at Barrow-in-Furness (54°04′N 3°10′W); inshore lifeboats are stationed at Barrow-in-Furness and at Saint Bees Head (54°31′N 3°38′W), where the lifeboat station is situated on the SE side of South Head.

For details of rescue organisation see 1.60.

Tidal streams
9.116

1   The streams off the coast between the Isle of Walney and Saint Bees Head are weak and rather uncertain. Near the land they set in approximately the direction of the coast.

Tidal streams are given on the charts and in *Admiralty Tidal Stream Atlas — Irish Sea and Bristol Channel.*

Directions
(continued from 9.24)

Principal marks
9.117

1   **Landmarks:**
Isle of Walney Lighthouse (54°03′N 3°11′W) (9.40).
Black Combe (54°15′N 3°20′W). The dark coloured hill with a smooth domed summit is a prominent mark.

Radio tower, conspicuous (metal framework; elevation 60 m) (54°18′·5N 3°24′·9W), from which obstruction lights are exhibited.

2   Lattice Tower, conspicuous, (54°19′·4N 3°24′·8W). The tower is situated within Eskmeals Firing Range (9.130).

Saint Bees Head (54°31′N 3°38′W) on which stands a light (9.108), is a perpendicular cliff of red sandstone having a flat summit, 95 m high.

Major lights:
Isle of Walney Light (54°03′N 3°11′W) (9.40).
Saint Bees Head Light (54°31′N 3°38′W) (9.108).

Other aids to navigation
9.118

1   See 9.21.

Morecambe Light Buoy to Saint Bees Head
9.119

1   From a position W of Morecambe Light Buoy (53°52′N 3°24′W) to a position W of Saint Bees Head (54°31′N 3°38′W), the route leads approximately 40 miles NNW, passing:

Clear of a well head (53°52′·5N 3°28′·1W), with a depth of 12·3 m over it and marked by a light buoy (special), thence:

ENE of the gas fields lying about 16 miles WSW of the Isle of Walney (54°05′N 3°15′W), and:

2   WSW of Barrow Wind Farm (54°00′N 3°18′W) (9.34), thence:

WSW of a dangerous wreck, the position of which is approximate, lying 1¾ cables W of Cockspec (54°06′N 3°18′W), rocky ground with detached seaweed-covered drying patches close SW and

1 mile SE extending 1¼ miles from the coast abreast Vickerstown (54°06′N 3°15′W), the highest part of the Isle of Walney, thence:

3 WSW of Haverigg Point (54°11′N 3°19′W) (9.121), thence:

WSW of Black Leg Rock (54°14′·5N 3°24′·7W) lying 1 mile off the coast. A patch with a depth of 4·3 m over it lies 5½ cables WNW of the rock. Thence:

4 WSW of Selker Light Buoy (starboard hand), moored 2½ miles WSW of Selker Point (54°17′N 3°25′W), marking Selker Rocks which dry, and detached rocky patches close W and S. The visible wreck of a fishing vessel (mast 1·4 m above chart datum) lies close SE of the rocks. Thence:

WSW of the entrance to Ravenglass Harbour (54°21′N 3°25′W) (9.127), thence:

WSW of Drigg Rock (54°20′·9N 3°28′·5W) (9.129), thence:

5 WSW of a buoy (starboard hand) marking the head of an outfall extending SW from Seascale village (54°24′N 3°29′W), thence:

WSW of a light buoy (W cardinal), marking a wreck with a swept depth of 8·3 m (54°24′·6N 3°33′·6W); two buoys (starboard hand), marking the head of an outfall extending SW from Sellafield Power Station, lie close SE; thence:

6 WSW of South Head, the S point of the promontory forming Saint Bees Head.

Clearing bearing 340° or greater of Saint Bees Head Light (9.108) clears W of the coastal dangers N of Haverigg Point. These dangers lie in the obscured sector of the light.

Useful marks
9.120
1 Offshore platform (53°57′·6N 3°40′·3W).
Hare Hill Beacon (54°03′·4N 3°13′·1W) (9.86).
Bootle Church (tower) (54°17′N 3°22′W).
Tide gauge (black and white stripes, radar reflector) (54°18′·3N 3°25′·6W).
Barn Scar Beacon (black, conical topmark) (54°22′·4N 3°28′·4W) standing on Barn Scar.

(Directions continue for Solway Firth at 10.35)

River Duddon estuary

Chart 1320
General information
9.121
1 The river Duddon flows through a wide estuary into the sea between the N end of the Isle of Walney and Haverigg Point (54°11′N 3°19′W), a low-lying point of land composed of sand dunes, 3 miles NW, emerging through Duddon Channel. A group of wind turbines stands 1 mile N of Haverigg Point.

2 Hodbarrow Point (54°11′N 3°15′W) is fronted by a sea wall which extends 1 mile W. The wall protects a red haematic iron ore mine which has workings under the seabed. The sea breaks over the wall in strong SW winds.

The estuary, which is encumbered by Duddon Sands extending 2 miles seaward of the line forming the entrance points, consists of low-lying ground on either side, much of it marshland, backed by higher ground.

9.122
1 **Submarine cable** crosses the river Duddon estuary from a position 8 cables NE of Hodbarrow Point in a SE direction to the opposite shore. The landing places of the cable are each marked by a beacon (special).
9.123
1 **Tidal streams** in the river Duddon estuary begin as follows:

Interval from HW Liverpool	Direction
−0610	In-going
−0015	Out-going

9.124
1 **Local knowledge.** Duddon Channel, which is subject to frequent changes, should not be attempted without local knowledge.

In the S approach to Duddon Bar (54°09′N 3°20′W) rocky ground and drying patches (9.119) lie in the obscured section of the Isle of Walney Light.

Foul ground extends for approximately 1 mile off the W coast of the Isle of Walney.

Millom
9.125
1 Millom (54°13′N 3°16′W), a small port, is situated on the W shore of the river Duddon estuary, 1 mile N of Hodbarrow Point. Hodbarrow Lagoon, close W of Hodbarrow Point, is a Site of Special Scientific Interest.

There is a ship-breaking operation at the port; vessels of up to 4·2 m draught can reach the breaking site alongside a pier on HW.

Scarth Channel
9.126
1 Scarth Channel, with depths of approximately 4·3 m at MHWS, leads E from the bar of the river Duddon (9.124) round the N end of the Isle of Walney to Barrow and is only used by shallow draught vessels over the HW period with local knowledge.

Chart 1346
Ravenglass Harbour
9.127
1 Ravenglass Harbour (54°21′N 3°25′W), is formed by the drying estuary of the rivers Esk, Mite and Irt.

The harbour dries completely for 3 hours either side of LW. Vessels up to 3·4 m draught can enter on HW.

The entrance is not easily distinguishable but may be identified by a concrete blockhouse, from which a light is exhibited, and leading marks (9.129) standing on the S side.

2 A nature reserve and gullery exists on the dunes at Drigg Point (54°21′N 3°26′W), the N entrance point of the harbour; see 1.58.

Eskmeals Viaduct spans the river Esk 8 cables within its entrance and a bridge spans the river Mite close NW of Ravenglass Village.

The village is the site of an historic Roman fort.
9.128
1 **Tidal streams** begin at the same time as those in the river Duddon estuary (9.121).

Maximum in-going spring rate from 4 to 6 kn.
9.129
1 **Directions.** Vessels should keep at least 2 miles offshore until the harbour entrance has been identified.

Drigg Rock, awash, but steep-to on its W side, lies in the approaches to the entrance, 1½ miles W of Drigg Point.

Leading marks:

Front mark (pyramid of white painted blocks) close S of concrete blockhouse.

Rear mark (white cone).

2   Vessels should approach on the line of the leading marks until 2 or 3 cables from the front mark. The channel then follows a winding course close to the S shore, but is unmarked and should not be entered without careful reference to the chart, or local knowledge.

Entrance should only be made at or near HW. On spring tides there are depths of 5·5 m in the entrance channel and as far as Ravenglass there are depths of approximately 4·9 m.

3   **Useful marks:**

Concrete blockhouse (white shutters) (54°20′N 3°25′W).

Lattice tower (54°19′·4N 3°24′·8W) (9.117).

Radio tower (54°18′·5N 3°24′·9W) (9.117).

Tide Gauge (54°18′·3N 3°25′·6W) (9.120).

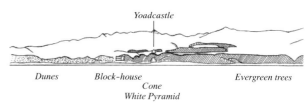

Yoadcastle

Dunes   *Block-house*   *Evergreen trees*
Cone
White Pyramid

Ravenglass Leading Marks (9.129)
(Original dated 1996)

(Drawing - Ravenglass Boating Association)

9.130

1   **Caution.** Eskmeals Firing Range covers the approaches to Ravenglass. Craft intending to enter Ravenglass should contact the Operations Room, who keep a listening watch on VHF when the range is in use, before approaching the channel. For further details see 1.15 and *Admiralty List of Radio Signals Volume 6(1)*.

NOTES

Chapter 10 - Solway Firth, South Coast of Scotland and Isle of Man

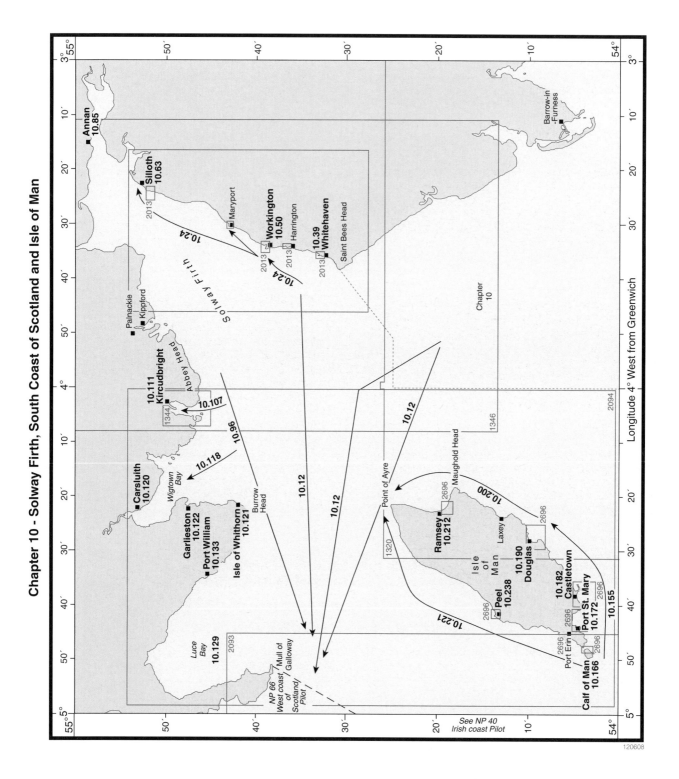

CHAPTER 10

SOLWAY FIRTH, SOUTH COAST OF SCOTLAND AND ISLE OF MAN

GENERAL INFORMATION

Chart 1826
Scope of the chapter
10.1

1   In this chapter are described the routes and passages between Saint Bees Head (54°31'N 3°38'W) and the Mull of Galloway (54°38'N 4°51'W).

Also described are the waters within the Solway Firth, Wigtown Bay and Luce Bay, and those around the Isle of Man, together with their ports and harbours.

2   The description includes offshore routes NE of the Isle of Man, see 10.20, the Solway Firth to the Mull of Galloway, see 10.22, and SW of the Isle of Man towards Liverpool Bay, see 10.154.

The chapter is divided into the following sections:
Saint Bees Head to the Mull of Galloway (10.8).
Isle of Man (10.137).

Topography
10.2

1   From Saint Bees Head to the Mull of Galloway the coast is deeply indented by the Solway Firth, Wigtown and Luce Bays. The entrances to all these bays are wide, and separated by bold headlands.

With the exception of the Solway Firth, the land within the coastline consists of high ground.

Mountains and hills occupy most of the surface of the Isle of Man, the highest point being Snaefell (10.18).

Exercise areas
10.3

1   **Submarine exercise areas.** Submarines frequently exercise both surfaced and dived in areas W of the Isle of Man and between the Isle of Man and the North Channel. A good lookout is to kept for them when passing through these waters. For further details on submarine exercises (Subfacts) see 1.14.

2   **Firing practice areas.** Kirkcudbright Range (54°47'N 4°00'W) and Luce Bay Bombing Range (54°44'N 4°46'W) (10.129), as shown on the chart. For further information on practice areas see 1.15.

Fishing
10.4

1   In July and August herring trawlers may be encountered in concentrations off the SW coast of the Isle of Man, and in August and September off the E and SE coasts of the island.

During the summer months strings of lobster pots may be encountered up to 2 miles off the coasts of the island, especially in the vicinity of Point of Ayre.

For details and types of fishing, and nets used, see *The Mariner's Handbook.*

High speed craft
10.5

1   High speed ferries operate between Liverpool and the Isle of Man and Belfast; between Liverpool and Dublin; and between Heysham and Belfast. See 1.8.

Tidal streams
10.6

1   The S-going stream from the North Channel divides W of the channel between the Isle of Man and the coast of Scotland and sets E through the channel and S between the Isle of Man and the Irish coast; the E-going branch again divides E of the channel and sets E to the Solway Firth and SE to Morecambe and Liverpool Bays. Similarly, the streams from Morecambe and Liverpool Bays and from the Solway Firth meet E of the channel; those from between the Isle of Man and the Irish coast meet them W of it.

2   The localities in which the streams separate and meet, especially the latter, may be indicated by eddies or ripples, or even tide-rips. See also 1.91.

Tidal streams are given on the chart and in *Admiralty Tidal Stream Atlas — Irish Sea and Bristol Channel.*

Rescue
10.7

1   For details of rescue organisation and locations of assets see 1.60 and text under Rescue.

SAINT BEES HEAD TO MULL OF GALLOWAY

GENERAL INFORMATION

Chart 1826
Area covered
10.8

1   In this section are described the offshore routes and coastal passages which lie between Saint Bees Head (54°31'N 3°38'W) and the Mull of Galloway, approximately 29 miles WNW, including the waters of the Solway Firth, together with the minor ports of Whitehaven, Workington and Silloth, and the coastal bays, harbours and anchorages situated on the S coast of Scotland between Abbey Head (54°46'N 3°58'W) and the Mull of Galloway.

2   It is arranged as follows:
Offshore Routes (10.12).
Solway Firth and Approaches (10.24).

Coastal Passage — Abbey Head to Mull of Galloway (10.96).

Topography
10.9

1   See 10.2.

Exercise areas
10.10

1   See 10.3.

Nature reserves
10.11

1   Caerlaverock (54°58'N 3°30'W) (Chart 1346).
The Scares (54°40'N 4°42'W), bird reserve.
Mull of Galloway (54°38'N 4°51'W), bird reserve.
For further information see Protection of wildlife (1.58).

OFFSHORE ROUTES

General information

Charts 1826, 2094, 1346
Routes
10.12

1 An offshore route from Morecambe Bay which passes NNW then WNW of King William Banks (54°27′N 4°08′W), lying off the NE coast of the Isle of Man, leads to a position SW of the Mull of Galloway (54°38′N 4°51′W).

2 From a position on the offshore route, SE of King William Banks, a clear weather route leads WNW to the vicinity of the Mull of Galloway, passing closer inshore to the Isle of Man and between the banks which lie off the NE tip of the island. The track between the banks has a minimum width of 2 miles with depths exceeding 20 m at its narrowest part.

For an offshore route which leads between the Solway Firth and the Mull of Galloway, see 10.22.

Topography
10.13

1 See 10.2.

Exercise areas
10.14

1 See 10.3.

Submarine pipeline
10.15

1 See 10.99.

Rescue
10.16

1 An all-weather lifeboat is stationed at Ramsey Harbour (54°19′N 4°23′W). For details of lifeboat see 1.73.

For details of all-weather lifeboat rescue services on the W coast of Scotland see *West of Scotland Pilot*; on the E coast of Ireland see *Irish Coast Pilot*.

For details of rescue organisation see 1.60.

Tidal streams and tide race
10.17

1 Between Point of Ayre and the Scottish mainland N tidal streams are given on the charts.

The tidal stream sets across Ballacash and King William Banks in both directions, but approximately in the direction of the channel between Ballacash and Bahama Banks.

See also *Admiralty Tidal Stream Atlas — Irish Sea and Bristol Channel*.

For details of a dangerous race off the Mull of Galloway, see 10.102.

Directions
(continued from 9.110)

Principal marks
10.18

1 **Landmarks:**
　　Saint Bees Head Lighthouse (54°31′N 3°38′W) (9.108).
　　Mull of Galloway Lighthouse (white round tower, 26 m in height) (54°38′N 4°51′W). The altitude of this light is such that it is frequently obscured by low cloud.

Mull of Galloway Lighthouse from SSE (10.18)
(Original dated 2001)

(Photograph - Air Images)

2 Snaefell (54°16′N 4°28′W), the highest point of the Isle of Man; on the summit, which is frequently covered by cloud, stands a lattice framework tower exhibiting obstruction lights. North Barrule, the prominent summit of the NE spur of Snaefell lies nearly 3 miles NE.

3 **Major lights:**
　　Saint Bees Head Light (54°31′N 3°38′W) (9.108).
　　Maughold Head Light (54°18′N 4°18′W) (10.204).
　　Point of Ayre Light (tall white tower, two red bands; 30 m in height) (54°25′N 4°22′W).
　　Mull of Galloway Light — as above.

Other aids to navigation
10.19

1 **Racons:**
　　Point of Ayre Lighthouse (54°25′N 4°22′W).
　　South Rock Light Float (54°24′·5N 5°21′·9W) (Chart 2093) (*Irish Coast Pilot*).
　　For further details see *Admiralty List of Radio Signals Volume 2*.

Outer route north-east of the Isle of Man
10.20

1 From a position approximately 8 miles SE of the E extremity of King William Banks (54°27′N 4°08′W), the continuation of the offshore route from Morecambe Bay leads NNW then WNW, keeping outside of the banks NE of the Isle of Man, to a position SW of the Mull of Galloway, a distance of about 44 miles, passing (with positions from Maughold Head Light (54°18′N 4°18′W) (10.204)):

2 WSW of Saint Bees Head (54°31′N 3°38′W) on which there is a prominent lighthouse (9.108), thence:
　　ENE and NNE of a light buoy (E cardinal) (54°26′N 4°00′W) moored at the E extremity of King William Banks, which extend over nearly 6 miles and are steep-to on their S side, thence:

3 NNE of King William Banks (11 miles NE) and Ballacash Bank (9 miles NNE) (10.21), thence:
　　NNE of Point of Ayre (54°25′N 4°22′W) (10.22), on which stands a prominent light (10.18), thence:
　　SSW of Burrow Head (54°41′N 4°24′W), thence:
　　SSW of the Mull of Galloway (54°38′N 4°51′W) on which stands a light (10.18), and from which a heavy race (10.102) extends S.

Inner route north-east of the Isle of Man
10.21

1 From a position 8 miles SE of the E extremity of King William Banks, a clear weather route for suitable vessels, through Ballacash Channel (54°25′N 5°15′W), leads approximately 42 miles WNW to a position SW of the Mull of Galloway, passing:

2

SSW of the light buoy (E cardinal) marking the E extremity of King William Banks, thence:

NNE of Bahama Bank (5 miles NE) marked at its SE end by Bahama Light Buoy (S cardinal) (6 miles ENE); the bank, with depths over it of less than 2 m, extends 7 miles SE from Whitestone Bank (see below) and consists of fine sand and pebbles; it is nearly steep-to on both sides. And:

SSW of Ballacash Bank (9 miles NNE), unmarked and steep-to on the N and S sides. And:

3

NNE of Whitestone Bank (7 miles N), marked by a light buoy (W cardinal) moored off its SW side, which extends 2½ miles SE of Point of Ayre (54°25′N 4°22′W) and on which the sea breaks, thence:

NNE of Point of Ayre as described at 10.22.

Cautions. An unmarked dangerous wreck lies 1 mile N of Point of Ayre; Strunakill Bank with depths of less than 10 m, and on which the sea breaks, lies 1 mile NW of the point.

The Solway Firth to the Mull of Galloway
10.22

1

From a position S of South Workington Light Buoy (54°37′N 3°38′W) which is moored at the S end of Workington Bank (10.37), and N of Saint Bees Head (9.117), an offshore route leads approximately 45 miles W to a position SW of the Mull of Galloway (54°38′N 4°51′W) passing:

2

S of Abbey Head (54°46′N 3°58′W) (10.24) with high ground close W, thence:

S of Little Ross (54°46′N 4°05′W), an island, on which stands a prominent lighthouse (10.105); the high ground of Meikle Ross (10.107) lies close W of the island, thence:

3

N of Point of Ayre (54°25′N 4°22′W), the N tip of the Isle of Man, on which stands a prominent lighthouse (10.18), thence:

S of Burrow Head (54°41′N 4°24′W) and with a heavy race (10.118) forming off the headland, thence:

4

S of Big Scare (54°40′N 4°42′W) (10.129), which lies in the entrance to Luce Bay, thence:

S of the Mull of Galloway, on which stands a prominent lighthouse (10.18) and S of a heavy race (10.102) which forms off the Mull.

Useful marks
10.23

1

Point of Ayre low light (red tower, lower part white on black base, 10 m in height) standing 2 cables NE of Point of Ayre high light (10.18). It is partially obscured between the bearings 335°–341°.

Hotel (dome) (54°20′·4N 4°23′·5W) (10.216).

Albert Tower (54°19′N 4°23′W) (10.216).

Mew Island Light (54°42′N 5°31′W) (Chart 2093) (see *Irish Coast Pilot*).

(Directions for the North Channel and Saint George's Channel are given in the Irish Coast Pilot; coastal directions NW of the Mull of Galloway are given in the West Coast of Scotland Pilot)

SOLWAY FIRTH AND APPROACHES

General information

Chart 1346
General description
10.24

1

The Solway Firth is entered between Saint Bees Head (54°31′N 3°38′W) (9.117) and Abbey Head (54°46′N 3°58′W), 19 miles NW; a large proportion of the firth is encumbered with continually shifting, drying sandbanks interspersed with channels. The upper part of the firth, above Dubmill Point (10.25), is a National Nature Reserve.

2

Navigable and buoyed channels lie on the SE side of the firth from its entrance as far as Annan (54°59′N 3°16′W), where navigation may be said to cease. These channels give access to the small ports of Whitehaven, Workington and Silloth.

3

Rough Firth and Urr Water which lie on the NW side, 6 miles above Abbey Head, provide much of the main yachting activity in the area.

Maryport (54°43′N 3°30′W), a small harbour on the SE side, contains a yacht marina.

Strong W winds raise a heavy sea within the firth which decreases when N of Workington (54°39′N 3°34′W).

Topography
10.25

1

On the SE side of the lower part of the firth the coastline N of Saint Bees Head, which is indented by several small bays, consists of cliffs fronted by rocky ledges and stones as far as Workington, backed by rising ground. There are numerous disused iron foundries with tall chimneys situated on this stretch of coast. The foreshore generally dries out to between 1 and 2 cables offshore.

2

North of Workington the coastline as far as Dubmill Point (54°48′N 3°26′W) is low, backed by gradually rising ground with the foreshore, which dries out to 5 cables offshore, consisting of stones and slag from the furnaces in the neighbourhood.

3

On the NW side the coastline, E of Abbey Head, is bold and rocky and backed by higher ground, with the exception of Auchencairn Bay (54°50′N 3°50′W) and Rough Firth where the coast recedes, but the land behind remains hilly rising to Bengairn, a mountain landmark visible for many miles. From Castlehill Point (54°51′N 3°47′W) the coast, for a distance of 4 miles ENE is backed by hills which gradually rise NE to Criffell, a mountain; thence the land slopes E to Southerness Point (54°52′·4N 3°35′·6W).

4

The immediate coastline on both sides of the upper part of the firth lying NE of a line joining Dubmill Point to Southerness Point (7 miles NW), is low-lying.

Moricambe Bay, the largest of the bays in the area, lies on the SE side of the firth 3 miles NE of Silloth (54°52′N 3°23′W).

5

Several rivers flow out from both sides of the firth. The river Nith (10.95), the largest, lies on the NW side N of Borron Point (54°54′N 3°34′W).

Wave recorder
10.26

1

A wave recorder light buoy (special) (54°41′·7N 3°48′·2W) is moored in the centre of the entrance to the Solway Firth.

Pilotage
10.27
1   Pilotage is compulsory for vessels entering the ports of Whitehaven, Workington, Silloth and Annan.

For Whitehaven, pilots board off the port; for Workington, Silloth or Annan, pilots board off Workington. The pilot boarding positions are shown on the chart.

Owing to the continually shifting sandbanks in the upper part of the firth the area is left blank on the charts, and navigation within it should not be attempted without a pilot or local knowledge.

Local knowledge
10.28
1   Navigation N of Maryport Roads (10.80) and the channels off the N shore should not be attempted without local knowledge.

Rescue
10.29
1   An all-weather lifeboat is stationed at Workington (54°39′N 3°34′W); inshore lifeboats are stationed at Silloth (54°52′N 3°24′W) and Kippford (54°53′N 3°49′W).

For details of rescue organisation see 1.60.

Tidal streams
10.30
1   Off the entrance to the Solway Firth, tidal streams are more or less rotary anti-clockwise; the strongest streams set NE and SW with a spring rate up to 2 kn.

Ripples or eddies may be encountered especially between 6 and 5 hours before HW Liverpool when the E-going stream meets the out-going stream from the firth.

As the firth is approached the in-going stream sets NE towards Three Fathoms Bank (54°41′N 3°40′W) and then N in the direction of the channel, the rate increasing to nearly 4 kn at springs.

Chart 2013
10.31
1   On the SE side of the firth, between Saint Bees Head and Dubmill Point, the tidal streams set mainly in the direction of the coast.

In English Channel, 5 miles N of Saint Bees Head, the in-going stream begins 5¼ hours before HW Liverpool and the out-going stream begins ¾ hour after HW at that port. The spring rate in each direction is 3 kn.

2   Tidal streams are given on the chart and in *Admiralty Tidal Stream Atlas — Irish Sea and Bristol Channel.*

For tidal streams affecting Silloth Channel, see 10.69.

Chart 1346
10.32
1   On the NW side of the firth, between Abbey Head (54°46′N 3°58′W) and Hestan Islet, about 6½ miles NE, the streams set in the direction of the coast. The in-going stream begins 5¾ hours before HW at Liverpool and the out-going stream begins ¼ hour after HW at that port. The spring rate in each direction is 3 kn.

Off Southerness Point the spring rate is 5 kn.
10.33
1   In the upper part of the Solway Firth the rate and range of the tidal stream is considerable and the rise from LW very rapid, especially near springs when there may be a bore.

The duration of the in-going stream E of Dumroof Bank (54°48′N 3°39′W) decreases rapidly.

Off Carlisle at the head of the firth, the duration of the in-going stream is not more than 3 hours.

Magnetic anomaly
10.34
1   There is a magnetic anomaly in English Channel (10.37) owing to slag being washed into the sea from the heaps near Workington (54°39′N 3°34′W).

Directions
(continued from 9.120)

Principal marks
10.35
1   **Landmarks:**

    Tower (54°31′·0N 3°36′·9W)

    Chimney (54°31′·7N 3°35′·9W), tall with black top, standing within a chemical works; a chimney which lies 1·3 miles E is also conspicuous.

    Radio Mast (54°33′·2N 3°34′·0W).

    Chimneys (54°34′·0N 3°34′·8W), two in number, standing at Micklam Brickworks. A radio mast (elevation 146 m) stands 3½ cables ESE.

    Chimney (54°38′N 3°34′W).

2   Chimney (grey with black top) (54°40′·0N 3°32′·6W), at Thames Board Mill; another chimney and a group of 9 wind turbines stand respectively 4 cables and 7 cables farther NNE.

    Chimney (54°40′·8N 3°31′·8W).

    Spire (54°43′N 3°30′W).

    Turret (54°43′·2N 3°29′·4W).

    Seacroft Farm, conspicuous, (54°47′·5N 3°26′·0W).

    Major light:

    Saint Bees Head Light (54°31′N 3°38′W) (9.108).

Seacroft Farm from W (10.35)

(Original dated 2001)

(Photograph - Air Images)

10.36
1   Vessels bound for ports in the Solway Firth should make for Saint Bees Head or the light buoy marking the S end of Workington Bank (54°39′N 3°39′W), thence follow English Channel (10.37).

Caution. Shifting sandbanks and channels, which are subject to frequent changes, encumber much of the Solway Firth, particularly in the upper part of the firth.

Chart 2013
English Channel
10.37
1   English Channel, the best navigable channel which is also buoyed, lies between the shoals which extend from the coast between Harrington (54°37′N 3°34′W) and Dubmill Point, and Workington Bank (see below), Three Fathoms Bank (54°41′N 3°40′W) (10.30) and Robin Rigg (54°45′N 3°39′W), where a windfarm, marked by light buoys (special), is under construction (2007). This channel has a

least depth of 10·5 m as far as Maryport Roads, thence the depths shoal quickly; the depths are subject to rapid and large variations.

2   From a position W of Saint Bees Head (54°31′N 3°38′W), the track to the pilot boarding position, for vessels calling at Workington, Silloth or Annan, leads NNE through English Channel for a distance of approximately 9 miles, passing:

WNW of the entrance to Whitehaven (54°33′N 3°36′W) with an outfall extending 1 mile seaward from the coast 1½ miles N thence:

3   ESE of Workington Bank (54°39′N 3°39′W), a sandbank, marked at its S end by South Workington Light Buoy (S cardinal) and at its N end by North Workington Light Buoy (N cardinal); a conspicuous chimney (10.35) stands on the mainland, opposite the bank, 1 mile S of Workington Harbour, thence:

WNW of the entrance to Workington Harbour and pilot boarding area.

Useful marks
10.38
1   West Pier Light, Whitehaven (54°33′N 3°36′W) (10.46).

South Pier Light, Workington (54°39′·1N 3°34′·6W) (10.56).

(Directions continue for Workington at 10.56 and for Silloth at 10.70; directions for Whitehaven are given at 10.46)

Whitehaven

Chart 2013 plan of Whitehaven Harbour
General information
10.39
1   **Position.** Whitehaven (54°33′N 3°36′W), a small port, consists of an artificial tidal harbour affording good shelter in all winds to vessels which can lie aground, and non-tidal basins in which vessels can lie afloat.

2   **Function.** The port is now primarily a fishing and leisure harbour. Substantial redevelopment of the harbour, including a new Sealock and improved facilities for the fishing industry, has recently taken place. There is a marina.

3   Whitehaven, which lies close E of the harbour, has a population of about 26 500.

Approach and entry. The approaches to the harbour lead from the open sea and are clear of danger; entry to the inner harbours is through a narrow channel leading from the harbour entrance to the Sealock.

4   **Port Authority.** Whitehaven Harbour Commissioners, Pears House, 1 Duke Street, Whitehaven, Cumbria CA28 7HW.

The Port Authority is represented by a General Manager, who also acts as Harbour Master.

Limiting conditions
10.40
1   The Sealock is 30 m long and 13·7 m wide, and allows access to the inner harbours approximately 3½ hours either

Whitehaven Harbour from NW (10.39)
(Original dated 2001)

(Photograph - Air Images)

299

side of HW, although on certain neap tides almost 24 hour access is available to shallow draught vessels.

The impounded water level is maintained at about 7·0 m; when the predicted height of tide is greater than 7·0 m both Sealock gates are opened, allowing vessels to pass through. Maximum LOA is 60 m.

10.41

1 Commercial vessels up to 60 m LOA and 5 m draught can be accommodated in the inner harbours by prior permission of the Harbour Master.

In Outer Harbour, vessels must be prepared to take the ground by prior permission of the Harbour Master.

Arrival information
10.42

1 **Port operations.** See *Admiralty List of Radio Signals Volume 6(1)*.

Outer anchorage. Anchorage may be obtained 5 cables W of the harbour entrance in depths of approximately 10 m, fine sand and shell.

Pilotage is compulsory for vessels of 50 m LOA and over. Vessels should forward their ETA messages at least 12 hours in advance to the local Agent or Harbour Master.

2 The pilot boards from the Workington pilot vessel *Derwent*, which is equipped with VHF, about ½ mile S of South Workington Light Buoy (10.22), as shown on the chart.

For further details on pilotage and communications, see *Admiralty List of Radio Signals Volume 6(1)*.

Tugs are not available.

Harbour
10.43

1 **General layout.** The harbour comprises Outer Harbour, which is tidal, and the inner harbours, which are entered through the Sealock.

Outer Harbour is entered between the heads of North Pier and West Pier; the harbour dries a short distance N of the entrance.

2 The inner harbours are contained within Old Quay and Old North Wall, a jetty which projects S from North Pier, and the Sealock; they are further divided into North, Inner and South Harbours, and Custom House and Queen's Docks.

North Harbour is used by fishing vessels; there are fish handling, refrigeration and distribution facilities as well as an ice plant and bunkering facilities.

3 Queen's Dock is still fitted with dock gates, but since the impounding of the inner harbours the gates are left open.

There are marinas in Inner Harbour, Queen's Dock and South Harbour.

10.44

1 **Traffic signals.** Signals (Diagram 10.44) are displayed from a tubular steel mast near the Sealock Control Room, a round white building with a conical slate roof situated on the N side of the Sealock.

10.45

1 **Tidal stream.** Eddies occur off the harbour entrance; they set away from the North Pierhead at all states of the tide.

Within Outer Harbour a weak tidal stream sets anti-clockwise at all states of the tide; it tends to set NE across the entrance to the Sealock.

Signal	Meaning
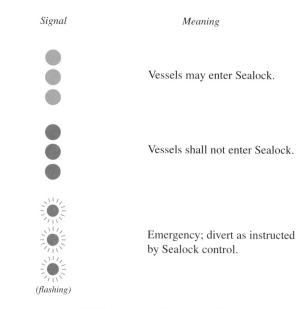	Vessels may enter Sealock.
	Vessels shall not enter Sealock.
(flashing)	Emergency; divert as instructed by Sealock control.

Whitehaven- traffic signals (10.44)

Directions for entering harbour
10.46

1 **Landmarks:**

Church Tower (54°33′N 3°35′W) (not shown on plan).

West Pier Light Tower, (conspicuous white round tower, 14 m in height) at the entrance to the harbour.

2 Mast (white tubular steel; elevation 42 m) (54°33′·0N 3°35′·6W) standing within the harbour.

Heritage Centre (white round tower, conical roof) (54°32′·9N 3°35′·7W) standing on the W side of South Harbour.

10.47

1 **Approach.** Vessels entering Outer Harbour should pass close to North Pierhead on account of the offshore eddies; see 10.45. A crescent-shaped bar extends SE from the inner side of West Pierhead, which should be given a wide berth.

2 **Entry** to the Sealock is by a channel, dredged to 1·0 m above chart datum in 1998, through Outer Harbour, thence passing N of the sealock approach structure, a series of dolphins joined by a catwalk, which extends W from the S side of the Sealock entrance. Lights are exhibited from the W end of the approach structure and from the N and S sides of the Sealock entrance, as shown on the chart.

Caution. A heavy sea is thrown across the harbour entrance in gales from between W and N.

10.48

1 **Useful marks:**

Light tower (white round tower, 6 m in height) standing at the head of North Pier.

Light beacon (starboard hand), marking the head of an outfall 4 cables SSW of West Pier Light Tower.

Port services
10.49

1 **Repairs:** deck and engine repairs can be carried out. There is a secure hard standing area, equipped with a 45 tonne mobile boathoist and a 1 tonne crane, at the N side of Queen's Dock.

2 **Other facilities:** issue of SSCC and SSCEC; disposal of waste oil; hospital 1 mile distant with helicopter landing facilities.

Supplies: fresh water; provisions; ice; diesel fuel at North Harbour.

Workington

Chart 2013 plan of Workington Harbour
General information
10.50
1 **Position.** Workington (54°39′N 3°34′W), the principal port of the County of Cumbria and the major deep-sea port between the rivers Clyde and Mersey, is situated at the mouth of the river Derwent and consists of a tidal harbour and a wet dock.
2 **Function.** The port is used principally for the import of chemicals, petroleum products, gypsum and timber; exports include scrap metal and rail track materials. There is a RoRo berth with ramp within the wet dock.

Workington has a population of about 25 500.

Approach and entry. Approach to the harbour is from English Channel; entry to Prince of Wales Dock is from a narrow channel which leads from the harbour entrance.
3 **Traffic.** In 2007 there were 74 ship calls with a total of 235 070 dwt.

Port Authority. The Port of Workington, Cumbria County Council, Harbour Office, Prince of Wales Dock, Workington, Cumbria CA14 2JH.

The Port Authority is represented by a Harbour Master.

Limiting conditions
10.51
1 **Depths.** There is a maintained depth of 1·8 m within the approach channel, the turning basin and Prince of Wales Dock.

Sea water is impounded in Prince of Wales Dock by sea gates allowing water levels to be maintained over LW. The sea gates are usually open 2 hours before HW to 1½ hours after.
2 Depths in the approach channel, turning basin and Prince of Wales Dock are liable to change owing to siltation; the Harbour Master should be consulted for the latest information.
3 **Maximum size of vessel handled.** Vessels of up to 12 000 dwt, 137·2 m in length having a beam of 20·1 m and draught 8·5 m can be accommodated on spring tides in Prince of Wales Dock.

For the latest information on maximum draught acceptance, the Harbour Master should be consulted prior to arrival.

Arrival information
10.52
1 **Port operations.** See *Admiralty List of Radio Signals Volume 6(1)*.

Outer anchorage. Vessels awaiting pratique or entry to the port anchor NW of the entrance, as shown on the chart. The holding is good but the anchorage is exposed to the prevailing SW winds.
2 **Pilotage** is compulsory for all vessels over 50 m LOA unless a Pilot Exemption Certificate is held. ETA of vessel

Workington from E (10.50)
(Original dated 2001)

(Photograph - Air Images)

should be forwarded to their local Agents at least 24 hours in advance.

The pilot boarding position lies off the harbour entrance, as shown on the chart.

3 Workington pilot vessel provides pilotage to Silloth and Annan; pilots for these ports are stationed at Silloth and board incoming vessels off Workington about 2 hours before HW at Silloth.

For further details on pilotage, see *Admiralty List of Radio Signals Volume 6(1).*

10.53

1 **Tugs.** A tug is available and its use is compulsory for vessels over 100 m LOA. Passenger vessels and vessels carrying dangerous substances are required to have a tug standing by on arrival and departure, regardless of size. The Port Authority reserves the right to appoint a tug to attend any vessel, at the discretion of the Harbour Master; 24 hours notice is required for the use of the tug. The Harbour Master should be consulted prior to arrival.

Harbour
10.54

1 **General layout.** The harbour comprises a wet dock, Prince of Wales Dock, which is used for commercial traffic, and a tidal harbour used principally by fishing vessels and small craft.

The harbour, through which the river Derwent runs out to the sea, is protected by South Pier, built of concrete, which extends 2½ cables NW from the S side of the river entrance, and North Jetty which projects 1 cable NW from N side of the river entrance.

2 In the immediate vicinity of the harbour, the land, which is low lying, has a great deal of on-going industrial development.

The ruins of John Pier which extend W from the shore, lie on the seaward side of South Pier.

Dredging. Owing to continual silting the approach channel and turning basin are maintained by frequent dredging.

3 **Traffic signals** (Diagram 10.54) are displayed from a steel framework pylon situated at the NW end of Prince of Wales Dock.

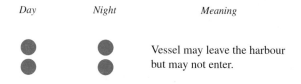

Day	Night	Meaning
		Vessel may leave the harbour but may not enter.

Workington - traffic signals (10.54)

10.55

1 **Tidal streams.** See 10.31. Eddies occur off the entrance to the harbour.

Directions for entering harbour
(continued from 10.38)
10.56

1 **Landmarks:**

South Pier Light (red square brick building, 6 m in height) (54°39'·1N 3°34'·6W), standing 1 cable within the head of South Pier.

Nine wind turbines, conspicuous, standing 2 to 6 cables NNE of the head of North Jetty (54°39'·1N 3°34'·2W).

10.57

1 **Leading lights.** From the pilot boarding position in English Channel the alignment (131¾°) of the leading lights leads into the harbour to a position about ¾ cable W of the head of North Jetty:

Front light (white pyramidal tower, orange band, 7 m in height) (54°38'·9N 3°34'·2W).

Rear light (similar structure, 9 m in height) (134 m from front light).

The track passes (with positions from South Pier Light (54°39'·1N 3°34'·7W):

2 NE of the head of South Pier (¾ cable WNW) on which stands a light (metal mast), thence:

NE of South Pier Light, thence:

SW of Bush Perch Light (metal mast) (1¼ cables E), thence into the turning basin.

On either side of the leading lights, lights in line, having the same alignment as the leading lights, indicate the approximate sides of the channel.

10.58

1 The turning basin, which is protected by North Jetty, with a light at its head (metal column, 4 m in height), links the entrance channel to Prince of Wales Dock.

2 The best time for entering Prince of Wales Dock is about ½ hour before HW, when the tidal stream setting across the entrance channel is weak and when the last of the in-going stream counteracts the stream coming down from the river Derwent; with an out-going stream, care is necessary to prevent the river stream catching a vessel on the port bow if the turn into the Turning Basin is not made early. In the Turning Basin itself there is little or no tidal stream and there is no difficulty in entering the dock.

Berths
10.59

1 **Prince of Wales Dock,** the wet dock, is entered from the Turning Basin through a gateway 21·3 m wide with depths of 9·3 m over the sill at HW springs.

The W portion of the dock is 97 m wide and the E portion 76 m wide; it has a total quay space of 772 m, with depths of 10 m at springs and 7 m at neaps.

2 Sufficient water is maintained in the dock to float the vessel of the deepest draught in the dock at that time.

There are 7 numbered berths, which include No 4 berth, a tanker terminal 132 m long, and a RoRo berth which lies at the NW end of No 6 berth.

10.60

1 **Riverside Wharf,** a tidal wharf on the S side of Prince of Wales Dock, is no longer used.

There are no commercial berths outside of the wet dock.

10.61

1 **Tidal Harbour and tidal dock.** The entrance to Tidal Harbour on the S side of the river entrance is crossed by a railway bridge which also crosses the river entrance. A half-tide channel leads from Turning Basin to Tidal Harbour, and at the bridge the passage has a width of 15 m and a vertical clearance of 1·8 m.

2 Tidal Harbour accommodates a number of small craft with short or lowering masts which can take the ground; it has a total quay space of 853 m with depths of 7 m on spring tides, and 4 m on neap tides.

The tidal dock, or Old Harbour, which has a slipway and quay, lies W of the entrance to the tidal harbour; it dries completely and is mainly used by local fishing craft.

For a berth within Tidal Harbour, the Harbour Master should be contacted.

Workington Leading Lights (131¾°) from WNW (10.57)

(Original dated 2001)

(Photograph - Air Images)

Port services
10.62

1   **Repairs**: hull, deck and engine repairs undertaken in the port; diver.

    Other facilities: issue of SSCC and SSCEC; hospital.

    Supplies: fuel and diesel oil by road; fresh water; stores and provisions.

    Communications: international airport at Manchester, 160 km distant.

    Harbour regulations: bye-laws are in force.

    Rescue: an all-weather lifeboat and an inshore lifeboat are based at the port. See 1.60 for details of rescue organisation.

Silloth Harbour

Chart 2013 plan of Silloth Docks and Approaches
General information
10.63

1   **Position.** Silloth Harbour (54°52′N 3°24′W), a small port which contains a tidal basin and wet dock, lies on the SE side of the Solway Firth 15 miles NNE of Workington.

    Function. The port is used mainly for the export and import of bulk cargoes which include grain, animal feeds, cement and fertilisers; general cargo is also handled.

    Silloth has a population of about 3000.

2   **Approach and entry** to the port from seawards is made through English and Silloth Channels; the wet dock is entered from the tidal basin.

    Traffic. In 2007 there were 76 ship calls with a total of 184 168 dwt.

    Port Authority. Associated British Ports, Dock Office, Silloth, Cumbria CA7 4JQ.

3   The port is jointly administered by the Port Manager and Harbour Master at Barrow-in-Furness; see 9.76.

    There is a resident Harbour Master at Silloth.

Limiting conditions
10.64

1   Vessels of up to 90 m length, 13·5 m beam and 6·0 m draught can be accommodated.

    The sea gates into New Dock (10.74), the wet dock, are usually open from 1½ before until ½ hour after HW.

    New Dock has a maintained depth of 4·0 m, but depths are liable to change owing to siltation. The Harbour Master should be consulted for the latest information.

Arrival information
10.65

1   **Port operations.** Communications can be made direct with Silloth Dock Office 2½ hours before to about 1 hour after HW Silloth, call sign: Silloth Harbour Radio.

    VTS. Vessels over 40 m LOA inbound for the Port of Silloth or the upper reaches of the Solway Firth are required to report to Silloth Harbour Radio. The position of the reporting point is shown on the chart.

2   **Outer anchorage.** See 10.80.

    Pilotage is provided by Workington pilot vessel (10.52) from Workington and is compulsory for all vessels over 50 m in length; Silloth Pilots also act as pilots for Annan.

Silloth from WNW (10.63)

(Original dated 2001)

(Photograph - Air Images)

Vessels should send their ETA messages to their agent or to the Harbour Master Silloth at least 12 hours before arrival.

10.66

1   Vessels navigating without a pilot must obtain information and instructions from the Harbour Master before entering the harbour.

For further information see *Admiralty List of Radio Signals Volume 6(1)*.

2   **Tugs** are not based in the port, and are not usually necessary; if required, they should be ordered from Workington or Barrow.

Regulations concerning entry. A vessel may enter or leave the port only with the specific approval of the Port Authority, calling SILLOTH HARBOUR RADIO on VHF.

Harbour

10.67

1   **General layout.** The harbour comprises Marshall Dock, a tidal basin which dries, and New Dock, a wet dock. They lie to the SW of the town.

New Dock, the commercial dock, with facilities for bulk storage, is entered from Marshall Dock through a gateway.

10.68

1   **Traffic signals** (Diagram 10.68) are shown from a tall lattice signal mast at the entrance to New Dock.

10.69

1   **Tidal streams.** For details of tidal streams at the entrance to Silloth Channel, see information on the chart.

Tidal flow across the port entrance limits commercial shipping entry to HW Silloth ± 30 minutes. In the channel tidal streams set strongly in the direction of the channel when banks are dry but weakly across the banks when they are covered; at springs they attain a rate of nearly 4 kn.

Day	*Night*	*Meaning*
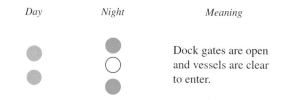		Dock gates are open and vessels are clear to enter.

Silloth traffic signals (10.68)

2   Off Silloth the in-going stream begins 4 hours before HW Liverpool and the out-going stream 1 hour after HW at that port.

A W-going stream beginning ¾ hour before HW may be experienced off the entrance to the tidal basin.

3   **Tidal heights** may vary from predictions given in *Admiralty Tide Tables* owing to local weather conditions. Strong SW winds may increase tidal heights by more than 1 m and a heavy swell may also be experienced.

Directions for entering harbour

(continued from 10.38)

10.70

1   **Landmark:**

Spire (54°52′·2N 3°23′·3W), NE of the docks, is prominent from off the port.

10.71

1   **Approach.** From the pilot boarding position off Workington the route to Silloth Harbour leads about 8 miles NNE towards Solway Light Buoy, mentioned below, then a further 7 miles NE through the buoyed Silloth Channel, passing (with positions from Lees Scar Light Beacon (54°51′·8N 3°24′·8W)):

2   WNW of a light buoy (starboard hand) (54°40′·3N 3°35′·8W) which marks the end of an outfall, thence:

WNW of a beacon (starboard hand) (54°42′·8N 3°31′·4W) marking the end of an outfall, thence:

WNW of the entrance to Maryport Harbour (54°43′N 3°30′W) (10.82), with a conspicuous spire in the town, thence:

3   WNW of Solway Light Buoy (starboard hand) (54°46′·8N 3°30′·1W), thence:

NW of Corner Light Buoy (starboard hand) (4 miles SW), moored off Ellison Scar, thence:

4   NW of Beckfoot Light Buoy (starboard hand) (2 miles SW) moored W of Catherine Scar at the NW edge of Beckfoot Flats, mainly sand. The flats, which lie between the harbour entrance and Dubmill Point 4½ miles SSW, dry to as far as 1½ miles offshore and are largely unsurveyed, but are known to contain areas of isolated large stones. Thence:

5   NW of Lees Scar Light Beacon (starboard hand) (white structure on piles; 4 m in height), which marks the NW edge of Beckfoot Flats.

The track continues NE for about ½ mile before altering ESE on to the alignment of the Silloth leading lights.

Caution. The line of Silloth Channel frequently changes and the buoys are laid for the aid of the pilots and do not necessarily mark the navigable channel; local knowledge is necessary.

10.72

1   **Leading lights.** The alignment (115¼°) of the leading lights (white masts, vertical strip lights, 80 m apart), standing at the head of New Dock, leads through Marshall Dock in a narrow channel with a passage width of 30 m. The channel is maintained at a depth below New Dock sill level by sluicing at spring tides.

10.73

1   **Useful marks:**

Maryport South Pier Light (metal framework tower) (54°43′·1N 3°30′·6W).

Dolphin light, exhibited from the outermost dolphin marking a groyne at the entrance to Marshall Dock at Silloth.

2   East Cote Light (white structure on piles, 12 m in height), standing 9 cables NE of the harbour entrance and visible throughout Silloth Channel between the bearings 046°- 058° thereby avoiding Beckfoot Flats (10.71).

Berths

10.74

1   **New Dock,** 200 m long and 122 m wide, and over 100 years old, is entered from Marshall Dock through a gateway 18·0 m wide at the top, 16·2 at the bottom, with a depth over the sill of 7·4 m at MHWS and 5·1 m at MHWN. The quay height is approximately 9·9 m above sill level.

2   The dock has 590 m of quay; see 10.64 regarding depths.

At the E end there is a 3 drum silo for bulk cement, a storage tank for molasses and facilities for the discharge of animal feeds; flour mills line the N side of the dock and general cargo (including livestock) is handled on the S side.

3   **Marshall Dock,** a tidal basin which has 366 m of quay, is 183 m long and 91·5 m wide. The dock is suitable for mooring craft which can take the ground, out of the line

for vessels entering New Dock. Mooring permits are issued by the Dock Superintendent Harbour Master.

Visiting craft/fishing vessels should enter New Dock for the duration of their stay.

Port services

10.75

1   **Repairs:** minor repairs only.

Supplies: fresh water; all types of fuel by road; provisions and stores.

Other facilities. Garbage disposal facilities are available. The reception of oily waste, noxious and harmful substances can be arranged through the ship's agent.

10.76

1   **Harbour regulations.** Bye-laws concerning vessels carrying petroleum spirit and carbide of calcium are similar to those in force at Barrow; see 9.97.

Anchorages and harbours on the south-east side of the Solway Firth

Charts 1346, 2013

General directions

10.77

1   Small craft should approach the ports lying on the SE side of the firth by following the directions given at 10.35 and 10.70.

No attempt should be made to cross the firth over the shoals and flats which encumber its centre without extensive recent local knowledge. Craft intending to cross the mouth of the firth are strongly recommended to do so to seaward of Two Feet Bank Light Buoy (W cardinal) which is moored off the W edge of Two Feet Bank (54°43′N 3°41′W).

Saltom Bay

10.78

1   Saltom Bay, between Saint Bees Head (54°31′N 3°38′W) and Whitehaven, 2½ miles N, is skirted by oyster grounds; depths of less than 5 m extend 5 cables offshore but the bay provides good anchorage, in offshore winds.

For anchorage off Whitehaven, see 10.42.

Harrington Harbour

10.79

1   Harrington Harbour (54°37′N 3°34′W), 4 miles N of Whitehaven, is no longer in commercial use and now has facilities only for sailing and fishing. The harbour dries completely. The outer and inner ends of the remains of a breakwater on the N side of the harbour are marked by beacons (port hand).

Maryport Roads

10.80

1   Maryport Roads are situated abreast Maryport (54°43′N 3°30′W) and afford shelter from all but W winds.

The outer road lies NW of the outermost shoal off Maryport; there is anchorage, as indicated on the chart, in depths of 12 m, sand, with Maryport South Pier Light (10.73) bearing 124°, distant 2¾ miles.

2   The inner road, with depths of from 5 to 7·5 m, lies between the 5 m depth contour which here runs parallel with, and 1 mile from, the coast, and a shoal with a least depth 3·5 m lying parallel with the coast 5 cables seaward of the 5 m depth contour.

Recommended berths, for vessels with suitable draught, are in depths of 7·5 m, sand and shingle, with Maryport South Pier Light bearing 107°, or 145°, distant 1 mile.

10.81

1   **Directions.** The anchorages should be approached from S through English Channel, keeping 1¾ miles W of the coast between Workington and Maryport near LW.

If approaching inner roads from N vessels should keep the extremity of Saint Bees Head (54°31′N 3°38′W) bearing 196°, and anchor in either of the recommended berths.

2   From the S, the line of bearing 095° of the turret of a house (54°43′·2N 3°29′·4W) leads E to an inner roads anchorage; vessels should anchor when Maryport South Pier Light is 1 mile distant.

Maryport Harbour
10.82

1   **General information.** Maryport Harbour (54°43′N 3°30′W) lies at the mouth of the river Ellen and is used by inshore fishing vessels and pleasure craft. There are two wet docks, one of which, Senhouse Dock, contains a large marina.

Directions:

Approach to the harbour is from English Channel passing W of a light beacon (starboard hand) marking the seaward end of an outfall 6 cables SW of South Pier head.

2   Entry is through a channel, dredged to 1 m above chart datum, passing between the heads of North and South Piers as far as Elizabeth Basin.

Strong E winds may cause a fall in the sea level. In March 1986 HW was on one occasion 0·7 m less than predicted owing to this effect.

Useful mark:

South Pier Light (metal framework tower) (54°43′·1N 3°30′·6W).

Spire (54°43′N 3°30′W), standing on the E side of Old Harbour.

3   Tower (54°43′·3N 3°29′·7W), part of a former Naval Battery placement 4 cables NE of the harbour.

Turret (54°43′·2N 3°29′·5W) of a conspicuous house, not shown on the plan chart, and partially obscured by trees.

4   **Berths:**

Maryport Marina, situated in Senhouse Dock, berths for craft up to 25 m LOA, 4 m draught at HW; minimum depth of 2·5 m in the dock, which is entered from Senhouse Basin through a gateway; sill 2·8 m above chart datum. Entry; HW ±2½ hours. Full range of facilities including a 60-tonne capacity boat lift and slipway.

5   Elizabeth Basin, a tidal basin, lies E of Senhouse Dock; Elizabeth Dock is entered through a gateway from the basin; sill 2·57 m above chart datum; entry into the dock is from 2½ hours before to ½ hour after HW; used as a wet dock and accommodates fishing boats.

North Harbour and Old Harbour, in the E part of the harbour, are completely silted up and are of use only to small boats.

Allonby Bay
10.83

1   **General information.** Allonby Bay lies between Maryport (54°43′N 3°30′W) and Dubmill Point, 5½ miles NNE. Its foreshore consists of sand, stones and rock and dries out to 4 cables offshore. The N part merges with Dubmill Scar and Ellison Scar, consisting of sandbanks and areas of isolated large stones which dry for a distance of 2¾ miles offshore and terminate at Far Sand Bank.

2   **Tidal streams.** There is negligible tidal stream in the bay from 2 hours after local HW until 2 hours before the next HW owing to the uncovering of the flats which extend from Dubmill Point between these times.

Anchorage. There is good anchorage in the S portion of the bay, in depths of between 2·5 and 5 m. When anchoring in the bay vessels should not bring Allonby Belfry (54°46′N 3°26′W) to bear more than 083° on account of foul ground N of this line.

Chart 1346
Moricambe Bay
10.84

1   Moricambe Bay (54°54′N 3°18′W) is an extensive inlet into which flow the rivers Waver and Wampool. On the N side of the bay stand a series of radio masts.

Cardurnock Flats, which front the coast N of the bay, contain several rocky outcrops. A half-tide channel crosses the flats from Powfoot Channel (10.87) and runs into the entrance of each river.

Annan
10.85

1   **General description.** Annan (54°59′N 3°16′W) is a small port and market town, little used except by fishing vessels, which lies 1 mile inside the mouth of the river Annan which flows into the firth at Barnkirk Point, or Annan Waterfoot, which is one of the most prominent features in this vicinity; the river is crossed by two bridges at the town.

2   A light beacon (special) stands at the head of a pipeline which extends a short distance from the shore close W of Barnkirk Point.

Annan has a population of about 9000.

Harbour Authority. Annan Harbour Trust, Council Offices, High Street, Annan, Dumfries and Galloway DG12 6AQ.

10.86

1   **Limiting conditions.** The river between the town and entrance is approximately ½ cable wide and is experiencing severe siltation; vessels of up to 55 m in length with a draught of 3 m have been able to reach Town Quay at HW. As the quay dries at LW, vessels must be able to take the ground.

10.87

1   **Pilotage** is compulsory, see 10.65; pilots board off Workington. For further details see *Admiralty List of Radio Signals Volume 6(1)*.

Powfoot Channel, which leads from Silloth to the river Annan entrance lies in an area of frequent change (10.27).

10.88

1   **Tidal stream.** In Powfoot Channel, the in-going stream begins 3 hours before HW Liverpool and the out-going stream 1 hour after HW at that port.

The maximum spring rate in each direction is 6 kn.

10.89

1   **Berths.** There are two quays on the river; Town Quay, 105 m long, with a depth alongside of 3·6 m at MHWS is restricted at its N end owing to siltation; Nivens Quay, 30 m long, is a private quay.

Supplies: fresh water; provisions; fuel by road tanker.

Anchorages and harbours on the north-west side of the Solway Firth

General directions
10.90

1   Directions for Kippford and Palnackie are given at 10.92 and 10.93. The approach to Sandyhills Bay and the river Nith, which lie in an area of frequent change (10.27) requires recent local knowledge.

Caution. See 10.77.

Hestan Island
10.91

1   During offshore winds there is sheltered anchorage, in a depth of 3 m, between Balcary Point (54°49′·6N 3°49′·5W), bold and rocky, and Hestan Island (5½ cables NE). There is a light (white metal framework tower) on the E end of the island.

Anchorage can also be found inward of Balcary Point or, if capable of taking the ground, small craft can moor inside Balcary Bay, mud and sand.

There is deeper water off the E side of the island.

Kippford
10.92

1   **General information.** Kippford (54°53′N 3°49′W), a yachting centre with sheltered moorings which dry, lies on the E side of Urr Water, which is navigable at MHWS by craft of 2·7 m draught as far as Palnackie (10.93).

The centre is also used by inshore fishing boats.

2   **Limiting conditions.** Rough Firth (Urr Estuary) channel is not navigable at LW ±3 hours.

Maximum size of craft visiting Kippford: 45·7 m LOA, draught 2·4 m and should be suitable for taking the ground.

Directions. From S keep any part of Rough Island (54°52′N 3°48′W) open of Castlehill Point (54°51′·2N 3°47′·3W) to clear Craig Roan (4¾ cables ESE), a rock which dries 6·0 m.

3   A channel, which follows the course of Urr Water, leads from seaward to Kippford, thence Palnackie, passing W of Rough Island and keeping close to the W side of Rough Firth where it deepens at Gibb's Hole, nearly 1 mile N of Almorness Point (54°50′·8N 3°48′·5W), before leading N towards Kippford. From Gibb's Hole inwards the channel is marked by privately maintained red floats which may not always indicate the deepest water but which should be left to port. Entrance to Kippford lies between two perches situated opposite the Solway Yacht Club start hut.

4   **Anchorage.** Sheltered anchorage is available off Hestan Island, see 10.91.

Berths. All moorings dry. A floating pontoon at Solway Yacht Club can be used at HW ±2½ hours. There are berths for visitors.

Repairs: boatyard; slipway.

Supplies: fresh water; provisions.

Palnackie
10.93

1   Palnackie (54°53′·5N 3°50′·3W), a small harbour which dries, is used by inshore fishing vessels and pleasure craft which can take the ground. It lies on the W side of Urr Water, 1½ miles above Kippford and 2 miles S of the small town of Dalbeattie. Vessels of up to 40 m LOA can be accommodated at the quay, which has a depth alongside of 4·0 m at MHWS. Facilities are limited.

Sandyhills Bay
10.94

1   Sandyhills Bay, 2½ miles NE of Castlehill Point (54°51′·2N 3°47′·3W), dries, but small craft can enter at HW and take the ground, mud and sand.

Chart 1346
River Nith and Glencaple Quay
10.95

1   **General information.** The approach to the river Nith lies between Borron Point (54°54′N 3°34′W) and Blackshaw Spit, at the SW end of Blackshaw Bank.

The river, tidal as far as Dumfries, 5½ miles within its entrance and now used mainly by small craft which can take the ground, is entered between Airds Point, 4 miles N of Borron Point, and Scar Point. The muddy estuary largely dries but the river is navigable to Dumfries at MHWS by craft of 1·0 m draught.

2   The river is partly confined on the W side by an embankment, which covers between Airds Point and Glencaple Quay, 1½ miles N. The channel in this area is marked on both sides by perches; the channel bed is composed of sand.

Local knowledge. The river Nith and its approaches lie in an area of frequent change (10.27). Good local knowledge is required; entry should be made on an in-going stream.

3   **Tidal streams** set N and S to and from the river. The in-going stream begins when the sands cover, and the out-going stream begins +0020 HW Liverpool.

The streams within the river set for only two hours in either direction.

Bore. A fast and powerful bore can run in the river and with spring tides can attain a speed of 15 kn with a frontal wave, and rise several feet within a few seconds.

4   **Berths.** Glencaple Quay can accept vessels with a draught of 3·5 m at MHWS; Kingholm Quay, where there is a tidal dock, on the E bank nearly 3 miles above Glencaple can take vessels of 3 m draught at MHWS. Facilities are limited at both berths.

A pier extends from the coast at Carsethorn, a small village on the W side of the estuary, 1 mile N of Borron Point.

COASTAL PASSAGE — ABBEY HEAD TO MULL OF GALLOWAY

General information

Charts 1826, 2094
Route
10.96

1   The route from Abbey Head (54°46′N 3°58′W) leads approximately 38 miles WSW to a position SW of the Mull of Galloway (54°38′N 4°51′W) at the S entrance to the North Channel (see *Irish Coast Pilot*), passing S of a heavy race which forms off the Mull.

Topography
10.97

1   The coastline in this area is greatly indented by Wigtown and Luce Bays, separated by The Machars, a long broad promontory, its axis running NNW/SSE, with high ground on its W side at the S end of which lies Burrow Head (54°41′N 4°24′W).

Kirkcudbright Bay, a small narrow bay, lies close E of Wigtown Bay.

2   Between Abbey Head and Gypsy Point (54°46′N 4°03′W), the E entrance point to Kirkcudbright Bay, the coast is bold and rocky; for a description of the Mull of Galloway see 10.105.

For features on the NW side of the Mull of Galloway see *West Coast of Scotland Pilot*.

Exercise areas
10.98
1 See 10.3.

Submarine pipeline
10.99
1 A charted submarine gas interconnector pipeline which passes NW of the Isle of Man, extends NE from the Irish Coast and is landed on the S coast of Scotland at the head of Brighouse Bay (54°47′N 4°07′W).

Rescue
10.100
1 There is no all-weather lifeboat coverage on this stretch of coast; an inshore lifeboat is stationed at Kirkcudbright (10.111).

For lifeboat rescue services on the E side of the North Channel see *West of Scotland Pilot* and on the W side of the Irish Sea see *Irish Coast Pilot*.

For details of rescue organisation see 1.60.

Tidal streams and heavy race
10.101
1 **Tidal streams** of the North Channel change direction round the Mull of Galloway and set E and W between the coast of Scotland and the Isle of Man.

At a position 3 miles S of the Mull of Galloway the streams begin nearly as in mid-channel in the North Channel, or nearly 2 hours later than along the coast N of the Mull.

Tidal streams are given on the chart and in *Admiralty Tidal Stream Atlas — Irish Sea and Bristol Channel*.
10.102
1 **Heavy race.** In consequence of the time difference and of the change in directions of the streams, a heavy race forms off the Mull of Galloway, extending nearly 3 miles S. During the E-going stream the race extends NNE towards the head of Luce Bay; during the W-going stream it extends SW and W.

The race is violent and may be dangerous to small vessels, especially with a strong wind against the stream.

Directions

Principal marks
10.103
1 **Landmarks:**
    Water Tower (54°46′·9N 4°01′·4W).
    Lookout Tower standing 2 cables SE of Torrs Point (54°47′N 4°04′W).
    Saint Ninian's Tower (54°41′·8N 4°21′·5W) (10.121).
2   Radio Mast (54°42′N 4°25′W).
    Mull of Galloway Lighthouse (54°38′N 4°51′W) (10.18).

Major Lights:
    Mull of Galloway Light (54°38′N 4°51′W) (10.18).
    Point of Ayre Light (54°25′N 4°22′W) (10.18).

Lookout Tower, Torrs Point from SW (10.103)
(Original dated 2001)

(Photograph - Air Images)

Other aids to navigation
10.104
1   **Racons:**

Point of Ayre Lighthouse (54°25′N 4°22′W).

South Rock Light Float (54°24′·5N 5°21′·9W) (Chart 2093) (*Irish Coast Pilot*).

For further details see *Admiralty List of Radio Signals Volume 2*.

Charts 1346, 2094
Passage
10.105
1   From a position SE of Abbey Head (54°46′N 3°58′W) to a position SW of the Mull of Galloway (54°38′N 4°51′W) the coastal route leads approximately 38 miles WSW, passing:

SSE of a dangerous wreck (position approximate) (54°45′N 3°59′W), thence:

SSE of Gipsy Point (54°46′N 4°03′W), thence:

2   SSE of Little Ross (54°46′N 4°05′W), an island, fringed by a steep-to ledge 60 m wide, lying at the W entrance to Kirkcudbright Bay. A light (white tower, 20 m in height) stands at the highest part of the island; a light beacon (10.115) stands 1¼ cables NNE of the light. West Quay, a slip, extends from the NW side of the island. Thence:

3   SSE of Burrow Head (54°41′N 4°24′W) and off which a heavy tide race (10.118) exists close S, thence:

4   SSE of The Scares (54°40′N 4°42′W) (10.129), lying in the middle of the entrance to Luce Bay and in the S portion of Luce Bay Bombing Range (10.129), thence:

5   SSE and SW of the Mull of Galloway (54°38′N 4°51′W), a bold and precipitous headland, steep-to on its S and W sides, which forms the W entrance point of Luce Bay and on which stands Mull of Galloway Light (10.18); it provides a good radar echo.

6   For a description of features NW of the Mull of Galloway see *West Coast of Scotland Pilot*.

Useful marks
10.106
1   Saint Bees Head Lighthouse (54°31′N 3°38′W) (9.108).

Maughold Head Light (54°18′N 4°18′W) (10.204).

Crammag Head Light (54°40′N 4°58′W) (see the *West Coast of Scotland Pilot*).

(Directions for the coastal passage NW of the Mull of Galloway are given in the West Coast of Scotland Pilot)

Kirkcudbright Bay

Chart 1344
General information
10.107
1   **General description.** Kirkcudbright Bay (pronounced K'coobri Bay) is entered between Gipsy Point (54°46′N 4°03′W) and the island of Little Ross, 1¼ miles W, and on which stands a prominent lighthouse (10.105). At the head of the bay the river Dee leads to the small port of Kirkcudbright (10.111).

The bay is sheltered from all except S winds; there are no offshore dangers in the approach with the exception of a detached 3·9 m patch, 2 cables W of Gipsy Point.

2   Little Ross is separated from the peninsula of Meikle Ross, high ground at the S end of a promontory forming the W side of Kirkcudbright Bay, by The Sound, a passage 1 cable wide. The passage, the N end of which becomes impassable at LW, is bounded on its W side by Richardson's Rock, parts of which are above water; Sugarloaf, an isolated pinnacle rock which dries, lies in the N approach to The Sound.

Mull of Galloway from E (10.105)

(Original dated 2001)

(Photograph - Air Images)

10.108

1   **Topography.** Much of the bay comprises low-lying wooded areas backed by rising ground; Milton Sands and Manxman's Lake, both of which dry, occupy the N half of the bay and are separated by the narrow channel of the river Dee. Saint Mary's Isle, a wooded peninsula, projects SW across Manxman's Lake.

10.109

1   **Tidal streams.** Off Kirkcudbright Bay, and in the entrance to the river Dee, the tidal stream begins as follows:

Interval from HW Liverpool	Direction
–0600	E-going; In-going in the river Dee entrance.
HW	W-going; Out-going in the river Dee entrance.

2   The maximum spring rate in each direction is approximately 4 kn.

Close inshore the E-going stream sets round Meikle Ross and Little Ross towards the river Dee entrance; the W-going stream across the bay is joined by the out-going stream from the river.

10.110

1   **Landmarks:**

Little Ross Lighthouse (54°46′N 4°05′W) and light beacon (10.105) standing on Little Ross at the W entrance to the bay.

Lookout Tower, standing near Torrs Point (10.103).

Lifeboat House, which is conspicuous from NW, standing 8 cables N of Torrs Point.

Kirkcudbright

10.111

1   **Position.** Kirkcudbright (54°50′N 4°03′W), a small port, lies on the river Dee, 3 miles within the bar (10.115).

Function. A fleet of about 20 fishing vessels, mainly engaged in scallop dredging, operates from Kirkcudbright. The port is also used by small commercial vessels importing rough salt and timber, and recreational craft.

Kirkcudbright has a population of about 3500.

2   **Port limits** enclose an area from a line joining the S side of the lifeboat slip to the S point of Senwick Bay, to the S side of Kirkcudbright Bridge.

Port Authority. Dumfries and Galloway Council, Council Offices, English Street, Dumfries DG1 2DD.

Marine enquiries should be addressed to the Harbour Master.

10.112

1   **Limiting conditions.** The largest vessel capable of reaching the port is one of 1500 dwt, length 67 m, having a draught of 5 m at MHWS.

10.113

1   **Pilotage** is not compulsory but is advisable, as local knowledge is essential; it is arranged through the Harbour Master. Vessels should forward their ETA 24 hours in advance. The pilot boards off the Lifeboat Station 8 cables N of Torrs Point (54°47′N 4°04′W).

For further details see *Admiralty List of Radio Signals Volume 6(1)*.

10.114

1   **Tidal streams** at Kirkcudbright are affected by the flow of water from the power station dam at Tongland, 2 miles above the town; on occasions there is no in-going stream, and even on spring tides it is very weak.

10.115

1   **Directions.** The bay is entered between Gipsy Point and Little Ross.

Caution. The buoys are moved as necessary to conform with changes in the channel. The characteristics of the light buoys and minor shore lights should not be relied on.

Leading lights. The alignment (201°), astern, of the leading lights on Little Ross (54°46′N 4°05′W) leads over the bar into the river Dee.

2   Front light (stone beacon, 10 m in height) (54°46′·1N 4°05′·0W).

Rear light (lighthouse) (10.105) (1¼ cables from front light).

From the lifeboat house (54°47′·7N 4°03′·7W) (10.110), from where a light is exhibited, the channel is marked by light buoys and light beacons.

3   Above No 17 Light Buoy there is a speed limit of 5 kn; vessels are swung before berthing.

Useful mark:

Sawmill on Gibbhill Point (54°50′N 4°04′W).

River Dee from SW (10.111)

(Original dated 2001)

(Photograph - Air Images)

Kircudbright from SE (10.116)

(Original dated 2001)

(Photograph - Air Images)

10.116

1   **Berths.** Town Quay (54°50′·3N 4°03′·1W), which has a length of 159 m and a depth alongside of 5·2 m at MHWS dries to a mud berth; there are no berths alongside for vessels which cannot take the ground.

There is a line of pontoons, for use by small craft, downstream from Town Quay. They are moored to piles and connected to the S bank by a floating walkway. The pile at each end and one in the middle are lit (starboard hand).

2   **Repairs and other facilities:** minor repairs; small hospital.

Supplies: fresh water; fuel by road tanker; provisions by prior arrangement.

Anchorages
10.117

1   There is anchorage in Ross Roads, between Little Ross (54°46′N 4°05′W) and Torrs Point (1 mile NE), but S winds cause an uneasy swell. An outfall extends 1½ cables SSW from the shore 1 cable SE of Torrs Point.

Vessels which can take the ground can find shelter in Ross Bay, sand, 5 cables N of Little Ross, or in Manxman's Lake where the bottom consists of sandy mud.

2   Anchorage can be obtained in The Sound, on the W side of Little Ross, SW of West Quay and clear of a disused submarine cable. This anchorage lies in the lee of a spit extending NW from the island and avoids the strong setting out-going stream through The Sound.

An anchorage also exists off Balmangan Woods, 1 mile N of Little Ross. A group of drying rocks, including Frenchman's Rock, lie 4 cables N of the anchorage and 2 cables off the W shore.

Wigtown Bay

Chart 2094
General information
10.118

1   **General description.** Wigtown Bay is entered between Meikle Ross (54°46′N 4°06′W) and Burrow Head (11 miles WSW). The NW and NE portions are occupied by extensive drying sands through which the river Cree flows.

2   Both coastlines of the bay are interspersed by numerous small indentations and rocky headlands backed by rising ground and areas of forestry. The mainly steep-to and rocky NE coastline is broken by the deep indentation of Fleet Bay (54°50′N 4°14′W); between the bay and Carsluith, 4 miles NW, the coast is backed by high well wooded land rising to a range of hills the highest of which is Cairnharrow.

3   A conspicuous caravan site (54°50′N 4°16′W) lies at the W entrance to Fleet Bay.

Fisheries. In the upper part of the bay, several salmon fisheries using stake nets extend small distances out from both sides of the coastline.

4   **Submarine gas pipeline.** See 10.123.

Tidal streams half way across the entrance to Wigtown Bay begin as follows:

Interval from HW Liverpool	Direction	Remarks
−6000	E	Sets ENE into the bay, then E.
HW	W	Sets W across the bay, then SW.

5   Maximum spring rate in each direction is approximately 4 kn.

Close inshore off Burrow Head the streams begin nearly 2 hours before these times, considerably earlier than elsewhere in the locality; these streams are local and are affected by eddies.

Further details are shown on the chart.

Race. There is a heavy race off Burrow Head when the W-going stream is opposed by a strong W wind.

Directions
10.119

1   **Landmarks:**
    Radio Mast (54°42′N 4°25′W).
    Water Tower (54°41′·3N 4°24′·2W).
    Saint Ninian's Tower (54°41′·8N 4°21′·5W) (10.121).

The S portion of the bay and its approaches are clear, except for charted dangers extending a short distance from the shore on either side.

It is however, inadvisable to proceed above Islands of Fleet (54°49′N 4°14′W) without local knowledge.

(Directions for Carsluith Quay are given 10.120)

Carsluith
10.120

1   **Position.** Carsluith Quarry Quay lies 1 mile S of Creetown (54°54′N 4°23′W).

Function. The quay is used for shipping stone from the granite quarry at Kirkmabreck, Creetown.

Quay Authority. Tarmac Roadstone (Scotland) Ltd, Morrington Quarry, Stepford Road, Dunscore, Dumfries DG2 0JW.

Marine matters should be addressed to the Area Production Manager.

2   **Limiting conditions.** The largest vessel accommodated (1991) was one of 3100 dwt, having a length of 120 m taking the ground from 3 hours after to 3 hours before HW.

Access to the quay is strictly tidal, movements being made from approximately 2 hours before HW.

Pilotage is available to take vessels to the quay. The pilot boards at the seaward entrance to the channel.

3   **Tidal streams.** In the NW part of Wigtown Bay the streams set inward and outward from the river Cree (54°54′N 4°24′W) which is tidal to within 1 mile of Newton Stewart (54°57′N 4°29′W).

Off Creetown the in-going stream begins 5½ hours before HW Liverpool and the out-going stream begins ½ hour before HW at that port.

4   The maximum spring rate in each direction is approximately 5 kn but the rate may be affected by freshets.

Directions. West Channel, the navigable channel to the quarry quay and on to Creetown, is entered 2 miles N of Eggerness Point (54°47′·4N 4°20′·6W) (10.122). It is marked on its starboard side by buoys and is bounded on its W side by Baldoon Sands.

5   The channel off the quay is about 150 m wide with space for swinging. Close S of Creetown, the channel, now bounded on its W side by Wigtown Sands leading to the

river Cree entrance, crosses towards the W bank of the river.

Berth. There is a single berth, approximately 30 m long with a further 20 m angled addition which projects W from the coast. It is well fendered.

There are no facilities.

Isle of Whithorn
10.121

1   **General information.** The Isle of Whithorn (54°42′N 4°22′W), in reality a peninsula on which stands Saint Ninian's Tower (see below), lies midway between the bold headlands of Burrow Head (10.105) and Cairn Head, 3 miles NNE.

The Isle of Whithorn Bay lies on the S side of the peninsula.

Function. Vessels of 500 dwt can be accommodated but fishing vessels and leisure craft mostly use the harbour.

2   **Harbour Authority.** Dumfries and Galloway Regional Council, Council Offices, English Street, Dumfries DG1 2DD.

The Harbour Authority is represented by the Wigtown Manager for marine matters. There is a resident Harbour Master who is employed on a part time basis.

Limiting conditions. There are depths of 5·5 m at MHWS within the harbour which dries at LW; vessels should be prepared to take the ground, soft mud on a hard bottom.

3   At half tide vessels with a draught of 2·5 m can enter.

The maximum size of vessel that the harbour can accommodate in suitable conditions at MHWS is one having a length of 66 m, beam 7·5 m and draught 5 m.

Harbour. The picturesque harbour is protected by a pier, from which a light is exhibited, constructed of reinforced concrete with a concrete surface extending approximately 76 m NW from the Isle of Whithorn.

4   Saint Ninian's Tower, a white structure with buildings nearby which is conspicuous from seaward except from SE, stands on the summit of the Isle of Whithorn peninsula near its SE end.

Directions. The harbour is entered from S on the alignment (335°) of leading lights (metal masts: orange diamond daymarks) situated close together at the head of the bay.

5   Vessels should give a wide berth to Screen Rocks, two small detached reefs which dry, lying at the W entrance to the bay and marked by a beacon (port hand).

Caution. The tidal stream sets towards Screen Rocks during the out-going tide.

Berths. There is anchorage in the bay S of the pier in depths of 6 m, sand; S winds bring in a heavy sea.

6   A berth 66 m in length exists alongside the pier.

Facilities are limited, except for small craft; metered electricity on the pier enables repair work to be carried out; the pier can be floodlit.

Supplies: fresh water; marine diesel by road tanker; provisions.

Garlieston
10.122

1   **General description.** Garlieston (54°47′N 4°22′W) a small town and tidal harbour, lies within Garlieston Bay, an inlet 5 cables wide which dries, situated W of Eggerness Point, a low-lying rocky point which protects it from N and NE winds.

A pier, from the head of which a light is exhibited, extends a short distance NNE then E from the shore at the SE end of the town.

Isle of Whithorn and St. Ninian's Tower from SE (10.121)
(Original dated 2001)

(Photograph - Air Images)

2   **Function.** On the commercial side, the port handles grain and fertiliser cargoes but fishing vessels and small craft also use the harbour.

Harbour Authority. Dumfries and Galloway Regional Council, Council Offices, English Street, Dumfries DG1 2DD.

Navigational matters concerning the harbour should be addressed to the Wigtown Manager. There is a resident Harbour Master who is employed on a part-time basis.

3   **Limiting conditions.** Vessels up to 1000 dwt can be accommodated at berth No 1; maximum beam 7·5 m, owing to siltation off the berth.

There are depths of 5·5 m at MHWS alongside the pier at which time the pier has a freeboard of only 0·6 m; as all berths dry out at LW vessels must be prepared to take the ground, soft mud bottom.

4   Cargo vessels should negotiate the entrance channel at HW ±1 hour.

Pilotage is not compulsory but is advisable for cargo vessels, and can be arranged by contacting the Harbour Master. The boarding position is approximately 1 mile offshore; the pilot vessel is equipped with VHF radio.

An ETA is required from cargo vessels giving as much notice as possible to the Harbour Master.

5   **Tug.** One small tug is available within the harbour.

Directions. Vessels with suitable draught enter the harbour by the Pouton Burn Channel which can be negotiated 3½ hours either side of HW. When approaching the pier, vessels should pass at least 1 cable off to avoid a rocky patch which lies ½ cable off the seaward end of the pier.

6   **Berths.** Anchorage in offshore winds can be obtained 5 cables SE of Garlieston Pier, sand and stones; a heavy swell in the locality is caused by SE winds.

There are three alongside berths on the pier; the longest berth being 85 m.

Small craft can berth inside the harbour alongside the pier wall.

Repairs: metered electricity on the pier for repairs; inner section of the pier has floodlighting; slipway.

Supplies: fresh water; diesel fuel by road tanker; provisions.

Minor bays
10.123

1   **Brighouse Bay** lies between Meikle Ross (54°46′N 4°06′W) and Borness Point, 2 miles NW, and is fringed by shelving rocks extending approximately 1 cable off the W point; the bay is prone to S winds and rough water.

Halftide Rock, which dries 4·5 m lies 2 cables offshore at Dunrod Point, the W entrance to the bay.

2   A gas interconnector pipeline (10.99) lands at the head of the bay, as shown on the chart.

Kirkandrews Bay lies 2 miles NW of Borness Point and is fronted by ledges, 2 to 3 cables wide, and is not suitable for anchorage except temporarily in offshore winds.

3   **Rigg Bay,** the shores of which are thickly wooded, lies close N of Sliddery Point (54°46′N 4°21′W). The S and N entrance points are foul, particularly the latter from which above-water rocks extend 2½ cables SE. The bottom of the bay consists of sand.

A rectangular concrete section of Mulberry Harbour from World War II, 25 m long and 15 m wide, lies stranded in a depth of 2·5 m at the entrance to the bay. It dries 3·9 m and is marked by a light-buoy (E cardinal).

Anchorages and harbours
10.124

1	**Islands of Fleet** (54°49′N 4°14′W) a group of four rocky islands which extend across the entrance to Fleet Bay provide anchorages in offshore winds, as shown on the chart. Between Barlocco Isle, the S isle which is connected with the coast by drying rocks, and Ardwall Isle, 4 cables NW, there is fair anchorage in depths of 4·6 m, sand; between Ardwall and the S islet of Murray's Isles, 4 cables WNW, there is good anchorage in depths of 3·7 m.

At LW, Ardwall Isle and Murray's Isles are connected by the sands of Fleet Bay.
10.125

1	**Portyerrock Bay**, NW of Cairn Head (54°43′N 4°21′W), provides shelter from S winds and good anchorage, as shown on the chart, in depths of approximately 10 to 12 m, sand, almost clear of the influence of tidal streams.
10.126

1	**Fleet Bay**, the whole of which dries, is entered between Ardwall Isle (54°49′N 4°14′W) and Garvellan Rocks which extend 3 cables from the coast, 1¾ miles NW. The bay is exposed to S winds. A caravan site stands on top of the cliffs above Garvellan Rocks.

At the head of the bay lies Fleet Canal leading to Port Macadam and Gatehouse of Fleet. The canal is approachable only by small craft using the contoured channel of Water of Fleet from seawards, which from off Sandgreen on the E shore, 1½ miles within the bay, is marked by perches carrying topmarks.

2	A by-pass bridge which crosses the canal below Gatehouse of Fleet has a vertical clearance of 3 m at MHWS. Craft which cannot negotiate the bridge can moor at mid-stream posts below the bridge.
10.127

1	**Creetown** (54°54′N 4°23′W), a small town, lies at the E entrance to the river Cree. In good weather and with a suitable tide small craft of 3·7 m draught can navigate as far as Creetown by continuing in the channel N of Carsluith (10.120).
10.128

1	**Wigtown** (54°52′N 4°26′W), a small town and small craft harbour, stands on an eminence lying on the NW side near the head of Wigtown Bay, approximately 2 miles SW of the entrance to the river Cree; the intervening ground is flat and marshy.

The river Bladnoch flows into the bay, 5 cables S of the town, through the old port of Wigtown which is now disused. Entrance to the harbour is through a channel, partly marked by perches and buoys, which follows the course of the river.

Luce Bay

General information
10.129

1	**General description.** Luce Bay is entered between Burrow Head (54°41′N 4°24′W) and the Mull of Galloway, 16 miles W (10.105). The Bay is exposed to an indraught owing to S winds which are frequent at all times of the year.

2	The Scares, a group of rocks virtually devoid of vegetation, lie in the middle of the entrance to the Bay.

They consist of Big Scare a steep-to rock 21 m high, the outermost of the group, lying 5½ miles ENE of the Mull of Galloway, and Little Scares a group of above-water and below-water rocks 7 cables NNE; the rocks, which form a bird reserve, are virtually inaccessible.

There is a bird reserve near the Mull of Galloway Light (10.18); it is owned by the Royal Society of the Protection of Birds which discourages access to it.

3	**Topography.** On the E side, N of Burrow Head, the coastline comprises a shingle beach backed by high land rising to Fell of Carleton, 6 cables inland, becoming flat farther N as far as the Mull of Sinniness (54°50′N 4°46′W) where the land within the Mull rises sharply N towards Knock Fell (Chart 2724) and E towards Mochrum Fell.

The head of the Bay consists of sandhills fronted by Luce Sands, nearly 6 miles in length, which dry out 5 cables. Two rivers, Water of Luce and Piltanton Burn flow through a common outlet at the E end of the Sands.

4	On the W side the coastline, which is generally rocky and stony with numerous indentations, is contained by the peninsula forming the S part of The Rhins of Galloway (see *West Coast of Scotland Pilot*) which terminates in the Mull of Galloway (10.105).

Firing practice area. There are several target floats moored in the Bay which are painted in distinctive colours; the area, which is a bombing range and shown on the chart, is marked by DZ light buoys, and at the N end there are also platforms each with an associated mooring buoy.

5	Within the limits of the range there is a large amount of potentially hazardous unexploded ordnance on the seabed, including an area centred on 54°45′·2N 4°49′·8W marked by light buoys (N S, E and W cardinal).

Bye-laws are in operation; information and assistance can be obtained from Test and Evaluation Establishment, West Freugh (54°51′N 4°57′W) (10.134); for further information on firing practice areas see *Annual Notice to Mariners Number 5*.

6	**Tidal stream** in the middle of the Bay is more or less rotary anti-clockwise; the strongest and weakest streams set as follows:

Interval from HW Liverpool	Direction	Rate	
		Sp	Np
+0555	ESE	¼	¼
−0315	NNE	1¼	¾
−0015	W	½	¼
+0245	SSW	1¼	¾

7	During the E-going stream an eddy sets W towards Cailness Point (54°41′N 4°52′W) then S along the coast to the Mull of Galloway.

On the E side of the Bay the streams follow the coast in both directions between Burrow Head and the Point of Lag, 5½ miles NNW.

In the NW part of the Bay the streams are probably weak and irregular.

Tidal stream information is shown on the chart.

Directions

Principal mark
10.130

1	**Landmarks:**
Mull of Galloway Lighthouse (54°38′N 4°51′W) (10.18).
Major light:
Mull of Galloway Light (54°38′N 4°51′W) (10.18).

Passage
10.131

1   From the W, the Mull of Galloway may be confidently approached as regards depth of water; however, due regard should be paid to the race (10.102), and, to a ridge with a least depth of 10 m which lies between 1 and 2 miles NE of the Mull and is indicated by an extensive area of disturbed water.

  From E, a race (10.118) exists S of Burrow Head (54°41′N 4°24′W); a detached shoal with depths of less than 6 m lies 1½ miles W of the headland.

2   Elsewhere Luce Bay is generally clear of dangers outside 4 cables offshore, the bottom consisting mainly of fine sand and shells, except near The Scares (10.129) where it is gravel and rock.

  Caution. An unmarked dangerous wreck (position approximate) lies 2½ miles E of Big Scare (54°40′N 4°42′W) (10.129) and Target Barge M3 constitutes a dangerous unmarked wreck in position 54°48′·3N 4°51′·4W.

Useful mark
10.132

1   Silos (54°41′·3N 4°53′·6W), on the S side of Drummore.

Port William
10.133

1   **General description.** Port William (54°45′·5N 4°35′·0W), a small resort with a harbour, lies 1¾ miles N of Barsalloch Point (10.135). The harbour consists of an L-shaped pier extending WNW from the shore, which dries alongside 1½ hours either side of LW, and a small stone breakwater to the N of it leaving an entrance about 20 m wide.

  Inshore fishing vessels and pleasure craft can enter the harbour after half-tide and berth alongside the inner face of the pier.

2   It is the only place on the E coast of Luce Bay which affords any shelter in S winds.

  Harbour Authority. Dumfries and Galloway Regional Council, Council Offices, English Street, Dumfries DG1 2DD.

  The Harbour Authority is represented by a resident Harbour Master who is employed on a part-time basis throughout the year.

3   **Limiting conditions.** The harbour can accommodate any vessel having a draught up to 3 m at MHWS which can take the ground, clay.

  Directions. The alignment (105°) of Port William Leading Lights leads to the harbour entrance.

    Front light (54°45′·7N 4°35′·3W) (metal mast, 6 m in height) standing on the head of the jetty.

    Rear light (130 m from front light) (bracket on building).

4   Entry is between the head of the pier and a beacon (port hand) situated at the head of the small breakwater.

  Repairs: minor repairs, small slipway.

  Supplies: fresh water; fuel; provisions.

  Anchorage. There is good anchorage in offshore winds, 3 to 4 cables W of the pierhead in depths of 7 m.

Drummore
10.134

1   **General description.** Drummore, a village on the W side of Drummore Bay, lies 1 mile NW of Cailness Point (54°41′N 4°52′W), a low lying point. The harbour at

Drummore has a quay, built under the shelter of the point E of the village, extending NW which is prolonged by a groyne extending for 46 m; a breakwater constructed of rock, 120 m long, extends NE from the shore towards the head of the quay leaving an entrance 50 m wide.

  Harbour Authority. Test and Evaluation Establishment, West Freugh, Stranraer DG9 9DN.

2   **Limiting conditions.** Vessels with a draught of up to 4·5 m can berth on the inner side of the quay at MHWS but the harbour dries, soft mud.

  Directions. The harbour is first approached from the E or NE, thence entered from NW. The bearing 220° of the church spire situated in the village, a building that is not easy to identify when more than 5 cables from the village, will assist the approach from NE until the alignment of the quay (NW-SE) is reached.

3   **Repairs:** minor repairs; small slipway.

  Supplies: fresh water; fuel; provisions.

  Anchorage. Drummore Bay affords good anchorage, with shelter from S and W winds, 5 cables offshore in depths of 4 to 5 m, sand.

  Other moorings can be obtained alongside the inner side of the rock built breakwater.

Anchorages
10.135

1   **Back Bay** between the Point of Cairndoon (54°43′N 4°31′W) and the Point of Lag, 1 mile NW, on which stands a beacon and from which point a stony ledge dries out to about 2 cables offshore. The bay provides anchorage in offshore winds.

2   **Monreith Bay** is entered between the Point of Lag and Barsalloch Point (54°44′N 4°34′W), 1¼ miles NW, which dries out to 1½ cables from the point; the shores of the bay are high and the foreshore is stony except for some fine sand off the village of Monreith.

  The bay provides good shelter from N and E winds.

3   **Auchenmalg Bay** lies close E of the Mull of Sinniness (54°50′N 4°46′W) and provides anchorage, in offshore winds, 3½ cables offshore in depths of 7 m.

  Crows Nest Bay lies 1½ miles NW of the Mull of Sinniness, the intervening coast being bold and rocky; Stair Haven lies on the E side of the bay, which provides anchorage in offshore winds.

4   **East Tarbet Bay** lies on the N side of the promontory forming the Mull of Galloway (10.105) which protects it from S; it is the most secure anchorage in Luce Bay. A landing place (10.136) is situated at the head of the bay.

5   The best anchorage is 2½ cables ENE of the landing place in depths of from 6 to 7 m, as shown on the chart.

  New England Bay (54°44′N 4°54′W) is skirted by large stones near the low-water line. It affords good anchorage, in offshore winds, in depths of 8 m.

6   **Chapel Rossan Bay** (54°46′N 4°56′W) affords good shelter from W winds. The S point of the bay is rocky and the N point stony; there are patches of stones with a least depth of 2·4 m over them which skirt the bay.

  Sandhead Bay, at the SW end of Luce Sands (10.129), provides good anchorage 1 mile offshore in depths of 7 m.

Landing place
10.136

1   A storehouse and landing place, used for supplying the lighthouse at the S end of the Mull of Galloway (54°38′N 4°51′W), are situated at the head of East Tarbet Bay close N.

ISLE OF MAN

GENERAL INFORMATION

Chart 2094
Area covered
10.137

1 This section describes the coastal waters and harbours of the Isle of Man, lying in the N part of the Irish Sea approximately equidistant from the shores of England and Northern Ireland, and an offshore route from the Calf of Man (54°03′N 4°49′W), a small island of the SW tip of the main island, to Liverpool Bay.

It is arranged as follows:

2 Offshore Route — Calf of Man to Liverpool Bay (10.146).
Calf of Man to Douglas (10.155).
Douglas to Point of Ayre (10.200).
Calf of Man to Point of Ayre — West coast (10.221).

Topography
10.138

1 The 221 square miles of the island consist largely of mountains and hills, the N part being low-lying and flat. The highest point, at 617 m, is Snaefell (54°16′N 4°28′W) (10.18). A valley cuts across the island from Douglas (54°09′N 4°28′W), the capital and main port, on the E coast to Peel (54°13′N 4°41′W), a small harbour, on the W. The coastline S of this valley is heavily indented by small bays.

Administration
10.139

1 The island is a dependency of the British Crown and is administered in accordance with its own laws by the Court of Tynwald (1.78).

The principal port and seat of government is Douglas (54°09′N 4°28′W).

The population of the island was 76 315 in 2001.

Harbour Authorities. Department of Transport (DOT) (Rheynn Arraghey), Harbours Division, Sea Terminal Building, Douglas, Isle of Man IM1 2RF. The harbours division is responsible for all harbours on the island.

2 Navigational matters should be addressed to the Director of Harbours at the above address:
Telephone: +44 (0)1624 686626
Email: enquiries@harbours.dot.gov.im

Trade. Principal exports of the island are fish, agricultural produce and livestock; the chief imports consist of petroleum products, fertilisers and container cargoes.

Submarine exercise areas
10.140

1 See 10.3.

Fishing
10.141

1 See 10.4; lobster pots are present at most times of the year up to 1 cable offshore between Orrisdale Head (54°18′N 4°35′W) S around the Calf of Man to Maughold Head (54°18′N 4°19′W). Whelk pots, similar to lobster

Chicken Rock Lighthouse, Calf of Man and Isle of Man from SW (10.138)
(Original dated 2001)

(Photograph - Air Images)

pots, may be encountered up to several miles offshore, particularly amongst the banks E of Point of Ayre (54°25′N 4°22′W).

Pilotage
10.142

1 Throughout all harbours of the Isle of Man, pilotage is available but not compulsory.

Tidal streams
10.143

1 During the in-going streams in Saint George's Channel and the North Channel the offshore tidal stream sets as follows:

Locality	Direction
NW coast; N part	NE
NW coast; S part	SW
SE coast; N part	S
SE coast; S part	NE

During the out-going streams the directions are reversed.

2 There is a large area of weak and irregular streams offshore SW of the Isle of Man. See 1.94.

The coastal streams, which extend up to 6 miles from the coast, meet and separate off Maughold Head (54°18′N 4°18′W) and off Contrary Head (54°13′N 4°43′W); they are modified by eddies and local conditions. See 10.227.

Tidal streams are given on the chart and in *Admiralty Tidal Stream Atlas — Irish Sea and Bristol Channel*, and also the relevant parts of this section.

Offshore routes
10.144

1 For details of an offshore route between a position SW of the Calf of Man and Liverpool Bay, see 10.146.

For details of an offshore route between a position SW of the Calf of Man (54°03′N 4°49′W) and a position off Mew Island (54°42′N 5°31′W), see *Irish Coast Pilot*.

An offshore route lies between Morecambe Bay and a position SW of the Mull of Galloway passing close NNE of the Isle of Man, for details see 10.12.

Rescue
10.145

1 All-weather lifeboats are stationed at:
Douglas (54°09′N 4°29′W).
Ramsey (54°19′N 4°23′W).
Peel (54°13′N 4°42′W).
Port Saint Mary (54°04′N 4°44′W).
Inshore lifeboats are stationed at:
Port Saint Mary.
Port Erin (54°05′N 4°46′W).
For further details of rescue organisation and assets see 1.60.

OFFSHORE ROUTE — CALF OF MAN TO LIVERPOOL BAY

General information

Charts 1826, 2094, 1981, 1951
Route
10.146

1 An offshore route for vessels proceeding from the North Channel (*Irish Coast Pilot*) towards Liverpool Bay passes SW of the Calf of Man (54°03′N 4°49′W).

The route from the Calf of Man to the vicinity of Bar Light Buoy (53°32′N 3°21′W), the pilot boarding area for vessels entering the river Mersey (8.85), leads ESE for a distance of approximately 60 miles.

Topography
10.147

1 For a description of the S coast of the Isle of Man, see 10.156; the coastline bordering the river Dee and the river Mersey estuaries is in general, low lying and indistinct. See 8.60.

Wrecks
10.148

1 Liverpool Bay; see 8.5.

Marine exploitation
10.149

1 Liverpool Bay; see 9.4.

Rescue
10.150

1 An all-weather lifeboat and an inshore lifeboat are stationed at Port Saint Mary (54°04′N 4°44′W).
For details of rescue organisation see 1.60.

Tidal streams
10.151

1 See 1.94. Tidal streams are given on the charts and in *Admiralty Tidal Stream Atlas — Irish Sea and Bristol Channel*.

Directions

Principal marks
10.152

1 **Landmarks:**
Chicken Rock Lighthouse (granite tower; 44 m in height) (54°02′N 4°50′W), conspicuous, standing on Chicken Rock (10.163).

Chicken Rock Lighthouse from S (10.152)
(Original dated 2001)

(Photograph - Air Images)

2 Calf of Man Lighthouse (disused) (white, 8-sided tower on granite building; 11 m in height) (54°03′N 4°50′W) standing on the Calf of Man (10.166).
Television Mast (54°04′·5N 4°44′·5W) (10.162).
King William's College (Tower) (54°05′N 4°38′W) (10.181).
Tower (54°03′·5N 4°37′·3W) (10.181).

3 **Major lights:**
Chicken Rock Light — as above.
Douglas Head Light (54°09′N 4°28′W) (10.162).

Other aids to navigation
10.153
1 **Racon:**
Bar Light Buoy (53°32′N 3°21′W).
For further details see *Admiralty List of Radio Signals Volume 2.*

Calf of Man to the Bar Light Buoy
10.154
1 For details of the offshore route between the North Channel and the Calf of Man, see *Irish Coast Pilot.*

From a position SW of the Calf of Man (54°03′N 4°49′W) to the vicinity of Bar Light Buoy (53°32′N 3°21′W) and the pilot boarding area for the river Mersey, the route leads approximately 60 miles ESE, in deep water, passing:
2 SSW of Chicken Rock (6 cables SW of the Calf of Man) on which stands a conspicuous lighthouse (10.152), thence:
SSW of Wart Bank (54°02′N 4°47′W) (10.163) with a least depth of 8·3 m, thence:
SSW of Langness Point (54°03′N 4°38′W) from where a light (white tower, 19 m in height) is exhibited close E; a prominent tower (10.181) lies 2½ cables NE of the light, thence:
3 SSW of South Morecambe Gas Field (53°51′N 3°35′W) (9.4) from where a flare is exhibited, thence:
To Bar Light Buoy, keeping clear of the platforms in the Douglas/Hamilton Oil/Gas Fields, as shown on the chart. See 9.4.

(Directions for entering the river Mersey are given at 8.92)

CALF OF MAN TO DOUGLAS

General information

Chart 2094
Route
10.155
1 From a position SW of Chicken Rock (54°02′N 4°50′W) to the vicinity of Douglas Head (54°09′N 4°28′W) the passage leads E then NE for a distance of about 19 miles, passing SE of Dreswick Point (10.163).

Topography
10.156
1 The Calf of Man (10.166) is an island which lies close off the SW extremity of the Isle of Man and separated from it by Calf Sound.

The S coast of the Isle of Man is indented by small bays whose low and uneven shores are skirted by rocks and ledges. At the W end, Spanish Head (54°03′N 4°46′W) lies at the S end of a peninsula which rises to Mull Hill, 1 mile inland, forming the SW extremity of the Isle of Man.
2 Langness Peninsula, T-shaped, which lies at the E end consists of rugged abrupt rocks of slate formation terminating at Langness Point (54°03′N 4°38′W) at the SW end of the peninsula and Saint Michael's Island at the NE end.

The SE coastline, low-lying at the S end, consists of cliffs which rise from 6 m to 119 m NE of Santon Head (54°06′N 4°33′W), then decrease in height and rise again towards Douglas Head (54°09′N 4°28′W) (10.163).

Historic wreck
10.157
1 An historic wreck is situated 2 cables SW of Langness Light (54°03′N 4°37′W). The wreck is protected against unauthorised interference. See 1.57 and *Annual Notice to Mariners Number 16.*

Submarine cable
10.158
1 A submarine cable is landed on the shore close W of Port Grenaugh (54°06′N 4°34′W); the cable links the Isle of Man with the English mainland.

Transfer of cargo operation
10.159
1 Transfer of liquid cargo operations occasionally take place in an area approximately 4 miles E of Douglas Head (54°09′N 4°28′W). Vessels engaged in these operations may be at anchor, or otherwise unable to manoeuvre, and should be given a wide berth.

Rescue
10.160
1 All-weather lifeboats are stationed at Port Saint Mary (54°04′N 4°44′W) and at Douglas (54°09′N 4°28′W); an inshore lifeboat is stationed at Port Saint Mary.
For details of rescue organisation see 1.60.

Natural conditions
10.161
1 **Tidal streams** W of the Calf of Man set N and S, but change direction off Chicken Rock (54°02′N 4°50′W) and set W and E between the Calf of Man and Langness Point (54°03′N 4°38′W). The spring rate in each direction is approximately 5 kn.
There is little stream close off the W and E sides of Calf of Man.
2 The in-going stream off the E side of Langness Peninsula begins 5¾ hours after HW Liverpool and the out-going stream begins 4¼ hours before HW at that port.
The maximum spring rate in each direction is 2¼ kn. farther seawards, rates of 5 kn have been experienced.
During the NE-going stream an eddy sets W towards Saint Michael's Island then S towards Dreswick Point.
Tidal streams between Derby Haven and Douglas Head (54°09′N 4°28′W), clear of the land, set NE and SW.
3 Near the land the NE-going stream sets for 3¼ hours and the SW-going stream sets for 9¼ hours. An eddy forms during the second half of the NE-going stream. The streams begin as follows:

Position	Interval from HW Liverpool	Direction
Santon Head (54°06′N 4°33′W)	+0515	NE
	−0400	SW
Douglas Head	−0610	NE
	−0300	SW

4 The maximum spring rate in each direction is 2¼ kn.
Tidal streams are given on the chart and in *Admiralty Tidal Streams Atlas — Irish Sea and Bristol Channel.*
Races. A race extends E from Chicken Rock during the E-going stream, and N from the rock on the W-going stream.

5   The E-going stream begins –0610 HW Liverpool; W-going stream begins HW Liverpool.

A race forms off Dreswick Point under certain weather conditions at springs. In a SW wind over a SW setting stream, the race, which is known locally as Langness Race, extends nearly 1 mile SE of the point and can be dangerous for small craft.

Directions

Principal marks
10.162
1   **Landmarks:**
On the S coast:
Chicken Rock Lighthouse (54°02′N 4°50′W) (10.152).
Calf of Man Lighthouse (disused) (54°03′N 4°50′W) (10.152).
Television Mast (elevation 133 m), conspicuous, (54°04′·5N 4°44′·5W), standing 57 m in height, and overlooking Port Saint Mary.

Television Mast, Port St. Mary (10.162)
(Original dated 1997)

(Photograph - Naval Party 1008)

2   King William's College (Tower) (54°05′N 4°38′W) (10.181).
On the SE coast:
Tower (54°03′·5N 4°37′·3W) (10.181).
Carnane Radio Mast, conspicuous (54°08′·4N 4°29′·6W), standing on a hill, exhibits obstruction lights; a second radio mast, also exhibiting obstruction lights, stands 2 miles farther W.
Douglas Head Hotel (tower) (54°08′·5N 4°28′·1W).
3   **Major lights:**
Chicken Rock Light (54°02′N 4°50′W) (10.152).
Douglas Head Light (white tower and buildings, 20 m in height) (54°09′N 4°28′W).

Douglas Head Light from NE (10.162)
(Original dated 1997)

(Photograph - Naval Party 1008)

Chicken Rock to Douglas Head
10.163
1   From a position SW of Chicken Rock (54°02′N 4°50′W) to a position SE of Douglas Head (54°09′N 4°28′W) the passage leads E then NE for a distance of about 19 miles, passing (with positions from Langness Light (54°03′N 4°37′W)):
S of Chicken Rock, 1½ m high, on which stands a light (10.152); a steep-to 13·7 m patch lies 1 cable SE; tide races (10.161) form off the rock, and:
2   Clear of a wreck with an unsurveyed clearance depth of 25 m (54°00′·7N 4°50′·3W), thence:
S of Wart Bank (5½ miles WSW) with a least depth of 8·3 m over it lying 1 mile S of Spanish Head (54°03′N 4°46′W) (10.156); precipitous cliffs lie close NW of the headland, and masts, part of the disused radio station of Cregneish and a beacon close NE stand on high ground NE of the headland. Thence:
3   S of Kallow Point (4 miles WNW) the W entrance point to Bay ny Carrickey, thence:
S of Scarlett Point (1½ miles WNW) the E entrance point of Bay ny Carrickey, thence:
S and SE of Dreswick Point, the S tip of Langness Peninsula, with a dangerous race (10.161) extending SE; Langness Light is exhibited from the point; an unmarked dangerous wreck lies close S, thence:
4   SE of foul ground with a least depth of 9·7 m over it which lies 7 cables SE of Saint Michael's Island (1½ miles NE), sometimes called Fort Island because of a ruined fort which stands at the NE end of the island; the island is joined to the NE part of Langness Peninsula by a causeway. A dangerous sea is often found over the foul ground during gales; Douglas Head Light (10.162) in sight at night clears this danger, thence:
5   SE of Santon Head (4 miles NE), 60 m high, with Baltic Rock, which dries, together with another rock with a depth of 1 m over it, close SE, lying close S of the headland, thence:
SE of Little Ness (6 miles NE) with rocks, which dry extending ¾ cable offshore, thence:
6   SE of Douglas Head (8 miles NE) on which stands a light (10.162). Douglas Head Hotel (10.162) stands 1½ cables SW. The Head has a bold appearance when seen from NE or SW and is fringed by a steep-to narrow ledge of rock.

10.164
1   **Caution.** Off the SE coastline Douglas Head Light is obscured when bearing more than 037°.

Useful marks
10.165
1   Thousla Rock Light Beacon (54°03′·7N 4°48′·0W) (10.168).
Milner's Tower (54°05′·5N 4°46′·6W) (10.228), visible to SE and seaward of the S coastline from Bay ny Carrickey to the N end of Langness Peninsula.

(Directions continue for the coastal passage at 10.204; directions for entry to Douglas are given at 10.194)

Calf of Man with Calf Sound

Calf of Man
10.166
1   **General description.** The Calf of Man (54°03′N 4°49′W) is an island which lies close off the SW extremity of the Isle of Man; it rises to an elevation of 125 m near its NW end and thence diminishes to the N coast which is

Calf of Man Lighthouse and disused lighthouses from W (10.166)
(Original dated 2001)

(Photograph - Air Images)

low and rocky; elsewhere the coastline is formed by cliffs of from 30 to 105 m in height.

2   The Buroo, a bold rocky cliff, with the appearance of an islet, lies at the S end of the island to which it is connected by a drying isthmus. It is perforated by a hole known as The Eye.

The Stack, is a rocky islet separated from the W extremity of the island by a narrow boat passage in which there is a submerged rock.

Tidal streams. See 10.161.

3   **Passage.** A passage, with a least depth of 24·5 m, lies between Chicken Rock (54°02′N 4°50′W) and the Calf of Man.

Useful marks:

    Two disused lighthouses, which lie close NE and SE of Calf of Man Lighthouse (also disused) (10.152), in line, lead over Chicken Rock.

10.167

1   **Landing places** are situated at South Harbour, a small inlet close E of The Buroo, at Grant's Harbour on the NE corner of the island, and at Cow Harbour on the N side of the island.

Chart 2696 plan of Calf Sound
Calf Sound
10.168

1   **General description.** The passage between the Calf of Man and the Isle of Man is divided into two channels by the low barren island of Kitterland; Calf Sound, the W

channel, is wider and deeper than Little Sound, which lies close E of Kitterland.

The Cletts, rocks, extend ¾ cable offshore from the Calf of Man near the S entrance to Calf Sound.

2   **Tidal streams** set strongly through Calf Sound, mainly in the direction of the channel.

The N-going stream begins −0145 HW Liverpool; the S-going stream begins +0345 HW Liverpool.

The maximum spring rate in each direction is approximately 3½ kn.

Landmarks:

3   Thousla Rock Light Beacon (8–sided concrete tapered pillar; 9 m in height) (54°03′·7N 4°48′·0W), conspicuous, standing on a rock of the same name, which dries, lying on the W side of Calf Sound near its N entrance.

4   Flagstaff, standing near the NE shore of Little Sound; monuments (prominent stone crosses, 1·2 m in height) stand about 110 m NW and 80 m SE of the flagstaff.

Local knowledge is required before attempting passage through Calf Sound or Little Sound.

Bay ny Carrickey

Chart 2696 plan of Bay ny Carrickey
General information
10.169

1   **General description.** Bay ny Carrickey is entered between Kallow Point (54°04′N 4°44′W) and Scarlett Point, 2½ miles E. The low and uneven shores of the bay are

skirted by rocks and ledges extending 2 cables offshore, with the exception of a sandy bight in the NW corner. The small harbour of Port Saint Mary (10.172) lies in the SW corner of the bay.

2   The Carrick, a rock, occupies the centre of the bay; a light (isolated danger; 8 m in height) is exhibited from the rock, which presents a good radar target.

A rock with a depth of 1·3 m over it lies 2½ cables NE of the light beacon.

The Carrick Light-beacon from S (low water) (10.169)
(Original dated 1997)

(Photograph - Naval Party 1008)

10.170
1   **Tidal streams.** The tidal stream in the bay sets between the shore and The Carrick. It sets clockwise on the in-going stream and anti-clockwise on the out-going stream, changing at about one hour before HW and LW, attaining a spring rate of up to 2 kn.

The rate of the NE-going stream is increased by SW gales; a rate estimated at 5 kn has been observed off the entrance to Port Saint Mary.

10.171
1   **Anchorage.** Bay ny Carrickey has poor holding owing to numerous patches of rock and hard sand; during offshore winds vessels usually anchor between Port Saint Mary and The Carrick in depths of approximately 6 m.

Port Saint Mary

General information
10.172
1   **Position.** Port Saint Mary (54°04′N 4°44′W), a small harbour which consists of a drying inner harbour and an outer harbour with alongside berths and moorings, lies in the SW corner of a bay of the same name situated on the W side of Bay ny Carrickey.

Function. The harbour is used by yachts, fishing vessels and, occasionally, by coasters and passenger vessels.

Port limits are bounded by lines drawn from The Carrick N to the coast and W to the root of Alfred Pier.

Approach and entry. Approached between SW and SE to pass between The Carrick (54°04′·3N 4°42′·7W) and the head of Alfred Pier (6¾ cables W).

Traffic. In 2007 there were 5 port calls with a total of 4044 dwt.

Port Authority. See 10.139. For local information there is a Port Manager at Port Saint Mary who is also responsible for the administration of Port Erin and Castletown Harbours.

Limiting conditions
10.173
1   **Tidal levels.** Mean spring range about 5·4 m; mean neap range about 3·2 m. See *Admiralty Tide Tables*.

Maximum size of vessel handled. The drying, hard sand, inner harbour can be entered by vessels drawing 3·7 m and 2·5 m at MHWS and MHWN respectively.

At Alfred Pier, vessels up to 60 m in length having a draught of up to 3·0 m can be accommodated. Occasionally, dependent on weather, vessels up to 65 m can be berthed alongside.

Arrival information
10.174
1   **Port radio.** Office hours only and when a vessel is expected.

Pilotage. See 10.142. For further details see *Admiralty List of Radio Signals Volume 6(1)*.

Harbour
10.175
1   **General layout.** The outer harbour is partly sheltered from NE by Carthure Rocks, rocky ledges which extend SE from Gansey Point and marked by a beacon (starboard hand); it is also sheltered from SE by Alfred Pier, which extends NE from the shore 2 cables NE of Kallow Point at the W entrance point to Bay ny Carrickey.

2   The inner harbour, which is quayed all round, is formed by two piers extending from the shore 1¾ cables W of Alfred Pier.

Tidal stream: see 10.170 for tidal streams in the bay.

Climate information: see information for Ronaldsway at 1.154.

Directions for entering harbour
10.176
1   Approaching from SE, the alignment (295°) of the lights (white towers, red band, 7 and 8 m in height) exhibited from the heads of Alfred Pier and the inner pier 2 cables NW, leads SSW of The Carrick (10.169).

2   Approaching from SW give Kallow Point and Alfred Pier a berth of at least 2 cables until the inner pierhead is open N of Alfred Pier.

On entering, pass ½ cable N of Alfred Pier to avoid a 3 m patch off the pierhead; if entering the inner harbour pass the inner pierhead close-to.

Basins and berths
10.177
1   **Anchorage** can be had in Chapel Bay, N/NE of Alfred Pier in 3 to 6 m.

Alongside berths are available at the outer end of Alfred Pier for maximum size of vessel (10.173), however, the pier is heavily used by the local fishing fleet and prior arrangement is essential. Smaller vessels with a draught not exceeding 2·5 m can berth at the inner end, which is kept free of fishing vessels between April and October.

2   Berths for craft which can take the ground are situated in the inner harbour.

Port St. Mary from ENE (10.177)
(Original dated 2001)

(Photograph - Air Images)

Visitors' moorings are laid during the summer season in the outer harbour, and off Chapel Bay. There are two slipways for small craft on the SW side of the outer harbour and one in the inner harbour.

Landing can be made at the head of the W pier by a ladder and at steps mid-way on its E side.

Port services
10.178
1   **Repairs:** small craft only.

Supplies: fresh water at Alfred Pier; diesel oil by road; provisions and stores in limited quantities.

Castletown Bay

Chart 2696 plan of Castletown Bay
General information
10.179
1   **Description.** Castletown Bay is entered between Scarlett Point (54°03'·7N 4°40'·0W) (10.169) and Langness Point (1¼ miles ESE), the SW tip of Langness Peninsula.

2   The Skerranes, rocks which dry, extend 1 cable SW from Langness Point. The NW side of the bay is bordered by drying rocks, of which Lheeah-rio Rocks, the outermost, are marked on their SE side by a light buoy (port hand); Boe Norris and Sandwick Boe, drying rocks, lie 4 and 5½ cables, respectively, farther NE.

There is a 5 m patch near the centre of the bay; in the SE part of the bay the bottom is foul and depths are uneven.

10.180
1   **Tidal streams.** Off the entrance to the bay an E-going eddy begins +0015 HW Liverpool, with a spring rate of 2½ kn, shortly after the commencement of the W-going stream off Langness. This eddy sets towards the W side of Langness Peninsula and divides; one branch sets S towards Langness Point and the other sets N and W round the bay.

There is a practically continuous S-going stream along the SE shore of the bay.
10.181
1   **Landmarks:**
Tower, built of stone and conspicuous, which stands towards the SW end of Langness Peninsula, 2½ cables NNE of Langness Light.
Tower, conspicuous, part of an hotel standing at the NE end of Langness Peninsula.
2   King William's College, with a conspicuous tall battlemented tower marked by an obstruction light (occasional), situated at the head of the bay.
Castle Rushen (54°04'·4N 4°39'·2W), a quadrangular building flanked by towers, standing near Castletown Harbour.
Major light:
Chicken Rock Light (54°02'N 4°50'W) (10.152) (Chart 2094).

Castletown Harbour
General information
10.182
1   **Position.** Castletown Harbour (54°04'N 4°39'W) lies on the NW side of Castletown Bay and consists of an outer and inner harbour, both of which dry.

Castletown from SE (10.182)
(Original dated 2001)

(Photograph - Air Images)

Function. The harbour is mainly used by pleasure craft, inshore fishing vessels and occasionally small coasters.

The population of Castletown, formerly the ancient capital of the Isle of Man, is about 3000.

2   **Port limits.** The outer limit is a line drawn between Scarlet Point and the Skerranes off Langness Point (10.179), encompassing the whole of Castletown Bay.

Port Authority. See 10.139. For local information, the Port Manager at Port Saint Mary is also responsible for the administration of Castletown Harbour.

Limiting conditions
10.183

1   **Maximum size of vessel handled:** inner harbour 55 m LOA, 8·2 m beam, 3·5 m draught on MHWS and 2·6 m draught on MHWN; outer harbour 55 m LOA, 3·8 m draught on MHWS and 2·7 m on MHWN. All vessels take the ground.

Local weather. The outer harbour is untenable with strong S to SE winds.

Arrival information
10.184

1   **Port radio:** 0900-1630 and when a vessel is expected.

Outer anchorage: SE of the light buoy marking Lheeah-rio Rocks in 13 to 18 m.

Pilotage. See 10.142.

For further details see *Admiralty List of Radio Signals Volume 6(1).*

Harbour
10.185

1   **General layout.** The outer harbour lies within New Pier, a breakwater, nearly 130 m long, and Irish Quay, a concrete faced pier. A landing hard (10.187) extends SE from the head of the breakwater.

The inner harbour is divided into three parts by a swing foot-bridge, which exhibits lights, and a fixed road bridge, both with a width between abutments of 8·7 m.

2   The narrow entrance to the inner harbour lies between Irish Quay and a light beacon, marking rocks on the E side.

Within the swing bridge the harbour is quayed all round; the middle portion of the harbour has a gravel bottom.

Climate information: see information for Ronaldsway at 1.154.

Directions for entering harbour
10.186

1   **Landmarks:** see 10.181.

On passing SE of the light buoy marking Lheeah-rio Rocks, the approximate alignment (323°) of the lights (white towers, red band, 9 and 4 m in height respectively) exhibited from the heads of New Pier and Irish Quay leads towards the harbour entrance, passing between Lheeah-rio and Boe Norris rocks. Vessels should keep NE of this alignment when approaching the harbour entrance giving the landing hard, extending SE from New Pier, a wide berth.

Basins and berths
10.187

1   **Berths.** Cargo handling takes place only at Umber Quay in the inner harbour. There is a lay-by berth on Irish Quay in the outer harbour. Both berths have a gravel bottom overlying rock.

The innermost part of the harbour, within the road bridge, has a bottom of gravel and mud and provides good accommodation for small craft. There is a slipway in the outer harbour.

2   **Landing.** Hard landing which extends SE from Castletown New Pier is usable by boats near LW.

Landing is also possible inside Castletown Bay, 2½ cables NE of Langness Point.

Port services
10.188

1   **Repairs:** marine engineer 1 mile distant.
Other facilities: oily waste by arrangement.
Supplies: fresh water; fuel by road; chandler 1 mile distant.

Derby Haven
10.189

1   **General information.** Derby Haven lies on the E side of the isthmus of Langness Peninsula. The bay is entered between Saint Michael's Island (54°04′N 4°36′W) and the coast 4 cables NW; gales from E bring in a heavy sea.
Ronaldsway Airport lies on the NW side of the bay, the shores of which are flat; N of the bay the runway lights extend seaward to the LW mark.

2   **Anchorage** may be found 1½ cables NW of the fort on Saint Michael's Island, in a depth of about 7 m where the holding is good, sand over marl.
Harbour. The head of the bay dries, and a portion has been converted into a sheltered harbour by a detached breakwater, 1¼ cables in length, constructed on a drying rocky ledge which projects some distance W of its N end; elsewhere the bottom consists of sand, mud, gravel and marl. The small resort of Derbyhaven fronts the head of the bay.

3   A light (white tower, green band) is exhibited from the S end of the breakwater; a beacon (port hand) stands ½ cable SSW of the light which marks the NE end of a drying rocky ledge.
Entry to the harbour is normally made between the S end of the breakwater and the beacon; the entrance is 55 m wide and has a depth of 4·9 m at MHWS, gradually shoaling within.

4   The N entrance, seldom used, has a similar width but a depth of 2·7 m MHWS; an outfall extends from the shore passing N of the breakwater.
Berths. There are mooring posts on the breakwater, and a landing slipway on its W side, near the N end. There are moorings in the bay off a jetty which extends NW from Saint Michael's Island.

Douglas Harbour
Chart 2696 plan of Douglas Bay
General information
10.190

1   **Position.** Douglas Harbour (54°09′N 4°28′W) lies at the mouth of the Douglas River where it enters the S end of Douglas Bay on the E coast of the Isle of Man.
Function. Douglas is the principal port for the Isle of Man; it handles RoRo vessels, coastal dry cargo ships and tankers and a considerable volume of passenger traffic, particularly in the summer months.

2   **Topography.** The frontage of the bay consists of a built-up area forming the town of Douglas and its suburb

Douglas Harbour from ESE (10.190)
(Original dated 2001)

(Photograph - Air Images)

Onchan. The foreshore at the head of the bay dries to 2 cables offshore and consists of gravel, sand and rock with below-water rocky ledges projecting a further 2 cables seaward.

Port limits are defined by a line drawn from Douglas Head (54°09′N 4°28′W) to Banks Howe (2¼ miles NE) (10.206).

3 For harbour control purposes a vessel control limit extends to 2¾ miles SE, 2½ miles SW and 4¼ miles NE from Douglas Head (54°08′·6N 4°28′·0W) (see Chart 2094).

Approach and entry. The harbour is approached and entered from the NE and entered on the alignment of a set of leading lights.

4 **Traffic.** In 2007, in addition to the regular ferry traffic, there were 27 ship calls with a total of 77 630 dwt.

Harbour Authority. For details see 10.139; for local information there is a duty Harbour Master at Douglas.

Limiting conditions
10.191

1 **Controlling depth.** The outer harbour has a maintained depth of 5·4 m.

Deepest and longest berth is the tanker berth on Battery Pier (10.198). The main RoRo berth is No 5 on the N side of King Edward VIII Pier (10.198).

Tidal levels: Mean spring range 6·1 m; mean neap range 3·0 m. See information in *Admiralty Tide Tables*.

Density of water: 1·025 g/cm^3 at all berths in Douglas Harbour.

2 **Maximum size of vessels handled:**

Cross channel RoRo ferries; 130·0 m LOA, draught 6·0 m.

Cargo vessels; 100·0 m LOA, draught 4·0 m.

Tankers: 85·0 m LOA, draught 5·5 m at MLWS, approximately 2500 dwt; larger vessels can be accepted by arrangement.

Arrival information
10.192

1 **Port operations.** Douglas Harbour Control operates an information service from a building situated at the root of Victoria Pier; a radar assistance service is available on request. Radar surveillance operates from Victoria Pier Head.

VTS. A VTS scheme with radar surveillance is maintained for the control of shipping. See *Admiralty List of Radio Signals Volume 6(1)*. Positions of reporting points are shown on the chart.

2 **Notice of ETA required.** Vessels should forward their ETA to Harbour Control at least 24 hours in advance.

Vessels should report their ETA 1 hour before arrival and again when 1 mile from the harbour entrance.

Outer anchorages. The holding in Douglas Bay is indifferent; gales between NE, through S to SW, bring a heavy swell into the bay. The following anchorages are recommended by the Harbours Division; Douglas Head bearing:

3 196°, 7·0 cables, in 11·0 m.
199°, 9·0 cables, in 13·0 m.
212°, 8·0 cables, in 14·0 m.
215°, 9·5 cables, in 15·0 m.

Care should be taken not to anchor near the submarine power cable extending NE and E from Port Skillion (54°08′·7N 4°27′·8W).

4 **Pilotage** is not compulsory, but a pilot is available on request; notice for a pilot is the same as for ETA. The pilot

boarding area is up to 1 mile ENE of No 1 Light Buoy or as directed by Harbour Control.

For further details see *Admiralty List of Radio Signals Volume 6(1)*.

Tugs. One small tug is available.

Harbour
10.193

1 **General layout.** Douglas Harbour consists of an outer harbour, containing the main commercial docks and in which vessels lie afloat, a middle harbour which mostly dries, and an inner wet dock marina into which the Douglas River flows. The harbour entrance, which faces NE, has a minimum width of 125 m.

Traffic signals. International Port Traffic Signals are exhibited from a mast at the head of Victoria Pier.

2 **Tidal streams.** The rate of tidal streams within Douglas Bay is much less than that off Douglas Head (10.161).

Across the harbour entrance an E-setting stream of 1½ kn may be experienced about 2 hours before HW springs, even when a N-setting stream is evident in the bay. At neap tides the E-setting stream is less than 1 kn and may be experienced 3 to 4 hours before HW.

3 **Tide rips** exist during the S-going stream in an area up to 3 cables NE to SE of the head of Princess Alexandra Pier. With strong winds between S and E the tide-rips may be dangerous to small boats.

Directions for entering harbour
10.194

1 **Landmarks:**

Douglas Head Hotel (tower) (54°08′·5N 4°28′·2W) (10.162).

Spherical tank standing at the root of the Princess Alexandra Pier (10.193).

Chimney, conspicuous, the position of which is approximate (54°09′N 4°30′W) (Chart 2094).

2 Refuge Tower (54°09′N 4°28′W), castellated and prominent, standing on the highest part of Conister Rock (10.195), N of the entrance to the harbour. A light, visible between the bearings of 234°-312°, is exhibited from the tower.

Church (spire), conspicuous, the most N group of towers and spires situated in the S part of the town, 7½ cables NW of the head of Victoria Pier.

3 Saint Ninian's Church tower, also conspicuous, standing 1·2 miles NNW of the pier.

Saint Ninian's Church tower from ESE (10.194)

(Original dated 1997)

(Photograph - Naval Party 1008)

Grandstand Tower from ESE (10.194)
(Original dated 1997)

(Photograph - Naval Party 1008)

Grandstand Tower, conspicuous (54°10′·1N 4°28′·7W).

Radio Tower, conspicuous (54°10′·1N 4°28′·5W).

Major light:

Douglas Head Light (54°09′N 4°28′W) (10.162).

10.195

1 **Leading lights:**

Front light (metal mast on concrete column, white and red triangular daymark point up) standing in the sea 1½ cables SSW of Victoria Pierhead.

Rear light (similar structure, daymark point down) (62 m SW of front light).

The alignment (229¼°) of the lights leads through Douglas Bay to the outer harbour entrance, passing (with positions from front light):

2 SE of Conister, or Saint Mary's Rock (2½ cables N), a detached drying ledge on which stands a refuge tower (10.194). Below-water rocky heads extending E and SE are marked by Nos 1 and 3 Light Buoys (starboard hand). Thence:

3 NW of a dolphin (2½ cables NE) which lies close NW off the head of Princess Alexandra Pier from which a light (red metal mast) is exhibited, thence:

Between the head of Victoria Pier (1½ cables NNE) from where a light (white column; 6 m in height) is exhibited, and the head of Battery Pier which also displays a light (white tower, red band).

Douglas Leading Lights from NE (10.195)
(Original dated 2001)

(Photograph - Air Images)

10.196

1   **Caution.** Care should be taken when entering the harbour after heavy rains which cause freshets in the river.

Useful marks
10.197

1   Gas-holder (green tank), close SSE of the rear leading light (10.195), is prominent and visible near the leading line.

    Sea Terminal Building (spire), standing at the root of Victoria Pier.

Basins and berths
10.198

1   **Outer harbour,** the main commercial harbour, is entered at its NE corner between the head of Victoria Pier, extending ESE to form the N side of the basin, and a round dolphin 60 m NNW of the head of Princess Alexandra Pier, a rubble mound breakwater which extends 160 m NE from the head of Battery Pier, the E side of the basin. King Edward VIII Pier extends ESE from the W side of the outer harbour to form the S side of the basin.

2   **Victoria Pier.** Cross-channel vessels are the main users of this pier; berthing can be arranged either side. A RoRo berth, with a maintained depth 4·4 m, lies on the inner section of the pier. Height of quay above sea level at the outer berths, 3 m at MHWS; 4·8 m at MHWN.

    Battery Pier, berth No 15, is used by tankers; depth alongside 5·4 m. The inner end of berth No 14 is used by small craft.

3   **King Edward VIII Pier** is also used by cross-channel vessels which can berth either side; a RoRo berth, with a maintained depth alongside of 5·4 m, lies on the N side of the pier.

    Middle harbour, which accepts small commercial vessels and mostly dries, is entered from E between the heads of King Edward VIII Pier and Fort Anne Jetty, 45 m S.

4   **Berths** 6, 7 and 8 lie along the N side of the basin and handle bulk cargoes from vessels up to 100 m in length, having a draught of up to 4·4 m at MHWS and which can take the ground, gravel over clay.

5   **Inner harbour,** entered via a flap gate and bascule bridge at the W end of the middle harbour, contains pontoon berths for small craft. It is entered at HW ±2 hours, but entry can be delayed owing to tidal conditions and strong E winds. A depth of 2·8 m is maintained at the sill. The Tongue, a narrow finger pier, separates North and South Quays. The bottom is gravel over clay.

Port services
10.199

1   **Repairs:** limited repair facilities only.

    Other facilities: divers; SSCC and SSCEC; Customs and Excise business for the Isle of Man is transacted at Douglas; hospital; slipway for small boats, usable at all states of the tide, close to Fort Anne Jetty.

    Supplies: fuel by road; fresh water; provisions and stores.

2   **Harbour regulations** are in force for the loading and discharging of gas and petroleum products; details may be obtained from Harbour Control.

    Landings. There are landing steps at all the piers in the outer harbour.

There is a landing place at Port Soderick (Chart 2094), within the harbour limits, 2½ miles SW of Douglas Head.

DOUGLAS TO POINT OF AYRE

General information

Chart 2094
Route
10.200

1   From a position SE of Douglas Head (54°09′N 4°28′W) to the vicinity N of Point of Ayre (54°25′N 4°22′W) the coastal passage continues NE thence NNE and NNW for a distance of about 20 miles, passing SE of Clay Head (54°12′N 4°23′W) and rounding Maughold (pronounced Maccull) Head (54°18′N 4°18′W).

Topography
10.201

1   The coast between Banks Howe (10.206) at the N entrance to Douglas Bay and Maughold Head, 10 miles NE, the E extremity of the island, consists of bold cliffs and is steep-to. The cliffs at Maughold Head rise to an elevation of 114 m. The coastline N of the headland towards Ramsey (54°19′N 4°23′W) is backed by high cliffs; thence for 3 miles farther N to Shellag Point, it consists of low clay cliffs fronted by a sandy beach and backed by low, undulating and well cultivated land.

2   The land rises abruptly to a height of 89 m close within Shellag Point and then slopes N for 1½ miles to Port Cranstal where it again becomes a plain; the E side of this higher ground forms the cliffs fronting the shore.

    From Shellag Point to Point of Ayre (54°25′N 4°22′W), the N extremity of the island, the coastline is low and fronted by a gravel beach.

Rescue
10.202

1   See 10.160. An all weather lifeboat is stationed at Ramsey (54°19′N 4°23′W).

    For details of rescue organisation see 1.60.

Natural conditions
10.203

1   **Tidal streams** near the land between Bank Howes and Maughold Head are similar to those described at 10.161.

    Off Maughold Head the NE-going stream begins 5 hours after HW Liverpool and the SW-going stream begins 4¼ hours before HW at that port.

    For tidal streams farther offshore see 10.143.

2   **Caution.** It is probable that a W set towards Maughold Head will be experienced between the locality in which the offshore streams meet and separate, and the headland, whilst the inshore streams are running NW and SW away from the headland.

3   Between Maughold Head and Point of Ayre the N-going coastal stream sets for 9 hours, and the S-going coastal stream for 3 hours; the streams are not strong but increase in strength off Point of Ayre.

    The NW/N-going stream begins 3¾ hours before HW Liverpool and the SE/S-going stream begins 5¼ hours after HW at that port.

4   Tidal streams off Point of Ayre and off-lying banks are given on the charts and in *Admiralty Tidal Stream Atlas — Irish Sea and Bristol Channel.*

    Race. An eddy forms W of Point of Ayre during the W-going stream, and SE of the point during the E-going stream; a race occurs off the point when these eddy streams meet the tidal streams.

Directions

(continued from 10.165)

Principal marks
10.204

1   **Landmarks:**

Radio Mast (54°08′·4N 4°29·6′W).
Church (spire), (54°09′N 4°29′W) (10.194).
Saint Ninian's Church (tower) (54°10′N 4°29′W) (10.194).
Television Mast (54°13′·4N 4°23′·9W) (10.208).

2   Albert Tower, conspicuous, (54°19′N 4°23′W) (10.216).
Hotel (Dome) (54°20′·4N 4°23′·5W) (10.216).

Major lights:

Douglas Head Light (54°09′N 4°28′W) (10.162).
Maughold Head Light (white tower, 23 m in height) (54°18′N 4°18′W).
Point of Ayre Light (54°25′N 4°22′W) (10.18).

Maughold Head Lighthouse from SE (10.204)
(Original dated 2001)

(Photograph – Air Images)

Other aids to navigation
10.205

1   **Racon:**

Point of Ayre Lighthouse (54°25′N 4°22′W) (10.18).
For further details see *Admiralty List of Radio Signals Volume 2.*

Passage
10.206

1   From a position SE of Douglas Head (54°09′N 4°28′W) the coastal passage to Point of Ayre, a distance of approximately 20 miles, initially continues NE, thence NNE and NNW after rounding Maughold Head, passing (with positions from Maughold Head (54°18′N 4°18′W)):

SE of Banks Howe (8½ miles SSW), with bold cliffs, thence:
SE and ESE of Clay Head (6½ miles SSW), thence:

2   ESE of Laxey Head (5 miles SSW) with a Television Mast (10.208) 5 cables W of the headland, thence:
ESE of Carrick Roayrt (3·9 miles SSW), a steep-to rock which dries, lying 1 cable off the shore, thence:
ESE and ENE of Maughold Head, from where a light (10.204) is exhibited. It consists of bold high cliffs and is steep-to, thence:

3   ENE of the entrance to Ramsey Harbour (54°19′N 4°23′W) with a pier (10.215) extending from the

shore 3 cables S; a conspicuous tower (10.216) stands 6½ cables S of the harbour, thence:
ENE of foul ground which lies parallel to the coast N of Shellag Point (5 miles NNW), thence:
WSW of Whitestone Bank Light Buoy (10.21) (6·9 miles NNW), thence:
ENE of Point of Ayre High Light (10.18).

4   **Clearing bearing.** Point of Ayre High Light bearing 225° and open W of the low light clears the off-lying Ballacash and King William Banks, as shown on the chart.
Caution. See 10.21.

Useful marks
10.207

1   Snaefell (54°16′N 4°28′W) (10.18).
Laxey Pierhead Light (white tower with red band, 4 m in height) (54°13′·5N 4°23′·2W); the light however, is obscured when bearing less than 318°.
Laxey Breakwater Light (white tower with green band, 4 m in height) (70 m SE of Pierhead light).
Ramsey Pierhead Lights (54°19′·4N 4°22′·4W) (10.218).

(Directions for an inshore route passing N of Point of Ayre and leading to the Mull of Galloway are given at 10.18; directions for the coastal passage on the West Coast of the Isle of Man are given at 10.228)

Laxey Bay

General information
10.208

1   **General description.** Laxey Bay is entered between Clay Head (54°12′N 4°23′W) and Laxey Head, nearly 2 miles N.
Topography. The bay, which in general is backed by high ground, is fronted by a narrow sandy beach with drying rocky ledges interspersed by sandy areas; in the N part of the bay lies the small harbour of Laxey.

2   **Landmark:**

Television Mast, 50 m in height, standing on high ground 4 cables W of the harbour entrance overlooking the bay.

Laxey Harbour
10.209

1   **General information.** Laxey Harbour (54°13′·5N 4°23′·3W), which dries, lies at the mouth of the Laxey River where it flows into the N corner of Laxey Bay, and is well sheltered under Laxey Head.
The harbour is formed by a breakwater extending SE from the SW entrance point of the river and by an L-shaped breakwater extending SSE and SSW from the shore on the NE side of the river mouth, forming an entrance 61 m wide facing SSW.

2   Lights are exhibited from both breakwater heads (10.207).
Within the entrance, a training wall, marked by beacons, runs along the NE side of the channel.
There is a resident Harbour Keeper who can provide local information. For Harbour Authority see 10.139.
Vessels up to 44 m LOA, draught 3·4 m can enter; there are depths alongside the pier of 4·9 m at MHWS.

3   **Caution.** Lobster pots and associated marking buoys are laid off the entrance to the harbour.
Berths. The harbour, no longer used for commercial traffic, is mainly used by inshore fishing vessels and pleasure craft, with moorings alongside the pier and in the

Point of Ayre, Lighthouse and Low Light from ESE (10.206)
(Original dated 2001)

(Photograph - Air Images)

small inner harbour. The longest berth is at the inner end
of the SE breakwater.

Yacht mooring buoys are laid in the S part of Laxey
Bay during the summer months.

Facilities are limited; slipway; fresh water.

Anchorage
10.210

1 Laxey Bay affords an anchorage, as shown on the chart,
during offshore winds in depths of 9 to 13 m, fine sand
and clay.

Landing — Port Cornaa
10.211

1 **Landing:** Port Cornaa, 3 miles N of Laxey Head
(54°14′N 4°23′W), is fronted by a steep shingle beach;
there is a creek which can be entered by small boats after
a rising half tide.

Ramsey Harbour

Charts 2094, 2696 plan of Ramsey Bay
General information
10.212

1 **Position.** Ramsey Harbour (54°19′N 4°23W), lies in the
SW part of Ramsey Bay, at the mouth of the Sulby River.

Function. Small commercial and fishing harbour also
used by pleasure craft. The main commercial traffic is from
the UK and Ireland and it is the only Manx port with
facilities to handle imports of bulk cement.

Port limits. The outer limit is a line drawn from Cor
Stack (54°18′·2N 4°19′·0W) (10.217) to Shellag Point,
4½ miles NW.

2 **Approach and entry.** The harbour is approached from E
and entered between two breakwaters extending E from the
shore.

Traffic. In 2007 there were 219 ship calls with a total
of 119 143 dwt.

Port Authority. There is a port manager and a harbour
keeper at Ramsey. The harbour office is open 0700-1600
daily and whenever a vessel is expected. See also 10.139.

Limiting conditions
10.213

1 **Depth.** The harbour dries and vessels should be prepared
to take the ground.

Deepest and longest berth: East Quay (10.219).

Tidal levels: mean spring range 6·5 m; mean neap range
3·6 m. See *Admiralty Tide Tables.*

Maximum size of vessel handled: 61 m LOA; draught
4·0 m at MHWS, 3·0 m at MHWN; 750 gt.

Local weather and sea state: strong E winds can make
entry difficult.

Arrival information
10.214

1 **Port operations.** Between the hours of 0700 and 1600
vessels can call Ramsey Harbour direct. Out of hours
vessels should contact Douglas Harbour Control (10.192) to
have their information relayed to Ramsey.

Ramsey from SSE (10.212)
(Original dated 2001)

(Photograph - Air Images)

2   **Outer anchorage.** An anchorage is shown on the chart 4 cables E of South Pier Light in a depth of 5·5 m, sand, clear of a foul area 4½ cables ENE of the South Pier Light; the holding is good but E winds send in a heavy sea. During prolonged E gales a small sandbank sometimes builds up 1 cable E of the harbour entrance.

3   **Pilotage** is not compulsory, but may be available if arranged in advance through the Port Manager.

    For further details see *Admiralty List of Radio Signals Volume 6(1)*.

Harbour
10.215
1   **General layout.** The harbour is entered between two roughly parallel breakwaters, North Pier and South Pier, which extend E from the shore for about 1½ cables. Within the entrance the harbour is divided into two parts by a swing bridge, exhibiting lights, which has a channel width of 25 m for vessels to pass through. The E part consists of two quays, East Quay and Town Quay. To the W of the bridge there are two basins, both drying.

    A sandy foreshore dries ½ cable seaward of the breakwater heads.

2   Queen's Pier (disused) extends nearly 4 cables ENE from the coast, 3 cables S of the harbour entrance. Landing is prohibited as the structure, part of which has been demolished, is unsafe. A dolphin, from where a light is exhibited, stands ½ cable N of the seaward end of the pier.

    Tidal streams set fairly strongly across the harbour entrance.

Directions for entering harbour
10.216
1   **Landmarks:**

    Albert Tower, a stone square structure, 14 m in height, standing at an elevation of 144 m on a hill, 6½ cables S of the harbour entrance.

    Crane, standing in the harbour area, and a building close to the shore, 2 cables SW of the harbour entrance. Both are conspicuous.

    Hotel (Chart 2094), prominent pale cream coloured building with a red dome, standing on the coast 1 mile N of the harbour entrance.

10.217
1   **Approach.** From S the approach through Ramsey Bay to the harbour entrance leads NW from the vicinity of Maughold Head (54°18′N 4°18′W), passing (with positions from the harbour entrance):

    NE of Cor Stack and Stack Mooar (2 and 2½ miles SE), two detached rocks, which lie close offshore, thence:

    NE of The Carrick (8½ cables SE), a drying rock marked by a beacon (port hand), thence:

2   NE of the dolphin (3¾ cables ESE) off the seaward end of Queen's Pier (10.215).

    From N the bay is clear except for charted dangers lying close to the coast.

    Two obstructions with a least depth 4·8 and 6·9 m over them lie 3½ cables NE and 8½ cables ENE, respectively, of the harbour entrance; a small patch of foul ground lies close NNE of the entrance.

Ramsey entrance from E (10.218)

(Original dated 2001)

(Photograph - Air Images)

10.218

1   **Entry.** The harbour channel is entered from E between North Pier, from the head of which a light (white tower, black base; 8 m in height) is exhibited, and South Pier which also exhibits a light (white tower, red band; 8 m in height) from its pierhead. A channel marker light is exhibited from the knuckle at the W end of South Pier.

   The width between the pierheads is 48·8 m and in the entrance channel between the piers there are depths of 6 m at MHWS; shoaler depths exist alongside the inner sections of each pier, see 10.219.

2   Within the E part of the harbour the channel leads S of a light beacon (dolphin; green metal post) which marks the toe of Mooragh Bank lying inside the entrance.

   It is unsafe to attempt to enter the harbour in strong E winds without obtaining advice from the Port Manager.

   Care is necessary when proceeding into the harbour after heavy rains which produce strong freshets in the river.

Berths

10.219

1   The commercial berths are on East Quay, immediately S of the inner end of the entrance channel, where there are cargo handling cranes. Town Quay is generally used by fishing vessels. Depths alongside are between 4·5 and 5·5 m at MHWS. The bottom is mud and gravel over clay.

2   The inner harbour and Old Harbour, NW of the swing bridge, are accessible at HW ±2 hours. There are moorings and alongside berths for craft which can take the ground.

   Seasonal unlit buoys (special) may be encountered within Ramsey Bay during May to October.

Port services

10.220

1   **Facilities:** minor repairs, slipway of 200 gt capacity; gridiron of length 40 m, breadth 7·5 m, 72 hours notice to the Port Manager required; hospital.

   Supplies: fresh water at quays; fuel from Douglas by road; small quantities of provisions.

CALF OF MAN TO POINT OF AYRE — WEST COAST

General information

Chart 2094

Routes

10.221

1   From a position SW of the Calf of Man (54°03′N 4°49′W) to a position N of Point of Ayre (54°25′N 4°22′W), the route leads N, thence NE and ENE for a distance of about 36 miles.

   An inshore route (10.232) for small vessels exists along the coast between Jurby Head and Point of Ayre.

Topography

10.222

1   Between Calf of Man (54°03′N 4°49′W) and Contrary Head (10 miles NNE) the coast is steep-to in many places with cliffs up to 160 m high backed by a mountain range, of which South Barrule (54°09′N 4°40′W) is the highest at 480 m. The only indentations are Port Erin (54°05′N

4°45'W) and Fleshwick Bay, 1¼ miles farther N. Elby Point (54°10'N 4°45'W) (10.230) is low lying.

2   Between Calf Sound (10.168) and Port Erin, several drying rocks project from the base of the cliffs and the coast is foul to a distance of 2 cables offshore.

North of Contrary Head the coastline gradually decreases in height as far as Jurby Head (54°21'N 4°33'W), where it becomes low-lying and somewhat featureless, but backed by the highest mountains on the island.

3   Between a position 2½ miles S of Orrisdale Head (54°18'N 4°35'W) and Point of Ayre the coast is fronted by a sand and shingle beach which dries to about 1 cable offshore.

Submarine exercise areas
10.223

1   See 10.3 and chart.

Unexploded ordnance area
10.224

1   There is an area of unexploded ordnance, associated with a former bombing range, off Jurby Head (54°21'N 4°33'W).

Shelter
10.225

1   As a lee shore the W coast of the Isle of Man, N of Peel Harbour (54°14'N 4°42'W), offers no shelter.

Rescue
10.226

1   An all-weather lifeboat is stationed at Peel Harbour (54°14'N 4°42'W) and an inshore lifeboat is stationed at Port Erin (54°05'N 4°45'W).

For details of rescue organisation see 1.60.

Tidal streams
10.227

1   Between Calf Sound (54°04'N 4°48'W) and Contrary Head (9¼ miles N) the streams set in approximately the direction of the coast. Close inshore they begin earlier than off Contrary Head, see below.

Between Bradda Head, 2 miles N of Calf Sound, and Niarbyl Isle, lying close off Elby Point (54°10'N 4°45'W), the stream is nearly always N-going, caused by an eddy which sets N during the S-going stream.

2   Between Niarbyl Isle and Contrary Head (3 miles farther N) the S-going stream begins 4½ hours after HW Liverpool and the N-going stream begins 1½ hours before HW Liverpool.

Off Contrary Head the streams are very weak but increase towards Niarbyl Isle where the spring rate is about 1 kn.

3   The SE-going and NW-going streams of the North Channel divide and meet off Contrary Head, setting as follows at the positions indicated:

Position	Interval from HW Liverpool	Direction	Max. Sp rate in kn
6 miles N of	+0610	NE by E	1
Contrary Head	HW	WSW	1¼
5 miles W of	+0610	SSE	1¼
Contrary Head	HW	NW by N	1¼

4   Between Contrary Head and Point of Ayre the streams set in approximately the direction of the coast beginning at the times shown above.

There is negligible stream off Saint Patrick's Isle (54°14'N 4°42'W), but farther NE the rate in both

directions increases and attains a rate of 2 kn off Jurby Head and 3 kn off Point of Ayre.

5   The stream sets nearly continuously E across Strunakill Bank (10.21), and between it and Point of Ayre.

For general tidal stream indications in the area see *Admiralty Tidal Stream Atlas — Irish Sea and Bristol Channel*.

Directions

Principal marks
10.228

1   **Landmarks:**
Excepting the summit of Snaefell (54°16'N 4°28'W) (10.18), when clear, most of the landmarks on this side of the island are confined to the SW part of the coastline as follows:
     Chicken Rock Lighthouse (54°02'N 4°50'W) (10.152).
2   Calf of Man Lighthouse (disused) (54°03'N 4°50'W) (10.152).
     Milner's Tower (square, round turret) (54°05'·6N 4°46'·7W), conspicuous from W, standing on the high cliffs close E of Bradda Head; the headland provides a good radar echo.
3   Corrins Folly (square stone tower) (54°12'·8N 4°42'·7W) standing a short distance NE of Contrary Head.
     Peel Castle (54°13'·5N 4°41'·9W) (10.241).
     Major lights:
     Point of Ayre Light (54°25'N 4°22'W) (10.18).
     Chicken Rock Light (54°02'N 4°50'W) (10.152).

Other aids to navigation
10.229

1   **Racons:**
     Point of Ayre Light (54°25'N 4°22'W) (10.18).
     South Rock Light Float (54°24'·5N 5°22'·0W) (Chart 2093) (*Irish Coast Pilot*).
For further details see *Admiralty List of Radio Signals Volume 2*.

Calf of Man to Contrary Head
10.230

1   From a position SW of Calf of Man (54°03'N 4°49'W) to the vicinity of Contrary Head (10 miles NNE) the route leads about 13 miles N, passing (with positions from Elby Point (54°10'N 4°45'W)):
     W of Chicken Rock (8¼ miles SSW) on which stands a conspicuous lighthouse (10.152), thence:
     W of the Calf of Man, thence:
2   W of Bradda Head (4¼ miles SSW), on which stands a conspicuous tower (10.228), thence:
     WNW of Elby Point, low and rocky; Niarbyl Isle lies on a rocky ledge which extends 3 cables WSW from the point. Thence:
     WNW of Contrary Head, with a conspicuous tower (10.228) standing close NE.

Contrary Head to Point of Ayre
10.231

1   From Contrary Head (54°13'N 4°43'W) to a position N of Point of Ayre (54°25'N 4°22'W) the route leads a further 20 miles NE, thence ENE, passing (with positions from Jurby Head (54°21'N 4°33'W)):
     NW of Saint Patrick's Isle (9¼ miles SW) at the entrance to Peel Harbour, on which stands a conspicuous tower (10.241), thence:
2   NW of Craig Rock (6¾ miles SW), surrounded by The Dogger, a sandbank. A wreck (position

approximate) with a swept depth 7 m lies
8¼ cables WSW of Craig Rock. Thence:
NW of Jurby Rock (4¼ cables W), with depths of
less than 3 m over it, thence:

3 NNW of Rue Point (4½ miles NE) with a spit, depths
less than 2 m, extending 4 cables offshore, thence:
NNW of Strunakill Bank (7 miles NE) (10.21),
extending from about ½ to 2¼ miles NW of Point
of Ayre.

10.232

1 **Inshore route.** A route for small vessels, which lies
farther inshore than that described at 10.231, passes
between Strunakill Bank and Point of Ayre. Vessels
following this route should take into account the sandbanks
which lie close offshore, particularly between Jurby Head
and Rue Point, and local weather conditions. Local
knowledge is necessary.

2 **Clearing bearings.** The line of bearing 202° of the W
end of the Calf of Man open W of Contrary Head passes
W of Craig Rock (54°16′N 4°40′W), but does not clear the
7 m wreck lying 8¼ cables WSW of the rock (10.231).

The alignment (071°) of Kirk Michael Church (tower)
(54°17′N 4°35′W) (10.233) with the N edge of the sand
cliffs of Glen Wyllin, 4 cables WSW of the church, passes
NW of Craig Rock.

Useful marks
10.233

1 Television mast (54°11′N 4°40′W), a prominent
four-sided framework structure standing on the
SW ridge of Slieau Whallian.
Television mast (50 m in height) (54°13′N 4°37′W),
336 m 3 miles E of Peel.
Power station chimney (54°13′N 4°42′W).

2 Kirk Michael Church (pinnacled tower) (54°17′N
4°35′W) with a valley on either side.
Control tower, part of a former bombing range,
standing at Jurby Head (54°21′N 4°33′W). It
assists in identifying the headland. The ruins of
Jurby Chapel stand on high ground close within
Jurby Head.

*(Directions for an inshore route passing N of Point of
Ayre leading to Morecambe Bay are given at 10.18;
directions for a coastal passage from
Douglas to Point of Ayre are given at 10.204)*

Port Erin

Charts 2094, 2696 plan of Port Erin
General information
10.234

1 Port Erin (54°05′N 4°45′W), a quiet seaside resort used
mainly by small craft and inshore fishing vessels, lies at
the head of Port Erin Bay on the low-lying neck of the
peninsula which forms the SW extremity of the Isle of
Man. Passenger vessels operate between here and Calf of
Man during the summer months and occasional cruise ships
visit, anchoring in the bay. The port also operates as a
dive centre.

2 The bay is sheltered by two headlands and a sandy
beach skirts its head. Although open to the W the bay
receives some protection from the ruins of a breakwater
which extends N from the S entrance point and is covered
at HW springs.

3 **Port Authority.** The Port St Mary Port Manager's
responsibilities include Port Erin, see also 10.139. Harbour
office hours are 0900–1630. There is no port radio and

vessels intending to enter the bay should call Douglas
while still well clear as it is a VHF shadow area.

Tidal information. Mean spring range 4·8 m; mean neap
range 2·6 m. Tidal streams are negligible. See information
in *Admiralty Tide Tables*.

Sea fisheries experimental area. The area extends from
the coast S of the harbour and is marked at its W edge by
three light buoys (special).

Directions for entering harbour
10.235

1 **Leading lights.** The alignment (099°) of leading lights,
standing near the shore at the head of the bay, leads into
the centre of the bay.
Front light (white tower, red band, 11 m in height)
(54°05′·2N 4°45′·6W).
Rear light (white column, red band and lantern, 4 m
in height) (39 m from front light).

2 The track passes about midway between the head of the
ruined breakwater, marked by a buoy (starboard hand), and
a 1·5 m patch (1½ cables N) close off the N shore.

The Sker, an above-water rock, lies 1¾ cables WNW of
the 1·5 m patch, close to the N shore, and is the only other
danger close to the approach.

Berths
10.236

1 **Alongside berths.** Raglan Pier, which dries to a sandy
bottom at its outer end, lies in the SE corner of the bay
and offers fair shelter. It can accommodate vessels with a
maximum draught of 3 m on neap tides. A light (white
tower, green band, 7 m in height) is exhibited from the
head of the pier.

2 A jetty, ½ cable W of the pier, has a least depth of
1·4 m at its outer steps.

Anchorage. The bay affords good anchorage except in
W winds, in depths of 5 to 8 m, sand and gravel.

Moorings. Visiting yachts can use two mooring buoys
situated between the ruined breakwater and Raglan Pier.

Port services
10.237

1 **Repairs:** minor repairs; slipway SE of pier.
Supplies: marine diesel by road, 24 hours notice; fresh
water at Raglan Pier; some provisions; stores from Port
St Mary.

Peel Harbour

Charts 2094, 2696 plan of Peel
General information
10.238

1 **Position.** Peel Harbour lies S of Saint Patrick's Isle
(54°14′N 4°42′W) at the entrance to the river Neb. It is
dominated by Peel Castle (10.241).

Function. Small commercial harbour, principally a
fishing port which exports fish and agricultural produce and
imports petroleum products and occasional general cargoes.

Harbour limits extend from Thistle Head (6 cables SW
from the harbour) NW for about 8 cables, thence ENE to
the coast 2½ miles from the harbour entrance.

2 **Approach and entry.** The port is approached from the
open waters of the Irish Sea and entered from ENE
between the head of the N breakwater and the head of a
groyne (1 cable S) (10.241) extending ENE from the
middle of the E quay.

Traffic. In 2007 there were 19 ship calls with a total of
71 029 dwt.

Harbour Authority. See 10.139; local information can be obtained from the Harbour Keeper. Harbour Office hours are 0800-1630.

Limiting conditions
10.239

1 **Outer harbour:** vessels of up to 85 m in length and a draught of up to 5·0 m can lie afloat alongside the breakwater at MLWS.

Maximum size of vessel handled: 112·5 m LOA, 5·8 m draught at the outer breakwater berth; 48·7 m LOA; draught 3·9 m at MHWS, 3·0 m at MHWN in the inner harbour.

The breakwater berth is untenable in strong winds from W through NW to NE.

Arrival information
10.240

1 **Port operations.** When a vessel is expected the port radio is manned, call sign: Peel Harbour; at other times vessels should contact Douglas (10.192).

For further details see *Admiralty List of Radio Signals Volume 6(1)*.

2 **Outer anchorage** exists 2¾ cables N of the breakwater light (10.242), in a depth of 10 m, sand. Vessels may be required to anchor elsewhere around the island should conditions not be favourable, particularly in strong winds from SW through N to NE.

Pilotage is not compulsory but may be available if arranged in advance.

Harbour
10.241

1 **Layout.** The harbour, which consists of an outer and inner harbour, is open to the N but is protected from S by the rising ground of Corrins Hill, leading to Contrary Head on the summit of which stands Corrins Folly (10.228).

2 Saint Patrick's Isle is joined to the W side of the harbour by a causeway. Peel Castle, which stands on the isle, dominates the entrance to the harbour. The walls of the castle are flanked by towers and enclose an area covered by ruins which include a conspicuous tall round tower and what is supposed to be the first Christian church erected on the Isle of Man; it also includes the ruins of the Cathedral Church of Man.

3 A mole extends 1¼ cable ENE from Saint Patrick's Isle; the E side of the harbour is formed by another mole, 110 m long, extending N from the E side of the river entrance. A groyne extends 140 m NE from a position near the middle of the mole.

4 Castle Jetty, which projects a short distance from the E side of Saint Patrick's Isle, affords some protection to the harbour.

Entry to the inner harbour is through a flap gate 12m wide and controlled by vessel traffic lights. The operation of the gate is automatic and retains a minimum depth of 2·5 m at the sill.

5 **Submarine cables** linking the Isle of Man and N.Ireland run NNE through the outer harbour from a position on the shore 2 cables E of the entrance to the inner harbour, thence NW towards the Irish Coast.

Tidal streams are negligible off Peel.

Directions for entering harbour
10.242

1 **Landmarks:**

Clock tower, red and square shaped, part of the remains of Saint Peter's church which stands near the centre of Peel.

2 Saint Germain's church tower, square, built of red stone, standing 2 cables farther E of Saint Peter's church.

Peel Castle (54°13'·6N 4°41'·9W) (10.241).

Power station chimney (54°13'·1N 4°41'·9W), red lights at top.

3 **Directions.** From open water, approach to the port can be made from between W and NNE. If approaching from NW, Peel is not always easy to identify as mist collects in its valley; if approaching from N vessels should be aware of Craig Rock (54°16'N 4°40'W) and the unmarked wreck (position approximate) lying WSW (10.231).

4 **Leading lights.** The alignment (207°) of Peel leading lights leads to the harbour entrance E of the breakwater head, from where a light (white tower, 8 m in height) is exhibited:

Front light (54°13'·6N 4°41'·7W) stands at the head of the groyne.

Rear light (on pumping station cupola) (1¼ cables from front light).

5 **Cautions.** An obstruction, consisting of concrete blocks protecting a sewer outfall with a least depth 4·9 m over it, lies ½ cable ENE of the head of the breakwater and a shoal patch with a least depth 4·7 m over it lies close S of the breakwater head.

6 **Useful marks:**

Light (white tower, red band) which surmounts an office building at the head of the E pier.

Light (white tower, three green bands; 4 m in height) standing at the head of Castle Jetty (10.241).

Berths
10.243

1 **Outer harbour.** There are depths of 4·3 to 5·5 m alongside the the outer half of the S side of the mole.

A tanker berth 91·5 m long, with a manifold connection 46 m from the head of the mole, has depths alongside of between 4·5 and 5·2 m. Vessels berth starboard side-to on arrival.

2 **Inner harbour** is quayed on both sides; moorings can be obtained alongside West Quay, the bottom consists of rock and gravel, elsewhere it is gravel and sand.

Port services
10.244

1 **Repairs:** small repairs can be carried out.

Supplies: fresh water; fuel by road; small quantities of supplies and provisions.

Anchorage
10.245

1 There is good holding off the entrance to Fleshwick Bay (54°06'·5N 4°45'·0W) in depths of 24 m.

Dangerous wrecks lie approximately 5 cables NNW of the anchorage as shown on the chart.

During offshore winds small craft may find shelter in the bay.

APPENDIX I

EXTRACT FROM MERSEY CHANNEL COLLISION RULES

SCHEDULE

PRELIMINARY

1. In these Rules, except where the context otherwise requires — "Collision Regulations" means the Merchant Shipping (Distress Signals and Prevention of Collisions) Regulations 1996 **(a)** made under section 21 of the Merchant Shipping Act 1979 **(b)** and, in relation to seaplanes, the Collision Regulations (Seaplanes) Order 1989 **(c)** made under section 418 (1) of the Merchant Shipping Act 1894 as extended by section 97 (1) of the Civil Aviation Act 1982 **(d)** and the several words and expressions to which meanings are assigned by the Collision Regulations shall have the same meanings as in those Regulations.

2. Every vessel navigating in any part of the River Mersey or in the sea channels or approaches thereto between the Rock Lighthouse and the furthest point seawards to which such sea channels or approaches respectively are for the time being buoyed on both sides shall comply with —
   (a) these Rules, and
   (b) the Collision Regulations, except in so far as compliance with these Rules requires otherwise.

RULES CONCERNING MARKS, LIGHTS, ETC.

3. (1) The lights prescribed by these Rules shall be exhibited from sunset to sunrise, from sunrise to sunset in restricted visibility and in all other circumstances when it is deemed necessary and during such other times no other lights shall be exhibited, except such lights as cannot be mistaken for the lights specified in these Rules or do not impair their visibility or distinctive character, or interfere with keeping a proper lookout.
   (2) The marks and shapes prescribed by these Rules shall be exhibited from sunrise to sunset.
   (3) The lights and shapes specified in these Rules shall comply with the provisions of the Collision Regulations.

4. A power driven vessel when being towed shall, if under power, notwithstanding anything contained in Rule 24 (e) of the Collision Regulations, exhibit the lights prescribed by Rule 23 of the Collision Regulations:
   Provided that a power driven floating crane shall not be required under this paragraph to exhibit the light prescribed by Rule 23 (a) (ii) of the Collision Regulations.

5. A power driven floating crane when under way shall exhibit the lights prescribed by Rule 23 (a) (i) (iii) and (iv) of the Collision Regulations, but shall not be required to carry the light prescribed by Rule 23 (a) (ii) thereof.

6. A vessel of 20 metres or over in length, when at anchor, shall in addition to the requirements of Rule 30 of the Collision Regulations, carry aft where it can best be seen one ball at a height of 4·5 metres lower than the forward ball.

7. (1) A vessel, when lying at, or attached to another vessel lying at, any Jetty or Stage to the northward of a line drawn from the south end of the Liverpool Landing Stage to the south end of the Woodside Ferry Stage, shall exhibit the lights prescribed by Rule 23 of the Collision Regulations or, as the case may be, Rule 25 thereof:
   Provided that a power driven floating crane shall not be required under this paragraph to exhibit the light prescribed by Rule 23 (a) (ii) of the Collision Regulations.
   (2) A vessel, when lying at any Jetty or Stage to the southward of the said line, or moored head and stern to buoys permanently fixed, shall exhibit where they can best be seen one white all round light forward and at or near the stern a second white all round light. The forward light shall be 4·5 metres above the after light provided that a vessel under 50 metres length may carry one such light only, fixed where it can best be seen.

8. A vessel exceeding 200 metres in length when under way or at anchor, shall, in addition to the lights prescribed by Rule 23 or Rule 30 of the Collision Regulations, exhibit where they can best be seen three red all round lights spaced vertically 2 metres apart.

9. A vessel wishing to warn ships of an unmarked underwater obstruction shall display the lights or shapes provided for in Rule 27 (b) and (d) of the Collision Regulations; additionally, such vessel may use her searchlight to warn on-coming ships as provided for in Rule 36 of the Collision Regulations.

STEERING AND SAILING RULES

10. For the purposes of Rule 9 of the Collision Regulations (navigation in narrow channels), the fairways of the River Mersey and the sea channels or approaches thereto between the Rock Lighthouse and the furthest point seawards to which such sea channels or approaches respectively are for the time being buoyed on both sides shall be taken to be narrow channels.

11. A vessel shall not navigate to come into or leave the Main (i.e The Queens and Crosby) Channel seaward of a line drawn on a true bearing of 071 degrees from the Rock Lighthouse (i.e. a line drawn from the Rock Lighthouse to the west pierhead of the Gladstone River Entrance) at such a time or in such a manner as to hamper traffic passing up and down the Main Channel.

12. A power driven vessel under way, when about to turn round, i.e. alter her course more than 12 points (135 degrees), shall indicate the same by four short and rapid blasts on the whistle followed, after a short interval, if turning with her head to starboard by one short blast or, if turning with her head to port by two short blasts. The giving of the signal so prescribed shall not relieve a vessel of her obligations under the Collision Regulations or these Rules:

Provided that a vessel of less than 50 metres in length shall not be required to give the signal so prescribed unless she is towing one or more vessels and the distance from her stern to the stern of the last vessel towed is 50 metres or more.

LAUNCHING OF VESSELS

13.(1) A shipbuilder or other person (hereinafter called "the shipbuilder") shall not launch a vessel into any part of the River Mersey to the northward of a straight line, drawn from Eastham Ferry Slip to the northwest corner of the North Dock at Garston, unless the requirements of this Rule have been complied with.

(2) At least three clear days before the date fixed for the launch the shipbuilder shall, in addition to giving any other notice required by law, give to the Secretary of The Mersey Docks and Harbour Company at the Port of Liverpool Building, Liverpool, notice in writing of the place, day and hour proposed for the launch.

(3) Upon receiving such notice The Mersey Docks and Harbour Company shall publish within the Port of Liverpool a notice to mariners giving particulars of the place, day and hour proposed for the launch, and prescribing the area which is to be kept clear as provided by these Rules (hereinafter called the "launching area"). The launching area shall be bounded on the shore side by the line of the shore between a point 600 metres or such distance as in the opinion of the Marine Surveyor to the said Company may be necessary, to the southward and another point 300 metres to the northward, of the river end of the launchway, and on the remaining three sides by straight lines so drawn as to include an area of a size sufficient, in the opinion of the said Marine Surveyor having regard to the vessel's tonnage and to other relevant circumstances, in the interests of safety of vessels using the river.

(4) At least three hours before the time proposed for the launch the shipbuilder shall mark the launching area by anchoring at each angle thereof in the river a mark boat suitably dressed with flags in rainbow fashion from stem to stern.

(5) Ten minutes before the time proposed for the launch the shipbuilder shall cause each mark boat to exhibit a red flag measuring 2 metres long by 1·5 metres broad and inscribed with the word "LAUNCH" (hereinafter called a "launching flag") in large white letters thereon, at such a height being not less than 6 metres above the hull of the mark boat, as to be clear of and to fly well above and distinct from all other flags thereon.

14. If the vessel is not launched within thirty minutes of the launching flags being first exhibited the shipbuilder shall take steps to prevent the vessel being launched upon that day.

15.(1) The shipbuilder shall cause each mark boat to continue to exhibit the launching flag until the vessel has been launched and is under control, or, if the vessel is not launched, until there remains no risk of the vessel coming off the launchway of her own accord.

(2) As soon as the vessel is under control or there remains no risk of the vessel coming off the launchway, the shipbuilder shall cause the mark boats to be withdrawn.

16. The shipbuilder shall take means to bring up the vessel which has been launched and to have her under control within the launching area.

17.(1) A vessel anchored or moored, prior to the day of the launch, within the launching area, or in such a position as to swing into it, shall be removed not later than 1 a.m. on the day of the launch.

(2) A vessel shall not on the day of the launch, except for a purpose in connection with the launch, be anchored or moored within the launching area, or in such a position as to swing into it, until after the mark boats have been withdrawn.

(3) A vessel shall not, except for the purpose of leaving the launching area or for a purpose in connection with the launch, be navigated within the launching area whilst the launching flags are exhibited.

(The above Rules were made by Order in Council on 20th December, 1978, and came into operation on 11th March, 1979).

EXTRACT FROM BYE-LAWS WITH RESPECT TO THE SPEED OF VESSELS NAVIGATING THE RIVER MERSEY AND THE SEA CHANNELS AND APPROACHES THERETO

A vessel shall not be navigated or manoeuvred in any part of the River Mersey, or in any of the sea channels or approaches to the river from the furthest point seaward to which such sea channels or approaches are or may be buoyed at speeds which will or are likely to—

(1) force open the gates or caissons of any of the works or property of the Mersey Docks and Harbour Company or walls, revetments, training banks, or other works or property (including vessels) of the Mersey Docks and Harbour Company; or

(3) cause damage to the banks of the River Mersey or sea channels or approaches as aforesaid; or

(4) cause damage to vessels lying alongside any jetty or stage belonging to the Mersey Docks and Harbour Company or to the moorings of such vessels.

The Master, Owner or other person having the command, charge or management for the time being of any vessel contravening the above mentioned Bye-law shall be liable to a penalty not exceeding Fifty pounds for each contravention.

APPENDIX II

TERRITORIAL WATERS ORDER IN COUNCIL, 1964

AT THE COURT AT BUCKINGHAM PALACE

The 25th day of September, 1964

Present,

THE QUEEN'S MOST EXCELLENT MAJESTY IN COUNCIL

Her Majesty, by virtue and in exercise of all the powers enabling Her in that behalf, is pleased, by and with the advice of her Privy Council, to order, and it is hereby ordered, as follows:

1. This Order may be cited as the Territorial Waters Order in Council 1964 and shall come into operation on 30th September 1964.

2. (1) Except as otherwise provided in Articles 3 and 4 of this Order, the baseline from which the breadth of the territorial sea adjacent to the United Kingdom, the Channel Islands and the Isle of Man is measured shall be low-water line along the coast, including the coast of all islands comprised in those territories.

(2) For the purposes of this Article a low-tide elevation which lies wholly or partly within the breadth of sea which would be territorial sea if all low-tide elevations were disregarded for the purpose of the measurement of the breadth thereof and if Article 3 of this Order were omitted shall be treated as an island.

3. (1) The baseline from which the breadth of the territorial sea is measured between Cape Wrath and the Mull of Kintyre shall consist of the series of straight lines drawn so as to join successively, in the order in which they are set out, the points identified by the co-ordinates of latitude and longitude in the first column of the Schedule to this Order, each being a point situate on low-water line and on or adjacent to the feature, if any, named in the second column of that Schedule opposite to the co-ordinates of latitude and longitude of the point in the first column.

(2) The provisions of paragraph (1) of this Article shall be without prejudice to the operation of Article 2 of this Order in relation to any island or low-tide elevation which for the purpose of that Article is treated as if it were an island, being an island or low-tide elevation which lies to the seaward of the baseline specified in paragraph (1) of this Article.

4. In the case of the sea adjacent to a bay, the baseline from which the breadth of the territorial sea is measured shall, subject to the provisions of Article 3 of this Order:

(a) if the bay has only one mouth and the distance between the low-water lines of the natural entrance points of the bay does not exceed 24 miles, be a straight line joining the said low-water lines;

(b) if, because of the presence of islands, the bay has more than one mouth and the distances between the low-water lines of the natural entrance points of each mouth added together do not exceed 24 miles, be a series of straight lines across each of the mouths drawn so as to join the said low-water lines;

(c) if neither paragraph (a) nor (b) of this Article applies, be a straight line 24 miles in length drawn from low-water line to low-water line within the bay in such a manner as to enclose the maximum area of water that is possible with a line of that length.

5. (1) In this Order:

the expression "bay" means an indentation of the coast such that its area is not less that of the semi-circle whose diameter is a line drawn across the mouth of the indentation, and for the purposes of this definition the area of an indentation shall be taken to be the area bounded by low-water line around the shore of the indentation and the straight line joining the low-water lines of its natural entrance points, and where, because of the presence of islands, an indentation has more than one mouth the length of the diameter of the semi-circle referred to shall be the sum of the lengths of the straight lines drawn across each of the mouths, and in calculating the area of an indentation the area of any islands lying within it shall be treated as part of the area of the indentation;

the expression "island" means a naturally formed area of land surrounded by water which is above water at mean high-water spring tides; and

the expression "low-tide elevation" means a naturally formed area of drying land surrounded by water which is below water at mean high-water spring tides.

(2) For the purpose of this Order, permanent harbour works which form an integral part of a harbour system shall be treated as forming part of the coast.

(3) The Interpretation Act 1889 (a) shall apply to the interpretation of this Order as it applies to the interpretation of an Act of Parliament.

6. This Order shall be published in the *London Gazette*, the *Edinburgh Gazette* and the *Belfast Gazette*.

W.G. AGNEW

(a) 52 and 53 Vict.c.63.

EXPLANATORY NOTE

(This Note is not part of the Order, but it is intended to indicate its general purport).

This Order establishes the baseline from which the breadth of the territorial sea adjacent to the United Kingdom, the Channel Islands and the Isle of Man is measured. This, generally, is low-water line round the coast, including the coast of all islands, but between Cape Wrath and the Mull of Kintyre a series of straight lines joining specified points lying generally on the seaward side of the islands lying off the coast are used, and where there are well defined bays elsewhere lines not exceeding 24 miles in length drawn across the bays are used.

TERRITORIAL SEA (AMENDMENT) ORDER 1998

For the schedule to the Territorial Waters Order in Council 1964 (**a**) there shall be substituted the schedule set out below:

SCHEDULE

POINTS BETWEEN CAPE WRATH AND LAGGAN JOINED BY GEODESICS TO FORM BASELINES

	Latitude North			Longitude West			Name of Feature
	°	′	″	°	′	″	
1.	58	37	40	5	00	13	Cape Wrath
2.	58	31	12	6	15	41	Lith–Sgeir
3.	58	30	44	6	16	55	Gealltuig
4.	58	29	09	6	20	17	Dell Rock
5.	58	18	28	6	47	45	Tiumpan Head
6.	58	17	36	6	52	43	Màs Sgeir
7.	58	17	09	6	55	20	Old Hill
8.	58	14	30	7	02	06	Gallan Head
9.	58	14	01	7	02	57	Islet SW of Gallan Head
10.	58	10	39	7	06	54	Eilean Molach
11.	57	59	08	7	17	42	Gasker
12.	57	41	19	7	43	13	Haskeir Eagach
13.	57	32	22	7	43	58	Huskeiran
14.	57	14	33	7	27	44	Rubha Ardvule
15.	57	00	50	7	31	42	Greuab Head
16.	56	58	07	7	33	24	Doirlinn Head
17.	56	56	57	7	34	17	Aird a' Chaolais
18.	56	56	05	7	34	55	Biruaslum
19.	56	49	21	7	39	32	Guarsay Mor
20.	56	48	00	7	39	57	Sron an Duin
21.	56	47	07	7	39	36	Skate Point
22.	56	19	17	7	07	02	Skerryvore
23.	56	07	58	6	38	00	Dubh Artach
24.	55	41	36	6	32	02	Frenchman's Rocks
25.	55	40	24	6	30	59	Orsay Island
26.	55	35	24	6	20	18	Mull of Oa
27.	55	17	57	5	47	54	Mull of Kintyre
28.	54	58	29	5	11	07	Laggan

The positions of points 1 to 28 are defined by co-ordinates of latitude and longitude on the Ordnance Survey of Great Britain (1936) Datum (OSGB 36).

The Territorial Waters (Amendment) Order 1996 (**b**) is hereby revoked.

N. H. Nicholls
Clerk of the Privy Council

EXPLANATORY NOTE
(This note is not part of the Order)

The Order amends the Schedule to the Territorial Waters Order in Council 1964 by adding a new baseline between Mull of Kintyre and Laggan, as well as making minor changes to points 5, 9 and 22, which result from the publication of a new, larger scale chart of the area.

(**a**) 1965 III, p.6452A; revised Schedules were substituted by the Territorial Waters (Amendment) Order in Council 1979 and the Territorial Sea (Amendment) Order 1996.
(**b**) SI 1996/1628

TERRITORIAL SEA ACT 1987

Be it enacted by the Queen's Most Excellent Majesty, by and with the advice and consent of the Lords Spiritual and Temporal, and Commons, in this present Parliament assembled, and by the Authority of the same, as follows:

1. (1) Subject to the provisions of this Act —

    (a) the breadth of the territorial sea adjacent to the United Kingdom for all purposes be 12 nautical miles; and

    (b) the baselines from which the breadth of that territorial sea is to be measured shall for all purposes be those established by Her Majesty by Order in Council.

(2) Her Majesty may, for the purpose of implementing any international agreement or otherwise, by Order in Council provide that any part of the territorial sea adjacent to the United Kingdom shall extend to such line other than that provided for by subsection (1) above as may be specified in the Order.

(3) In any legal proceedings a certificate issued by or under the authority of the Secretary of State stating the location of any baseline established under subsection (1) above shall be conclusive of what is stated in the certificate.

(4) As from the coming into force of this section the Territorial Waters Order in Council 1964 and the Territorial Waters (Amendment) Order 1998 shall have effect for all purposes as if they were Orders in Council made by virtue of subsection (1) (b) above: and subsection (5) below shall apply to those Orders as it applies to any other instrument.

(5) Subject to the provisions of this Act, any enactment or instrument which (whether past or made before or after the coming into force of this section) contains a reference (however worded) to the territorial sea adjacent to, or to any part of, the United Kingdom shall be construed in accordance with this section and with any provision made, or having effect as if made, under this section.

(6) Without prejudice to the operation of subsection (5) above in relation to a reference to the baselines from which the breadth of the territorial sea adjacent to the United Kingdom is measured, nothing in that subsection shall require any reference in any enactment or instrument to a specified distance to be construed as a reference to a distance equal to the breadth of that territorial sea.

(7) In this section "nautical miles" means international nautical miles of 1,852 m.

2. (1) Except in so far as Her Majesty may by Order of Council otherwise provide, nothing in section 1 above shall affect the operation of any enactment contained in a local Act passed before the date on which that section comes into force.

(2) Nothing in section 1 above, or in any Order in Council under that section or subsection (1) above, shall affect the operation of so much of any enactment passed or instrument made before the date on which that section comes into force as for the time being settles the limits within which any harbour authority or port health authority has jurisdiction or is able to exercise any power.

(3) Where any area which is not part of the territorial sea adjacent to the United Kingdom becomes part of that sea by virtue of section 1 above or an Order in Council under that section, subsection (2) of section 1 of the Continental Shelf Act 1964 (vesting and exercise of rights with respect to coal) shall continue, on and after the date on which section 1 above of that Order comes into force, to have effect with respect to coal in that area as if the area were not part of the territorial sea.

(4) Nothing in section 1 above, or in any Order in Council under that section, shall affect —

    (a) any regulations made under section 6 of the Petroleum (Production) Act 1934 before the date on which that section or Order comes into force; or

    (b) any licences granted under the said Act of 1934 before that date or granted on or after that date in pursuance of regulations made under that section before that date.

(5) In this section —

    "coal" has the same meaning as in the Coal Industry Nationalisation Act 1946;

    "harbour authority" means a harbour authority within the meaning of the Harbours Act 1964 or the Harbours Act (Northern Ireland) 1970; and

    "port health authority" means a port health authority for the purposes of the Public health (Control of Disease) Act 1984.

3. (1) The enactment mentioned in Schedule 1 to this Act shall have effect with the amendments there specified (being minor amendments and amendments consequential on the provisions of this Act).

(2) Her Majesty may by Order in Council —

    (a) make, in relation to any enactment passed or instrument made before the date on which section 1 above comes into force, any amendment corresponding to any of those made by Schedule 1 to this Act;

    (b) amend subsection (1) of section 36 of the Wildlife and Countryside Act 1981 (marine nature reserves) so as to include such other parts of the territorial sea adjacent to Great Britain as may be specified in the Order in the waters and parts of the sea which, by virtue of paragraph 6 of Schedule 1 to this Act, may be designated under that section;

    (c) amend paragraph 1 of Article 20 of the Nature Conservation and Amenity Lands (Northern Ireland) Order 1985 (marine nature reserves) so as to include such other parts of the territorial sea adjacent to Northern Ireland as may be specified in the Order in the waters and parts of the sea which, by virtue of paragraph 9 of Schedule 1 to this Act, may be designated under that Article.

(3) Her Majesty may by Order in Council make such modifications of the effect of any Order in Council under section 1 (7) of the Continental Shelf Act 1964 (designated areas) as appear to Her to be necessary or expedient in consequence of any provision made by or under this Act.

(4) The enactments mentioned in Schedule 2 to this Act are hereby repealed to the extent specified in the third column of that Schedule.

4. (1) This Act may be sited as the Territorial Sea Act 1987.

(2) This Act shall come into force on such day as Her Majesty may by Order in Council appoint, and different days may be appointed for different provisions and for different purposes.

(3) This Act extends to Northern Ireland.

(4) Her Majesty may by Order in Council direct that any of the provisions of this Act shall extend, with such exceptions, adaptations and modifications (if any) as may be specified in the Order, to any of the Channel Islands or to the Isle of Man.

APPENDIX III

THE TERRITORIAL SEA ACT 1987 (ISLE OF MAN) ORDER 1991

AT THE COURT OF BUCKINGHAM PALACE

The 24th day of July 1991

Present,

THE QUEEN'S MOST EXCELLENT MAJESTY IN COUNCIL

Her Majesty, in pursuance of section 4 (4) of the Territorial Sea Act 1987 (**a**), is pleased, by and with the advice of Her Privy Council, to order, and it is hereby ordered as follows:

1. The Order may be cited as the Territorial Sea Act 1987 (Isle of Man) Order 1991 and shall come into force on 2nd September 1991.

2. The Territorial Sea Act 1987 shall extend to the Isle of Man with the exceptions, adaptations and modifications specified in the Schedule to this Order.

G.I. de Deney

(a) 1987 c.49.

SCHEDULE

EXCEPTIONS, ADAPTATIONS AND MODIFICATIONS IN THE EXTENSION OF THE TERRITORIAL SEA ACT 1987 TO THE ISLE OF MAN

1. Any reference to an enactment shall be construed, unless the contrary intention appears, as a reference to it as it has effect in the Isle of Man.

2. In section 1 —

    (a) in subsections (1) (a), (2), (5) and (6), for "United Kingdom" there shall be substituted "Isle of Man";

    (b) in subsection (1), there shall be added at the end the following provision:

    "Provided that where the baselines from which the breadth of the territorial sea adjacent to the Isle of Man is measured are less than 24 nautical miles from the baselines from which the breadth of the territorial sea adjacent to the United Kingdom is measured the seaward limit of the territorial sea adjacent to the Isle of Man shall be the median line,";

    (c) in subsection (3), for "Secretary of State" there shall be substituted "Governor";

    (d) in subsection (4), for "coming into force of this section" there shall be substituted "extension of this section to the Isle of Man";

    (e) in subsections (5) and (6), after "enactment" there shall be inserted "contained in an Act of Parliament", and

    (f) in subsection (7), after "section" there shall be inserted "'median line' is a line every point of which is equidistant from the nearest points of the baselines from which the breadth of the territorial sea adjacent to the Isle of Man and the United Kingdom respectively is measured and".

3. In section 2 —

    (a) subsection (1) shall be omitted;

    (b) for subsections (2) to (4) there shall be substituted the following subsections;

    "(2) Nothing in section 1 above, or in any Order in Council under that section, shall affect the operation of any provision relating to sea fisheries made by or under any enactment contained in an Act of Parliament.

    (3) Where any area which is not part of the territorial sea adjacent to the Isle of Man becomes part of that sea by virtue of section 1 above or an Order in Council under that section, any rights with respect to coal which were, immediately before the extension of this Act to the Isle of Man, vested in and exercisable by the British Coal Corporation by virtue of section 1 (2) of the Continental Shelf Act 1964 (**a**) shall continue to be so vested and exercisable after the date of that extension as if the area were not part of the territorial sea:

    Provided that those rights may be transferred to, or to a person nominated by, the Government of the Isle of Man on such terms as may be agreed between that Government and the British Coal Corporation or any successor in title to the British Coal Corporation.

    (4) Nothing in section 1 above, or in any Order in Council made under that section, shall affect any licences granted under the Petroleum (Production) Act 1934 (**b**) before the extension of this Act to the Isle of Man or the coming into force of that Order.", and

    (c) in subsection (5), the definitions of "harbour authority" and "port health authority" shall be omitted.

4. Section 3 shall be omitted.

5. In section 4, subsections (2) to (4) shall be omitted.

6. Schedule 1 shall be omitted.

7. In schedule 2, the entries relating to the Customs and Excise Management Act 1979 (**c**) and the Alcoholic Liquor Duties Act 1979 (**d**) shall be omitted.

(**a**) 1964 c.29.
(**b**) 1934 c.36, as extended by section 1 (3) of the Continental Shelf Act 1964.
(**c**) 1979 c.2.
(**d**) 1979 c.4.

EXPLANATORY NOTE

(This note is not part of the Order)

    This Order extends the Territorial Sea Act 1987 to the Isle of Man with the exceptions, adaptations and modifications specified in the Schedule to the Order.

Distances table - West coasts of England and Wales

Notes.

1. For further information and notes on distances, see *Admiralty Distance Tables Atlantic Ocean* Table 1b and Index Chart 1b.
2. 5 miles S of BISHOP ROCK
3. 5½ miles W of FASTNET
4. 3 miles W of LONGSHIPS
5. 5½ miles SW of MULL OF KINTYRE
6. 5 miles N of ÎLE d'OUESSANT
7. 6½ miles W of SMALLS
8. 6 miles SE of TUSKAR ROCK

From \ To	Belfast	Bideford	BISHOP ROCK (Note 2)	Bristol	Cardiff	Clyde, Firth of	Cork	Douglas (IOM)	Dublin	FASTNET (Note 3)	Fishguard	Holyhead	Liverpool	LONGSHIPS (Note 4)	Milford Haven	MULL OF KINTYRE (Note 5)	OUESSANT, ÎLE d' (Note 6)	SMALLS (Note 7)	Swansea	TUSKAR ROCK (Note 8)	Workington
Barrow-in-Furness	100	227	295	254	256	139	240	42	106	296	148	64	28	271	179	121	369	173	231	155	43
Belfast		249	314	277	279	68	256	78	101	311	175	98	120	293	202	37	391	193	254	170	79
Bideford			116	45	47	298	157	208	162	202	93	161	218	88	50	273	186	71	33	92	247
BISHOP ROCK (Note 2)				157	159	363	138	276	217	151	163	230	286	29	126	338	90	122	144	144	316
Bristol					3	326	189	236	189	237	121	189	246	129	78	301	227	99	32	120	275
Cardiff						327	190	237	191	239	122	191	247	131	80	302	229	100	33	122	277
Clyde, Firth of							304	122	149	359	223	145	160	341	251	50	439	241	302	219	119
Cork								220	159	61	127	176	232	139	117	280	229	91	166	85	261
Douglas (IOM)									76	276	130	48	54	252	161	102	350	155	213	135	43
Dublin										214	89	52	99	197	110	124	295	98	166	73	118
FASTNET (Note 3)											181	231	287	162	168	335	236	143	215	140	316
Fishguard												83	140	137	45	199	235	42	97	44	169
Holyhead													53	205	114	122	303	108	166	91	87
Liverpool														262	171	142	360	165	222	146	68
LONGSHIPS (Note 4)															100	317	98	99	116	124	291
Milford Haven																226	198	26	55	45	200
MULL OF KINTYRE (Note 5)																	415	217	278	194	100
OUESSANT, ÎLE d' (Note 6)																		197	214	223	389
SMALLS (Note 7)																			76	26	194
Swansea																				97	252
TUSKAR ROCK (Note 8)																					176

341

INDEX

NOTES

NOTES

NOTES

PUBLICATIONS OF THE
UNITED KINGDOM HYDROGRAPHIC OFFICE

A complete list of Sailing Directions, Charts and other works published by the United Kingdom Hydrographic Office, together with a list of Agents for their sale, is contained in the *Catalogue of Admiralty Charts and Publications*, published annually. The list of Admiralty Distributors is also on the UKHO website (www.ukho.gov.uk), or it can be obtained from:

The United Kingdom Hydrographic Office,
Admiralty Way,
Taunton, Somerset
TA1 2DN

Produced in the United Kingdom
by UKHO